◆§ ॐ◆

THE
MAJOR
ENGLISH
ROMANTIC
POETS

WILLIAM H. MARSHALL is Professor of English at the University of Pennsylvania. A member of the Modern Language Association, the Modern Humanities Research Association, and the American Association of University Professors, Dr. Marshall received his B.A. and M.A. at the University of Virginia (Phi Beta Kappa) and his Ph.D. at the University of Pennsylvania. A Byron specialist, Professor Marshall is the author of *The Structure of Byron's Major Poems* and of *Byron, Shelley, Hunt, and the Liberal.* Dr. Marshall has written numerous essays and articles on literary figures, past and present, including Donne, Milton, Spenser, Dickens, Samuel Butler, Meredith, Charlotte Brontë, and T. S. Eliot. Professor Marshall is the editor of *The Major Victorian Poets,* a companion volume to *The Major English Romantic Poets,* also published by *Washington Square Press.*

Other books by William H. Marshall

Byron, Shelley, Hunt, and The Liberal
The Major Victorian Poets, an Anthology
The Structure of Byron's Major Poems

THE MAJOR ENGLISH ROMANTIC POETS

An Anthology

Edited and with Biographical
and Critical Introductions by
WILLIAM H. MARSHALL

WASHINGTON SQUARE PRESS, INC. • NEW YORK
1966

Acknowledgments

ERNEST BENN, LTD.—for the selected poems of Percy Bysshe Shelley, reprinted from *The Complete Works of Percy Bysshe Shelley*, eds. Roger Ingpen and Walter E. Peck. London: Ernest Benn, 1926-30, and are reprinted by permission of Ernest Benn, Ltd.

THE CLARENDON PRESS—for the selected poems of Samuel Taylor Coleridge, reprinted from *The Complete Poetical Works of Samuel Taylor Coleridge*, ed. Ernest Hartley Coleridge. Oxford: The Clarendon Press, 1912, 1957, and are reprinted by permission of The Clarendon Press.

THE CLARENDON PRESS—for the selected poems of John Keats, reprinted from *The Poetical Works of John Keats*, ed. H. W. Garrod. Oxford: The Clarendon Press, second edition, 1958, and are reprinted by permission of the Clarendon Press.

THE CLARENDON PRESS—for the selected poems of William Wordsworth, reprinted from *The Poetical Works of William Wordsworth*, eds. Ernest de Selincourt and Helen Darbshire. Oxford: The Clarendon Press, 1940-49, and from *The Prelude, or Growth of a Poet's Mind*, eds. Ernest de Selincourt and Helen Darbshire. Oxford: The Clarendon Press, second edition, 1959, and are reprinted by permission of the Clarendon Press.

JOHN MURRAY—for the selected poems of Lord Byron, reprinted from *The Works of Lord Byron: Poetry*, ed. Ernest H. Coleridge. London: John Murray, 1898-1904, and are reprinted by permission of John Murray.

TO
My Mother and Father

Preface

THIS ANTHOLOGY is designed to fulfill several needs: first, to make readily and inexpensively available the most significant poems of the major English Romantic poets; secondly, to put before the student and the interested reader the reliable standard texts of these poems; finally, though not less significantly, to present the body of material in terms of the major ideas that have been advanced in recent years about the nature of Romanticism and the Romantic Movement.

In selecting the poems included here I have made every effort to bring together those which represent the best work of each poet and, at the same time, reveal him in relation to the age in which he lived and the cultural movement of which he was a significant part. The book offers a variety of representative poems sufficient for the general reader and a coverage adequate for the student making a survey of major English Romantic poetry. In addition, it represents for the more advanced student most of the major poems of medium length and, in either their entirety or significant portions, those longer poems with which he will be intensively concerned. In all instances I have been guided not by the inclusions in earlier anthologies but by what appears to me to have intrinsic merit; thus, for example, I have included a later canto of Byron's *Don Juan* rather than the more frequently anthologized first and second cantos. In placing Coleridge before the slightly senior Wordsworth, I have followed the usual practice of others, but only because it seems suitable: Coleridge's indisputably major poems antedate those of Wordsworth by several years, and, more significantly, Coleridge's thinking places him closer to the core of the Romantic Movement. In the case of each of the five poets I have arranged the poems in the order of composition, so far as this can be determined.

For each poem included in this anthology, I have used the

edition of the poet's work which is generally considered standard; it is my hope that in this way I might avoid the most common and serious weakness of literary anthologies—the inaccurate text, one frequently representing something very far indeed from what the author originally wrote. The editions used are: *The Complete Poetical Works of Samuel Taylor Coleridge*, ed. Ernest Hartley Coleridge (2 vols. Oxford: The Clarendon Press, 1912, 1957); *The Poetical Works of William Wordsworth*, eds. Ernest de Selincourt and Helen Darbishire (5 vols. Oxford: The Clarendon Press, 1940-49); William Wordsworth, *The Prelude, or Growth of a Poet's Mind*, eds. Ernest de Selincourt and Helen Darbishire (Oxford: The Clarendon Press, second edition, 1959); *The Works of Lord Byron: Poetry*, ed. Ernest Hartley Coleridge (7 vols. London: John Murray, 1898-1903); *The Complete Works of Percy Bysshe Shelley*, eds. Roger Ingpen and Walter E. Peck (10 vols. London: Ernest Benn, 1926-30); *The Poetical Works of John Keats*, ed. H. W. Garrod (Oxford: The Clarendon Press, second edition, 1958).

During the last several decades certain scholars have made significant contributions to our understanding of Romanticism: among others Arthur O. Lovejoy, René Wellek, Jacques Barzun, and more recently, M. H. Abrams and Morse Peckham. Various strong differences appear among their ideas, but in characteristically Romantic fashion we can reconcile most of these differences and recognize that together they have redirected our thinking about the nature of Romanticism and its relation to ourselves. Despite this fact, the influence of these critics has not yet been felt as it should have been in works prepared for the student and the intelligent general reader. In the six introductions which I have written for this anthology I have attempted to remedy this situation as far as circumstances permit: Although the evaluation of the Romantic Movement and of each of the five poets is my own, I am obviously indebted to those whose fresh examination of Romanticism has illuminated a subject previously quite dark.

Each of my introductions falls into two sections, the first, historical or biographical and the second, critical. Of these the first, dealing largely in fact, should be of some use to nearly all readers; the second is primarily for the advanced student. In dealing with each poet I have attempted to present something of the poet's own view of his art and its place in the larger

world. It is my hope that students will find each of these
aspects useful in approaching the poems and in understanding
the way in which the particular poet was a Romantic.
Ultimately, of course, all statements must be tested against the
poems themselves, and if in this process the introductions
stimulate differences of response and strong discussion rather
than merely dogmatic acceptance, they will have achieved one
of their major purposes.

> —WILLIAM H. MARSHALL
> *University of Pennsylvania*
> *Philadelphia, Pennsylvania*
> *February 15, 1963*

Contents

The Romantic Movement

THE ENGLISH ROMANTIC MOVEMENT belongs to the early nineteenth century. There is general agreement that its first major literary expression was William Wordsworth and Samuel Taylor Coleridge's *Lyrical Ballads,* published in 1798, for the second edition of which Wordsworth wrote a Preface, a kind of manifesto for the new poetry, that appeared in 1800. The date of the close of the Romantic Movement in England is less certainly a matter of accord. To some, accepting the implications of the terms used to name phases of social history, it might seem to be 1837, the year that Victoria became Queen; to others, recalling the long twilight years of William Wordsworth, it might more suitably be 1850, the year of his death; to still others, aware that most of Wordsworth's and nearly all of Coleridge's significant poetry was first written before middle life, it might be placed as early as 1824, the year in which Lord Byron died for the cause of Greek Independence. There are those who merely emphasize the fact to which nearly all agree, that the English Romantic Movement occurred during, and was presumably related to, a period of European upheaval, and any chronological limits imposed upon our idea of the Movement must be conceived of in terms of what was happening, socially and intellectually, in Europe itself. And this fact seems to be the most appropriate point from which to depart.

In October 1760, George II, King of England since 1727, died, leaving the throne to his twenty-two-year-old grandson. After his ascension, George III set forth upon a course designed to re-establish the absolutism which the Monarchy had lost in the Revolution of 1688. During the fifty-one years that he actively ruled—until, by the Regency Act of 1811, the then old King was declared incompetent and his son the Prince of Wales, later George IV, was made Prince Regent of England—

George III pursued this course of absolutism, though it was to conclude in failure, to cause England to lose her American colonies, and probably to hasten just those political and social developments which the King himself so violently feared. But George III, as conscientious and perhaps as stupid as Byron was to describe him in *The Vision of Judgment*, was never to understand the times in which he lived or the intellectual and social forces that were subtly at work in much of Europe. Neither was he to understand that for the first time in Western history the basic assumptions of the intelligentsia were shifting in a way that, during the two centuries following George's ascension, was to alter the history of the world and to affect the viewpoints and reactions of most men. George III was a product of his time, and as such he thought of the universe, reflected in man's activities and in his political and social structures, as orderly and unchanging, essentially a kind of grand mechanism.

This kind of absolutism, intellectual and social, of course dominated the minds ruling France as well as those ruling England. What George III intended to do, Louis XIV (1643-1715) had achieved and Louis XV (1715-1774) had sustained; however, the young man who came to the French throne in 1774 as Louis XVI was weaker than his forebears and ultimately unable to preserve a political and social system which, in its rigidity, had long outlived its usefulness. The French Revolution, beginning in 1789, is usually—and rightly—regarded as the episode marking the breakdown of the ancient order and the turning point toward the modern. But such a generalization, though eminently useful for establishing images of history in the human mind, can be enormously deceiving if accepted too literally. Though it has been proposed that the Revolution was the initial expression of the Romantic impulse, there is more reason to believe that in itself the French Revolution marks the end, and presumably the failure, of the Enlightenment—that period in intellectual history preceding the Romantic, of which the Revolution itself was the most significant political result.

In the wake of the breakdown of the single standard of faith which had moved most Medieval men as if they were one, European intellectuals developed various conceptions of the nature of the universe and man's place therein which for the most part, shared at least certain qualities. Responding principally to Isaac Newton's law of universal gravitation (1687), they used what was called "physics" as the basis for their philosophic systems, just as their Medieval forebears had used theology. In this way they conceived of, and in their various ways explained, the universe as a giant machine, whose unchanging operations, no matter how complicated, could be understood by man through the clear exercise of his reason. The Enlightenment, as the total movement of many diverse parts is called, thereby preserved the Medieval view of an orderly universe by putting reason and experience in the place that faith had once held; standards and values—the differences between good and evil, high and low—would seem to remain firm without the necessity of resting upon religious assumptions. What many could not foresee, though it may seem totally obvious to us, is that the methods of Enlightenment thinkers—empirical inquiry and logical exploration—would lead to assertions undermining the very standards and values that they had hoped to sustain.

Voltaire (1694-1778) and Jean-Jacques Rousseau (1712-1778), both social critics though in many ways antithetical, were part of the same movement. Their writings were of primary importance in influencing those intellectuals among the leaders of the oppressed and voiceless peasants and bourgeois of France. Much of the French Revolution was carried on in the name of Reason, the quality more exalted, of course, than any other by the Enlightenment; however, before the revolutionary activity abated, France experienced and Europe witnessed one of the most irrational and savage episodes in human history. The Revolution succeeded in bringing down an order which drew its support from fixed conceptions of the universe and society. It demonstrated the ultimate weakness of the many systems of thought influencing it which conceived of man merely as a mechanism; yet it brought forth nothing, either in intellectual or political systems, to replace that which it had destroyed. The French Revolution left Western European man much in the position of the speaker in Matthew Arnold's poem "Dover Beach," written nearly three generations later, long after the Romantic Movement in England had supposedly come to an end:

The Sea of Faith
Was once, too, at the full, and round earth's shore

Lay like the folds of a bright girdle furled.
But now I only hear
Its melancholy, long, withdrawing roar,
Retreating, to the breath
Of the night-wind, down the vast edges drear
And naked shingles of the world.

Ah, love, let us be true
To one another! for the world, which seems
To lie before us like a land of dreams,
So various, so beautiful, so new,
Hath really neither joy, nor love, nor light,
Nor certitude, nor peace, nor help for pain;
And we are here as on a darkling plain
Swept with confused alarms of struggle and flight,
Where ignorant armies clash by night.

The impact of the French Revolution upon England was obviously enormous. Most significant, perhaps, is its temporary alteration of the course of British political development. To many Englishmen who had taken a sympathetic view of the Colonists' position during the American Revolution, the very different movement in France, which its leaders would carry on as a war of liberation beyond French soil, represented a threat to individual liberty, property, constitutional government, and religion—an entire way of life characterized as British. From 1793 until the second fall of Napoleon, in 1815, Britain was intermittently at war with France; an entire generation grew up, much as in our own times, without certitude or peace. The war caused confusion in the public mind concerning the nature of constitutionally guaranteed freedom and gave the Tory government, supported in turn by the King and the Prince Regent, what excuse it needed for repressive measures, such as the periodic suspension of *habeas corpus*, the Seditious Meetings Act, and the Treasonable Practices Act. Though these and similar measures intensified the zeal of many working for internal reform, they seriously impeded progress: The trafficking in slaves was made illegal in 1807, but Catholic Emancipation did not become a reality until 1829, or the abolition of slavery itself until 1833.

Another force at work during these years, contributing heavily to the confusion in public life and private minds, was

the industrialization of England. This force was rapidly producing large new urban groups: the factory-owners, who now
joined the merchants as part of the middle classes, and the
factory-workers, who, more often than not during these years,
were badly exploited by their employers. Neither of these
groups, often at odds with each other, possessed sufficient channels to express their needs and wants. Parliament was to remain
the instrument of power of the agrarian aristocracy until the
passage of the first Reform Bill in 1832, and even this bill only
gave representation to a limited number of the upper middle
class. The workers were to remain for decades without a parliamentary voice; they had to depend for expression upon
demonstrations—which might bring the army down upon
them and result in violence or even massacre—or upon the
few men in Parliament who sympathized with their plight, such
as Sir Francis Burdett, or a small number of courageous jour-
nalists of advanced opinions, such as William Cobbett of *The
Political Register* and the brothers John and Leigh Hunt of
The Examiner. There were many repressive measures against
the English workers, notably the Frame-Breakers Act of 1812,
which provided the death penalty for those workers who broke
the machines that had forced them into technological unem-
ployment. It was not until 1833, the year following the enact-
ment of the Reform Bill, that the first Factory Act was passed.
This act provided minimal safeguards for children working in
the textile industries.

The Napoleonic Era came to an end at the Belgian town
of Waterloo, on June 18, 1815. Napoleon abdicated for the
second and final time and, in keeping with the decree of the
victors, he was exiled to St. Helena, a solitary island in the
South Atlantic. Here he was to remain until his death in 1821,
an ambiguous symbol to poet and peasant alike.

Reconstruction began, undertaken by those who would deny
the irreversible quality in human history; in the name of
"legitimacy," the Congress of Vienna imposed upon Europe a
peace settlement generally designed to re-establish the social
order that had existed before the French Revolution. The
Bourbons were restored to France in the person of Louis
XVIII, Lombardy and Venice became part of the Austrian
Empire, the rest of Italy was divided into numerous small
states, and Belgium and the Netherlands were united as one

kingdom. The authoritarian mind, from which the Treaty of Vienna emanated, influenced policies in matters not directly affected by the settlement. For example, when the Greeks began their struggle for independence against the decaying Ottoman Empire in 1821, the major powers withheld or on occasion prevented support for the Greeks, respecting the supposed "legitimacy" involved. It did not matter that, like the other peoples of Western Europe, they were Christians. For four years the only significant support given the revolution outside of Greece itself came from the Greek Committee. This committee was formed in London in 1823 by men who were identified with a consistent anti-Tory position. In 1827, it was only after the near-collapse of the Greek effort that Great Britain, Russia and France were sufficiently moved to intervene on behalf of Greece, which became independent in 1832.

By this time, however, the forces that had shaped the Treaty of Vienna were for the most part seriously weakened. In 1830, the Tory government of England fell, and with the passage of the Reform Bill two years later the middle classes at least began to achieve political power commensurate with their growing wealth. Also in 1830, Louis Philippe, Duke of Orleans, a radical member of a younger branch of the Bourbon family which was supported by the growing bourgeoisie, replaced Charles X, brother of Louis XVIII, on the throne of France. And this same year the Belgians successfully rebelled against the Dutch king and won their independence.

Europe in part reflected the change that, during the thirties, was passing over England. The society of Regency England (1811-1820), which Byron had known and immortalized in the final cantos of *Don Juan*, showed far less vitality during the reign of George IV (1820-1830) and in the following decade was yielding to the London businessman, in whose image a way of life and an Empire were to be constructed during the reign of Victoria. Wordsworth's rustics were in many instances being slowly displaced by machines; some were seeking economic salvation in the cities, and even if, unlike Luke in the poem "Michael," they survived morally, as most did, their values were irreversibly altered. Certainly, in time all were to feel the impact of the spread of the railway, the first line of which was opened beween Liverpool and Manchester that same year, 1830.

Of the five major poets identified with this era, at its close only Coleridge and Wordsworth remained. Coleridge, once a journalist championing freedom against the Tory repressions in the early years of the French Revolution, had grown steadily more conservative; rejecting his youthful Unitarianism for moderate Anglicanism and turning for the most part from poetry to metaphysics, he had become gradually detached from his own times, and in the two decades preceding his death in 1834 he was doing the work, principally in theology and in criticism, that was to exert a major influence on the remainder of his century and on ours. Wordsworth, who—more than most Englishmen of his time—was involved in and disillusioned by the French Revolution, had always been an agrarianist; as he witnessed the urban encroachment upon the English countryside, increasingly he came to distrust mankind in the mass, and his belief in the need for leadership, implicit even in his early critical theory, became the basis for an unswerving political position. He consistently associated leadership with the present order of society and during the last twenty years of his long life defied the forces of change in whatever form they might come to him.

But these men represented the older generation. The younger poets had died well before the close of the era which was hereafter to be associated with them: John Keats died in 1821, Percy Bysshe Shelley in 1822 and George Gordon Byron in 1824. Each had responded to the conditions of his age. There was a difference, however, for these men did not experience the intense disillusionment caused by the failure of the French Revolution. For this reason, perhaps, it was easier for them to maintain a consistent position than it was for the older poets. Keats was never committed to an organized social philosophy, though he was always intellectually preoccupied with the relation between life and art; Shelley affirmed certain highly related social and political ideals throughout his life; and Byron remained somewhat detached from the world around him, though on occasion he spoke in the House of Lords (*against* the Frame-Breakers Act and *for* Catholic Emancipation) and finally sacrificed his life and fortune on behalf of Greek freedom.

To return to the point of departure, it is of course impossible to point with precision to the end of the Romantic Movement

—presumably it came during the 1830's—but the question is really of slight importance. What is of major significance is the nature of the intellectual force dramatically at work during the era—Romanticism—and the degree to which it continued to be active through the later nineteenth century and into our own.

II

ROMANTICISM has frequently been defined in terms of one of its possible qualities—a return to nature, an increase in personal poetry, primitivism, or a disregard for literary genres and the "rules" of classic composition. In each instance there is an element of truth, however partial, but the impression that any of these statements might give is that Romanticism was somehow a kind of accident occurring in the early nineteenth century quite independent of any other forces; consequently, the effects of the entire movement might be wiped away merely with a reversion to "classicism." Such an impression is in most instances unintentional, for it implies a denial of the essentially irreversible nature of the historical process. During the last few decades certain literary critics and historians of ideas have worked intensely upon the problem of Romanticism, so that, despite their disagreement in particular areas, they have developed a general view of Romanticism which comprehends and interrelates those qualities in terms of which Romanticism has so frequently been defined.

From the remarks in the preceding section, it should be rather clear that Romanticism emerged as the failure of the Enlightenment became apparent to Western European thinkers. The process was, of course, not sudden, and when we deal with the philosophic minds of any age, we must make allowance for variation, among both individuals and cultural groups. Certainly during the last two decades of the eighteenth century belief in an ordered, beneficent and entirely meaningful universe was sustained only with increasing difficulties by conceiving of that universe in mechanistic terms.

During the eighteenth century in England not all literature was recognizably Popean or Johnsonian. Many works appearing throughout the century dealt in large measure with man in his natural condition, human emotion, or the creative activities of the mind—such poems as James Thomson's "The Seasons" (1726-1730), Edward Young's "Night Thoughts" (1742), Robert Blair's "The Grave" (1743), William Collins' "Odes" (1746), Thomas Warton's "The Pleasures of Melancholy" (1747), Thomas Gray's "Elegy Written in a Country Churchyard" (1750), and Mark Akenside's "The Pleasures of the Imagination" (1757); such novels as Horace Walpole's

Gothic work, *The Castle of Otranto* (1764), Henry Mac-
kenzie's sentimental *The Man of Feeling* (1771), and William
Beckford's Oriental tale, *Vathek* (1786). These were of course
to exert their measure of influence upon the English Romantic
writers of the nineteenth century; however, we cannot conclude
from this that the writers of these poems and novels were early
members, or even specific forerunners, of the Romantic Movement. Quite simply, for the most part they subscribed to the
mechanistic philosophy that lay at the heart of the Enlightenment, and in their work they were, in large measure, either
placing human emotion within the framework thus provided
or emotionally escaping from the rigidity of the philosophy
without rejecting its basic assumptions. Romanticism appears
only when this rejection occurs, which, for the majority of
intellectuals, was very near the end of the eighteenth century.

What had been a way of looking at things for more than a
century—a rationalism shared by most good minds which had
been the basis for theories and practices of art, music, literature, manners, even interior decoration—now appeared to find
little justification in the growing awareness that the universe
and man's experiences therein were essentially not static and
mechanically dependable but ever evolving and, like an organism, filled with unsuspected and diverse possibilities. The
collapse of the common sense of things left the early nineteenth-century thinker little to fall back upon but his own
evaluation of experience in terms that would vary from those
of other men.

During the Middle Ages, the Renaissance, and the Enlightenment, it had been possible to create a literature which
drew its metaphors and analogies from a fixed image of the
universe which all thinking men (in the Middle Ages, virtually
all men) would understand and poetically accept, such as the
order of virtues and vices implicit in both the meaning and
structure of Edmund Spenser's *The Faerie Queene*, the
geocentric cosmography employed in different ways by John
Donne in "The Second Anniversary" and John Milton in
Paradise Lost, or the great clock—the mechanism to which
various rationalist writers compared the universe. In the early
nineteenth century, however, this was no longer really possible
for most of the major literary figures. Allegory—the use of
symbols in a work of art in such a way that each symbol
represents only one quality and the fixed arrangement of the

symbols reflects the universal order of the qualities for which they stand—long a principal method in literature, as in John Bunyan's prose narrative *The Pilgrim's Progress* (1678), gave way to an employment of symbols in such a way that the relation of the symbols to each other remained fluid and each symbol carried an indefinite number of possible meanings. In effect, most literary artists could not still write the didactic work in which the reality was derived from a system of commonly accepted standards. In the place of this earlier type of work there frequently appeared the descriptive poem bearing occasional philosophic reflections that had no structural relation to the poem itself and were ultimately merely decorative, such as the first two cantos of Byron's *Childe Harold's Pilgrimage*. The mimetic function that earlier poetry had served now ceased to be really meaningful to many literary figures, for in any given case if the poet felt that he no longer understood the nature and structure of the universe, he could hardly write a poem imitating and explaining these.

At the beginning of the nineteenth century, therefore, each thinking, creative mind was in large measure left in isolation. In such a situation, what was a man to do? Only to exploit the possibilities of that very isolation, to construct out of his own experiences a body of values by which he could become reconciled to what seemed to him the failure of the older, externally imposed system. Stated another way, assuming that the self is the only possible source for understanding reality, he might move from an image of an integrated self to an image of an integrated and meaningful universe. There were those who, abandoning the rationalist view of a machine-like universe, were then unable to construct for themselves a body of values. These figures reveal in their thought and work what Morse Peckham has significantly called Negative Romanticism; Byron clearly offers the outstanding example in his time. Others, expressing what has similarly been called Positive Romanticism, were able to construct a system of values through which they could find meaning in their own experiences and in the larger universe: Coleridge in his æsthetic position, particularly revealed in his proposals about symbolic truth, or Shelley in his later idealism.

Thus, near the heart of Romanticism lies a kind of subjectivism, but this should not be regarded, as some of the anti-Romantic writers of more than a generation ago proposed,

merely as a kind of escapism. Instead, for many thinkers in the
early nineteenth century, this kind of subjectivism offered the
only courageous way of dealing with life: to pretend that one
could still find meaning in the rationalism of the Enlightenment when this indeed was not so was itself a form of escapism.
As M. H. Abrams has meaningfully pointed out, the poets at
the beginning of the nineteenth century not only for the most
part abandoned the mimetic in their work, but turned to the
expressive: Rather than reflect the nature of the outer world,
as it had done for ages past, poetry now served to express what
the poet would regard as his own inner light. For the first time
a truly personal literature developed, a literature based upon
the conscious belief of some, and the unconscious sense of
others, that only if the sense and its experiences were understood could there be a substratum for an understanding of,
and a belief in, outer reality. In the *Biographia Literaria*
(1817), no doubt the most important single critical work of
the English Romantic Movement, Samuel Taylor Coleridge
made the proposition that was implicit in much of the major
poetry of his own time: "We begin with the I KNOW MY-
SELF, in order to end with the absolute I AM. We proceed
from the SELF, in order to lose and find all self in GOD." For
Coleridge, the poet employing Imagination, the highest human
capacity and, in fact, Coleridge's basis for his claim to be a
poet, reflects divine creativity; from the reality of the former
he derives the basis for belief in the latter. Always implied is
the idea of the transcendental poet, the poet as prophet, which
is variously expressed in Romantic writings, particularly in
Wordsworth's and Shelley's rather precise statements.

It is not surprising, therefore, to find among the works of the
five major English Romantic poets an impressive number of
personal, in fact clearly biographical, poems. It is important, in
establishing a context for reading and interpreting these works,
to understand the times and circumstances of those who wrote
them. But one of the unfortunate by-products of Romanticism
has been the development of the tendency on the part of some
critics to consider a personal poem *entirely* within the biographical context. For these critics the poem assumes significance because it reveals the poet as a personality, whereas
in actuality a knowledge of the poet is important because it
offers an instrument, which we might choose on occasion to
discard later, for an initial approach to the poem. Ultimately,

of course, a Romantic poem, like any work of art, constitutes a reality in itself, which must be comprehended on its own terms. We must not assume that because any one of these poems takes the form of a personal record, it is necessarily a spontaneous confession written in a moment of emotional intensity; we must not, in other words, fail to make the distinction between the *occasion* of the poem, the situation described therein, on one hand, and the *meaning* and *structure*, on the other. Nor, in many instances, should we take the self denoted by the pronoun *I* as the poet's own being. Even in an autobiographical work, the poem itself determines the degree to which the speaker can be literally identified with the *whole* personality of the poet. In other instances, the problem is less subtle. The speaker in *The Rime of the Ancient Mariner*, for example, must be first taken for what the total poem makes him out to be—an old sailor who has endured an extraordinarily horrible experience, from which he has emerged with both a sense of guilt and an emotional need to find a basis for believing in the essential goodness of a universe in which such an experience is possible. In Byron's "The Prisoner of Chillon," the speaker, unlike the Mariner in bearing no guilt, moves from faith in himself to faith in the world. In neither instance is the speaker in the poem identifiable with the poet who wrote it, though he might make statements reflecting attitudes of the poet.

These two poems, like others cast as third-person narratives or dramas—such as Shelley's *Alastor* or *Prometheus Unbound*—concern the central problem for the Romantic thinker: the reconstruction of a basis for certitude after the failure, sometimes brought on by an act or experience, of an older system of belief. Since the patterns of movement may at first seem similar, it is important to make a distinction between what in earlier literature is concerned with the fall from grace and regeneration, such as the story of the Redcrosse Knight's escape from Despayre in the first book of *The Faerie Queene*, and those accounts of doubt and reaffirmation given in various forms by the Romantic poets. In the earlier literature, the only variable is the individual soul living in a just and meaningful creation in which he must find his place: His story is essentially one of departure and return. In Romantic literature, all things outside the individual self seem variable: The course is the rejection of one set of values and the subjective reconstitution of another. In the earlier literature, spiritual salvation is an absolute condition to which the individual soul aspires and which he can achieve with finality: It is a state of *being*. In Romantic literature personal salvation is attained so long as the individual self continues to find a basis for affirmation: It is a state of constant *becoming*. There is for the Romantic thinker, unlike his predecessor in the Enlightenment, no such thing as an absolute goal or achievable perfection, but only the continual act of seeking, a process itself. Demogorgon's final speech in *Prometheus Unbound* makes it clear that for man himself Promethean regeneration is a state that is never final. To think in terms of conceivable and attainable absolutes, of states of *being* rather than of *becoming*, would be to imagine the universe as a mechanism rather than as an organism, evolving and filled with unsuspected potential. This would be, in effect, to accept once more the primary assumptions of the Enlightenment, the rejection of which made the Romantic thinkers what they were. The paradox of imperfection, by which man believes that though he can never achieve perfection he must continually move toward it if he is to find self-realization, is an essential aspect of Romanticism.

For present purposes there remains little except to deal explicitly with that question which preceded the opening of this section: whether Romanticism ceased to find expression in, say, 1830, or persisted beyond what we have long called the Romantic Movement. At this point the answer is perhaps rather obvious. In its positive forms Romanticism has accepted the human dilemma for what it is, paradoxically making man's imperfection the basis for continual act and affirmation; in its negative form it has left man without certitude. The principal manifestation of Romanticism in literature is to be found in those works concerned with the search for reality by means of the quest for self-identity or full self-expression. The major English Victorian poets were therefore Romantic. Alfred Tennyson's poetry frequently deals with the problem of sustaining the image of the self through disillusionment, uncertainty, and pain: "The Lady of Shalott" reveals failure, "In Memoriam," ultimate triumph. Robert Browning concerned himself with the unending process of personal realization, which was necessarily based upon acceptance of the paradox of imperfection. Matthew Arnold was fundamentally interested in the problem of intellectual isolation, a problem indeed familiar to Arnold's predecessors. In the major novels of the nineteenth century, we find an increasing use of dramatic or interior monologue, in which the protagonist records experiences with the hope that, both in terms of the experiences recorded and by the very act of recording them, he can put together the pieces of his life and thereby derive an image of universal order: Charlotte Brontë's *Jane Eyre*, Charles Dickens' *David Copperfield*, and William Makepeace Thackeray's *Henry Esmond*. Later, the patterns by which the novel as a form serves this essentially Romantic function become more complex and varied. The record of the quest for self-identity is a dominant form of the twentieth-century novel, exemplarily found perhaps in James Joyce's *Ulysses*. In other areas of intellectual activity, philosophies built upon the assumption that reality begins with the self and modern psychology, we find, if not partial expressions of, movements that are clearly related to what we mean by Romanticism.

It is reasonable to say that the Romantic Movement occurred in the early nineteenth century if by this we are referring to the initial impulse of a cultural force and wish only to isolate the period of this impulse from those of later expressions of the same force. Quite clearly, Romanticism continues to express itself as dynamically and variously today as it did more than a century and a half ago. For this reason the five poets presented here have more to say to us than we might sometimes suspect.

THE
MAJOR
ENGLISH
ROMANTIC
POETS

Samuel Taylor Coleridge

1772=1834

Samuel Taylor Coleridge

SAMUEL TAYLOR COLERIDGE was born October 21, 1772, the tenth child of John Coleridge, Vicar of Ottery St. Mary in Devon. The boy first attended his father's own school, for it was planned that he should be prepared for ultimate ordination in the Church of England. In October 1781, however, John Coleridge died, and the following year Samuel entered Christ's Hospital, the London school for orphan boys. His life as a "blue coat boy" lasted nine years, until the summer of 1791. The Master of the Upper Grammar School at Christ's Hospital, the Reverend James Boyer, a strict and conscientious man, took a particular interest in Coleridge's intellectual development and directed him in ways which, though perhaps not fully apparent to the boy, were to seem essential to Coleridge the poet and critic. "I learnt from him, that Poetry . . . had a logic of its own, as severe as that of science," Coleridge recorded many years later in the first chapter of the *Biographia Literaria* (1817). Much of his mature activity was directed toward the explanation and illustration of this proposition.

In February 1791, Samuel Taylor Coleridge was elected to a sizarship at Jesus College, Cambridge, where he proceeded the following October. All considered, his years at Cambridge were without great value. He was interested in politics, taking the anti-Tory position and opposing the war with France, but he was also preoccupied with thoughts of Mary Evans, whom he had met before he came to Cambridge. His use of opium, though quite limited, is supposed to have begun at this time, and his debts accumulated over the several years he spent at Cambridge. In much that he did, a high degree of indecision was apparent. Probably the most unfortunate episode, sometimes regarded as comic rather than grotesque, was Coleridge's enlistment, in December 1793, in the 15th Light Dragoons under the name "Silas Tomkyn Comberbache," preserving

3

thereby the initials by which history was to know him. After an extraordinarily unsuccessful military career and through the intercession of friends who had become aware of his folly, Coleridge was discharged in April 1794 and returned to Cambridge.

Two months later, visiting Oxford, Coleridge met Robert Southey. Both were enthusiastic young intellectuals intent upon reform and social justice. It is not at all surprising that out of their association came the idea for "Pantisocracy," a utopian community to be established along the banks of the Susquehanna in America; here the participants would share the physical work and rewards as well as each other's ideas. Southey was at this time engaged to Edith Fricker, and it was planned that she would accompany him to Pantisocracy; to the utopian planners it seemed only convenient that Coleridge should become pledged to Edith's sister Sara. Leaving Cambridge in December 1794 (though he allowed his name to remain on the registry until the following June), Coleridge went to London, where there followed a period of agonizing indecision. In October 1795, under further pressure from Southey and with some renewed hope that Pantisocracy would become a reality, Coleridge proceeded to Bristol and married Sara Fricker. The following month Southey and Edith were married, but by this time Pantisocracy could no longer be regarded as a meaningful possibility, and soon after this realization Southey departed for Lisbon.

Samuel and Sara Coleridge spent the first weeks of their marriage at Clevedon, near the Bristol Channel, the occasion for the two poems "The Eolian Harp" and "Reflections on Having Left a Place of Retirement." Like the speaker in the latter of these, Coleridge felt compelled to return to the world of "honourable toil" and "to fight the bloodless fight" for justice and freedom. By December 1795, he was making plans to publish a newspaper, *The Watchman*, which was to serve as guardian of public liberty against the infringements of the Tory ministry; the next month he was journeying to various cities to procure subscriptions, which he received in numbers insufficient for publication to begin in February, as he had planned. *The Watchman* appeared for the first time in March and, with the tenth number, for the last time in May 1796, leaving its writer and editor with new debts and an even more intense sense of failure and uncertainty. Coleridge's first volume of verse, *Poems on Various Subjects,* was published during this time; however, it did nothing to ease his financial situation, which was rendered more difficult by the birth of his first child, David Hartley, in September 1796. An attack of neuralgia two months later is supposed to have increased his habitual use of laudanum which, nevertheless, still remained moderate. In January 1797, the Coleridges settled in a cottage at Stowey, provided for them by the poet's friend and patron Thomas Poole, and here—as thinker, poet, and momentarily Unitarian preacher—Coleridge was to spend the most important period of his life.

Coleridge had met William Wordsworth in 1795, but their acquaintance was no more than casual until March 1797, when Thomas Poole took a house at Alfoxden, near the Bristol Channel and but a few miles from Stowey, for Wordsworth and his sister, Dorothy. Except for Coleridge's brief sojourn to Shrewsbury, Shropshire, which William Hazlitt was to record years later in his memorable essay "My First Acquaintance with Poets," Wordsworth and Coleridge were close to each other until the late summer of 1798. Although the two poets were of diverse, if not antithetical, temperaments, for this short period their differences made them complementary to each other. Coleridge achieved his highest level of poetic activity, lasting several months, and Wordsworth, aided by Coleridge and Dorothy, moved from the intellectual despair brought on by his disillusioning experiences in France during the Revolution to a point of reaffirmation. The most significant result of the association of the two poets was the *Lyrical Ballads,* published in 1798, a volume principally containing Wordsworth's poems, though Coleridge contributed "The Rime of the Ancient Mariner," "The Foster-Mother's Tale," "The Nightingale," and "The Dungeon." As the Advertisement for the first edition explained, the poems in the volume were experimental, both in content and metrics. But the explanation was insufficient. Even though in time the small first edition was exhausted, the unprepared reading public remained, if not hostile, at least unenthusiastic, so that Wordsworth felt the need to write his historic Preface to the second edition, which was published in 1800.

In the late spring of 1798, after the Wordsworths had terminated their lease at Alfoxden and Coleridge had said farewell for a time to Sara and their children, the three com-

panions set forth for Germany. It was becoming apparent that
the Coleridge marriage was no stronger than the scheme for
Pantisocracy from which it had emerged, and in time it was to
terminate just as unhappily. Their temporary separation during
Coleridge's German tour intensified existing strains, which became even more apparent after the death of their second son,
Berkeley, in February 1799. But Germany does not represent
merely personal failure in the life of Coleridge. Soon separating
from the Wordsworths because he wished to learn German,
he continued studying, thinking and conversing, and in July
1799 he returned to England, immersed in the ideas of the
German Transcendentalists. Although scholars have differed
strongly on the degree to which Coleridge was influenced by
the German critics, it is clear that his own development as a
critic was at least accelerated by his firm introduction to
German culture. Coleridge was not in any total sense original
as a critic; nevertheless, though the ideas of the German
philosophers doubtless influenced his own, they were synthesized in his mind and emerged as we find them in the
Biographia Literaria and the *Philosophical Lectures*, among
various other works characteristically English and "Coleridgean."

After his return to England, Coleridge achieved a reconciliation with Robert Southey, from whom, understandably perhaps, there had been some estrangement; then he rejoined his
family at Stowey. Soon he met Sara Hutchinson—the sister of
Wordsworth's fiancée, Mary—who was for many years to
become the object of Coleridge's intense but hopeless love.
He settled in London, where he wrote for *The Morning Post*
during the first four months of 1800 and translated Schiller's
play *Wallenstein* into two parts, *The Piccolomini* and *The
Death of Wallenstein*, both published but without financial
success later that year.

Coleridge's health had never been good. At the age of six he
had run away from home and spent the night on the damp
ground, and from this time forth he had been subject to recurring attacks of a rheumatic nature. By 1800, physical decline,
assisted no doubt by the increasing use of opium, was becoming apparent. In the summer of that year he was in Keswick,
Cumberland, where his family lodged with Southey at Greta
Hall. The Wordsworths were at nearby Grasmere, but the
"Annus Mirabilis" of 1797-98 was now over, and there were

new strains arising from Coleridge's growing attraction to Sara
Hutchinson, who kept house for a brother living near Durham.
Coleridge addressed to her, as a letter in April 1802, the early
form of the poem that we know as "Dejection: An Ode." He
had begun to doubt his poetic powers, and indeed he was to
write little poetry of absolute quality in the three decades that
remained. The causes for his lack of creativity have been assigned to various factors, such as his growing interest in metaphysics, his use of opium, and his shift from early revolutionary
enthusiasm, which began in 1802, when Napoleon ceased to
appear to him as a political savior. Coleridge's marriage was
now entering its last unhappy phase. In fact, while he traveled
he left his wife at Greta Hall, where she was to remain after
the separation—an ironic reminder to Robert Southey of
earlier and pleasanter days.

Restlessness and bad health moved Coleridge to consider
the value of another journey abroad, and in time he settled
upon Malta, where he arrived in May 1804. The following
January he was appointed to a government post, as acting
Public Secretary. He was in Naples in December 1805, escaping to Rome the following month, only ten days before the
arrival of French forces; in Rome he again eluded the French,
who, he believed, sought his arrest for remarks he had recently
made about Napoleon in *The Morning Post.* Coleridge arrived back in England in August 1806, much worse in condition and appearance for his once-intended therapeutic journey.

The years following Coleridge's return from Southern
Europe are generally regarded as constituting the lowest and
loneliest period of his personal life. He proceeded, rather in-
directly, to Greta Hall, where he persuaded Mrs. Coleridge,
somewhat hesitant because of public opinion, to agree to a
separation. During these years his relations with the Wordsworths continued to be strained, in part because the differences
in temperament between the two poets were increasingly apparent and certainly because Coleridge's persisting love for Sara
Hutchinson created a most difficult situation. During 1811 and
1812 there was deep estrangement which, though followed by a
reconciliation, left a permanent mark on the relationship between the two poets. Coleridge was once more involved in a
journalistic venture, this time in the form of a weekly called
The Friend, which appeared for twenty-seven irregular numbers in 1809 and 1810 before it failed, leaving Coleridge with

debts of several hundred pounds. He himself wrote most of the copy for this journal, of which the avowed purpose was to "uphold those truths and those merits, which are founded in the nobler and more permanent parts of our nature." During these years Coleridge's use of opium had become a serious affliction.

In April 1816, after the intercession on his behalf by friends, Samuel Taylor Coleridge came to stay for a month at the house of Dr. James Gillman at Highgate. He hoped that the medical man might be able to relieve him of his addiction to opium and restore him to health. Here he remained for the last eighteen years of his life, never cured of his addiction, though yielding to it in comparative moderation. He appeared to be prematurely old to the many who came to hear him talk and to learn from him, but his great intellect remained active to the last. "The Sage of Highgate" died July 25, 1834.

Ironically, Coleridge did much of his major work during the decade following his return from Malta and particularly during the eighteen years passed at the house of James Gillman. His play *Remorse*, a revision of a much earlier work entitled *Osorio*, ran for twenty performances at the Drury Lane Theatre in the winter of 1813. More impressive certainly are the literary lectures, particularly the ones on Shakespeare and on the problems of philosophy, which he gave from 1808 onward. Although the volume which included "Christabel," "Kubla Khan, a Vision" and "The Pains of Sleep" was published in 1816 and fresh poems were added to the various new editions of his work, Coleridge's major activity during these years was philosophic and critical. His work had overtones of his now firm conservatism in politics and the trinitarianism in religion to which he had fully returned. Of these works, the most important are the *Biographia Literaria*, published in 1817, a seemingly disjointed but actually complex and highly ordered statement of the foundations for all Coleridgean criticism, and the *Aids to Reflection*, published in 1825, which develops the metaphysical and theological implications of the view of organic unity dominating Coleridge's literary criticism. In other words, in his later years Coleridge presented what in time came to be regarded as the *rationale* for much of the major Romantic poetry, including of course his own.

II

Throughout his critical writings Coleridge offered various definitions of a poem. Of these perhaps the most direct occurs in the fourteenth chapter of the *Biographia Literaria:*

> A poem is that species of composition, which is opposed to works of science, by proposing for its *immediate* object pleasure, not truth; and from all other species (having *this* object in common with it) it is discriminated by proposing to itself such delight from the *whole,* as is compatible with a distinct gratification from each component part.

In his Shakespearean criticism Coleridge emphasized that the pleasure conveyed by poetry is essentially *intellectual.* Thus, it becomes apparent that the mind operates at two levels, that dealing with finite things, obviously the lower level, and that concerned with ideas. Elsewhere Coleridge made the distinction explicit between the *Understanding,* whose province is bound by time and space, and the *Reason,* with which man apprehends higher, transcending truth. Of those forms of composition directed toward man's higher intellectual capacities, collectively called the Reason, a poem is unlike all others in that the pleasure it brings arises from the reader's necessary response to the total work rather than merely to any part. The unity of the poem is, in fact, essential, for, properly brought together, the various parts of the poem are no longer distinguishable, and the poem itself has become a reality that can be apprehended only in its own terms.

How does a poem come to be? In various places Coleridge insisted that what many had regarded as poetry was mere verse. The works of Alexander Pope, Coleridge remarked in the first chapter of the *Biographia Literaria,* were "characterized not so much by poetic thoughts, as by thoughts *translated* into the language of poetry." The function of the poet is not merely mechanical, a fitting of words to lines, as practiced by the English classical poets of the preceding century. Instead, the poetic act is as organic as the response to poetry which it anticipates: "The poet, described in *ideal* perfection, brings the whole soul of man into activity, with the subordination of its faculties to each other, according to their relative worth and dignity." The power by which the poet fuses all elements is what Coleridge called *imagination*, as distinguished from *fancy*. In its highest form imagination, possessed only by the poet, "dissolves, diffuses, dissipates, in order to recreate"; whereas fancy merely allows the mind to consider impressions such as the elements of memory outside of "the order of time and space." The difference between the two in Coleridge's view is, to use a rather fundamental analogy, like the difference between chemical and physical change: In the imagination, as in chemical action, elements brought together will be synthesized, producing what is a composite of *all* of these elements but neither reducible to nor definable as any one in particular; in the operation of the fancy, as in physical change, the elements entering the process may alter in size or shape, distribution or importance within the accumulation, but each retains its essential distinctness and integrity. The imagination reconciles what in a world of mere time and space might appear to be opposing forces, thereby creating the total unity that constitutes the poem. For Coleridge the seat of the imagination is in the unconscious part of the mind. Thus, though one using fancy and operating at a conscious level knows what he does and has full control over an essentially mechanical process, the poet, reacting to the force deep within him, creates a work that far surpasses the merely mechanical aspect of its structure or the intentional aspect of its creation. The poet apprehends and in his poem communicates to other men essential and transcending truth, which they cannot understand for themselves. In so doing he presumably gives to his poem qualities drawn from the unconscious part of his mind, of which he would never consciously be aware.

Quite obviously, Coleridge defined a poem in terms of substance as well as form. The relation between the idea from which the poem springs and the words of a poem is organic: In the ideal poem the words are of the best possible choice for the expression of the idea; to alter the words, in sequence or number, is to weaken the poem—in effect to destroy it as an ideal poem. It is in this sense that the pleasure which the reader derives is necessarily conditioned by an awareness of the whole rather than of the component parts. Or, pursued further, if one element cannot be substituted for another within the poem, then certainly the poem itself cannot be translated into a prose statement of its meaning without losing all of the qualities which distinguish it from what Coleridge called "science." To use Coleridge's distinction, a true poem is "not a copy, but an imitation, of nature"; science or a paraphrase of the poem is merely a copy.

Once more the implications are rather apparent: To be a poem, a work of literature must transcend the temporal and spatial limits of the experience from which it has been derived. "It is for the Biographer, not the Poet, to give the *accidents of individual Life*," Coleridge wrote to William Wordsworth in 1815. "Whatever is not representative, generic, may be indeed most poetically exprest, but it is not Poetry." In the *Biographia Literaria*, published two years later, Coleridge went further, proposing that one "promise of genius is the choice of subjects very remote from the private interests and circumstances of the writer himself. At least I have found, that where the subject is taken immediately from the author's personal sensations and experiences, the excellence of a particular poem is but an equivocal mark, and often a fallacious pledge, of genuine poetic power." Despite this assertion, among the most esteemed poems of Samuel Taylor Coleridge are seven which are quite clearly personal: "The Eolian Harp," "Reflections on Having Left a Place of Retirement," "This Lime-tree Bower my Prison," "Frost at Midnight," "Fears in Solitude," "Dejection: An Ode" and "The Pains of Sleep." Coleridge himself would quite readily meet any objection by proposing that in each case the subject was not "taken *immediately* from the author's personal sensations and experiences" (italics mine) but passed through the deep well of the imagination, emerging as "representative" and "generic." Thus, the poem now far transcends the limits of the particular experience with which it appears to deal; it has a being of its own as distinct and real as that of the experience itself. Demonstration far surpasses assertion in critical matters, however, and for this purpose the first of these poems, "The Eolian Harp," may serve.

The title of the poem refers to the instrument produced by stretching strings in or across a box in such a way that, placed in a window or another exposed position, it yields harmonic sounds when the wind passes through it. Implicit in the title is the idea of that which is passive, can be moved, and is perceivable—imaged by the harp—and of that which is active, moves, and can be imagined or conceived—imaged by the wind

—and of the harmony produced when these two come together. The occasion described is the retreat of the speaker and
his bride shortly after their marriage. This retreat is symbolized
by the "white-flower'd Jasmin, and the broad-leav'd Myrtle"
with which the speaker opens his description of their cottage.
The harp and the wind also have a symbolic as well as merely
environmental relation to the couple. The woman "Sara," like
the harp, exists at the level of perception: Her feminine potential, the passive quality in her association with her husband,
can only be realized by the love of her husband, just as the
harp's musical potential can be actualized only by the force
of the wind. The mundane thoughts of the woman receive
significance only from the imaginings, conceptions and faith of
her husband. Thus, two dominant themes suggested in the title
are established in the poem: (1) the passive, the actual, the
perceivable and the female, expressed primarily by the presence
of the woman Sara and symbolized by the eolian harp; (2) the
active, the potential, the conceptual or imaginative and the
male, expressed primarily by the speaker's awareness of himself
and by the ideas concerning the life-force which are in his own
mind and symbolized by the harp-moving wind. In terms of
these two motifs, the poem divides into five phases: (I) lines
1-25, (II) 26-33, (III) 34-43, (IV) 44-48, (V) 49-64; the first
and third phase express motif (1), the second and fourth motif
(2), and the fifth constitutes the resolution of the two motifs.
Though not expressly so, the poem implicitly follows the structure of the ode, having two strophes, two antistrophes and the
epode.

Thus, in the first phase of the poem (lines 1-25), the
speaker describes the actual and perceivable scene that faces
him, dominated by "My pensive Sara" and the harp, "that
simplest Lute." Both are passive and feminine, Sara as a bride
and the harp "by the desultory breeze caress'd,/ Like some coy
maid half yielding to her lover." The passive "clouds, that late
were rich with light" and the reflective "star of eve" frame the
scene. The actual, "the world so hush'd," implies a potential
of sound and movement. In the second phase of the poem
(lines 26-33), the speaker affirms the potential just implied:
"the mute still air/ Is Music slumbering on her instrument."
This symbolizes the active, universal force, "the one Life
within us and abroad," the "soul" of "motion" and the essence
of reality, "A light in sound, a sound-like power in light,/

Rhythm in all thought." It is of course significant that during the second phase of the poem the woman Sara, appearing in the first phase, is not present in the speaker's thoughts. In the third phase (lines 34-43), the speaker, once more describing the scene of which Sara is the center, makes explicit the theme of passivity. It is first the passivity of sense—"I stretch my limbs at noon,/ Whilst through my half-clos'd eye-lids I behold/ The sunbeams dance, like diamonds, on the main"— which suggests in turn the passivity of mind as the speaker "tranquil muse[s] upon tranquillity," and thoughts and "idle flitting phantasies" pass over his "indolent and passive brain." Once more the speaker considers the eolian harp, the object of "wild and various random gales," to which his thoughts, "uncall'd and undetain'd" by his receptive mind, are compared. Hence, one of the symbolic values of the harp, the intellectual faculty, implied in the first phase of the poem by the association of the harp and "pensive Sara," is made explicit in the third. The relation between nature, as the setting of the first phase of the poem, and the mind, as the setting of the third, is clarified in the fourth (lines 44-48). In this phase nature is compared to the harp in order to emphasize not its actual and perceivable state but the potential heights to which the soul, or vital principle, of each form in nature can carry that form:

> And what if all of animated nature
> Be but organic Harps diversely fram'd,
> That tremble into thought, as o'er them sweeps
> Plastic and vast, one intellectual breeze,
> At once the Soul of each, and God of all?

The final section of the poem (lines 49-64) resolves the differences between the two motifs. Once more the speaker describes the actual scene, as he did in the first and third phases, but now, by the contemplation of the harp in both its decorative and symbolic functions, he has reached the point in his meditations where he can propose that faith is the mover of the mind, as the wind is the mover of the harp: The individual thinker, like the speaker himself in these very contemplations, is one of the many "organic Harps diversely fram'd." That his mind has been moved by faith in a force transcending the limits of his particular thoughts and his particular situation, that he has been able to fuse the two motifs, is demonstrated, he asserts, by his possession of "Peace, and this Cot, and thee, heart-honour'd Maid!"

"The Eolian Harp" is ideally Coleridgean. Its occasion is personal, but it should be clear that the relation between the speaker in the poem and "Sara," their marriage itself, is not simply what the poet Coleridge was recollecting or celebrating from his own life but, like the harp in the window of the idealized couple's cottage, both a fact and a symbol, the point of departure for the construction of a complicated poetic unit.

The number of Coleridge's poems which by his own standards could be considered successful may seem limited. The reasons are several. First, the Coleridge canon is restricted since his major activity as a poet covered only a few years at the turn of the century. Secondly, Coleridge did not immediately free himself from the effects of his own eighteenth-century background: In some of the poems of his early period there are traces of badly weakened devices, such as the personification of abstract qualities and formal apostrophe, which are characteristic of an earlier poetry and which seem strangely inappropriate to Coleridge's subjects and treatment. Finally, some poems clearly show the effects of writing hurriedly upon an occasion in such a way that the particulars of the occasion are never assimilated into the organic structure of the poem. The fundamental idea in Coleridge's criticism is organicism, the essence of which is qualitative, so that, judged by his own basic standards, by the quality of his achievement rather than by the frequency with which any quality is achieved, Coleridge is a major poet.

The most striking instance of qualitative achievement is to be found in the so-called *magic triad*, by which to many persons Coleridge is entirely known: "The Rime of the Ancient Mariner," "Kubla Khan" and "Christabel." Unlike many of his other major poems, these demand the ultimate response in the reader, "that willing suspension of disbelief that constitutes poetic faith." The poet does not ask that his reader believe but merely that he cease to disbelieve. Poetic faith consists, Coleridge remarked in a discussion of a Shakespearean scene, "not in the mind's judging it to be a forest, but in its remission of the judgment that it is not a forest." Of course, this ultimate response limits the degree to which the reader can apply the standards of logic and ordinary prose-meanings to the poems in question. Moreover, two of the poems in the triad, "Kubla Khan" and "Christabel," were not finished, a fact which may complicate any evaluation of them in terms of organic unity; the result is that any attempt to isolate the verbal "meaning" of these poems, a practice in itself not consistent with Coleridgean criteria, is particularly futile.

"The Rime of the Ancient Mariner" occupies a special place among Coleridge's poems. It demands poetic faith, but at the same time it possesses organic unity and even contains a complete story. Among the rather realistic scenes of the Mariner's encounter with the Wedding Guest, the old sailor himself recounts an episode abounding in the supernatural. The tendency of some readers may be to try to make this story comprehensible in terms of ordinary experience, reducing it to what appears at first sight to be its moral message as enunciated by the Mariner in the third from final stanza—"He prayeth best, who loveth best/ All things both great and small"—or by interpreting it *merely* as Coleridge's expression of his own sense of guilt or of failure at the supposed loss of his poetic powers. Either interpretation involves an oversimplification: The first overlooks the fact that, whatever else it may be, "The Rime of the Ancient Mariner" is a dramatic monologue within a frame; that as a consequence, the utterances by the Mariner, moral or otherwise, must be regarded first in terms of the larger structure of the poem rather than taken at face value. The second confuses the history of the poem—part of which might well be Coleridge's use of the poem for personal expression— and the poem itself as a distinct reality existing outside of historical time and revealing meaning, structure and value.

In responding to the various individual interpretations of "The Rime of the Ancient Mariner" or of any other major Coleridgean poem, the reader must not fall into the error of believing that one interpretation alone is possible. If he does, he is then reading the poem as an allegory, which is, in Coleridge's words, "nothing but a translation of abstract notions into a picture-language which is itself nothing but an abstraction from objects of the senses." Instead, the reader should regard the poem as a complex work of symbolism operating at many levels and revealing indefinite possibilities of meaning, an absolutely integrated whole, each of whose dynamic parts— the symbol itself—continually assumes new force and value because of its relation to the total structure. The reader's own response, then, continually assumes new scope and intensity, and he experiences the pleasure which Coleridge believed is the essential gift of poetry.

Samuel Taylor Coleridge

THE EOLIAN HARP

COMPOSED AT CLEVEDON, SOMERSETSHIRE

My pensive Sara! thy soft cheek reclined
Thus on mine arm, most soothing sweet it is
To sit beside our Cot, our Cot o'ergrown
With white-flower'd Jasmin, and the broad-leav'd Myrtle,
(Meet emblems they of Innocence and Love!)   5
And watch the clouds, that late were rich with light,
Slow saddening round, and mark the star of eve
Serenely brilliant (such should Wisdom be)
Shine opposite! How exquisite the scents
Snatch'd from yon bean-field! and the world so hush'd   10
The stilly murmur of the distant Sea
Tells us of silence.
                And that simplest Lute,
Placed length-ways in the clasping casement, hark!
How by the desultory breeze caress'd,
Like some coy maid half yielding to her lover,   15
It pours such sweet upbraiding, as must needs
Tempt to repeat the wrong! And now, its strings
Boldlier swept, the long sequacious notes
Over delicious surges sink and rise,
Such a soft floating witchery of sound   20
As twilight Elfins make, when they at eve
Voyage on gentle gales from Fairy-Land,
Where Melodies round honey-dropping flowers,
Footless and wild, like birds of Paradise,
Nor pause, nor perch, hovering on untam'd wing!   25
O! the one Life within us and abroad,
Which meets all motion and becomes its soul,
A light in sound, a sound-like power in light,
Rhythm in all thought, and joyance every where—
Methinks, it should have been impossible   30
Not to love all things in a world so fill'd;
Where the breeze warbles, and the mute still air
Is Music slumbering on her instrument.

   And thus, my Love! as on the midway slope
Of yonder hill I stretch my limbs at noon,   35

Whilst through my half-clos'd eye-lids I behold
The sunbeams dance, like diamonds, on the main,
And tranquil muse upon tranquillity;
Full many a thought uncall'd and undetain'd,
And many idle flitting phantasies,   40
Traverse my indolent and passive brain,
As wild and various as the random gales
That swell and flutter on this subject Lute!
    And what if all of animated nature
Be but organic Harps diversely fram'd,   45
That tremble into thought, as o'er them sweeps
Plastic and vast, one intellectual breeze,
At once the Soul of each, and God of all?
    But thy more serious eye a mild reproof
Darts, O belovéd Woman! nor such thoughts   50
Dim and unhallow'd dost thou not reject,
And biddest me walk humbly with my God.
Meek Daughter in the family of Christ!
Well hast thou said and holily disprais'd
These shapings of the unregenerate mind;   55
Bubbles that glitter as they rise and break
On vain Philosophy's aye-babbling spring.
For never guiltless may I speak of him,
The Incomprehensible! save when with awe
I praise him, and with Faith that inly *feels*;   60
Who with his saving mercies healéd me,
A sinful and most miserable man,
Wilder'd and dark, and gave me to possess
Peace, and this Cot, and thee, heart-honour'd Maid!
   [1795]

REFLECTIONS ON HAVING LEFT A PLACE OF RETIREMENT

SERMONI PROPRIORA.—HOR.

Low was our pretty Cot: our tallest Rose
Peep'd at the chamber-window. We could hear
At silent noon, and eve, and early morn,
The Sea's faint murmur. In the open air
Our Myrtles blossom'd; and across the porch   5

Thick Jasmins twined: the little landscape round
Was green and woody, and refresh'd the eye.
It was a spot which you might aptly call
The Valley of Seclusion! Once I saw
(Hallowing his Sabbath-day by quietness)   10
A wealthy son of Commerce saunter by,
Bristowa's citizen: methought, it calm'd
His thirst of idle gold, and made him muse
With wiser feelings: for he paus'd, and look'd
With a pleas'd sadness, and gaz'd all around,   15
Then eyed our Cottage, and gaz'd round again,
And sigh'd, and said, it was a Blesséd Place.
And we were bless'd. Oft with patient ear
Long listening to the viewless sky-lark's note
(Viewless, or haply for a moment seen   20
Gleaming on sunny wings) in whisper'd tones
I've said to my Belovéd, 'Such, sweet Girl!
The inobtrusive song of Happiness,
Unearthly minstrelsy! then only heard
When the Soul seeks to hear; when all is hush'd,   25
And the Heart listens!'
                              But the time, when first
From that low Dell, steep up the stony Mount
I climb'd with perilous toil and reach'd the top,
Oh! what a goodly scene! Here the bleak mount,
The bare bleak mountain speckled thin with sheep;   30
Grey clouds, that shadowing spot the sunny fields;
And river, now with bushy rocks o'er-brow'd,
Now winding bright and full, with naked banks;
And seats, and lawns, the Abbey and the wood,
And cots, and hamlets, and faint city-spire;   35
The Channel there, the Islands and white sails,
Dim coasts, and cloud-like hills, and shoreless Ocean—
It seem'd like Omnipresence! God, methought,
Had built him there a Temple: the whole World
Seem'd imag'd in its vast circumference: 40
No wish profan'd my overwhelméd heart.
Blest hour! It was a luxury,—to be!

Ah! quiet Dell! dear Cot, and Mount sublime!
I was constrain'd to quit you. Was it right,
While my unnumber'd brethren toil'd and bled,   45

That I should dream away the entrusted hours
On rose-leaf beds, pampering the coward heart
With feelings all too delicate for use?
Sweet is the tear that from some Howard's eye
Drops on the cheek of one he lifts from earth: 50
And he that works me good with unmov'd face,
Does it but half: he chills me while he aids,
My benefactor, not my brother man!
Yet even this, this cold beneficence
Praise, praise it, O my Soul! oft as thou scann'st   55
The sluggard Pity's vision-weaving tribe!
Who sigh for Wretchedness, yet shun the Wretched,
Nursing in some delicious solitude
Their slothful loves and dainty sympathies!
I therefore go, and join head, heart, and hand,   60
Active and firm, to fight the bloodless fight
Of Science, Freedom, and the Truth in Christ.

Yet oft when after honourable toil
Rests the tir'd mind, and waking loves to dream,
My spirit shall revisit thee, dear Cot!   65
Thy Jasmin and thy window-peeping Rose,
And Myrtles fearless of the mild sea-air.
And I shall sigh fond wishes—sweet Abode!
Ah!—had none greater! And that all had such!
It might be so—but the time is not yet.   70
Speed it, O Father! Let thy Kingdom come!
[1795]

ODE TO THE DEPARTING YEAR

ARGUMENT

The Ode commences with an address to the Divine Providence that regulates into one vast harmony all the events of time, however calamitous some of them may appear to mortals. The second Strophe calls on men to suspend their private joys and sorrows, and devote them for a while to the cause of human nature in general. The first Epode speaks of the Empress of Russia, who

died of an apoplexy on the 17th of November 1796; having just
concluded a subsidiary treaty with the Kings combined against
France. The first and second Antistrophe describe the Image of
the Departing Year, etc., as in a vision. The second Epode
prophesies, in anguish of spirit, the downfall of this country.

I

Spirit who sweepest the wild Harp of Time!
  It is most hard, with an untroubled ear
  Thy dark inwoven harmonies to hear!
Yet, mine eye fix'd on Heaven's unchanging clime
Long had I listen'd, free from mortal fear,   5
  With inward stillness, and a bowéd mind;
  When lo! its folds far waving on the wind,
I saw the train of the Departing Year!
  Starting from my silent sadness
  Then with no unholy madness,   10
Ere yet the enter'd cloud foreclos'd my sight,
I rais'd the impetuous song, and solemnis'd his flight.

II

  Hither, from the recent tomb,
  From the prison's direr gloom,
  From Distemper's midnight anguish;   15
And thence, where Poverty doth waste and languish;
  Or where, his two bright torches blending,
  Love illumines Manhood's maze;
  Or where o'er cradled infants bending,
  Hope has fix'd her wishful gaze;   20
  Hither, in perplexéd dance,
Ye Woes! ye young-eyed Joys! advance!
  By Time's wild harp, and by the hand
  Whose indefatigable sweep
  Raises its fateful strings from sleep,   25
I bid you haste, a mix'd tumultuous band!
  From every private bower,
    And each domestic hearth,
  Haste for one solemn hour;
And with a loud and yet a louder voice,   30

O'er Nature struggling in portentous birth,
    Weep and rejoice!
Still echoes the dread Name that o'er the earth
Let slip the storm, and woke the brood of Hell:
    And now advance in saintly Jubilee   35
Justice and Truth! They too have heard thy spell,
    They too obey thy name, divinest Liberty!

                                III

I mark'd Ambition in his war-array!
    I heard the mailéd Monarch's troublous cry—
'Ah! wherefore does the Northern Conqueress stay!   40
Groans not her chariot on its onward way?'
    Fly, mailéd Monarch, fly!
    Stunn'd by Death's twice' mortal mace,
    No more on Murder's lurid face
The insatiate Hag shall gloat with drunken eye!   45
    Manes of the unnumber'd slain!
    Ye that gasp'd on Warsaw's plain!
    Ye that erst at Ismail's tower,
When human ruin choked the streams,
    Fell in Conquest's glutted hour,   50
Mid women's shrieks and infants' screams!
    Spirits of the uncoffin'd slain,
        Sudden blasts of triumph swelling,
    Oft, at night, in misty train,
        Rush around her narrow dwelling!   55
The exterminating Fiend is fled—
    (Foul her life, and dark her doom)
Mighty armies of the dead
    Dance, like death-fires, round her tomb!
Then with prophetic song relate,   60
Each some Tyrant-Murderer's fate!

                                IV

Departing Year! 'twas on no earthly shore
    My soul beheld thy Vision! Where alone,
    Voiceless and stern, before the cloudy throne.
Aye Memory sits: thy robe inscrib'd with gore,   65

With many an unimaginable groan
  Thou storied'st thy sad hours! Silence ensued,
  Deep silence o'er the ethereal multitude,
Whose locks with wreaths, whose wreaths with glories
    shone.
  Then, his eye wild ardours glancing,   70
  From the choiréd gods advancing,
The Spirit of the Earth made reverence meet,
And stood up, beautiful, before the cloudy seat.

                         v

  Throughout the blissful throng,
  Hush'd were harp and song: 75
Till wheeling round the throne the Lampads seven.
  (The mystic Words of Heaven)
  Permissive signal make:
The fervent Spirit bow'd, then spread his wings and spake!
  'Thou in stormy blackness throning   80
  Love and uncreated Light,
  By the Earth's unsolaced groaning,
  Seize thy terrors, Arm of might!
  By Peace with proffer'd insult scared,
    Masked Hate and envying Scorn!   85
    By years of Havoc yet unborn!
And Hunger's bosom to the frost-winds bared!
  But chief by Afric's wrongs,
    Strange, horrible, and foul!
  By what deep guilt belongs   90
To the deaf Synod, 'full of gifts and lies!
By Wealth's insensate laugh! by Torture's howl!
    Avenger, rise!
  For ever shall the thankless Island scowl,
  Her quiver full, and with unbroken bow?   95
Speak! from thy storm-black Heaven O speak aloud!
    And on the darkling foe
Open thine eye of fire from some uncertain cloud!
  O dart the flash! O rise and deal the blow!
The Past to thee, to thee the Future cries!   100
  Hark! how wide Nature joins her groans below!
    Rise, God of Nature! rise.'

VI

The voice had ceas'd, the Vision fled;
Yet still I gasp'd and reel'd with dread.
And ever, when the dream of night   105
Renews the phantom to my sight,
Cold sweat-drops gather on my limbs;
    My ears throb hot; my eye-balls start;
My brain with horrid tumult swims;
    Wild is the tempest of my heart;   110
And my thick and struggling breath
Imitates the toil of death!
No stranger agony confounds
    The Soldier on the war-field spread,
When all foredone with toil and wounds,   115
    Death-like he dozes among heaps of dead!
(The strife is o'er, the day-light fled,
    And the night-wind clamours hoarse!
See! the startling wretch's head
    Lies pillow'd on a brother's corse!)   120

VII

Not yet enslaved, not wholly vile,
O Albion! O my mother Isle!
Thy valleys, fair as Eden's bowers
Glitter green with sunny showers;
Thy grassy uplands' gentle swells   125
    Echo to the bleat of flocks;
(Those grassy hills, those glittering dells
    Proudly ramparted with rocks)
And Ocean mid his uproar wild
Speaks safety to his Island-child!   130
Hence for many a fearless age
Has social Quiet lov'd thy shore;
    Nor ever proud Invader's rage
Or sack'd thy towers, or stain'd thy fields with gore.

VIII

Abandon'd of Heaven! mad Avarice thy guide,   135
At cowardly distance, yet kindling with pride—
Mid thy herds and thy corn-fields secure thou hast stood,
And join'd the wild yelling of Famine and Blood!
The nations curse thee! They with eager wondering
    Shall hear Destruction, like a vulture, scream!   140
    Strange-eyed Destruction! who with many a dream
Of central fires through nether seas up-thundering
    Soothes her fierce solitude; yet as she lies
    By livid fount, or red volcanic stream,
    If ever to her lidless dragon-eyes,   145
    O Albion! thy predestin'd ruins rise,
The fiend-hag on her perilous couch doth leap,
Muttering distemper'd triumph in her charméd sleep.

IX

    Away, my soul, away!
    In vain, in vain the Birds of warning sing—   150
And hark! I hear the famish'd brood of prey
Flap their lank pennons on the groaning wind!
    Away, my soul, away!
    I unpartaking of the evil thing,
    With daily prayer and daily toil   155
    Soliciting for food my scanty soil,
    Have wail'd my country with a loud Lament.
Now I recentre my immortal mind
    In the deep Sabbath of meek self-content;
Cleans'd from the vaporous passions that bedim   160
God's Image, sister of the Seraphim.
    [1796]

THIS LIME-TREE BOWER MY PRISON

[ADDRESSED TO CHARLES LAMB, OF THE INDIA HOUSE, LONDON]

In the June of 1797 some long-expected friends paid a visit to the
author's cottage; and on the morning of their arrival, he met with

an accident, which disabled him from walking during the whole
time of their stay. One evening, when they had left him for a few
hours, he composed the following lines in the garden-bower.

Well, they are gone, and here must I remain,
This lime-tree bower my prison! I have lost
Beauties and feelings, such as would have been
Most sweet to my remembrance even when age
Had dimm'd mine eyes to blindness! They, meanwhile,   5
Friends, whom I never more may meet again,
On springy heath, along the hill-top edge,
Wander in gladness, and wind down, perchance,
To that still roaring dell, of which I told;
The roaring dell, o'erwooded, narrow, deep,   10
And only speckled by the mid-day sun;
Where its slim trunk the ash from rock to rock
Flings arching like a bridge;—that branchless ash,
Unsunn'd and damp, whose few poor yellow leaves
Ne'er tremble in the gale, yet tremble still,   15
Fann'd by the water-fall! and there my friends
Behold the dark green file of long lank weeds
That all at once (a most fantastic sight!)
Still nod and drip beneath the dripping edge
Of the blue clay-stone.

           Now, my friends emerge   20
Beneath the wide wide Heaven—and view again
The many-steepled tract magnificent
Of hilly fields and meadows, and the sea,
With some fair bark, perhaps, whose sails light up
The slip of smooth clear blue betwixt two Isles   25
Of purple shadow! Yes! they wander on
In gladness all; but thou, methinks, most glad,
My gentle-hearted Charles! for thou hast pined
And hunger'd after Nature, many a year,
In the great City pent, winning thy way   30
With sad yet patient soul, through evil and pain
And strange calamity! Ah! slowly sink
Behind the western ridge, thou glorious Sun!
Shine in the slant beams of the sinking orb,
Ye purple heath-flowers! richlier burn, ye clouds!   35

Live in the yellow light, ye distant groves!
And kindle, thou blue Ocean! So my friend
Struck with deep joy may stand, as I have stood,
Silent with swimming sense; yea, gazing round
On the wide landscape, gaze till all doth seem   40
Less gross than bodily; and of such hues
As veil the Almighty Spirit, when yet he makes
Spirits perceive his presence.

A delight
Comes sudden on my heart, and I am glad
As I myself were there! Nor in this bower,   45
This little lime-tree bower, have I not mark'd
Much that has sooth'd me. Pale beneath the blaze
Hung the transparent foliage; and I watch'd
Some broad and sunny leaf, and lov'd to see
The shadow of the leaf and stem above   50
Dappling its sunshine! And that walnut-tree
Was richly ting'd, and a deep radiance lay
Full on the ancient ivy, which usurps
Those fronting elms, and now, with blackest mass
Makes their dark branches gleam a lighter hue   55
Through the late twilight: and though now the bat
Wheels silent by, and not a swallow twitters,
Yet still the solitary humble-bee
Sings in the bean-flower! Henceforth I shall know
That Nature ne'er deserts the wise and pure;   60
No plot so narrow, be but Nature there,
No waste so vacant, but may well employ
Each faculty of sense, and keep the heart
Awake to Love and Beauty! and sometimes
'Tis well to be bereft of promis'd good,   65
That we may lift the soul, and contemplate
With lively joy the joys we cannot share.
My gentle-hearted Charles! when the last rook
Beat its straight path along the dusky air
Homewards, I blest it! deeming its black wing   70
(Now a dim speck, now vanishing in light)
Had cross'd the mighty Orb's dilated glory,
While thou stood'st gazing; or, when all was still,
Flew creeking o'er thy head, and had a charm

For thee, my gentle-hearted Charles, to whom   75
No sound is dissonant which tells of Life.
     [1797]

THE RIME OF THE ANCIENT MARINER

IN SEVEN PARTS

ARGUMENT

How a Ship having passed the Line was driven by storms to the
cold Country towards the South Pole; and how from thence she
made her course to the tropical Latitude of the Great Pacific
Ocean; and of the strange things that befell; and in what manner
the Ancyent Marinere came back to his own Country.

PART I

*An ancient
Mariner meet-
eth three Gal-
lants bidden
to a wedding-
feast, and de-
taineth one.*

It is an ancient Mariner,
And he stoppeth one of three.
'By thy long grey beard and glittering eye,
Now wherefore stopp'st thou me?

The Bridegroom's doors are opened wide,   5
And I am next of kin;
The guests are met, the feast is set:
May'st hear the merry din.'

*The Wedding-
Guest is spell-
bound by the
eye of the old
seafaring man,
and con-
strained to
hear his tale.*

He holds him with his skinny hand,
'There was a ship,' quoth he.   10
'Hold off! unhand me, grey-beard loon!'
Eftsoons his hand dropt he.

He holds him with his glittering eye—
The Wedding-Guest stood still,
And listens like a three years' child: 15
The Mariner hath his will.

The Wedding-Guest sat on a stone:
He cannot choose but hear;
And thus spake on that ancient man,
The bright-eyed Mariner.   20

The Mariner
tells how the
ship sailed
southward
with a good
wind and fair
weather, till it
reached the
line.

'The ship was cheered, the harbour cleared,
Merrily did we drop
Below the kirk, below the hill,
Below the lighthouse top.

The Sun came up upon the left,   25
Out of the sea came he!
And he shone bright, and on the right
Went down into the sea.

Higher and higher every day,
Till over the mast at noon—'   30
The Wedding-Guest here beat his breast,
For he heard the loud bassoon.

The Wedding-
Guest heareth
the bridal
music; but
the Mariner
continueth
his tale.

The bride hath paced into the hall,
Red as a rose is she;
Nodding their heads before her goes   35
The merry minstrelsy.

The Wedding-Guest he beat his breast,
Yet he cannot choose but hear;
And thus spake on that ancient man,
The bright-eyed Mariner.   40

The ship
driven by a
storm toward
the south pole.

'And now the STORM-BLAST came, and he
Was tyrannous and strong:
He struck with his o'ertaking wings,
And chased us south along.

With sloping masts and dipping prow,   45
As who pursued with yell and blow
Still treads the shadow of his foe,
And forward bends his head,
The ship drove fast, loud roared the blast,
And southward aye we fled.   50

And now there came both mist and snow,
And it grew wondrous cold:
And ice, mast-high, came floating by,
As green as emerald.

The land of
ice, and of
fearful sounds
where no
living thing
was to be seen.

And through the drifts the snowy clifts   55
Did send a dismal sheen:
Nor shapes of men nor beasts we ken—
The ice was all between.

The ice was here, the ice was there,
The ice was all around: 60
It cracked and growled, and roared and
    howled,
Like noises in a swound!

Till a great
sea-bird,
called the
Albatross,
came through
the snow-fog,
and was
received with
great joy and
hospitality.

At length did cross an Albatross,
Through the fog it came;
As if it had been a Christian soul,   65
We hailed it in God's name.

It ate the food it ne'er had eat,
And round and round it flew.
The ice did split with a thunder-fit;
The helmsman steered us through!   70

And lo! the
Albatross
proveth a bird
of good omen,
and followeth
the ship as it
returned
northward
through fog
and floating
ice.

And a good south wind sprung up behind;
The Albatross did follow,
And every day, for food or play,
Came to the mariner's hollo!

In mist or cloud, on mast or shroud,   75
It perched for vespers nine;
Whiles all the night, through fog-smoke
    white,
Glimmered the white Moon-shine.'

The ancient
Mariner
inhospitably
killeth the
pious bird of
good omen.

'God save thee, ancient Mariner!
From the fiends, that plague thee thus!—   80
Why look'st thou so?'—With my cross-
    bow
I shot the ALBATROSS.

PART II

The Sun now rose upon the right:
Out of the sea came he,
Still hid in mist, and on the left 85
Went down into the sea.

And the good south wind still blew behind,
But no sweet bird did follow,
Nor any day for food or play
Came to the mariners' hollo! 90

His shipmates cry out against the ancient Mariner, for killing the bird of good luck.

And I had done a hellish thing,
And it would work 'em woe:
For all averred, I had killed the bird
That made the breeze to blow.
Ah wretch! said they, the bird to slay, 95
That made the breeze to blow!

But when the fog cleared off, they justify the same, and thus make themselves accomplices in the crime.

Nor dim nor red, like God's own head,
The glorious Sun uprist:
Then all averred, I had killed the bird
That brought the fog and mist. 100
'Twas right, said they, such birds to slay,
That bring the fog and mist.

The fair breeze continues; the ship enters the Pacific Ocean, and sails northward, even till it reaches the Line.

The fair breeze blew, the white foam flew,
The furrow followed free;
We were the first that ever burst 105
Into that silent sea.

The ship hath been suddenly becalmed.

Down dropt the breeze, the sails dropt down,
'Twas sad as sad could be;
And we did speak only to break
The silence of the sea! 110

All in a hot and copper sky,
The bloody Sun, at noon,
Right up above the mast did stand,
No bigger than the Moon.

Day after day, day after day,   115
We stuck, nor breath nor motion;
As idle as a painted ship
Upon a painted ocean.

And the Albatross begins to be avenged.

Water, water, every where,
And all the boards did shrink;   120
Water, water, every where,
Nor any drop to drink.

The very deep did rot: O Christ!
That ever this should be!
Yea, slimy things did crawl with legs   125
Upon the slimy sea.

About, about, in reel and rout
The death-fires danced at night;
The water, like a witch's oils,
Burnt green, and blue and white.   130

A Spirit had followed them; one of the invisible inhabitants of this planet, neither departed souls nor angels; concerning whom the learned Jew, Josephus, and the Platonic Constantinopolitan, Michael Psellus, may be consulted. They are very numerous, and there is no climate or element without one or more.

And some in dreams assured were
Of the Spirit that plagued us so;
Nine fathom deep he had followed us
From the land of mist and snow.

And every tongue, through utter drought,   135
Was withered at the root;
We could not speak, no more than if
We had been choked with soot.

The shipmates, in their sore distress, would fain throw the whole guilt on the ancient Mariner: in sign whereof they hang the dead sea-bird round his neck

Ah! well a-day! what evil looks
Had I from old and young!   140
Instead of the cross, the Albatross
About my neck was hung.

PART III

There passed a weary time. Each throat
Was parched, and glazed each eye.
A weary time! a weary time!   145
How glazed each weary eye,
When looking westward, I beheld
A something in the sky.

*The ancient
Mariner be-
holdeth a sign
in the element
afar off.*

At first it seemed a little speck,
And then it seemed a mist;   150
It moved and moved, and took at last
A certain shape, I wist.

A speck, a mist, a shape, I wist!
And still it neared and neared:
As if it dodged a water-sprite,   155
It plunged and tacked and veered.

*At its nearer
approach, it
seemeth him
to be a ship;
and at a dear
ransom he
freeth his
speech from
the bonds of
thirst.*

With throats unslaked, with black lips
    baked,
We could nor laugh nor wail;
Through utter drought all dumb we stood!
I bit my arm, I sucked the blood,   160
And cried, A sail! a sail!

With throats unslaked, with black lips
    baked,
Agape they heard me call:
A flash of joy; Gramercy! they for joy did grin,
And all at once their breath drew in,   165
As they were drinking all.

*And horror
follows. For
can it be a
ship that
comes onward
without wind
or tide?*

See! see! (I cried) she tacks no more!
Hither to work us weal;
Without a breeze, without a tide,
She steadies with upright keel!   170

The western wave was all a-flame.
The day was well nigh done!
Almost upon the western wave

Rested the broad bright Sun;
When that strange shape drove suddenly   175
Betwixt us and the Sun.

It seemeth
him but the
skeleton of
a ship.

And straight the Sun was flecked with bars,
(Heaven's Mother send us grace!)
As if through a dungeon-grate he peered
With broad and burning face.   180

Alas! (thought I, and my heart beat loud)
And its ribs
are seen as
bars on the
face of the
setting Sun.
How fast she nears and nears!
Are those her sails that glance in the Sun,
Like restless gossameres?

The Spectre-
Woman and
her Death-
mate, and no
other on
board the
skeleton ship.
Are those her ribs through which the Sun   185
Did peer, as through a grate?
And is that Woman all her crew?
Is that a DEATH? and are there two?
Is DEATH that woman's mate?

Like vessel,
like crew!
Her lips were red, her looks were free,   190
Her locks were yellow as gold:
Death and
Life-in-Death
have diced for
the ship's
crew, and she
(the latter)
winneth the
ancient
Mariner.
Her skin was as white as leprosy,
The Night-mare LIFE-IN-DEATH was she,
Who thicks man's blood with cold.

The naked hulk alongside came,   195
And the twain were casting dice;
'The game is done! I've won! I've won!'
Quoth she, and whistles thrice.

No twilight
within the
courts of the
Sun.
The Sun's rim dips; the stars rush out:
At one stride comes the dark;   200
With far-heard whisper, o'er the sea,
Off shot the spectre-bark.

At the rising
of the Moon,
We listened and looked sideways up!
Fear at my heart, as at a cup,
My life-blood seemed to sip!   205
The stars were dim, and thick the night,
The steersman's face by his lamp gleamed
      white;

From the sails the dew did drip—
Till clomb above the eastern bar
The hornéd Moon, with one bright star   210
Within the nether tip.

One after one, by the star-dogged Moon,
Too quick for groan or sigh,
Each turned his face with a ghastly pang,
And cursed me with his eye.   215

Four times fifty living men,
(And I heard nor sigh nor groan)
With heavy thump, a lifeless lump,
They dropped down one by one.

The souls did from their bodies fly,—   220
They fled to bliss or woe!
And every soul, it passed me by,
Like the whizz of my cross-bow!

PART IV

'I fear thee, ancient Mariner!
I fear thy skinny hand!   225
And thou art long, and lank, and brown,
As is the ribbed sea-sand.

I fear thee and thy glittering eye,
And thy skinny hand, so brown.'—
Fear not, fear not, thou Wedding-Guest!   230
This body dropt not down.

Alone, alone, all, all alone,
Alone on a wide wide sea!
And never a saint took pity on
My soul in agony.   235

The many men, so beautiful!
And they all dead did lie:
And a thousand thousand slimy things
Lived on; and so did I.

Margin notes:

One after another.

His shipmates drop down dead.

But Life-in-Death begins her work on the ancient Mariner.

The Wedding-Guest feareth that a Spirit is talking to him;

But the ancient Mariner assureth him of his bodily life, and proceedeth to relate his horrible penance.

He despiseth the creatures of the calm,

And envieth
that *they*
should live,
and so many
lie dead.

I looked upon the rotting sea,   240
And drew my eyes away;
I looked upon the rotting deck,
And there the dead men lay.

I looked to heaven, and tried to pray;
But or ever a prayer had gusht,   245
A wicked whisper came, and made
My heart as dry as dust.

I closed my lids, and kept them close,
And the balls like pulses beat;
For the sky and the sea, and the sea and the
     sky   250
Lay like a load on my weary eye,
And the dead were at my feet.

But the curse
liveth for him
in the eye of
the dead men.

The cold sweat melted from their limbs,
Nor rot nor reek did they:
The look with which they looked on me   255
Had never passed away.

An orphan's curse would drag to hell
A spirit from on high;
But oh! more horrible than that
Is the curse in a dead man's eye!   260
Seven days, seven nights, I saw that curse,
And yet I could not die.

In his lone-
liness and
fixedness he
yearneth to-
wards the
journeying
Moon, and the
stars that still
sojourn, yet
still move
onward; and
every where
the blue sky
belongs to

The moving Moon went up the sky,
And no where did abide:
Softly she was going up,   265
And a star or two beside—

Her beams bemocked the sultry main,
Like April hoar-frost spread;
But where the ship's huge shadow lay,
The charméd water burnt alway   270
A still and awful red.

them, and is their appointed rest, and their native country and their own
natural homes, which they enter unannounced, as lords that are certainly expected and yet there is a silent joy at their arrival.

By the light
of the Moon he
beholdeth
God's crea-
tures of the
great calm.

Beyond the shadow of the ship,
I watched the water-snakes:
They moved in tracks of shining white,
And when they reared, the elfish light   275
Fell off in hoary flakes.

Within the shadow of the ship
I watched their rich attire:
Blue, glossy green, and velvet black,
They coiled and swam; and every track   280
Was a flash of golden fire.

Their beauty
and their
happiness.

He blesseth
them in his
heart.

O happy, living things! no tongue
Their beauty might declare:
A spring of love gushed from my heart,
And I blessed them unaware: 285
Sure my kind saint took pity on me,
And I blessed them unaware.

The spell
begins to
break.

The self-same moment I could pray;
And from my neck so free
The Albatross fell off, and sank   290
Like lead into the sea.

PART V

Oh sleep! it is a gentle thing.
Beloved from pole to pole!
To Mary Queen the praise be given!
She sent the gentle sleep from Heaven,   295
That slid into my soul.

By grace of
the holy
Mother, the
ancient
Mariner is
refreshed with
rain.

The silly buckets on the deck,
That had so long remained,
I dreamt that they were filled with dew;
And when I awoke, it rained.   300

My lips were wet, my throat was cold,
My garments all were dank;
Sure I had drunken in my dreams,
And still my body drank.

I moved, and could not feel my limbs: 305
I was so light—almost
I thought that I had died in sleep,
And was a blessèd ghost.

He heareth
sounds and
seeth strange
sights and
commotions in
the sky and
the element.

And soon I heard a roaring wind:
It did not come anear;   310
But with its sound it shook the sails,
That were so thin and sere.

The upper air burst into life!
And a hundred fire-flags sheen,
To and fro they were hurried about!   315
And to and fro, and in and out,
The wan stars danced between.

And the coming wind did roar more loud,
And the sails did sigh like sedge;
And the rain poured down from one black
    cloud;   320
The Moon was at its edge.

The thick black cloud was cleft, and still
The Moon was at its side:
Like waters shot from some high crag,
The lightning fell with never a jag,   325
A river steep and wide.

The bodies of
the ship's crew
are inspired,
[inspirited,
S. L.] and the
ship moves
on;

The loud wind never reached the ship,
Yet now the ship moved on!
Beneath the lightning and the Moon
The dead men gave a groan.   330

They groaned, they stirred, they all uprose,
Nor spake, nor moved their eyes;
It had been strange, even in a dream,
To have seen those dead men rise.

The helmsman steered, the ship moved on; 335
Yet never a breeze up-blew;
The mariners all 'gan work the ropes,
Where they were wont to do;

They raised their limbs like lifeless tools—
We were a ghastly crew.   340

The body of my brother's son
Stood by me, knee to knee:
The body and I pulled at one rope,
But he said nought to me.

'I fear thee, ancient Mariner!'   345
Be calm, thou Wedding-Guest!
'Twas not those souls that fled in pain,
Which to their corses came again,
But a troop of spirits blest:

For when it dawned—they dropped their
    arms,   350
And clustered round the mast;
Sweet sounds rose slowly through their
    mouths,
And from their bodies passed.

Around, around, flew each sweet sound,
Then darted to the Sun;   355
Slowly the sounds came back again,
Now mixed, now one by one.

Sometimes a-dropping from the sky
I heard the sky-lark sing;
Sometimes all little birds that are,   360
How they seemed to fill the sea and air
With their sweet jargoning!

And now 'twas like all instruments,
Now like a lonely flute;
And now it is an angel's song,   365
That makes the heavens be mute.

It ceased; yet still the sails made on
A pleasant noise till noon,
A noise like of a hidden brook
In the leafy month of June,   370

But not by the souls of the men, nor by dæmons of earth or middle air, but by a blessed troop of angelic spirits, sent down by the invocation of the guardian saint.

That to the sleeping woods all night
Singeth a quiet tune.

Till noon we quietly sailed on,
Yet never a breeze did breathe:
Slowly and smoothly went the ship,   375
Moved onward from beneath.

The lonesome
Spirit from
the south-pole
carries on the
ship as far as
the Line, in
obedience to
the angelic
troop, but still
requireth
vengeance.

Under the keel nine fathom deep,
From the land of mist and snow,
The spirit slid: and it was he
That made the ship to go.   380
The sails at noon left off their tune,
And the ship stood still also.

The Sun, right up above the mast,
Had fixed her to the ocean:
But in a minute she 'gan stir,   385
With a short uneasy motion—
Backwards and forwards half her length
With a short uneasy motion.

Then like a pawing horse let go,
She made a sudden bound: 390
It flung the blood into my head,
And I fell down in a swound.

The Polar
Spirit's fellow-
dæmons, the
invisible in-
habitants of
the element,
take part in
his wrong;
and two of
them relate,
one to the
other, that
penance long
and heavy for
the ancient
Mariner hath
been accorded
to the Polar
Spirit, who
returneth
southward.

How long in that same fit I lay,
I have not to declare;
But ere my living life returned,   395
I heard and in my soul discerned
Two voices in the air.

'Is it he?' quoth one, 'Is this the man?
By him who died on cross,
With his cruel bow he laid full low   400
The harmless Albatross.

The spirit who bideth by himself
In the land of mist and snow,
He loved the bird that loved the man
Who shot him with his bow.'   405

The other was a softer voice,
As soft as honey-dew:
Quoth he, 'The man hath penance done,
And penance more will do.'

PART VI

FIRST VOICE

'But tell me, tell me! speak again,   410
Thy soft response renewing—
What makes that ship drive on so fast?
What is the ocean doing?'

SECOND VOICE

'Still as a slave before his lord,
The ocean hath no blast;   415
His great bright eye most silently
Up to the Moon is cast—

If he may know which way to go;
For she guides him smooth or grim.
See, brother, see! how graciously   420
She looketh down on him.'

FIRST VOICE

The Mariner
hath been
cast into a
trance; for the
angelic power
causeth the
vessel to drive
northward
faster than
human life
could endure.

'But why drives on that ship so fast,
Without or wave or wind?'

SECOND VOICE

'The air is cut away before,
And closes from behind.   425

Fly, brother, fly! more high, more high!
Or we shall be belated:
For slow and slow that ship will go,
When the Mariner's trance is abated.'

The super-
natural motion
is retarded;
the Mariner
awakes, and
his penance
begins anew.

I woke, and we were sailing on   430
As in a gentle weather:
'Twas night, calm night, the moon was
     high;
The dead men stood together.

All stood together on the deck,
For a charnel-dungeon fitter: 435
All fixed on me their stony eyes,
That in the Moon did glitter.

The pang, the curse, with which they died,
Had never passed away:
I could not draw my eyes from theirs,   440
Nor turn them up to pray.

The curse is
finally ex-
piated.

And now this spell was snapt: once more
I viewed the ocean green,
And looked far forth, yet little saw
Of what had else been seen—   445

Like one, that on a lonesome road
Doth walk in fear and dread,
And having once turned round walks on,
And turns no more his head;
Because he knows, a frightful fiend   450
Doth close behind him tread.

But soon there breathed a wind on me,
Nor sound nor motion made:
Its path was not upon the sea,
In ripple or in shade.   455

It raised my hair, it fanned my cheek
Like a meadow-gale of spring—
It mingled strangely with my fears,
Yet it felt like a welcoming.

Swiftly, swiftly flew the ship,   460
Yet she sailed softly too:
Sweetly, sweetly blew the breeze—
On me alone it blew.

And the
ancient
Mariner be-
holdeth his
native
country.

Oh! dream of joy! is this indeed
The light-house top I see?   465
Is this the hill? is this the kirk?
Is this mine own countree?

We drifted o'er the harbour-bar,
And I with sobs did pray—
O let me be awake, my God!   470
Or let me sleep alway.

The harbour-bay was clear as glass,
So smoothly it was strewn!
And on the bay the moonlight lay,
And the shadow of the Moon.   475

The rock shone bright, the kirk no less,
That stands above the rock:
The moonlight steeped in silentness
The steady weathercock.

And the bay was white with silent light,   480
Till rising from the same,
The angelic
spirits leave
the dead
bodies,
Full many shapes, that shadows were,
In crimson colours came.

And appear in
their own
forms of light.
A little distance from the prow
Those crimson shadows were: 485
I turned my eyes upon the deck—
Oh, Christ! what saw I there!

Each corse lay flat, lifeless and flat,
And, by the holy rood!
A man all light, a seraph-man,   490
On every corse there stood.

This seraph-band, each waved his hand:
It was a heavenly sight!
They stood as signals to the land,
Each one a lovely light;   495

This seraph-band, each waved his hand,
No voice did they impart—

No voice; but oh! the silence sank
Like music on my heart.

But soon I heard the dash of oars,   500
I heard the Pilot's cheer;
My head was turned perforce away
And I saw a boat appear.

The Pilot and the Pilot's boy,
I heard them coming fast: 505
Dear Lord in Heaven! it was a joy
The dead men could not blast.

I saw a third—I heard his voice:
It is the Hermit good!
He singeth loud his godly hymns   510
That he makes in the wood.
He'll shrieve my soul, he'll wash away
The Albatross's blood.

PART VII

The Hermit of the Wood.

This Hermit good lives in that wood
Which slopes down to the sea.   515
How loudly his sweet voice he rears!
He loves to talk with marineres
That come from a far countree.

He kneels at morn, and noon, and eve—
He hath a cushion plump: 520
It is the moss that wholly hides
The rotted old oak-stump.

The skiff-boat neared: I heard them talk,
'Why, this is strange, I trow!
Where are those lights so many and fair, 525
That signal made but now?'

Approacheth the ship with wonder.

'Strange, by my faith!' the Hermit said—
'And they answered not our cheer!

The planks looked warped! and see those
    sails,
How thin they are and sere!   530
I never saw aught like to them,
Unless perchance it were

Brown skeletons of leaves that lag
My forest-brook along;
When the ivy-tod is heavy with snow,   535
And the owlet whoops to the wolf below,
That eats the she-wolf's young.'

'Dear Lord! it hath a fiendish look—
(The Pilot made reply)
I am a-feared'—'Push on, push on!'   540
Said the Hermit cheerily.

The boat came closer to the ship,
But I nor spake nor stirred;
The boat came close beneath the ship,
And straight a sound was heard.   545

*The ship
suddenly
sinketh.*

Under the water it rumbled on,
Still louder and more dread:
It reached the ship, it split the bay;
The ship went down like lead.

*The ancient
Mariner is
saved in the
Pilot's boat.*

Stunned by that loud and dreadful sound, 550
Which sky and ocean smote,
Like one that hath been seven days
    drowned
My body lay afloat;
But swift as dreams, myself I found
Within the Pilot's boat.   555

Upon the whirl, where sank the ship,
The boat spun round and round;
And all was still, save that the hill
Was telling of the sound.

I moved my lips—the Pilot shrieked   560
And fell down in a fit;

The holy Hermit raised his eyes,
And prayed where he did sit.

I took the oars: the Pilot's boy,
Who now doth crazy go,   565
Laughed loud and long, and all the while
His eyes went to and fro.
'Ha! ha!' quoth he, 'full plain I see,
The Devil knows how to row.'

And now, all in my own countree,   570
I stood on the firm land!
The Hermit stepped forth from the boat,
And scarcely he could stand.

The ancient
Mariner
earnestly en-
treateth the
Hermit to
shrieve him;
and the
penance of
life falls on
him.

'O shrieve me, shrieve me, holy man!'
The Hermit crossed his brow.   575
'Say quick,' quoth he, 'I bid thee say—
What manner of man art thou?'

Forthwith this frame of mine was wrenched
With a woful agony,
Which forced me to begin my tale;   580
And then it left me free.

And ever and
anon through
out his future
life an agony
constraineth
him to travel
from land to
land;

Since then, at an uncertain hour,
That agony returns:
And till my ghastly tale is told,
This heart within me burns.   585

I pass, like night, from land to land;
I have strange power of speech;
That moment that his face I see,
I know the man that must hear me:
To him my tale I teach.   590

What loud uproar bursts from that door!
The wedding-guests are there:
But in the garden-bower the bride
And bride-maids singing are:
And hark the little vesper bell,   595
Which biddeth me to prayer!

O Wedding-Guest! this soul hath been
Alone on a wide wide sea:
So lonely 'twas, that God himself
Scarce seemed there to be.   600

O sweeter than the marriage-feast,
'Tis sweeter far to me,
To walk together to the kirk
With a goodly company!—

To walk together to the kirk,   605
And all together pray,
While each to his great Father bends,
Old men, and babes, and loving friends
And youths and maidens gay!

And to teach,
by his own
example, love
and reverence
to all things
that God made
and loveth.

Farewell, farewell! but this I tell   610
To thee, thou Wedding-Guest!
He prayeth well, who loveth well
Both man and bird and beast.

He prayeth best, who loveth best
All things both great and small;   615
For the dear God who loveth us,
He made and loveth all.

The Mariner, whose eye is bright,
Whose beard with age is hoar,
Is gone: and now the Wedding-Guest   620
Turned from the bridegroom's door.

He went like one that hath been stunned,
And is of sense forlorn:
A sadder and a wiser man,
He rose the morrow morn.   625
        [1797–1798]

CHRISTABEL

PART I

'Tis the middle of night by the castle clock,
And the owls have awakened the crowing cock;
Tu—whit!——Tu—whoo!
And hark, again; the crowing cock,
How drowsily it crew.   5

Sir Leoline, the Baron rich,
Hath a toothless mastiff bitch;
From her kennel beneath the rock
She maketh answer to the clock,
Four for the quarters, and twelve for the hour;   10
Ever and aye, by shine and shower,
Sixteen short howls, not over loud;
Some say, she sees my lady's shroud.

Is the night chilly and dark?
The night is chilly, but not dark.   15
The thin gray cloud is spread on high,
It covers but not hides the sky.
The moon is behind, and at the full;
And yet she looks both small and dull.
The night is chill, the cloud is gray: 20
'Tis a month before the month of May,
And the Spring comes slowly up this way.

The lovely lady, Christabel,
Whom her father loves so well,
What makes her in the wood so late,   25
A furlong from the castle gate?
She had dreams all yesternight
Of her own betrothéd knight;
And she in the midnight wood will pray
For the weal of her lover that's far away.   30

She stole along, she nothing spoke,
The sighs she heaved were soft and low,

And naught was green upon the oak
But moss and rarest misletoe:
She kneels beneath the huge oak tree,   35
And in silence prayeth she.

The lady sprang up suddenly,
The lovely lady, Christabel!
It moaned as near, as near can be,
But what it is she cannot tell.   40
On the other side it seems to be,
Of the huge, broad-breasted, old oak tree.

The night is chill; the forest bare;
Is it the wind that moaneth bleak?
There is not wind enough in the air   45
To move away the ringlet curl
From the lovely lady's cheek—
There is not wind enough to twirl
The one red leaf, the last of its clan,
That dances as often as dance it can,   50
Hanging so light, and hanging so high,
On the topmost twig that looks up at the sky.

Hush, beating heart of Christabel!
Jesu, Maria, shield her well!
She folded her arms beneath her cloak,   55
And stole to the other side of the oak.
        What sees she there?

There she sees a damsel bright,
Drest in a silken robe of white,
That shadowy in the moonlight shone: 60
The neck that made that white robe wan,
Her stately neck, and arms were bare;
Her blue-veined feet unsandal'd were,
And wildly glittered here and there
The gems entangled in her hair.   65
I guess, 'twas frightful there to see
A lady so richly clad as she—
Beautiful exceedingly!

Mary mother, save me now!
(Said Christabel,) And who art thou?   70

The lady strange made answer meet,
And her voice was faint and sweet:—
Have pity on my sore distress,
I scarce can speak for weariness:
Stretch forth thy hand, and have no fear!   75
Said Christabel, How camest thou here?
And the lady, whose voice was faint and sweet,
Did thus pursue her answer meet:—

My sire is of a noble line,
And my name is Geraldine: 80
Five warriors seized me yestermorn,
Me, even me, a maid forlorn:
They choked my cries with force and fright,
And tied me on a palfrey white.
The palfrey was as fleet as wind,   85
And they rode furiously behind.
They spurred amain, their steeds were white:
And once we crossed the shade of night.
As sure as Heaven shall rescue me,
I have no thought what men they be;   90
Nor do I know how long it is
(For I have lain entranced I wis)
Since one, the tallest of the five,
Took me from the palfrey's back,
A weary woman, scarce alive.   95
Some muttered words his comrades spoke:
He placed me underneath this oak;
He swore they would return with haste;
Whither they went I cannot tell—
I thought I heard, some minutes past,   100
Sounds as of a castle bell.
Stretch forth thy hand (thus ended she),
And help a wretched maid to flee.

Then Christabel stretched forth her hand,
And comforted fair Geraldine: 105
O well, bright dame; may you command
The service of Sir Leoline;

And gladly our stout chivalry
Will he send forth and friends withal
To guide and guard you safe and free 110
Home to your noble father's hall.

She rose: and forth with steps they passed
That strove to be, and were not, fast.
Her gracious stars the lady blest,
And thus spake on sweet Christabel: 115
All our household are at rest,
The hall as silent as the cell;
Sir Leoline is weak in health,
And may not well awakened be,
But we will move as if in stealth, 120
And I beseech your courtesy,
This night, to share your couch with me.

They crossed the moat, and Christabel
Took the key that fitted well;
A little door she opened straight, 125
All in the middle of the gate;
The gate that was ironed within and without,
Where an army in battle array had marched out.
The lady sank, belike through pain,
And Christabel with might and main 130
Lifted her up, a weary weight,
Over the threshold of the gate:
Then the lady rose again,
And moved, as she were not in pain.

So free from danger, free from fear, 135
They crossed the court: right glad they were.
And Christabel devoutly cried
To the lady by her side,
Praise we the Virgin all divine
Who hath rescued thee from thy distress! 140
Alas, alas! said Geraldine,
I cannot speak for weariness.
So free from danger, free from fear,
They crossed the court: right glad they were.

Outside her kennel, the mastiff old   145
Lay fast asleep, in moonshine cold.
The mastiff old did not awake,
Yet she an angry moan did make!
And what can ail the mastiff bitch?
Never till now she uttered yell   150
Beneath the eye of Christabel.
Perhaps it is the owlet's scritch:
For what can ail the mastiff bitch?

They passed the hall, that echoes still,
Pass as lightly as you will!   155
The brands were flat, the brands were dying,
Amid their own white ashes lying;
But when the lady passed, there came
A tongue of light, a fit of flame;
And Christabel saw the lady's eye,   160
And nothing else saw she thereby,
Save the boss of the shield of Sir Leoline tall,
Which hung in a murky old niche in the wall.
O softly tread, said Christabel,
My father seldom sleepth well.   165

Sweet Christabel her feet doth bare,
And jealous of the listening air
They steal their way from stair to stair,
Now in glimmer, and now in gloom,
And now they pass the Baron's room,   170
As still as death, with stifled breath!
And now have reached her chamber door;
And now doth Geraldine press down
The rushes of the chamber floor.

The moon shines dim in the open air,   175
And not a moonbeam enters here.
But they without its light can see
The chamber carved so curiously,
Carved with figures strange and sweet,
All made out of the carver's brain,   180
For a lady's chamber meet:
The lamp with twofold silver chain
Is fastened to an angel's feet.

The silver lamp burns dead and dim;
But Christabel the lamp will trim.   185
She trimmed the lamp, and made it bright,
And left it swinging to and fro,
While Geraldine, in wretched plight,
Sank down upon the floor below.

O weary lady, Geraldine,   190
I pray you, drink this cordial wine!
It is a wine of virtuous powers;
My mother made it of wild flowers.

And will your mother pity me,
Who am a maiden most forlorn?   195
Christabel answered—Woe is me!
She died the hour that I was born.
I have heard the grey-haired friar tell
How on her death-bed she did say,
That she should hear the castle-bell   200
Strike twelve upon my wedding-day.
O mother dear! that thou wert here!
I would, said Geraldine, she were!

But soon with altered voice, said she—
'Off, wandering mother! Peak and pine!   205
I have power to bid thee flee.'
Alas! what ails poor Geraldine?
Why stares she with unsettled eye?
Can she the bodiless dead espy?
And why with hollow voice cries she,   210
'Off, woman, off! this hour is mine—
Though thou her guardian spirit be,
Off, woman, off! 'tis given to me.'

Then Christabel knelt by the lady's side,
And raised to heaven her eyes so blue—   215
Alas! said she, this ghastly ride—
Dear lady! it hath wildered you!
The lady wiped her moist cold brow,
And faintly said, ' 'tis over now!'

Again the wild-flower wine she drank: 220
Her fair large eyes 'gan glitter bright,
And from the floor whereon she sank,
The lofty lady stood upright:
She was most beautiful to see,
Like a lady of a far countrée.   225

And thus the lofty lady spake—
'All they who live in the upper sky,
Do love you, holy Christabel!
And you love them, and for their sake
And for the good which me befel,   230
Even I in my degree will try,
Fair maiden, to requite you well.
But now unrobe yourself; for I
Must pray, ere yet in bed I lie.'

Quoth Christabel, So let it be!   235
And as the lady bade, did she.
Her gentle limbs did she undress,
And lay down in her loveliness.

But through her brain of weal and woe
So many thoughts moved to and fro,   240
That vain it were her lids to close;
So half-way from the bed she rose,
And on her elbow did recline
To look at the lady Geraldine.

Beneath the lamp the lady bowed,   245
And slowly rolled her eyes around;
Then drawing in her breath aloud,
Like one that shuddered, she unbound
The cincture from beneath her breast:
Her silken robe, and inner vest,   250
Dropt to her feet, and full in view,
Behold! her bosom and half her side——
A sight to dream of, not to tell!
O shield her! shield sweet Christabel!

Yet Geraldine nor speaks nor stirs;   255
Ah! what a stricken look was hers!

Deep from within she seems half-way
To lift some weight with sick assay,
And eyes the maid and seeks delay;
Then suddenly, as one defied,   260
Collects herself in scorn and pride,
And lay down by the Maiden's side!—
And in her arms the maid she took,
            Ah wel-a-day!
And with low voice and doleful look   265
These words did say:
'In the touch of this bosom there worketh a spell,
Which is lord of thy utterance, Christabel!
Thou knowest to-night, and wilt know to-morrow,
This mark of my shame, this seal of my sorrow;   270
            But vainly thou warrest,
            For this is alone in
            Thy power to declare,
            That in the dim forest
            Thou heard'st a low moaning,   275
And found'st a bright lady, surpassingly fair;
And didst bring her home with thee in love and in charity,
To shield her and shelter her from the damp air.'

                    THE CONCLUSION TO PART I

It was a lovely sight to see
The lady Christabel, when she   280
Was praying at the old oak tree.
            Amid the jaggéd shadows
            Of mossy leafless boughs,
            Kneeling in the moonlight,
            To make her gentle vows;   285
Her slender palms together prest,
Heaving sometimes on her breast;
Her face resigned to bliss or bale—
Her face, oh call it fair not pale,
And both blue eyes more bright than clear,   290
Each about to have a tear.

With open eyes (ah woe is me!)
Asleep, and dreaming fearfully,

Fearfully dreaming, yet, I wis,
Dreaming that alone, which is—   295
O sorrow and shame! Can this be she,
The lady, who knelt at the old oak tree?
And lo! the worker of these harms,
That holds the maiden in her arms,
Seems to slumber still and mild,   300
As a mother with her child.

A star hath set, a star hath risen,
O Geraldine! since arms of thine
Have been the lovely lady's prison.
O Geraldine! one hour was thine—   305
Thou'st had thy will! By tairn and rill,
The night-birds all that hour were still.
But now they are jubilant anew,
From cliff and tower, tu—whoo! tu—whoo!
Tu—whoo! tu—whoo! from wood and fell!   310

And see! the lady Christabel
Gathers herself from out her trance;
Her limbs relax, her countenance
Grows sad and soft; the smooth thin lids
Close o'er her eyes; and tears she sheds—   315
Large tears that leave the lashes bright!
And oft the while she seems to smile
As infants at a sudden light!

Yea, she doth smile, and she doth weep,
Like a youthful hermitess,   320
Beauteous in a wilderness,
Who, praying always, prays in sleep.
And, if she move unquietly,
Perchance, 'tis but the blood so free
Comes back and tingles in her feet.   325
No doubt, she hath a vision sweet.
What if her guardian spirit 'twere,
What if she knew her mother near?
But this she knows, in joys and woes,
That saints will aid if men will call: 330
For the blue sky bends over all!
    [1797]

PART II

Each matin bell, the Baron saith,
Knells us back to a world of death.
These words Sir Leoline first said,
When he rose and found his lady dead: 335
These words Sir Leoline will say
Many a morn to his dying day!

And hence the custom and law began
That still at dawn the sacristan,
Who duly pulls the heavy bell,   340
Five and forty beads must tell
Between each stroke—a warning knell,
Which not a soul can choose but hear
From Bratha Head to Wyndermere.

Saith Bracy the bard, So let it knell!   345
And let the drowsy sacristan
Still count as slowly as he can!
There is no lack of such, I ween,
As well fill up the space between.
In Langdale Pike and Witch's Lair,   350
And Dungeon-ghyll so foully rent,
With ropes of rock and bells of air
Three sinful sextons' ghosts are pent,
Who all give back, one after t'other,
The death-note to their living brother;   355
And oft too, by the knell offended,
Just as their one! two! three! is ended,
The devil mocks the doleful tale
With a merry peal from Borodale.

The air is still! through mist and cloud   360
That merry peal comes ringing loud;
And Geraldine shakes off her dread,
And rises lightly from the bed;
Puts on her silken vestments white,
And tricks her hair in lovely plight,   365
And nothing doubting of her spell

Awakens the lady Christabel.
'Sleep you, sweet lady Christabel?
I trust that you have rested well.'

And Christabel awoke and spied   370
The same who lay down by her side—
O rather say, the same whom she
Raised up beneath the old oak tree!
Nay, fairer yet! and yet more fair!
For she belike hath drunken deep   375
Of all the blessedness of sleep!
And while she spake, her looks, her air
Such gentle thankfulness declare,
That (so it seemed) her girded vests
Grew tight beneath her heaving breasts.   380
'Sure I have sinn'd!' said Christabel,
'Now heaven be praised if all be well!'
And in low faltering tones, yet sweet,
Did she the lofty lady greet
With such perplexity of mind   385
As dreams too lively leave behind.

So quickly she rose, and quickly arrayed
Her maiden limbs, and having prayed
That He, who on the cross did groan,
Might wash away her sins unknown,   390
She forthwith led fair Geraldine
To meet her sire, Sir Leoline.

The lovely maid and the lady tall
Are pacing both into the hall,
And pacing on through page and groom,   395
Enter the Baron's presence-room.

The Baron rose, and while he prest
His gentle daughter to his breast,
With cheerful wonder in his eyes
The lady Geraldine espies,   400
And gave such welcome to the same,
As might beseem so bright a dame!

But when he heard the lady's tale,
And when she told her father's name,
Why waxed Sir Leoline so pale,   405
Murmuring o'er the name again,
Lord Roland de Vaux of Tryermaine?

Alas! they had been friends in youth;
But whispering tongues can poison truth;
And constancy lives in realms above;
And life is thorny; and youth is vain;   410
And to be wroth with one we love
Doth work like madness in the brain.
And thus it chanced, as I divine,
With Roland and Sir Leoline.   415
Each spake words of high disdain
And insult to his heart's best brother:
They parted—ne'er to meet again!
But never either found another
To free the hollow heart from paining—   420
They stood aloof, the scars remaining,
Like cliffs which had been rent asunder;
A dreary sea now flows between;—
But neither heat, nor frost, nor thunder,
Shall wholly do away, I ween,   425
The marks of that which once hath been.

Sir Leoline, a moment's space,
Stood gazing on the damsel's face:
And the youthful Lord of Tryermaine
Came back upon his heart again.   430

O then the Baron forgot his age,
His noble heart swelled high with rage;
He swore by the wounds in Jesu's side
He would proclaim it far and wide,
With trump and solemn heraldry,   435
That they, who thus had wronged the dame,
Were base as spotted infamy!
'And if they dare deny the same,
My herald shall appoint a week,
And let the recreant traitors seek   440
My tourney court—that there and then

I may dislodge their reptile souls
From the bodies and forms of men!'
He spake: his eye in lightning rolls!
For the lady was ruthlessly seized; and he kenned   445
In the beautiful lady the child of his friend!

And now the tears were on his face,
And fondly in his arms he took
Fair Geraldine, who met the embrace,
Prolonging it with joyous look.   450
Which when she viewed, a vision fell
Upon the soul of Christabel,
The vision of fear, the touch and pain!
She shrunk and shuddered, and saw again—
(Ah, woe is me! Was it for thee,   455
Thou gentle maid! such sights to see?)

Again she saw that bosom old,
Again she felt that bosom cold,
And drew in her breath with a hissing sound:
Whereat the Knight turned wildly round,   460
And nothing saw, but his own sweet maid
With eyes upraised, as one that prayed.

The touch, the sight, had passed away,
And in its stead that vision blest,
Which comforted her after-rest   465
While in the lady's arms she lay,
Had put a rapture in her breast,
And on her lips and o'er her eyes
Spread smiles like light!
                             With new surprise,
'What ails then my belovéd child?'   470
The Baron said—His daughter mild
Made answer, 'All will yet be well!'
I ween, she had no power to tell
Aught else: so mighty was the spell.

Yet he, who saw this Geraldine,   475
Had deemed her sure a thing divine:
Such sorrow with such grace she blended,
As if she feared she had offended

Sweet Christabel, that gentle maid!
And with such lowly tones she prayed   480
She might be sent without delay
Home to her father's mansion.
      'Nay!
Nay, by my soul!' said Leoline.
"Ho! Bracy the bard, the charge be thine!
Go thou, with music sweet and loud,   485
And take two steeds with trappings proud,
And take the youth whom thou lov'st best
To bear thy harp, and learn thy song,
And clothe you both in solemn vest,
And over the mountains haste along,   490
Lest wandering folk, that are abroad,
Detain you on the valley road.

'And when he has crossed the Irthing flood,
My merry bard! he hastes, he hastes
Up Knorren Moor, through Halegarth Wood,   495
And reaches soon that castle good
Which stands and threatens Scotland's wastes.

"Bard Bracy! bard Bracy! your horses are fleet,
Ye must ride up the hall, your music so sweet,
More loud than your horses' echoing feet!   500
And loud and loud to Lord Roland call,
Thy daughter is safe in Langdale hall!
Thy beautiful daughter is safe and free—
Sir Leoline greets thee thus through me!
He bids thee come without delay   505
With all thy numerous array
And take thy lovely daughter home:
And he will meet thee on the way
With all his numerous array
White with their panting palfreys' foam: 510
And, by mine honour! I will say,
That I repent me of the day
When I spake words of fierce disdain
To Roland de Vaux of Tryermaine!—
—For since that evil hour hath flown,   515
Many a summer's sun hath shone;

Yet ne'er found I a friend again
Like Roland de Vaux of Tryermaine.

The lady fell, and clasped his knees,
Her face upraised, her eyes o'erflowing;   520
And Bracy replied, with faltering voice,
His gracious Hail on all bestowing!—
'Thy words, thou sire of Christabel,
Are sweeter than my harp can tell;
Yet might I gain a boon of thee,   525
This day my journey should not be,
So strange a dream hath come to me,
That I had vowed with music loud
To clear yon wood from thing unblest,
Warned by a vision in my rest!   530
For in my sleep I saw that dove,
That gentle bird, whom thou dost love,
And call'st by thy own daughter's name—
Sir Leoline! I saw the same
Fluttering, and uttering fearful moan,   535
Among the green herbs in the forest alone.
Which when I saw and when I heard,
I wonder'd what might ail the bird;
For nothing near it could I see,
Save the grass and green herbs underneath the old tree.   540

'And in my dream methought I went
To search out what might there be found;
And what the sweet bird's trouble meant,
That thus lay fluttering on the ground.
I went and peered, and could descry   545
No cause for her distressful cry;
But yet for her dear lady's sake
I stooped, methought, the dove to take,
When lo! I saw a bright green snake
Coiled around its wings and neck.   550
Green as the herbs on which it couched,
Close by the dove's its head it crouched;
And with the dove it heaves and stirs,
Swelling its neck as she swelled hers!
I woke; it was the midnight hour,   555
The clock was echoing in the tower;

But though my slumber was gone by,
This dream it would not pass away—
It seems to live upon my eye!
And thence I vowed this self-same day   560
With music strong and saintly song
To wander through the forest bare,
Lest aught unholy loiter there.'

Thus Bracy said: the Baron, the while,
Half-listening heard him with a smile;   565
Then turned to Lady Geraldine,
His eyes made up of wonder and love;
And said in courtly accents fine,
'Sweet maid, Lord Roland's beauteous dove,
With arms more strong than harp or song,   570
Thy sire and I will crush the snake!'
He kissed her forehead as he spake,
And Geraldine in maiden wise
Casting down her large bright eyes,
With blushing cheek and courtesy fine   575
She turned her from Sir Leoline;
Softly gathering up her train,
That o'er her right arm fell again;
And folded her arms across her chest,
And couched her head upon her breast,   580
And looked askance at Christabel——
Jesu, Maria, shield her well!

A snake's small eye blinks dull and shy;
And the lady's eyes they shrunk in her head,
Each shrunk up to a serpent's eye,   585
And with somewhat of malice, and more of dread,
At Christabel she looked askance!—
One moment—and the sight was fled!
But Christabel in dizzy trance
Stumbling on the unsteady ground   590
Shuddered aloud, with a hissing sound;
And Geraldine again turned round,
And like a thing, that sought relief,
Full of wonder and full of grief,
She rolled her large bright eyes divine   595
Wildly on Sir Leoline.

The maid, alas! her thoughts are gone,
She nothing sees—no sight but one!
The maid, devoid of guile and sin,
I know not how, in fearful wise,   600
So deeply had she drunken in
That look, those shrunken serpent eyes,
That all her features were resigned
To this sole image in her mind:
And passively did imitate   605
That look of dull and treacherous hate!
And thus she stood, in dizzy trance,
Still picturing that look askance
With forced unconscious sympathy
Full before her father's view——   610
As far as such a look could be
In eyes so innocent and blue!

And when the trance was o'er, the maid
Paused awhile, and inly prayed:
Then falling at the Baron's feet,   615
'By my mother's soul do I entreat
That thou this woman send away!'
She said: and more she could not say:
For what she knew she could not tell,
O'er-mastered by the mighty spell.   620

Why is thy cheek so wan and wild,
Sir Leoline? Thy only child
Lies at thy feet, thy joy, thy pride,
So fair, so innocent, so mild;
The same, for whom thy lady died!   625
O by the pangs of her dear mother
Think thou no evil of thy child!
For her, and thee, and for no other,
She prayed the moment ere she died:
Prayed that the babe for whom she died,   630
Might prove her dear lord's joy and pride!
     That prayer her deadly pangs beguiled,
          Sir Leoline!
And wouldst thou wrong thy only child,
          Her child and thine?   635

Within the Baron's heart and brain
If thoughts, like these, had any share,
They only swelled his rage and pain,
And did but work confusion there.
His heart was cleft with pain and rage, 640
His cheeks they quivered, his eyes were wild,
Dishonoured thus in his old age;
Dishonoured by his only child,
And all his hospitality
To the wronged daughter of his friend 645
By more than woman's jealousy
Brought thus to a disgraceful end—
He rolled his eye with stern regard
Upon the gentle minstrel bard,
And said in tones abrupt, austere— 650
'Why, Bracy! dost thou loiter here?
I bade thee hence!' The bard obeyed;
And turning from his own sweet maid,
The agéd knight, Sir Leoline,
Led forth the lady Geraldine! 655
[1800]

THE CONCLUSION TO PART II

A little child, a limber elf,
Singing, dancing to itself,
A fairy thing with red round cheeks,
That always finds, and never seeks,
Makes such a vision to the sight 660
As fills a father's eyes with light;
And pleasures flow in so thick and fast
Upon his heart, that he at last
Must needs express his love's excess
With words of unmeant bitterness. 665
Perhaps 'tis pretty to force together
Thoughts so all unlike each other;
To mutter and mock a broken charm,
To dally with wrong that does no harm.
Perhaps 'tis tender too and pretty 670
At each wild word to feel within

A sweet recoil of love and pity.
And what, if in a world of sin
(O sorrow and shame should this be true!)
Such giddiness of heart and brain   675
Comes seldom save from rage and pain,
So talks as it's most used to do.
    [1801]

FROST AT MIDNIGHT

The Frost performs its secret ministry,
Unhelped by any wind. The owlet's cry
Came loud—and hark, again! loud as before.
The inmates of my cottage, all at rest,
Have left me to that solitude, which suits   5
Abstruser musings: save that at my side
My cradled infant slumbers peacefully.
'Tis calm indeed! so calm, that it disturbs
And vexes meditation with its strange
And extreme silentness. Sea, hill, and wood,   10
This populous village! Sea, and hill, and wood,
With all the numberless goings-on of life,
Inaudible as dreams! the thin blue flame
Lies on my low-burnt fire, and quivers not;
Only that film, which fluttered on the grate,   15
Still flutters there, the sole unquiet thing.
Methinks, its motion in this hush of nature
Gives it dim sympathies with me who live,
Making it a companionable form,
Whose puny flaps and freaks the idling Spirit   20
By its own moods interprets, every where
Echo or mirror seeking of itself,
And makes a toy of Thought.

                   But O! how oft,
How oft, at school, with most believing mind,
Presageful, have I gazed upon the bars.   25
To watch that fluttering *stranger!* and as oft
With unclosed lids, already had I dreamt

Of my sweet birth-place, and the old church-tower,
Whose bells, the poor man's only music, rang
From morn to evening, all the hot Fair-day,   30
So sweetly, that they stirred and haunted me
With a wild pleasure, falling on mine ear
Most like articulate sounds of things to come!
So gazed I, till the soothing things, I dreamt,
Lulled me to sleep, and sleep prolonged my dreams!   35
And so I brooded all the following morn,
Awed by the stern preceptor's face, mine eye
Fixed with mock study on my swimming book:
Save if the door half opened, and I snatched
A hasty glance, and still my heart leaped up,   40
For still I hoped to see the *stranger's* face,
Townsman, or aunt, or sister more beloved,
My play-mate when we both were clothed alike!

Dear Babe, that sleepest cradled by my side,
Whose gentle breathings, heard in this deep calm,   45
Fill up the intersperséd vacancies
And momentary pauses of the thought!
My babe so beautiful! it thrills my heart
With tender gladness, thus to look at thee,
And think that thou shalt learn far other lore,   50
And in far other scenes! For I was reared
In the great city, pent 'mid cloisters dim,
And saw nought lovely but the sky and stars.
But *thou*, my babe! shalt wander like a breeze
By lakes and sandy shores, beneath the crags   55
Of ancient mountain, and beneath the clouds,
Which image in their bulk both lakes and shores
And mountain crags: so shalt thou see and hear
The lovely shapes and sounds intelligible
Of that eternal language,, which thy God   60
Utters, who from eternity doth teach
Himself in all, and all things in himself.
Great universal Teacher! he shall mould
Thy spirit, and by giving make it ask.

Therefore all seasons shall be sweet to thee,   65
Whether the summer clothe the general earth
With greenness, or the redbreast sit and sing

Betwixt the tufts of snow on the bare branch
Of mossy apple-tree, while the nigh thatch
Smokes in the sun-thaw; whether the eave-drops fall   70
Heard only in the trances of the blast,
Or if the secret ministry of frost
Shall hang them up in silent icicles,
Quietly shining to the quiet Moon.
    [1798]

FRANCE: AN ODE

I

Ye Clouds! that far above me float and pause,
    Whose pathless march no mortal may controul!
    Ye Ocean-Waves! that, wheresoe'er ye roll,
Yield homage only to eternal laws!
Ye Woods! that listen to the night-birds singing,   5
    Midway the smooth and perilous slope reclined,
Save when your own imperious branches swinging,
    Have made a solemn music of the wind!
Where, like a man beloved of God,
Through glooms, which never woodman trod,   10
    How oft, pursuing fancies holy,
My moonlight way o'er flowering weeds I wound,
    Inspired, beyond the guess of folly,
By each rude shape and wild unconquerable sound!
O ye loud Waves! and O ye Forests high!   15
    And O ye Clouds that far above me soared!
Thou rising Sun! thou blue rejoicing Sky!
    Yea, every thing that is and will be free!
    Bear witness for me, wheresoe'er ye be,
    With what deep worship I have still adored   20
    The spirit of divinest Liberty.

II

When France in wrath her giant-limbs upreared,
    And with that oath, which smote air, earth, and sea,

Stamped her strong foot and said she would be free,
Bear witness for me, how I hoped and feared!   25
With what a joy my lofty gratulation
    Unawed I sang, amid a slavish band:
And when to whelm the disenchanted nation,
    Like fiends embattled by a wizard's wand,
        The Monarchs marched in evil day,   30
        And Britain joined the dire array;
Though dear her shores and circling ocean,
Though many friendships, many youthful loves
    Had swoln the patriot emotion
And flung a magic light o'er all her hills and groves;   35
Yet still my voice, unaltered, sang defeat
    To all that braved the tyrant-quelling lance,
And shame too long delayed and vain retreat!
For ne'er, O Liberty! with partial aim
I dimmed thy light or damped thy holy flame;   40
    But blessed the paeans of delivered France,
And hung my head and wept at Britain's name.

III

'And what,' I said, 'though Blasphemy's loud scream
    With that sweet music of deliverance strove!
    Though all the fierce and drunken passions wove   45
A dance more wild than e'er was maniac's dream!
    Ye storms, that round the dawning East assembled,
The Sun was rising, though ye hid his light!'
    And when, to soothe my soul, that hoped and trembled,
The dissonance ceased, and all seemed calm and bright; 50
    When France her front deep-scarr'd and gory
    Concealed with clustering wreaths of glory;
        When, insupportably advancing,
    Her arm made mockery of the warrior's ramp;
        While timid looks of fury glancing.   55
Domestic treason, crushed beneath her fatal stamp,
Writhed like a wounded dragon in his gore;
    Then I reproached my fears that would not flee;
'And soon,' I said, 'shall Wisdom teach her lore
In the low huts of them that toil and groan!   60
And, conquering by her happiness alone,
    Shall France compel the nations to be free,

Till Love and Joy look round, and call the Earth their
　own.'

IV

Forgive me, Freedom! O forgive those dreams!
　I hear thy voice, I hear thy loud lament,　　　　　　65
　From bleak Helvetia's icy caverns sent—
I hear thy groans upon her blood-stained streams!
　Heroes, that for your peaceful country perished,
And ye that, fleeing, spot your mountain-snows
　With bleeding wounds; forgive me, that I cherished　70
One thought that ever blessed your cruel foes!
　To scatter rage, and traitorous guilt,
　Where Peace her jealous home had built;
　A patriot-race to disinherit
Of all that made their stormy wilds so dear;　　　　　　75
　And with inexpiable spirit
To taint the bloodless freedom of the mountaineer—
O France, that mockest Heaven, adulterous, blind,
　And patriot only in pernicious toils!
Are these thy boasts, Champion of human kind?　　　　80
　To mix with Kings in the low lust of sway,
Yell in the hunt, and share the murderous prey;
To insult the shrine of Liberty with spoils
　From freemen torn; to tempt and to betray?

V

The Sensual and the Dark rebel in vain,　　　　　　　85
　Slaves by their own compulsion! In mad game
They burst their manacles and wear the name
　Of Freedom, graven on a heavier chain!
O Liberty! with profitless endeavour
Have I pursued thee, many a weary hour;　　　　　　　90
　But thou nor swell'st the victor's strain, nor ever
Didst breathe thy soul in forms of human power.
　Alike from all, howe'er they praise thee,
　(Nor prayer, nor boastful name delays thee)
　　Alike from Priestcraft's harpy minions,　　　　　　95
And factious Blasphemy's obscener slaves,
　　Thou speedest on thy subtle pinions,

The guide of homeless winds, and playmate of the waves!
And there I felt thee!—on that sea-cliff's verge,
   Whose pines, scarce travelled by the breeze above,   100
Had made one murmur with the distant surge!
Yes, while I stood and gazed, my temples bare,
And shot my being through earth, sea, and air,
   Possessing all things with intensest love,
    O Liberty! my spirit felt thee there.   105
[1798]

LEWTI

OR THE CIRCASSIAN LOVE-CHAUNT

At midnight by the stream I roved,
To forget the form I loved.
Image of Lewti! from my mind
Depart; for Lewti is not kind.
The Moon was high, the moonlight gleam   5
   And the shadow of a star
Heaved upon Tamaha's stream;
   But the rock shone brighter far,
The rock half sheltered from my view
By pendent boughs of tressy yew.—   10
So shines my Lewti's forehead fair,
Gleaming through her sable hair.
Image of Lewti! from my mind
Depart; for Lewti is not kind.

I saw a cloud of palest hue,   15
   Onward to the moon it passed;
Still brighter and more bright it grew,
With floating colours not a few,
   Till it reached the moon at last:
Then the cloud was wholly bright,   20
With a rich and amber light!
And so with many a hope I seek,
   And with such joy I find my Lewti;
And even so my pale wan cheek
   Drinks in as deep a flush of beauty!   25

Nay, treacherous image! leave my mind,
If Lewti never will be kind.

The little cloud—it floats away,
  Away it goes; away so soon!
Alas! it has no power to stay: 30
Its hues are dim, its hues are grey—
  Away it passes from the moon!
How mournfully it seems to fly,
  Ever fading more and more,
To joyless regions of the sky—   35
  And now 'tis whiter than before!
As white as my poor cheek will be,
  When, Lewti! on my couch I lie,
A dying man for love of thee.
Nay, treacherous image! leave my mind— 40
And yet, thou didst not look unkind.

I saw a vapour in the sky,
Thin, and white, and very high;
I ne'er beheld so thin a cloud:
  Perhaps the breezes that can fly   45
  Now below and now above,
Have snatched aloft the lawny shroud
  Of Lady fair—that died for love.
For maids, as well as youths, have perished
From fruitless love too fondly cherished. 50
Nay, treacherous image! leave my mind—
For Lewti never will be kind.

Hush! my heedless feet from under
  Slip the crumbling banks for ever:
Like echoes to a distant thunder,   55
  They plunge into the gentle river.
The river-swans have heard my tread,
And startle from their reedy bed.
O beauteous birds! methinks ye measure
  Your movements to some heavenly tune! 60
O beauteous birds! 'tis such a pleasure
  To see you move beneath the moon,
I would it were your true delight
To sleep by day and wake all night.

I know the place where Lewti lies,   65
When silent night has closed her eyes:
  It is a breezy jasmine-bower,
The nightingale sings o'er her head:
  Voice of the Night! had I the power
That leafy labyrinth to thread,   70
And creep, like thee, with soundless tread,
I then might view her bosom white
Heaving lovely to my sight,
As these two swans together heave
On the gently-swelling wave.   75

Oh! that she saw me in a dream,
  And dreamt that I had died for care;
All pale and wasted I would seem,
  Yet fair withal, as spirits are!
I'd die indeed, if I might see   80
Her bosom heave, and heave for me!
Soothe, gentle image! soothe my mind!
To-morrow Lewti may be kind.
      [1798]

FEARS IN SOLITUDE

WRITTEN IN APRIL 1798, DURING THE ALARM OF AN INVASION

A green and silent spot, amid the hills,
A small and silent dell! O'er stiller place
No singing sky-lark ever poised himself.
The hills are heathy, save that swelling slope,
Which hath a gay and gorgeous covering on,   5
All golden with the never-bloomless furze,
Which now blooms most profusely: but the dell,
Bathed by the mist, is fresh and delicate
As vernal corn-field, or the unripe flax,
When, through its half-transparent stalks, at eve,   10
The level sunshine glimmers with green light.
Oh! 'tis a quiet spirit-healing nook!
Which all, methinks, would love; but chiefly he,

The humble man, who, in his youthful years,
Knew just so much of folly, as had made   15
His early manhood more securely wise!
Here he might lie on fern or withered heath,
While from the singing lark (that sings unseen
The minstrelsy that solitude loves best),
And from the sun, and from the breezy air,   20
Sweet influences trembled o'er his frame;
And he, with many feelings, many thoughts,
Made up a meditative joy, and found
Religious meanings in the forms of Nature!
And so, his senses gradually wrapt   25
In a half sleep, he dreams of better worlds,
And dreaming hears thee still, O singing lark,
That singest like an angel in the clouds!

My God! it is a melancholy thing
For such a man, who would full fain preserve   30
His soul in calmness, yet perforce must feel
For all his human brethren—O my God!
It weighs upon the heart, that he must think
What uproar and what strife may now be stirring
This way or that way o'er these silent hills—   35
Invasion, and the thunder and the shout,
And all the crash of onset; fear and rage,
And undetermined conflict—even now,
Even now, perchance, and in his native isle:
Carnage and groans beneath this blessed sun!   40
We have offended, Oh! my countrymen!
We have offended very grievously,
And been most tyrannous. From east to west
A groan of accusation pierces Heaven!
The wretched plead against us; multitudes   45
Countless and vehement, the sons of God,
Our brethren! Like a cloud that travels on,
Steamed up from Cairo's swamps of pestilence,
Even so, my countrymen! have we gone forth
And borne to distant tribes slavery and pangs,   50
And, deadlier far, our vices, whose deep taint
With slow perdition murders the whole man,
His body and his soul! Meanwhile, at home,
All individual dignity and power

Engulfed in Courts, Committees, Institutions,   55
Associations and Societies,
A vain, speech-mouthing, speech-reporting Guild,
One Benefit-Club for mutual flattery,
We have drunk up, demure as at a grace,
Pollutions from the brimming cup of wealth;   60
Contemptuous of all honourable rule,
Yet bartering freedom and the poor man's life
For gold, as at a market! The sweet words
Of Christian promise, words that even yet
Might stem destruction, were they wisely preached,   65
Are muttered o'er by men, whose tones proclaim
How flat and wearisome they feel their trade:
Rank scoffers some, but most too indolent
To deem them falsehoods or to know their truth.
Oh! blasphemous! the Book of Life is made   70
A superstitious instrument, on which
We gabble o'er the oaths we mean to break;
For all must swear—all and in every place,
College and wharf, council and justice-court;
All, all must swear, the briber and the bribed,   75
Merchant and lawyer, senator and priest,
The rich, the poor, the old man and the young;
All, all make up one scheme of perjury,
That faith doth reel; the very name of God
Sounds like a juggler's charm; and, bold with joy,   80
Forth from his dark and lonely hiding-place,
(Portentous sight!) the owlet Atheism,
Sailing on obscene wings athwart the noon,
Drops his blue-fringéd lids, and holds them close,
And hooting at the glorious sun in Heaven,   85
Cries out, 'Where is it?'

                           Thankless too for peace,
(Peace long preserved by fleets and perilous seas)
Secure from actual warfare, we have loved
To swell the war-whoop, passionate for war!
Alas! for ages ignorant of all   90
Its ghastlier workings, (famine or blue plague,
Battle, or siege, or flight through wintery snows,)
We, this whole people, have been clamorous
For war and bloodshed; animating sports,

The which we pay for as a thing to talk of,   95
Spectators and not combatants! No guess
Anticipative of a wrong unfelt,
No speculation on contingency,
However dim and vague, too vague and dim
To yield a justifying cause; and forth,   100
(Stuffed out with big preamble, holy names,
And adjurations of the God in Heaven,)
We send our mandates for the certain death
Of thousands and ten thousands! Boys and girls,
And women, that would groan to see a child   105
Pull off an insect's leg, all read of war,
The best amusement for our morning meal!
The poor wretch, who has learnt his only prayers
From curses, who knows scarcely words enough
To ask a blessing from his Heavenly Father,   110
Becomes a fluent phraseman, absolute
And technical in victories and defeats,
And all our dainty terms for fratricide;
Terms which we trundle smoothly o'er our tongues
Like mere abstractions, empty sounds to which   115
We join no feeling and attach no form!
As if the soldier died without a wound;
As if the fibres of this godlike frame
Were gored without a pang; as if the wretch,
Who fell in battle, doing bloody deeds,   120
Passed off to Heaven, translated and not killed;
As though he had no wife to pine for him,
No God to judge him! Therefore, evil days
Are coming on us, O my countrymen!
And what if all-avenging Providence,   125
Strong and retributive, should make us know
The meaning of our words, force us to feel
The desolation and the agony
Of our fierce doings?
                        Spare us yet awhile,
Father and God! O! spare us yet awhile!   130
Oh! let not English women drag their flight
Fainting beneath the burthen of their babes,
Of the sweet infants, that but yesterday
Laughed at the breast! Sons, brothers, husbands, all
Who ever gazed with fondness on the forms   135

Which grew up with you round the same fire-side,
And all who ever heard the sabbath-bells
Without the infidel's scorn, make yourselves pure!
Stand forth! be men! repel an impious foe,
Impious and false, a light yet cruel race,   140
Who laugh away all virtue, mingling mirth
With deeds of murder; and still promising
Freedom, themselves too sensual to be free,
Poison life's amities, and cheat the heart
Of faith and quiet hope, and all that soothes,   145
And all that lifts the spirit! Stand we forth;
Render them back upon the insulted ocean,
And let them toss as idly on its waves
As the vile sea-weed, which some mountain-blast
Swept from our shores! And oh! may we return   150
Not with a drunken triumph, but with fear,
Repenting of the wrongs with which we stung
So fierce a foe to frenzy!

                   I have told,
O Britons! O my brethren! I have told
Most bitter truth, but without bitterness.   155
Nor deem my zeal or factious or mistimed;
For never can true courage dwell with them,
Who, playing tricks with conscience, dare not look
At their own vices. We have been too long
Dupes of a deep delusion! Some, belike,   160
Groaning with restless enmity, expect
All change from change of constituted power;
As if a Government had been a robe,
On which our vice and wretchedness were tagged
Like fancy-points and fringes, with the robe   165
Pulled off at pleasure. Fondly these attach
A radical causation to a few
Poor drudges of chastising Providence,
Who borrow all their hues and qualities
From our own folly and rank wickedness,   170
Which gave them birth and nursed them. Others, mean-
    while,
Dote with a mad idolatry; and all
Who will not fall before their images,
And yield them worship, they are enemies

Even of their country!
                     Such have I been deemed.—   175
But, O dear Britain! O my Mother Isle!
Needs must thou prove a name most dear and holy
To me, a son, a brother, and a friend,
A husband, and a father! who revere
All bounds of natural love, and find them all   180
Within the limits of thy rocky shores.
O native Britain! O my Mother Isle!
How shouldst thou prove aught else but dear and holy
To me, who from thy lakes and mountain-hills,
Thy clouds, thy quiet dales, thy rocks and seas,   185
Have drunk in all my intellectual life,
All sweet sensations, all ennobling thoughts,
All adoration of the God in nature,
All lovely and all honourable things,
Whatever makes this mortal spirit feel   190
The joy and greatness of its future being?
There lives nor form nor feeling in my soul
Unborrowed from my country! O divine
And beauteous island! thou hast been my sole
And most magnificent temple, in the which   195
I walk with awe, and sing my stately songs,
Loving the God that made me!—
                     May my fears,
My filial fears, be vain! and may the vaunts
And menace of the vengeful enemy
Pass like the gust, that roared and died away   200
In the distant tree: which heard, and only heard
In this low dell, bowed not the delicate grass.

But now the gentle dew-fall sends abroad
The fruit-like perfume of the golden furze:
The light has left the summit of the hill,   205
Though still a sunny gleam lies beautiful,
Aslant the ivied beacon. Now farewell,
Farewell, awhile, O soft and silent spot!
On the green sheep-track, up the heathy hill,
Homeward I wind my way; and lo! recalled   210
From bodings that have well-nigh wearied me,
I find myself upon the brow, and pause

Startled! And after lonely sojourning
In such a quiet and surrounded nook,
This burst of prospect, here the shadowy main,   215
Dim-tinted, there the mighty majesty
Of that huge amphitheatre of rich
And elmy fields, seems like society—
Conversing with the mind, and giving it
A livelier impulse and a dance of thought!   220
And now, belovéd Stowey! I behold
Thy church-tower, and, methinks, the four huge elms
Clustering, which mark the mansion of my friend;
And close behind them, hidden from my view,
Is my own lowly cottage, where my babe   225
And my babe's mother dwell in peace! With light
And quickened footsteps thitherward I tend.
Remembering thee, O green and silent dell!
And grateful, that by nature's quietness
And solitary musings, all my heart   230
Is softened, and made worthy to indulge
Love, and the thoughts that yearn for human kind.
     [1798]

THE NIGHTINGALE

A CONVERSATION POEM, APRIL, 1798

No cloud, no relique of the sunken day
Distinguishes the West, no long thin slip
Of sullen light, no obscure trembling hues.
Come, we will rest on this old mossy bridge!
You see the glimmer of the stream beneath,   5
But hear no murmuring: it flows silently,
O'er its soft bed of verdure. All is still,
A balmy night! and though the stars be dim,
Yet let us think upon the vernal showers
That gladden the green earth, and we shall find   10
A pleasure in the dimness of the stars.
And hark! the Nightingale begins its song,
'Most musical, most melancholy' bird!

A melancholy bird? Oh! idle thought!
In Nature there is nothing melancholy.   15
But some night-wandering man whose heart was pierced
With the remembrance of a grievous wrong,
Or slow distemper, or neglected love,
(And so, poor wretch! filled all things with himself,
And made all gentle sounds tell back the tale   20
Of his own sorrow) he, and such as he,
First named these notes a melancholy strain.
And many a poet echoes the conceit;
Poet who hath been building up the rhyme
When he had better far have stretched his limbs   25
Beside a brook in mossy forest-dell,
By sun or moon-light, to the influxes
Of shapes and sounds and shifting elements
Surrendering his whole spirit, of his song
And of his fame forgetful! so his fame   30
Should share in Nature's immortality,
A venerable thing! and so his song
Should make all Nature lovelier, and itself
Be loved like Nature! But 'twill not be so;
And youths and maidens most poetical,   35
Who lose the deepening twilights of the spring
In ball-rooms and hot theatres, they still
Full of meek sympathy must heave their sighs
O'er Philomela's pity-pleading strains.

My Friend, and thou, our Sister! we have learnt   40
A different lore: we may not thus profane
Nature's sweet voices, always full of love
And joyance! 'Tis the merry Nightingale
That crowds, and hurries, and precipitates
With fast thick warble his delicious notes,   45
As he were fearful that an April night
Would be too short for him to utter forth
His love-chant, and disburthen his full soul
Of all its music!
                    And I know a grove
Of large extent, hard by a castle huge,   50
Which the great lord inhabits not; and so
This grove is wild with tangling underwood,
And the trim walks are broken up, and grass,

Thin grass and king-cups grow within the paths.
But never elsewhere in one place I knew   55
So many nightingales; and far and near,
In wood and thicket, over the wide grove,
They answer and provoke each other's song,
With skirmish and capricious passagings,
And murmurs musical and swift jug jug,   60
And one low piping sound more sweet than all—
Stirring the air with such a harmony,
That should you close your eyes, you might almost
Forget it was not day! On moonlight bushes,
Whose dewy leaflets are but half-disclosed,   65
You may perchance behold them on the twigs,
Their bright, bright eyes, their eyes both bright and full,
Glistening, while many a glow-worm in the shade
Lights up her love-torch.
                          A most gentle Maid,
Who dwelleth in her hospitable home   70
Hard by the castle, and at latest eve
(Even like a Lady vowed and dedicate
To something more than Nature in the grove)
Glides through the pathways; she knows all their notes,
That gentle Maid! and oft, a moment's space,   75
What time the moon was lost behind a cloud,
Hath heard a pause of silence; till the moon
Emerging, hath awakened earth and sky
With one sensation, and those wakeful birds
Have all burst forth in choral minstrelsy,   80
As if some sudden gale had swept at once
A hundred airy harps! And she hath watched
Many a nightingale perch giddily
On blossomy twig still swinging from the breeze,
And to that motion tune his wanton song   85
Like tipsy Joy that reels with tossing head.

Farewell, O Warbler! till to-morrow eve,
And you, my friends! farewell, a short farewell!
We have been loitering long and pleasantly,
And now for our dear homes.—That strain again!   90
Full fain it would delay me! My dear babe,
Who, capable of no articulate sound,
Mars all things with his imitative lisp,

How he would place his hand beside his ear,
His little hand, the small forefinger up,   95
And bid us listen! And I deem it wise
To make him Nature's play-mate. He knows well
The evening-star; and once, when he awoke
In most distressful mood (some inward pain
Had made up that strange thing, an infant's dream—)   100
I hurried with him to our orchard-plot,
And he beheld the moon, and, hushed at once,
Suspends his sobs, and laughs most silently,
While his fair eyes, that swam with undropped tears,
Did glitter in the yellow moon-beam! Well!—   105
It is a father's tale: But if that Heaven
Should give me life, his childhood shall grow up
Familiar with these songs, that with the night
He may associate joy.—Once more, farewell,
Sweet Nightingale! once more, my friends! farewell.   110
    [1798]

KUBLA KHAN

In Xanadu did Kubla Khan
A stately pleasure dome decree:
Where Alph, the sacred river, ran
Through caverns measureless to man
    Down to a sunless sea.   5
So twice five miles of fertile ground
With walls and towers were girdled round:
And there were gardens bright with sinuous rills,
Where blossomed many an incense-bearing tree;
And here were forests ancient as the hills,   10
Enfolding sunny spots of greenery.

But oh! that deep romantic chasm which slanted
Down the green hill athwart a cedarn cover!
A savage place! as holy and enchanted
As e'er beneath a waning moon was haunted   15
By woman wailing for her demon-lover!
'And from this chasm, with ceaseless turmoil seething,

As if this earth in fast thick pants were breathing,
A mighty fountain momently was forced:
Amid whose swift half-intermitted burst   20
Huge fragments vaulted like rebounding hail,
Or chaffy grain beneath the thresher's flail:
And 'mid these dancing rocks at once and ever
It flung up momently the sacred river.
Five miles meandering with a mazy motion   25
Through wood and dale the sacred river ran,
Then reached the caverns measureless to man,
And sank in tumult to a lifeless ocean:
And 'mid this tumult Kubla heard from far
Ancestral voices prophesying war!   30
   The shadow of the dome of pleasure
   Floated midway on the waves;
   Where was heard the mingled measure
   From the fountain and the caves.
It was a miracle of rare device,   35
A sunny pleasure-dome with caves of ice!

   A damsel with a dulcimer
   In a vision once I saw:
   It was an Abyssinian maid,
   And on her dulcimer she played,   40
   Singing of Mount Abora.
   Could I revive within me
   Her symphony and song,
   To such a deep delight 'twould win me,
That with music loud and long,   45
I would build that dome in air,
That sunny dome! those caves of ice!
And all who heard should see them there,
And all should cry, Beware! Beware!
His flashing eyes, his floating hair!   50
Weave a circle round him thrice,
And close your eyes with holy dread,
For he on honey-dew hath fed,
And drunk the milk of Paradise.
  [1798]

DEJECTION: AN ODE

Late, late yestreen I saw the new Moon,
With the old Moon in her arms;
And I fear, I fear, my Master dear!
We shall have a deadly storm.
                    Ballad of Sir Patrick Spence.

I

Well! If the Bard was weather-wise, who made
    The grand old ballad of Sir Patrick Spence,
    This night, so tranquil now, will not go hence
Unroused by winds, that ply a busier trade
Than those which mould yon cloud in lazy flakes,   5
Or the dull sobbing draft, that moans and rakes
Upon the strings of this Æolian lute,
        Which better far were mute.
    For lo! the New-moon winter-bright!
    And overspread with phantom light,   10
    (With swimming phantom light o'erspread
    But rimmed and circled by a silver thread)
I see the old Moon in her lap, foretelling
    The coming-on of rain and squally blast.
And oh! that even now the gust were swelling,   15
    And the slant night-shower driving loud and fast!
Those sounds which oft have raised me, whilst they awed,
        And sent my soul abroad,
Might now perhaps their wonted impulse give,
Might startle this dull pain, and make it move and live! 20

II

A grief without a pang, void, dark, and drear,
    A stifled, drowsy, unimpassioned grief,
    Which finds no natural outlet, no relief,
        In word, or sigh, or tear—
O Lady! in this wan and heartless mood,   25
To other thoughts by yonder throstle woo'd,
    All this long eve, so balmy and serene,

Have I been gazing on the western sky,
And its peculiar tint of yellow green:
And still I gaze—and with how blank an eye!   30
And those thin clouds above, in flakes and bars,
That give away their motion to the stars;
Those stars, that glide behind them or between,
Now sparkling, now bedimmed, but always seen:
Yon crescent Moon, as fixed as if it grew   35
In its own cloudless, starless lake of blue;
I see them all so excellently fair,
I see, not feel, how beautiful they are!

III

My genial spirits fail;
And what can these avail   40
To lift the smothering weight from off my breast?
It were a vain endeavour,
Though I should gaze for ever
On that green light that lingers in the west:
I may not hope from outward forms to win   45
The passion and the life, whose fountains are within.

IV

O Lady! we receive but what we give,
And in our life alone does Nature live:
Ours is her wedding garment, ours her shroud!
And would we aught behold, of higher worth,   50
Than that inanimate cold world allowed
To the poor loveless ever-anxious crowd,
Ah! from the soul itself must issue forth
A light, a glory, a fair luminous cloud
Enveloping the Earth—   55
And from the soul itself must there be sent
A sweet and potent voice, of its own birth,
Of all sweet sounds the life and element!

V

O pure of heart! thou need'st not ask of me
What this strong music in the soul may be!   60

What, and wherein it doth exist,
This light, this glory, this fair luminous mist,
This beautiful and beauty-making power.
    Joy, virtuous Lady! Joy that ne'er was given,
Save to the pure, and in their purest hour,   65
Life, and Life's effluence, cloud at once and shower,
Joy, Lady! is the spirit and the power,
Which wedding Nature to us gives in dower
    A new Earth and new Heaven,
Undreamt of by the sensual and the proud—   70
Joy is the sweet voice, Joy the luminous cloud—
    We in ourselves rejoice!
And thence flows all that charms or ear or sight,
    All melodies the echoes of that voice,
All colours a suffusion from that light.   75

VI

There was a time when, though my path was rough,
    This joy within me dallied with distress,
And all misfortunes were but as the stuff
    Whence Fancy made me dreams of happiness:
For hope grew round me, like the twining vine,   80
And fruits, and foliage, not my own, seemed mine.
But now afflictions bow me down to earth:
Nor care I that they rob me of my mirth;
    But oh! each visitation
Suspends what nature gave me at my birth,   85
    My shaping spirit of Imagination.
For not to think of what I needs must feel,
    But to be still and patient, all I can;
And haply by abstruse research to steal
    From my own nature all the natural man—   90
    This was my sole resource, my only plan:
Till that which suits a part infects the whole,
And now is almost grown the habit of my soul.

VII

Hence, viper thoughts, that coil around my mind,
    Reality's dark dream!   95

I turn from you, and listen to the wind,
   Which long has raved unnoticed. What a scream
Of agony by torture lengthened out
That lute sent forth! Thou Wind, that rav'st without,
   Bare crag, or mountain-tairn, or blasted tree,   100
Or pine-grove whither woodman never clomb,
Or lonely house, long held the witches' home,
   Methinks were fitter instruments for thee,
Mad Lutanist! who in this month of showers,
Of dark-brown gardens, and of peeping flowers,   105
Mak'st Devils' yule, with worse than wintry song,
The blossoms, buds, and timorous leaves among.
   Thou Actor, perfect in all tragic sounds!
Thou mighty Poet, e'en to frenzy bold!
     What tell'st thou now about?   110
     'Tis of the rushing of an host in rout,
With groans, of trampled men, with smarting wounds—
At once they groan with pain, and shudder with the cold!
But hush! there is a pause of deepest silence!
   And all that noise, as of a rushing crowd,   115
With groans, and tremulous shudderings—all is over—
   It tells another tale, with sounds less deep and loud!
     A tale of less affright,
     And tempered with delight,
As Otway's self had framed the tender lay,—   120
     'Tis of a little child
     Upon a lonesome wild,
Not far from home, but she hath lost her way:
And now moans low in bitter grief and fear,
And now screams loud, and hopes to make her mother
     hear.   125

VIII

'Tis midnight, but small thoughts have I of sleep:
Full seldom may my friend such vigils keep!
Visit her, gentle Sleep! with wings of healing,
   And may this storm be but a mountain-birth,
May all the stars hang bright above her dwelling,   130
   Silent as though they watched the sleeping Earth!
     With light heart may she rise,
     Gay fancy, cheerful eyes,

Joy lift her spirit, joy attune her voice;
To her may all things live, from pole to pole,   135
Their life the eddying of her living soul!
  O simple spirit, guided from above,
Dear Lady! friend devoutest of my choice,
Thus mayest thou ever, evermore rejoice.

[1802]

HYMN BEFORE SUN-RISE, IN THE VALE OF CHAMOUNI

Hast thou a charm to stay the morning-star
In his steep course? So long he seems to pause
On thy bald awful head, O sovran BLANC,
The Arve and Arveiron at thy base
Rave ceaselessly; but thou, most awful Form!   5
Risest from forth thy silent sea of pines,
How silently! Around thee and above
Deep is the air and dark, substantial, black,
An ebon mass: methinks thou piercest it,
As with a wedge! But when I look again,   10
It is thine own calm home, thy crystal shrine,
Thy habitation from eternity!
O dread and silent Mount! I gazed upon thee,
Till thou, still present to the bodily sense,
Didst vanish from my thought: entranced in prayer   15
I worshipped the Invisible alone.

  Yet, like some sweet beguiling melody,
So sweet, we know not we are listening to it,
Thou, the meanwhile, wast blending with my Thought,
Yea, with my Life and Life's own secret joy: 20
Till the dilating Soul, enrapt, transfused,
Into the mighty vision passing—there
As in her natural form, swelled vast to Heaven!

  Awake, my soul! not only passive praise
Thou owest! not alone these swelling tears,   25
Mute thanks and secret ecstasy! Awake,

Voice of sweet song! Awake, my heart, awake!
Green vales and icy cliffs, all join my Hymn.

Thou first and chief, sole sovereign of the Vale!
O struggling with the darkness all the night,   30
And visited all night by troops of stars.
Or when they climb the sky or when they sink:
Companion of the morning-star at dawn,
Thyself Earth's rosy star, and of the dawn
Co-herald: wake, O wake, and utter praise!   35
Who sank thy sunless pillars deep in Earth?
Who filled thy countenance with rosy light?
Who made thee parent of perpetual streams?

And you, ye five wild torrents fiercely glad!
Who called you forth from night and utter death,   40
From dark and icy caverns called you forth,
Down those precipitous, black, jaggéd rocks,
For ever shattered and the same for ever?
Who gave you your invulnerable life,
Your strength, your speed, your fury, and your joy,   45
Unceasing thunder and eternal foam?
And who commanded (and the silence came),
Here let the billows stiffen, and have rest?

Ye Ice-falls! ye that from the mountain's brow
Adown enormous ravines slope amain—   50
Torrents, methinks, that heard a mighty voice,
And stopped at once amid their maddest plunge!
Motionless torrents! silent cataracts!
Who made you glorious as the Gates of Heaven
Beneath the keen full moon? Who bade the sun   55
Clothe you with rainbows? Who, with living flowers
Of loveliest blue, spread garlands at your feet?—
God! let the torrents, like a shout of nations,
Answer! and let the ice-plains echo, God!
God! Sing ye meadow-streams with gladsome voice!   60
Ye pine-groves, with your soft and soul-like sounds!
And they too have a voice, yon piles of snow,
And in their perilous fall shall thunder, God!

Ye living flowers that skirt the eternal frost!
Ye wild goats sporting round the eagle's nest!   65
Ye eagles, play-mates of the mountain-storm!
Ye lightnings, the dread arrows of the clouds!
Ye signs and wonders of the element!
Utter forth God, and fill the hills with praise!

Thou too, hoar Mount! with thy sky-pointing peaks, 70
Oft from whose feet the avalanche, unheard,
Shoots downward, glittering through the pure serene
Into the depth of clouds, that veil thy breast—
Thou too again, stupendous Mountain! thou
That as I raise my head, awhile bowed low   75
In adoration, upward from thy base
Slow travelling with dim eyes suffused with tears,
Solemnly seemest, like a vapoury cloud,
To rise before me—Rise, O ever rise,
Rise like a cloud of incense from the Earth!   80
Thou kingly Spirit throned among the hills,
Thou dread ambassador from Earth to Heaven,
Great Hierarch! tell thou the silent sky,
And tell the stars, and tell yon rising sun
Earth, with her thousand voices, praises GOD.   85
          [1802]

THE PAINS OF SLEEP

Ere on my bed my limbs I lay,
It hath not been my use to pray
With moving lips or bended knees;
But silently, by slow degrees,
My spirit I to Love compose,   5
In humble trust mine eye-lids close,
With reverential resignation,
No wish conceived, no thought exprest,
Only a sense of supplication;
A sense o'er all my soul imprest   10
That I am weak, yet not unblest,
Since in me, round me, every where
Eternal Strength and Wisdom are.

But yester-night I prayed aloud
In anguish and in agony,   15
Up-starting from the fiendish crowd
Of shapes and thoughts that tortured me:
A lurid light, a trampling throng,
Sense of intolerable wrong,
And whom I scorned, those only strong!   20
Thirst of revenge, the powerless will
Still baffled, and yet burning still!
Desire with loathing strangely mixed
On wild or hateful objects fixed.
Fantastic passions! maddening brawl!   25
And shame and terror over all!
Deeds to be hid which were not hid,
Which all confused I could not know
Whether I suffered, or I did:
For all seemed guilt, remorse or woe,   30
My own or others still the same
Life-stifling fear, soul-stifling shame.

So two nights passed: the night's dismay
Saddened and stunned the coming day.
Sleep, the wide blessing, seemed to me   35
Distemper's worst calamity.
The third night, when my own loud scream
Had waked me from the fiendish dream,
O'ercome with sufferings strange and wild,
I wept as I had been a child;   40
And having thus by tears subdued
My anguish to a milder mood,
Such punishments, I said, were due
To natures deepliest stained with sin,—
For aye entempesting anew   45
The unfathomable hell within,
The horror of their deeds to view,
To know and loathe, yet wish and do!
Such griefs with such men well agree,
But wherefore, wherefore fall on me?   50
To be beloved is all I need,
And whom I love, I love indeed.
    [1808]

TIME, REAL AND IMAGINARY

AN ALLEGORY

On the wide level of a mountain's head,
(I knew not where, but 'twas some faery place)
Their pinions, ostrich-like, for sails out-spread,
Two lovely children run an endless race,
      A sister and a brother!   5
      This far outstripp'd the other;
   Yet ever runs she with reverted face,
   And looks and listens for the boy behind:
      For he, alas! is blind!
O'er rough and smooth with even step he passed,   10
And knows not whether he be first or last.
   [1812]

YOUTH AND AGE

Verse, a breeze mid blossoms straying,
Where Hope clung feeding, like a bee—
Both were mine! Life went a-maying
    With Nature, Hope, and Poesy,
      When I was young!   5

When I was young?—Ah, woful When!
Ah! for the change 'twixt Now and Then!
This breathing house not built with hands,
This body that does me grievous wrong,
O'er aery cliffs and glittering sands,   10
How lightly then it flashed along:—
Like those trim skiffs, unknown of yore,
On winding lakes and rivers wide,
That ask no aid of sail or oar,
That fear no spite of wind or tide!   15
Nought cared this body for wind or weather
When Youth and I lived in't together.

Flowers are lovely; Love is flower-like;
Friendship is a sheltering tree;
O! the joys, that came down shower-like,   20
Of Friendship, Love, and Liberty,
                    Ere I was old!

Ere I was old? Ah woful Ere,
Which tells me, Youth's no longer here!
O Youth! for years so many and sweet,   25
'Tis known, that Thou and I were one,
I'll think it but a fond conceit—
It cannot be that Thou art gone!
Thy vesper-bell hath not yet toll'd:—
And thou wert aye a masker bold!   30
What strange disguise hast now put on,
To make believe, that thou art gone?
I see these locks in silvery slips,
This drooping gait, this altered size:
But Spring-tide blossoms on thy lips,   35
And tears take sunshine from thine eyes!
Life is but thought: so think I will
That Youth and I are house-mates still.

Dew-drops are the gems of morning,
But the tears of mournful eve!   40
Where no hope is, life's a warning
That only serves to make us grieve,
                    When we are old:

That only serves to make us grieve
With oft and tedious taking-leave,   45
Like some poor nigh-related guest,
That may not rudely be dismist;
Yet hath outstay'd his welcome while,
And tells the jest without the smile.
    [1823–1832]

William Wordsworth

1770–1850

William Wordsworth

WILLIAM WORDSWORTH was born in the town of Cocker-mouth, Cumberland, on April 7, 1770. The second of five children of John and Ann Wordsworth, he was most closely associated during his life with his only sister, Dorothy, who was a year younger than he. In 1778, the mother of the Wordsworth children died, and William and Dorothy were separated for some years. Richard, the eldest child, and William were sent to a school in Hawkshead, a town not far to the south. A sensitive and independent boy, William Wordsworth absorbed from his intense activities at the school—sports, reading, solitary wanderings—something of that self-awareness which was to inform much of his major poetry. In October 1787, he entered St. John's College, Cambridge, from which he received his B. A. degree in January 1791. Much of his real education, emerging from his emotional and intellectual responses to experience, remained still ahead of him.

During the long vacation in 1790, Wordsworth had visited France, then in the second year of the Revolution that was rapidly becoming a matter of conscience and decision for most of the intellectuals of England. He returned to Cambridge to take his degree, and then, after visiting London and Wales, he spent the early autumn of 1791 at Cambridge, reading extensively but pursuing no definite plans. Deeply under the influence of the writings of Jean-Jacques Rousseau and others who had given intellectual foundations to the movements which coalesced as the French Revolution, William Wordsworth went back to France in November 1791 and remained there for more than a year, until his situation became clearly dangerous. This experience in France, bringing disillusionment in the Revolution and the subsequent quest for an object of reaffirmation, constitutes the major intellectual and emotional fact of Wordsworth's life—he was later to give poetic testimony to this in *The Prelude*. It led him toward the intellectual awareness of the nature of poetry and of the social role of the poet, which he was to explain in his Preface to the second edition of *Lyrical Ballads* (1800)—an idea that in itself contributed perhaps more than has been suspected to the conservatism, the belief in a firmly structured society, which Wordsworth was to hold in his later years. Some have proposed that the most influential aspect of this period in France was Wordsworth's relationship with Annette Vallon, a young woman of Blois, who bore him a daughter, Anne Caroline, in December 1792, about the time that Wordsworth returned to England. He fully intended to marry Annette as soon as he could safely come back to France; however, in February 1793 the war was declared which was to last between their two countries with but slight interruption until 1815. Obviously the experience had an emotional impact upon Wordsworth which was, in subtle and indirect ways, to affect his life and his poetry. One of the principal results was reflected in the burdening sense of guilt that doubtless afflicted Wordsworth as he emerged as a public figure and a staunch defender of the established order in the years that followed. But to propose that the image of Annette Vallon lies crucially at the center of the meaning and the allusions in Wordsworth's major poetry, such as in the recurrent use of the theme of desertion in the narrative poems, is greatly to overstate the case.

In 1793, Wordsworth prepared and published his first major poems, "Descriptive Sketches" and "An Evening Walk," both typical of the meditative poems about nature that prevailed toward the end of the eighteenth century. The advance of the Reign of Terror rendered his earlier hopes in the Revolution entirely untenable, and for a period of several years he was threatened with a despair that is perhaps characteristic of the intellectual's movement from illusion through disillusion toward what might be ultimate reaffirmation. For a short while Wordsworth was influenced by the rationalism of William Godwin. In Godwin's circle from 1793 to 1795 he found kindred minds, some of which had already begun grappling with the problems caused by the failure of the Revolution in France.

In 1795, Wordsworth received a legacy of £900 and established a home with Dorothy, first at Racedown Lodge, Dorset, then at Alfoxden, Somerset. Here the Wordsworths came to know Samuel Taylor Coleridge and were closely associated with him in what has subsequently been known as the "Annus Mirabilis" of the two poets. The most direct result of their association was the first edition of the *Lyrical Ballads*, published in 1798, and only less direct were their declarations of literary position, first by Wordsworth in the Preface to the second edition of that book, published in 1800, and then by Coleridge in his *Biographia Literaria*, published in 1817. Wordsworth made the major contribution to the *Lyrical Ballads*, both in volume and in the number of titles, which included many of the poems which have since been identified with his most active and successful period as a poet. Although Coleridge's contribution to the second edition was slightly increased, this volume, unlike the anonymous first edition, bore Wordsworth's though not Coleridge's name. In the short-lived period of intense literary association, Wordsworth clearly became the dominant personality. It is fallacious to assume, however, as some have done, that Wordsworth's ideas about poetry were derived almost entirely from Coleridge, or even that Wordsworth himself, too literally identified with the speaker in the poem "The Tables Turned," was essentially an anti-intellectualist. It has been rather clearly demonstrated that though Wordsworth remained basically an empiricist, remote from a systematizing philosopher, he was an active, extensive reader, whose ideas, though in part derived from others, assumed a form characteristic of his own mind and experience.

William and Dorothy Wordsworth passed the winter of 1798-1799 in Germany. In England once more, they settled in Dove Cottage at Grasmere, a Cumberland town not far from Wordsworth's birthplace in the heart of the Lake District that he loved. Wordsworth became engaged to Mary Hutchinson, whom he was to marry in 1802, shortly after he and Dorothy visited Annette Vallon and Wordsworth's daughter during a temporary cessation of hostilities between England and France.

In the five years following his marriage, Wordsworth moved rather apparently to the conservative political position which he was to hold for the remainder of his life. What effect marriage and permanent settlement had upon this situation none can say. Nor can the significance of the resulting diminution of Dorothy's influence upon him be measured; though Dorothy

Wordsworth remained a member of the household, the place that she had held as her brother's intellectual companion was, necessarily, hers no longer. However, Mary, though bringing stability to the home, for the most part lacked those powers which Dorothy had exercised, after Wordsworth's disillusionment in the French Revolution, to bring about the relationship which inspired the "Lines Composed a Few Miles above Tintern Abbey." The journey to France in 1802 and the Coronation of Napoleon as Emperor simply confirmed Wordsworth's hopelessness for France. He was deeply affected when his younger brother, Captain John Wordsworth, went down with his ship, the *Abergavenny*, in February 1805. The reaction that he experienced clearly intensified the emotional forces that were already at work within him; the poems "Ode to Duty" and "Character of the Happy Warrior," written from 1804 to 1806, offer some testimony to the nature of these forces. Wordsworth moved toward a definition of England's present in terms of the past rather than of the future, and he came to identify that national interest with that of the powerful property-holding classes. By 1807, he was assuming a position of religious orthodoxy. Although through much of his later writing Wordsworth revealed persisting intellectual and emotional sympathies with the lower rural classes, these were essentially characteristic of an agrarian conservative, who deplored the effects of industrialism upon these people, rather than of a radical reformer. During the many remaining years of Wordsworth's life, the opinions to which he moved from 1802 to 1807 simply became more firmly established.

The question necessarily arises concerning the way in which Wordsworth's motion toward traditionalism and conservatism affected the quality of his poetry. Although his yearly productivity from 1807 onward was not diminished, the quality of the work composed before that date, in the estimate of nearly all critics who have made a judgment, clearly exceeds that of the work that followed. The proposition that his later political position, supposedly derived from a growing distrust of mankind, has a direct or even parallel relation to the diminution of quality in his poetry, rests in itself upon circumstantial evidence. *The Prelude*, which stands apart from Wordsworth's other work, may suggest a solution to the problem.

During the years from 1798 to 1805, Wordsworth wrote the first draft of *The Prelude*, or *Growth of a Poet's Mind*, the long autobiographical poem which, carrying the speaker through the disillusioning experiences with the French Revolution, concludes in an affirmation of the transcending powers of poetry itself. Wordsworth did not publish the poem, however, and during the remaining years of his life he made revisions in it, attempting to reflect the changes in his views after 1805. Though the tone of the version of *The Prelude* published after Wordsworth's death in 1850 is clearly more conservative than that of the draft finished in 1805, it is apparent that he did not succeed in removing the traces of his 1798 position toward life and art. Essentially this was impossible, for the assumption underlying the very meaning and structure of the poem is that of indefinite growth and change in the mind of man, denying by implication fixity in the universe itself. Such an assumption would really have no meaningful place in the system of beliefs of the later Wordsworth, but to make the poem conform to these beliefs would be to destroy the poem itself; thus *The Prelude* was not published during the poet's life. The other major poems, whose meaning and structure rest upon the essentially Romantic assumption of the unending growth and change of the self, were composed, and for the most part published, before 1807. It is these poems which, largely though not entirely, achieve the complexity that is not found in much of his later work and have long been regarded as Wordsworth's most successful compositions. In the years that followed 1807, abundant though his writing was, Wordsworth wrote poetry that essentially rested upon the assumption of fixity and permanence and infrequently revealed the dynamic force of his earlier work.

During the ensuing years the Wordsworths moved twice, in neither instance very far. First, in 1808, they moved to Allan Bank; then, in 1814, to Rydal Mount, where the poet was to spend the remainder of his life. To some, Wordsworth's last years have seemed a kind of long twilight, devoid of major incident and any of the stimulation of his early years. Wordsworth became more involved in Tory politics: In 1813 he was appointed Distributor of Stamps for Westmoreland and in 1818 Justice of the Peace. Throughout these years he consistently opposed such measures as Parliamentary Reform. In 1820, he journeyed with Mary and Dorothy to visit Annette Vallon and their daughter, now married, whose existence was to be kept from the public until long after Wordsworth's death. In 1828, he traveled with Coleridge to the Rhine Valley. Four years later Dorothy was mysteriously stricken and was to remain thereafter an invalid, losing even intellectual powers in the years preceding her death in 1855. The death of others followed, including Coleridge in 1834, Southey in 1843, and finally Wordsworth's daughter Dora in 1847. The growing isolation during the last several decades of Wordsworth's life, probably intensified by his certitude about all imaginable matters, became at length utter loneliness. Ironically, public recognition came late, making faint beginnings in 1817, the year that Coleridge's *Biographia Literaria*—ostensibly written in justification of Wordsworth's early poems— was published, and culminating in 1843, when Wordsworth followed Southey as Poet Laureate. What solace any of this brought to his later years must remain uncertain. He died at the age of eighty, on April 23, 1850.

II

Of Wordsworth's critical writings, the best known and most significant is the Preface to the second edition of the *Lyrical Ballads*. The occasion for the Preface was the republication, with changes and additions, of the volume of 1798, which had suffered so much from the critics that Wordsworth regarded the justification of at least his own contributions as necessary. Wordsworth's other critical essays, composed and published on various occasions during his many remaining years, principally make explicit the implications in the Preface of 1800 and in some instances, carry these explicit assertions to their logical conclusions.

The purpose of his poems, Wordsworth proposed, was to re-create "situations from common life" by describing them "in a selection of language really used by men," over which he cast "a certain colouring of the imagination"; thus, in the poems these situations would pass beyond what they were in life, revealing thereby "the primary laws of our nature." The poet's material was taken from "humble and rustic life" because here the "elementary feelings co-exist in a state of greater simplicity" than in more sophisticated life, and the language, regularly used with the recurring experience and feeling characteristic of the rustic life, is more permanent and philosophic than the artificial language conventionally used by writers of verse. But the poet's material itself is only instrumental: It stimulates "the spontaneous overflow of powerful feelings" which, somewhat later in the essay, Wordsworth equated to "good poetry." Only "a man who, being possessed of more than usual organic sensibility, had also thought long and deeply" can react to simple experience in such a way that his images of the experience are refined to produce the feelings essential to poetry. Quite obviously, in Wordsworth's proposals the emphasis is subjective. In the poems described "the feeling . . . developed gives importance to the action and situation, and not the action and situation to the feeling." The Poet (the capital is significantly Wordsworth's), though "a man speaking to men," is nevertheless one who exists apart from them,

> . . . a man, it is true, endowed with more lively sensibility, more enthusiasm and tenderness, who has a greater knowledge of human nature, and a more comprehensive soul, than are supposed to be common among mankind; a man pleased with his own passions and volitions, and who rejoices more than other men in the spirit of life that is in him; delighting to contemplate similar volitions and passions as manifested in the goings-on of the Universe, and habitually impelled to create them where he does not find them. To these qualities he has added a disposition to be affected more than other men by absent things as if they were present; an ability of conjuring up in himself passions, which are indeed far from being the same as those produced by real events, yet (especially in those parts of the general sympathy which are pleasing and delightful) do more nearly resemble the passions produced by real events, than anything which, from the motions of their own minds merely, other men are accustomed to feel in themselves:—whence, and from practice, he has acquired a greater readiness and power in expressing what he thinks and feels, and especially those thoughts and feelings which, by his own choice, or from the structure of his own mind, arise in him without immediate external excitement.

The Poet's role, then, is not merely to create an imitation of experience but, from the emotional force of his imagination, to create in his own mind and for other men a reality where there was none before. Poetry is indeed "the spontaneous overflow of powerful feelings," but not because of the direct stimulation of the experience about which the Poet writes. Any man may have an immediate emotional reaction to an experience, but only when this reaction is "recollected in tranquillity" by the Poet in the way that develops the "powerful feelings" does it constitute the essence of good poetry:

> . . . the emotion is contemplated till, by a species of re-action, the tranquillity gradually disappears, and an emotion, kindred to that which was before the subject of contemplation, is gradually produced, and does itself actually exist in the mind. In this mood successful composition generally begins, and in a mood similar to this it is carried on; but the emotion, of whatever kind, and in whatever degree, from various causes, is qualified by various pleasures, so that in describing any passions whatsoever, which are voluntarily described, the mind will, upon the whole, be in a state of enjoyment.

The "overflow of powerful feelings" in all ways transcends the emotional reaction that directly follows the initial experience. A good poem timelessly reveals the essence of that experience, and in so doing achieves an enduring reality of its own that is totally distinct from the existence of the experience. This derives from the mind of the Poet rather than from either the materials originally contemplated by the Poet or the nonessential qualities added to the poem, such as "harmonious metrical language."

Like the other major Romantic Poets, Wordsworth was concerned here primarily with the question of the reality of the self and its responses to experience rather than with the question of value and meaning in the universe outside the self; at least, from the answer to the first question he would infer the response to the second. From the point of view of these proposals, Wordsworth was as much interested in the power of art to carry man beyond the revelation of nature as the classical poets were, and it becomes absurd to insist, as some anti-Romantic critics have done in our own century, that Wordsworth reduced man to the level of raw nature, barbarity and mindlessness. "The human mind is capable of being excited without the application of gross and violent stimulants," he wrote at one point in the Preface, "and he must have a very faint perception of its beauty and dignity who does not know this, and who does not further know, that one being is elevated above another in proportion as he possesses this capability." The Poet is clearly the most exalted of men; in the traditional image of the priest or the prophet, he brings to man that truth which he cannot find for himself (the basis of Wordsworth's later view of a firmly structured society is apparent in these early utterances). The truth is essentially concerned with timelessness, or put another way, with the succession through experience of the phases of the self, in a world that would otherwise seem alien and meaningless:

> My heart leaps up when I behold
> A rainbow in the sky:
> So was it when my life began;
> So is it now I am a man;
> So be it when I shall grow old,
> > Or let me die!
> The Child is father of the Man;
> And I could wish my days to be
> Bound each to each by natural piety.

Each man is an accumulation of all of his moments, every one of which is ideally enriched by the recollection in tranquillity of those which have preceded. The forms of nature, like the "rainbow in the sky," give him a feeling, though not necessarily an understanding, of the unity of his moments, of the continuity of his being. But only the Poet can comprehend and give form to the full implications of his tranquil recollections.

The question arises whether we can adequately judge an author's work by his own æsthetic principles. Obviously a poem must ultimately offer its own standards for judgment, and perhaps it is more meaningful to suggest that an author's explicit æsthetic principles must be tested by his own literary performance. Yet the æsthetic doctrines may serve usefully as an instrument for approaching the poems, but, once inside a work, we may choose to discard the instrument and proceed by a method that the work itself suggests or imposes. Such is particularly the case with Wordsworth's poems and the proposals made in the Preface of 1800. Although in many

of the poems of the later years the awareness of self that lies
at the heart of the 1800 essay is nowhere to be found, Wordsworth's esteemed poems for the most part bear directly or in-
directly upon the concern with the quest for meaning and
continuity in the self that underlies the activity of the Poet
and the endurance of man.

Among the short poems "The Solitary Reaper" is an example. In this poem the speaker, revealed as a Poet himself,
transcends the limits of a given experience in time, carrying
with him the reality of the moment when the young girl herself is no longer before him:

> Whate'er the theme the Maiden sang
> As if her song could have no ending;
> I saw her singing at her work,
> And o'er the sickle bending:—
> I listened, motionless and still;
> And, as I mounted up the hill,
> The music in my heart I bore,
> Long after it was heard no more.

The short work "I Wandered Lonely as a Cloud" is a more
precise example, essentially a poem about poetry itself. The
first three stanzas appear to be concerned with the daffodils,
but in the fourth the speaker records his own "recollection in
tranquillity" to the point that "powerful feelings" emerge
from his spirit, and the image of the daffodils, which he has
actually sketched in the first three stanzas, is timelessly re-
created:

> For oft, when on my couch I lie
> In vacant or in pensive mood,
> They flash upon that inward eye
> Which is the bliss of solitude;
> And then my heart with pleasure fills,
> And dances with the daffodils.

The longer poem, "Lines Composed a Few Miles above
Tintern Abbey," perhaps offers Wordsworth's most rounded
expression of the theme of personal continuity. In the first of
four movements (lines 1-57), the speaker, returning to the

scene on the Wye River after five years, recalls his earlier visit
and attempts to describe what his image of "these beauteous
forms" has meant to him during the interim:

> But oft, in lonely rooms, and 'mid the din
> Of towns and cities, I have owed to them
> In hours of weariness, sensations sweet,
> Felt in the blood, and felt along the heart;
> And passing even into my purer mind,
> With tranquil restoration:—feelings too
> Of unremembered pleasure: such, perhaps,
> As have no slight or trivial influence
> On that best portion of a good man's life,
> His little, nameless, unremembered, acts
> Of kindness and of love.

In the second movement (lines 58-83), he recollects an even
earlier phase of his being, extreme youth, a period in which his
responses, though spontaneous and uninhibited, were bound
by the senses and conditioned entirely by unassimilated emotions: The forms of nature "were then to me/ An appetite; a
feeling and a love," which were unconditioned by long and
deep meditation. In contrast, the present, described by the
speaker in the third movement (lines 84-111) of the poem,
brings a fusion of mind and feeling within the self, from which
emerges, in the speaker's contemplation of nature, a poetic
awareness of the essential goodness of the universe and the
unity of life. By continuous tranquil recollections of past moments, the speaker has constructed in the present a meaningful
image of the self from which he can derive a belief in both
universal harmony and the reality of the future. Thus, in the
fourth movement (lines 112-159), he turns to address his
sister, standing beside him. In her he sees the image of himself
at this place five years before, but he foresees as well his present
self imaged in his sister five years hence; should he then be
dead, she—in tranquillity and in solitude recollecting this
moment with him—will create in her own mind an image that
will achieve a reality surpassing that which the present experience has for her, just as he now has given in his mind a
reality to the past that it did not have at the moment when
he physically experienced it.

The obvious subjectivity of "Tintern Abbey" is implied in "Michael" and a number of the other poems less directly concerned with the forces underlying the poetizing process. In "Michael," interest is first directed to the responses of the speaker himself, apparently a Poet telling the story, then to the responses of those within the story that he tells. Here significance is attached not to the sheep-fold but to the feelings of Michael that are called forth by recollection of all that the sheep-fold has come to symbolize to him. The fold serves, in other words, as the principal instrument by which he binds his "days each to each." The protagonist in "The Old Cumberland Beggar," through natural and intense feeling, has become emotionally one with the land over which he passes, and arouses in those around him the natural feelings by which they too can bind their days together:

> While from door to door,
> This old Man creeps, the villagers in him
> Behold a record which together binds
> Past deeds and offices of charity
> Else unremembered, and so keeps alive
> The kindly mood in hearts which lapse of years,
> And that half-wisdom half-experience gives,
> Make slow to feel, and by sure steps resign
> To selfishness and cold oblivious cares.
> Among the farms and solitary huts,
> Hamlets and thinly-scattered villages,
> Where'er the aged Beggar takes his rounds,
> The mild necessity of use compels
> To acts of love; and habit does the work
> Of reason; yet prepares that after-joy
> Which reason cherishes.

In "Ode. Intimations of Immortality from Recollections of Early Childhood," Wordsworth explored the ultimate implications of his subjectivism and the theme of personal continuity: The speaker, establishing the unity of his days in life, infers the reality of a self that transcends the limits of this life. This is the most striking instance of his use of the concept, and it probably constitutes his most complex poem. Although certainly not all of Wordsworth's major poems are so ordered, the majority concern, in characteristically Romantic fashion, the nature of the self and its quest, amid change and growth, for a sense of reality with which, to a degree varying in each instance, the speaker infuses nature and his own experiences.

William Wordsworth

THE REVERIE OF POOR SUSAN

At the corner of Wood Street, when daylight appears,
Hangs a Thrush that sings loud, it has sung for three years:
Poor Susan has passed by the spot, and has heard
In the silence of morning the song of the Bird.

'Tis a note of enchantment; what ails her? She sees   5
A mountain ascending, a vision of trees;
Bright volumes of vapour through Lothbury glide,
And a river flows on through the vale of Cheapside.

Green pastures she views in the midst of the dale,
Down which she so often has tripped with her pail;   10
And a single small cottage, a nest like a dove's,
The one only dwelling on earth that she loves.

She looks, and her heart is in heaven: but they fade,
The mist and the river, the hill and the shade:
The stream will not flow, and the hill will not rise,   15
And the colours have all passed away from her eyes!
[1797]

THE OLD CUMBERLAND BEGGAR

The class of Beggars, to which the Old Man here described
belongs, will probably soon be extinct. It consisted of poor, and,
mostly, old and infirm persons, who confined themselves to a
stated round in their neighbourhood, and had certain fixed days,
on which, at different houses, they regularly received alms, sometimes in money, but mostly in provisions.

I saw an aged Beggar in my walk;
And he was seated, by the highway side,
On a low structure of rude masonry
Built at the foot of a huge hill, that they
Who lead their horses down the steep rough road   5

May thence remount at ease. The aged Man
Had placed his staff across the broad smooth stone
That overlays the pile; and, from a bag
All white with flour, the dole of village dames,
He drew his scraps and fragments, one by one;   10
And scanned them with a fixed and serious look
Of idle computation. In the sun,
Upon the second step of that small pile,
Surrounded by those wild unpeopled hills,
He sat, and ate his food in solitude: 15
And ever, scattered from his palsied hand,
That, still attempting to prevent the waste,
Was baffled still, the crumbs in little showers
Fell on the ground; and the small mountain birds,
Not venturing yet to peck their destined meal,   20
Approached within the length of half his staff.

    Him from my childhood have I known; and then
He was so old, he seems not older now;
He travels on, a solitary Man,
So helpless in appearance, that for him   25
The sauntering Horseman throws not with a slack
And careless hand his alms upon the ground,
But stops,—that he may safely lodge the coin
Within the old Man's hat; nor quits him so,
But still, when he has given his horse the rein,   30
Watches the aged Beggar with a look
Sidelong, and half-reverted. She who tends
The toll-gate, when in summer at her door
She turns her wheel, if on the road she sees
The aged Beggar coming, quits her work,   35
And lifts the latch for him that he may pass.
The post-boy, when his rattling wheels o'ertake
The aged Beggar in the woody lane,
Shouts to him from behind; and, if thus warned
The old man does not change his course, the boy   40
Turns with less noisy wheels to the roadside,
And passes gently by, without a curse
Upon his lips or anger at his heart.

    He travels on, a solitary Man;
His age has no companion. On the ground   45

His eyes are turned, and, as he moves along,
They move along the ground; and, evermore,
Instead of common and habitual sight
Of fields with rural works, of hill and dale,
And the blue sky, one little span of earth   50
Is all his prospect. Thus, from day to day.
Bow-bent, his eyes for ever on the ground,
He plies his weary journey; seeing still,
And seldom knowing that he sees, some straw,
Some scattered leaf, or marks which, in one track, 55
The nails of cart or chariot-wheel have left
Impressed on the white road,—in the same line,
At distance still the same. Poor Traveller!
His staff trails with him; scarcely do his feet
Disturb the summer dust; he is so still   60
In look and motion, that the cottage curs,
Ere he has passed the door, will turn away,
Weary of barking at him. Boys and girls,
The vacant and the busy, maids and youths,
The urchins newly breeched—all pass him by: 65
Him even the slow-paced waggon leaves behind.

But deem not this Man useless—Statesmen! ye
Who are so restless in your wisdom, ye
Who have a broom still ready in your hands
To rid the world of nuisances; ye proud,   70
Heart-swoln, while in your pride ye contemplate
Your talents, power, or wisdom, deem him not
A burthen of the earth! 'Tis Nature's law
That none, the meanest of created things,
Of forms created the most vile and brute,   75
The dullest or most noxious, should exist
Divorced from good—a spirit and pulse of good,
A life and soul, to every mode of being
Inseparably linked. Then be assured
That least of all can aught—that ever owned   80
The heaven-regarding eye and front sublime
Which man is born to—sink, howe'er depressed,
So low as to be scorned without a sin;
Without offence to God cast out of view;
Like the dry remnant of a garden-flower   85
Whose seeds are shed, or as an implement

Worn out and worthless. While from door to door,
This old Man creeps, the villagers in him
Behold a record which together binds
Past deeds and offices of charity   90
Else unremembered, and so keeps alive
The kindly mood in hearts which lapse of years,
And that half-wisdom half-experience gives,
Make slow to feel, and by sure steps resign
To selfishness and cold oblivious cares.   95
Among the farms and solitary huts,
Hamlets and thinly-scattered villages,
Where'er the aged Beggar takes his rounds,
The mild necessity of use compels
To acts of love; and habit does the work   100
Of reason; yet prepares that after-joy
Which reason cherishes. And thus the soul,
By that sweet taste of pleasure unpursued,
Doth find herself insensibly disposed
To virtue and true goodness. Some there are,   105
By their good works exalted, lofty minds,
And meditative, authors of delight
And happiness, which to the end of time
Will live, and spread, and kindle: even such minds
In childhood, from this solitary Being,   110
Or from like wanderer, haply have received
(A thing more precious far than all that books
Or the solicitudes of love can do!)
That first mild touch of sympathy and thought,
In which they found their kindred with a world   115
Where want and sorrow were. The easy man
Who sits at his own door,—and, like the pear
That overhangs his head from the green wall,
Feeds in the sunshine; the robust and young,
The prosperous and unthinking, they who live   120
Sheltered, and flourish in a little grove
Of their own kindred;—all behold in him
A silent monitor, which on their minds
Must needs impress a transitory thought
Of self-congratulation, to the heart   125
Of each recalling his peculiar boons,
His charters and exemptions; and, perchance,
Though he to no one give the fortitude

And circumspection needful to preserve
His present blessings, and to husband up   130
The respite of the season, he, at least,
And 'tis no vulgar service, makes them felt.

Yet further.————Many, I believe, there are
Who live a life of virtuous decency,
Men who can hear the Decalogue and feel   135
No self-reproach; who of the moral law
Established in the land where they abide
Are strict observers; and not negligent
In acts of love to those with whom they dwell,
Their kindred, and the children of their blood.   140
Praise be to such, and to their slumbers peace!
—But of the poor man ask, the abject poor;
Go, and demand of him, if there be here
In this cold abstinence from evil deeds,
And these inevitable charities,   145
Wherewith to satisfy the human soul?
No—man is dear to man; the poorest poor
Long for some moments in a weary life
When they can know and feel that they have been,
Themselves, the fathers and the dealers-out   150
Of some small blessings; have been kind to such
As needed kindness, for this single cause,
That we have all of us one human heart.
—Such pleasure is to one kind Being known,
My neighbour, when with punctual care, each week,   155
Duly as Friday comes, though pressed herself
By her own wants, she from her store of meal
Takes one unsparing handful for the scrip
Of this old Mendicant, and, from her door
Returning with exhilarated heart,   160
Sits by her fire, and builds her hope in heaven.

Then let him pass, a blessing on his head!
And while in that vast solitude to which
The tide of things has borne him, he appears
To breathe and live but for himself alone,   165
Unblamed, uninjured, let him bear about
The good which the benignant law of Heaven
Has hung around him: and, while life is his,

Still let him prompt the unlettered villagers
To tender offices and pensive thoughts.   170
—Then let him pass, a blessing on his head!
And, long as he can wander, let him breathe
The freshness of the valleys; let his blood
Struggle with frosty air and winter snows;
And let the chartered wind that sweeps the heath   175
Beat his grey locks against his withered face.
Reverence the hope whose vital anxiousness
Gives the last human interest to his heart.
May never HOUSE, misnamed of INDUSTRY,
Make him a captive!—for that pent-up din,   180
Those life-consuming sounds that clog the air,
Be his the natural silence of old age!
Let him be free of mountain solitudes;
And have around him, whether heard or not,
The pleasant melody of woodland birds.   185
Few are his pleasures: if his eyes have now
Been doomed so long to settle upon earth
That not without some effort they behold
The countenance of the horizontal sun,
Rising or setting, let the light at least   190
Find a free entrance to their languid orbs,
And let him, where and when he will, sit down
Beneath the trees, or on a grassy bank
Of highway side, and with the little birds
Share his chance-gathered meal; and, finally,   195
As in the eye of Nature he has lived,
So in the eye of Nature let him die!
　　[1797]

GOODY BLAKE AND HARRY GILL

A TRUE STORY

Oh! what's the matter? what's the matter?
What is't that ails young Harry Gill?
That evermore his teeth they chatter,

Chatter, chatter, chatter still!
Of waistcoats Harry has no lack,   5
Good duffle grey, and flannel fine;
He has a blanket on his back,
And coats enough to smother nine.

In March, December, and in July,
'Tis all the same with Harry Gill;   10
The neighbours tell, and tell you truly,
His teeth they chatter, chatter still.
At night, at morning, and at noon,
'Tis all the same with Harry Gill;
Beneath the sun, beneath the moon,   15
His teeth they chatter, chatter still!

Young Harry was a lusty drover,
And who so stout of limb as he?
His cheeks were red as ruddy clover;
His voice was like the voice of three.   20
Old Goody Blake was old and poor;
Ill fed she was, and thinly clad;
And any man who passed her door
Might see how poor a hut she had.

All day she spun in her poor dwelling: 25
And then her three hours' work at night,
Alas! 'twas hardly worth the telling,
It would not pay for candle-light.
Remote from sheltered village-green,
On a hill's northern side she dwelt,   30
Where from sea-blasts the hawthorns lean,
And hoary dews are slow to melt.

By the same fire to boil their pottage,
Two poor old Dames, as I have known,
Will often live in one small cottage;   35
But she, poor Woman! housed alone.
'Twas well enough, when summer came,
The long, warm, lightsome summer-day,
Then at her door the *canty* Dame
Would sit, as any linnet, gay.   40

But when the ice our streams did fetter,
Oh then how her old bones would shake!
You would have said, if you had met her,
'Twas a hard time for Goody Blake.
Her evenings then were dull and dead: 45
Sad case it was, as you may think,
For very cold to go to bed;
And then for cold not sleep a wink.

O joy for her! whene'er in winter
The winds at night had made a rout;   50
And scattered many a lusty splinter
And many a rotten bough about.
Yet never had she, well or sick,
As every man who knew her says,
A pile beforehand, turf or stick,   55
Enough to warm her for three days.

Now, when the frost was past enduring,
And made her poor old bones to ache,
Could any thing be more alluring
Than an old hedge to Goody Blake?   60
And, now and then, it must be said,
When her old bones were cold and chill,
She left her fire, or left her bed,
To seek the hedge of Harry Gill.

Now Harry he had long suspected   65
This trespass of old Goody Blake;
And vowed that she should be detected—
That he on her would vengeance take.
And oft from his warm fire he'd go,
And to the fields his road would take;   70
And there, at night, in frost and snow,
He watched to seize old Goody Blake.

And once, behind a rick of barley,
Thus looking out did Harry stand:
The moon was full and shining clearly,   75
And crisp with frost the stubble land.
—He hears a noise—he's all awake—
Again?—on tip-toe down the hill

He softy creeps—'tis Goody Blake;
She's at the hedge of Harry Gill!   80

Right glad was he when he beheld her:
Stick after stick did Goody pull:
He stood behind a bush of elder,
Till she had filled her apron full.
When with her load she turned about,   85
The by-way back again to take;
He started forward, with a shout,
And sprang upon poor Goody Blake.

And fiercely by the arm he took her,
And by the arm he held her fast,   90
And fiercely by the arm he shook her,
And cried, "I've caught you then at last!"
Then Goody, who had nothing said,
Her bundle from her lap let fall;
And, kneeling on the sticks, she prayed   95
To God that is the judge of all.

She prayed, her withered hand uprearing,
While Harry held her by the arm—
"God! who art never out of hearing,
O may he never more be warm!"   100
The cold, cold moon above her head,
Thus on her knees did Goody pray;
Young Harry heard what she had said:
And icy cold he turned away.

He went complaining all the morrow   105
That he was cold and very chill:
His face was gloom, his heart was sorrow,
Alas! that day for Harry Gill!
That day he wore a riding-coat,
But not a whit the warmer he: 110
Another was on Thursday brought,
And ere the Sabbath he had three.

'Twas all in vain, a useless matter,
And blankets were about him pinned;
Yet still his jaws and teeth they clatter,   115

Like a loose casement in the wind.
And Harry's flesh it fell away;
And all who see him say, 'tis plain,
That, live as long as live he may,
He never will be warm again.   120

No word to any man he utters,
A-bed or up, to young or old;
But ever to himself he mutters,
"Poor Harry Gill is very cold."
A-bed or up, by night or day;   125
His teeth they chatter, chatter still.
Now think, ye farmers all, I pray,
Of Goody Blake and Harry Gill!
            [1798]

SIMON LEE

THE OLD HUNTSMAN

With an incident in which he was concerned.

In the sweet shire of Cardigan,
Not far from pleasant Ivor-hall,
An old Man dwells, a little man,—
'Tis said he once was tall.
Full five-and-thirty years he lived   5
A running huntsman merry;
And still the centre of his cheek
Is red as a ripe cherry.

No man like him the horn could sound,
And hill and valley rang with glee   10
When Echo bandied, round and round,
The halloo of Simon Lee.
In those proud days, he little cared
For husbandry or tillage;
To blither tasks did Simon rouse   15
The sleepers of the village.

He all the country could outrun,
Could leave both man and horse behind;
And often, ere the chase was done,
He reeled, and was stone-blind.
And still there's something in the world   20
At which his heart rejoices;
For when the chiming hounds are out,
He dearly loves their voices!

But, oh the heavy change!—bereft   25
Of health, strength, friends, and kindred, see!
Old Simon to the world is left
In liveried poverty.
His Master's dead,—and no one now
Dwells in the Hall of Ivor;
Men, dogs, and horses, all are dead;   30
He is the sole survivor.

And he is lean and he is sick;
His body, dwindled and awry,
Rests upon ankles swoln and thick;   35
His legs are thin and dry.
One prop he has, and only one,
His wife, an aged woman,
Lives with him, near the waterfall,
Upon the village Common.   40

Beside their moss-grown hut of clay,
Not twenty paces from the door,
A scrap of land they have, but they
Are poorest of the poor.
This scrap of land he from the heath   45
Enclosed when he was stronger;
But what to them avails the land
Which he can till no longer?

Oft, working by her Husband's side,
Ruth does what Simon cannot do;
For she, with scanty cause for pride,   50
Is stouter of the two.
And, though you with your utmost skill
From labour could not wean them,

'Tis little, very little—all   55
That they can do between them.

Few months of life has he in store
As he to you will tell,
For still, the more he works, the more
Do his weak ankles swell.   60
My gentle Reader, I perceive
How patiently you've waited,
And now I fear that you expect
Some tale will be related.

O Reader! had you in your mind   65
Such stores as silent thought can bring,
O gentle Reader! you would find
A tale in every thing.
What more I have to say is short,
And you must kindly take it: 70
It is no tale; but, should you think,
Perhaps a tale you'll make it.

One summer-day I chanced to see
This old Man doing all he could
To unearth the root of an old tree,   75
A stump of rotten wood.
The mattock tottered in his hand;
So vain was his endeavour,
That at the root of the old tree
He might have worked for ever.   80

"You're overtasked, good Simon Lee,
Give me your tool," to him I said;
And at the word right gladly he
Received my proffered aid.
I struck, and with a single blow   85
The tangled root I severed,
At which the poor old Man so long
And vainly had endeavoured.

The tears into his eyes were brought,
And thanks and praises seemed to run   90
So fast out of his heart, I thought

They never would have done.
—I've heard of hearts unkind, kind deeds
With coldness still returning;
Alas! the gratitude of men   95
Hath oftener left me mourning.
    [1798]

EXPOSTULATION AND REPLY

"Why, William, on that old grey stone,
Thus for the length of half a day,
Why, William, sit you thus alone,
And dream your time away?

"Where are your books?—that light bequeathed   5
To Beings else forlorn and blind!
Up! up! and drink the spirit breathed
From dead men to their kind.

"You look round on your Mother Earth,
As if she for no purpose bore you;   10
As if you were her first-born birth,
And none had lived before you!"

One morning thus, by Esthwaite lake,
When life was sweet, I knew not why,
To me my good friend Matthew spake,   15
And thus I made reply:

"The eye—it cannot choose but see;
We cannot bid the ear be still;
Our bodies feel, where'er they be,
Against or with our will.   20

"Nor less I deem that there are Powers
Which of themselves our minds impress;
That we can feed this mind of ours
In a wise passiveness.

"Think you, 'mid all this mighty sum   25
Of things for ever speaking,
That nothing of itself will come,
But we must still be seeking?

"—Then ask not wherefore, here, alone,
Conversing as I may,   30
I sit upon this old grey stone,
And dream my time away."
    [1798]

THE TABLES TURNED

AN EVENING SCENE ON THE SAME SUBJECT

Up! up! my Friend, and quit your books;
Or surely you'll grow double:
Up! up! my Friend, and clear your looks;
Why all this toil and trouble?

The sun, above the mountain's head,   5
A freshening lustre mellow
Through all the long green fields has spread,
His first sweet evening yellow.

Books! 'tis a dull and endless strife:
Come, hear the woodland linnet,   10
How sweet his music! on my life,
There's more of wisdom in it.

And hark! how blithe the throstle sings!
He, too, is no mean preacher:
Come forth into the light of things,   15
Let Nature be your Teacher.

She has a world of ready wealth,
Our minds and hearts to bless—
Spontaneous wisdom breathed by health,
Truth breathed by cheerfulness.   20

One impulse from a vernal wood
May teach you more of man,
Of moral evil and of good,
Than all the sages can.

Sweet is the lore which Nature brings;   25
Our meddling intellect
Mis-shapes the beauteous forms of things:—
We murder to dissect.

Enough of Science and of Art;
Close up those barren leaves;
Come forth, and bring with you a heart   30
That watches and receives.
[1798]

LINES

COMPOSED A FEW MILES ABOVE TINTERN ABBEY, ON REVISITING
THE BANKS OF THE WYE DURING A TOUR. JULY 13, 1798

Five years have past; five summers, with the length
Of five long winters! and again I hear
These waters, rolling from their mountain-springs
With a soft inland murmur.—Once again
Do I behold these steep and lofty cliffs,   5
That on a wild secluded scene impress
Thoughts of more deep seclusion; and connect
The landscape with the quiet of the sky.
The day is come when I again repose
Here, under this dark sycamore, and view   10
These plots of cottage-ground, these orchard-tufts,
Which at this season, with their unripe fruits,
Are clad in one green hue, and lose themselves
'Mid groves and copses. Once again I see
These hedge-rows, hardly hedge-rows, little lines   15
Of sportive wood run wild: these pastoral farms,
Green to the very door; and wreaths of smoke
Sent up, in silence, from among the trees!
With some uncertain notice, as might seem

Of vagrant dwellers in the houseless woods,   20
Or of some Hermit's cave, where by his fire
The Hermit sits alone.

                    These beauteous forms,
Through a long absence, have not been to me
As is a landscape to a blind man's eye:
But oft, in lonely rooms, and 'mid the din   25
Of towns and cities, I have owed to them
In hours of weariness, sensations sweet,
Felt in the blood, and felt along the heart;
And passing even into my purer mind,
With tranquil restoration:—feelings too   30
Of unremembered pleasure: such, perhaps,
As have no slight or trivial influence
On that best portion of a good man's life,
His little, nameless, unremembered, acts
Of kindness and of love. Nor less, I trust,   35
To them I may have owed another gift,
Of aspect more sublime; that blessed mood
In which the burthen of the mystery,
In which the heavy and the weary weight
Of all this unintelligible world,   40
Is lightened:—that serene and blessed mood,
In which the affections gently lead us on,—
Until, the breath of this corporeal frame
And even the motion of our human blood
Almost suspended, we are laid asleep   45
In body, and become a living soul:
While with an eye made quiet by the power
Of harmony, and the deep power of joy,
We see into the life of things.
                             If this
Be but a vain belief, yet, oh! how oft—   50
In darkness and amid the many shapes
Of joyless daylight; when the fretful stir
Unprofitable, and the fever of the world,
Have hung upon the beatings of my heart—
How oft, in spirit, have I turned to thee,   55
O sylvan Wye! thou wanderer thro' the woods,
How often has my spirit turned to thee!

And now, with gleams of half-extinguished thought,
With many recognitions dim and faint,
And somewhat of a sad perplexity,
The picture of the mind revives again: 60
While here I stand, not only with the sense
Of present pleasure, but with pleasing thoughts
That in this moment there is life and food
For future years. And so I dare to hope,   65
Though changed, no doubt, from what I was when first
I came among these hills; when like a roe
I bounded o'er the mountains, by the sides
Of the deep rivers, and the only streams,
Wherever nature led: more like a man   70
Flying from something that he dreads than one
Who sought the thing he loved. For nature then
(The coarser pleasures of my boyish days,
And their glad animal movements all gone by)
To me was all in all.—I cannot paint   75
What then I was. The sounding cataract
Haunted me like a passion: the tall rock,
The mountain, and the deep and gloomy wood,
Their colours and their forms, were then to me
An appetite; a feeling and a love,   80
That had no need of a remoter charm,
By thought supplied, nor any interest
Unborrowed from the eye.—That time is past,
And all its aching joys are now no more,
And all its dizzy raptures. Not for this   85
Faint I, nor mourn nor murmur; other gifts
Have followed: for such loss, I would believe,
Abundant recompense. For I have learned
To look on nature, not as in the hour
Of thoughtless youth; but hearing oftentimes   90
The still, sad music of humanity,
Nor harsh nor grating, though of ample power
To chasten and subdue. And I have felt
A presence that disturbs me with the joy
Of elevated thoughts; a sense sublime   95
Of something far more deeply interfused,
Whose dwelling is the light of setting suns,
And the round ocean and the living air,
And the blue sky, and in the mind of man:

A motion and a spirit, that impels   100
All thinking things, all objects of all thought,
And rolls through all things. Therefore am I still
A lover of the meadows and the woods,
And mountains; and of all that we behold
From this green earth; of all the mighty world   105
Of eye, and ear,—both what they half create,
And what perceive; well pleased to recognise
In nature and the language of the sense
The anchor of my purest thoughts, the nurse,
The guide, the guardian of my heart, and soul   110
Of all my moral being.
                                        Nor perchance,
If I were not thus taught, should I the more
Suffer my genial spirits to decay:
For thou art with me here upon the banks
Of this fair river; thou my dearest Friend,   115
My dear, dear Friend; and in thy voice I catch
The language of my former heart, and read
My former pleasures in the shooting lights
Of thy wild eyes. Oh! yet a little while
May I behold in thee what I was once,   120
My dear, dear Sister! and this prayer I make,
Knowing that Nature never did betray
The heart that loved her; 'tis her privilege,
Through all the years of this our life, to lead
From joy to joy: for she can so inform   125
The mind that is within us, so impress
With quietness and beauty, and so feed
With lofty thoughts, that neither evil tongues,
Rash judgments, nor the sneers of selfish men,
Nor greetings where no kindness is, nor all   130
The dreary intercourse of daily life,
Shall e'er prevail against us, or disturb
Our cheerful faith, that all which we behold
Is full of blessings. Therefore let the moon
Shine on thee in thy solitary walk;   135
And let the misty mountain-winds be free
To blow against thee: and, in after years,
When these wild ecstasies shall be matured
Into a sober pleasure; when thy mind
Shall be a mansion for all lovely forms,   140

Thy memory be as a dwelling-place
For all sweet sounds and harmonies; oh! then,
If solitude, or fear, or pain, or grief,
Should be thy portion, with what healing thoughts
Of tender joy wilt thou remember me,   145
And these my exhortations! Nor, perchance—
If I should be where I no more can hear
Thy voice, nor catch from thy wild eyes these gleams
Of past existence—wilt thou then forget
That on the banks of this delightful stream   150
We stood together; and that I, so long
A worshipper of Nature, hither came
Unwearied in that service: rather say
With warmer love—oh! with far deeper zeal
Of holier love. Nor wilt thou then forget,   155
That after many wanderings, many years
Of absence, these steep woods and lofty cliffs,
And this green pastoral landscape, were to me
More dear, both for themselves and for thy sake!
[1798]

WE ARE SEVEN

————A simple Child,
That lightly draws its breath,
And feels its life in every limb,
What should it know of death?

I met a little cottage Girl: 5
She was eight years old, she said;
Her hair was thick with many a curl
That clustered round her head.

She had a rustic, woodland air,
And she was wildly clad: 10
Her eyes were fair, and very fair;
—Her beauty made me glad.

"Sisters and brothers, little Maid,
How many may you be?"
"How many? Seven in all," she said,   15
And wondering looked at me.

"And where are they? I pray you tell."
She answered, "Seven are we;
And two of us at Conway dwell,
And two are gone to sea.   20

"Two of us in the church-yard lie,
My sister and my brother;
And, in the church-yard cottage, I
Dwell near them with my mother."

"You say that two at Conway dwell,   25
And two are gone to sea,
Yet ye are seven! I pray you tell,
Sweet Maid, how this may be."

Then did the little Maid reply,   30
"Seven boys and girls are we;
Two of us in the church-yard lie,
Beneath the church-yard tree."

"You run about, my little Maid,
Your limbs they are alive;
If two are in the church-yard laid,   35
Then ye are only five."

"Their graves are green, they may be seen,"
The little Maid replied,
"Twelve steps or more from my mother's door,
And they are side by side.   40

"My stockings there I often knit,
My kerchief there I hem;
And there upon the ground I sit,
And sing a song to them.

                                               45
"And often after sun-set, Sir,
When it is light and fair,

I take my little porringer,
And eat my supper there.

"The first that died was sister Jane;
In bed she moaning lay,   50
Till God released her of her pain;
And then she went away.

"So in the church-yard she was laid;
And, when the grass was dry,
Together round her grave we played,   55
My brother John and I.

"And when the ground was white with snow,
And I could run and slide,
My brother John was forced to go,
And he lies by her side."   60

"How many are you, then," said I,
"If they two are in heaven?"
Quick was the little Maid's reply,
"O Master! we are seven."

"But they are dead; those two are dead!   65
Their spirits are in heaven!"
'Twas throwing words away; for still
The little Maid would have her will,
And said, "Nay, we are seven!"
   [1798]

LUCY GRAY;

OR, SOLITUDE

Oft I had heard of Lucy Gray:
And, when I crossed the wild,
I chanced to see at break of day
The solitary child.

No mate, no comrade Lucy knew;   5
She dwelt on a wide moor,
—The sweetest thing that ever grew
Beside a human door!

You yet may spy the fawn at play,
The hare upon the green;   10
But the sweet face of Lucy Gray
Will never more be seen.

"To-night will be a stormy night—
You to the town must go;
And take a lantern, Child, to light   15
Your mother through the snow."

"That, Father! will I gladly do:
'Tis scarcely afternoon—
The minster-clock has just struck two,
And yonder is the moon!"   20

At this the Father raised his hook,
And snapped a faggot-band;
He plied his work;—and Lucy took
The lantern in her hand.

Not blither is the mountain roe: 25
With many a wanton stroke
Her feet disperse the powdery snow,
That rises up like smoke.

The storm came on before its time:
She wandered up and down;   30
And many a hill did Lucy climb:
But never reached the town.

The wretched parents all that night
Went shouting far and wide;
But there was neither sound nor sight   35
To serve them for a guide.

At day-break on a hill they stood
That overlooked the moor;

And thence they saw the bridge of wood,
A furlong from their door.   40

They wept—and, turning homeward, cried,
"In heaven we all shall meet;"
—When in the snow the mother spied
The print of Lucy's feet.

Then downwards from the steep hill's edge   45
They tracked the footmarks small;
And through the broken hawthorn hedge,
And by the long stone-wall;

And then an open field they crossed:
The marks were still the same;   50
They tracked them on, nor ever lost;
And to the bridge they came.

They followed from the snowy bank
Those footmarks, one by one,
Into the middle of the plank;   55
And further there were none!

—Yet some maintain that to this day
She is a living child;
That you may see sweet Lucy Gray
Upon the lonesome wild.   60

O'er rough and smooth she trips along,
And never looks behind;
And sings a solitary song
That whistles in the wind.
    [1799]

STRANGE FITS OF PASSION HAVE I KNOWN

Strange fits of passion have I known:
And I will dare to tell,
But in the Lover's ear alone,
What once to me befell.

When she I loved looked every day   5
Fresh as a rose in June,
I to her cottage bent my way,
Beneath an evening-moon.

Upon the moon I fixed my eye,
All over the wide lea;   10
With quickening pace my horse drew nigh
Those paths so dear to me.

And now we reached the orchard-plot;
And, as we climbed the hill,
The sinking moon to Lucy's cot   15
Came near, and nearer still.

In one of those sweet dreams I slept,
Kind Nature's gentlest boon!
And all the while my eyes I kept
On the descending moon.   20

My horse moved on; hoof after hoof
He raised, and never stopped:
When down behind the cottage roof,
At once, the bright moon dropped.

What fond and wayward thoughts will slide   25
Into a Lover's head!
"O mercy!" to myself I cried,
"If Lucy should be dead!"
          [1799]

A SLUMBER DID MY SPIRIT SEAL

A slumber did my spirit seal;
    I had no human fears:
She seemed a thing that could not feel
    The touch of earthly years.

No motion has she now, nor force;   5
   She neither hears nor sees;
Rolled round in earth's diurnal course,
   With rocks, and stones, and trees.
    [1799]

SHE DWELT AMONG THE UNTRODDEN WAYS

She dwelt among the untrodden ways
   Beside the springs of Dove,
A Maid whom there were none to praise
   And very few to love:

A violet by a mossy stone   5
   Half hidden from the eye!
—Fair as a star, when only one
   Is shining in the sky.

She lived unknown, and few could know
   When Lucy ceased to be;   10
But she is in her grave, and, oh,
   The difference to me!
    [1799]

THREE YEARS SHE GREW IN SUN AND SHOWER

Three years she grew in sun and shower,
Then Nature said, "A lovelier flower
On earth was never sown;
This Child I to myself will take;
She shall be mine, and I will make   5
A Lady of my own.

"Myself will to my darling be
Both law and impulse: and with me
The Girl, in rock and plain,

In earth and heaven, in glade and bower,   10
Shall feel an overseeing power
To kindle or restrain.

"She shall be sportive as the fawn
That wild with glee across the lawn
Or up the mountain springs;   15
And her's shall be the breathing balm,
And her's the silence and the calm
Of mute insensate things.

"The floating clouds their state shall lend
To her; for her the willow bend;   20
Nor shall she fail to see
Even in the motions of the Storm
Grace that shall mould the Maiden's form
By silent sympathy.

"The stars of midnight shall be dear   25
To her; and she shall lean her ear
In many a secret place
Where rivulets dance their wayward round,
And beauty born of murmuring sound
Shall pass into her face.   30

"And vital feelings of delight
Shall rear her form to stately height,
Her virgin bosom swell;
Such thoughts to Lucy I will give
While she and I together live   35
Here in this happy dell."

Thus Nature spake—The work was done—
How soon my Lucy's race was run!
She died, and left to me
This heath, this calm, and quiet scene;   40
The memory of what has been,
And never more will be.
        [1799]

RUTH

When Ruth was left half desolate,
Her Father took another Mate;
And Ruth, not seven years old,
A slighted child, at her own will
Went wandering over dale and hill,
In thoughtless freedom, bold.

And she had made a pipe of straw,
And music from that pipe could draw
Like sounds of winds and floods;
Had built a bower upon the green,
As if she from her birth had been
An infant of the woods.

Beneath her father's roof, alone
She seemed to live; her thoughts her own;
Herself her own delight;
Pleased with herself, nor sad, nor gay;
And, passing thus the live-long day,
She grew to woman's height.

There came a Youth from Georgia's shore—
A military casque he wore,
With splendid feathers drest;
He brought them from the Cherokees;
The feathers nodded in the breeze,
And made a gallant crest.

From Indian blood you deem him sprung:
But no! he spake the English tongue,
And bore a soldier's name;
And, when America was free
From battle and from jeopardy,
He 'cross the ocean came.

With hues of genius on his cheek
In finest tones the Youth could speak:
—While he was yet a boy,

The moon, the glory of the sun,   35
And streams that murmur as they run,
Had been his dearest joy.

He was a lovely Youth! I guess
The panther in the wilderness
Was not so fair as he;   40
And, when he chose to sport and play,
No dolphin ever was so gay
Upon the tropic sea.

Among the Indians he had fought,
And with him many tales he brought
Of pleasure and of fear: 45
Such tales as told to any maid
By such a Youth, in the green shade,
Were perilous to hear.

He told of girls—a happy rout!   50
Who quit their fold with dance and shout,
Their pleasant Indian town,
To gather strawberries all day long;
Returning with a choral song
When daylight is gone down.

He spake of plants that hourly change   55
Their blossoms, through a boundless range
Of intermingling hues;
With budding, fading, faded flowers
They stand the wonder of the bowers
From morn to evening dews.   60

He told of the magnolia, spread
High as a cloud, high over head!
The cypress and her spire;
—Of flowers that with one scarlet gleam
Cover a hundred leagues, and seem   65
To set the hills on fire.

The Youth of green savannahs spake,
And many an endless, endless lake,
With all its fairy crowds

Of islands, that together lie   70
As quietly as spots of sky
Among the evening clouds.

"How pleasant," then he said, "it were
A fisher or a hunter there,
In sunshine or in shade   75
To wander with an easy mind;
And build a household fire, and find
A home in every glade!

"What days and what bright years! Ah me!
Our life were life indeed, with thee   80
So passed in quiet bliss,
And all the while," said he, "to know
That we were in a world of woe,
On such an earth as this!"

And then he sometimes interwove   85
Fond thoughts about a father's love:
"For there," said he, "are spun
Around the heart such tender ties,
That our own children to our eyes
Are dearer than the sun.   90

"Sweet Ruth! and could you go with me
My helpmate in the woods to be,
Our shed at night to rear;
Or run, my own adopted bride,
A sylvan huntress at my side,   95
And drive the flying deer!

"Beloved Ruth!"—No more he said.
The wakeful Ruth at midnight shed
A solitary tear:
She thought again—and did agree   100
With him to sail across the sea,
And drive the flying deer.

"And now, as fitting is and right,
We in the church our faith will plight,
A husband and a wife."   105

Even so they did; and I may say
That to sweet Ruth that happy day
Was more than human life.

Through dream and vision did she sink,
Delighted all the while to think   110
That on those lonesome floods,
And green savannahs, she should share
His board with lawful joy, and bear
His name in the wild woods.

But, as you have before been told,   115
This Stripling, sportive, gay, and bold,
And, with his dancing crest,
So beautiful, through savage lands
Had roamed about, with vagrant bands
Of Indians in the West.   120

The wind, the tempest roaring high,
The tumult of a tropic sky,
Might well be dangerous food
For him, a Youth to whom was given
So much of earth—so much of heaven,   125
And such impetuous blood.

Whatever in those climes he found
Irregular in sight or sound
Did to his mind impart
A kindred impulse, seemed allied   130
To his own powers, and justified
The workings of his heart.

Nor less, to feed voluptuous thought,
The beauteous forms of nature wrought,
Fair trees and gorgeous flowers;   135
The breezes their own languor lent;
The stars had feelings, which they sent
Into those favored bowers.

Yet, in his worst pursuits, I ween
That sometimes there did intervene   140
Pure hopes of high intent:

For passions linked to forms so fair
And stately, needs must have their share
Of noble sentiment.

But ill he lived, much evil saw,   145
With men to whom no better law
Nor better life was known;
Deliberately, and undeceived,
Those wild men's vices he received,
And gave them back his own.   150

His genius and his moral frame
Were thus impaired, and he became
The slave of low desires:
A Man who without self-control
Would seek what the degraded soul   155
Unworthily admires.

And yet he with no feigned delight
Had wooed the Maiden, day and night
Had loved her, night and morn:
What could he less than love a Maid   160
Whose heart with so much nature played?
So kind and so forlorn!

Sometimes, most earnestly, he said,
"O Ruth! I have been worse than dead;
False thoughts, thoughts bold and vain,   165
Encompassed me on every side
When I, in confidence and pride,
Had crossed the Atlantic main.

"Before me shone a glorious world—
Fresh as a banner bright, unfurled   170
To music suddenly:
I looked upon those hills and plains,
And seemed as if let loose from chains,
To live at liberty.

"No more of this; for now, by thee   175
Dear Ruth! more happily set free
With nobler zeal I burn;

My soul from darkness is released,
Like the whole sky when to the east
The morning doth return."   180

Full soon that better mind was gone;
No hope, no wish remained, not one,—
They stirred him now no more;
New objects did new pleasure give,
And once again he wished to live   185
As lawless as before.

Meanwhile, as thus with him it fared,
They for the voyage were prepared,
And went to the sea-shore,
But, when they thither came, the Youth   190
Deserted his poor Bride, and Ruth
Could never find him more.

God help thee, Ruth!—Such pains she had,
That she in half a year was mad,
And in a prison housed;   195
And there, with many a doleful song
Made of wild words, her cup of wrong
She fearfully caroused.

Yet sometimes milder hours she knew,
Nor wanted sun, nor rain, nor dew,   200
Nor pastimes of the May;
—They all were with her in her cell;
And a clear brook with cheerful knell
Did o'er the pebbles play.

When Ruth three seasons thus had lain,   205
There came a respite to her pain;
She from her prison fled;
But of the Vagrant none took thought;
And where it liked her best she sought
Her shelter and her bread.   210

Among the fields she breathed again:
The master-current of her brain
Ran permanent and free;

And, coming to the Banks of Tone,
There did she rest; and dwell alone   215
Under the greenwood tree.

The engines of her pain, the tools
That shaped her sorrow, rocks and pools,
And airs that gently stir
The vernal leaves—she loved them still;   220
Nor ever taxed them with the ill
Which had been done to her.

A Barn her *winter* bed supplies;
But, till the warmth of summer skies
And summer days is gone,   225
(And all do in this tale agree)
She sleeps beneath the greenwood tree,
And other home hath none.

An innocent life, yet far astray!
And Ruth will, long before her day,   230
Be broken down and old:
Sore aches she needs must have! but less
Of mind, than body's wretchedness,
From damp, and rain, and cold.

If she is prest by want of food,   235
She from her dwelling in the wood
Repairs to a road-side;
And there she begs at one steep place
Where up and down with easy pace
The horsemen-travellers ride.   240

That oaten pipe of hers is mute,
Or thrown away; but with a flute
Her loneliness she cheers:
This flute, made of a hemlock stalk,
At evening in his homeward walk   245
The Quantock woodman hears.

I, too, have passed her on the hills
Setting her little water-mills
By spouts and fountains wild—

Such small machinery as she turned   250
Ere she had wept, ere she had mourned,
A young and happy Child!

Farewell! and when thy days are told,
Ill-fated Ruth, in hallowed mould
Thy corpse shall buried be,   255
For thee a funeral bell shall ring,
And all the congregation sing
A Christian psalm for thee.
        [1799]

MATTHEW

In the School of ————— is a tablet, on which are inscribed, in
gilt letters, the Names of the several persons who have been
Schoolmasters there since the foundation of the School, with the
time at which they entered upon and quitted their office. Opposite to one of those Names the Author wrote the following
lines.

If Nature, for a favourite child,
In thee hath tempered so her clay,
That every hour thy heart runs wild,
Yet never once doth go astray,

Read o'er these lines; and then review   5
This tablet, that thus humbly rears
In such diversity of hue
Its history of two hundred years.

—When through this little wreck of fame,
Cipher and syllable! thine eye   10
Has travelled down to Matthew's name,
Pause with no common sympathy.

And, if a sleeping tear should wake,
Then be it neither checked nor stayed:
For Matthew a request I make   15
Which for himself he had not made.

Poor Matthew, all his frolics o'er,
Is silent as a standing pool;
Far from the chimney's merry roar,
And murmur of the village school.   20

The sighs which Matthew heaved were sighs
Of one tired out with fun and madness;
The tears which came to Matthew's eyes
Were tears of light, the dew of gladness.

Yet, sometimes, when the secret cup   25
Of still and serious thought went round,
It seemed as if he drank it up—
He felt with spirit so profound.

—Thou soul of God's best earthly mould!
Thou happy Soul! and can it be   30
That these two words of glittering gold
Are all that must remain of thee?
    [1799]

THE TWO APRIL MORNINGS

We walked along, while bright and red
Uprose the morning sun;
And Matthew stopped, he looked, and said,
"The will of God be done!"

A village schoolmaster was he,   5
With hair of glittering grey;
As blithe a man as you could see
On a spring holiday.

And on that morning, through the grass,
And by the steaming rills,
We travelled merrily, to pass   10
A day among the hills.

"Our work," said I, "was well begun,
Then, from thy breast what thought,
Beneath so beautiful a sun,   15
So sad a sigh has brought?"

A second time did Matthew stop;
And fixing still his eye
Upon the eastern mountain-top,
To me he made reply: 20

"Yon cloud with that long purple cleft
Brings fresh into my mind
A day like this which I have left
Full thirty years behind.

"And just above yon slope of corn   25
Such colours, and no other,
Were in the sky, that April morn,
Of this the very brother.

"With rod and line I sued the sport
Which that sweet season gave,   30
And, to the churchyard come, stopped short
Beside my daughter's grave.

"Nine summers had she scarcely seen,
The pride of all the vale;
And then she sang;—she would have been   35
A very nightingale.

"Six feet in earth my Emma lay;
And yet I loved her more,
For so it seemed, than till that day
I e'er had loved before.   40

"And, turning from her grave, I met,
Beside the churchyard yew,
A blooming Girl, whose hair was wet
With points of morning dew.

"A basket on her head she bare;   45
Her brow was smooth and white:
To see a child so very fair,
It was a pure delight!

"No fountain from its rocky cave
E'er tripped with foot so free;   50
She seemed as happy as a wave
That dances on the sea.

"There came from me a sigh of pain
Which I could ill confine;
I looked at her, and looked again: 55
And did not wish her mine!"

Matthew is in his grave, yet now,
Methinks, I see him stand,
As at that moment, with a bough
Of wilding in his hand.   60

[1799]

IT WAS AN APRIL MORNING

It was an April morning: fresh and clear
The Rivulet, delighting in its strength,
Ran with a young man's speed; and yet the voice
Of waters which the winter had supplied
Was softened down into a vernal tone.   5
The spirit of enjoyment and desire,
And hopes and wishes, from all living things
Went circling, like a multitude of sounds.
The budding groves seemed eager to urge on
The steps of June; as if their various hues   10
Were only hindrances that stood between
Them and their object; but, meanwhile, prevailed
Such an entire contentment in the air
That every naked ash, and tardy tree
Yet leafless, showed as if the countenance   15
With which it looked on this delightful day

Were native to the summer.—Up the brook
I roamed in the confusion of my heart,
Alive to all things and forgetting all.
At length I to a sudden turning came   20
In this continuous glen, where down a rock
The Stream, so ardent in its course before,
Sent forth such sallies of glad sound, that all
Which I till then had heard, appeared the voice
Of common pleasure: beast and bird, the lamb,   25
The shepherd's dog, the linnet and the thrush,
Vied with this waterfall, and made a song,
Which, while I listened, seemed like the wild growth
Or like some natural produce of the air,
That could not cease to be. Green leaves were here;   30
But 'twas the foliage of the rocks—the birch,
The yew, the holly, and the bright green thorn,
With hanging islands of resplendent furze:
And, on a summit, distant a short space,
By any who should look beyond the dell,   35
A single mountain-cottage might be seen.
I gazed and gazed, and to myself I said,
"Our thoughts at least are ours; and this wild nook,
My EMMA, I will dedicate to thee."
——Soon did the spot become my other home,   40
My dwelling, and my out-of-doors abode.
And, of the Shepherds who have seen me there,
To whom I sometimes in our idle talk
Have told this fancy, two or three, perhaps,
Years after we are gone and in our graves,   45
When they have cause to speak of this wild place,
May call it by the name of EMMA'S DELL.
      [1800]

TIS SAID, THAT SOME HAVE DIED FOR LOVE

'Tis said, that some have died for love:
And here and there a church-yard grave is found
In the cold north's unhallowed ground,
Because the wretched man himself had slain,

His love was such a grievous pain.   5
And there is one whom I five years have known;
He dwells alone
Upon Helvellyn's side:
He loved—the pretty Barbara died;
And thus he makes his moan: 10
Three years had Barbara in her grave been laid
When thus his moan he made:

"Oh, move, thou Cottage, from behind that oak!
Or let the aged tree uprooted lie,
That in some other way yon smoke   15
May mount into the sky!
The clouds pass on; they from the heavens depart:
I look—the sky is empty space;
I know not what I trace;
But when I cease to look, my hand is on my heart.   20

"O! what a weight is in these shades! Ye leaves,
That murmur once so dear, when will it cease?
Your sound my heart of rest bereaves,
It robs my heart of peace.
Thou Thrush, that singest loud—and loud and free,   25
Into yon row of willows flit,
Upon that alder sit;
Or sing another song, or choose another tree.

"Roll back, sweet Rill! back to thy mountain-bounds,
And there for ever be thy waters chained!   30
For thou dost haunt the air with sounds
That cannot be sustained;
If still beneath that pine-tree's ragged bough
Headlong yon waterfall must come,
Oh let it then be dumb!   35
Be anything, sweet Rill, but that which thou art now.

"Thou Eglantine, so bright with sunny showers,
Proud as a rainbow spanning half the vale,
Thou one fair shrub, oh! shed thy flowers,
And stir not in the gale.   40
For thus to see thee nodding in the air,
To see thy arch thus stretch and bend,

Thus rise and thus descend,—
Disturbs me till the sight is more than I can bear."

The Man who makes this feverish complaint   45
Is one of giant stature, who could dance
Equipped from head to foot in iron mail.
Ah gentle Love! if ever thought was thine
To store up kindred hours for me, thy face
Turn from me, gentle Love! nor let me walk   50
Within the sound of Emma's voice, nor know
Such happiness as I have known to-day.
        [1800]

MICHAEL

A PASTORAL POEM

If from the public way you turn your steps
Up the tumultuous brook of Green-head Ghyll,
You will suppose that with an upright path
Your feet must struggle; in such bold ascent
The pastoral mountains front you, face to face.   5
But, courage! for around that boisterous brook
The mountains have all opened out themselves,
And made a hidden valley of their own.
No habitation can be seen; but they
Who journey thither find themselves alone   10
With a few sheep, with rocks and stones, and kites
That overhead are sailing in the sky.
It is in truth an utter solitude;
Nor should I have made mention of this Dell
But for one object which you might pass by,   15
Might see and notice not. Beside the brook
Appears a straggling heap of unhewn stones!
And to that simple object appertains
A story—unenriched with strange events,
Yet not unfit, I deem, for the fireside,   20
Or for the summer shade. It was the first
Of those domestic tales that spake to me
Of Shepherds, dwellers in the valleys, men

Whom I already loved;—not verily
For their own sakes, but for the fields and hills   25
Where was their occupation and abode.
And hence this Tale, while I was yet a Boy
Careless of books, yet having felt the power
Of Nature, by the gentle agency
Of natural objects, led me on to feel   30
For passions that were not my own, and think
(At random and imperfectly indeed)
On man, the heart of man, and human life.
Therefore, although it be a history
Homely and rude, I will relate the same   35
For the delight of a few natural hearts;
And, with yet fonder feeling, for the sake
Of youthful Poets, who among these hills
Will be my second self when I am gone.

Upon the forest-side in Grasmere Vale   40
There dwelt a Shepherd, Michael was his name;
An old man, stout of heart, and strong of limb.
His bodily frame had been from youth to age
Of an unusual strength: his mind was keen,
Intense, and frugal, apt for all affairs,   45
And in his shepherd's calling he was prompt
And watchful more than ordinary men.
Hence had he learned the meaning of all winds,
Of blasts of every tone; and oftentimes,
When others heeded not, He heard the South   50
Make subterraneous music, like the noise
Of bagpipers on distant Highland hills.
The Shepherd, at such warning, of his flock
Bethought him, and he to himself would say,
"The winds are now devising work for me!"   55
And, truly, at all times, the storm, that drives
The traveller to a shelter, summoned him
Up to the mountains: he had been alone
Amid the heart of many thousand mists,
That came to him, and left him, on the heights.   60
So lived he till his eightieth year was past.
And grossly that man errs, who should suppose
That the green valleys, and the streams and rocks,
Were things indifferent to the Shepherd's thoughts.

Fields, where with cheerful spirits he had breathed   65
The common air; hills, which with vigorous step
He had so often climbed; which had impressed
So many incidents upon his mind
Of hardship, skill or courage, joy or fear;
Which, like a book, preserved the memory   70
Of the dumb animals, whom he had saved,
Had fed or sheltered, linking to such acts
The certainty of honourable gain;
Those fields, those hills—what could they less? had laid
Strong hold on his affections, were to him   75
A pleasurable feeling of blind love,
The pleasure which there is in life itself.

    His days had not been passed in singleness.
His Helpmate was a comely matron, old—
Though younger than himself full twenty years.   80
She was a woman of a stirring life,
Whose heart was in her house: two wheels she had
Of antique form; this large, for spinning wool;
That small, for flax; and if one wheel had rest,
It was because the other was at work.   85
The Pair had but one inmate in their house,
An only Child, who had been born to them
When Michael, telling o'er his years, began
To deem that he was old,—in shepherd's phrase,
With one foot in the grave. This only Son,   90
With two brave sheep-dogs tried in many a storm,
The one of an inestimable worth,
Made all their household. I may truly say,
That they were as a proverb in the vale
For endless industry. When day was gone,   95
And from their occupations out of doors
The Son and Father were come home, even then,
Their labour did not cease; unless when all
Turned to the cleanly supper-board, and there,
Each with a mess of pottage and skimmed milk,   100
Sat round the basket piled with oaten cakes,
And their plain home-made cheese. Yet when the meal
Was ended, Luke (for so the Son was named)
And his old Father both betook themselves
To such convenient work as might employ   105

Their hands by the fire-side; perhaps to card
Wool for the Housewife's spindle, or repair
Some injury done to sickle, flail, or scythe,
Or other implement of house or field.

Down from the ceiling, by the chimney's edge,   110
That in our ancient uncouth country style
With huge and black projection overbrowed
Large space beneath, as duly as the light
Of day grew dim the Housewife hung a lamp;
An aged utensil, which had performed   115
Service beyond all others of its kind.
Early at evening did it burn—and late,
Surviving comrade of uncounted hours,
Which, going by from year to year, had found,
And left the couple neither gay perhaps   120
Nor cheerful, yet with objects and with hopes,
Living a life of eager industry.
And now, when Luke had reached his eighteenth year,
There by the light of this old lamp they sate,
Father and Son, while far into the night   125
The Housewife plied her own peculiar work,
Making the cottage through the silent hours
Murmur as with the sound of summer flies.
This light was famous in its neighbourhood,
And was a public symbol of the life   130
That thrifty Pair had lived. For, as it chanced,
Their cottage on a plot of rising ground
Stood single, with large prospect, north and south,
High into Easedale, up to Dunmail-Raise,
And westward to the village near the lake;   135
And from this constant light, so regular,
And so far seen, the House itself, by all
Who dwelt within the limits of the vale,
Both old and young, was named THE EVENING STAR.

Thus living on through such a length of years,   140
The Shepherd, if he loved himself, must needs
Have loved his Helpmate; but to Michael's heart
This son of his old age was yet more dear—
Less from instinctive tenderness, the same
Fond spirit that blindly works in the blood of all—   145

Than that a child, more than all other gifts
That earth can offer to declining man,
Brings hope with it, and forward-looking thoughts,
And stirrings of inquietude, when they
By tendency of nature needs must fail.   150
Exceeding was the love he bare to him,
His heart and his heart's joy! For often-times
Old Michael, while he was a babe in arms,
Had done him female service, not alone
For pastime and delight, as is the use   155
Of fathers, but with patient mind enforced
To acts of tenderness; and he had rocked
His cradle, as with a woman's gentle hand.

And in a later time, ere yet the Boy
Had put on boy's attire, did Michael love,   160
Albeit of a stern unbending mind,
To have the Young-one in his sight, when he
Wrought in the field, or on his shepherd's stool
Sate with a fettered sheep before him stretched
Under the large old oak, that near his door   165
Stood single, and, from matchless depth of shade,
Chosen for the Shearer's covert from the sun,
Thence in our rustic dialect was called
The Clipping Tree, a name which yet it bears.
There, while they two were sitting in the shade,   170
With others round them, earnest all and blithe,
Would Michael exercise his heart with looks
Of fond correction and reproof bestowed
Upon the Child, if he disturbed the sheep
By catching at their legs, or with his shouts   175
Scared them, while they lay still beneath the shears.

And when by Heaven's good grace they boy grew up
A healthy Lad, and carried in his cheek
Two steady roses that were five years old;
Then Michael from a winter coppice cut   180
With his own hands a sapling, which he hooped
With iron, making it throughout in all
Due requisites a perfect shepherd's staff,
And gave it to the Boy; wherewith equipt
He as a watchman oftentimes was placed   185

At gate or gap, to stem or turn the flock;
And, to his office prematurely called,
There stood the urchin, as you will divine,
Something between a hindrance and a help;
And for this cause not always, I believe,   190
Receiving from his Father hire of praise;
Though nought was left undone which staff, or voice
Or looks, or threatening gestures, could perform.

But soon as Luke, full ten years old, could stand
Against the mountain blasts; and to the heights,   195
Not fearing toil, nor length of weary ways,
He with his Father daily went, and they
Were as companions, why should I relate
That objects which the Shepherd loved before
Were dearer now? that from the Boy there came   200
Feelings and emanations—things which were
Light to the sun and music to the wind;
And that the old Man's heart seemed born again?

Thus in his Father's sight the Boy grew up:
And now, when he had reached his eighteenth year,   205
He was his comfort and his daily hope.

While in this sort the simple household lived
From day to day, to Michael's ear there came
Distressful tidings. Long before the time
Of which I speak, the Shepherd had been bound   210
In surety for his brother's son, a man
Of an industrious life, and ample means;
But unforeseen misfortunes suddenly
Had prest upon him; and old Michael now
Was summoned to discharge the forfeiture,   215
A grievous penalty, but little less
Than half his substance. This unlooked-for claim,
At the first hearing, for a moment took
More hope out of his life than he supposed
That any old man ever could have lost.   220
As soon as he had armed himself with strength
To look his trouble in the face, it seemed
The Shepherd's sole resource to sell at once
A portion of his patrimonial fields.

Such was his first resolve; he thought again,   225
And his heart failed him. "Isabel," said he,
Two evenings after he had heard the news,
"I have been toiling more than seventy years,
And in the open sunshine of God's love
Have we all lived; yet if these fields of ours   230
Should pass into a stranger's hand, I think
That I could not lie quiet in my grave.
Our lot is a hard lot; the sun himself
Has scarcely been more diligent than I;
And I have lived to be a fool at last   235
To my own family. An evil man
That was, and made an evil choice, if he
Were false to us; and, if he were not false,
There are ten thousand to whom loss like this
Had been no sorrow. I forgive him;—but   240
'Twere better to be dumb than to talk thus.

    "When I began, my purpose was to speak
Of remedies and of a cheerful hope.
Our Luke shall leave us, Isabel; the land
Shall not go from us, and it shall be free;   245
He shall possess it, free as is the wind
That passes over it. We have, thou know'st,
Another kinsman—he will be our friend
In this distress. He is a prosperous man,
Thriving in trade—and Luke to him shall go,   250
And with his kinsman's help and his own thrift
He quickly will repair this loss, and then
He may return to us. If here he stay,
What can be done? Where every one is poor,
What can be gained?"
                    At this the old Man paused,   255
And Isabel sat silent, for her mind
Was busy, looking back into past times.
There's Richard Bateman, thought she to herself,
He was a parish-boy—at the church-door
They made a gathering for him, shillings, pence,   260
And halfpennies, wherewith the neighbours bought
A basket, which they filled with pedlar's wares;
And, with this basket on his arm, the lad

Went up to London, found a master there,
Who, out of many, chose the trusty boy   265
To go and overlook his merchandise
Beyond the seas; where he grew wondrous rich,
And left estates and monies to the poor,
And, at his birth-place, built a chapel floored
With marble, which he sent from foreign lands.   270
These thoughts, and many others of like sort,
Passed quickly through the mind of Isabel,
And her face brightened. The old Man was glad,
And thus resumed:—"Well, Isabel! this scheme
These two days has been meat and drink to me.   275
Far more than we have lost is left us yet.
—We have enough—I wish indeed that I
Were younger;—but this hope is a good hope.
Make ready Luke's best garments, of the best
Buy for him more, and let us send him forth   280
To-morrow, or the next day, or to-night:
—If he *could* go, the Boy should go to-night."

Here Michael ceased, and to the fields went forth
With a light heart. The Housewife for five days
Was restless morn and night, and all day long   285
Wrought on with her best fingers to prepare
Things needful for the journey of her son.
But Isabel was glad when Sunday came
To stop her in her work; for, when she lay
By Michael's side, she through the last two nights   290
Heard him, how he was troubled in his sleep:
And when they rose at morning she could see
That all his hopes were gone. That day at noon
She said to Luke, while they two by themselves
Were sitting at the door, "Thou must not go: 295
We have no other Child but thee to lose,
None to remember—do not go away,
For if thou leave thy Father he will die."
The Youth made answer with a jocund voice;
And Isabel, when she had told her fears,   300
Recovered heart. That evening her best fare
Did she bring forth, and all together sat
Like happy people round a Christmas fire.

With daylight Isabel resumed her work;
And all the ensuing week the house appeared   305
As cheerful as a grove in Spring: at length
The expected letter from their kinsman came,
With kind assurances that he would do
His utmost for the welfare of the Boy;
To which, requests were added, that forthwith   310
He might be sent to him. Ten times or more
The letter was read over; Isabel
Went forth to show it to the neighbours round;
Nor was there at that time on English land
A prouder heart than Luke's. When Isabel   315
Had to her house returned, the old Man said,
"He shall depart to-morrow." To this word
The Housewife answered, talking much of things
Which, if at such short notice he should go,
Would surely be forgotten. But at length   320
She gave consent, and Michael was at ease.

    Near the tumultuous brook of Green-head Ghyll,
In that deep valley, Michael had designed
To build a Sheep-fold; and, before he heard
The tidings of his melancholy loss,   325
For this same purpose he had gathered up
A heap of stones, which by the streamlet's edge
Lay thrown together, ready for the work.
With Luke that evening thitherward he walked:
And soon as they had reached the place he stopped,   330
And thus the old Man spake to him:—"My son,
To-morrow thou wilt leave me: with full heart
I look upon thee, for thou art the same
That wert a promise to me ere thy birth,
And all thy life hast been my daily joy.   335
I will relate to thee some little part
Of our two histories; 'twill do thee good
When thou art from me, even if I should touch
On things thou canst not know of.——After thou
First cam'st into the world—as oft befalls   340
To new-born infants—thou didst sleep away
Two days, and blessings from thy Father's tongue
Then fell upon thee. Day by day passed on,
And still I loved thee with increasing love.

Never to living ear came sweeter sounds   345
Than when I heard thee by our own fire-side
First uttering, without words, a natural tune;
While thou, a feeding babe, didst in thy joy
Sing at thy Mother's breast. Month followed month,
And in the open fields my life was passed   350
And on the mountains; else I think that thou
Hadst been brought up upon thy Father's knees.
But we were playmates, Luke: among these hills,
As well thou knowest, in us the old and young
Have played together, nor with me didst thou   355
Lack any pleasure which a boy can know."
Luke had a manly heart; but at these words
He sobbed aloud. The old Man grasped his hand,
And said, "Nay, do not take it so—I see
That these are things of which I need not speak.   360
—Even to the utmost I have been to thee
A kind and a good Father: and herein
I but repay a gift which I myself
Received at others' hands; for, though now old
Beyond the common life of man, I still   365
Remember them who loved me in my youth.
Both of them sleep together: here they lived,
As all their Forefathers had done; and when
At length their time was come, they were not loth
To give their bodies to the family mould.   370
I wished that thou should'st live the life they lived,
But 'tis a long time to look back, my Son,
And see so little gain from threescore years.
These fields were burthened when they came to me;
Till I was forty years of age, not more   375
Than half of my inheritance was mine.
I toiled and toiled; God blessed me in my work,
And till these three weeks past the land was free.
—It looks as if it never could endure
Another Master. Heaven forgive me, Luke,   380
If I judge ill for thee, but it seems good
That thou should'st go."
                              At this the old Man paused;
Then, pointing to the stones near which they stood,
Thus after a short silence, he resumed:
"This was a work for us; and now, my Son,   385

It is a work for me. But, lay one stone—
Here, lay it for me, Luke, with thine own hands.
Nay, Boy, be of good hope;—we both may live
To see a better day. At eighty-four
I still am strong and hale;—do thou thy part;   390
I will do mine.—I will begin again
With many tasks that were resigned to thee:
Up to the heights, and in among the storms,
Will I without thee go again, and do
All works which I was wont to do alone,   395
Before I knew thy face.—Heaven bless thee, Boy!
Thy heart these two weeks has been beating fast
With many hopes; it should be so—yes—yes—
I knew that thou couldst never have a wish
To leave me, Luke: thou hast been bound to me   400
Only by links of love: when thou art gone,
What will be left to us!—But I forget
My purposes. Lay now the corner-stone,
As I requested; and hereafter, Luke,
When thou art gone away, should evil men   405
Be thy companions, think of me, my Son,
And of this moment; hither turn thy thoughts,
And God will strengthen thee: amid all fear
And all temptation, Luke, I pray that thou
May'st bear in mind the life thy Fathers lived,   410
Who, being innocent, did for that cause
Bestir them in good deeds. Now, fare thee well—
When thou return'st, thou in this place wilt see
A work which is not here: a covenant
'Twill be between us; but, whatever fate   415
Befall thee, I shall love thee to the last,
And bear thy memory with me to the grave."

    The Shepherd ended here; and Luke stooped down,
And, as his Father had requested, laid
The first stone of the Sheep-fold. At the sight   420
The old Man's grief broke from him; to his heart
He pressed his Son, he kissed him and wept;
And to the house together they returned.
—Hushed was that House in peace, or seeming peace,
Ere the night fell:—with morrow's dawn the Boy   425
Began his journey, and when he had reached

The public way, he put on a bold face;
And all the neighbours, as he passed their doors,
Came forth with wishes and with farewell prayers,
That followed him till he was out of sight.   430

A good report did from their Kinsman come,
Of Luke and his well-doing: and the Boy
Wrote loving letters, full of wondrous news,
Which, as the Housewife phrased it, were throughout
"The prettiest letters that were ever seen."   435
Both parents read them with rejoicing hearts.
So, many months passed on: and once again
The Shepherd went about his daily work
With confident and cheerful thoughts; and now
Sometimes when he could find a leisure hour   440
He to that valley took his way, and there
Wrought at the Sheep-fold. Meantime Luke began
To slacken in his duty; and, at length,
He in the dissolute city gave himself
To evil courses: ignominy and shame   445
Fell on him, so that he was driven at last
To seek a hiding-place beyond the seas.

There is a comfort in the strength of love;
'Twill make a thing endurable, which else
Would overset the brain, or break the heart: 450
I have conversed with more than one who well
Remember the old Man, and what he was
Years after he had heard this heavy news.
His bodily frame had been from youth to age
Of an unusual strength. Among the rocks   455
He went, and still looked up to sun and cloud,
And listened to the wind; and, as before,
Performed all kinds of labour for his sheep,
And for the land, his small inheritance.
And to that hollow dell from time to time   460
Did he repair, to build the Fold of which
His flock had need. 'Tis not forgotten yet
The pity which was then in every heart
For the old Man—and 'tis believed by all
That many and many a day he thither went,   465
And never lifted up a single stone.

There, by the Sheep-fold, sometimes he was seen
Sitting alone, or with his faithful Dog,
Then old, beside him, lying at his feet.
The length of full seven years, from time to time,   470
He at the building of this Sheep-fold wrought,
And left the work unfinished when he died.
Three years, or little more, did Isabel
Survive her Husband: at her death the estate
Was sold, and went into a stranger's hand.   475
The Cottage which was named the EVENING STAR
Is gone—the ploughshare has been through the ground
On which it stood; great changes have been wrought
In all the neighbourhood:—yet the oak is left
That grew beside their door; and the remains   480
Of the unfinished Sheep-fold may be seen
Beside the boisterous brook of Green-head Ghyll.

[1800]

I TRAVELLED AMONG UNKNOWN MEN

I travelled among unknown men,
    In lands beyond the sea;
Nor, England! did I know till then
    What love I bore to thee.

'Tis past, that melancholy dream!   5
    Nor will I quit thy shore
A second time; for still I seem
    To love thee more and more.

Among thy mountains did I feel
    The joy of my desire;   10
And she I cherished turned her wheel
    Beside an English fire.

Thy mornings showed, thy nights concealed,
    The bowers where Lucy played;
And thine too is the last green field   15
    That Lucy's eyes surveyed.

[1801]

TO THE CUCKOO

O blithe New-comer! I have heard,
I hear thee and rejoice.
O Cuckoo! shall I call thee Bird,
Or but a wandering Voice?

While I am lying on the grass   5
Thy twofold shout I hear,
From hill to hill it seems to pass
At once far off, and near.

Though babbling only to the Vale,
Of sunshine and of flowers,   10
Thou bringest unto me a tale
Of visionary hours.

Thrice welcome, darling of the Spring!
Even yet thou art to me
No bird, but an invisible thing,   15
A voice, a mystery;

The same whom in my schoolboy days
I listened to; that Cry
Which made me look a thousand ways
In bush, and tree, and sky.   20

To seek thee did I often rove
Through woods and on the green;
And thou wert still a hope, a love;
Still longed for, never seen.

And I can listen to thee yet;   25
Can lie upon the plain
And listen, till I do beget
That golden time again.

O blessèd Bird! the earth we pace
Again appears to be   30
An unsubstantial, faery place;
That is fit home for Thee!
    [1802]

MY HEART LEAPS UP

My heart leaps up when I behold
    A rainbow in the sky:
So was it when my life began;
So is it now I am a man;
So be it when I shall grow old,   5
    Or let me die!
The Child is father of the Man;
And I could wish my days to be
Bound each to each by natural piety.
[1802]

TO THE SMALL CELANDINE

Pansies, lilies, kingcups, daisies,
Let them live upon their praises;
Long as there's a sun that sets,
Primroses will have their glory;
Long as there are violets,   5
They will have a place in story:
There's a flower that shall be mine,
'Tis the little Celandine.

Eyes of some men travel far
For the finding of a star;   10
Up and down the heavens they go,
Men that keep a mighty rout!
I'm as great as they, I trow,
Since the day I found thee out,
Little Flower—I'll make a stir,   15
Like a sage astronomer.

Modest, yet withal an Elf
Bold, and lavish of thyself;
Since we needs must first have met
I have seen thee, high and low,   20

Thirty years or more, and yet
'Twas a face I did not know;
Thou hast now, go where I may,
Fifty greetings in a day.

Ere a leaf is on a bush,   25
In the time before the thrush
Has a thought about her nest,
Thou wilt come with half a call,
Spreading out thy glossy breast
Like a careless Prodigal;   30
Telling tales about the sun,
When we've little warmth, or none.

Poets, vain men in their mood!
Travel with the multitude:
Never heed them; I aver   35
That they all are wanton wooers;
But the thrifty cottager,
Who stirs little out of doors,
Joys to spy thee near her home;
Spring is coming, Thou art come!   40

Comfort have thou of thy merit,
Kindly, unassuming Spirit!
Careless of thy neighbourhood,
Thou dost show thy pleasant face
On the moor, and in the wood,   45
In the lane;—there's not a place,
Howsoever mean it be,
But 'tis good enough for thee.

Ill befall the yellow flowers,
Children of the flaring hours!   50
Buttercups, that will be seen,
Whether we will see or no;
Others, too, of lofty mien;
They have done as worldlings do,
Taken praise that should be thine,   55
Little, humble Celandine.

Prophet of delight and mirth,
Ill-requited upon earth;
Herald of a mighty band,
Of a joyous train ensuing,   60
Serving at my heart's command,
Tasks that are no tasks renewing,
I will sing, as doth behove,
Hymns in praise of what I love!
[1802]

RESOLUTION AND INDEPENDENCE

I

There was a roaring in the wind all night;
The rain came heavily and fell in floods;
But now the sun is rising calm and bright;
The birds are singing in the distant woods;
Over his own sweet voice the Stock-dove broods;   5
The Jay makes answer as the Magpie chatters;
And all the air is filled with pleasant noise of waters.

II

All things that love the sun are out of doors;
The sky rejoices in the morning's birth;
The grass is bright with rain-drops;—on the moors   10
The hare is running races in her mirth;
And with her feet she from the plashy earth
Raises a mist; that, glittering in the sun,
Runs with her all the way, wherever she doth run.

III

I was a Traveller then upon the moor;   15
I saw the hare that raced about with joy;
I heard the woods and distant waters roar;
Or heard them not, as happy as a boy:
The pleasant season did my heart employ:

My old remembrances went from me wholly;   20
And all the ways of men, so vain and melancholy.

IV

But, as it sometimes chanceth, from the might
Of joy in minds that can no further go,
As high as we have mounted in delight
In our dejection do we sing as low;   25
To me that morning did it happen so;
And fears and fancies thick upon me came;
Dim sadness—and blind thoughts, I knew not, nor could
    name.

V

I heard the sky-lark warbling in the sky;
And I bethought me of the playful hare: 30
Even such a happy Child of earth am I;
Even as these blissful creatures do I fare;
Far from the world I walk, and from all care;
But there may come another day to me—
Solitude, pain of heart, distress, and poverty.   35

VI

My whole life I have lived in pleasant thought,
As if life's business were a summer mood;
As if all needful things would come unsought
To genial faith, still rich in genial good;
But how can He expect that others should   40
Build for him, sow for him, and at his call
Love him, who for himself will take no heed at all?

VII

I thought of Chatterton, the marvellous Boy,
The sleepless Soul that perished in his pride;
Of Him who walked in glory and in joy   45
Following his plough, along the mountain-side:
By our own spirits are we deified:
We Poets in our youth begin in gladness;
But thereof come in the end despondency and madness.

VIII

Now, whether it were by peculiar grace,   50
A leading from above, a something given,
Yet it befell that, in this lonely place,
When I with these untoward thoughts had striven,
Beside a pool bare to the eye of heaven
I saw a Man before me unawares: 55
The oldest man he seemed that ever wore gray hairs.

IX

As a huge stone is sometimes seen to lie
Couched on the bald top of an eminence;
Wonder to all who do the same espy,
By what means it could thither come, and whence;   60
So that it seems a thing endued with sense:
Like a sea-beast crawled forth, that on a shelf
Of rock or sand reposeth, there to sun itself;

X

Such seemed this Man, not all alive nor dead,
Nor all asleep—in his extreme old age: 65
His body was bent double, feet and head
Coming together in life's pilgrimage;
As if some dire constraint of pain, or rage
Of sickness felt by him in times long past,
A more than human weight upon his frame had cast.   70

XI

Himself he propped, limbs, body, and pale face,
Upon a long grey staff of shaven wood:
And, still as I drew near with gentle pace,
Upon the margin of the moorish flood
Motionless as a cloud the old Man stood,   75
That heareth not the loud winds when they call;
And moveth all together, if it move at all.

XII

At length, himself unsettling, he the pond
Stirred with his staff, and fixedly did look
Upon the muddy water, which he conned, 80
As if he had been reading a book:
And now a stranger's privilege I took;
And, drawing to his side, to him did say,
"This morning gives us promise of a glorious day."

XIII

A gentle answer did the old Man make, 85
In courteous speech which forth he slowly drew:
And him with further words I thus bespake,
"What occupation do you there pursue?
This is a lonesome place for one like you."
Ere he replied, a flash of mild surprise 90
Broke from the sable orbs of his yet-vivid eyes.

XIV

His words came feebly, from a feeble chest,
But each in solemn order followed each,
With something of a lofty utterance drest—
Choice word and measured phrase, above the reach 95
Of ordinary men; a stately speech;
Such as grave Livers do in Scotland use,
Religious men, who give to God and man their dues.

XV

He told, that to these waters he had come
To gather leeches, being old and poor: 100
Employment hazardous and wearisome!
And he had many hardships to endure:
From pond to pond he roamed, from moor to moor;
Housing, with God's good help, by choice or chance;
And in this way he gained an honest maintenance. 105

XVI

The old Man still stood talking by my side;
But now his voice to me was like a stream
Scarce heard; nor word from word could I divide;
And the whole body of the Man did seem
Like one whom I had met with in a dream;   110
Or like a man from some far region sent,
To give me human strength, by apt admonishment.

XVII

My former thoughts returned: the fear that kills;
And hope that is unwilling to be fed;
Cold, pain, and labour, and all fleshly ills;   115
And mighty Poets in their misery dead.
—Perplexed, and longing to be comforted,
My question eagerly did I renew,
"How is it that you live, and what is it you do?"

XVIII

He with a smile did then his words repeat;   120
And said that, gathering leeches, far and wide
He travelled; stirring thus about his feet
The waters of the pools where they abide.
"Once I could meet with them on every side;
But they have dwindled long by slow decay;   125
Yet still I persevere, and find them where I may."

XIX

While he was talking thus, the lonely place,
The old Man's shape, and speech—all troubled me:
In my mind's eye I seemed to see him pace
About the weary moors continually,   130
Wandering about alone and silently.
While I these thoughts within myself pursued,
He, having made a pause, the same discourse renewed.

XX

And soon with this he other matter blended,
Cheerfully uttered, with demeanour kind,   135
But stately in the main; and when he ended,
I could have laughed myself to scorn to find
In that decrepit Man so firm a mind.
"God," said I, "be my help and stay secure;
I'll think of the Leech-gatherer on the lonely moor!"   140
   [1802]

I GRIEVED FOR BUONAPARTE

I grieved for Buonaparté with a vain
And an unthinking grief! The tenderest mood
Of that Man's mind—what can it be? what food
Fed his first hopes? what knowledge could he gain?
'Tis not in battles that from youth we train   5
The Governor who must be wise and good,
And temper with the sternness of the brain
Thoughts motherly, and meek as womanhood.
Wisdom doth live with children round her knees:
Books, leisure, perfect freedom, and the talk   10
Man holds with week-day man in the hourly walk
Of the mind's business: these are the degrees
By which true Sway doth mount; this is the stalk
True Power doth grow on; and her rights are these.
   [1802]

COMPOSED BY THE SEA-SIDE, NEAR CALAIS, AUGUST, 1802

Fair Star of evening, Splendour of the west,
Star of my Country!—on the horizon's brink
Thou hangest, stooping, as might seem, to sink
On England's bosom; yet well pleased to rest,
Meanwhile, and be to her a glorious crest   5
Conspicuous to the Nations. Thou, I think,

Shouldst be my Country's emblem; and shouldst wink,
Bright Star! with laughter on her banners, drest
In thy fresh beauty. There! that dusky spot
Beneath thee, that is England; there she lies.   10
Blessings be on you both! one hope, one lot,
One life, one glory!—I, with many a fear
For my dear Country, many heartfelt sighs,
Among men who do not love her, linger here.

       [1802]

CALAIS, AUGUST, 1802

Is it a reed that's shaken by the wind,
Or what is it that ye go forth to see?
Lords, lawyers, statesmen, squires of low degree,
Men known, and men unknown, sick, lame, and blind,
Post forward all, like creatures of one kind,   5
With first-fruit offerings crowd to bend the knee
In France, before the new-born Majesty.
'Tis ever thus. Ye men of prostrate mind,
A seemly reverence may be paid to power;
But that's a loyal virtue, never sown   10
In haste, nor springing with a transient shower:
When truth, when sense, when liberty were flown,
What hardship had it been to wait an hour?
Shame on you, feeble Heads, to slavery prone!

       [1802]

COMPOSED NEAR CALAIS, ON THE ROAD LEADING TO ARDRES, AUGUST 7, 1802

Jones! as from Calais southward you and I
Went pacing side by side, this public Way
Streamed with the pomp of a too-credulous day.
When faith was pledged to new-born Liberty:

A homeless sound of joy was in the sky: 5
From hour to hour the antiquated Earth
Beat like the heart of Man: songs, garlands, mirth,
Banners, and happy faces, far and nigh!
And now, sole register that these things were,
Two solitary greetings have I heard,   10
"Good morrow, Citizen!" a hollow word,
As if a dead man spake it! Yet despair
Touches me not, though pensive as a bird
Whose vernal coverts winter hath laid bare.

    [1802]

IT IS A BEAUTEOUS EVENING

It is a beauteous evening, calm and free,
The holy time is quiet as a Nun
Breathless with adoration; the broad sun
Is sinking down in its tranquillity;
The gentleness of heaven broods o'er the Sea: 5
Listen! the mighty Being is awake,
And doth with his eternal motion make
A sound like thunder—everlastingly.
Dear Child! dear Girl! that walkest with me here,
If thou appear untouched by solemn thought,   10
Thy nature is not therefore less divine:
Thou liest in Abraham's bosom all the year;
And worshipp'st at the Temple's inner shrine,
God being with thee when we know it not.

    [1802]

ON THE EXTINCTION OF THE VENETIAN REPUBLIC

Once did She hold the gorgeous east in fee;
And was the safeguard of the west: the worth
Of Venice did not fall below her birth,
Venice, the eldest Child of Liberty.

She was a maiden City, bright and free;   5
No guile seduced, no force could violate;
And, when she took unto herself a Mate,
She must espouse the everlasting Sea.
And what if she had seen those glories fade,
Those titles vanish, and that strength decay;   10
Yet shall some tribute of regret be paid
When her long life hath reached its final day:
Men are we, and must grieve when even the Shade
Of that which once was great, is passed away.

       [1802]

COMPOSED IN THE VALLEY NEAR DOVER, ON THE DAY OF LANDING

Here, on our native soil, we breathe once more.
The cock that crows, the smoke that curls, that sound
Of bells;—those boys who in yon meadow-ground
In white-sleeved shirts are playing; and the roar
Of the waves breaking on the chalky shore;—   5
All, all are English. Oft have I looked round
With joy in Kent's green vales; but never found
Myself so satisfied in heart before.
Europe is yet in bonds; but let that pass,
Thought for another moment. Thou art free,   10
My Country! and 'tis joy enough and pride
For one hour's perfect bliss, to tread the grass
Of England once again, and hear and see,
With such a dear Companion at my side.

       [1802]

SEPTEMBER, 1802. NEAR DOVER

Inland, within a hollow vale, I stood;
And saw, while sea was calm and air was clear,
The coast of France—the coast of France how near!
Drawn almost into frightful neighbourhood.

I shrunk; for verily the barrier flood   5
Was like a lake, or river bright and fair,
A span of waters; yet what power is there!
What mightiness for evil and for good!
Even so doth God protect us if we be
Virtuous and wise. Winds blow, and waters roll,   10
Strength to the brave, and Power, and Deity;
Yet in themselves are nothing! One decree
Spake laws to *them*, and said that by the soul
Only, the Nations shall be great and free.
    [1802]

COMPOSED UPON WESTMINSTER BRIDGE, SEPTEMBER 3, 1802

Earth has not anything to show more fair:
Dull would he be of soul who could pass by
A sight so touching in its majesty:
This City now doth, like a garment, wear
The beauty of the morning; silent, bare,   5
Ships, towers, domes, theatres, and temples lie
Open unto the fields, and to the sky;
All bright and glittering in the smokeless air.
Never did sun more beautifully steep
In his first splendour, valley, rock, or hill;   10
Ne'er saw I, never felt, a calm so deep!
The river glideth at his own sweet will:
Dear God! the very houses seem asleep;
And all that mighty heart is lying still!
    [1802]

WRITTEN IN LONDON, SEPTEMBER, 1802

O Friend! I know not which way I must look
For comfort, being, as I am, opprest,
To think that now our life is only drest
For show; mean handy-work of craftsman, cook,

Or groom!—We must run glittering like a brook   5
In the open sunshine, or we are unblest:
The wealthiest man among us is the best:
No grandeur now in nature or in book
Delights us. Rapine, avarice, expense,
This is idolatry; and these we adore: 10
Plain living and high thinking are no more:
The homely beauty of the good old cause
Is gone; our peace, our fearful innocence,
And pure religion breathing household laws.
    [1802]

LONDON, 1802

Milton! thou shouldst be living at this hour:
England hath need of thee: she is a fen
Of stagnant waters: altar, sword, and pen,
Fireside, the heroic wealth of hall and bower,
Have forfeited their ancient English dower   5
Of inward happiness. We are selfish men;
Oh! raise us up, return to us again;
And give us manners, virtue, freedom, power.
Thy soul was like a Star, and dwelt apart;
Thou hadst a voice whose sound was like the sea: 10
Pure as the naked heavens, majestic, free,
So didst thou travel on life's common way,
In cheerful godliness; and yet thy heart
The lowliest duties on herself did lay.
    [1802]

GREAT MEN HAVE BEEN AMONG US

Great men have been among us; hands that penned
And tongues that uttered wisdom—better none:
The later Sidney, Marvel, Harrington,
Young Vane, and others who called Milton friend.
These moralists could act and comprehend: 5

They knew how genuine glory was put on;
Taught us how rightfully a nation shone
In splendour: what strength was, that would not bend
But in magnanimous meekness. France, 'tis strange,
Hath brought forth no such souls as we had then.   10
Perpetual emptiness! unceasing change!
No single volume paramount, no code,
No master spirit, no determined road;
But equally a want of books and men!
     [1802]

TO THE DAISY

Bright Flower! whose home is everywhere,
Bold in maternal Nature's care,
And all the long year through the heir
    Of joy and sorrow;
Methinks that there abides in thee   5
Some concord with humanity,
Given to no other flower I see
    The forest thorough!

Is it that Man is soon deprest?
A thoughtless Thing! who, once unblest,   10
Does little on his memory rest,
    Or on his reason,
And Thou would'st teach him how to find
A shelter under every wind,
A hope for times that are unkind   15
    And every season?

Thou wander'st the wide world about,
Uncheck'd by pride or scrupulous doubt,
With friends to greet thee, or without,
    Yet pleased and willing;
Meek, yielding to the occasion's call,   20
And all things suffering from all,
Thy function apostolical
    In peace fulfilling.
    [1802]

TO A SKY-LARK

Up with me; up with me into the clouds!
   For thy song, Lark, is strong;
Up with me, up with me into the clouds!
   Singing, singing,
With clouds and sky about thee ringing,   5
   Lift me, guide me till I find
That spot which seems so to thy mind!

I have walked through wildernesses dreary,
And to-day my heart is weary;
Had I now the wings of a Faery,   10
Up to thee would I fly.
There is madness about thee, and joy divine
In that song of thine;
Lift me, guide me high and high
To thy banqueting place in the sky.   15

     Joyous as morning,
  Thou art laughing and scorning;
  Thou hast a nest for thy love and thy rest,
  And, though little troubled with sloth,
  Drunken Lark! thou would'st be loth   20
  To be such a traveller as I.
  Happy, happy Liver,
  With a soul as strong as a mountain river
  Pouring out praise to the almighty Giver,
  Joy and jollity be with us both!   25

Alas! my journey, rugged and uneven,
Through prickly moors or dusty ways must wind:
But hearing thee, or others of thy kind,
As full of gladness and as free of heaven,
I, with my fate contented, will plod on,   30
And hope for higher raptures, when life's day is done.
    [1802]

TO THE DAISY

In youth from rock to rock I went,
From hill to hill in discontent
Of pleasure high and turbulent,
   Most pleased when most uneasy;
But now my own delights I make,—   5
My thirst at every rill can slake,
And gladly Nature's love partake
   Of Thee, sweet Daisy!

Thee Winter in the garland wears
That thinly decks his few grey hairs;   10
Spring parts the clouds with softest airs,
   That she may sun thee;
Whole Summer-fields are thine by right;
And Autumn, melancholy Wight!
Doth in thy crimson head delight   15
   When rains are on thee.

In shoals and bands, a morrice train,
Thou greet'st the traveller in the lane;
Pleased at his greeting thee again;
   Yet nothing daunted,   20
Nor grieved if thou be set at nought:
And oft alone in nooks remote
We meet thee, like a pleasant thought,
   When such are wanted.

Be violets in their secret mews   25
The flowers the wanton Zephyrs choose;
Proud be the rose, with rains and dews
   Her head impearling,
Thou liv'st with less ambitious aim,
Yet hast not gone without thy fame;   30
Thou art indeed by many a claim
   The Poet's darling.

If to a rock from rains he fly,
Or, some bright day of April sky,

Imprisoned by hot sunshine lie   35
   Near the green holly,
And wearily at length should fare;
He needs but look about, and there
Thou art!—a friend at hand, to scare
   His melancholy.   40

A hundred times, by rock or bower,
Ere thus I have lain couched an hour,
Have I derived from thy sweet power
   Some apprehension;
Some steady love; some brief delight;   45
Some memory that had taken flight;
Some chime of fancy wrong or right;
   Or stray invention.

If stately passions in me burn,
And one chance look to Thee should turn,   50
I drink out of an humbler urn
   A lowlier pleasure;
The homely sympathy that heeds
The common life our nature breeds;
A wisdom fitted to the needs   55
   Of hearts at leisure.

Fresh-smitten by the morning ray,
When thou art up, alert and gay,
Then, cheerful Flower! my spirits play
   With kindred gladness: 60
And when, at dusk, by dews opprest
Thou sink'st, the image of thy rest
Hath often eased my pensive breast
   Of careful sadness.

And all day long I number yet,   65
All seasons through, another debt,
Which I, wherever thou art met,
   To thee am owing;
An instinct call it, a blind sense;
A happy, genial influence,   70
Coming one knows not how, or whence,
   Nor whither going.

Child of the Year! that round dost run
Thy pleasant course,—when day's begun
As ready to salute the sun   75
  As lark or leveret,
Thy long-lost praise thou shalt regain;
Nor be less dear to future men
Than in old time;—thou not in vain
  Art Nature's favourite.   80
    [1802]

YARROW UNVISITED

From Stirling castle we had seen
The mazy Forth unravelled;
Had trod the banks of Clyde, and Tay,
And with the Tweed had travelled;
And when we came to Clovenford,   5
Then said my *"winsome Marrow,"*
"Whate'er betide, we'll turn aside,
And see the Braes of Yarrow."

"Let Yarrow folk, *frae* Selkirk town,
Who have been buying, selling,   10
Go back to Yarrow, 'tis their own;
Each maiden to her dwelling!
On Yarrow's banks let herons feed,
Hares couch, and rabbits burrow!
But we will downward with the Tweed,   15
Nor turn aside to Yarrow.

"There's Galla Water, Leader Haughs,
Both lying right before us;
And Dryborough, where with chiming Tweed
The lintwhites sing in chorus;   20
There's pleasant Tiviot-dale, a land
Made blithe with plough and harrow:
Why throw away a needful day
To go in search of Yarrow?

"What's Yarrow but a river bare,   25
That glides the dark hills under?
There are a thousand such elsewhere
As worthy of your wonder."
—Strange words they seemed of slight and scorn;
My True-love sighed for sorrow;   30
And looked me in the face, to think
I thus could speak of Yarrow!

"Oh! green," said I, "are Yarrow's holms,
And sweet is Yarrow flowing!
Fair hangs the apple frae the rock,   35
But we will leave it growing.
O'er hilly path, and open Strath,
We'll wander Scotland thorough;
But, though so near, we will not turn
Into the dale of Yarrow.   40

"Let beeves and home-bred kine partake
The sweets of Burn-mill meadow;
The swan on still St. Mary's Lake
Float double, swan and shadow!
We will not see them; will not go,   45
To-day, nor yet to-morrow;
Enough if in our hearts we know
There's such a place as Yarrow.

"Be Yarrow stream unseen, unknown!
It must, or we shall rue it: 50
We have a vision of our own;
Ah! why should we undo it?
The treasured dreams of times long past,
We'll keep them, winsome Marrow!
For when we're there, although 'tis fair,   55
    'Twill be another Yarrow!

"If Care with freezing years should come,
And wandering seem but folly,—
Should we be loth to stir from home,
And yet be melancholy;   60
Should life be dull, and spirits low,
'Twill soothe us in our sorrow,

That earth hath something yet to show,
The bonny holms of Yarrow!"
[1803]

ODE

INTIMATIONS OF IMMORTALITY FROM RECOLLECTIONS OF EARLY CHILDHOOD

The Child is father of the Man;
And I could wish my days to be
Bound each to each by natural piety.

I

There was a time when meadow, grove, and stream,
The earth, and every common sight,
    To me did seem
    Apparelled in celestial light,
The glory and the freshness of a dream.
It is not now as it hath been of yore;—   5
    Turn wheresoe'er I may,
      By night or day,
The things which I have seen I now can see no more.

II

    The Rainbow comes and goes,   10
    And lovely is the Rose,
    The Moon doth with delight
Look round her when the heavens are bare;
    Waters on a starry night
    Are beautiful and fair;   15
  The sunshine is a glorious birth;
 But yet I know, where'er I go,
That there hath past away a glory from the earth.

III

Now, while the birds thus sing a joyous song,
  And while the young lambs bound   20
      As to the tabor's sound,
To me alone there came a thought of grief:
A timely utterance gave that thought relief,
      And I again am strong:
The cataracts blow their trumpets from the steep;   25
No more shall grief of mine the season wrong;
I hear the Echoes through the mountains throng,
The Winds come to me from the fields of sleep,
      And all the earth is gay;
          Land and sea   30
      Give themselves up to jollity,
        And with the heart of May
      Doth every Beast keep holiday;—
        Thou Child of Joy,
Shout round me, let me hear thy shouts, thou happy   35
        Shepherd-boy!

IV

Ye blessèd Creatures, I have heard the call
  Ye to each other make; I see
The heavens laugh with you in your jubilee;
  My heart is at your festival,
    My head hath its coronal,   40
The fulness of your bliss, I feel—I feel it all.
      Oh evil day! if I were sullen
      While Earth herself is adorning,
        This sweet May-morning,
      And the Children are culling   45
        On every side,
      In a thousand valleys far and wide,
      Fresh flowers; while the sun shines warm,
And the Babe leaps up on his Mother's arm:—
      I hear, I hear, with joy I hear!   50
      —But there's a Tree, of many, one,
A single Field which I have looked upon,

Both of them speak of something that is gone:
    The Pansy at my feet
    Doth the same tale repeat: 55
Whither is fled the visionary gleam?
Where is it now, the glory and the dream?

          v

Our birth is but a sleep and a forgetting:
The Soul that rises with us, our life's Star,
    Hath had elsewhere its setting,   60
      And cometh from afar:
    Not in entire forgetfulness,
    And not in utter nakedness,
But trailing clouds of glory do we come
    From God, who is our home: 65
Heaven lies about us in our infancy!
Shades of the prison-house begin to close
    Upon the growing Boy,
      But He
Beholds the light, and whence it flows,   70
    He sees it in his joy;
The Youth, who daily farther from the east
    Must travel, still is Nature's Priest,
    And by the vision splendid
    Is on his way attended;   75
At length the Man perceives it die away,
And fade into the light of common day.

          vi

Earth fills her lap with pleasures of her own;
Yearnings she hath in her own natural kind,
And, even with something of a Mother's mind,   80
    And no unworthy aim,
    The homely Nurse doth all she can
To make her Foster-child, her Inmate Man,
    Forget the glories he hath known,
And that imperial palace whence he came.   85

VII

Behold the Child among his new-born blisses,
A six years' Darling of a pigmy size!
See, where 'mid work of his own hand he lies,
Frettied by sallies of his mother's kisses,
With light upon him from his father's eyes!   90
See, at his feet, some little plan or chart,
Some fragment from his dream of human life,
Shaped by himself with newly-learned art;
      A wedding or a festival,
      A mourning or a funeral;   95
        And this hath now his heart,
      And unto this he frames his song:
        Then will he fit his tongue
To dialogues of business, love, or strife;
      But it will not be long   100
      Ere this be thrown aside,
      And with new joy and pride
The little Actor cons another part;
Filling from time to time his "humorous stage"
With all the Persons, down to palsied Age,   105
That Life brings with her in her equipage;
      As if his whole vocation
      Were endless imitation.

VIII

Thou, whose exterior semblance doth belie
      Thy Soul's immensity;   110
Thou best Philosopher, who yet dost keep
Thy heritage, thou Eye among the blind,
That, deaf and silent, read'st the eternal deep,
Haunted for ever by the eternal mind,—
      Mighty Prophet! Seer blest!   115
      On whom those truths do rest,
Which we are toiling all our lives to find,
In darkness lost, the darkness of the grave;
Thou, over whom thy Immortality
Broods like the Day, a Master o'er a Slave,   120
A Presence which is not to be put by;

Thou little Child, yet glorious in the might
Of heaven-born freedom on thy being's height,
Why with such earnest pains dost thou provoke
The years to bring the inevitable yoke,   125
Thus blindly with thy blessedness at strife?
Full soon thy Soul shall have her earthly freight,
And custom lie upon thee with a weight,
Heavy as frost, and deep almost as life!

IX

  O joy! that in our embers   130
  Is something that doth live,
  That nature yet remembers
  What was so fugitive!
The thought of our past years in me doth breed
Perpetual benediction: not indeed   135
For that which is most worthy to be blest;
Delight and liberty, the simple creed
Of Childhood, whether busy or at rest,
With new-fledged hope still fluttering in his breast:—
  Not for these I raise   140
  The song of thanks and praise;
  But for those obstinate questionings
  Of sense and outward things,
  Fallings from us, vanishings;
  Blank misgivings of a Creature   145
Moving about in worlds not realised,
High instincts before which our mortal Nature
Did tremble like a guilty Thing surprised:
  But for those first affections,
  Those shadowy recollections,   150
  Which, be they what they may,
Are yet the fountain light of all our day,
Are yet a master light of all our seeing;
  Uphold us, cherish, and have power to make
Our noisy years seem moments in the being   155
Of the eternal Silence: truths that wake,
  To perish never;
Which neither listlessness, nor mad endeavour,
  Nor Man nor Boy,
Nor all that is at enmity with joy,   160

Can utterly abolish or destroy!
          Hence in a season of calm weather
          Though inland far we be,
Our Souls have sight of that immortal sea
          Which brought us hither,   165
          Can in a moment travel thither,
And see the Children sport upon the shore,
And hear the mighty waters rolling evermore.

                              X

Then sing, ye Birds, sing, sing a joyous song!
          And let the young Lambs bound   170
          As to the tabor's sound!
We in thought will join your throng,
          Ye that pipe and ye that play,
          Ye that through your hearts to-day
          Feel the gladness of the May!   175
What though the radiance which was once so bright
Be now for ever taken from my sight,
          Though nothing can bring back the hour
Of splendour in the grass, of glory in the flower;
          We will grieve not, rather find   180
          Strength in what remains behind;
          In the primal sympathy
          Which having been must ever be;
          In the soothing thoughts that spring
          Out of human suffering;   185
          In the faith that looks through death,
In years that bring the philosophic mind.

                              XI

And O, ye Fountains, Meadows, Hills, and Groves,
Forebode not any severing of our loves!
Yet in my heart of hearts I feel your might;   190
I only have relinquished one delight
To live beneath your more habitual sway.
I love the Brooks which down their channels fret,
Even more than when I tripped lightly as they;
The innocent brightness of a new-born Day   195
          Is lovely yet;

The Clouds that gather round the setting sun
Do take a sober colouring from an eye
That hath kept watch o'er man's mortality;
Another race hath been, and other palms are won.   200
Thanks to the human heart by which we live,
Thanks to its tenderness, its joys, and fears,
To me the meanest flower that blows can give
Thoughts that do often lie too deep for tears.

[1802–04]

SHE WAS A PHANTOM OF DELIGHT

She was a Phantom of delight
When first she gleamed upon my sight;
A lovely Apparition, sent
To be a moment's ornament;
Her eyes as stars of Twilight fair;   5
Like Twilight's, too, her dusky hair;
But all things else about her drawn
From May-time and the cheerful Dawn;
A dancing Shape, an Image gay,
To haunt, to startle, and way-lay.   10

I saw her upon nearer view,
A Spirit, yet a Woman too!
Her household motions light and free,
And steps of virgin-liberty;
A countenance in which did meet   15
Sweet records, promises as sweet;
A Creature not too bright or good
For human nature's daily food;
For transient sorrows, simple wiles,
Praise, blame, love, kisses, tears, and smiles.   20

And now I see with eye serene
The very pulse of the machine;
A Being breathing thoughtful breath,
A Traveller between life and death;
The reason firm, the temperate will,   25

Endurance, foresight, strength, and skill;
A perfect Woman, nobly planned,
To warn, to comfort, and command;
And yet a Spirit still, and bright
With something of angelic light.   30
    [1804]

I WANDERED LONELY AS A CLOUD

I wandered lonely as a cloud
That floats on high o'er vales and hills,
When all at once I saw a crowd,
A host, of golden daffodils;
Beside the lake, beneath the trees,   5
Fluttering and dancing in the breeze.

Continuous as the stars that shine
And twinkle on the milky way,
They stretched in never-ending line
Along the margin of a bay: 10
Ten thousand saw I at a glance,
Tossing their heads in sprightly dance.

The waves beside them danced; but they
Out-did the sparkling waves in glee:
A poet could not but be gay,   15
In such a jocund company:
I gazed—and gazed—but little thought
What wealth the show to me had brought:

For oft, when on my couch I lie
In vacant or in pensive mood,   20
They flash upon that inward eye
Which is the bliss of solitude;
And then my heart with pleasure fills,
And dances with the daffodils.
    [1804]

ODE TO DUTY

"Jam non consilio bonus, sed more eò perductus, ut non tantum
rectè facere possim, sed nisi rectè facere non possim."

Stern Daughter of the Voice of God!
O Duty! if that name thou love
Who art a light to guide, a rod
To check the erring, and reprove;
Thou, who art victory and law   5
When empty terrors overawe;
From vain temptations dost set free;
And calm'st the weary strife of frail humanity!

There are who ask not if thine eye
Be on them; who, in love and truth,   10
Where no misgiving is, rely
Upon the genial sense of youth;
Glad Hearts! without reproach or blot;
Who do thy work, and know it not:
Oh! if through confidence misplaced   15
They fail, thy saving arms, dread Power! around them cast.

Serene will be our days and bright,
And happy will our nature be,
When love is an unerring light,
And joy its own security.   20
And they a blissful course may hold
Even now, who, not unwisely bold,
Live in the spirit of this creed;
Yet seek thy firm support, according to their need.

I, loving freedom, and untried;   25
No sport of every random gust,
Yet being to myself a guide,
Too blindly have reposed my trust:
And oft, when in my heart was heard
Thy timely mandate, I deferred   30
The task, in smoother walks to stray;
But thee I now would serve more strictly, if I may.

Through no disturbance of my soul,
Or strong compunction in me wrought,
I supplicate for thy control;   35
But in the quietness of thought:
Me this unchartered freedom tires;
I feel the weight of chance-desires:
My hopes no more must change their name,
I long for a repose that ever is the same.   40

[Yet not the less would I throughout
Still act according to the voice
Of my own wish; and feel past doubt
That my submissiveness was choice:
Not seeking in the school of pride   45
For "precepts over dignified,"
Denial and restraint I prize
No farther than they breed a second Will more wise.]
Stern Lawgiver! yet thou dost wear
The Godhead's most benignant grace;   50
Nor know we anything so fair
As is the smile upon thy face:
Flowers laugh before thee on their beds
And fragrance in thy footing treads;
Thou dost preserve the stars from wrong;   55
And the most ancient heavens, through Thee, are fresh
    and strong.

To humbler functions, awful Power!
I call thee: I myself commend
Unto thy guidance from this hour;
Oh, let my weakness have an end!   60
Give unto me, made lowly wise,
The spirit of self-sacrifice;
The confidence of reason give;
And in the light of truth thy Bondman let me live!
    [1804]

STEPPING WESTWARD

"What, you are stepping westward?"—"Yea."
—'Twould be a wildish destiny,
If we, who thus together roam
In a strange Land, and far from home,
Were in this place the guests of Chance: 5
Yet who would stop, or fear to advance,
Though home or shelter he had none,
With such a sky to lead him on?

The dewy ground was dark and cold;
Behind, all gloomy to behold;   10
And stepping westward seemed to be
A kind of heavenly destiny:
I liked the greeting; 'twas a sound
Of something without place or bound;
And seemed to give spiritual right   15
To travel through that region bright.

The voice was soft, and she who spake
Was walking by her native lake:
The salutation had to me
The very sound of courtesy: 20
Its power was felt; and while my eye
Was fixed upon the glowing Sky,
The echo of the voice enwrought
A human sweetness with the thought
Of travelling through the world that lay   25
Before me in my endless way.
    [1805]

THE SOLITARY REAPER

Behold her, single in the field,
Yon solitary Highland Lass!
Reaping and singing by herself;

Stop here, or gently pass!
Alone she cuts and binds the grain,   5
And sings a melancholy strain;
O listen! for the Vale profound
Is overflowing with the sound.

No Nightingale did ever chaunt
More welcome notes to weary bands   10
Of travellers in some shady haunt,
Among Arabian sands:
A voice so thrilling ne'er was heard
In spring-time from the Cuckoo-bird,
Breaking the silence of the seas   15
Among the farthest Hebrides.

Will no one tell me what she sings?—
Perhaps the plaintive numbers flow
For old, unhappy, far-off things,
And battles long ago: 20
Or is it some more humble lay,
Familiar matter of to-day?
Some natural sorrow, loss, or pain,
That has been, and may be again?

Whate'er the theme, the Maiden sang   25
As if her song could have no ending;
I saw her singing at her work,
And o'er the sickle bending:—
I listened, motionless and still;
And, as I mounted up the hill,   30
The music in my heart I bore,
Long after it was heard no more.
[1805]

ELEGIAC STANZAS

SUGGESTED BY A PICTURE OF PEELE CASTLE, IN A STORM, PAINTED BY SIR GEORGE BEAUMONT

I was thy neighbour once, thou rugged Pile!
Four summer weeks I dwelt in sight of thee:

I saw thee every day; and all the while
Thy Form was sleeping on a glassy sea.

So pure the sky, so quiet was the air!   5
So like, so very like, was day to day!
Whene'er I looked, thy Image still was there;
It trembled, but it never passed away.

How perfect was the calm! it seemed no sleep;
No mood, which season takes away, or brings: 10
I could have fancied that the mighty Deep
Was even the gentlest of all gentle Things.

Ah! THEN, if mine had been the Painter's hand,
To express what then I saw; and add the gleam,
The light that never was, on sea or land,   15
The consecration, and the Poet's dream;

I would have planted thee, thou hoary Pile
Amid a world how different from this!
Beside a sea that could not cease to smile:
On tranquil land, beneath a sky of bliss.   20

Thou shouldst have seemed a treasure-house divine
Of peaceful years; a chronicle of heaven:—
Of all the sunbeams that did ever shine
The very sweetest had to thee been given.

A Picture had it been of lasting ease,   25
Elysian quiet, without toil or strife;
No motion but the moving tide, a breeze,
Or merely silent Nature's breathing life.

Such, in the fond illusion of my heart,
Such Picture would I at that time have made: 30
And seen the soul of truth in every part,
A stedfast peace that might not be betrayed.

So once it would have been,—'tis so no more;
I have submitted to a new control:
A power is gone, which nothing can restore;   35
A deep distress hath humanised my Soul.

Not for a moment could I now behold
A smiling sea, and be what I have been:
The feeling of my loss will ne'er be old;
This, which I know, I speak with mind serene.   40

Then, Beaumont, Friend! who would have been the
    Friend,
If he had lived, of Him whom I deplore,
This work of thine I blame not, but commend;
This sea in anger, and that dismal shore.

O 'tis a passionate Work!—yet wise and well,   45
Well chosen is the spirit that is here;
That Hulk which labours in the deadly swell,
This rueful sky, this pageantry of fear!

And this huge Castle, standing here sublime,
I love to see the look with which it braves,   50
Cased in the unfeeling armour of old time,
The lightning, the fierce wind, and trampling waves.

Farewell, farewell the heart that lives alone,
Housed in a dream, at distance from the Kind!
Such happiness, wherever it be known,   55
Is to be pitied; for 'tis surely blind.

But welcome fortitude, and patient cheer,
And frequent sights of what is to be borne!
Such sights, or worse, as are before me here.—
Not without hope we suffer and we mourn.   60
        [1805]

CHARACTER OF THE HAPPY WARRIOR

Who is the happy Warrior? Who is he
That every man in arms should wish to be?
—It is the generous Spirit, who, when brought
Among the tasks of real life, hath wrought
Upon the plan that pleased his boyish thought: 5

Whose high endeavours are an inward light
That makes the path before him always bright:
Who, with a natural instinct to discern
What knowledge can perform, is diligent to learn;
Abides by this resolve, and stops not there,   10
But makes his moral being his prime care;
Who, doomed to go in company with Pain,
And Fear, and Bloodshed, miserable train!
Turns his necessity to glorious gain;
In face of these doth exercise a power   15
Which is our human nature's highest dower;
Controls them and subdues, transmutes, bereaves
Of their bad influence, and their good receives:
By objects which might force the soul to abate
Her feeling, rendered more compassionate;   20
Is placable—because occasions rise
So often that demand such sacrifice;
More skilful in self-knowledge, even more pure,
As tempted more; more able to endure,
As more exposed to suffering and distress;   25
Thence, also, more alive to tenderness.
—'Tis he whose law is reason; who depends
Upon that law as on the best of friends;
Whence, in a state where men are tempted still
To evil for a guard against worse ill,   30
And what in quality or act is best
Doth seldom on a right foundation rest,
He labours good on good to fix, and owes
To virtue every triumph that he knows:
—Who, if he rise to station of command,   35
Rises by open means; and there will stand
On honourable terms, or else retire,
And in himself possess his own desire;
Who comprehends his trust, and to the same
Keeps faithful with a singleness of aim;   40
And therefore does not stoop, nor lie in wait
For wealth, or honours, or for worldly state;
Whom they must follow; on whose head must fall,
Like showers of manna, if they come at all:
Whose powers shed round him in the common strife,   45
Or mild concerns of ordinary life,
A constant influence, a peculiar grace;

But who, if he be called upon to face
Some awful moment to which Heaven has joined
Great issues, good or bad for human kind,   50
Is happy as a Lover; and attired
With sudden brightness, like a Man inspired;
And, through the heat of conflict, keeps the law
In calmness made, and sees what he foresaw;
Or if an unexpected call succeed,   55
Come when it will, is equal to the need:
—He who, though thus endued as with a sense
And faculty for storm and turbulence,
Is yet a Soul whose master-bias leans
To homefelt pleasures and to gentle scenes;   60
Sweet images! which, whereso'er he be,
Are at his heart; and such fidelity
It is his darling passion to approve;
More brave for this, that he hath much to love:—
'Tis, finally, the Man, who lifted high,   65
Conspicuous object in a Nation's eye,
Or left unthought-of in obscurity,—
Who, with a toward or untoward lot,
Prosperous or adverse, to his wish or not—
Plays, in the many games of life, that one   70
Where what he most doth value must be won:
Whom neither shape of danger can dismay,
Nor thought of tender happiness betray;
Who, not content that former worth stand fast,
Looks forward, persevering to the last,   75
From well to better, daily self-surpast:
Who, whether praise of him must walk the earth
For ever, and to noble deeds give birth,
Or he must fall, to sleep without his fame,
And leave a dead unprofitable name—   80
Finds comfort in himself and in his cause;
And, while the mortal mist is gathering, draws
His breath in confidence of Heaven's applause:
This is the happy Warrior; this is He
That every Man in arms should wish to be.   85
[1805–06]

THE WORLD IS TOO MUCH WITH US

The world is too much with us; late and soon,
Getting and spending, we lay waste our powers:
Little we see in Nature that is ours;
We have given our hearts away, a sordid boon!
This Sea that bares her bosom to the moon;   5
The winds that will be howling at all hours,
And are up-gathered now like sleeping flowers;
For this, for everything, we are out of tune;
It moves us not.—Great God! I'd rather be
A Pagan suckled in a creed outworn;   10
So might I, standing on this pleasant lea,
Have glimpses that would make me less forlorn;
Have sight of Proteus rising from the sea;
Or hear old Triton blow his wreathèd horn.
    [1806]

THOUGHT OF A BRITON ON THE SUBJUGATION OF SWITZERLAND

Two Voices are there; one is of the sea,
One of the mountains; each a mighty Voice:
In both from age to age thou didst rejoice,
They were thy chosen music, Liberty!
There came a Tyrant, and with holy glee   5
Thou fought'st against him; but hast vainly striven:
Thou from thy Alpine holds at length art driven,
Where not a torrent murmurs heard by thee.
Of one deep bliss thine ear hath been bereft:
Then cleave, O cleave to that which still is left;   10
For, high-souled Maid, what sorrow would it be
That Mountain floods should thunder as before,
And Ocean bellow from his rocky shore,
And neither awful Voice be heard by thee!
    [1806]

AT THE GRAVE OF BURNS, 1803

SEVEN YEARS AFTER HIS DEATH

I shiver, Spirit fierce and bold,
At thought of what I now behold:
As vapours breathed from dungeons cold
    Strike pleasure dead,
So sadness comes from out the mould   **5**
    Where Burns is laid.

And have I then thy bones so near,
And thou forbidden to appear?
As if it were thyself that's here
    I shrink with pain;   **10**
And both my wishes and my fear
    Alike are vain.

Off weight—nor press on weight!—away
Dark thoughts!—they came, but not to stay;
With chastened feelings would I pay   **15**
    The tribute due
To him, and aught that hides his clay
    From mortal view.

Fresh as the flower, whose modest worth
He sang, his genius "glinted" forth,   **20**
Rose like a star that touching earth,
    For so it seems,
Doth glorify its humble birth
    With matchless beams.

The piercing eye, the thoughtful brow,   **25**
The struggling heart, where be they now?—
Full soon the Aspirant of the plough,
    The prompt, the brave,
Slept, with the obscurest, in the low
    And silent grave.   **30**

I mourned with thousands, but as one
More deeply grieved, for He was gone

Whose light I hailed when first it shone,
    And showed my youth
How Verse may build a princely throne   35
    On humble truth.

Alas! where'er the current tends,
Regret pursues and with it blends,—
Huge Criffel's hoary top ascends
    By Skiddaw seen,—   40
Neighbours we were, and loving friends
    We might have been;

True friends though diversely inclined;
But heart with heart and mind with mind,
Where the main fibres are entwined,   45
    Through Nature's skill,
May even by contraries be joined
    More closely still.

The tear will start, and let it flow;
Thou "poor Inhabitant below,"   50
At this dread moment—even so—
    Might we together
Have sate and talked where gowans blow,
    Or on wild heather.

What treasures would have then been placed   55
Within my reach; of knowledge graced
By fancy what a rich repast!
    But why go on?—
Oh! spare to sweep, thou mournful blast,
    His grave grass-grown.   60

There, too, a Son, his joy and pride,
(Not three weeks past the Stripling died,)
Lies gathered to his Father's side,
    Soul-moving sight!
Yet one to which is not denied   65
    Some sad delight.

For *he* is safe, a quiet bed
Hath early found among the dead,

Harboured where none can be misled,
  Wronged, or distrest;   70
And surely here it may be said
  That such are blest.

And oh for Thee, by pitying grace
Checked oft-times in a devious race,
May He, who halloweth the place   75
  Where Man is laid,
Receive thy Spirit in the embrace
  For which it prayed!

Sighing I turned away; but ere
Night fell I heard, or seemed to hear,   80
Music that sorrow comes not near,
  A ritual hymn,
Chanted in love that casts out fear
  By Seraphim.
          [1803–07]

COMPOSED BY THE SIDE OF GRASMERE LAKE

Clouds, lingering yet, extend in solid bars
Through the grey west; and lo! these waters, steeled
By breezeless air to smoothest polish, yield
A vivid repetition of the stars;
Jove, Venus, and the ruddy crest of Mars   5
Amid his fellows beauteously revealed
At happy distance from earth's groaning field,
Where ruthless mortals wage incessant wars.
Is it a mirror?—or the nether Sphere
Opening to view the abyss in which she feeds   10
Her own calm fires?—But list! a voice is near;
Great Pan himself low-whispering through the reeds,
"Be thankful, thou; for, if unholy deeds
Ravage the world, tranquillity is here!"
          [1807]

YARROW VISITED

SEPTEMBER, 1814

And is this—Yarrow?—*This* the Stream
Of which my fancy cherished,
So faithfully, a waking dream?
An image that hath perished!
O that some Minstrel's harp were near,   5
To utter notes of gladness,
And chase this silence from the air,
That fills my heart with sadness!

Yet why?—a silvery current flows
With uncontrolled meanderings;   10
Nor have these eyes by greener hills
Been soothed, in all my wanderings.
And, through her depths, Saint Mary's Lake
Is visibly delighted;
For not a feature of those hills   15
Is in the mirror slighted.

A blue sky bends o'er Yarrow vale,
Save where that pearly whiteness
Is round the rising sun diffused,
A tender hazy brightness;   20
Mild dawn of promise! that excludes
All profitless dejection;
Though not unwilling here to admit
A pensive recollection.

Where was it that the famous Flower   25
Of Yarrow Vale lay bleeding?
His bed perchance was yon smooth mound
On which the herd is feeding:
And haply from this crystal pool,
Now peaceful as the morning,   30
The Water-wraith ascended thrice—
And gave his doleful warning.

Delicious is the Lay that sings
The haunts of happy Lovers,
The path that leads them to the grove,   35
The leafy grove that covers:
And Pity sanctifies the Verse
That paints, by strength of sorrow,
The unconquerable strength of love;
Bear witness, rueful Yarrow!   40

But thou, that didst appear so fair
To fond imagination,
Dost rival in the light of day
Her delicate creation:
Meek loveliness is round thee spread,   45
A softness still and holy;
The grace of forest charms decayed,
And pastoral melancholy.

That region left, the vale unfolds
Rich groves of lofty stature,   50
With Yarrow winding through the pomp
Of cultivated nature;
And, rising from those lofty groves,
Behold a Ruin hoary!
The shattered front of Newark's Towers,   55
Renowned in Border story.

Fair scenes for childhood's opening bloom,
For sportive youth to stray in;
For manhood to enjoy his strength;
And age to wear away in!   60
Yon cottage seems a bower of bliss,
A covert for protection
Of tender thoughts, that nestle there—
The brood of chaste affection.

How sweet, on this autumnal day,   65
The wild-wood fruits to gather,
And on my True-love's forehead plant
A crest of blooming heather!
And what if I enwreathed my own!
'Twere no offence to reason;   70

The sober Hills thus deck their brows
To meet the wintry season.

I see—but not by sight alone,
Loved Yarrow, have I won thee;
A ray of fancy still survives—   75
Her sunshine plays upon thee!
Thy ever-youthful waters keep
A course of lively pleasure;
And gladsome notes my lips can breathe,
Accordant to the measure.   80

The vapours linger round the Heights,
They melt, and soon must vanish;
One hour is theirs, nor more is mine—
Sad thought, which I would banish,
But that I know, where'er I go,   85
Thy genuine image, Yarrow!
Will dwell with me—to heighten joy,
And cheer my mind in sorrow.
            [1814]

from THE RIVER DUDDON

A SERIES OF SONNETS

III

How shall I paint thee?—Be this naked stone
My seat, while I give way to such intent;
Pleased could my verse, a speaking monument,
Make to the eyes of men thy features known.
But as of all those tripping lambs not one   5
Outruns his fellows, so hath Nature lent
To thy beginning nought that doth present
Peculiar ground for hope to build upon.
To dignify the spot that gives thee birth
No sign of hoar Antiquity's esteem   10
Appears, and none of modern Fortune's care;

Yet thou thyself hast round thee shed a gleam
Of brilliant moss, instinct with freshness rare;
Prompt offering to thy Foster-mother, Earth!

IV

Take, cradled Nursling of the mountain, take
This parting glance, no negligent adieu!
A Protean change seems wrought while I pursue
The curves, a loosely-scattered chain doth make;
Or rather thou appear'st a glistering snake,   5
Silent, and to the gazer's eye untrue,
Thridding with sinuous lapse the rushes, through
Dwarf willows gliding, and by ferny brake.
Starts from a dizzy steep the undaunted Rill
Robed instantly in garb of snow-white foam;   10
And laughing dares the Adventurer, who hath clomb
So high, a rival purpose to fulfil;
Else let the dastard backward wend, and roam,
Seeking less bold achievement, where he will!
        [1806–20]

from ECCLESIASTICAL SONNETS

CONCLUSION

Why sleeps the future, as a snake enrolled,
Coil within coil, at noon-tide? For the WORD
Yields, if with unpresumptuous faith explored,
Power at whose touch the sluggard shall unfold
His drowsy rings. Look forth!—that Stream behold,   5
THAT STREAM upon whose bosom we have passed
Floating at ease while nations have effaced
Nations, and Death has gathered to his fold
Long lines of mighty Kings—look forth, my Soul!
(Nor in this vision be thou slow to trust)   10
The living Waters, less and less by guilt
Stained and polluted, brighten as they roll,
Till they have reached the eternal City—built
For the perfected Spirits of the just!
        [1821]

TO A SKYLARK

Ethereal minstrel! pilgrim of the sky!
Dost thou despise the earth where cares abound?
Or, while the wings aspire, are heart and eye
Both with thy nest upon the dewy ground?
Thy nest which thou canst drop into at will,   5
Those quivering wings composed, that music still!

Leave to the nightingale her shady wood;
A privacy of glorious light is thine;
Whence thou dost pour upon the world a flood
Of harmony, with instinct more divine;   10
Type of the wise who soar, but never roam;
True to the kindred points of Heaven and Home!
    [1825]

YARROW REVISITED

The gallant Youth, who many have gained,
    Or seeks, a "winsome Marrow,"
Was but an Infant in the lap
    When first I looked on Yarrow;
Once more, by Newark's Castle-gate   5
    Long left without a warder,
I stood, looked, listened, and with Thee,
    Great Minstrel of the Border!

Grave thoughts ruled wide on that sweet day,
    Their dignity installing   10
In gentle bosoms, while sere leaves
    Were on the bough, or falling;
But breezes played, and sunshine gleamed—
    The forest to embolden;
Reddened the fiery hues, and shot   15
    Transparence through the golden.

For busy thoughts the Stream flowed on
   In foamy agitation;
And slept in many a crystal pool
   For quiet contemplation: 20
No public and no private care
   The freeborn mind enthralling,
We made a day of happy hours,
   Our happy days recalling.

Brisk Youth appeared, the Morn of Youth,   25
   With freaks of graceful folly,—
Life's temperate Noon, her sober Eve,
   Her Night not melancholy;
Past, present, future, all appeared
   In harmony united,   30
Like guests that meet, and some from far,
   By cordial love invited.

And if, as Yarrow, through the woods
   And down the meadow ranging,
Did meet us with unaltered face,   35
   Though we were changed and changing;
If, *then*, some natural shadows spread
   Our inward prospect over,
The soul's deep valley was not slow
   Its brightness to recover.   40

Eternal blessings on the Muse,
   And her divine employment!
The blameless Muse, who trains her Sons
   For hope and calm enjoyment;
Albeit sickness, lingering yet,   45
   Has o'er their pillow brooded;
And Care waylays their steps—a Sprite
   Not easily eluded.

For thee, O Scott! compelled to change
   Green Eildon-hill and Cheviot   50
For warm Vesuvio's vine-clad slopes;
   And leave thy Tweed and Tiviot
For mild Sorrento's breezy waves;
   May classic Fancy, linking

With native Fancy her fresh aid,   55
   Preserve thy heart from sinking!

Oh! while they minister to thee,
   Each vying with the other,
May Health return to mellow Age,
   With Strength, her venturous brother;   60
And Tiber, and each brook and rill
   Renowned in song and story,
With unimagined beauty shine,
   Nor lose one ray of glory!

For Thou, upon a hundred streams,   65
   By tales of love and sorrow,
Of faithful love, undaunted truth,
   Hast shed the power of Yarrow:
And streams unknown, hills yet unseen,
   Wherever they invite Thee,   70
At parent Nature's grateful call,
   With gladness must requite Thee.

A gracious welcome shall be thine,
   Such looks of love and honour
As thy own Yarrow gave to me   75
   When first I gazed upon her;
Beheld what I had feared to see,
   Unwilling to surrender
Dreams treasured up from early days,
   The holy and the tender.   80

And what, for this frail world, were all
   That mortals do or suffer,
Did no responsive harp, no pen,
   Memorial tribute offer?
Yea, what were mighty Nature's self?   85
   Her features, could they win us,
Unhelped by the poetic voice
   That hourly speaks within us?

Nor deem that localised Romance
   Plays false with our affections;   90

Unsanctifies our tears—made sport
  For fanciful dejections:
Ah, no! the visions of the past
  Sustain the heart in feeling
Life as she is—our changeful Life,   95
  With friends and kindred dealing.

Bear witness, Ye, whose thoughts that day
  In Yarrow's groves were centred;
Who through the silent portal arch
  Of mouldering Newark enter'd;   100
And clomb the winding stair that once
  Too timidly was mounted
By the "last Minstrel," (not the last!)
  Ere he his Tale recounted.

Flow on for ever, Yarrow Stream!   105
  Fulfil thy pensive duty,
Well pleased that future Bards should chant
  For simple hearts thy beauty:
To dream-light dear while yet unseen,
  Dear to the common sunshine,   110
And dearer still, as now I feel,
  To memory's shadowy moonshine!
    [1831]

from THE PRELUDE

OR, GROWTH OF A POET'S MIND

(First edition, 1850)

BOOK TWELFTH

IMAGINATION AND TASTE, HOW IMPAIRED AND RESTORED

Long time have human ignorance and guilt
Detained us, on what spectacles of woe
Compelled to look, and inwardly oppressed

With sorrow, disappointment, vexing thoughts,
Confusion of the judgment, zeal decayed, 5
And, lastly, utter loss of hope itself
And things to hope for! Not with these began
Our song, and not with these our song must end.—
Ye motions of delight, that haunt the sides
Of the green hills; ye breezes and soft airs, 10
Whose subtle intercourse with breathing flowers,
Feelingly watched, might teach Man's haughty race
How without injury to take, to give
Without offence; ye who, as if to show
The wondrous influence of power gently used, 15
Bend the complying heads of lordly pines,
And, with a touch, shift the stupendous clouds
Through the whole compass of the sky; ye brooks,
Muttering along the stones, a busy noise
By day, a quiet sound in silent night; 20
Ye waves, that out of the great deep steal forth
In a calm hour to kiss the pebbly shore,
Not mute, and then retire, fearing no storm;
And you, ye groves, whose ministry it is
To interpose the covert of your shades, 25
Even as a sleep, between the heart of man
And outward troubles, between man himself,
Not seldom, and his own uneasy heart:
Oh! that I had a music and a voice
Harmonious as your own, that I might tell 30
What ye have done for me. The morning shines,
Nor heedeth Man's perverseness; Spring returns,—
I saw the Spring return, and could rejoice,
In common with the children of her love,
Piping on boughs, or sporting on fresh fields, 35
Or boldly seeking pleasure nearer heaven
On wings that navigate cerulean skies.
No neither were complacency, nor peace,
Nor tender yearnings, wanting for my good
Through these distracted times; in Nature still 40
Glorying, I found a counterpoise in her,
Which, when the spirit of evil reached its height,
Maintained for me a secret happiness.

This narrative, my Friend! hath chiefly told
Of intellectual power, fostering love,   **45**
Dispensing truth, and, over men and things,
Where reason yet might hesitate, diffusing
Prophetic sympathies of genial faith:
So was I favoured—such my happy lot—
Until that natural graciousness of mind   **50**
Gave way to overpressure from the times
And their disastrous issues. What availed,
When spells forbade the voyager to land,
That fragrant notice of a pleasant shore
Wafted, at intervals, from many a bower   **55**
Of blissful gratitude and fearless love?
Dare I avow that wish was mine to see,
And hope that future times *would* surely see,
The man to come, parted, as by a gulph,
From him who had been; that I could no more   **60**
Trust the elevation which had made me one
With the great family that still survives
To illuminate the abyss of ages past,
Sage, warrior, patriot, hero; for it seemed
That their best virtues were not free from taint   **65**
Of something false and weak, that could not stand
The open eye of Reason. Then I said,
'Go to the Poets; they will speak to thee
More perfectly of purer creatures;—yet
If reason be nobility in man,   **70**
Can aught be more ignoble than the man
Whom they delight in, blinded as he is
By prejudice, the miserable slave
Of low ambition or distempered love?'

      In such strange passion, if I may once more   **75**
Review the past, I warred against myself—
A bigot to a new idolatry—
Like a cowled monk who hath forsworn the world,
Zealously laboured to cut off my heart
From all the sources of her former strength;   **80**
And as, by simple waving of a wand,
The wizard instantaneously dissolves
Palace or grove, even so could I unsoul
As readily by syllogistic words

Those mysteries of being which have made,   85
And shall continue evermore to make,
Of the whole human race one brotherhood.

What wonder, then, if, to a mind so far
Perverted, even the visible Universe
Fell under the dominion of a taste   90
Less spiritual, with microscopic view
Was scanned, as I had scanned the moral world?

O Soul of Nature! excellent and fair!
That didst rejoice with me, with whom I, too,
Rejoiced through early youth, before the winds   95
And roaring waters, and in lights and shades
That marched and countermarched about the hills
In glorious apparition, Powers on whom
I daily waited, now all eye and now
All ear; but never long without the heart   100
Employed, and man's unfolding intellect:
O Soul of Nature! that, by laws divine
Sustained and governed, still dost overflow
With an impassioned life, what feeble ones
Walk on this earth! how feeble have I been   105
When thou wert in thy strength! Nor this through stroke
Of human suffering, such as justifies
Remissness and inaptitude of mind,
But through presumption; even in pleasure pleased
Unworthily, disliking here, and there   110
Liking; by rules of mimic art transferred
To things above all art; but more,—for this,
Although a strong infection of the age,
Was never much my habit—giving way
To a comparison of scene with scene,   115
Bent overmuch on superficial things,
Pampering myself with meagre novelties
Of colour and proportion; to the moods
Of time and season, to the moral power,
The affections and the spirit of the place,   120
Insensible. Nor only did the love
Of sitting thus in judgment interrupt
My deeper feelings, but another cause,
More subtle and less easily explained,

That almost seems inherent in the creature,   125
A twofold frame of body and of mind.
I speak in recollection of a time
When the bodily eye, in every stage of life
The most despotic of our senses, gained
Such strength in *me* as often held my mind   130
In absolute dominion. Gladly here,
Entering upon abstruser argument,
Could I endeavour to unfold the means
Which Nature studiously employs to thwart
This tyranny, summons all the senses each   135
To counteract the other, and themselves,
And make them all, and the objects with which all
Are conversant, subservient in their turn
To the great ends of Liberty and Power.
But leave we this: enough that my delights   140
(Such as they were) were sought insatiably.
Vivid the transport, vivid though not profound;
I roamed from hill to hill, from rock to rock,
Still craving combinations of new forms,
New pleasure, wider empire for the sight,   145
Proud of her own endowments, and rejoiced
To lay the inner faculties asleep.
Amid the turns and counterturns, the strife
And various trials of our complex being,
As we grow up, such thraldom of that sense   150
Seems hard to shun. And yet I knew a maid,
A young enthusiast, who escaped these bonds;
Her eye was not the mistress of her heart;
Far less did rules prescribed by passive taste,
Or barren intermeddling subtleties,   155
Perplex her mind; but, wise as women are
When genial circumstances hath favoured them,
She welcomed what was given, and craved no more;
Whate'er the scene presented to her view,
That was the best, to that she was attuned   160
By her benign simplicity of life,
And through a perfect happiness of soul,
Whose variegated feelings were in this
Sisters, that they were each some new delight.
Birds in the bower, and lambs in the green field,   165
Could they have known her, would have loved; methought

Her very presence such a sweetness breathed,
That flowers, and trees, and even the silent hills,
And every thing she looked on, should have had
An intimation how she bore herself   170
Towards them and to all creatures. God delights
In such a being; for her common thoughts
Are piety, her life is gratitude.

  Even like this maid, before I was called forth
From the retirement of my native hills,   175
I loved whate'er I saw: nor lightly loved,
But most intensely; never dreamt of aught
More grand, more fair, more exquisitely framed
Than those few nooks to which my happy feet
Were limited. I had not at that time   180
Lived long enough, nor in the least survived
The first diviner influence of this world,
As it appears to unaccustomed eyes.
Worshipping then among the depth of things,
As piety ordained; could I submit   185
To measured admiration, or to aught
That should preclude humility and love?
I felt, observed, and pondered; did not judge,
Yea, never thought of judging; with the gift
Of all this glory filled and satisfied.   190
And afterwards, when through the gorgeous Alps
Roaming, I carried with me the same heart:
In truth, the degradation—howsoe'er
Induced, effect, in whatsoe'er degree,
Of custom that prepares a partial scale   195
In which the little oft outweighs the great;
Or any other cause that hath been named;
Or lastly, aggravated by the times
And their impassioned sounds, which well might make
The milder minstrelsies of rural scenes   200
Inaudible—was transient; I had known
Too forcibly, too early in my life,
Visitings of imaginative power
For this to last: I shook the habit off
Entirely and for ever, and again   205
In Nature's presence stood, as now I stand,
A sensitive being, a creative soul.

There are in our existence spots of time,
That with distinct pre-eminence retain
A renovating virtue, whence, depressed   210
By false opinion and contentious thought,
Or aught of heavier or more deadly weight,
In trivial occupations, and the round
Of ordinary intercourse, our minds
Are nourished and invisibly repaired;   215
A virtue, by which pleasure is enhanced,
That penetrates, enables us to mount,
When high, more high, and lifts us up when fallen.
This efficacious spirit chiefly lurks
Among those passages of life that give   220
Profoundest knowledge to what point, and how,
The mind is lord and master—outward sense
The obedient servant of her will. Such moments
Are scattered everywhere, taking their date
From our first childhood. I remember well,   225
That once, while yet my inexperienced hand
Could scarcely hold a bridle, with proud hopes
I mounted, and we journeyed towards the hills:
An ancient servant of my father's house
Was with me, my encourager and guide: 230
We had not travelled long, ere some mischance
Disjoined me from my comrade; and, through fear
Dismounting, down the rough and stony moor
I led my horse, and, stumbling on, at length
Came to a bottom, where in former times   235
A murderer had been hung in iron chains.
The gibbet-mast had mouldered down, the bones
And iron case were gone; but on the turf,
Hard by, soon after that fell deed was wrought,
Some unknown hand had carved the murderer's name. 240
The monumental letters were inscribed
In times long past; but still, from year to year,
By superstition of the neighbourhood,
The grass is cleared away, and to this hour
The characters are fresh and visible: 245
A casual glance had shown them, and I fled,
Faltering and faint, and ignorant of the road:
Then, reascending the bare common, saw
A naked pool that lay beneath the hills,

The beacon on the summit, and, more near,   250
A girl, who bore a pitcher on her head,
And seemed with difficult steps to force her way
Against the blowing wind. It was, in truth,
An ordinary sight; but I should need
Colours and words that are unknown to man,   255
To paint the visionary dreariness
Which, while I looked all round for my lost guide,
Invested moorland waste, and naked pool,
The beacon crowning the lone eminence,
The female and her garments vexed and tossed   260
By the strong wind. When, in the blessed hours
Of early love, the loved one at my side,
I roamed, in daily presence of this scene,
Upon the naked pool and dreary crags,
And on the melancholy beacon fell   265
A spirit of pleasure and youth's golden gleam;
And think ye not with radiance more sublime
For these remembrances, and for the power
They had left behind? So feeling comes in aid
Of feeling, and diversity of strength   270
Attends us, if but once we have been strong.
Oh! mystery of man, from what a depth
Proceed thy honours. I am lost, but see
In simple childhood something of the base
On which thy greatness stands; but this I feel,   275
That from thyself it comes, that thou must give,
Else never canst receive. The days gone by
Return upon me almost from the dawn
Of life: the hiding-places of man's power
Open; I would approach them, but they close.   280
I see by glimpses now; when age comes on,
May scarcely see at all; and I would give,
While yet we may, as far as words can give,
Substance and life so what I feel, enshrining,
Such is my hope, the spirit of the Past   285
For future restoration.—Yet another
Of these memorials:—
           One Christmas-time,
On the glad eve of its dear holidays,
Feverish, and tired, and restless, I went forth
Into the fields, impatient for the sight   290

Of those led palfreys that should bear us home;
My brothers and myself. There rose a crag,
That, from the meeting-point of two highways
Ascending, overlooked them both, far stretched;
Thither, uncertain on which road to fix   295
My expectation, thither I repaired,
Scout-like, and gained the summit; 'twas a day
Tempestuous, dark, and wild, and on the grass
I sate half-sheltered by a naked wall;
Upon my right hand couched a single sheep,   300
Upon my left a blasted hawthorn stood;
With those companions at my side, I watched,
Straining my eyes intensely, as the mist
Gave intermitting prospect of the copse
And plain beneath. Ere we to school returned,—   305
That dreary time,—ere we had been ten days
Sojourners in my father's house, he died,
And I and my three brothers, orphans then,
Followed his body to the grave. The event,
With all the sorrow that it brought, appeared   310
A chastisement; and when I called to mind
That day so lately past, when from the crag
I looked in such anxiety of hope;
With trite reflections of morality,
Yet in the deepest passion, I bowed low   315
To God, Who thus corrected my desires;
And, afterwards, the wind and sleety rain,
And all the business of the elements,
The single sheep, and the one blasted tree,
And the bleak music from that old stone wall,   320
The noise of wood and water, and the mist
That on the line of each of those two roads
Advanced in such indisputable shapes;
All these were kindred spectacles and sounds
To which I oft repaired, and thence would drink,   325
As at a fountain; and on winter nights,
Down to this very time, when storm and rain
Beat on my roof, or, haply, at noon-day,
While in a grove I walk, whose lofty trees,
Laden with summer's thickest foliage, rock   330
In a strong wind, some working of the spirit,
Some inward agitations thence are brought,

Whate'er their office, whether to beguile
Thoughts over busy in the course they took,
Or animate an hour of vacant ease.   335

BOOK THIRTEENTH

IMAGINATION AND TASTE, HOW IMPAIRED AND RESTORED—CONCLUDED

From Nature doth emotion come, and moods
Of calmness equally are Nature's gift:
This is her glory; these two attributes
Are sister horns that constitute her strength.
Hence Genius, born to thrive by interchange   5
Of peace and excitation, finds in her
His best and purest friend; from her receives
That energy by which he seeks the truth,
From her that happy stillness of the mind
Which fits him to receive it when unsought.   10

    Such benefit the humblest intellects
Partake of, each in their degree; 'tis mine
To speak, what I myself have known and felt;
Smooth task! for words find easy way, inspired
By gratitude, and confidence in truth.   15
Long time in search of knowledge did I range
The field of human life, in heart and mind
Benighted; but, the dawn beginning now
To re-appear, 'twas proved that not in vain
I had been taught to reverence a Power   20
That is the visible quality and shape
And image of right reason; that matures
Her processes by steadfast laws; gives birth
To no impatient or fallacious hopes,
No heat of passion or excessive zeal,   25
No vain conceits; provokes to no quick turns
Of self-applauding intellect; but trains
To meekness, and exalts by humble faith;
Holds up before the mind intoxicate
With present objects, and the busy dance   30

Of things that pass away, a temperate show
Of objects that endure; and by this course
Disposes her, when over-fondly set
On throwing off incumbrances, to seek
In man, and in the frame of social life,   35
Whate'er there is desirable and good
Of kindred permanence, unchanged in form
And function, or, through strict vicissitude
Of life and death, revolving. Above all
Were re-established now those watchful thoughts   40
Which, seeing little worthy or sublime
In what the Historian's pen so much delights
To blazon—power and energy detached
From moral purpose—early tutored me
To look with feelings of fraternal love   45
Upon the unassuming things that hold
A silent station in this beauteous world.

      Thus moderated, thus composed, I found
Once more in Man an object of delight,
Of pure imagination, and of love;   50
And, as the horizon of my mind enlarged,
Again I took the intellectual eye
For my instructor, studious more to see
Great truths, than touch and handle little ones.
Knowledge was given accordingly; my trust   55
Became more firm in feelings that had stood
The test of such a trial; clearer far
My sense of excellence—of right and wrong:
The promise of the present time retired
Into its true proportion; sanguine schemes,   60
Ambitious projects, pleased me less; I sought
For present good in life's familiar face,
And built thereon my hopes of good to come.

      With settling judgments now of what would last
And what would disappear; prepared to find   65
Presumption, folly, madness, in the men
Who thrust themselves upon the passive world
As Rulers of the world; to see in these,
Even when the public welfare is their aim,
Plans without thought, or built on theories   70

Vague and unsound; and having brought the books
Of modern statists to their proper test,
Life, human life, with all its sacred claims
Of sex and age, and heaven-descended rights,
Mortal, or those beyond the reach of death;   75
And having thus discerned how dire a thing
Is worshipped in that idol proudly named
'The Wealth of Nations,' where alone that wealth
Is lodged, and how increased; and having gained
A more judicious knowledge of the worth   80
And dignity of individual man,
No composition of the brain, but man
Of whom we read, the man whom we behold
With our own eyes—I could not but inquire—
Not with less interest than heretofore,   85
But greater, though in spirit more subdued—
Why is this glorious creature to be found
One only in ten thousand? What one is,
Why may not millions be? What bars are thrown
By Nature in the way of such a hope?   90
Our animal appetites and daily wants,
Are these obstructions insurmountable?
If not, then others vanish into air.
'Inspect the basis of the social pile:
Inquire,' said I, 'how much of mental power   95
And genuine virtue they possess who live
By bodily toil, labour exceeding far
Their due proportion, under all the weight
Of that injustice which upon ourselves
Ourselves entail.' Such estimate to frame   100
I chiefly looked (what need to look beyond?)
Among the natural abodes of men,
Fields with their rural works; recalled to mind
My earliest notices; with these compared
The observations made in later youth,   105
And to that day continued.—For, the time
Had never been when throes of mighty Nations
And the world's tumult unto me could yield,
How far soe'er transported and possessed,
Full measure of content; but still I craved   110
An intermingling of distinct regards
And truths of individual sympathy

Nearer ourselves. Such often might be gleaned
From the great City, else it must have proved
To me a heart-depressing wilderness;   115
But much was wanting: therefore did I turn
To you, ye pathways, and ye lonely roads;
Sought you enriched with everything I prized,
With human kindnesses and simple joys.

    Oh! next to one dear state of bliss, vouchsafed   120
Alas! to few in this untoward world,
The bliss of walking daily in life's prime
Through field or forest with the maid we love,
While yet our hearts are young, while yet we breathe
Nothing but happiness, in some lone nook,   125
Deep vale, or any where, the home of both,
From which it would be misery to stir:
Oh! next to such enjoyment of our youth,
In my esteem, next to such dear delight,
Was that of wandering on from day to day   130
Where I could meditate in peace, and cull
Knowledge that step by step might lead me on
To wisdom; or, as lightsome as a bird
Wafted upon the wind from distant lands,
Sing notes of greeting to strange fields or groves,   135
Which lacked not voice to welcome me in turn:
And, when that pleasant toil had ceased to please,
Converse with men, where if we meet a face
We almost meet a friend, on naked heaths
With long long ways before, by cottage bench,   140
Or well-spring where the weary traveller rests.

    Who doth not love to follow with his eye
The windings of a public way? the sight,
Familiar object as it is, hath wrought
On my imagination since the morn   145
Of childhood, when a disappearing line,
One daily present to my eyes, that crossed
The naked summit of a far-off hill
Beyond the limits that my feet had trod,
Was like an invitation into space   150
Boundless, or guide into eternity.
Yes, something of the grandeur which invests

The mariner who sails the roaring sea
Through storm and darkness, early in my mind
Surrounded, too, the wanderers of the earth;
Grandeur as much, and loveliness far more.   155
Awed have I been by strolling Bedlamites;
From many other uncouth vagrants (passed
In fear) have walked with quicker step; but why
Take note of this? When I began to enquire,   160
To watch and question those I met, and speak
Without reserve to them, the lonely roads
Were open schools in which I daily read
With most delight the passions of mankind,
Whether by words, looks, sighs, or tears, revealed;   165
There saw into the depth of human souls,
Souls that appear to have no depth at all
To careless eyes. And—now convinced at heart
How little those formalities, to which
With overweening trust alone we give   170
The name of Education, have to do
With real feeling and just sense; how vain
A correspondence with the talking world
Proves to the most; and called to make good search
If man's estate, by doom of Nature yoked   175
With toil, be therefore yoked with ignorance;
If virtue be indeed so hard to rear,
And intellectual strength so rare a boon—
I prized such walks still more, for there I found
Hope to my hope, and to my pleasure peace   180
And steadiness, and healing and repose
To every angry passion. There I heard,
From mouths of men obscure and lowly, truths
Replete with honour; sounds in unison
With loftiest promises of good and fair.   185

   There are who think that strong affection, love
Known by whatever name, is falsely deemed
A gift, to use a term which they would use,
Of vulgar nature; that its growth requires
Retirement, leisure, language purified   190
By manners studied and elaborate;
That whoso feels such passion in its strength
Must live within the very light and air

Of courteous usages refined by art.
True is it, where oppression worse than death   195
Salutes the being at his birth, where grace
Of culture hath been utterly unknown,
And poverty and labour in excess
From day to day pre-occupy the ground
Of the affections, and to Nature's self   200
Oppose a deeper nature; there, indeed,
Love cannot be; nor does it thrive with ease
Among the close and overcrowded haunts
Of cities, where the human heart is sick,
And the eye feeds it not, and cannot feed.   205
—Yes, in those wanderings deeply did I feel
How we mislead each other; above all,
How books mislead us, seeking their reward
From judgments of the wealthy Few, who see
By artificial lights; how they debase   210
The Many for the pleasure of those Few;
Effeminately level down the truth
To certain general notions, for the sake
Of being understood at once, or else
Through want of better knowledge in the heads   215
That framed them; flattering self-conceit with words,
That, while they most ambitiously set forth
Extrinsic differences, the outward marks
Whereby society has parted man
From man, neglect the universal heart.   220

Here, calling up to mind what then I saw,
A youthful traveller, and see daily now
In the familiar circuit of my home,
Here might I pause, and bend in reverence
To Nature, and the power of human minds,   225
To men as they are men within themselves.
How oft high service is performed within,
When all the external man is rude in show,—
Not like a temple rich with pomp and gold,
But a mere mountain chapel, that protects   230
Its simple worshippers from sun and shower.
Of these, said I, shall be my song; of these,
If future years mature me for the task,
Will I record the praises, making verse

Deal boldly with substantial things; in truth 235
And sanctity of passion, speak of these,
That justice may be done, obeisance paid
Where it is due: thus haply shall I teach,
Inspire, through unadulterated ears
Pour rapture, tenderness, and hope,—my theme 240
No other than the very heart of man,
As found among the best of those who live,
Not unexalted by religious faith,
Nor uninformed by books, good books, though few,
In Nature's presence: thence may I select 245
Sorrow, that is not sorrow, but delight;
And miserable love, that is not pain
To hear of, for the glory that redounds
Therefrom to human kind, and what we are.
Be mine to follow with no timid step 250
Where knowledge leads me: it shall be my pride
That I have dared to tread this holy ground,
Speaking no dream, but things oracular;
Matter not lightly to be heard by those
Who to the letter of the outward promise 255
Do read the invisible soul; by men adroit
In speech, and for communion with the world
Accomplished; minds whose faculties are then
Most active when they are most eloquent,
And elevated most when most admired. 260
Men may be found of other mould than these,
Who are their own upholders, to themselves
Encouragement, and energy, and will,
Expressing liveliest thoughts in lively words
As native passion dictates. Others, too, 265
There are among the walks of homely life
Still higher, men for contemplation framed,
Shy, and unpractised in the strife of phrase;
Meek men, whose very souls perhaps would sink
Beneath them, summoned to such intercourse: 270
Theirs is the language of the heavens, the power,
The thought, the image, and the silent joy:
Words are but under-agents in their souls;
When they are grasping with their greatest strength,
They do not breathe among them: this I speak 275
In gratitude to God, Who feeds our hearts

For His own service; knoweth, loveth us,
When we are unregarded by the world.

Also, about this time did I receive
Convictions still more strong than heretofore,   280
Not only that the inner frame is good,
And graciously composed, but that, no less,
Nature for all conditions wants not power
To consecrate, if we have eyes to see,
The outside of her creatures, and to breathe   285
Grandeur upon the very humblest face
Of human life. I felt that the array
Of act and circumstance, and visible form,
Is mainly to the pleasure of the mind
What passion makes them; that meanwhile the forms   290
Of Nature have a passion in themselves,
That intermingles with those works of man
To which she summons him; although the works
Be mean, have nothing lofty of their own;
And that the Genius of the Poet hence   295
May boldly take his way among mankind
Wherever Nature leads; that he hath stood
By Nature's side among the men of old,
And so shall stand for ever. Dearest Friend!
If thou partake the animating faith   300
That Poets, even as Prophets, each with each
Connected in a mighty scheme of truth,
Have each his own peculiar faculty,
Heaven's gift, a sense that fits him to perceive
Objects unseen before, thou wilt not blame   305
The humblest of this band who dares to hope
That unto him hath also been vouchsafed
An insight that in some sort he possesses,
A privilege whereby a work of his,
Proceeding from a source of untaught things   310
Creative and enduring, may become
A power like one of Nature's. To a hope
Not less ambitious once among the wilds
Of Sarum's Plain, my youthful spirit was raised;
There, as I ranged at will the pastoral downs   315
Trackless and smooth, or paced the bare white roads
Lengthening in solitude their dreary line,

Time with his retinue of ages fled
Backwards, nor checked his flight until I saw
Our dim ancestral Past in vision clear;   320
Saw multitudes of men, and, here and there,
A single Briton clothed in wolf-skin vest,
With shield and stone-axe, stride across the wold;
The voice of spears was heard, the rattling spear
Shaken by arms of mighty bone, in strength,   325
Long mouldered, of barbaric majesty.
I called on Darkness—but before the word
Was uttered, midnight darkness seemed to take
All objects from my sight; and lo! again
The Desert visible by dismal flames;   330
It is the sacrificial altar, fed
With living men—how deep the groans! the voice
Of those that crowd the giant wicker thrills
The monumental hillocks, and the pomp
Is for both worlds, the living and the dead.   335
At other moments (for through that wide waste
Three summer days I roamed) where'er the Plain
Was figured o'er with circles, lines, or mounds,
That yet survive, a work, as some divine,
Shaped by the Druids, so to represent   340
Their knowledge of the heavens, and image forth
The constellations; gently was I charmed
Into a waking dream, a reverie
That, with believing eyes, where'er I turned,
Beheld long-bearded teachers, with white wands   345
Uplifted, pointing to the starry sky,
Alternately, and plain below, while breath
Of music swayed their motions, and the waste
Rejoiced with them and me in those sweet sounds.

This for the past, and things that may be viewed   350
Or fancied in the obscurity of years
From monumental hints: and thou, O Friend!
Pleased with some unpremeditated strains
That served those wanderings to beguile, hast said
That then and there my mind had exercised   355
Upon the vulgar forms of present things,
The actual world of our familiar days,
Yet higher power; had caught from them a tone,

An image, and a character, by books
Not hitherto reflected. Call we this   360
A partial judgment—and yet why? for *then*
We were as strangers; and I may not speak
Thus wrongfully of verse, however rude,
Which on thy young imagination, trained
In the great City, broke like light from far.   365
Moreover, each man's Mind is to herself
Witness and judge; and I remember well
That in life's every-day appearances
I seemed about this time to gain clear sight
Of a new world—a world, too, that was fit   370
To be transmitted, and to other eyes
Made visible; as ruled by those fixed laws
Whence spiritual dignity originates,
Which do both give it being and maintain
A balance, an ennobling interchange   375
Of action from without and from within;
The excellence, pure function, and best power
Both of the object seen, and eye that sees.

[1798–1805; revised, 1805–50]

George Gordon, Lord Byron

1788–1824

George Gordon, Lord Byron

GEORGE GORDON BYRON was born in London on January 22, 1788. His ancestors on his father's side were the Buruns, contemporaries and supporters of William the Conqueror, and on his mother's, the Gordons of Gight, an estate on the River Ythan thirty miles north of Aberdeen. A degree of violence marks the history of each family. William, the fifth Lord Byron, from whom the poet inherited his title in 1798, was known as "The Wicked Lord"; in his youth he was considered a rake, in his middle years he killed his neighbor and distant kinsman William Chaworth in a duel, and in his last years he became the recluse about whom legends grew that were to outlive him by generations. William Byron's brother and the poet's grandfather, Admiral John Byron, known as "Foulweather Jack," experienced in his youth shipwreck off Patagonia, which he recorded many years later in the *Narrative of the Honourable John Byron* (1768). The behavior of John, the Admiral's son and the poet's father, known as "Mad Jack" Byron, was sufficiently bad that before his death even the rakish old officer saw fit to disinherit him. Jack Byron eloped with the Marchioness of Carmarthen, marrying her after her husband had obtained a divorce from her by act of Parliament; of this marriage the surviving child was Ada Augusta, born in 1783. After Mrs. Byron's death the following year, "Mad Jack" sought another woman of means, and within a year and a half he met and married Catherine Gordon, the survivor of a long line of rather violent Scottish lairds. Within months his extravagance had reduced her moderate fortune to little indeed and, some time before the poet's birth, Jack Byron was forced to flee to France to avoid his creditors. Mrs. Byron joined him briefly, only to return to

London for the birth of their child. In 1789, mother and son moved to Aberdeen, where they could live more moderately than in London and, except for short periods, she and her husband remained separated until his death in 1791.

The child had been born with a clubbed right foot, an affliction that was to cause him suffering at least as intensely psychological as physical. In his early years his mother showed him an ambivalence that has become almost legendary, alternately abusing and petting him. They lived upon limited money in restricted quarters where George's early training was received from the nurse Agnes Gray, whose Calvinistic teachings had enduring emotional impact upon the boy; however, in later life he did his best to refute intellectually the doctrine of predestination. His regular schooling assumed various forms, culminating in four years at Harrow, from 1801 to 1805.

In 1794, the grandson of "The Wicked Lord" was killed in battle, and George Gordon Byron became heir apparent to the title and to Newstead Abbey in Nottinghamshire, the family seat, which was now in ruins and denuded of its forests. Four years later he became the sixth Lord Byron. His imagination was stimulated by Newstead Abbey when he first saw it, but for many of the remaining years of his minority the estate was leased, and on his holidays Byron came home to a house rented by his mother in Southwell, a town fourteen miles from Nottingham. At Newstead, which he frequently visited during these years, he met Mary Chaworth, grandniece of the man whom Byron's grandfather had killed. Two years older than Byron, she was the first woman in whom he became seriously interested, and her marriage to John Musters in 1808 caused Byron deep suffering then and, in recollection, for years afterward.

Byron entered Trinity College, Cambridge, in the autumn of 1805. Here his career was unspectacular, perhaps in part because in those years there was little in the English universities to inspire an intelligent and well-read young man, certainly because in Byron himself there were very mixed motives without any synthesizing sense of purpose. He kept a bear for a pet, who, he remarked, "should sit for a fellowship"; he became reluctantly involved in the normal social activities of aristocratic undergraduates; and before he had left Cambridge, he was heavily in debt.

In 1806, the year following his matriculation, Byron privately printed a volume of verse entitled *Fugitive Pieces*, but the reaction among those friends to whom he distributed copies was so adverse that he recalled and burned all but a few; the work was revised and once more privately put in print, this time as *Poems on Various Occasions*. In 1807, *Hours of Idleness* was published; this was the volume that, the following year, was to draw the severe criticism from *The Edinburgh Review* that in turn called forth Byron's scathing attack in the satirical poem "English Bards and Scotch Reviewers," published in 1809.

Following the practice of young men of the nobility, Byron, though very much in debt, set forth after taking his degree in 1809 for the grand tour. He visited Portugal, Spain, Gibraltar, Malta, Greece, and Albania, and then, after the customary year had passed, he extended his tour, remaining in the vicinity of Athens from October 1810 to the spring of 1811. During these two years he wrote the first two cantos of *Childe Harold's Pilgrimage*, constituting little more than a record of his experiences and a description of his responses to them. In addition, he thoroughly assimilated the background for both the Oriental Tales that he was to write several years later and other works, including parts of *Don Juan*, that lay in the more remote future. Many of his occasional poems, frequently taking the form of short lyrics, resulted directly from these travels; the most famous of these is doubtless the poem "Maid of Athens," which Byron wrote to Theresa Macri, the youngest daughter of the widow of a former British Vice-Consul, at whose house the poet lodged after his first arrival in Athens, on Christmas Day 1809.

Following his return to London in July 1811, Byron turned over the manuscript of the first two cantos of *Childe Harold* to Robert Charles Dallas, a relation by marriage to the Byrons. Dallas submitted the poem to the publisher John Murray, who accepted it as soon as Byron had agreed to modify several passages. The poem was published in March 1812, and almost at once the first edition sold out; within days George Gordon Byron was one of England's best known poets, the principal literary lion of Regency London.

He was particularly active in the Whig Society, which gathered principally at Holland House. When he had taken his seat in the House of Lords in March 1809, Byron declared his intention to become a member of neither party; yet his sympathies, from the few times that he was present to vote, were clearly for the Whigs. For a while he had some ambition for a career in Parliament, but this diminished as his experiences became more varied, so that after the publication of *Childe Harold* he was identified with the society rather than the politics of the Whigs.

Within this milieu many of the indiscretions occurred which were to color Byron's reputation from his time to ours. Among these was his relationship with Mrs. Augusta Byron Leigh—the daughter of "Mad Jack" Byron by his first wife, thus Byron's half-sister—which, though it did not persist beyond 1814, was in all likelihood the cause of Byron's marital tragedy in 1816. Whatever has been said in condemnation of the pair, the fact that they did not know each other until Augusta was grown and Byron nearly so may offer a degree of psychological extenuation. And certainly, despite the enormous number of books and articles which were written through the nineteenth century and into the twentieth on the reasons for the separation between Lord and Lady Byron— the so-called Byron Controversy—the importance of the affair in the composition of the poems has been exaggerated and in the reader's response to them it is negligible.

In 1812, Byron met Miss Anne Isabella Milbanke, only child of a wealthy family of Seaham, near Durham. She was several years younger than Byron, a woman of mathematical interests and evangelical impulses, perhaps less suited to one of Byron's temperament than anyone else could be. She rejected the poet's first proposal, made in 1812, but two years later she accepted his second, only after she had persuaded herself that he was essentially redeemable. They were married at Seaham on January 2, 1815, and by April had settled in London, where they remained through their tempestuous year of marriage. In December, a daughter, named Augusta Ada, was born. In January 1816, Lady Byron set out with the child to join her parents at Kirkby Mallory, the estate of an uncle in Leicestershire. Although the parting seemed congenial, Lady Byron never returned; once with her parents, she sent first to determine if Byron were sane, then to petition for separation. After accusations and strong expressions on both sides (of which the poem "Fare Thee Well," published at the time, is a peculiar instance), the separation papers were signed, and in April 1816, Lord Byron left England for what were to be the remaining eight years of his life.

Despite the complications and distractions during the years of initial fame from 1812 to 1815, Byron continued to write. Of some importance are the three tales directly reflecting his Oriental experiences—"The Giaour," "The Bride of Abydos," "The Corsair"—soon followed by two others, "Lara" and "The Siege of Corinth." Although none of these approaches high literary quality, together they constitute the work of a period important in Byron's artistic development, carrying him from the excessively personal and somewhat disorganized work best represented by the first two cantos of *Childe Harold's Pilgrimage* to the more complexly structured poems of the middle years, 1816 through 1819, and toward *Don Juan*. The fact that at this time he still affected a lack of seriousness regarding his literary work and, in cavalier fashion, gave away copyrights, doubtless explains some of the limitations in quality.

Although he owned his ancestral estate as well as one other large property at the time of his departure, Byron was heavily in debt. Of greater personal significance to him was the fact that those who had exalted him in 1812 generally rejected him in 1816, and though in later years he was perhaps to exaggerate the obloquy directed toward him, it was indeed a lonely man who sailed from Dover in April. The image has been distorted, initially by Byron himself and later by others, so that a situation which was first approached too sentimentally is now often regarded too cynically. Clearly, Byron suffered from 1816 as he had not done before, and his work entered a new phase, revealed in the major poems which he wrote after his departure from England; yet we can never ascertain the exact relation between the two facts.

Byron crossed Belgium, passing over the year-old battlefield at Waterloo, and sailed up the Rhine to Switzerland. At Geneva he met Percy Bysshe Shelley and soon established himself and his entourage in the Villa Diodati, overlooking Lake Geneva. Here, somewhat under the literary influence of Shelley, Byron wrote the third canto of *Childe Harold's Pilgrimage*, a complex work which has but nominal relation to the first two cantos. Somewhat later he wrote "The Prisoner of Chillon," which is actually his first dramatic monologue, and before he left Switzerland he began *Manfred*, his first

drama, which he finished in Venice in February 1817 and
John Murray published later that year. The indirect refer-
ences in the play to the probable causes for his separation from
Lady Byron created a sensational response in England and
from that day to this have drawn attention from the essential
literary values of the work. On a sojourn to Florence from
Venice he wrote "The Lament of Tasso," another major dramatic monologue and, once more in Venice, he composed the
fourth and final canto of *Childe Harold's Pilgrimage.* In spite
of the rumors current at the time and the legend that has
grown since then that Byron's life in Venice was devoted to
dissipation, his literary activity was prodigious. In the latter
part of 1817, he wrote "Beppo," a total departure in form
from his earlier work; in the tradition of the Italian mock-
heroic poem in *ottava rima,* which had recently been introduced to the English, "Beppo" is the precursor of *Don Juan.*
Other poems followed rapidly: "Mazeppa" in 1818, the first
two cantos of *Don Juan* in 1818 and 1819, and the subsequent
fourteen cantos during the few years that remained of Byron's
life. In 1819, he wrote "The Prophecy of Dante," a relatively
long dramatic monologue, and from 1820 to 1822 he composed seven more plays: *Marino Faliero, Doge of Venice; Sar-
danapalus; The Two Foscari; Cain, a Mystery; Heaven and
Earth, a Mystery; Werner, or The Inheritance;* and the incomplete *Deformed Transformed*—of which perhaps only the
two "Mysteries" reveal significant literary quality. In 1821,
Byron composed "The Vision of Judgment," a travesty of
the official poem by the Poet Laureate, Robert Southey, on
the death of George III in 1820.

Byron's attachment to the Countess Teresa Guiccioli drew
him to Ravenna in 1819. Two years later he and Teresa
moved to Pisa, where they were near the Shelleys and surrounded by a small circle of friends and admirers. In an im-
pulsive moment Byron had proposed (and Shelley had then
nourished the suggestion) that the radical journalist and poet
Leigh Hunt, a particular friend to Shelley, join them in Italy,
where he could edit a periodical that would become the principal outlet for the writings of all three. For various reasons
Hunt delayed his arrival until the summer of 1822, by which
time Byron's interest in the project had significantly cooled.
After Hunt reached Pisa, Shelley settled him and his large
family in the first floor of Byron's Casa Lanfranchi and then

began the short journey by water to his own home some miles from Pisa itself; he was drowned crossing the Gulf of Spezia. Byron and Hunt, alone and ultimately incompatible, moved to Genoa several months after Shelley's death. In time the proposed periodical, *The Liberal*, appeared and, despite public reaction that was at first heated but then indifferent and enormous editorial difficulties, lasted for four quarterly numbers; it contained, among lesser known works, Byron's "The Vision of Judgment," for which the publisher was indicted by the Government, and William Hazlitt's essay "My First Acquaintance with Poets."

By early 1823, Byron had grown thoroughly tired not only of Hunt and *The Liberal* but of an existence that in all ways seemed pointless. He was therefore easily susceptible to the overtures of the London Greek Committee, to which he was elected in May 1823. Further involvement was rapid, and in July Byron sailed for Greece. Though a representative of the Committee, he was in his own person an English Lord and a famous poet, who was bringing supplies and hope to the Greeks in their struggle against the Turks. The months that Byron spent in western Greece drained his strength and spirits as well as his purse. The Greeks were divided into large factions, each seeking Byron's support, and though he was probably the only man who at this time could have reconciled them to each other, he had for the moment little success. His position became increasingly more discouraging. Perhaps the final irony of Byron's life is that instead of finding the "soldier's grave" which he prophesied for himself in his poem "On This Day I Complete My Thirty-sixth Year," he died of a severe fever in a small house in the swamps of Missolonghi, on April 19, 1824.

In England as well as in Greece Byron was universally mourned. A boy of fourteen years named Alfred Tennyson wandered sorrowfully into the woods when he heard the news and carved "Byron is dead" into a tree. In his own lifetime Byron had become a legend. Through the years that followed his death, his friends came to his support against his enemies' attacks upon his memory, principally over the question of the marriage, and on neither side was there moderation. Later in the century, as the new prosperous middle classes grew, Byron became a symbol for something that existed outside the pale of the righteous but was at the same time unspeakably attractive; for others, a minority, his fascination could be openly avowed. It has been in comparatively recent years that scholars, penetrating the legend, have been able to render his biography with balance and perspective.

II

Byron's position as a poet has been somewhat less firmly settled. Consciously he was a classicist, regarding Alexander Pope as "the best of poets" and his own contemporaries as "all in the wrong, one as much as another . . . upon a wrong revolutionary poetical system, or systems." There can be little doubt that in some of his early writings, notably the satire "English Bards and Scotch Reviewers," Byron was writing in imitation of Pope and his school, but a close examination reveals that although this poem is trenchant in its attack upon individual wrongs in the literary world, it lacks a unifying conception of the ideal that these abuses violate and remains, throughout, a work of many parts mechanically joined.

Underlying the kind of literary art which we identify with Augustan England, specifically with Alexander Pope, is the acceptance of an ideal rather than real order, which is ironically affirmed in satire by an attack upon some form of disorder. Byron himself was unable to accept any such order. He existed apart from any tradition of belief. Although his religious training was composed of Calvinism superimposed upon Anglicanism, he was never long exposed to an atmosphere permeated by religious absolutism; he was familiar with but emotionally unaffected by Renaissance Humanism, and his interest in the writers of the Enlightenment represented an intellectual acquisition rather than an emotional expression. Nor was he in his own lifetime to become part of positions developing in and characteristic of the nineteenth century: the bourgeois *rationale* emerging from the teachings of Jeremy Bentham and James Mill, the intellectualist ideals of reformers like Shelley, or the evolutionism culminating with the publication in 1859 of Charles Darwin's *On the Origin of Species*. Byron recognized the inadequacies of the systems of thought that he knew, but in his writings, both public and private, he offered no substitutes for them. Throughout his life he was unable to discover an intellectual basis for absolutism, but at the same time he found relativism emotionally repellent. Thus, as an avowed classicist Byron consistently failed.

In time, however, he achieved something far greater. Caught between skepticism and the will to believe, he recognized his early failure as a classicist and for a while composed works that were either highly personal and demanded no significant affirmation, such as the first two cantos of *Childe Harold,* or essentially escapist and usually popular, such as the tales written during the London years of fame. Then, beginning in 1816, Byron, though he perhaps did not really understand his philosophic position, was able to reconcile his emotional absolutism with his intellectual relativism as the basis for his literary art. In a group of poems—the third canto of *Childe Harold,* "The Prisoner of Chillon," the drama *Manfred,* "The Lament of Tasso," and "Mazeppa"—he dramatized the ironic situation of those who are unable to reconcile themselves to universal and personal imperfection.

The protagonists are of two kinds. Some fail in their efforts to find unity and meaning in the world, in part by reconstituting their visions of that world, and, consequently, they cease to struggle toward resolution. After his failure to draw a meaningful response from Astarte, Manfred loses the will to live. The speaker in the third canto of *Childe Harold* has created the image of Harold with which to identify his own sorrow, by transferring his emotional suffering to another; however, he cannot sustain the image and falls back upon his own insecurity and pain. Other protagonists appear to succeed only because in their minds they alter the world to some degree so that it conforms to the various images they hold of themselves. Therefore, the dominant quality of the poems in which these protagonists appear is irony, developed through the discrepancy between the inner vision of the protagonist and outer reality. The form particularly suited to this kind of literary work is the dramatic monologue, which Byron used extensively during these middle years. "Mazeppa" serves as perhaps the clearest illustration. An old Polish Hetman, Mazeppa has been serving under King Charles XII of Sweden, and now, following the Russian victory at Pultowa, the King and Mazeppa hide in the cold night with a small band of followers as the Russians move about in search of them. Ostensibly to soothe his King, Mazeppa tells a story which, in reality, is calculated to bring hope to Mazeppa himself by intensifying his belief that somehow he is the special object of providential care. Representing a normal though ultimately ironic human procedure under the circumstances, Mazeppa's tale is one concerned with an ordeal he survived many years before, of which the resemblance to the present situation is always implicit and even once asserted. Mazeppa's tale *in itself* may be regarded as entertaining or as pointless, but *within its frame* it is ironic, and by this irony the poem itself is dramatically sustained.

Thus, in his middle years Byron became an *ironist*: he saw clearly the limits of man's capacity and the absurdity of human activities, but he made this vision the foundation for his art. By exposing man's weaknesses, he was not implicitly proposing a constructive substitute in human behavior, an ideal, as the satirist does; irony became for him, in other words, an end in itself rather than a means to satiric achievement. When Byron began working on *Don Juan*, therefore, he carried into his new poem viewpoints and techniques that he had been developing over the last few years. The irony of the poem is in no way calculated to, and certainly does not serve as the instrument for persuading the reader to abandon folly and fulfill an accepted ideal. It simply emphasizes further that life, reflecting nothing of the ideal, is a kaleidoscope of many fragmentary parts, a fact which, pleasant or not, must be accepted as the basis for any subsequent action. For this reason *Don Juan* has been called one of the truly great modern poems. Those who have failed to understand that there are implications in the fragmentary nature of *Don Juan* have fallen too readily into the belief, which Byron himself ironically did much to encourage, that the poem is merely a spontaneous effusion without structure or meaning.

The plot of *Don Juan* is simple and, insofar as it survives the speaker's digressions, it is lineal, directly recounting the activities of the protagonist. Don Juan is raised in Seville by his mother, the opinionated and dominant Donna Inez. At sixteen he becomes the lover of Donna Julia, a woman of twenty-three who is married to a man of fifty. One night the lovers are discovered; in the scandal that ensues Julia goes to a convent, and Juan is sent forth on a tour. He is the sole survivor of a shipwreck; washed upon an island shore, he is nursed back to health by the lovely Haidée, with whom he lives in total happiness until the pirate Lambro, Haidée's father, who has been presumed dead, returns to the island. Juan is captured and sent into slavery, and Haidée dies of grief. Purchased by the favorite wife of the Sultan, who would of course conceal her acquisition from her husband, Juan is disguised as a woman and hidden temporarily in the harem at Ismail. He refuses to become the Sultana's lover, but he is rescued from what otherwise would have been death when the Russian army arrives and successfully attacks the city. Juan, who distinguishes himself during the battle, is sent to St. Petersburg to tell the Empress Catherine of the victory. He becomes the principal adviser and ultimately the lover of Catherine; however, in time he grows tired of life in St. Petersburg, and the Empress sends him upon a mission to England. Here Juan is accepted by the aristocracy, particularly because of his own background and his marital eligibility. The poem ends abruptly after fourteen stanzas of the seventeenth canto.

It is at once apparent that the narrative in *Don Juan* is insufficient to sustain a poem of more than fifteen thousand lines; we must look elsewhere. In the protagonist we look for a figure of heroic proportions, but what we find is totally ironic: Drawn from a tradition of strong heroes, Don Juan, like the Anglicized form so emphatically given his name (it explicitly rhymes with "true one" and "new one"), is merely a parody of his supposed self, chosen not because of the tradition but for the rhyming potential that his name possesses. The insubstantial being of the protagonist constitutes the central irony of the poem.

What remains? The seeming myriad of masks assumed by the speaker in the poem or, preferably perhaps, the speakers. For sustained intervals the narrative and its protagonist are unceremoniously cast aside, and, in sequence or sometimes in conflict with each other, the various masks or speakers appear. Some readers complain that *Don Juan* lacks consistency. It does if it is read literally, as a narrative told directly by Byron the poet. Here it is important, even more than in the dramatic monologues like "Mazeppa," to make a firm distinction between the speaker at any point in the poem and the poet himself. At one instant the speaker who emerges is naïve, prudish, even stupid, perhaps frightened by the implications of what he is saying; at another, he is worldly, callously humorous, perhaps cynical, determined to make explicit the shocking implications of his remarks. The wary reader, though becoming involved as he responds to the ambiguities in the poem, must in part exist outside the poem as well, always conscious of the dramatic irony characterizing the utterance of the speaker at any point. Nor should this same reader trust the narrative: at a moment of heightened tension in the action, the speaker may interrupt and comment most inappropriately; the tension is relieved. In the later cantos of *Don Juan*, particularly the eleventh through the sixteenth, which deal with Juan's experiences in England, the plot is even more distended than in others, so that the characteristic irony of the work is more abundantly developed. For this reason, despite the frequency with which the earlier cantos have been reprinted, many modern critics regard the English cantos as superior.

Don Juan may be seen as a vast literary joke. It is humorous in its means but, beneath the knavish leer, serious in its implications. It is the most nearly perfect expression, in which form and substance are consonant, of that particular Romantic position to which Byron moved.

George Gordon, Lord Byron

MAID OF ATHENS, ERE WE PART
Ζωή μου, σᾶς ἀγαπῶ.

1

Maid of Athens, ere we part,
Give, oh give me back my heart!
Or, since that has left my breast,
Keep it now, and take the rest!
Hear my vow before I go,   5
Ζωή μου, σᾶς ἀγαπῶ.[1]

2

By those tresses unconfined,
Wooed by each Ægean wind;
By those lids whose jetty fringe
Kiss thy soft cheeks' blooming tinge;   10
By those wild eyes like the roe,
Ζωή μου, σᾶς ἀγαπῶ.

3

By that lip I long to taste;
By that zone-encircled waist;
By all the token-flowers that tell   15
What words can never speak so well;
By love's alternate joy and woe,
Ζωή μου, σᾶς ἀγαπῶ.

4

Maid of Athens! I am gone:
Think of me, sweet! when alone.   20
Though I fly to Istambol,
Athens holds my heart and soul:
Can I cease to love thee? No!
Ζωή μου, σᾶς ἀγαπῶ.
[1810]

---
[1] "My life, I love you!" (Byron's translation in a note)

SHE WALKS IN BEAUTY

I

She walks in Beauty, like the night
  Of cloudless climes and starry skies;
And all that's best of dark and bright
  Meet in her aspect and her eyes:
Thus mellowed to that tender light   5
  Which Heaven to gaudy day denies.

II

One shade the more, one ray the less,
  Had half impaired the nameless grace
Which waves in every raven tress,
  Or softly lightens o'er her face;   10
Where thoughts serenely sweet express,
  How pure, how dear their dwelling-place.

III

And on that cheek, and o'er that brow,
  So soft, so calm, yet eloquent,
The smiles that win, the tints that glow,   15
  But tell of days in goodness spent,
A mind at peace with all below,
  A heart whose love is innocent!
    [1814]

STANZAS FOR MUSIC

1

I speak not, I trace not, I breathe not thy name,
There is grief in the sound, there is guilt in the fame;
But the tear which now burns on my cheek may impart
The deep thoughts that dwell in that silence of heart.

2

Too brief for our passion, too long for our peace,   5
Were those hours—can their joy or their bitterness cease?
We repent, we abjure, we will break from our chain,—
We will part, we will fly to—unite it again!

3

Oh! thine be the gladness, and mine be the guilt!
Forgive me, adored one!—forsake, if thou wilt;—   10
But the heart which is thine shall expire undebased
And *man* shall not break it—whatever *thou* mayst.

4

And stern to the haughty, but humble to thee,
This soul, in its bitterest blackness, shall be:
And our days seem as swift, and our moments more sweet,   15
With thee by my side, than with worlds at our feet.

5

One sigh of thy sorrow, one look of thy love,
Shall turn me or fix, shall reward or reprove;
And the heartless may wonder at all I resign—
Thy lip shall reply, not to them, but to *mine*.   20
[1814]

WHEN WE TWO PARTED

1

When we two parted
    In silence and tears,
Half broken-hearted
    To sever for years,

Pale grew thy cheek and cold,   5
  Colder thy kiss;
Truly that hour foretold
  Sorrow to this.

2

The dew of the morning
  Sunk chill on my brow—   10
It felt like the warning
  Of what I feel now.
Thy vows are all broken,
  And light is thy fame:
I hear thy name spoken,   15
  And share in its shame.

3

They name thee before me,
  A knell to mine ear;
A shudder comes o'er me—
  Why wert thou so dear?   20
They know not I knew thee,
  Who knew thee too well:—
Long, long shall I rue thee,
  Too deeply to tell.

4

In secret we met—   25
  In silence I grieve,
That thy heart could forget,
  Thy spirit deceive.
If I should meet thee
  After long years,   30
How should I greet thee?—
  With silence and tears.

[1816]

FARE THEE WELL

Fare thee well! and if for ever,
   Still for ever, fare thee well:
Even though unforgiving, never
   'Gainst thee shall my heart rebel.
Would that breast were bared before thee   5
   Where thy head so oft hath lain,
While that placid sleep came o'er thee
   Which thou ne'er canst know again:
Would that breast, by thee glanced over,
   Every inmost thought could show!   10
Then thou would'st at last discover
   'Twas not well to spurn it so.
Though the world for this commend thee—
   Though it smile upon the blow,
Even its praises must offend thee,   15
   Founded on another's woe:
Though my many faults defaced me,
   Could no other arm be found,
Than the one which once embraced me,
   To inflict a cureless wound?   20
Yet, oh yet, myself deceive not—
   Love may sink by slow decay,
But by sudden wrench, believe not
   Hearts can thus be torn away:
Still thine own its life retaineth—   25
   Still must mine, though bleeding, beat;
And the undying thought which paineth
   Is—that we no more may meet.
These are words of deeper sorrow
   Than the wail above the dead;   30
Both shall live—but every morrow
   Wake us from a widowed bed.
And when thou would'st solace gather—
   When our child's first accents flow—
Wilt thou teach her to say "Father!"   35
   Though his care she must forego?
When her little hands shall press thee—
   When her lip to thine is pressed—

Think of him whose prayer shall bless thee—
  Think of him thy love *had* blessed!   40
Should her lineaments resemble
  Those thou never more may'st see,
Then thy heart will softly tremble
  With a pulse yet true to me.
All my faults perchance thou knowest—   45
  All my madness—none can know—
All my hopes—where'er thou goest—
  Wither—yet with *thee* they go.
Every feeling hath been shaken;
  Pride—which not a world could bow—   50
Bows to thee—by thee forsaken,
  Even my soul forsakes me now.
But 'tis done—all words are idle—
  Words from me are vainer still;
But the thoughts we cannot bridle   55
  Force their way without the will.
Fare thee well! thus disunited—
  Torn from every nearer tie—
Seared in heart—and lone—and blighted—
  More than this I scarce can die.   60

     [1816]

CHILDE HAROLD'S PILGRIMAGE

CANTO THE THIRD

I

Is thy face like thy mother's, my fair child!
  ADA! sole daughter of my house and heart?
When last I saw thy young blue eyes they smiled,
  And then we parted,—not as now we part,
  But with a hope.—
              Awaking with a start,   5
The waters heave around me; and on high
  The winds lift up their voices: I depart,
  Whither I know not; but the hour's gone by,
When Albion's lessening shores could grieve or glad mine
    eye.

II

Once more upon the waters! yet once more!   10
  And the waves bound beneath me as a steed
  That knows his rider. Welcome to their roar!
  Swift be their guidance, wheresoe'er it lead!
  Though the strained mast should quiver as a reed,
  And the rent canvass fluttering strew the gale,   15
  Still must I on; for I am as a weed,
  Flung from the rock, on Ocean's foam, to sail
Where'er the surge may sweep, the tempest's breath prevail.

III

In my youth's summer I did sing of One,
  The wandering outlaw of his own dark mind;   20
  Again I seize the theme, then but begun,
  And bear it with me, as the rushing wind
  Bears the cloud onwards: in that Tale I find
  The furrows of long thought, and dried-up tears,
  Which, ebbing, leave a sterile track behind,   25
  O'er which all heavily the journeying years
Plod the last sands of life,—where not a flower appears.

IV

Since my young days of passion—joy, or pain—
  Perchance my heart and harp have lost a string—
  And both may jar: it may be, that in vain   30
  I would essay as I have sung to sing;
  Yet, though a dreary strain, to this I cling;
  So that it wean me from the weary dream
  Of selfish grief or gladness—so it fling
  Forgetfulness around me—it shall seem   35
To me, though to none else, a not ungrateful theme.

V

He, who grown agèd in this world of woe,
  In deeds, not years, piercing the depths of life,
  So that no wonder waits him—nor below

Can Love or Sorrow, Fame, Ambition, Strife,   40
Cut to his heart again with the keen knife
Of silent, sharp endurance—he can tell
Why Thought seeks refuge in lone caves, yet rife
With airy images, and shapes which dwell
Still unimpaired, though old, in the Soul's haunted cell.   45

VI

'Tis to create, and in creating live
A being more intense that we endow
With form our fancy, gaining as we give
The life we image, even as I do now—
What am I? Nothing: but not so art thou,   50
Soul of my thought! with whom I traverse earth,
Invisible but gazing, as I glow
Mixed with thy spirit, blended with thy birth,
And feeling still with thee in my crushed feelings' dearth.

VII

Yet must I think less wildly:—I *have* thought   55
Too long and darkly, till my brain became,
In its own eddy boiling and o'erwrought,
A whirling gulf of phantasy and flame:
And thus, untaught in youth my heart to tame,
My springs of life were poisoned. 'Tis too late: 60
Yet am I changed; though still enough the same
In strength to bear what Time can not abate,
And feed on bitter fruits without accusing Fate.

VIII

Something too much of this:—but now 'tis past,
And the spell closes with its silent seal—   65
Long absent HAROLD re-appears at last;
He of the breast which fain no more would feel,
Wrung with the wounds which kill not, but ne'er heal;
Yet Time, who changes all, had altered him
In soul and aspect as in age: years steal   70
Fire from the mind as vigour from the limb;
And Life's enchanted cup but sparkles near the brim.

IX

His had been quaffed too quickly, and he found
  The dregs were wormwood; but he filled again,
  And from a purer fount, on holier ground,   75
  And deemed its spring perpetual—but in vain!
  Still round him clung invisibly a chain
  Which galled for ever, fettering though unseen,
  And heavy though it clanked not; worn with pain,
  Which pined although it spoke not, and grew keen,   80
Entering with every step he took through many a scene.

X

Secure in guarded coldness, he had mixed
  Again in fancied safety with his kind,
  And deemed his spirit now so firmly fixed
  And sheathed with an invulnerable mind,   85
  That, if no joy, no sorrow lurked behind;
  And he, as one, might 'midst the many stand
  Unheeded, searching through the crowd to find
  Fit speculation—such as in strange land
He found in wonder-works of God and Nature's hand.   90

XI

But who can view the ripened rose, nor seek
  To wear it? who can curiously behold
  The smoothness and the sheen of Beauty's cheek,
  Nor feel the heart can never all grow old?
  Who can contemplate Fame through clouds unfold   95
  The star which rises o'er her steep, nor climb?
  Harold, once more within the vortex, rolled
  On with the giddy circle, chasing Time,
Yet with a nobler aim than in his Youth's fond prime.

XII

But soon he knew himself the most unfit   100
  Of men to herd with Man, with whom he held
  Little in common; untaught to submit

His thoughts to others, though his soul was quelled
In youth by his own thoughts; still uncompelled,
He would not yield dominion of his mind   105
To Spirits against whom his own rebelled,
Proud though in desolation—which could find
A life within itself, to breathe without mankind.

XIII

Where rose the mountains, there to him were friends;
Where rolled the ocean, thereon was his home;   110
Where a blue sky, and glowing clime, extends,
He had the passion and the power to roam;
The desert, forest, cavern, breaker's foam,
Were unto him companionship; they spake
A mutual language, clearer than the tome   115
Of his land's tongue, which he would oft forsake
For Nature's pages glassed by sunbeams on the lake.

XIV

Like the Chaldean, he could watch the stars,
Till he had peopled them and being bright
As their own beams; and earth, and earth-born jars,   120
And human frailties, were forgotten quite:
Could he have kept his spirit to that flight
He had been happy; but this clay will sink
Its spark immortal, envying it the light
To which it mounts, as if to break the link   125
That keeps us from yon heaven which woos us to its brink.

XV

But in Man's dwelling he became a thing
Restless and worn, and stern and wearisome,
Drooped as a wild-born falcon with clipt wing,
To whom the boundless air alone were home: 130
Then came his fit again, which to o'ercome,
As eagerly the barred-up bird will beat
His breast and beak against his wiry dome
Till the blood tinge his plumage—so the heat
Of his impeded Soul would through his bosom eat.   135

XVI

Self-exiled Harold wanders forth again,
   With nought of Hope left—but with less of gloom;
   The very knowledge that he lived in vain,
   That all was over on this side the tomb,
   Had made Despair a smilingness assume,   140
   Which, though 'twere wild,—as on the plundered
      wreck
   When mariners would madly meet their doom
   With draughts intemperate on the sinking deck;—
Did yet inspire a cheer, which he forbore to check.

XVII

Stop!—for thy tread is on an Empire's dust!   145
   An Earthquake's spoil is sepulchred below!
   Is the spot marked with no colossal bust?
   Nor column trophied for triumphal show?
   None; but *the moral's truth* tells simpler so.—
   As the ground was before, thus let it be;—   150
   How that red rain hath made the harvest grow!
   And is this all the world has gained by thee,
Thou first and last of Fields! king-making Victory?

XVIII

And Harold stands upon this place of skulls,
   The grave of France, the deadly Waterloo!   155
   How in an hour the Power which gave annuls
   Its gifts, transferring fame as fleeting too!—
   In "pride of place" here last the Eagle flew;
   Then tore with bloody talon the rent plain,
   Pierced by the shaft of banded nations through;   160
   Ambition's life and labours all were vain—
He wears the shattered links of the World's broken chain.

XIX

Fit retribution! Gaul may champ the bit
   And foam in fetters;—but is Earth more free?
   Did nations combat to make One submit?   165

Or league to teach all Kings true Sovereignty?
What! shall reviving Thraldom again be
The patched-up Idol of enlightened days?
Shall we, who struck the Lion down, shall we
Pay the Wolf homage? proffering lowly gaze   170
And servile knees to Thrones? No! prove before ye praise!

XX

If not, o'er one fallen Despot boast no more!
In vain fair cheeks were furrowed with hot tears
For Europe's flowers long rooted up before
The trampler of her vineyards; in vain, years   175
Of death, depopulation, bondage, fears,
Have all been borne, and broken by the accord
Of roused-up millions: all that most endears
Glory, is when the myrtle wreathes a Sword,
Such as Harmodius drew in Athens' tyrant Lord.   180

XXI

There was a sound of revelry by night,
And Belgium's Capital had gathered then
Her Beauty and her Chivalry—and bright
The lamps shone o'er fair women and brave men;
A thousand hearts beat happily; and when   185
Music arose with its voluptuous swell,
Soft eyes looked love to eyes which spake again,
And all went merry as a marriage bell;
But hush! hark! a deep sound strikes like a rising knell!

XXII

Did ye not hear it?—No—'twas but the Wind,   190
Or the car rattling o'er the stony street;
On with the dance! let joy be unconfined;
No sleep till morn, when Youth and Pleasure meet
To chase the glowing Hours with flying feet—
But hark!—that heavy sound breaks in once more,   195
As if the clouds its echo would repeat;
And nearer—clearer—deadlier than before!
Arm! Arm! it is—it is—the cannon's opening roar!

XXIII

Within a windowed niche of that high hall
  Sate Brunswick's fated Chieftain; he did hear   200
  That sound the first amidst the festival,
  And caught its tone with Death's prophetic ear;
  And when they smiled because he deemed it near,
  His heart more truly knew that peal too well
  Which stretched his father on a bloody bier,   205
  And roused the vengeance blood alone could quell;
He rushed into the field, and, foremost fighting, fell.

XXIV

Ah! then and there was hurrying to and fro—
  And gathering tears, and tremblings of distress,
  And cheeks all pale, which but an hour ago   210
  Blushed at the praise of their own loveliness—
  And there were sudden partings, such as press
  The life from out young hearts, and choking sighs
  Which ne'er might be repeated; who could guess
  If ever more should meet those mutual eyes,   215
Since upon night so sweet such awful morn could rise!

XXV

And there was mounting in hot haste—the steed,
  The mustering squadron, and the clattering car,
  Went pouring forward with impetuous speed,
  And swiftly forming in the ranks of war—   220
  And the deep thunder peal on peal afar;
  And near, the beat of the alarming drum
  Roused up the soldier ere the Morning Star;
  While thronged the citizens with terror dumb,
Or whispering, with white lips—"The foe! They come! 225
  they come!"

XXVI

And wild and high the "Cameron's Gathering" rose!
  The war-note of Lochiel, which Albyn's hills

Have heard, and heard, too, have her Saxon foes:—
How in the noon of night that pibroch thrills,
Savage and shrill! But with the breath which fills   230
Their mountain-pipe, so fill the mountaineers
With the fierce native daring which instils
The stirring memory of a thousand years,
And Evan's—Donald's fame rings in each clansman's ears!

XXVII

And Ardennes waves above them her green leaves,   235
Dewy with Nature's tear-drops, as they pass—
Grieving, if aught inanimate e'er grieves,
Over the unreturning brave,—alas!
Ere evening to be trodden like the grass
Which now beneath them, but above shall grow   240
In its next verdure, when this fiery mass
Of living Valour, rolling on the foe
And burning with high Hope, shall moulder cold and low.

XXVIII

Last noon beheld them full of lusty life;—
Last eve in Beauty's circle proudly gay;   245
The Midnight brought the signal-sound of strife,
The Morn the marshalling in arms,—the Day
Battle's magnificently-stern array!
The thunder-clouds close o'er it, which when rent
The earth is covered thick with other clay   250
Which her own clay shall cover, heaped and pent,
Rider and horse,—friend,—foe,—in one red burial blent!

XXIX

Their praise is hymned by loftier harps than mine;
Yet one I would select from that proud throng,
Partly because they blend me with his line,   255
And partly that I did his Sire some wrong,
And partly that bright names will hallow song;
And his was of the bravest, and when showered
The death-bolts deadliest the thinned files along,
Even where the thickest of War's tempest lowered,   260

They reached no nobler breast than thine, young, gallant
   Howard!

xxx

There have been tears and breaking hearts for thee,
   And mine were nothing, had I such to give;
   But when I stood beneath the fresh green tree,
   Which living waves where thou didst cease to live,   265
   And saw around me the wide field revive
   With fruits and fertile promise, and the Spring
   Come forth her work of gladness to contrive,
   With all her reckless birds upon the wing,
I turned from all she brought to those she could not bring. 270

xxxi

I turned to thee, to thousands, of whom each
   And one as all a ghastly gap did make
   In his own kind and kindred, whom to teach
   Forgetfulness were mercy for their sake;
   The Archangel's trump, not Glory's, must awake   275
   Those whom they thirst for; though the sound of Fame
   May for a moment soothe, it cannot slake
   The fever of vain longing, and the name
So honoured but assumes a stronger, bitterer claim.

xxxii

They mourn, but smile at length—and, smiling, mourn: 280
   The tree will wither long before it fall;
   The hull drives on, though mast and sail be torn;
   The roof-tree sinks, but moulders on the hall
   In massy hoariness; the ruined wall
   Stands when its wind-worn battlements are gone;   285
   The bars survive the captive they enthral;
   The day drags through though storms keep out the sun;
And thus the heart will break, yet brokenly live on:

xxxiii

Even as a broken Mirror, which the glass
   In every fragment multiplies—and makes
                                                           290

A thousand images of one that was,
The same—and still the more, the more it breaks;
And thus the heart will do which not forsakes,
Living in shattered guise; and still, and cold,
And bloodless, with its sleepless sorrow aches,   295
Yet withers on till all without is old,
Showing no visible sign, for such things are untold.

XXXIV

There is a very life in our despair,
    Vitality of poison,—a quick root
    Which feeds these deadly branches; for it were   300
As nothing did we die; but Life will suit
Itself to Sorrow's most detested fruit,
Like to the apples on the Dead Sea's shore,
All ashes to the taste: Did man compute
Existence by enjoyment, and count o'er   305
Such hours 'gainst years of life,—say, would he name
    threescore?

XXXV

The Psalmist numbered out the years of man:
    They are enough; and if thy tale be true,
    Thou, who didst grudge him even that fleeting span,
More than enough, thou fatal Waterloo!   310
Millions of tongues record thee, and anew
Their children's lips shall echo them, and say—
"Here, where the sword united nations drew,
Our countrymen were warring on that day!"
And this is much—and all—which will not pass away.   315

XXXVI

There sunk the greatest, nor the worst of men,
    Whose Spirit, antithetically mixed,
    One moment of the mightiest, and again
On little objects with like firmness fixed;
Extreme in all things! hadst thou been betwixt,   320
Thy throne had still been thine, or never been;
For Daring made thy rise as fall: thou seek'st

Even now to re-assume the imperial mien,
And shake again the world, the Thunderer of the scene!

XXXVII

Conqueror and Captive of the Earth art thou!   325
   She trembles at thee still, and thy wild name
   Was ne'er more bruited in men's minds than now
   That thou art nothing, save the jest of Fame,
   Who wooed thee once, thy Vassal, and became
   The flatterer of thy fierceness—till thou wert   330
   A God unto thyself; nor less the same
   To the astounded kingdoms all inert,
Who deemed thee for a time whate'er thou didst assert.

XXXVIII

Oh, more or less than man—in high or low—
   Battling with nations, flying from the field;   335
   Now making monarchs' necks thy footstool, now
   More than thy meanest soldier taught to yield;
   An Empire thou couldst crush, command, rebuild.
   But govern not thy pettiest passion, nor,
   However deeply in men's spirits skilled,   340
   Look through thine own, not curb the lust of War,
Nor learn that tempted Fate will leave the loftiest Star.

XXXIX

Yet well thy soul hath brooked the turning tide
   With that untaught innate philosophy,
   Which, be it Wisdom, Coldness, or deep Pride,   345
   Is gall and wormwood to an enemy.
   When the whole host of hatred stood hard by,
   To watch and mock thee shrinking, thou hast smiled
   With a sedate and all-enduring eye;—
   When Fortune fled her spoiled and favourite child,   350
He stood unbowed beneath the ills upon him piled.

XL

Sager than in thy fortunes; for in them
   Ambition steeled thee on too far to show

That just habitual scorn, which could contemn
   Men and their thoughts; 'twas wise to feel, not so   355
   To wear it ever on thy lip and brow,
   And spurn the instruments thou wert to use
   Till they were turned unto thine overthrow:
   'Tis but a worthless world to win or lose;
So hath it proved to thee, and all such lot who choose.   360

XLI

If, like a tower upon a headlong rock,
   Thou hadst been made to stand or fall alone,
   Such scorn of man had helped to brave the shock;
   But men's thoughts were the steps which paved thy
      throne,
   Their admiration thy best weapon shone;   365
   The part of Philip's son was thine, not then
   (Unless aside thy Purple had been thrown)
   Like stern Diogenes to mock at men—
For sceptred Cynics Earth were far too wide a den.

XLII

But Quiet to quick bosoms is a Hell,   370
   And *there* hath been thy bane; there is a fire
   And motion of the Soul which will not dwell
   In its own narrow being, but aspire
   Beyond the fitting medium of desire;
   And, but once kindled, quenchless evermore,   375
   Preys upon high adventure, nor can tire
   Of aught but rest; a fever at the core,
Fatal to him who bears, to all who ever bore.

XLIII

This makes the madmen who have made men mad
   By their contagion; Conquerors and Kings,   380
   Founders of sects and systems, to whom add
   Sophists, Bards, Statesmen, all unquiet things
   Which stir too strongly the soul's secret springs,
   And are themselves the fools to those they fool;
   Envied, yet how unenviable! what stings   385

Are theirs! One breast laid open were a school
Which would unteach Mankind the lust to shine or rule:

XLIV

Their breath is agitation, and their life
A storm whereon they ride, to sink at last,
And yet so nursed and bigoted to strife,   390
That should their days, surviving perils past,
Melt to calm twilight, they feel overcast
With sorrow and supineness, and so die;
Even as a flame unfed, which runs to waste
With its own flickering, or a sword laid by,   395
Which eats into itself, and rusts ingloriously.

XLV

He who ascends to mountain-tops, shall find
The loftiest peaks most wrapt in clouds and snow;
He who surpasses or subdues mankind,
Must look down on the hate of those below.   400
Though high *above* the Sun of Glory glow,
And far *beneath* the Earth and Ocean spread,
Round him are icy rocks, and loudly blow
Contending tempests on his naked head,
And thus reward the toils which to those summits led.   405

XLVI

Away with these! true Wisdom's world will be
Within its own creation, or in thine,
Maternal Nature! for who teems like thee,
Thus on the banks of thy majestic Rhine?
There Harold gazes on a work divine,   410
A blending of all beauties; streams and dells,
Fruit, foliage, crag, wood, cornfield, mountain, vine,
And chiefless castles breathing stern farewells
From gray but leafy walls, where Ruin greenly dwells.

XLVII

And there they stand, as stands a lofty mind,   415
Worn, but unstooping to the baser crowd,

All tenantless, save to the crannying Wind,
Or holding dark communion with the Cloud.
There was a day when they were young and proud;
Banners on high, and battles passed below;   420
But they who fought are in a bloody shroud,
And those which waved are shredless dust ere now,
And the bleak battlements shall bear no future blow.

XLVIII

Beneath these battlements, within those walls,
Power dwelt amidst her passions; in proud state   425
Each robber chief upheld his arméd halls,
Doing his evil will, nor less elate
Than mightier heroes of a longer date.
What want these outlaws conquerors should have
But History's purchased page to call them great?   430
A wider space—an ornamented grave?
Their hopes were not less warm, their souls were full as
    brave.

XLIX

In their baronial feuds and single fields,
What deeds of prowess unrecorded died!
And Love, which lent a blazon to their shields,   435
With emblems well devised by amorous pride,
Through all the mail of iron hearts would glide;
But still their flame was fierceness, and drew on
Keen contest and destruction near allied,
And many a tower for some fair mischief won,   440
Saw the discoloured Rhine beneath its ruin run.

L

But Thou, exulting and abounding river!
Making thy waves a blessing as they flow
Through banks whose beauty would endure for ever
Could man but leave thy bright creation so,   445
Nor its fair promise from the surface mow
With the sharp scythe of conflict,—then to see

Thy valley of sweet waters, were to know
Earth paved like Heaven—and to seem such to me,
Even now what wants thy stream?—that it should Lethe   450
    be.

LI

A thousand battles have assailed thy banks,
    But these and half their fame have passed away,
    And Slaughter heaped on high his weltering ranks:
    Their very graves are gone, and what are they?
    Thy tide washed down the blood of yesterday,   455
    And all was stainless, and on thy clear stream
    Glassed, with its dancing light, the sunny ray;
    But o'er the blacken'd memory's blighting dream
Thy waves would vainly roll, all sweeping as they seem.

LII

Thus Harold inly said, and passed along,   460
    Yet not insensible to all which here
    Awoke the jocund birds to early song
    In glens which might have made even exile dear:
    Though on his brow were graven lines austere,
    And tranquil sternness, which had ta'en the place   465
    Of feelings fierier far but less severe—
    Joy was not always absent from his face,
But o'er it in such scenes would steal with transient trace.

LIII

Nor was all Love shut from him, though his days
    Of Passion had consumed themselves to dust.   470
    It is in vain that we would coldly gaze
    On such as smile upon us; the heart must
    Leap kindly back to kindness, though Disgust
    Hath weaned it from all worldlings: thus he felt,
    For there was soft Remembrance, and sweet Trust   475
    In one fond breast, to which his own would melt,
And in its tenderer hour on that his bosom dwelt.

LIV

And he had learned to love,—I know not why,
  For this in such as him seems strange of mood,—
The helpless looks of blooming Infancy,   480
  Even in its earliest nurture; what subdued,
To change like this, a mind so far imbued
  With scorn of man, it little boots to know;
But thus it was; and though in solitude
  Small power the nipped affections have to grow,   485
In him this glowed when all beside had ceased to glow.

LV

And there was one soft breast, as hath been said,
  Which unto his was bound by stronger ties
Than the church links withal; and—though unwed,
  That love was pure—and, far above disguise,   490
Had stood the test of mortal enmities
  Still undivided, and cemented more
By peril, dreaded most in female eyes;
  But this was firm, and from a foreign shore
Well to that heart might his these absent greetings pour! 495

1

The castled Crag of Drachenfels
Frowns o'er the wide and winding Rhine,
Whose breast of waters broadly swells
Between the banks which bear the vine,
And hills all rich with blossomed trees,   500
And fields which promise corn and wine,
And scattered cities crowning these,
Whose far white walls along them shine,
Have strewed a scene, which I should see
With double joy wert *thou* with me.   505

2

And peasant girls, with deep blue eyes,
And hands which offer early flowers,

Walk smiling o'er this Paradise;
Above, the frequent feudal towers
Through green leaves lift their walls of gray;   510
And many a rock which steeply lowers,
And noble arch in proud decay,
Look o'er this vale of vintage-bowers;
But one thing want these banks of Rhine,—
Thy gentle hand to clasp in mine!   515

3

I send the lilies given to me—
Though long before thy hand they touch,
I know that they must withered be,
But yet reject them not as such;
For I have cherished them as dear,   520
Because they yet may meet thine eye,
And guide thy soul to mine even here,
When thou behold'st them drooping nigh,
And know'st them gathered by the Rhine,
And offered from my heart to thine!   525

4

The river nobly foams and flows—
The charm of this enchanted ground,
And all its thousand turns disclose
Some fresher beauty varying round:
The haughtiest breast its wish might bound   530
Through life to dwell delighted here;
Nor could on earth a spot be found
To Nature and to me so dear—
Could thy dear eyes in following mine
Still sweeten more these banks of Rhine!   535

LVI

By Coblentz, on a rise of gentle ground,
  There is a small and simple Pyramid,
  Crowning the summit of the verdant mound;
  Beneath its base are Heroes' ashes hid—
  Our enemy's—but let not that forbid   540

Honour to Marceau! o'er whose early tomb
Tears, big tears, gushed from the rough soldier's lid,
Lamenting and yet envying such a doom,
Falling for France, whose rights he battled to resume.

LVII

Brief, brave, and glorious was his young career,—   545
   His mourners were two hosts, his friends and foes;
And fitly may the stranger lingering here
   Pray for his gallant Spirit's bright repose;—
For he was Freedom's Champion, one of those,
   The few in number, who had not o'erstept   550
The charter to chastise which she bestows
   On such as wield her weapons; he had kept
The whiteness of his soul—and thus men o'er him wept.

LVIII

Here Ehrenbreitstein, with her shattered wall
   Black with the miner's blast, upon her height   555
Yet shows of what she was, when shell and ball
   Rebounding idly on her strength did light:—
A Tower of Victory! from whence the flight
   Of baffled foes was watched along the plain:
But Peace destroyed what War could never blight,   560
   And laid those proud roofs bare to Summer's rain—
On which the iron shower for years had poured in vain.

LIX

Adieu to thee, fair Rhine! How long delighted
   The stranger fain would linger on his way!
Thine is a scene alike where souls united   565
   Or lonely Contemplation thus might stray;
And could the ceaseless vultures cease to prey
   On self-condemning bosoms, it were here,
Where Nature, nor too sombre nor too gay,
   Wild but not rude, awful yet not austere,   570
Is to the mellow Earth as Autumn to the year.

LX

Adieu to thee again! a vain adieu!
 There can be no farewell to scene like thine;
 The mind is coloured by thy every hue;
 And if reluctantly the eyes resign   575
 Their cherished gaze upon thee, lovely Rhine!
'Tis with the thankful glance of parting praise;
 More mighty spots may rise—more glaring shine,
 But none unite in one attaching maze
The brilliant, fair, and soft,—the glories of old days, 580

LXI

The negligently grand, the fruitful bloom
 Of coming ripeness, the white city's sheen,
 The rolling stream, the precipice's gloom,
 The forest's growth, and Gothic walls between,—
 The wild rocks shaped, as they had turrets been, 585
In mockery of man's art; and these withal
 A race of faces happy as the scene,
 Whose fertile bounties here extend to all,
Still springing o'er thy banks, though Empires near them
 fall.

LXII

But these recede. Above me are the Alps,   590
 The Palaces of Nature, whose vast walls
 Have pinnacled in clouds their snowy scalps,
 And throned Eternity in icy halls
 Of cold Sublimity, where forms and falls
The Avalanche—the thunderbolt of snow!   595
 All that expands the spirit, yet appals,
 Gather around these summits, as to show
How Earth may pierce to Heaven, yet leave vain man
 below.

LXIII

But ere these matchless heights I dare to scan,
 There is a spot should not be passed in vain,— 600

Morat! the proud, the patriot field! where man
May gaze on ghastly trophies of the slain,
Nor blush for those who conquered on that plain;
Here Burgundy bequeathed his tombless host,
A bony heap, through ages to remain,   605
Themselves their monument;—the Stygian coast
Unsepulchred they roamed, and shrieked each wandering
    ghost.

LXIV

While Waterloo with Cannæ's carnage vies,
    Morat and Marathon twin names shall stand;
    They were true Glory's stainless victories,   610
    Won by the unambitious heart and hand
    Of a proud, brotherly, and civic band,
    All unbought champions in no princely cause
    Of vice-entailed Corruption; they no land
    Doomed to bewail the blasphemy of laws   615
Making Kings' rights divine, by some Draconic clause.

LXV

By a lone wall a lonelier column rears
    A gray and grief-worn aspect of old days;
    'Tis the last remnant of the wreck of years,
    And looks as with the wild-bewildered gaze   620
    Of one to stone converted by amaze,
    Yet still with consciousness; and there it stands
    Making a marvel that it not decays,
    When the coeval pride of human hands,
Levelled Aventicum, hath strewed her subject lands.   625

LXVI

And there—oh! sweet and sacred be the name!—
    Julia—the daughter—the devoted—gave
    Her youth to Heaven; her heart, beneath a claim
    Nearest to Heaven's, broke o'er a father's grave.
    Justice is sworn 'gainst tears, and hers would crave   630
    The life she lived in—but the Judge was just—

And then she died on him she could not save.
Their tomb was simple, and without a bust,
And held within their urn one mind—one heart—one
    dust.

LXVII

But these are deeds which should not pass away,   635
    And names that must not wither, though the Earth
Forgets her empires with a just decay,
    The enslavers and the enslaved—their death and birth;
    The high, the mountain-majesty of Worth
Should be—and shall, survivor of its woe,   640
    And from its immortality, look forth
    In the sun's face, like yonder Alpine snow,
Imperishably pure beyond all things below.

LXVIII

Lake Leman woos me with its crystal face,
    The mirror where the stars and mountains view   645
    The stillness of their aspect in each trace
Its clear depth yields of their far height and hue:
    There is too much of Man here, to look through
With a fit mind the might which I behold;
    But soon in me shall Loneliness renew   650
    Thoughts hid, but not less cherished than of old,
Ere mingling with the herd had penned me in their fold.

LXIX

To fly from, need not be to hate, mankind:
    All are not fit with them to stir and toil,
    Nor is it discontent to keep the mind   655
Deep in its fountain, lest it overboil
    In the hot throng, where we become the spoil
Of our infection, till too late and long
    We may deplore and struggle with the coil,
    In wretched interchange of wrong for wrong   660
Midst a contentious world, striving where none are strong.

LXX

There, in a moment, we may plunge our years
   In fatal penitence, and in the blight
   Of our own Soul turn all our blood to tears,
   And colour things to come with hues of Night;   665
   The race of life becomes a hopeless flight
   To those that walk in darkness: on the sea
   The boldest steer but where their ports invite—
   But there are wanderers o'er Eternity
Whose bark drives on and on, and anchored ne'er shall be. 670

LXXI

Is it not better, then, to be alone,
   And love Earth only for its earthly sake?
   By the blue rushing of the arrowy Rhone,
   Or the pure bosom of its nursing Lake,
   Which feeds it as a mother who doth make   675
   A fair but froward infant her own care,
   Kissing its cries away as these awake;—
   Is it not better thus our lives to wear,
Than join the crushing crowd, doomed to inflict or bear?

LXXII

I live not in myself, but I become   680
   Portion of that around me; and to me
   High mountains are a feeling, but the hum
   Of human cities torture: I can see
   Nothing to loathe in Nature, save to be
   A link reluctant in a fleshly chain,   685
   Classed among creatures, when the soul can flee,
   And with the sky—the peak—the heaving plain
Of Ocean, or the stars, mingle—and not in vain.

LXXIII

And thus I am absorbed, and this is life:—
   I look upon the peopled desert past,   690
   As on a place of agony and strife,

Where, for some sin, to Sorrow I was cast,
To act and suffer, but remount at last
With a fresh pinion; which I feel to spring,
Though young, yet waxing vigorous as the Blast   695
Which it would cope with, on delighted wing,
Spurning the clay-cold bonds which round our being cling.

LXXIV

And when, at length, the mind shall be all free
From what it hates in this degraded form,
Reft of its carnal life, save what shall be   700
Existent happier in the fly and worm,—
When Elements to Elements conform;
And dust is as it should be, shall I not
Feel all I see less dazzling but more warm?
The bodiless thought? the Spirit of each spot?   705
Of which, even now, I share at times the immortal lot?

LXXV

Are not the mountains, waves, and skies, a part
Of me and of my Soul, as I of them?
Is not the love of these deep in my heart
With a pure passion? should I not contemn   710
All objects, if compared with these? and stem
A tide of suffering, rather than forego
Such feelings for the hard and worldly phlegm
Of those whose eyes are only turned below,
Gazing upon the ground, with thoughts which dare not 715
    glow?

LXXVI

But this is not my theme; and I return
To that which is immediate, and require
Those who find contemplation in the urn,
To look on One, whose dust was once all fire,—
A native of the land where I respire   720
The clear air for a while—a passing guest,
Where he became a being,—whose desire
Was to be glorious; 'twas a foolish quest,
The which to gain and keep, he sacrificed all rest.

LXXVII

Here the self-torturing sophist, wild Rousseau,   725
   The apostle of Affliction, he who threw
   Enchantment over Passion, and from Woe
   Wrung overwhelming eloquence, first drew
   The breath which made him wretched; yet he knew
   How to make Madness beautiful, and cast   730
   O'er erring deeds and thoughts, a heavenly hue
   Of words, like sunbeams, dazzling as they past
The eyes, which o'er them shed tears feelingly and fast.

LXXVIII

His love was Passion's essence—as a tree
   On fire by lightning; with ethereal flame   735
   Kindled he was, and blasted; for to be
   Thus, and enamoured, were in him the same.
   But his was not the love of living dame,
   Nor of the dead who rise upon our dreams,
   But of ideal Beauty, which became   740
   In him existence, and o'erflowing teems
Along his burning page, distempered though it seems.

LXXIX

This breathed itself to life in Julie, *this*
   Invested her with all that's wild and sweet;
   This hallowed, too, the memorable kiss   745
   Which every morn his fevered lip would greet,
   From hers, who but with friendship his would meet;
   But to that gentle touch, through brain and breast
   Flashed the thrilled Spirit's love-devouring heat;
   In that absorbing sigh perchance more blest   750
Than vulgar minds may be with all they seek possest.

LXXX

His life was one long war with self-sought foes,
   Or friends by him self-banished; for his mind
   Had grown Suspicion's sanctuary, and chose,

For its own cruel sacrifice, the kind,   755
'Gainst whom he raged with fury strange and blind.
But he was phrensied,—wherefore, who may know?
Since cause might be which Skill could never find;
But he was phrensied by disease or woe,
To that worst pitch of all, which wears a reasoning show. 760

LXXXI

For then he was inspired, and from him came,
  As from the Pythian's mystic cave of yore,
  Those oracles which set the world in flame,
  Nor ceased to burn till kingdoms were no more:
  Did he not this for France? which lay before   765
  Bowed to the inborn tyranny of years?
  Broken and trembling to the yoke she bore,
  Till by the voice of him and his compeers,
Roused up too much wrath which follows o'ergrown fears?

LXXXII

They made themselves a fearful monument!   770
  The wreck of old opinions—things which grew,
  Breathed from the birth of Time: the veil they rent,
  And what behind it lay, all earth shall view.
  But good with ill they also overthrew,
  Leaving but ruins, wherewith to rebuild   775
  Upon the same foundation, and renew
  Dungeons and thrones, which the same hour refilled,
As heretofore, because Ambition was self-willed.

LXXXIII

But this will not endure, nor be endured!
  Mankind have felt their strength, and made it felt.   780
  They might have used it better, but, allured
  By their new vigour, sternly have they dealt
  On one another; Pity ceased to melt
  With her once natural charities. But they,
  Who in Oppression's darkness caved had dwelt,   785
  They were not eagles, nourished with the day;
What marvel then, at times, if they mistook their prey?

LXXXIV

What deep wounds ever closed without a scar?
   The heart's bleed longest, and but heal to wear
   That which disfigures it; and they who war   790
   With their own hopes, and have been vanquished, bear
Silence, but not submission: in his lair
Fixed Passion holds his breath, until the hour
Which shall atone for years; none need despair:
   It came—it cometh—and will come,—the power   795
To punish or forgive—in one we shall be slower.

LXXXV

Clear, placid Leman! thy contrasted lake,
   With the wild world I dwelt in, is a thing
   Which warns me, with its stillness, to forsake
Earth's troubled waters for a purer spring.   800
This quiet sail is as a noiseless wing
To waft me from distraction; once I loved
Torn Ocean's roar, but thy soft murmuring
Sounds sweet as if a Sister's voice reproved,
That I with stern delights should e'er have been so moved. 805

LXXXVI

It is the hush of night, and all between
   Thy margin and the mountains, dusk, yet clear,
   Mellowed and mingling, yet distinctly seen,
Save darkened Jura, whose capt heights appear
Precipitously steep; and drawing near,   810
There breathes a living fragrance from the shore,
Of flowers yet fresh with childhood; on the ear
Drops the light drip of the suspended oar,
Or chirps the grasshopper one good-night carol more.

LXXXVII

He is an evening reveller, who makes   815
   His life an infancy, and sings his fill;
   At intervals, some bird from out the brakes
Starts into voice a moment, then is still.

There seems a floating whisper on the hill,
But that is fancy—for the Starlight dews   820
All silently their tears of Love instil,
Weeping themselves away, till they infuse
Deep into Nature's breast the spirit of her hues.

LXXXVIII

Ye Stars! which are the poetry of Heaven!
If in your bright leaves we would read the fate   825
Of men and empires,—'tis to be forgiven,
That in our aspirations to be great,
Our destinies o'erleap their mortal state,
And claim a kindred with you; for ye are
A Beauty and a Mystery, and create   830
In us such love and reverence from afar,
That Fortune,—Fame,—Power,—Life, have named them-
selves a Star.

LXXXIX

All Heaven and Earth are still—though not in sleep,
But breathless, as we grow when feeling most;
And silent, as we stand in thoughts too deep:—   835
All Heaven and Earth are still: From the high host
Of stars, to the lulled lake and mountain-coast,
All is concentered in a life intense,
Where not a beam, nor air, nor leaf is lost,
But hath a part of Being, and a sense   840
Of that which is of all Creator and Defence.

XC

Then stirs the feeling infinite, so felt
In solitude, where we are *least* alone;
A truth, which through our being then doth melt,
And purifies from self: it is a tone,   845
The soul and source of Music, which makes known
Eternal harmony, and sheds a charm
Like to the fabled Cytherea's zone,
Binding all things with beauty;—'twould disarm
The spectre Death, had he substantial power to harm.   850

XCI

Not vainly did the early Persian make
   His altar the high places, and the peak
   Of earth-o'ergazing mountains, and thus take
   A fit and unwalled temple, there to seek
   The Spirit, in whose honour shrines are weak   855
   Upreared of human hands. Come, and compare
   Columns and idol-dwellings—Goth or Greek—
   With Nature's realms of worship, earth and air—
Nor fix on fond abodes to circumscribe thy prayer!

XCII

The sky is changed!—and such a change! Oh Night,   860
   And Storm, and Darkness, ye are wondrous strong,
   Yet lovely in your strength, as is the light
   Of a dark eye in Woman! Far along,
   From peak to peak, the rattling crags among
   Leaps the live thunder! Not from one lone cloud,   865
   But every mountain now hath found a tongue,
   And Jura answers, through her misty shroud,
Back to the joyous Alps, who call to her aloud!

XCIII

And this is in the Night:—Most glorious Night!
   Thou wert not sent for slumber! let me be   870
   A sharer in thy fierce and far delight,—
   A portion of the tempest and of thee!
   How the lit lake shines, a phosphoric sea,
   And the big rain comes dancing to the earth!
   And now again 'tis black,—and now, the glee   875
   Of the loud hills shakes with its mountain-mirth,
As if they did rejoice o'er a young Earthquake's birth.

XCIV

Now, where the swift Rhone cleaves his way between
   Heights which appear as lovers who have parted
   In hate, whose mining depths so intervene,   880
   That they can meet no more, though broken-hearted:

Though in their souls, which thus each other thwarted,
Love was the very root of the fond rage
Which blighted their life's bloom, and then departed:—
Itself expired, but leaving them an age   885
Of years all winters,—war within themselves to wage:

XCV

Now, where the quick Rhone thus hath cleft his way,
The mightiest of the storms hath ta'en his stand:
For here, not one, but many, make their play,
And fling their thunder-bolts from hand to hand,   890
Flashing and cast around: of all the band,
The brightest through these parted hills hath forked
His lightnings,—as if he did understand,
That in such gaps as Desolation worked,
There the hot shaft should blast whatever therein lurked. 895

XCVI

Sky—Mountains—River—Winds—Lake—Lightnings!
    ye!
With night, and clouds, and thunder—and a Soul
To make these felt and feeling, well may be
Things that have made me watchful; the far roll
Of your departing voices, is the knoll   900
Of what in me is sleepless,—if I rest.
But where of ye, O Tempests! is the goal?
Are ye like those within the human breast?
Or do ye find, at length, like eagles, some high nest?

XCVII

Could I embody and unbosom now   905
That which is most within me,—could I wreak
My thoughts upon expression, and thus throw
Soul—heart—mind—passions—feelings—strong or
    weak—
All that I would have sought, and all I seek,
Bear, know, feel—and yet breathe—into one word,   910

And that one word were Lightning, I would speak;
But as it is, I live and die unheard,
With a most voiceless thought, sheathing it as a sword.

XCVIII

The Morn is up again, the dewy Morn,
   With breath all incense, and with cheek all bloom—   915
Laughing the clouds away with playful scorn,
And living as if earth contained no tomb,—
And glowing into day: we may resume
The march of our existence: and thus I,
Still on thy shores, fair Leman! may find room   920
And food for meditation, nor pass by
Much, that may give us pause, if pondered fittingly.

XCIX

Clarens! sweet Clarens birthplace of deep Love!
   Thine air is the young breath of passionate Thought;
Thy trees take root in Love; the snows above,   925
The very Glaciers have his colours caught,
And Sun-set into rose-hues sees them wrought
By rays which sleep there lovingly: the rocks,
The permanent crags, tell here of Love, who sought
In them a refuge from the worldly shocks,   930
Which stir and sting the Soul with Hope that woos, then
   mocks.

C

Clarens! by heavenly feet thy paths are trod,—
   Undying Love's, who here ascends a throne
To which the steps are mountains; where the God
Is a pervading Life and Light,—so shown   935
Not on those summits solely, nor alone
In the still cave and forest; o'er the flower
His eye is sparkling, and his breath hath blown,
His soft and summer breath, whose tender power
Passes the strength of storms in their most desolate hour.   940

CI

All things are here of *Him;* from the black pines,
　Which are his shade on high, and the loud roar
　Of torrents, where he listeneth, to the vines
　Which slope his green path downward on the shore,
　Where the bowed Waters meet him, and adore,   945
　Kissing his feet with murmurs; and the Wood,
　The covert of old trees, with trunks all hoar,
　But light leaves, young as joy, stands where it stood,
Offering to him, and his, a populous solitude.

CII

A populous solitude of bees and birds,   950
　And fair-formed and many-coloured things,
　Who worship him with notes more sweet than words,
　And innocently open their glad wings,
　Fearless and full of life: the gush of springs,
　And fall of lofty fountains, and the bend   955
　Of stirring branches, and the bud which brings
　The swiftest thought of Beauty, here extend
Mingling—and made by Love—unto one mighty end.

CIII

He who hath loved not, here would learn that lore,
　And make his heart a spirit; he who knows   960
　That tender mystery, will love the more;
　For this is Love's recess, where vain men's woes,
　And the world's waste, have driven him far from those,
　For 'tis his nature to advance or die;
　He stands not still, but or decays, or grows   965
　Into a boundless blessing, which may vie
With the immortal lights, in its eternity!

CIV

'Twas not for fiction chose Rousseau this spot,
　Peopling it with affections; but he found
　It was the scene which Passion must allot   970

To the Mind's purified beings; 'twas the ground
Where early Love his Psyche's zone unbound,
And hallowed it with loveliness: 'tis lone,
And wonderful, and deep, and hath a sound,
And sense, and sight of sweetness; here the Rhone   975
Hath spread himself a couch, the Alps have reared a
    throne.

CV

Lausanne! and Ferney! ye have been the abodes
    Of Names which unto you bequeathed a name;
    Mortals, who sought and found, by dangerous roads,
    A path to perpetuity of Fame: 980
    They were gigantic minds, and their steep aim
    Was, Titan-like, on daring doubts to pile
    Thoughts which should call down thunder, and the
        flame
    Of Heaven again assailed—if Heaven, the while,
On man and man's research could deign do more than   985
    smile.

CVI

The one was fire and fickleness, a child
    Most mutable in wishes, but in mind
    A wit as various,—gay, grave, sage, or wild,—
    Historian, bard, philosopher, combined;
    He multiplied himself among mankind,   990
    The Proteus of their talents: But his own
    Breathed most in ridicule,—which, as the wind,
    Blew where it listed, laying all things prone,—
Now to o'erthrow a fool, and now to shake a throne.

CVII

The other, deep and slow, exhausting thought,   995
    And hiving wisdom with each studious year,
    In meditation dwelt—with learning wrought,
    And shaped his weapon with an edge severe,

Sapping a solemn creed with solemn sneer;
The lord of irony,—that master-spell,   1000
Which stung his foes to wrath, which grew from fear
And doomed him to the zealot's ready Hell,
Which answers to all doubts so eloquently well.

CVIII

Yet, peace be with their ashes,—for by them,
If merited, the penalty is paid;   1005
It is not ours to judge,—far less condemn;
The hour must come when such things shall be made
Known unto all,—or hope and dread allayed
By slumber, on one pillow, in the dust,
Which, thus much we are sure, must lie decayed;   1010
And when it shall revive, as is our trust,
'Twill be to be forgiven—or suffer what is just.

CIX

But let me quit Man's works, again to read
His Maker's, spread around me, and suspend
This page, which from my reveries I feed,   1015
Until it seems prolonging without end.
The clouds above me to the white Alps tend,
And I must pierce them, and survey whate'er
May be permitted, as my steps I bend
To their most great and growing region, where   1020
The earth to her embrace compels the powers of air.

CX

Italia too! Italia! looking on thee,
Full flashes on the Soul the light of ages,
Since the fierce Carthaginian almost won thee,
To the last halo of the Chiefs and Sages   1025
Who glorify thy consecrated pages;
Thou wert the throne and grave of empires; still,
The fount at which the panting Mind assuages
Her thirst of knowledge, quaffing there her fill,
Flows from the eternal source of Rome's imperial hill.   1030

CXI

Thus far have I proceeded in a theme
    Renewed with no kind auspices:—to feel
    We are not what we have been, and to deem
    We are not what we should be,—and to steel
    The heart against itself; and to conceal,   1035
    With a proud caution, love, or hate, or aught,—
    Passion or feeling, purpose, grief, or zeal,—
    Which is the tyrant Spirit of our thought,
Is a stern task of soul:—No matter,—it is taught.

CXII

And for these words, thus woven into song,   1040
    It may be that they are a harmless wile,—
    The colouring of the scenes which fleet along,
    Which I would seize, in passing, to beguile
    My breast, or that of others, for a while.
    Fame is the thirst of youth,—but I am not   1045
    So young as to regard men's frown or smile,
    As loss or guerdon of a glorious lot;—
I stood and stand alone,—remembered or forgot.

CXIII

I have not loved the World, nor the World me;
    I have not flattered its rank breath, nor bowed   1050
    To its idolatries a patient knee,
    Nor coined my cheek to smiles,—nor cried aloud
    In worship of an echo: in the crowd
    They could not deem me one of such—I stood
    Among them, but not of them—in a shroud   1055
    Of thoughts which were not their thoughts, and still
        could,
Had I not filed my mind, which thus itself subdued.

CXIV

I have not loved the World, nor the World me,—
    But let us part fair foes; I do believe,

Though I have found them not, that there may be   1060
Words which are things,—hope which will not deceive,
And Virtues which are merciful, nor weave
Snares for the failing; I would also deem
O'er others' griefs that some sincerely grieve—
That two, or one, are almost what they seem,—   1065
That Goodness is no name—and Happiness no dream.

CXV

My daughter! with thy name this song begun!
  My daughter! with thy name thus much shall end!—
  I see thee not—I hear thee not—but none
Can be so wrapt in thee; Thou art the Friend   1070
To whom the shadows of far years extend:
Albeit my brow thou never should'st behold,
My voice shall with thy future visions blend,
And reach into thy heart,—when mine is cold,—
A token and a tone, even from thy father's mould.   1075

CXVI

To aid thy mind's developement,—to watch
  Thy dawn of little joys,—to sit and see
  Almost thy very growth,—to view thee catch
Knowledge of objects,—wonders yet to thee!
To hold thee lightly on a gentle knee,   1080
And print on thy soft cheek a parent's kiss,—
This, it should seem, was not reserved for me—
Yet this was in my nature:—as it is,
I know not what is there, yet something like to this.

CXVII

Yet, though dull Hate as duty should be taught,   1085
  I know that thou wilt love me: though my name
  Should be shut from thee, as a spell still fraught
With desolation, and a broken claim:
Though the grave closed between us,—'twere the same,
I know that thou wilt love me—though to drain   1090
My blood from out thy being were an aim,
And an attainment,—all would be in vain,—
Still thou would'st love me, still that more than life retain.

CXVIII

The child of Love! though born in bitterness,
   And nurtured in Convulsion; Of thy sire   1095
   These were the elements,—and thine no less.
As yet such are around thee,—but thy fire
Shall be more tempered, and thy hope far higher!
Sweet by thy cradled slumbers! O'er the sea
And from the mountains where I now respire,   1100
   Fain would I waft such blessing upon thee,
As—with a sigh—I deem thou might'st have been to me!
    [1816]

SONNET ON CHILLON

Eternal Spirit of the chainless Mind!
   Brightest in dungeons, Liberty! thou art:
   For there thy habitation is the heart—
The heart which love of thee alone can bind;
And when thy sons to fetters are consigned—   5
   To fetters, and the damp vault's dayless gloom,
   Their country conquers with their martyrdom,
And Freedom's fame finds wings on every wind.
Chillon! thy prison is a holy place,
   And thy sad floor an altar—for 'twas trod,   10
Until his very steps have left a trace
   Worn, as if thy cold pavement were a sod,
By Bonnivard!—May none those marks efface!
   For they appeal from tyranny to God.
    [1816]

THE PRISONER OF CHILLON

I

My hair is grey, but not with years,
Nor grew it white
    In a single night,
As men's have grown from sudden fears:
My limbs are bowed, though not with toil,   5
   But rusted with a vile repose,
For they have been a dungeon's spoil,
   And mine has been the fate of those
To whom the goodly earth and air
Are banned, and barred—forbidden fare;   10
But this was for my father's faith
I suffered chains and courted death;
That father perished at the stake
For tenets he would not forsake;
And for the same his lineal race   15
In darkness found a dwelling place;
We were seven—who now are one,
   Six in youth, and one in age,
Finished as they had begun,
   Proud of Persecution's rage;   20
One in fire, and two in field,
Their belief with blood have sealed,
Dying as their father died,
For the God their foes denied;—
Three were in a dungeon cast,   25
Of whom this wreck is left the last.

II

There are seven pillars of Gothic mould,
In Chillon's dungeons deep and old,
There are seven columns, massy and grey,
Dim with a dull imprisoned ray,   30
A sunbeam which hath lost its way,
And through the crevice and the cleft
Of the thick wall is fallen and left;

Creeping o'er the floor so damp,
Like a marsh's meteor lamp: 35
And in each pillar there is a ring,
    And in each ring there is a chain;
That iron is a cankering thing,
    For in these limbs its teeth remain,
With marks that will not wear away,   40
Till I have done with this new day,
Which now is painful to these eyes,
Which have not seen the sun so rise
For years—I cannot count them o'er,
I lost their long and heavy score   45
When my last brother drooped and died,
And I lay living by his side.

                        III

They chained us each to a column stone,
And we were three—yet, each alone;
We could not move a single pace,   50
We could not see each other's face,
But with that pale and livid light
That made us strangers in our sight:
And thus together—yet apart,
Fettered in hand, but joined in heart,   55
'Twas still some solace in the dearth
Of the pure elements of earth,
To hearken to each other's speech,
And each turn comforter to each
With some new hope, or legend old,   60
Or song heroically bold;
But even these at length grew cold.
Our voices took a dreary tone,
An echo of the dungeon stone,
    A grating sound, not full and free,   65
    As they of yore were wont to be:
    It might be fancy—but to me
They never sounded like our own.

IV

I was the eldest of the three,
 And to uphold and cheer the rest   **70**
 I ought to do—and did my best—
And each did well in his degree.
 The youngest, whom my father loved,
Because our mother's brow was given
To him, with eyes as blue as heaven—   **75**
 For him my soul was sorely moved:
And truly might it be distressed
To see such bird in such a nest;
For he was beautiful as day—
 (When day was beautiful to me   **80**
 As to young eagles, being free)—
 A polar day, which will not see
A sunset till its summer's gone,
 Its sleepless summer of long light,
The snow-clad offspring of the sun: **85**
 And thus he was as pure and bright,
And in his natural spirit gay,
With tears for nought but others' ills,
And then they flowed like mountain rills,
Unless he could assuage the woe   **90**
Which he abhorred to view below.

V

The other was as pure of mind,
But formed to combat with his kind;
Strong in his frame, and of a mood
Which 'gainst the world in war had stood,   **95**
And perished in the foremost rank
 With joy:—but not in chains to pine:
His spirit withered with their clank,
 I saw it silently decline—
 And so perchance in sooth did mine: **100**
But yet I forced it on to cheer
Those relics of a home so dear.
He was a hunter of the hills,
 Had followed there the deer and wolf;

To him this dungeon was a gulf,　　　　　105
And fettered feet the worst of ills.

VI

Lake Leman lies by Chillon's walls:
A thousand feet in depth below
Its massy waters meet and flow;
Thus much the fathom-line was sent　　　110
From Chillon's snow-white battlement,
　　Which round about the wave inthralls:
A double dungeon wall and wave
Had made—and like a living grave.
Below the surface of the lake　　　　　115
The dark vault lies wherein we lay:
We heard it ripple night and day;
　　Sounding o'er our heads it knocked;
And I have felt the winter's spray
Wash through the bars when winds were high　120
And wanton in the happy sky;
　　And then the very rock hath rocked,
　　And I have felt it shake, unshocked,
Because I could have smiled to see
The death that would have set me free.　　125

VII

I said my nearer brother pined,
I said his mighty heart declined,
He loathed and put away his food;
It was not that 'twas coarse and rude,
For we were used to hunter's fare,　　　130
And for the like had little care:
The milk drawn from the mountain goat
Was changed for water from the moat,
Our bread was such as captives' tears
Have moistened many a thousand years,　　135
Since man first pent his fellow men
Like brutes within an iron den;
But what were these to us or him?
These wasted not his heart or limb;
My brother's soul was of that mould　　　140

Which in a palace had grown cold,
Had his free breathing been denied
The range of the steep mountain's side;
But why delay the truth?—he died.
I saw, and could not hold his head,   145
Nor reach his dying hand—nor dead,—
Though hard I strove, but strove in vain,
To rend and gnash my bonds in twain.
He died—and they unlocked his chain,
And scooped for him a shallow grave   150
Even from the cold earth of our cave.
I begged them, as a boon, to lay
His corse in dust whereon the day
Might shine—it was a foolish thought,
But then within my brain it wrought,   155
That even in death his freeborn breast
In such a dungeon could not rest.
I might have spared my idle prayer—
They coldly laughed—and laid him there:
The flat and turfless earth above   160
The being we so much did love;
His empty chain above it leant,
Such Murder's fitting monument!

VIII

But he, the favourite and the flower,
Most cherished since his natal hour,   165
His mother's image in fair face,
The infant love of all his race,
His martyred father's dearest thought,
My latest care, for whom I sought
To hoard my life, that his might be   170
Less wretched now, and one day free;
He, too, who yet had held untired
A spirit natural or inspired—
He, too, was struck, and day by day
Was withered on the stalk away.   175
Oh, God! it is a fearful thing
To see the human soul take wing
In any shape, in any mood:
I've seen it rushing forth in blood,

I've seen it on the breaking ocean   180
Strive with a swoln convulsive motion,
I've seen the sick and ghastly bed
Of Sin delirious with its dread:
But these were horrors—this was woe
Unmixed with such—but sure and slow: 185
He faded, and so calm and meek,
So softly worn, so sweetly weak,
So tearless, yet so tender—kind,
And grieved for those he left behind;
With all the while a cheek whose bloom   190
Was as a mockery of the tomb,
Whose tints as gently sunk away
As a departing rainbow's ray;
An eye of most transparent light,
That almost made the dungeon bright;   195
And not a word of murmur—not
A groan o'er his untimely lot,—
A little talk of better days,
A little hope my own to raise,
For I was sunk in silence—lost   200
In this last loss, of all the most;
And then the sighs he would suppress
Of fainting Nature's feebleness,
More slowly drawn, grew less and less:
I listened, but I could not hear;   205
I called, for I was wild with fear;
I knew 'twas hopeless, but my dread
Would not be thus admonishéd;
I called, and thought I heard a sound—
I burst my chain with one strong bound,   210
And rushed to him:—I found him not,
I only stirred in this black spot,
I only lived, *I* only drew
The accursed breath of dungeon-dew;
The last, the sole, the dearest link   215
Between me and the eternal brink,
Which bound me to my failing race,
Was broken in this fatal place.
One on the earth, and one beneath—
My brothers—both had ceased to breathe: 220
I took that hand which lay so still,

Alas! my own was full as chill;
I had not strength to stir, or strive,
But felt that I was still alive—
A frantic feeling, when we know   225
That what we love shall ne'er be so.
    I know not why
    I could not die,
I had no earthly hope—but faith,
And that forbade a selfish death.   230

IX

What next befell me then and there
    I know not well—I never knew—
First came the loss of light, and air,
    And then of darkness too:
I had no thought, no feeling—none—   235
Among the stones I stood a stone,
And was, scarce conscious what I wist,
As shrubless crags within the mist;
For all was blank, and bleak, and grey;
It was not night—it was not day;   240
It was not even the dungeon-light,
So hateful to my heavy sight,
But vacancy absorbing space,
And fixedness—without a place;
There were no stars—no earth—no time—   245
No check—no change—no good—no crime—
But silence, as a stirless breath
Which neither was of life nor death;
A sea of stagnant idleness,
Blind, boundless, mute, and motionless!   250

X

A light broke in upon my brain,—
    It was the carol of a bird;
It ceased, and then it came again,
    The sweetest song ear ever heard,
And mine was thankful till my eyes   255
Ran over with the glad surprise,
And they that moment could not see

I was the mate of misery;
But then by dull degrees came back
My senses to their wonted track;   260
I saw the dungeon walls and floor
Close slowly round me as before,
I saw the glimmer of the sun
Creeping as it before had done,
But through the crevice where it came   265
That bird was perched, as fond and tame,
    And tamer than upon the tree;
A lovely bird, with azure wings,
And song that said a thousand things,
    And seemed to say them all for me!   270
I never saw its like before,
I ne'er shall see its likeness more:
It seemed like me to want a mate,
But was not half so desolate,
And it was come to love me when   275
None lived to love me so again,
And cheering from my dungeon's brink,
Had brought me back to feel and think.
I know not if it late were free,
    Or broke its cage to perch on mine,   280
But knowing well captivity,
    Sweet bird! I could not wish for thine!
Or if it were, in wingéd guise,
A visitant from Paradise;
For—Heaven forgive that thought! the while   285
Which made me both to weep and smile—
I sometimes deemed that it might be
My brother's soul come down to me;
But then at last away it flew,
And then 'twas mortal well I knew,   290
For he would never thus have flown—
And left me twice so doubly lone,—
Lone—as the corse within its shroud,
Lone—as a solitary cloud,
    A single cloud on a sunny day,   295
While all the rest of heaven is clear,
A frown upon the atmosphere,
That hath no business to appear
    When skies are blue, and earth is gay.

XI

A kind of change came in my fate,   300
My keepers grew compassionate;
I know not what had made them so,
They were inured to sights of woe,
But so it was:—my broken chain
With links unfastened did remain,   305
And it was liberty to stride
Along my cell from side to side,
And up and down, and then athwart,
And tread it over every part;
And round the pillars one by one,   310
Returning where my walk begun,
Avoiding only, as I trod,
My brothers' graves without a sod;
For if I thought with heedless tread
My step profaned their lowly bed,   315
My breath came gaspingly and thick,
And my crushed heart felt blind and sick.

XII

I made a footing in the wall,
    It was not therefrom to escape,
For I had buried one and all,   320
    Who loved me in a human shape;
And the whole earth would henceforth be
A wider prison unto me:
No child—no sire—no kin had I,
No partner in my misery;   325
I thought of this, and I was glad,
For thought of them had made me mad;
But I was curious to ascend
To my barred windows, and to bend
Once more, upon the mountains high,   330
The quiet of a loving eye.

XIII

I saw them—and they were the same,
They were not changed like me in frame;

I saw their thousand years of snow
On high—their wide long lake below,   335
And the blue Rhone in fullest flow;
I heard the torrents leap and gush
O'er channelled rock and broken bush;
I saw the white-walled distant town,
And whiter sails go skimming down;   340
And then there was a little isle,
Which in my very face did smile,
    The only one in view;
A small green isle, it seemed no more,
Scarce broader than my dungeon floor,   345
But in it there were three tall trees,
And o'er it blew the mountain breeze,
And by it there were waters flowing,
And on it there were young flowers growing,
    Of gentle breath and hue.   350
The fish swam by the castle wall,
And they seemed joyous each and all;
The eagle rode the rising blast,
Methought he never flew so fast
As then to me he seemed to fly;   355
And then new tears came in my eye,
And I felt troubled—and would fain
I had not left my recent chain;
And when I did descend again,
The darkness of my dim abode   360
Fell on me as a heavy load;
It was as is a new-dug grave,
Closing o'er one we sought to save,—
And yet my glance, too much opprest,
Had almost need of such a rest.   365

XIV

It might be months, or years, or days—
    I kept no count, I took no note—
I had no hope my eyes to raise,
    And clear them of their dreary mote;
At last men came to set me free;   370
    I asked not why, and recked not where;
It was at length the same to me,

Fettered or fetterless to be,
  I learned to love despair.
And thus when they appeared at last,   375
And all my bonds aside were cast,
These heavy walls to me had grown
A hermitage—and all my own!
And half I felt as they were come
To tear me from a second home: 380
With spiders I had friendship made,
And watched them in their sullen trade,
Had seen the mice by moonlight play,
And why should I feel less than they?
We were all inmates of one place,   385
And I, the monarch of each race,
Had power to kill—yet, strange to tell!
In quiet we had learned to dwell;
My very chains and I grew friends,
So much a long communion tends   390
To make us what we are:—even I
Regained my freedom with a sigh.
    [1816]

MANFRED:

A DRAMATIC POEM

DRAMATIS PERSONÆ

MANFRED
CHAMOIS HUNTER
ABBOT OF ST. MAURICE
MANUEL
HERMAN

WITCH OF THE ALPS
ARIMANES
NEMESIS
THE DESTINIES
SPIRITS, ETC.

The Scene of the Drama is amongst the Higher Alps—partly in the Castle of Manfred, and partly in the Mountains.

ACT I.

SCENE I. MANFRED *alone. Scene, a Gothic Gallery. Time, Midnight.*

MAN. The lamp must be replenished, but even then
It will not burn so long as I must watch:
My slumbers—if I slumber—are not sleep,
But a continuance of enduring thought,
Which then I can resist not: in my heart   5
There is a vigil, and these eyes but close
To look within; and yet I live, and bear
The aspect and the form of breathing men.
But Grief should be the Instructor of the wise;
Sorrow is Knowledge: they who know the most   10
Must mourn the deepest o'er the fatal truth,
The Tree of Knowledge is not that of Life.
Philosophy and science, and the springs
Of Wonder, and the wisdom of the World,
I have essayed, and in my mind there is   15
A power to make these subject to itself—
But they avail not: I have done men good,
And I have met with good even among men—
But this availed not: I have had my foes,
And none have baffled, many fallen before me—   20
But this availed not:—Good—or evil—life—
Powers, passions—all I see in other beings,
Have been to me as rain unto the sands,
Since that all-nameless hour. I have no dread,
And feel the curse to have no natural fear,   25
Nor fluttering throb, that beats with hopes or wishes,
Or lurking love of something on the earth.
Now to my task.—
                          Mysterious Agency!
Ye Spirits of the unbounded Universe!
Whom I have sought in darkness and in light—
Ye, who do compass earth about, and dwell   30
In subtler essence—ye, to whom the tops
Of mountains inaccessible are haunts,

And Earth's and Ocean's caves familiar things—
I call upon ye by the written charm   35
Which gives me power upon you—Rise! Appear!
                                        [A pause.]

They come not yet.—Now by the voice of him
Who is the first among you—by this sign,
Which makes you tremble—by the claims of him
Who is undying,—Rise! Appear!——Appear!   40
                                        [A pause.]

If it be so.—Spirits of Earth and Air,
Ye shall not so elude me! By a power,
Deeper than all yet urged, a tyrant-spell,
Which had its birthplace in a star condemned,
The burning wreck of a demolished world,   45
A wandering hell in the eternal Space;
By the strong curse which is upon my Soul,
The thought which is within me and around me,
I do compel ye to my will.—Appear!
[A star is seen at the darker end of the gallery: it is
     stationary; and a voice is heard singing.]

FIRST SPIRIT.

Mortal! to thy bidding bowed,   50
From my mansion in the cloud,
Which the breath of Twilight builds,
And the Summer's sunset gilds
With the azure and vermilion,
Which is mixed for my pavilion;   55
Though thy quest may be forbidden,
On a star-beam I have ridden,
To thine adjuration bowed:
Mortal—by thy wish avowed!

Voice of the SECOND SPIRIT.

Mont Blanc is the Monarch of mountains;   60
     They crowned him long ago
On a throne of rocks, in a robe of clouds,
     With a Diadem of snow.
Around his waist are forests braced,
     The Avalanche in his hand;   65

But ere it fall, that thundering ball
  Must pause for my command.
The Glacier's cold and restless mass
  Moves onward day by day;
But I am he who bids it pass,
  Or with its ice delay.   70
I am the Spirit of the place,
  Could make the mountain bow
And quiver to his caverned base—
  And what with me would'st *Thou?*   75

Voice of the THIRD SPIRIT.

In the blue depth of the waters,
  Where the wave hath no strife,
Where the Wind is a stranger,
  And the Sea-snake hath life,
Where the Mermaid is decking   80
  Her green hair with shells,
Like the storm on the surface
  Came the sound of thy spells;
O'er my calm Hall of Coral
  The deep Echo rolled—   85
To the Spirit of Ocean
  Thy wishes unfold!

FOURTH SPIRIT.

Where the slumbering Earthquake
  Lies pillowed on fire,
And the lakes of bitumen
  Rise boilingly higher;   90
Where the roots of the Andes
  Strike deep in the earth,
As their summits to heaven
  Shoot soaringly forth;
I have quitted my birthplace,   95
  Thy bidding to bide—
Thy spell hath subdued me,
  Thy will be my guide!

Fifth Spirit.

I am the Rider of the wind,   100
    The Stirrer of the storm;
The hurricane I left behind
    Is yet with lightning warm;
To speed to thee, o'er shore and sea   105
    I swept upon the blast:
The fleet I met sailed well—and yet
    'Twill sink ere night be past.

Sixth Spirit.

My dwelling is the shadow of the Night,
Why doth thy magic torture me with light?

Seventh Spirit.

The Star which rules thy destiny   110
Was ruled, ere earth began, by me:
It was a World as fresh and fair
As e'er revolved round Sun in air;
Its course was free and regular,
Space bosomed not a lovelier star.   115
The Hour arrived—and it became
A wandering mass of shapeless flame,
A pathless Comet, and a curse,
The menace of the Universe;
Still rolling on with innate force,   120
Without a sphere, without a course,
A bright deformity on high,
The monster of the upper sky!
And Thou! beneath its influence born—
Thou worm! whom I obey and scorn—   125
Forced by a Power (which is not thine,
And lent thee but to make thee mine)
For this brief moment to descend,
Where these weak Spirits round thee bend
And parley with a thing like thee—   130
What would'st thou, Child of Clay! with me?

The Seven Spirits.

Earth—ocean—air—night—mountains—winds—thy Star,
    Are at thy beck and bidding, Child of Clay!
Before thee at thy quest their Spirits are—
    What would'st thou with us, Son of mortals—say?   135
Man. Forgetfulness——
First Spirit.   Of what—of whom—and why?
    Man. Of that which is within me; read it there—
Ye know it—and I cannot utter it.
    Spirit. We can but give thee that which we possess:
Ask of us subjects, sovereignty, the power   140
O'er earth—the whole, or portion—or a sign
Which shall control the elements, whereof
We are the dominators,—each and all,
These shall be thine.
    Man.   Oblivion—self-oblivion!
Can ye not wring from out the hidden realms   145
Ye offer so profusely—what I ask?
    Spirit. It is not in our essence, in our skill;
But—thou may'st die.
    Man.   Will Death bestow it on me?
    Spirit. We are immortal, and do not forget;
We are eternal; and to us the past   150
Is, as the future, present. Art thou answered?
    Man. Ye mock me—but the Power which brought ye
    here
Hath made you mine. Slaves, scoff not at my will!
The Mind—the Spirit—the Promethean spark,
The lightning of my being, is as bright,   155
Pervading, and far darting as your own,
And shall not yield to yours, though cooped in clay!
Answer, or I will teach you what I am.
    Spirit. We answer—as we answered; our reply
Is even in thine own words.
    Man.   Why say ye so?   160
    Spirit. If, as thou say'st, thine essence be as ours,
We have replied in telling thee, the thing
Mortals call death hath nought to do with us.
    Man. I then have called ye from your realms in vain;
Ye cannot, or ye will not, aid me.   165

SPIRIT.   Say—
What we possess we offer; it is thine:
Bethink ere thou dismiss us; ask again;
Kingdom, and sway, and strength, and length of days—
    MAN. Accurséd! what have I to do with days?
They are too long already.—Hence—begone!   170
        SPIRIT. Yet pause: being here, our will would do thee
            service;
Bethink thee, is there then no other gift
Which we can make not worthless in thine eyes?
    MAN. No, none: yet stay—one moment, ere we part,
I would behold ye face to face. I hear   175
Your voices, sweet and melancholy sounds,
As Music on the waters; and I see
The steady aspect of a clear large Star;
But nothing more. Approach me as ye are,
Or one—or all—in your accustomed forms.   180
    SPIRIT. We have no forms, beyond the elements
Of which we are the mind and principle:
But choose a form—in that we will appear.
    MAN. I have no choice; there is no form on earth
Hideous or beautiful to me. Let him,   185
Who is most powerful of ye, take such aspect
As unto him may seem most fitting—Come!
    SEVENTH SPIRIT (*appearing in the shape of a beautiful*
                female figure) Behold!
    MAN.   Oh God! if it be thus, and *thou*
Art not a madness and a mockery,
I yet might be most happy. I will clasp thee,   190
And we again will be——
                            [*The figure vanishes.*]
                    My heart is crushed!
                            [MANFRED *falls senseless.*]

(*A voice is heard in the Incantation which follows.*)

        When the Moon is on the wave,
            And the glow-worm in the grass,
        And the meteor on the grave,
            And the wisp on the morass;   195
        When the falling stars are shooting,
        And the answered owls are hooting,

And the silent leaves are still
In the shadow of the hill,
Shall my soul be upon thine, 200
With a power and with a sign.

Though thy slumber may be deep,
Yet thy Spirit shall not sleep;
There are shades which will not vanish,
There are thoughts thou canst not banish; 205
By a Power to thee unknown,
Thou canst never be alone;
Thou art wrapt as with a shroud,
Thou art gathered in a cloud;
And for ever shalt thou dwell 210
In the spirit of this spell.

Though thou seest me not pass by,
Thou shalt feel me with thine eye
As a thing that, though unseen,
Must be near thee, and hath been; 215
And when in that secret dread
Thou hast turned around thy head,
Thou shalt marvel I am not
As thy shadow on the spot,
And the power which thou dost feel 220
Shall be what thou must conceal.

And a magic voice and verse
Hath baptized thee with a curse;
And a Spirit of the air
Hath begirt thee with a snare; 225
In the wind there is a voice
Shall forbid thee to rejoice;
And to thee shall Night deny
All the quiet of her sky;
And the day shall have a sun, 230
Which shall make thee wish it done.

From thy false tears I did distil
An essence which hath strength to kill;
From thy own heart I then did wring
The black blood in its blackest spring; 235

From thy own smile I snatched the snake,
For there it coiled as in a brake;
From thy own lip I drew the charm
Which gave all these their chiefest harm;
In proving every poison known,　　　　　　　　240
I found the strongest was thine own.

By the cold breast and serpent smile,
By thy unfathomed gulfs of guile,
By that most seeming virtuous eye,
By the shut soul's hypocrisy;　　　　　　　　245
By the perfection of thine art
Which passed for human thine own heart;
By thy delight in others' pain,
And by thy brotherhood of Cain,
I call upon thee! and compel　　　　　　　　250
Thyself to be thy proper Hell!

And on thy head I pour the vial
Which doth devote thee to this trial;
Nor to slumber, nor to die,
Shall be in thy destiny;　　　　　　　　255
Though thy death shall still seem near
To thy wish, but as a fear;
Lo! the spell now works around thee,
And the clankless chain hath bound thee;
O'er thy heart and brain together　　　　　　　　260
Hath the word been passed—now wither!

SCENE II. *The Mountain of the Jungfrau. Time,
Morning.* MANFRED *alone upon the cliffs.*

MAN. The spirits I have raised abandon me,
The spells which I have studied baffle me,
The remedy I recked of tortured me;
I lean no more on superhuman aid;
It hath no power upon the past, and for　　　　　5
The future, till the past be gulfed in darkness,
It is not of my search.—My Mother Earth!
And thou fresh-breaking Day, and you, ye Mountains,
Why are ye beautiful? I cannot love ye.

And thou, the bright Eye of the Universe, 10
That openest over all, and unto all
Art a delight—thou shin'st not on my heart.
And you, ye crags, upon whose extreme edge
I stand, and on the torrent's brink beneath
Behold the tall pines dwindled as to shrubs 15
In dizziness of distance; when a leap,
A stir, a motion, even a breath, would bring
My breast upon its rocky bosom's bed
To rest for ever—wherefore do I pause?
I feel the impulse—yet I do not plunge; 20
I see the peril—yet do not recede;
And my brain reels—and yet my foot is firm:
There is a power upon me which withholds,
And makes it my fatality to live,—
If it be life to wear within myself 25
This barrenness of Spirit, and to be
My own Soul's sepulchre, for I have ceased
To justify my deeds unto myself—
The last infirmity of evil. Aye,
Thou winged and cloud-cleaving minister, 30
                    [*An Eagle passes.*]
Whose happy flight is highest into heaven,
Well may'st thou swoop so near me—I should be
Thy prey, and gorge thine eaglets; thou art gone
Where the eye cannot follow thee; but thine
Yet pierces downward, onward, or above, 35
With a pervading vision.—Beautiful!
How beautiful is all this visible world!
How glorious in its action and itself!
But we, who name ourselves its sovereigns, we,
Half dust, half deity, alike unfit 40
To sink or soar, with our mixed essence make
A conflict of its elements, and breathe
The breath of degradation and of pride,
Contending with low wants and lofty will,
Till our Mortality predominates, 45
And men are—what they name not to themselves,
And trust not to each other. Hark! the note,
       [*The Shepherd's pipe in the distance is heard.*]
The natural music of the mountain reed—
For here the patriarchal days are not

A pastoral fable—pipes in the liberal air,   50
Mixed with the sweet bells of the sauntering herd;
My soul would drink those echoes. Oh, that I were
The viewless spirit of a lovely sound,
A living voice, a breathing harmony,   55
A bodiless enjoyment—born and dying
With the blest tone which made me!

      Enter from below a CHAMOIS HUNTER.

    CHAMOIS HUNTER.   Even so
This way the Chamois leapt: her nimble feet
Have baffled me; my gains to-day will scarce
Repay my break-neck travail.—What is here?   60
Who seems not of my trade, and yet hath reached
A height which none even of our mountaineers,
Save our best hunters, may attain: his garb
Is goodly, his mien manly, and his air
Proud as a free-born peasant's, at this distance: 65
I will approach him nearer.
    MAN. (*not perceiving the other*). To be thus—
Grey-haired with anguish, like these blasted pines,
Wrecks of a single winter, barkless, branchless,
A blighted trunk upon a curséd root,
Which but supplies a feeling to Decay—   70
And to be thus, eternally but thus,
Having been otherwise! Now furrowed o'er
With wrinkles, ploughed by moments, not by years
And hours, all tortured into ages—hours
Which I outlive!—Ye toppling crags of ice!   75
Ye Avalanches, whom a breath draws down
In mountainous o'erwhelming, come and crush me!
I hear ye momently above, beneath,
Crash with a frequent conflict; but ye pass,
And only fall on things that still would live;
On the young flourishing forest, or the hut   80
And hamlet of the harmless villager.
    C. HUN. The mists begin to rise from up the valley;
I'll warn him to descend, or he may chance
To lose at once his way and life together.
    MAN. The mists boil up around the glaciers; clouds   85
Rise curling fast beneath me, white and sulphury,

Like foam from the roused ocean of deep Hell,
Whose every wave breaks on a living shore,
Heaped with the damned like pebbles.—I am giddy.
   C. Hun. I must approach him cautiously; if near,   90
A sudden step will startle him, and he
Seems tottering already.
   Man.   Mountains have fallen,
Leaving a gap in the clouds, and with the shock
Rocking their Alpine brethren; filling up
The ripe green valleys with Destruction's splinters;   95
Damming the rivers with a sudden dash,
Which crushed the waters into mist, and made
Their fountains find another channel—thus,
Thus, in its old age, did Mount Rosenberg—
Why stood I not beneath it?
   C. Hun.   Friend! have a care,   100
Your next step may be fatal!—for the love
Of Him who made you, stand not on that brink!
   Man. (*not hearing him*). Such would have been for me
       a fitting tomb;
My bones had then been quiet in their depth;
They had not then been strewn upon the rocks   105
For the wind's pastime—as thus—thus they shall be—
In this one plunge.—Farewell, ye opening Heavens!
Look not upon me thus reproachfully—
You were not meant for me—Earth! take these atoms!
     [As Manfred *is in act to spring from the cliff, the*
           Chamois Hunter *seizes and retains him with a*
           sudden grasp.]
   C. Hun. Hold, madman!—though aweary of thy life, 110
Stain not our pure vales with thy guilty blood;
Away with me——I will not quit my hold.
   Man. I am most sick at heart—nay, grasp me not—
I am all feebleness—the mountains whirl
Spinning around me——I grow blind——What art thou? 115
   C. Hun. I'll answer that anon.—Away with me——
The clouds grow thicker——there—now lean on me—
Place your foot here—here, take this staff, and cling
A moment to that shrub—now give me your hand,
And hold fast by my girdle—softly—well—   120
The Chalet will be gained within an hour:
Come on, we'll quickly find a surer footing,

And something like a pathway, which the torrent
Hath washed since winter.—Come, 'tis bravely done—
You should have been a hunter.—Follow me.   125
   [As they descend the rocks with difficulty, the scene
   closes.]

ACT II.

Scene I. *A Cottage among the Bernese Alps.* Manfred
and the Chamois Hunter.

C. Hun. No—no—yet pause—thou must not yet go
   forth:
Thy mind and body are alike unfit
To trust each other, for some hours, at least;
When thou art better, I will be thy guide—
But whither?
   Man.   It imports not: I do know   5
My route full well, and need no further guidance.
   C. Hun. Thy garb and gait bespeak thee of high
   lineage—
One of the many chiefs, whose castled crags
Look o'er the lower valleys—which of these
May call thee lord? I only know their portals;   10
My way of life leads me but rarely down
To bask by the huge hearths of those old halls,
Carousing with the vassals; but the paths,
Which step from out our mountains to their doors,
I know from childhood—which of these is thine?   15
   Man. No matter.
   C. Hun.   Well, Sir, pardon me the question,
And be of better cheer. Come, taste my wine;
'Tis of an ancient vintage; many a day
'T has thawed my veins among our glaciers, now
Let it do thus for thine—Come, pledge me fairly!   20
   Man. Away, away! there's blood upon the brim!
Will it then never—never sink in the earth?
   C. Hun. What dost thou mean? thy senses wander
   from thee.

MAN. I say 'tis blood—my blood! the pure warm
    stream
Which ran in the veins of my fathers, and in ours   25
When we were in our youth, and had one heart,
And loved each other as we should not love,
And this was shed: but still it rises up,
Colouring the clouds, that shut me out from Heaven,
Where thou art not—and I shall never be.   30
    C. HUN. Man of strange words, and some half-mad-
    dening sin,
Which makes thee people vacancy, whate'er
Thy dread and sufferance be, there's comfort yet—
The aid of holy men, and heavenly patience——
    MAN. Patience—and patience! Hence—that word was
    made   35
For brutes of burthen, not for birds of prey!
Preach it to mortals of a dust like thine,—
I am not of thine order.
    C. HUN.   Thanks to Heaven!
I would not be of thine for the free fame
Of William Tell; but whatsoe'er thine ill,   40
It must be borne, and these wild starts are useless.
    MAN. Do I not bear it?—Look on me—I live.
    C. HUN. This is convulsion, and no healthful life.
    MAN. I tell thee, man! I have lived many years,
Many long years, but they are nothing now   45
To those which I must number: ages—ages—
Space and eternity—and consciousness,
With the fierce thirst of death—and still unslaked!
    C. HUN. Why on thy brow the seal of middle age
Hath scarce been set; I am thine elder far.   50
    MAN. Think'st thou existence doth depend on time?
It doth; but actions are our epochs: mine
Have made my days and nights imperishable,
Endless, and all alike, as sands on the shore,
Innumerable atoms; and one desert,   55
Barren and cold, on which the wild waves break,
But nothing rests, save carcasses and wrecks,
Rocks, and the salt-surf weeds of bitterness.
    C. HUN. Alas! he's mad—but yet I must not leave him.
    MAN. I would I were—for then the things I see   60
Would be but a distempered dream.

C. Hun.   What is it
That thou dost see, or think thou look'st upon?
    Man. Myself, and thee—a peasant of the Alps—
Thy humble virtues, hospitable home,
And spirit patient, pious, proud, and free;   65
Thy self-respect, grafted on innocent thoughts;
Thy days of health, and nights of sleep; thy toils,
By danger dignified, yet guiltless; hopes
Of cheerful old age and a quiet grave,
With cross and garland over its green turf,   70
And thy grandchildren's love for epitaph!
This do I see—and then I look within—
It matters not—my Soul was scorched already!
    C. Hun. And would'st thou then exchange thy lot for
        mine?
    Man. No, friend! I would not wrong thee, nor ex-   75
        change
My lot with living being: I can bear—
However wretchedly, 'tis still to bear—
In life what others could not brook to dream,
But perish in their slumber.
    C. Hun.   And with this—
This cautious feeling for another's pain,   80
Canst thou be black with evil?—say not so.
Can one of gentle thoughts have wreaked revenge
Upon his enemies?
    Man.   Oh! no, no, no!
My injuries came down on those who loved me—
On those whom I best loved: I never quelled   85
An enemy, save in my just defence—
But my embrace was fatal.
    C. Hun.   Heaven give thee rest
And Penitence restore thee to thyself;
My prayers shall be for thee.
    Man.   I need them not,
But can endure thy pity. I depart—   90
'Tis time—farewell!—Here's gold, and thanks for thee—
No words—it is thy due.—Follow me not—
I know my path—the mountain peril's past:
And once again I charge thee, follow not!
                                        [Exit Manfred.]

SCENE II. *A lower Valley in the Alps. A Cataract.*

Enter MANFRED.

It is not noon—the Sunbow's rays still arch
The torrent with the many hues of heaven,
And roll the sheeted silver's waving column
O'er the crag's headlong perpendicular,
And fling its lines of foaming light along,   5
And to and fro, like the pale courser's tail,
The Giant steed, to be bestrode by Death,
As told in the Apocalypse. No eyes
But mine now drink this sight of loveliness;
I should be sole in this sweet solitude,   10
And with the Spirit of the place divide
The homage of these waters.—I will call her.
   [MANFRED *takes some of the water into the palm of*
       his hand and flings it into the air, muttering the
       adjuration. After a pause, the WITCH OF THE
       ALPS *rises beneath the arch of the sunbow of the*
       torrent.]
Beautiful Spirit! with thy hair of light,
And dazzling eyes of glory, in whose form
The charms of Earth's least mortal daughters grow   15
To an unearthly stature, in an essence
Of purer elements; while the hues of youth,—
Carnationed like a sleeping Infant's cheek,
Rocked by the beating of her mother's heart,
Or the rose tints, which Summer's twilight leaves   20
Upon the lofty Glacier's virgin snow,
The blush of earth embracing with her Heaven,—
Tinge thy celestial aspect, and make tame
The beauties of the Sunbow which bends o'er thee.
Beautiful Spirit! in thy calm clear brow,   25
Wherein is glassed serenity of Soul,
Which of itself shows immortality,
I read that thou wilt pardon to a Son
Of Earth, whom the abstruser powers permit
At times to commune with them—if that he   30
Avail him of his spells—to call thee thus,

And gaze on thee a moment.
    WITCH.   Son of Earth!
I know thee, and the Powers which give thee power!
I know thee for a man of many thoughts,
And deeds of good and ill, extreme in both,   35
Fatal and fated in thy sufferings.
I have expected this—what would'st thou with me?
    MAN. To look upon thy beauty—nothing further.
The face of the earth hath maddened me, and I
Take refuge in her mysteries, and pierce   40
To the abodes of those who govern her—
But they can nothing aid me. I have sought
From them what they could not bestow, and now
I search no further.
    WITCH.   What could be the quest
Which is not in the power of the most powerful,   45
The rulers of the invisible?
    MAN.   A boon;—
But why should I repeat it? 'twere in vain.
    WITCH. I know not that; let thy lips utter it.
    MAN. Well, though it torture me, 'tis but the same;
My pang shall find a voice. From my youth upwards   50
My Spirit walked not with the souls of men,
Nor looked upon the earth with human eyes;
The thirst of their ambition was not mine,
The aim of their existence was not mine;
My joys—my griefs—my passions—and my powers,   55
Made me a stranger; though I wore the form,
I had no sympathy with breathing flesh,
Nor midst the Creatures of Clay that girded me
Was there but One who——but of her anon.
I said with men, and with the thoughts of men,   60
I held but slight communion; but instead,
My joy was in the wilderness,—to breathe
The difficult air of the iced mountain's top,
Where the birds dare not build—nor insect's wing
Flit o'er the herbless granite; or to plunge   65
Into the torrent, and to roll along
On the swift whirl of the new-breaking wave
Of river-stream, or Ocean, in their flow.
In these my early strength exulted; or
To follow through the night the moving moon,   70

The stars and their development; or catch
The dazzling lightnings till my eyes grew dim;
Or to look, list'ning, on the scattered leaves,
While Autumn winds were at their evening song.
These were my pastimes, and to be alone;   75
For if the beings, of whom I was one,—
Hating to be so,—crossed me in my path,
I felt myself degraded back to them,
And was all clay again. And then I dived,
In my lone wanderings, to the caves of Death,   80
Searching its cause in its effect; and drew
From withered bones, and skulls, and heaped up dust,
Conclusions most forbidden. Then I passed
The nights of years in sciences untaught,
Save in the old-time; and with time and toil,   85
And terrible ordeal, and such penance
As in itself hath power upon the air,
And spirits that do compass air and earth,
Space, and the peopled Infinite, I made
Mine eyes familiar with Eternity,   90
Such as, before me, did the Magi, and
He who from out their fountain-dwellings raised
Eros and Anteros, at Gadara,
As I do thee;—and with my knowledge grew
The thirst of knowledge, and the power and joy   95
Of this most bright intelligence, until——
   Witch. Proceed.
   Man.   Oh! I but thus prolonged my words,
Boasting these idle attributes, because
As I approach the core of my heart's grief—
But—to my task. I have not named to thee   100
Father or mother, mistress, friend, or being,
With whom I wore the chain of human ties;
If I had such, they seemed not such to me—
Yet there was One——
   Witch.   Spare not thyself—proceed.
   Man. She was like me in lineaments—her eyes—   105
Her hair—her features—all, to the very tone
Even of her voice, they said were like to mine;
But softened all, and tempered into beauty:
She had the same lone thoughts and wanderings,
The quest of hidden knowledge, and a mind   110

To comprehend the Universe; nor these
Alone, but with them gentler powers than mine,
Pity, and smiles, and tears—which I had not;
And tenderness—but that I had for her;
Humility—and that I never had.   115
Her faults were mine—her virtues were her own—
I loved her, and destroyed her!
    WITCH.   With thy hand?
    MAN. Not with my hand, but heart, which broke her
        heart;
It gazed on mine, and withered. I have shed
Blood, but not hers—and yet her blood was shed;   120
I saw—and could not stanch it.
    WITCH.   And for this—
A being of the race thou dost despise—
The order, which thine own would rise above,
Mingling with us and ours,—thou dost forego
The gifts of our great knowledge, and shrink'st back   125
To recreant mortality—Away!
    MAN. Daughter of Air! I tell thee, since that hour—
But words are breath—look on me in my sleep,
Or watch my watchings—Come and sit by me!
My solitude is solitude no more,   130
But peopled with the Furies;—I have gnashed
My teeth in darkness till returning morn,
Then cursed myself till sunset;—I have prayed
For madness as a blessing—'tis denied me.
I have affronted Death—but in the war   135
Of elements the waters shrunk from me,
And fatal things passed harmless; the cold hand
Of an all-pitiless Demon held me back,
Back by a single hair, which would not break.
In Fantasy, Imagination, all   140
The affluence of my soul—which one day was
A Crœsus in creation—I plunged deep,
But, like an ebbing wave, it dashed me back
Into the gulf of my unfathomed thought.
I plunged amidst Mankind—Forgetfulness   145
I sought in all, save where 'tis to be found—
And that I have to learn—my Sciences,
My long pursued and superhuman art,
Is mortal here: I dwell in my despair—

And live—and live for ever.
    WITCH.   It may be   150
That I can aid thee.
    MAN.   To do this thy power
Must wake the dead, or lay me low with them.
Do so—in any shape—in any hour—
With any torture—so it be the last.
    WITCH. That is not in my province; but if thou   155
Wilt swear obedience to my will, and do
My bidding, it may help thee to thy wishes.
    MAN. I will not swear—Obey! and whom? the Spirits
Whose presence I command, and be the slave
Of those who served me—Never!
    WITCH.   Is this all?   160
Hast thou no gentler answer?—Yet bethink thee,
And pause ere thou rejectest.
    MAN.   I have said it.
    WITCH. Enough! I may retire then—say!
    MAN.   Retire!
        [The WITCH disappears.]
    MAN (alone). We are the fools of Time and Terror;
    Days
Steal on us, and steal from us; yet we live,   165
Loathing our life, and dreading still to die.
In all the days of this detested yoke—
This vital weight upon the struggling heart,
Which sinks with sorrow, or beats quick with pain,
Or joy that ends in agony or faintness—   170
In all the days of past and future—for
In life there is no present—we can number
How few—how less than few—wherein the soul
Forbears to pant for death, and yet draws back
As from a stream in winter, though the chill   175
Be but a moment's. I have one resource
Still in my science—I can call the dead,
And ask them what it is we dread to be:
The sternest answer can but be the Grave,
And that is nothing: if they answer not——   180
The buried Prophet answered to the Hag
Of Endor; and the Spartan Monarch drew
From the Byzantine maid's unsleeping spirit
An answer and his destiny—he slew

That which he loved, unknowing what he slew,   185
And died unpardoned—though he called in aid
The Phyxian Jove, and in Phigalia roused
The Arcadian Evocators to compel
The indignant shadow to depose her wrath,
Or fix her term of vengeance—she replied   190
In words of dubious import, but fulfilled.
If I had never lived, that which I love
Had still been living; had I never loved,
That which I love would still be beautiful,
Happy and giving happiness. What is she?   195
What is she now?—a sufferer for my sins—
A thing I dare not think upon—or nothing.
Within few hours I shall not call in vain—
Yet in this hour I dread the thing I dare:
Until this hour I never shrunk to gaze   200
On spirit, good or evil—now I tremble,
And feel a strange cold thaw upon my heart.
But I can act even what I most abhor,
And champion human fears.—The night approaches.
                                        [*Exit.*]

SCENE III. *The summit of the Jungfrau Mountain.*

Enter FIRST DESTINY.

The Moon is rising broad, and round, and bright;
And here on snows, where never human foot
Of common mortal trod, we nightly tread,
And leave no traces: o'er the savage sea,
The glassy ocean of the mountain ice,   5
We skim its rugged breakers, which put on
The aspect of a tumbling tempest's foam,
Frozen in a moment—a dead Whirlpool's image:
And this most steep fantastic pinnacle,
The fretwork of some earthquake—where the clouds   10
Pause to repose themselves in passing by—
Is sacred to our revels, or our vigils;
Here do I wait my sisters, on our way
To the Hall of Arimanes—for to-night
Is our great festival—'tis strange they come not.   15

A Voice without, singing.

The Captive Usurper,
　Hurled down from the throne,
Lay buried in torpor,
　Forgotten and lone;
I broke through his slumbers,   20
　I shivered his chain,
I leagued him with numbers—
　He's Tyrant again!
With the blood of a million he'll answer my care,
With a Nation's destruction—his flight and despair!   25

Second Voice, without.

The Ship sailed on, the Ship sailed fast,
But I left not a sail, and I left not a mast;
There is not a plank of the hull or the deck,
And there is not a wretch to lament o'er his wreck;
Save one, whom I held, as he swam, by the hair,   30
And he was a subject well worthy my care;
A traitor on land, and a pirate at sea—
But I saved him to wreak further havoc for me!

FIRST DESTINY, *answering.*

The City lies sleeping;
　The morn, to deplore it,   35
May dawn on it weeping:
　Sullenly, slowly,
The black plague flew o'er it—
　Thousands lie lowly;
Tens of thousands shall perish;   40
　The living shall fly from
The sick they should cherish;
　But nothing can vanquish
The touch that they die from.
　Sorrow and anguish,   45
And evil and dread,
　Envelope a nation;
The blest are the dead,

Who see not the sight
 Of their own desolation;   **50**
This work of a night—
This wreck of a realm—this deed of my doing—
For ages I've done, and shall still be renewing!

Enter the Second *and* Third Destinies.

The Three.

Our hands contain the hearts of men,
 Our footsteps are their graves;   **55**
We only give to take again
 The Spirits of our slaves!

First Des. Welcome!—Where's Nemesis?
Second Des.   At some
  great work;
But what I know not, for my hands were full.
 Third Des. Behold she cometh.

Enter Nemesis.

 First Des.   Say, where hast thou been? **60**
My Sisters and thyself are slow to-night.
 Nem. I was detained repairing shattered thrones—
Marrying fools, restoring dynasties—
Avenging men upon their enemies,
And making them repent their own revenge;   **65**
Goading the wise to madness; from the dull
Shaping out oracles to rule the world
Afresh—for they were waxing out of date,
And mortals dared to ponder for themselves,
To weigh kings in the balance—and to speak   **70**
Of Freedom, the forbidden fruit.—Away!
We have outstayed the hour—mount we our clouds!
            [Exeunt.]

SCENE IV. *The Hall of Arimanes.* ARIMANES *on his Throne, a Globe of Fire, surrounded by the* SPIRITS.

Hymn of the SPIRITS.

Hail to our Master!—Prince of Earth and Air!
  Who walks the clouds and waters—in his hand
The sceptre of the Elements, which tear
  Themselves to chaos at his high command!
He breatheth—and a tempest shakes the sea;   5
  He speaketh—and the clouds reply in thunder;
He gazeth—from his glance the sunbeams flee;
  He moveth—Earthquakes rend the world asunder.
Beneath his footsteps the Volcanoes rise;
  His shadow is the Pestilence: his path   10
The comets herald through the crackling skies;
  And Planets turn to ashes at his wrath.
To him War offers daily sacrifice;
  To him Death pays his tribute; Life is his,
With all its Infinite of agonies—   15
  And his the Spirit of whatever is!

Enter the DESTINIES *and* NEMESIS.

FIRST DES. Glory to Arimanes! on the earth
His power increaseth—both my sisters did
His bidding, nor did I neglect my duty!
  SECOND DES. Glory to Arimanes! we who bow   20
The necks of men, bow down before his throne!
  THIRD DES. Glory to Arimanes! we await
His nod!
  NEM. Sovereign of Sovereigns; we are thine,
And all that liveth, more or less, is ours,
And most things wholly so; still to increase   25
Our power, increasing thine, demands our care,
And we are vigilant. Thy late commands
Have been fulfilled to the utmost.

Enter MANFRED.

A Spirit.   What is here?
A mortal!—Thou most rash and fatal wretch,
Bow down and worship!
    Second Spirit.   I do know the man—   30
A Magian of great power, and fearful skill!
    Third Spirit. Bow down and worship, slave!—What
      know'st thou not
Thine and our Sovereign?—Tremble, and obey!
    All the Spirits. Prostrate thyself, and thy condemnéd
      clay,
Child of the Earth! or dread the worst.
    Man.   I know it;   35
And yet ye see I kneel not.
    Fourth Spirit.   'Twill bè taught thee.
    Man. 'Tis taught already;—many a night on the earth,
On the bare ground, have I bowed down my face,
And strewed my head with ashes; I have known
The fulness of humiliation—for   40
I sunk before my vain despair, and knelt
To my own desolation.
    Fifth Spirit.   Dost thou dare
Refuse to Arimanes on his throne
What the whole earth accords, beholding not
The terror of his Glory?—Crouch! I say.   45
    Man. Bid *him* bow down to that which is above him,
The overruling Infinite—the Maker
Who made him not for worship—let him kneel,
And we will kneel together.
    The Spirits.   Crush the worm!
Tear him in pieces!—
    First Des.   Hence! Avaunt!—he's mine.   50
Prince of the Powers Invisible! This man
Is of no common order, as his port
And presence here denote: his sufferings
Have been of an immortal nature—like
Our own; his knowledge, and his powers and will, 55
As far as is compatible with clay,
Which clogs the ethereal essence, have been such
As clay hath seldom borne; his aspirations
Have been beyond the dwellers of the earth,
And they have only taught him what we know—   60
That knowledge is not happiness, and science

But an exchange of ignorance for that
Which is another kind of ignorance.
This is not all—the passions, attributes
Of Earth and Heaven, from which no power, nor being,   65
Nor breath from the worm upwards is exempt,
Have pierced his heart; and in their consequence
Made him a thing—which—I who pity not,
Yet pardon those who pity. He is mine—
And thine it may be; be it so, or not—   70
No other Spirit in this region hath
A soul like his—or power upon his soul.
   Nem. What doth he here then?
   First Des.   Let *him* answer that.
   Man. Ye know what I have known; and without
     power
I could not be amongst ye: but there are   75
Powers deeper still beyond—I come in quest
Of such, to answer unto what I seek.
   Nem. What would'st thou?
   Man.   Thou canst not reply to me.
Call up the dead—my question is for them.
   Nem. Great Arimanes, doth thy will avouch   80
The wishes of this mortal?
   Ari.   Yea.
   Nem.   Whom wouldst thou
Uncharnel?
   Man.   One without a tomb—call up
Astarte.

NEMESIS.

Shadow! or Spirit!
   Whatever thou art,   85
Which still doth inherit
   The whole or a part
Of the form of thy birth,
   Of the mould of thy clay,
Which returned to the earth,   90
   Re-appear to the day!
Bear what thou borest,
   The heart and the form,

And the aspect thou worest
Redeem from the worm.   95
Appear!—Appear!—Appear!
Who sent thee there requires thee here!
[*The Phantom of* ASTARTE *rises and stands in the
midst.*]
MAN. Can this be death? there's bloom upon her
cheek;
But now I see it is no living hue,
But a strange hectic—like the unnatural red   100
Which Autumn plants upon the perished leaf.
It is the same! Oh, God! that I should dread
To look upon the same—Astarte!—No,
I cannot speak to her—but bid her speak—
Forgive me or condemn me.   105

NEMESIS.

By the Power which hath broken
The grave which enthralled thee,
Speak to him who hath spoken,
Or those who have called thee!
MAN.   She is silent,
And in that silence I am more than answered.   110
NEM. My power extends no further. Prince of Air!
It rests with thee alone—command her voice.
ARI. Spirit—obey this sceptre!
NEM.   Silent still!
She is not of our order, but belongs
To the other powers. Mortal! thy quest is vain,   115
And we are baffled also.
MAN.   Hear me, hear me—
Astarte! my belovéd! speak to me:
I have so much endured—so much endure—
Look on me! the grave hath not changed thee more
Than I am changed for thee. Thou lovedst me   120
Too much, as I loved thee: we were not made
To torture thus each other—though it were
The deadliest sin to love as we have loved.
Say that thou loath'st me not—that I do bear
This punishment for both—that thou wilt be   125
One of the blesséd—and that I shall die;

For hitherto all hateful things conspire
To bind me in existence—in a life
Which makes me shrink from Immortality—
A future like the past. I cannot rest. 130
I know not what I ask, nor what I seek:
I feel but what thou art, and what I am;
And I would hear yet once before I perish
The voice which was my music—Speak to me!
For I have called on thee in the still night, 135
Startled the slumbering birds from the hushed boughs,
And woke the mountain wolves, and made the caves
Acquainted with thy vainly echoed name,
Which answered me—many things answered me—
Spirits and men—but thou wert silent all. 140
Yet speak to me! I have outwatched the stars,
And gazed o'er heaven in vain in search of thee.
Speak to me! I have wandered o'er the earth,
And never found thy likeness—Speak to me!
Look on the fiends around—they feel for me: 145
I fear them not, and feel for thee alone.
Speak to me! though it be in wrath;—but say—
I reck not what—but let me hear thee once—
This once—once more!
    PHANTOM OF ASTARTE. Manfred!
    MAN.   Say on, say on—
I live but in the sound—it is thy voice! 150
    PHAN. Manfred! To-morrow ends thine earthly ills.
Farewell!
    MAN. Yet one word more—am I forgiven?
    PHAN. Farewell!
    MAN.   Say, shall we meet again?
    PHAN.   Farewell!
    MAN. One word for mercy! Say thou lovest me.
    PHAN. Manfred!
              [*The Spirit of* ASTARTE *disappears.*]
    NEM.   She's gone, and will not be recalled: 155
Her words will be fulfilled. Return to the earth.
    A SPIRIT. He is convulsed—This is to be a mortal,
And seek the things beyond mortality.
    ANOTHER SPIRIT. Yet, see, he mastereth himself, and
      makes
His torture tributary to his will. 160

Had he been one of us, he would have made
An awful Spirit.
    NEM.   Hast thou further question
Of our great Sovereign, or his worshippers?
    MAN. None.   **165**
    NEM.   Then for a time farewell.
    MAN. We meet then! Where? On the earth?—
Even as thou wilt: and for the grace accorded
I now depart a debtor. Fare ye well!
                               [*Exit* MANFRED.]
           (*Scene closes.*)

ACT III.

SCENE I. *A Hall in the Castle of Manfred.*

MANFRED *and* HERMAN.

    MAN. What is the hour?
    HER.   It wants but one till sunset,
And promises a lovely twilight.
    MAN.   Say,
Are all things so disposed of in the tower
As I directed?
    HER.   All, my Lord, are ready:
Here is the key and casket.
    MAN.   It is well:
Thou mayst retire.   **5**
                             [*Exit* HERMAN.]
    MAN (*alone*).   There is a calm upon me—
Inexplicable stillness! which till now
Did not belong to what I knew of life.
If that I did not know Philosophy
To be of all our vanities the motliest,   **10**
The merest word that ever fooled the ear
From out the schoolman's jargon, I should deem
The golden secret, the sought "Kalon," found,
And seated in my soul. It will not last,
But it is well to have known it, though but once: **15**

It hath enlarged my thoughts with a new sense,
And I within my tablets would note down
That there is such a feeling. Who is there?

Re-enter HERMAN.

HER. My Lord, the Abbot of St. Maurice craves
To greet your presence.

Enter the ABBOT OF ST. MAURICE.

ABBOT.   Peace be with Count Manfred!   20
MAN. Thanks, holy father! welcome to these walls;
Thy presence honours them, and blesseth those
Who dwell within them.
ABBOT.   Would it were so, Count!—
But I would fain confer with thee alone.
MAN. Herman, retire.—What would my reverend
    guest?   25
ABBOT. Thus, without prelude:—Age and zeal—my
    office—
And good intent must plead my privilege;
Our near, though not acquainted neighbourhood,
May also be my herald. Rumours strange,
And of unholy nature, are abroad,   30
And busy with thy name—a noble name
For centuries: may he who bears it now
Transmit it unimpaired!
MAN.   Proceed,—I listen.
ABBOT. 'Tis said thou holdest converse with the things
Which are forbidden to the search of man;   35
That with the dwellers of the dark abodes,
The many evil and unheavenly spirits
Which walk the valley of the Shade of Death,
Thou communest. I know that with mankind,
Thy fellows in creation, thou dost rarely   40
Exchange thy thoughts, and that thy solitude
Is as an Anchorite's—were it but holy.
MAN. And what are they who do avouch these things?
ABBOT. My pious brethren—the scaréd peasantry—
Even thy own vassals—who do look on thee   45
With most unquiet eyes. Thy life's in peril!
MAN. Take it.
ABBOT.   I come to save, and not destroy:

I would not pry into thy secret soul;
But if these things be sooth, there still is time
For penitence and pity: reconcile thee   50
With the true church, and through the church to Heaven.
    MAN. I hear thee. This is my reply—whate'er
I may have been, or am, doth rest between
Heaven and myself—I shall not choose a mortal
To be my mediator—Have I sinned   55
Against your ordinances? prove and punish!
    ABBOT. My son! I did not speak of punishment,
But penitence and pardon;—with thyself
The choice of such remains—and for the last,
Our institutions and our strong belief   60
Have given me power to smooth the path from sin
To higher hope and better thoughts; the first
I leave to Heaven,—"Vengeance is mine alone!"
So saith the Lord, and with all humbleness
His servant echoes back the awful word.   65
    MAN. Old man! there is no power in holy men,
Nor charm in prayer, nor purifying form
Of penitence, nor outward look, nor fast,
Nor agony—nor, greater than all these,
The innate tortures of that deep Despair,   70
Which is Remorse without the fear of Hell,
But all in all sufficient to itself
Would make a hell of Heaven—can exorcise
From out the unbounded spirit the quick sense
Of its own sins—wrongs—sufferance—and revenge   75
Upon itself; there is no future pang
Can deal that justice on the self-condemned
He deals on his own soul.
    ABBOT.   All this is well;
For this will pass away, and be succeeded
By an auspicious hope, which shall look up   80
With calm assurance to that blessed place,
Which all who seek may win, whatever be
Their earthly errors, so they be atoned:
And the commencement of atonement is
The sense of its necessity. Say on—   85
And all our church can teach thee shall be taught;
And all we can absolve thee shall be pardoned.
    MAN. When Rome's sixth Emperor was near his last,

The victim of a self-inflicted wound,
To shun the torments of a public death   90
From senates once his slaves, a certain soldier,
With show of loyal pity, would have stanched
The gushing throat with his officious robe;
The dying Roman thrust him back, and said—
Some empire still in his expiring glance—   95
"It is too late—is this fidelity?"
    ABBOT. And what of this?
    MAN.   I answer with the Roman—
"It is too late!"
    ABBOT.   It never can be so,
To reconcile thyself with thy own soul,
And thy own soul with Heaven. Hast thou no hope?   100
'Tis strange—even those who do despair above,
Yet shape themselves some fantasy on earth,
To which frail twig they cling, like drowning men.
    MAN. Aye—father! I have had those early visions,
And noble aspirations in my youth,   105
To make my own the mind of other men,
The enlightener of nations; and to rise
I knew not whither—it might be to fall;
But fall, even as the mountain-cataract,
Which having leapt from its more dazzling height,   110
Even in the foaming strength of its abyss,
(Which casts up misty columns that become
Clouds raining from the re-ascended skies,)
Lies low but mighty still.—But this is past,
My thoughts mistook themselves.
    ABBOT.   And wherefore so?   115
    MAN. I could not tame my nature down; for he
Must serve who fain would sway; and soothe, and sue,
And watch all time, and pry into all place,
And be a living Lie, who would become
A mighty thing amongst the mean—and such   120
The mass are; I disdained to mingle with
A herd, though to be leader—and of wolves.
The lion is alone, and so am I.
    ABBOT. And why not live and act with other men?
    MAN. Because my nature was averse from life;   125
And yet not cruel; for I would not make,
But find a desolation. Like the Wind,

The red-hot breath of the most lone Simoom,
Which dwells but in the desert, and sweeps o'er
The barren sands which bear no shrubs to blast,   130
And revels o'er their wild and arid waves,
And seeketh not, so that it is not sought,
But being met is deadly,—such hath been
The course of my existence; but there came
Things in my path which are no more.
  ABBOT.   Alas!   135
I 'gin to fear that thou art past all aid
From me and from my calling; yet so young,
I still would——
  MAN.   Look on me! there is an order
Of mortals on the earth, who do become
Old in their youth, and die ere middle age,   140
Without the violence of warlike death;
Some perishing of pleasure—some of study—
Some worn with toil, some of mere weariness,—
Some of disease—and some insanity—
And some of withered, or of broken hearts;   145
For this last is a malady which slays
More than are numbered in the lists of Fate,
Taking all shapes, and bearing many names.
Look upon me! for even of all these things
Have I partaken; and of all these things,   150
One were enough; then wonder not that I
Am what I am, but that I ever was,
Or having been, that I am still on earth.
  ABBOT. Yet, hear me still——
  MAN.   Old man! I do respect
Thine order, and revere thine years; I deem   155
Thy purpose pious, but it is in vain:
Think me not churlish; I would spare thyself,
Far more than me, in shunning at this time
All further colloquy—and so—farewell.
             [Exit MANFRED.]

  ABBOT. This should have been a noble creature: he   160
Hath all the energy which would have made
A goodly frame of glorious elements,
Had they been wisely mingled; as it is,
It is an awful chaos—Light and Darkness—
And mind and dust—and passions and pure thoughts   165

Mixed, and contending without end or order,—
All dormant or destructive. He will perish—
And yet he must not—I will try once more,
For such are worth redemption; and my duty
Is to dare all things for a righteous end.   170
I'll follow him—but cautiously, though surely.

                                        [*Exit* ABBOT.]

          SCENE II. *Another Chamber.*

          MANFRED *and* HERMAN.

    HER. My Lord, you bade me wait on you at sunset:
He sinks behind the mountain.
    MAN.   Doth he so?
I will look on him.
          [MANFRED *advances to the Window of the Hall.*]
                    Glorious Orb! the idol
Of early nature, and the vigorous race
Of undiseased mankind, the giant sons   5
Of the embrace of Angels, with a sex
More beautiful than they, which did draw down
The erring Spirits who can ne'er return.—
Most glorious Orb! that wert a worship, ere
The mystery of thy making was revealed!   10
Thou earliest minister of the Almighty,
Which gladdened, on their mountain tops, the hearts
Of the Chaldean shepherds, till they poured
Themselves in orisons! Thou material God!
And representative of the Unknown—   15
Who chose thee for his shadow! Thou chief Star!
Centre of many stars! which mak'st our earth
Endurable, and temperest the hues
And hearts of all who walk within thy rays!
Sire of the seasons! Monarch of the climes,   20
And those who dwell in them! for near or far,
Our inborn spirits have a tint of thee
Even as our outward aspects;—thou dost rise,
And shine, and set in glory. Fare thee well!
I ne'er shall see thee more. As my first glance   25
Of love and wonder was for thee, then take

My latest look: thou wilt not beam on one
To whom the gifts of life and warmth have been
Of a more fatal nature. He is gone—
I follow.   [Exit MANFRED.]

SCENE III. *The Mountains. The Castle of Manfred at
some distance. A Terrace before a Tower. Time, Twilight.*

HERMAN, MANUEL, *and other dependants of* MANFRED.

HER. 'Tis strange enough! night after night, for years,
He hath pursued long vigils in this tower,
Without a witness. I have been within it,—
So have we all been oft-times; but from it,
Or its contents, it were impossible   5
To draw conclusions absolute, of aught
His studies tend to. To be sure, there is
One chamber where none enter: I would give
The fee of what I have to come these three years,
To pore upon its mysteries.
    MANUEL.   'Twere dangerous;   10
Content thyself with what thou know'st already.
    HER. Ah! Manuel! thou art elderly and wise,
And couldst say much; thou hast dwelt within the castle—
How many years is't?
    MANUEL.   Ere Count Manfred's birth,
I served his father, whom he nought resembles.   15
    HER. There be more sons in like predicament!
But wherein do they differ?
    MANUEL.   I speak not
Of features or of form, but mind and habits;
Count Sigismund was proud, but gay and free,—
A warrior and a reveller; he dwelt not   20
With books and solitude, nor made the night
A gloomy vigil, but a festal time,
Merrier than day; he did not walk the rocks
And forest like a wolf, nor turn aside
From men and their delights.
    HER.   Beshrew the hour,   25
But those were jocund times! I would that such
Would visit the old walls again; they look

As if they had forgotten them.

MANUEL. These walls
Must change their chieftain first. Oh! I have seen
Some strange things in them, Herman.

HER. Come, be friendly; 30
Relate me some to while away our watch:
I've heard thee darkly speak of an event
Which happened hereabouts, by this same tower.

MANUEL. That was a night indeed! I do remember
'Twas twilight, as it may be now, and such 35
Another evening:—yon red cloud, which rests
On Eigher's pinnacle, so rested then,—
So like that it might be the same; the wind
Was faint and gusty, and the mountain snows
Began to glitter with the climbing moon; 40
Count Manfred was, as now, within his tower,—
How occupied, we knew not, but with him
The sole companion of his wanderings
And watchings—her, whom of all earthly things
That lived, the only thing he seemed to love,— 45
As he, indeed, by blood was bound to do,
The Lady Astarte, his——

Hush! who comes here?

Enter the ABBOT.

ABBOT. Where is your master?

HER. Yonder in the tower.

ABBOT. I must speak with him.

MANUEL. 'Tis impossible;
He is most private, and must not be thus 50
Intruded on.

ABBOT. Upon myself I take
The forfeit of my fault, if fault there be—
But I must see him.

HER. Thou hast seen him once
This eve already.

ABBOT. Herman! I command thee,
Knock, and apprize the Count of my approach. 55

HER. We dare not.

ABBOT. Then it seems I must be herald
Of my own purpose.

MANUEL.   Reverend father, stop—
I pray you pause.
    ABBOT.   Why so?
    MANUEL.   But step this way,
And I will tell you further.   [Exeunt.]

SCENE IV. *Interior of the Tower.*

MANFRED *alone.*

The stars are forth, the moon above the tops
Of the snow-shining mountains.—Beautifull
I linger yet with Nature, for the Night
Hath been to me a more familiar face
Than that of man; and in her starry shade   5
Of dim and solitary loveliness,
I learned the language of another world.
I do remember me, that in my youth,
When I was wandering,—upon such a night
I stood within the Coliseum's wall,   10
'Midst the chief relics of almighty Rome;
The trees which grew along the broken arches
Waved dark in the blue midnight, and the stars
Shone through the rents of ruin; from afar
The watch-dog bayed beyond the Tiber; and   15
More near from out the Cæsars' palace came
The owl's long cry, and, interruptedly,
Of distant sentinels the fitful song
Begun and died upon the gentle wind.
Some cypresses beyond the time-worn breach   20
Appeared to skirt the horizon, yet they stood
Within a bowshot. Where the Cæsars dwelt,
And dwell the tuneless birds of night, amidst
A grove which springs through levelled battlements,
And twines its roots with the imperial hearths,   25
Ivy usurps the laurel's place of growth;
But the gladiators' bloody Circus stands,
A noble wreck in ruinous perfection,
While Cæsar's chambers, and the Augustan halls,
Grovel on earth in indistinct decay.—   30
And thou didst shine, thou rolling Moon, upon

All this, and cast a wide and tender light,
Which softened down the hoar austerity
Of rugged desolation, and filled up,
As 'twere anew, the gaps of centuries;   35
Leaving that beautiful which still was so,
And making that which was not—till the place
Became religion, and the heart ran o'er
With silent worship of the Great of old,—
The dead, but sceptred, Sovereigns, who still rule   40
Our spirits from their urns.
                      'Twas such a night!
'Tis strange that I recall it at this time;
But I have found our thoughts take wildest flight
Even at the moment when they should array
Themselves in pensive order.

Enter the ABBOT.

ABBOT.   My good Lord!   45
I crave a second grace for this approach;
But yet let not my humble zeal offend
By its abruptness—all it hath of ill
Recoils on me; its good in the effect
May light upon your head—could I say *heart*—   50
Could I touch *that*, with words or prayers, I should
Recall a noble spirit which hath wandered,
But is not yet all lost.
MAN.   Thou know'st me not;
My days are numbered, and my deeds recorded:
Retire, or 'twill be dangerous—Away!   55
ABBOT. Thou dost not mean to menace me?
MAN.   Not I!
I simply tell thee peril is at hand,
And would preserve thee.
ABBOT.   What dost thou mean?
MAN.   Look there!
What dost thou see?
ABBOT.   Nothing.
MAN.   Look there, I say,
And steadfastly;—now tell me what thou seest?   60
ABBOT. That which should shake me,—but I fear it
   not:

I see a dusk and awful figure rise,
Like an infernal god, from out the earth;
His face wrapt in a mantle, and his form
Robed as with angry clouds: he stands between   65
Thyself and me—but I do fear him not.
    Man. Thou hast no cause—he shall not harm thee—
      but
His sight may shock thine old limbs into palsy.
I say to thee—Retire!
    Abbot.   And I reply—   70
Never—till I have battled with this fiend:—
What doth he here?
    Man.   Why—aye—what doth he here?
I did not send for him,—he is unbidden.
    Abbot. Alas! lost Mortal! what with guests like these
Hast thou to do? I tremble for thy sake:
Why doth he gaze on thee, and thou on him?   75
Ah! he unveils his aspect: on his brow
The thunder-scars are graven; from his eye
Glares forth the immortality of Hell—
Avaunt!—
    Man. Pronounce—what is thy mission?
    Spirit.   Come!
    Abbot. What art thou, unknown being? answer!—
      speak!   80
    Spirit. The genius of this mortal.—Come! 'tis time.
    Man. I am prepared for all things, but deny
The Power which summons me. Who sent thee here?
    Spirit. Thou'lt know anon—Come! come!
    Man.   I have commanded
Things of an essence greater far than thine,   85
And striven with thy masters. Get thee hence!
    Spirit. Mortal! thine hour is come—Away! I say.
    Man. I knew, and know my hour is come, but not
To render up my soul to such as thee:
Away! I'll die as I have lived—alone.   90
    Spirit. Then I must summon up my brethren.—Rise!
              [*Other* Spirits *rise up.*]
    Abbot. Avaunt! ye evil ones!—Avaunt! I say,—
Ye have no power where Piety hath power,
And I do charge ye in the name—
    Spirit.   Old man!

We know ourselves, our mission, and thine order;   95
Waste not thy holy words on idle uses,
It were in vain: this man is forfeited.
Once more—I summon him—Away! Away!
      MAN. I do defy ye,—though I feel my soul
Is ebbing from me, yet I do defy ye;   100
Nor will I hence, while I have earthly breath
To breathe my scorn upon ye—earthly strength
To wrestle, though with spirits; what ye take
Shall be ta'en limb by limb.
      SPIRIT.   Reluctant mortal!
Is this the Magian who would so pervade   105
The world invisible, and make himself
Almost our equal? Can it be that thou
Art thus in love with life? the very life
Which made thee wretched?
      MAN.   Thou false fiend, thou liest!
My life is in its last hour,—*that* I know,   110
Nor would redeem a moment of that hour;
I do not combat against Death, but thee
And thy surrounding angels; my past power
Was purchased by no compact with thy crew,
But by superior science—penance, daring,   115
And length of watching, strength of mind, and skill
In knowledge of our Fathers—when the earth
Saw men and spirits walking side by side,
And gave ye no supremacy: I stand
Upon my strength—I do defy—deny—   120
Spurn back, and scorn ye!—
      SPIRIT.   But thy many crimes
Have made thee——
      MAN.   What are they to such as thee?
Must crimes be punished but by other crimes,
And greater criminals?—Back to thy hell!
Thou hast no power upon me, *that* I feel;   125
Thou never shalt possess me, *that* I know:
What I have done is done; I bear within
A torture which could nothing gain from thine:
The Mind which is immortal makes itself
Requital for its good or evil thoughts,—   130
Is its own origin of ill and end—
And its own place and time: its innate sense,

When stripped of this mortality, derives
No colour from the fleeting things without,
But is absorbed in sufferance or in joy,   135
Born from the knowledge of its own desert.
Thou didst not tempt me, and thou couldst not tempt me;
I have not been thy dupe, nor am thy prey—
But was my own destroyer, and will be
My own hereafter.—Back, ye baffled fiends!   140
The hand of Death is on me—but not yours!
                              [The DEMONS disappear.]
    ABBOT. Alas! how pale thou art—thy lips are white—
And thy breast heaves—and in thy gasping throat
The accents rattle: Give thy prayers to Heaven—
Pray—albeit but in thought,—but die not thus.   145
    MAN. 'Tis over—my dull eyes can fix thee not;
But all things swim around me, and the earth
Heaves as it were beneath me. Fare thee well—
Give me thy hand.
    ABBOT.   Cold—cold—even to the heart—
But yet one prayer—Alas! how fares it with thee?   150
    MAN. Old man! 'tis not so difficult to die.
                              [MANFRED expires.]
    ABBOT. He's gone—his soul hath ta'en its earthless
        flight;
Whither? I dread to think—but he is gone.
    [1816–17]

SO WE'LL GO NO MORE A-ROVING

1

So we'll go no more a-roving
    So late into the night,
Though the heart be still as loving,
    And the moon be still as bright.

2

For the sword outwears its sheath,   5
    And the soul wears out the breast,

And the heart must pause to breathe,
And Love itself have rest.

3

Though the night was made for loving
And the day returns too soon,   10
Yet we'll go no more a-roving
By the light of the moon.
[1817]

MAZEPPA

I

'Twas after dread Pultowa's day,
When Fortune left the loyal Swede—
Around a slaughtered army lay,
No more to combat and to bleed.
The power and glory of the war,   5
Faithless as their vain votaries, men,
Had passed to the triumphant Czar,
And Moscow's walls were safe again—
Until a day more dark and drear,
And a more memorable year,   10
Should give to slaughter and to shame
A mightier host and haughtier name;
A greater wreck, a deeper fall,
A shock to one—a thunderbolt to all.

II

Such was the hazard of the die;   15
The wounded Charles was taught to fly
By day and night through field and flood,
Stained with his own and subjects' blood;
For thousands fell that flight to aid:
And not a voice was heard to upbraid   20
Ambition in his humbled hour,

When Truth had nought to dread from Power.
His horse was slain, and Gieta gave
His own—and died the Russians' slave.
This, too, sinks after many a league   25
Of well-sustained, but vain fatigue;
And in the depth of forests darkling,
The watch-fires in the distance sparkling—
    The beacons of surrounding foes—
A King must lay his limbs at length.   30
    Are these the laurels and repose
For which the nations strain their strength?
They laid him by a savage tree,
In outworn Nature's agony;
His wounds were stiff, his limbs were stark;   35
The heavy hour was chill and dark;
The fever in his blood forbade
A transient slumber's fitful aid:
And thus it was; but yet through all,
Kinglike the monarch bore his fall,   40
And made, in this extreme of ill,
His pangs the vassals of his will:
All silent and subdued were they,
As once the nations round him lay.

III

A band of chiefs!—alas! how few,   45
    Since but the fleeting of a day
Had thinned it; but this wreck was true
    And chivalrous: upon the clay
Each sate him down, all sad and mute,
    Beside his monarch and his steed;   50
For danger levels man and brute,
    And all are fellows in their need.
Among the rest, Mazeppa made
His pillow in an old oak's shade—
Himself as rough, and scarce less old,   55
The Ukraine's Hetman, calm and bold;
But first, outspent with this long course,
The Cossack prince rubbed down his horse,
And made for him a leafy bed,
    And smoothed his fetlocks and his mane,   60

And slacked his girth, and stripped his rein,
And joyed to see how well he fed;
For until now he had the dread
His wearied courser might refuse
To browse beneath the midnight dews: 65
But he was hardy as his lord,
And little cared for bed and board;
But spirited and docile too,
Whate'er was to be done, would do.
Shaggy and swift, and strong of limb,   70
All Tartar-like he carried him;
Obeyed his voice, and came to call,
And knew him in the midst of all:
Though thousands were around,—and Night,
Without a star, pursued her flight,—   75
That steed from sunset until dawn
His chief would follow like a fawn.

IV

This done, Mazeppa spread his cloak,
And laid his lance beneath his oak,
Felt if his arms in order good   80
The long day's march had well withstood—
If still the powder filled the pan,
    And flints unloosened kept their lock—
His sabre's hilt and scabbard felt,
And whether they had chafed his belt;   85
And next the venerable man,
From out his havresack and can,
    Prepared and spread his slender stock;
And to the Monarch and his men
The whole or portion offered then   90
With far less of inquietude
Than courtiers at a banquet would.
And Charles of this his slender share
With smiles partook a moment there,
To force of cheer a greater show,   95
And seem above both wounds and woe;—
And then he said—"Of all our band,
Though firm of heart and strong of hand,

In skirmish, march, or forage, none
Can less have said or more have done   100
Than thee, Mazeppa! On the earth
So fit a pair had never birth,
Since Alexander's days till now,
As thy Bucephalus and thou:
All Scythia's fame to thine should yield   105
For pricking on o'er flood and field."
Mazeppa answered—"Ill betide
The school wherein I learned to ride!"
Quoth Charles—"Old Hetman, wherefore so,
Since thou hast learned the art so well?"   110
Mazeppa said—" 'Twere long to tell;
And we have many a league to go,
With every now and then a blow,
And ten to one at least the foe,
Before our steeds may graze at ease,   115
Beyond the swift Borysthenes:
And, Sire, your limbs have need of rest,
And I will be the sentinel
Of this your troop."—"But I request,"
Said Sweden's monarch, "thou wilt tell   120
This tale of thine, and I may reap,
Perchance, from this the boon of sleep;
For at this moment from my eyes
The hope of present slumber flies."

"Well, Sire, with such a hope, I'll track   125
My seventy years of memory back:
I think 'twas in my twentieth spring,—
Aye 'twas,—when Casimir was king—
John Casimir,—I was his page
Six summers, in my earlier age: 130
A learnéd monarch, faith! was he,
And most unlike your Majesty;
He made no wars, and did not gain
New realms to lose them back again;
And (save debates in Warsaw's diet)   135
He reigned in most unseemly quiet;
Not that he had no cares to vex;
He loved the Muses and the Sex;
And sometimes these so froward are,

They made him wish himself at war;   140
But soon his wrath being o'er, he took
Another mistress—or new book:
And then he gave prodigious fêtes—
All Warsaw gathered round his gates
To gaze upon his splendid court,   145
And dames, and chiefs, of princely port.
He was the Polish Solomon,
So sung his poets, all but one,
Who, being unpensioned, made a satire,
And boasted that he could not flatter.   150
It was a court of jousts and mimes,
Where every courtier tried at rhymes;
Even I for once produced some verses,
And signed my odes 'Despairing Thyrsis.'
There was a certain Palatine,   155
    A Count of far and high descent,
Rich as a salt or silver mine;
And he was proud, ye may divine,
    As if from Heaven he had been sent;
He had such wealth in blood and ore   160
    As few could match beneath the throne;
And he would gaze upon his store,
And o'er his pedigree would pore,
Until by some confusion led,
Which almost looked like want of head,   165
    He thought their merits were his own.
His wife was not of this opinion;
    His junior she by thirty years,
Grew daily tired of his dominion;
    And, after wishes, hopes, and fears,   170
    To Virtue a few farewell tears,
A restless dream or two—some glances
At Warsaw's youth—some songs, and dances,
Awaited but the usual chances,
Those happy accidents which render   175
The coldest dames so very tender,
To deck her Count with titles given,
'Tis said, as passports into Heaven;
But, strange to say, they rarely boast
Of these, who have deserved them most.   180

V

"I was a goodly stripling then;
  At seventy years I so may say,
That there were few, or boys or men,
  Who, in my dawning time of day,
Of vassal or of knight's degree,   185
Could vie in vanities with me;
For I had strength—youth—gaiety,
A port, not like to this ye see,
But smooth, as all is rugged now;
  For Time, and Care, and War, have ploughed   190
My very soul from out my brow;
  And thus I should be disavowed
By all my kind and kin, could they
Compare my day and yesterday;
This change was wrought, too, long ere age   195
Had ta'en my features for his page:
With years, ye know, have not declined
My strength—my courage—or my mind,
Or at this hour I should not be
Telling old tales beneath a tree,   200
With starless skies my canopy.
  But let me on: Theresa's form—
Methinks it glides before me now,
Between me and yon chestnut's bough,
  The memory is so quick and warm;   205
And yet I find no words to tell
The shape of her I loved so well:
She had the Asiatic eye,
  Such as our Turkish neighbourhood
  Hath mingled with our Polish blood,   210
Dark as above us is the sky;
But through it stole a tender light,
Like the first moonrise of midnight;
Large, dark, and swimming in the stream,
Which seemed to melt to its own beam;   215
All love, half languor, and half fire,
Like saints that at the stake expire,
And lift their raptured looks on high,
As though it were a joy to die.

A brow like a midsummer lake,   220
   Transparent with the sun therein,
When waves no murmur dare to make,
   And heaven beholds her face within.
A cheek and lip—but why proceed?
   I loved her then, I love her still;   225
And such as I am, love indeed
   In fierce extremes—in good and ill.
But still we love even in our rage,
And haunted to our very age
With the vain shadow of the past,—   230
As is Mazeppa to the last.

VI

"We met—we gazed—I saw, and sighed;
She did not speak, and yet replied;
There are ten thousand tones and signs
We hear and see, but none defines—   235
Involuntary sparks of thought,
Which strike from out the heart o'erwrought,
And form a strange intelligence,
Alike mysterious and intense,
Which link the burning chain that binds,   240
Without their will, young hearts and minds;
Conveying, as the electric wire,
We know not how, the absorbing fire.
I saw, and sighed—in silence wept,
And still reluctant distance kept,   245
Until I was made known to her,
And we might then and there confer
Without suspicion—then, even then,
   I longed, and was resolved to speak;
But on my lips they died again,   250
   The accents tremulous and weak,
Until one hour.—There is a game,
   A frivolous and foolish play,
   Wherewith we while away the day;
It is—I have forgot the name—   255
And we to this, it seems, were set,
By some strange chance, which I forget:
I recked not if I won or lost,

It was enough for me to be
  So near to hear, and oh! to see   260
The being whom I loved the most.
I watched her as a sentinel,
(May ours this dark night watch as well!)
  Until I saw, and thus it was,
That she was pensive, nor perceived   265
Her occupation, nor was grieved
Nor glad to lose or gain; but still
Played on for hours, as if her will
Yet bound her to the place, though not
That hers might be the winning lot.   270
  Then through my brain the thought did pass,
Even as a flash of lightning there,
That there was something in her air
Which would not doom me to despair;
And on the thought my words broke forth,   275
  All incoherent as they were;
Their eloquence was little worth,
But yet she listened—'tis enough—
  Who listens once will listen twice;
  Her heart, be sure, is not of ice—   280
And one refusal no rebuff.

VII

"I loved, and was beloved again—
  They tell me, Sire, you never knew
  Those gentle frailties; if 'tis true,
I shorten all my joy or pain;   285
To you 'twould seem absurd as vain;
But all men are not born to reign,
Or o'er their passions, or as you
Thus o'er themselves and nations too.
I am—or rather was—a Prince,   290
  A chief of thousands, and could lead
  Them on where each would foremost bleed;
But could not o'er myself evince
The like control—But to resume:
  I loved, and was beloved again;   295
In sooth, it is a happy doom,
  But yet where happiest ends in pain.—

We met in secret, and the hour
Which led me to that lady's bower
Was fiery Expectation's dower.   300
My days and nights were nothing—all
Except that hour which doth recall,
In the long lapse from youth to age,
  No other like itself: I'd give
  The Ukraine back again to live   305
It o'er once more, and be a page,
The happy page, who was the lord
Of one soft heart, and his own sword,
And had no other gem nor wealth,
Save Nature's gift of Youth and Health.   310
We met in secret—doubly sweet,
Some say, they find it so to meet;
I know not that—I would have given
  My life but to have called her mine
In the full view of Earth and Heaven;   315
  For I did oft and long repine
That we could only meet by stealth.

VIII

"For lovers there are many eyes,
  And such there were on us; the Devil
  On such occasions should be civil—   320
The Devil!—I'm loth to do him wrong,
  It might be some untoward saint,
Who would not be at rest too long,
  But to his pious bile gave vent—
But one fair night, some lurking spies   325
Surprised and seized us both.
The Count was something more than wroth—
I was unarmed; but if in steel,
All cap-à-pie from head to heel,
What 'gainst their numbers could I do?   330
'Twas near his castle, far away
  From city or from succour near,
And almost on the break of day;
I did not think to see another,
  My moments seemed reduced to few;   335
And with one prayer to Mary Mother,

And, it may be, a saint or two,
As I resigned me to my fate,
They led me to the castle gate:
    Theresa's doom I never knew,   340
Our lot was henceforth separate.
An angry man, ye may opine,
Was he, the proud Count Palatine;
And he had reason good to be,
    But he was most enraged lest such   345
    An accident should chance to touch
Upon his future pedigree;
Nor less amazed, that such a blot
His noble 'scutcheon should have got,
While he was highest of his line;   350
    Because unto himself he seemed
    The first of men, nor less he deemed
In others' eyes, and most in mine.
'Sdeath! with a page—perchance a king
Had reconciled him to the thing;   355
But with a stripling of a page—
I felt—but cannot paint his rage.

IX

" 'Bring forth the horse!'—the horse was brought!
In truth, he was a noble steed,
    A Tartar of the Ukraine breed,   360
Who looked as though the speed of thought
Were in his limbs; but he was wild,
    Wild as the wild deer, and untaught,
With spur and bridle undefiled—
    'Twas but a day he had been caught;   365
And snorting, with erected mane,
And struggling fiercely, but in vain,
In the full foam of wrath and dread
To me the desert-born was led:
They bound me on, that menial throng,   370
Upon his back with many a thong;
They loosed him with a sudden lash—
Away!—away!—and on we dash!—
Torrents less rapid and less rash.

X

"Away!—away!—My breath was gone,   375
I saw not where he hurried on:
'Twas scarcely yet the break of day,
And on he foamed—away!—away!
The last of human sounds which rose,
As I was darted from my foes,   380
Was the wild shout of savage laughter,
Which on the wind came roaring after
A moment from that rabble rout:
With sudden wrath I wrenched my head,
    And snapped the cord, which to the mane   385
    Had bound my neck in lieu of rein,
And, writhing half my form about,
Howled back my curse; but 'midst the tread,
The thunder of my courser's speed,
Perchance they did not hear nor heed: 390
It vexes me—for I would fain
Have paid their insult back again.
I paid it well in after days:
There is not of that castle gate,
Its drawbridge and portcullis' weight,   395
Stone—bar—moat—bridge—or barrier left;
Nor of its fields a blade of grass,
    Save what grows on a ridge of wall,
    Where stood the hearth-stone of the hall;
And many a time ye there might pass,   400
Nor dream that e'er the fortress was.
I saw its turrets in a blaze,
Their crackling battlements all cleft,
    And the hot lead pour down like rain
From off the scorched and blackening roof,   405
Whose thickness was not vengeance-proof.
    They little thought that day of pain,
When launched, as on the lightning's flash,
They bade me to destruction dash,
    That one day I should come again,   410
With twice five thousand horse, to thank
    The Count for his uncourteous ride.
They played me then a bitter prank,

When, with the wild horse for my guide,
They bound me to his foaming flank: 415
At length I played them one as frank—
For Time at last sets all things even—
  And if we do but watch the hour,
  There never yet was human power
Which could evade, if unforgiven,   420
The patient search and vigil long
Of him who treasures up a wrong.

XI

"Away!—away!—my steed and I,
  Upon the pinions of the wind!
  All human dwellings left behind,   425
We sped like meteors through the sky,
When with its crackling sound the night
Is chequered with the Northern light.
Town—village—none were on our track,
  But a wild plain of far extent,   430
And bounded by a forest black;
  And, save the scarce seen battlement
On distant heights of some strong hold,
Against the Tartars built of old,
No trace of man. The year before   435
A Turkish army had marched o'er;
And where the Spahi's hoof hath trod,
The verdure flies the bloody sod:
The sky was dull, and dim, and gray,
  And a low breeze crept moaning by—   440
  I could have answered with a sigh—
But fast we fled,—away!—away!—
And I could neither sigh nor pray;
Any my cold sweat-drops fell like rain
Upon the courser's bristling mane;   445
But, snorting still with rage and fear,
He flew upon his far career:
At times I almost thought, indeed,
He must have slackened in his speed;
But no—my bound and slender frame   450
  Was nothing to his angry might,
And merely like a spur became:

Each motion which I made to free
My swoln limbs from their agony
  Increased his fury and affright: 455
I tried my voice,—'twas faint and low—
But yet he swerved as from a blow;
And, starting to each accent, sprang
As from a sudden trumpet's clang:
Meantime my cords were wet with gore,   460
Which, oozing through my limbs, ran o'er;
And in my tongue the thirst became
A something fierier far than flame.

XII

"We neared the wild wood—'twas so wide,
I saw no bounds on either side: 465
'Twas studded with old sturdy trees,
That bent not to the roughest breeze
Which howls down from Siberia's waste,
And strips the forest in its haste,—
But these were few and far between,   470
Set thick with shrubs more young and green,
Luxuriant with their annual leaves,
Ere strown by those autumnal eves
That nip the forest's foliage dead,
Discoloured with a lifeless red,   475
Which stands thereon like stiffened gore
Upon the slain when battle's o'er;
And some long winter's night hath shed
Its frost o'er every tombless head—
So cold and stark—the raven's beak   480
May peck unpierced each frozen cheek:
'Twas a wild waste of underwood,
And here and there a chestnut stood,
The strong oak, and the hardy pine;
  But far apart—and well it were,   485
Or else a different lot were mine—
  The boughs gave way, and did not tear
My limbs; and I found strength to bear
My wounds, already scarred with cold;
My bonds forbade to loose my hold.   490
We rustled through the leaves like wind,—

Left shrubs, and trees, and wolves behind;
By night I heard them on the track,
Their troop came hard upon our back,
With their long gallop, which can tire   495
The hound's deep hate, and hunter's fire:
Where'er we flew they followed on,
Nor left us with the morning sun;
Behind I saw them, scarce a rood,
At day-break winding through the wood,   500
And through the night had heard their feet
Their stealing, rustling step repeat.
Oh! how I wished for spear or sword,
At least to die amidst the horde,
And perish—if it must be so—   505
At bay, destroying many a foe!
When first my courser's race begun,
I wished the goal already won;
But now I doubted strength and speed:
Vain doubt; his swift and savage breed   510
Had nerved him like the mountain-roe—
Nor faster falls the blinding snow
Which whelms the peasant near the door
Whose threshold he shall cross no more,
Bewildered with the dazzling blast,   515
Than through the forest-paths he passed—
Untired, untamed, and worse than wild—
All furious as a favoured child
Balked of its wish; or—fiercer still—
A woman piqued—who has her will!   520

XIII

"The wood was passed; 'twas more than noon,
But chill the air, although in June;
Or it might be my veins ran cold—
Prolonged endurance tames the bold;
And I was then not what I seem,   525
But headlong as a wintry stream,
And wore my feelings out before
I well could count their causes o'er:
And what with fury, fear, and wrath,
The tortures which beset my path—   530

Cold—hunger—sorrow—shame—distress—
Thus bound in Nature's nakedness;
Sprung from a race whose rising blood
When stirred beyond its calmer mood,
And trodden hard upon, is like   535
The rattle-snake's, in act to strike—
What marvel if this worn-out trunk
Beneath its woes a moment sunk?
The earth gave way, the skies rolled round,
I seemed to sink upon the ground;   540
But erred—for I was fastly bound.
My heart turned sick, my brain grew sore,
And throbbed awhile, then beat no more:
The skies spun like a mighty wheel;
I saw the trees like drunkards reel,   545
And a slight flash sprang o'er my eyes,
Which saw no farther. He who dies
Can die no more than I died,
O'ertortured by that ghastly ride.
I felt the blackness come and go,   550
     And strove to wake; but could not make
My senses climb up from below:
I felt as on a plank at sea,
When all the waves that dash o'er thee,
At the same time upheave and whelm,   555
And hurl thee towards a desert realm.
My undulating life was as
The fancied lights that flitting pass
Our shut eyes in deep midnight, when
Fever begins upon the brain;   560
But soon it passed, with little pain,
     But a confusion worse than such:
     I own that I should deem it much,
Dying, to feel the same again;
And yet I do suppose we must   565
Feel far more ere we turn to dust!
No matter! I have bared my brow
Full in Death's face—before—and now.

XIV

"My thoughts came back. Where was I? Cold,

And numb, and giddy: pulse by pulse   570
Life reassumed its lingering hold,
And throb by throb,—till grown a pang
    Which for a moment would convulse,
    My blood reflowed, though thick and chill;
My ear with uncouth noises rang,   575
    My heart began once more to thrill;
My sight returned, though dim; alas!
And thickened, as it were, with glass.
Methought the dash of waves was nigh;
There was a gleam too of the sky,   580
Studded with stars;—it is no dream;
The wild horse swims the wilder stream!
The bright broad river's gushing tide
Sweeps, winding onward, far and wide,
And we are half-way, struggling o'er   585
To yon unknown and silent shore.
The waters broke my hollow trance,
And with a temporary strength
    My stiffened limbs were rebaptized.
My courser's broad breast proudly braves,   590
And dashes off the ascending waves,
And onward we advance!
We reach the slippery shore at length,
    A haven I but little prized,
For all behind was dark and drear,   595
And all before was night and fear.
How many hours of night or day
In those suspended pangs I lay,
I could not tell; I scarcely knew
If this were human breath I drew.   600

xv

"With glossy skin, and dripping mane,
    And reeling limbs, and reeking flank,
The wild steed's sinewy nerves still strain
    Up the repelling bank.
We gain the top: a boundless plain   605
Spreads through the shadow of the night,
    And onward, onward, onward—seems,
    Like precipices in our dreams,

To stretch beyond the sight;
And here and there a speck of white,   610
   Or scattered spot of dusky green,
In masses broke into the light,
As rose the moon upon my right:
   But nought distinctly seen
In the dim waste would indicate   615
The omen of a cottage gate;
No twinkling taper from afar
Stood like a hospitable star;
Not even an ignis-fatuus rose
To make him merry with my woes: 620
   That very cheat had cheered me then!
Although detected, welcome still,
Reminding me, through every ill,
   Of the abodes of men.

XVI

"Onward we went—but slack and slow;   625
   His savage force at length o'erspent,
The drooping courser, faint and low,
   All feebly foaming went:
A sickly infant had had power
To guide him forward in that hour!   630
   But, useless all to me,
His new-born tameness nought availed—
My limbs were bound; my force had failed,
   Perchance, had they been free.
With feeble effort still I tried   635
To rend the bonds so starkly tied,
   But still it was in vain;
My limbs were only wrung the more,
And soon the idle strife gave o'er,
   Which but prolonged their pain.   640
The dizzy race seemed almost done,
Although no goal was nearly won:
Some streaks announced the coming sun—
   How slow, alas! he came!
Methought that mist of dawning gray   645
Would never dapple into day,
How heavily it rolled away!

Before the eastern flame
Rose crimson, and deposed the stars,
And called the radiance from their cars,   650
And filled the earth, from his deep throne,
With lonely lustre, all his own.

XVII

"Uprose the sun; the mists were curled
Back from the solitary world
Which lay around—behind—before.   655
What booted it to traverse o'er
Plain—forest—river? Man nor brute,
Nor dint of hoof, nor print of foot,
Lay in the wild luxuriant soil—
No sign of travel, none of toil—   660
The very air was mute:
And not an insect's shrill small horn,
Nor matin bird's new voice was borne
From herb nor thicket. Many a wersi,
Panting as if his heart would burst,   665
The weary brute still staggered on;
And still we were—or seemed—alone:
At length, while reeling on our way,
Methought I heard a courser neigh,
From out yon tuft of blackening firs.   670
Is it the wind those branches stirs?
No, no! from out the forest prance
    A trampling troop; I see them come!
In one vast squadron they advance!
    I strove to cry—my lips were dumb!   675
The steeds rush on in plunging pride;
But where are they the reins to guide?
A thousand horse, and none to ride!
With flowing tail, and flying mane,
Wide nostrils never stretched by pain,   680
Mouths bloodless to the bit or rein,
And feet that iron never shod,
And flanks unscarred by spur or rod,
A thousand horse, the wild, the free,
Like waves that follow o'er the sea,   685
    Came thickly thundering on,

As if our faint approach to meet!
The sight re-nerved my courser's feet,
A moment staggering, feebly fleet,
A moment, with a faint low neigh,   690
    He answered, and then fell!
With gasps and glazing eyes he lay,
    And reeking limbs immoveable,
        His first and last career is done!
On came the troop—they saw him stoop,   695
    They saw me strangely bound along
    His back with many a bloody thong.
They stop—they start—they snuff the air,
Gallop a moment here and there,
Approach, retire, wheel round and round,   700
Then plunging back with sudden bound,
Headed by one black mighty steed,
Who seemed the Patriarch of his breed,
    Without a single speck or hair
Of white upon his shaggy hide;   705
They snort—they foam—neigh—swerve aside,
And backward to the forest fly,
By instinct, from a human eye.
    They left me there to my despair,
Linked to the dead and stiffening wretch,   710
Whose lifeless limbs beneath me stretch,
Relieved from that unwonted weight,
From whence I could not extricate
Nor him nor me—and there we lay,
    The dying on the dead!   715
I little deemed another day
    Would see my houseless, helpless head.

"And there from morn to twilight bound,
I felt the heavy hours toil round,
With just enough of life to see   720
My last of suns go down on me,
In hopeless certainty of mind,
That makes us feel at length resigned
To that which our foreboding years
Present the worst and last of fears: 725
Inevitable—even a boon,
Nor more unkind for coming soon,

Yet shunned and dreaded with such care,
As if it only were a snare
   That Prudence might escape: 730
At times both wished for and implored,
At times sought with self-pointed sword,
Yet still a dark and hideous close
To even intolerable woes,
   And welcome in no shape.   735
And, strange to say, the sons of pleasure,
They who have revelled beyond measure
In beauty, wassail, wine, and treasure,
Die calm, or calmer, oft than he
Whose heritage was Misery.   740
For he who hath in turn run through
All that was beautiful and new,
   Hath nought to hope, and nought to leave;
And, save the future, (which is viewed
Not quite as men are base or good,   745
But as their nerves may be endued,)
   With nought perhaps to grieve:
The wretch still hopes his woes must end,
And Death, whom he should deem his friend,
Appears, to his distempered eyes,   750
Arrived to rob him of his prize,
The tree of his new Paradise.
To-morrow would have given him all,
Repaid his pangs, repaired his fall;
To-morrow would have been the first   755
Of days no more deplored or curst,
But bright, and long, and beckoning years,
Seen dazzling through the mist of tears,
Guerdon of many a painful hour;
To-morrow would have given him power   760
To rule—to shine—to smite—to save—
And must it dawn upon his grave?

XVIII

"The sun was sinking—still I lay
   Chained to the chill and stiffening steed!
I thought to mingle there our clay;   765
   And my dim eyes of death had need,

No hope arose of being freed.
I cast my last looks up the sky,
    And there between me and the sun
I saw the expecting raven fly,   770
Who scarce would wait till both should die,
    Ere his repast begun;
He flew, and perched, then flew once more,
And each time nearer than before;
I saw his wing through twilight flit,   775
And once so near me he alit
    I could have smote, but lacked the strength;
But the slight motion of my hand,
And feeble scratching of the sand,
The exerted throat's faint struggling noise,   780
Which scarcely could be called a voice,
    Together scared him off at length.
I know no more—my latest dream
    Is something of a lovely star
    Which fixed my dull eyes from afar,   785
And went and came with wandering beam,
And of the cold—dull—swimming—dense
Sensation of recurring sense,
And then subsiding back to death,
And then again a little breath,   790
A little thrill—a short suspense,
    An icy sickness curdling o'er
My heart, and sparks that crossed my brain—
A gasp—a throb—a start of pain,
    A sigh—and nothing more.   795

                        XIX

"I woke—where was I?—Do I see
A human face look down on me?
And doth a roof above me close?
Do these limbs on a couch repose?
Is this a chamber where I lie?
And is it mortal yon bright eye,   800
That watches me with gentle glance?
    I closed my own again once more,
As doubtful that my former trance
    Could not as yet be o'er.   805

A slender girl, long-haired, and tall,
Sate watching by the cottage wall.
The sparkle of her eye I caught,
Even with my first return of thought;
For ever and anon she threw   810
    A prying, pitying glance on me
    With her black eyes so wild and free:
I gazed, and gazed, until I knew
    No vision it could be,—
But that I lived, and was released   815
From adding to the vulture's feast:
And when the Cossack maid beheld
My heavy eyes at length unsealed,
She smiled—and I essayed to speak,
    But failed—and she approached, and made   820
    With lip and finger signs that said,
I must not strive as yet to break
The silence, till my strength should be
Enough to leave my accents free;
And then her hand on mine she laid,   825
And smoothed the pillow for my head,
And stole along on tiptoe tread,
    And gently oped the door, and spake
In whispers—ne'er was voice so sweet!
Even music followed her light feet.   830
    But those she called were not awake,
And she went forth; but, ere she passed,
Another look on me she cast,
    Another sign she made, to say,
That I had nought to fear, that all   835
Were near, at my command or call,
    And she would not delay
Her due return:—while she was gone,
Methought I felt too much alone.

XX

"She came with mother and with sire—   840
What need of more?—I will not tire
With long recital of the rest,
Since I became the Cossack's guest.
They found me senseless on the plain,

They bore me to the nearest hut,   845
They brought me into life again—
Me—one day o'er their realm to reign!
    Thus the vain fool who strove to glut
His rage, refining on my pain,
    Sent me forth to the wilderness,   850
Bound—naked—bleeding—and alone,
To pass the desert to a throne,—
    What mortal his own doom may guess?
    Let none despond, let none despair!
To-morrow the Borysthenes   855
May see our coursers graze at ease
Upon his Turkish bank,—and never
Had I such welcome for a river
    As I shall yield when safely there.
Comrades, good night!"—The Hetman threw   860
    His length beneath the oak-tree shade,
    With leafy couch already made—
A bed nor comfortless nor new
To him, who took his rest whene'er
The hour arrived, no matter where: 865
    His eyes the hastening slumbers steep.
And if ye marvel Charles forgot
To thank his tale, *he* wondered not,—
    The King had been an hour asleep!
    [1818]

THE VISION OF JUDGMENT

I

Saint Peter sat by the celestial gate:
    His keys were rusty, and the lock was dull,
So little trouble had been given of late;
    Not that the place by any means was full,
But since the Gallic era "eighty-eight"   5
    The Devils had ta'en a longer, stronger pull,
And "a pull altogether," as they say
At sea—which drew most souls another way.

II

The Angels all were singing out of tune,
    And hoarse with having little else to do,   10
Excepting to wind up the sun and moon,
    Or curb a runaway young star or two,
Or wild colt of a comet, which too soon
    Broke out of bounds o'er the ethereal blue,
Splitting some planet with its playful tail,   15
As boats are sometimes by a wanton whale.

III

The Guardian Seraphs had retired on high,
    Finding their charges past all care below;
Terrestrial business filled nought in the sky
    Save the Recording Angel's black bureau;   20
Who found, indeed, the facts to multiply
    With such rapidity of vice and woe,
That he had stripped off both his wings in quills,
And yet was in arrear of human ills.

IV

His business so augmented of late years,   25
    That he was forced, against his will, no doubt,
(Just like those cherubs, earthly ministers,)
    For some resource to turn himself about,
And claim the help of his celestial peers,
    To aid him ere he should be quite worn out   30
By the increased demand for his remarks:
Six Angels and twelve Saints were named his clerks.

V

This was a handsome board—at least for Heaven;
    And yet they had even then enough to do,
So many Conquerors' cars were daily driven,   35
    So many kingdoms fitted up anew;
Each day, too, slew its thousands six or seven,
    Till at the crowning carnage, Waterloo,

They threw their pens down in divine disgust—
The page was so besmeared with blood and dust.   40

VI

This by the way; 'tis not mine to record
   What Angels shrink from: even the very Devil
On this occasion his own work abhorred,
   So surfeited with the infernal revel:
Though he himself had sharpened every sword,   45
   It almost quenched his innate thirst of evil.
(Here Satan's sole good work deserves insertion—
'Tis, that he has both Generals in reversion.)

VII

Let's skip a few short years of hollow peace,
   Which peopled earth no better, Hell as wont,   50
And Heaven none—they form the tyrant's lease,
   With nothing but new names subscribed upon 't;
'Twill one day finish: meantime they increase,
   "With seven heads and ten horns," and all in front,
Like Saint John's foretold beast; but ours are born   55
Less formidable in the head than horn.

VIII

In the first year of Freedom's second dawn
   Died George the Third; although no tyrant, one
Who shielded tyrants, till each sense withdrawn
   Left him nor mental nor external sun: 60
A better farmer ne'er brushed dew from lawn,
   A worse king never left a realm undone!
He died—but left his subjects still behind,
One half as mad—and t'other no less blind.

IX

He died! his death made no great stir on earth: 65
   His burial made some pomp; there was profusion
Of velvet—gilding—brass—and no great dearth
   Of aught but tears—save those shed by collusion:

For these things may be bought at their true worth;
 Of elegy there was the due infusion——   70
Bought also; and the torches, cloaks and banners,
Heralds, and relics of old Gothic manners,

x

Formed a sepulchral melodrame. Of all
 The fools who flocked to swell or see the show,
Who cared about the corpse? The funeral   75
 Made the attraction, and the black the woe,
There throbbed not there a thought which pierced the
    pall;
 And when the gorgeous coffin was laid low,
It seemed the mockery of hell to fold
The rottenness of eighty years in gold.   80

XI

So mix his body with the dust! It might
 Return to what it *must* far sooner, were
The natural compound left alone to fight
 Its way back into earth, and fire, and air;
But the unnatural balsams merely blight   85
 What Nature made him at his birth, as bare
As the mere million's base unmummied clay——
Yet all his spices but prolong decay.

XII

He's dead——and upper earth with him has done;
 He's buried; save the undertaker's bill,   90
Or lapidary scrawl, the world is gone
 For him, unless he left a German will:
But where's the proctor who will ask his son?
 In whom his qualities are reigning still,
Except that household virtue, most uncommon,   95
Of constancy to a bad, ugly woman.

XIII

"God save the king!" It is a large economy
 In God to save the like; but if he will

Be saving, all the better; for not one am I
  Of those who think damnation better still: 100
I hardly know too if not quite alone am I
  In this small hope of bettering future ill
By circumscribing, with some slight restriction,
The eternity of Hell's hot jurisdiction.

XIV

I know this is unpopular; I know   105
  'Tis blasphemous; I know one may be damned
For hoping no one else may e'er be so;
  I know my catechism; I know we're crammed
With the best doctrines till we quite o'erflow;
  I know that all save England's Church have shammed, 110
And that the other twice two hundred churches
And synagogues have made a *damned* bad purchase.

XV

God help us all! God help me too! I am,
  God knows, as helpless as the Devil can wish,
And not a whit more difficult to damn,   115
  Than is to bring to land a late-hooked fish,
Or to the butcher to purvey the lamb;
  Not that I'm fit for such a noble dish,
As one day will be that immortal fry
Of almost every body born to die.   120

XVI

Saint Peter sat by the celestial gate,
  And nodded o'er his keys: when, lo! there came
A wondrous noise he had not heard of late—
  A rushing sound of wind, and stream, and flame;
In short, a roar of things extremely great,   125
  Which would have made aught save a Saint exclaim;
But he, with first a start and then a wink,
Said, "There's another star gone out, I think!"

XVII

But ere he could return to his repose,
    A Cherub flapped his right wing o'er his eyes—   130
At which Saint Peter yawned, and rubbed his nose:
    "Saint porter," said the angel, "prithee rise!"
Waving a goodly wing, which glowed, as glows
    An earthly peacock's tail, with heavenly dyes:
To which the saint replied, "Well, what's the matter?   135
Is Lucifer come back with all this clatter?"

XVIII

"No," quoth the Cherub: "George the Third is dead."
    "And who *is* George the Third?" replied the apostle:
"*What George? what Third?*" "The King of England,"
    said
The angel. "Well! he won't find kings to jostle   140
Him on his way; but does he wear his head?
    Because the last we saw here had a tustle,
And ne'er would have got into Heaven's good graces,
Had he not flung his head in all our faces.

XIX

"He was—if I remember—King of France;   145
    That head of his, which could not keep a crown
On earth, yet ventured in my face to advance
    A claim to those of martyrs—like my own:
If I had had my sword, as I had once
    When I cut ears off, I had cut him down;   150
But having but my keys, and not my brand,
I only knocked his head from out his hand.

XX

"And then he set up such a headless howl,
    That all the Saints came out and took him in;
And there he sits by Saint Paul, cheek by jowl;   155
    That fellow Paul—the parvenù! The skin
Of Saint Bartholomew, which makes his cowl
    In heaven, and upon earth redeemed his sin,

So as to make a martyr, never sped
Better than did this weak and wooden head.   160

XXI

"But had it come up here upon its shoulders,
    There would have been a different tale to tell:
The fellow-feeling in the Saint's beholders
    Seems to have acted on them like a spell;
And so this very foolish head Heaven solders   165
    Back on its trunk: it may be very well,
And seems the custom here to overthrow
Whatever has been wisely done below."

XXII

The Angel answered, "Peter! do not pout:
    The King who comes has head and all entire,   170
And never knew much what it was about—
    He did as doth the puppet—by its wire,
And will be judged like all the rest, no doubt:
    My business and your own is not to inquire
Into such matters, but to mind our cue—   175
Which is to act as we are bid to do."

XXIII

While thus they spake, the angelic caravan,
    Arriving like a rush of mighty wind,
Cleaving the fields of space, as doth the swan
    Some silver stream (say Ganges, Nile, or Inde,   180
Or Thames, or Tweed), and midst them an old man
    With an old soul, and both extremely blind,
Halted before the gate, and, in his shroud,
Seated their fellow-traveller on a cloud.

XXIV

But bringing up the rear of this bright host   185
    A Spirit of a different aspect waved
His wings, like thunder-clouds above some coast
    Whose barren beach with frequent wrecks is paved;

His brow was like the deep when tempest-tossed;
   Fierce and unfathomable thoughts engraved   190
Eternal wrath on his immortal face,
And where he gazed a gloom pervaded space.

XXV

As he drew near, he gazed upon the gate
   Ne'er to be entered more by him or Sin,
With such a glance of supernatural hate,   195
   As made Saint Peter wish himself within;
He pottered with his keys at a great rate,
   And sweated through his Apostolic skin:
Of course his perspiration was but ichor,
Or some such other spiritual liquor.   200

XXVI

The very Cherubs huddled all together,
   Like birds when soars the falcon; and they felt
A tingling to the tip of every feather,
   And formed a circle like Orion's belt
Around their poor old charge; who scarce knew whither   205
   His guards had led him, though they gently dealt
With royal Manes (for by many stories,
And true, we learn the Angels all are Tories).

XXVII

As things were in this posture, the gate flew
   Asunder, and the flashing of its hinges   210
Flung over space an universal hue
   Of many-coloured flame, until its tinges
Reached even our speck of earth, and made a new
   Aurora borealis spread its fringes
O'er the North Pole; the same seen, when ice-bound,   215
By Captain Parry's crew, in "Melville's Sound."

XXVIII

And from the gate thrown open issued beaming
   A beautiful and mighty Thing of Light,

Radiant with glory, like a banner streaming
   Victorious from some world-o'erthrowing fight: 220
My poor comparisons must needs be teeming
   With earthly likenesses, for here the night
Of clay obscures our best conceptions, saving
Johanna Southcote, or Bob Southey raving.

XXIX

'Twas the Archangel Michael: all men know   225
   The make of Angels and Archangels, since
There's scarce a scribbler has not one to show,
   From the fiends' leader to the Angels' Prince.
There also are some altar-pieces, though
   I really can't say that they much evince   230
One's inner notions of immortal spirits;
But let the connoisseurs explain *their* merits.

XXX

Michael flew forth in glory and in good;
   A goodly work of him from whom all Glory
And Good arise; the portal past—he stood;   235
   Before him the young Cherubs and Saints hoary—
(I say young, begging to be understood
   By looks, not years; and should be very sorry
To state, they were not older than St. Peter,
But merely that they seemed a little sweeter).   240

XXXI

The Cherubs and the Saints bowed down before
   That arch-angelic Hierarch, the first
Of Essences angelical who wore
   The aspect of a god; but this ne'er nursed
Pride in his heavenly bosom, in whose core   245
   No thought, save for his Maker's service, durst
Intrude, however glorified and high;
He knew him but the Viceroy of the sky.

XXXII

He and the sombre, silent Spirit met—
    They knew each other both for good and ill;   250
Such was their power, that neither could forget
    His former friend and future foe; but still
There was a high, immortal, proud regret
    In either's eye, as if 'twere less their will
Than destiny to make the eternal years   255
Their date of war, and their "Champ Clos" the spheres.

XXXIII

But here they were in neutral space: we know
    From Job, that Satan hath the power to pay
A heavenly visit thrice a-year or so;
    And that the "Sons of God," like those of clay,   260
Must keep him company; and we might show
    From the same book, in how polite a way
The dialogue is held between the Powers
Of Good and Evil—but 'twould take up hours.

XXXIV

And this is not a theologic tract,   265
    To prove with Hebrew and with Arabic,
If Job be allegory or a fact,
    But a true narrative; and thus I pick
From out the whole but such and such an act
    As sets aside the slightest thought of trick.   270
'Tis every tittle true, beyond suspicion,
And accurate as any other vision.

XXXV

The spirits were in neutral space, before
    The gate of Heaven; like eastern thresholds is
The place where Death's grand cause is argued o'er,   275
    And souls despatched to that world or to this;
And therefore Michael and the other wore
    A civil aspect: though they did not kiss,

Yet still between his Darkness and his Brightness
There passed a mutual glance of great politeness.   280

XXXVI

The Archangel bowed, not like a modern beau,
    But with a graceful oriental bend,
Pressing one radiant arm just where below
    The heart in good men is supposed to tend;
He turned as to an equal, not too low;   285
    But kindly; Satan met his ancient friend
With more hauteur, as might an old Castilian
Poor Noble meet a mushroom rich civilian.

XXXVII

He merely bent his diabolic brow
    An instant; and then raising it, he stood   290
In act to assert his right or wrong, and show
    Cause why King George by no means could or should
Make out a case to be exempt from woe
    Eternal, more than other kings, endued
With better sense and hearts, whom History mentions,   295
Who long have "paved Hell with their good intentions."

XXXVIII

Michael began: "What wouldst thou with this man,
    Now dead, and brought before the Lord? What ill
Hath he wrought since his mortal race began,
    That thou canst claim him? Speak! and do thy will,   300
If it be just: if in this earthly span
    He hath been greatly failing to fulfil
His duties as a king and mortal, say,
And he is thine; if not—let him have way."

XXXIX

"Michael!" replied the Prince of Air, "even here   305
    Before the gate of Him thou servest, must
I claim my subject: and will make appear
    That as he was my worshipper in dust,

So shall he be in spirit, although dear
   To thee and thine, because nor wine nor lust   310
Were of his weaknesses; yet on the throne
He reigned o'er millions to serve me alone.

XL

"Look to our earth, or rather mine; it was,
   Once, more thy master's; but I triumph not
In this poor planet's conquest; nor, alas!   320
   Need he thou servest envy me my lot:
With all the myriads of bright worlds which pass
   In worship round him, he may have forgot
Yon weak creation of such paltry things:
I think few worth damnation save their kings,   320

XLI

"And these but as a kind of quit-rent, to
   Assert my right as Lord: and even had
I such an inclination, 'twere (as you
   Well know) superfluous; they are grown so bad,
That Hell has nothing better left to do   325
   Than leave them to themselves: so much more mad
And evil by their own internal curse,
Heaven cannot make them better, nor I worse.

XLII

"Look to the earth, I said, and say again:
   When this old, blind, mad, helpless, weak, poor worm 330
Began in youth's first bloom and flush to reign,
   The world and he both wore a different form,
And much of earth and all the watery plain
   Of Ocean called him king: through many a storm
His isles had floated on the abyss of Time;   335
For the rough virtues chose them for their clime.

XLIII

"He came to his sceptre young; he leaves it old:
   Look to the state in which he found his realm,
And left it; and his annals too behold,

How to a minion first he gave the helm;   340
How grew upon his heart a thirst for gold,
   The beggar's vice, which can but overwhelm
The meanest hearts; and for the rest, but glance
Thine eye along America and France.

XLIV

" 'Tis true, he was a tool from first to last   345
   (I have the workmen safe); but as a tool
So let him be consumed. From out the past
   Of ages, since mankind have known the rule
Of monarchs—from the bloody rolls amassed
   Of Sin and Slaughter—from the Cæsars' school,   350
Take the worst pupil; and produce a reign
More drenched with gore, more cumbered with the slain.

XLV

"He ever warred with freedom and the free:
   Nations as men, home subjects, foreign foes,
So that they uttered the word 'Liberty!'
   Found George the Third their first opponent. Whose   355
History was ever stained as his will be
   With national and individual woes?
I grant his household abstinence; I grant
His neutral virtues, which most monarchs want;   360

XLVI

"I know he was a constant consort; own
   He was a decent sire, and middling lord.
All this is much, and most upon a throne;
   As temperance, if at Apicius' board,
Is more than at an anchorite's supper shown.   365
   I grant him all the kindest can accord;
And this was well for him, but not for those
Millions who found him what Oppression chose.

XLVII

"The New World shook him off; the Old yet groans
   Beneath what he and his prepared, if not   370

Completed: he leaves heirs on many thrones
    To all his vices, without what begot
Compassion for him—his tame virtues; drones
    Who sleep, or despots who have now forgot
A lesson which shall be re-taught them, wake   375
Upon the thrones of earth; but let them quake!

XLVIII

"Five millions of the primitive, who hold
    The faith which makes ye great on earth, implored
A part of that vast all they held of old,—
    Freedom to worship—not alone your Lord,   380
Michael, but you, and you, Saint Peter! Cold
    Must be your souls, if you have not abhorred
The foe to Catholic participation
In all the license of a Christian nation.

XLIX

"True! he allowed them to pray God; but as   385
    A consequence of prayer, refused the law
Which would have placed them upon the same base
    With those who did not hold the Saints in awe."
But here Saint Peter started from his place
    And cried, "You may the prisoner withdraw: 390
Ere Heaven shall ope her portals to this Guelph,
While I am guard, may I be damned myself!

L

"Sooner will I with Cerberus exchange
    My office (and his is no sinecure)
Than see this royal Bedlam-bigot range   395
    The azure fields of Heaven, of that be sure!"
"Saint!" replied Satan, "you do well to avenge
    The wrongs he made your satellites endure;
And if to this exchange you should be given,
I'll try to coax our Cerberus up to Heaven!"   400

LI

Here Michael interposed: "Good Saint! and Devil!
   Pray, not so fast; you both outrun discretion.
Saint Peter! you were wont to be more civil:
   Satan! excuse this warmth of his expression,
And condescension to the vulgar's level:
   Even Saints sometimes forget themselves in session.   405
Have you got more to say?"—"No."—"If you please,
I'll trouble you to call your witnesses."

LII

Then Satan turned and waved his swarthy hand,
   Which stirred with its electric qualities   410
Clouds farther off than we can understand,
   Although we find him sometimes in our skies;
Infernal thunder shook both sea and land
   In all the planets—and Hell's batteries
Let off the artillery, which Milton mentions   415
As one of Satan's most sublime inventions.

LIII

This was a signal unto such damned souls
   As have the privilege of their damnation
Extended far beyond the mere controls
   Of worlds past, present, or to come; no station   420
Is theirs particularly in the rolls
   Of Hell assigned; but where their inclination
Or business carries them in search of game,
They may range freely—being damned the same.

LIV

They are proud of this—as very well they may,   425
   It being a sort of knighthood, or gilt key
Stuck in their loins; or like to an "entré"
   Up the back stairs, or such free-masonry.
I borrow my comparisons from clay,
   Being clay myself. Let not those spirits be   430

Offended with such base low likenesses;
We know their posts are nobler far than these.

LV

When the great signal ran from Heaven to Hell—
  About ten million times the distance reckoned
From our sun to its earth, as we can tell   435
  How much time it takes up, even to a second,
For every ray that travels to dispel
  The fogs of London, through which, dimly beaconed,
The weathercocks are gilt some thrice a year,
If that the *summer* is not too severe: 440

LVI

I say that I can tell—'twas half a minute;
  I know the solar beams take up more time
Ere, packed up for their journey, they begin it;
  But then their Telegraph is less sublime,
And if they ran a race, they would not win it   445
  'Gainst Satan's couriers bound for their own clime.
The sun takes up some years for every ray
To reach its goal—the Devil not half a day.

LVII

Upon the verge of space, about the size
  Of half-a-crown, a little speck appeared   450
(I've seen a something like it in the skies
  In the Ægean, ere a squall); it neared,
And, growing bigger, took another guise;
  Like an aërial ship it tacked, and steered,
Or *was* steered (I am doubtful of the grammar   455
Of the last phrase, which makes the stanza stammer;

LVIII

But take your choice): and then it grew a cloud;
  And so it was—a cloud of witnesses.
But such a cloud! No land ere saw a crowd
  Of locusts numerous as the heavens saw these;   460

They shadowed with their myriads Space; their loud
   And varied cries were like those of wild geese,
(If nations may be likened to a goose),
And realised the phrase of "Hell broke loose."

LIX

Here crashed a sturdy oath of stout John Bull,   465
   Who damned away his eyes as heretofore:
There Paddy brogued "By Jasus!"—"What's your wull?"
   The temperate Scot exclaimed: the French ghost swore
In certain terms I shan't translate in full,
   As the first coachman will; and 'midst the war,   470
The voice of Jonathan was heard to express,
"Our President is going to war, I guess."

LX

Besides there were the Spaniard, Dutch, and Dane,
   In short, an universal shoal of shades
From Otaheite's isle to Salisbury Plain,   475
   Of all climes and professions, years and trades,
Ready to swear against the good king's reign,
   Bitter as clubs in cards are against spades:
All summoned by this grand "subpœna," to
Try if kings mayn't be damned like me or you.   480

LXI

When Michael saw this host, he first grew pale,
   As Angels can; next, like Italian twilight,
He turned all colours—as a peacock's tail,
   Or sunset streaming through a Gothic skylight
In some old abbey, or a trout not stale,   485
   Or distant lightning on the horizon by night,
Or a fresh rainbow, or a grand review
Of thirty regiments in red, green, and blue.

LXII

Then he addressed himself to Satan: "Why—
   My good old friend, for such I deem you, though   490

Our different parties make us fight so shy,
　I ne'er mistake you for a *personal* foe;
Our difference is *political*, and I
　Trust that, whatever may occur below,
You know my great respect for you: and this   495
Makes me regret whate'er you do amiss—

LXIII

"Why, my dear Lucifer, would you abuse
　My call for witnesses? I did not mean
That you should half of Earth and Hell produce;
　'Tis even superfluous, since two honest, clean,   500
True testimonies are enough: we lose
　Our Time, nay, our Eternity, between
The accusation, and defence: if we
Hear both, 'twill stretch our immortality."

LXIV

Satan replied, "To me the matter is   505
　Indifferent, in a personal point of view:
I can have fifty better souls than this
　With far less trouble than we have gone through
Already; and I merely argued his
　Late Majesty of Britain's case with you   510
Upon a point of form: you may dispose
Of him; I've kings enough below, God knows!"

LXV

Thus spoke the Demon (late called "multifaced"
　By multo-scribbling Southey). "Then we'll call
One or two persons of the myriads placed   515
　Around our congress, and dispense with all
The rest," quoth Michael: "Who may be so graced
　As to speak first? there's choice enough—who shall
It be?" Then Satan answered, "There are many;
But you may choose Jack Wilkes as well as any."   520

LXVI

A merry, cock-eyed, curious-looking Sprite
  Upon the instant started from the throng,
Dressed in a fashion now forgotten quite;
  For all the fashions of the flesh stick long
By people in the next world; where unite   525
  All the costumes since Adam's, right or wrong,
From Eve's fig-leaf down to the petticoat,
Almost as scanty, of days less remote.

LXVII

The Spirit looked around upon the crowds
  Assembled, and exclaimed, "My friends of all   530
The spheres, we shall catch cold amongst these clouds;
  So let's to business: why this general call?
If those are freeholders I see in shrouds,
  And 'tis for an election that they bawl,
Behold a candidate with unturned coat!   535
Saint Peter, may I count upon your vote?"

LXVIII

"Sir," replied Michael, "you mistake; these things
  Are of a former life, and what we do
Above is more august; to judge of kings
  Is the tribunal met: so now you know."   540
"Then I presume those gentlemen with wings,"
  Said Wilkes, "are Cherubs; and that soul below
Looks much like George the Third, but to my mind
A good deal older—bless me! is he blind?"

LXIX

"He is what you behold him, and his doom   545
  Depends upon his deeds," the Angel said;
"If you have aught to arraign in him, the tomb
  Gives license to the humblest beggar's head
To lift itself against the loftiest."—"Some,"
  Said Wilkes, "don't wait to see them laid in lead,   550

For such a liberty—and I, for one,
Have told them what I thought beneath the sun."

LXX

"Above the sun repeat, then, what thou hast
    To urge against him," said the Archangel. "Why,"
Replied the spirit, "since old scores are past,   555
    Must I turn evidence? In faith, not I.
Besides, I beat him hollow at the last,
    With all his Lords and Commons: in the sky
I don't like ripping up old stories, since
His conduct was but natural in a prince.   560

LXXI

"Foolish, no doubt, and wicked, to oppress
    A poor unlucky devil without a shilling;
But then I blame the man himself much less
    Than Bute and Grafton, and shall be unwilling
To see him punished here for their excess,   565
    Since they were both damned long ago, and still in
Their place below: for me, I have forgiven,
And vote his *habeas corpus* into Heaven."

LXXII

"Wilkes," said the Devil, "I understand all this;
    You turned to half a courtier ere you died,   570
And seem to think it would not be amiss
    To grow a whole one on the other side
Of Charon's ferry; you forget that *his*
    Reign is concluded; whatsoe'er betide,
He won't be sovereign more: you've lost your labour,   575
For at the best he will but be your neighbour.

LXXIII

"However, I knew what to think of it,
    When I beheld you in your jesting way,
Fitting and whispering round about the spit
    Where Belial, upon duty for the day,   580

With Fox's lard was basting William Pitt,
His pupil; I knew what to think, I say:
That fellow even in Hell breeds farther ills;
I'll have him gagged—'twas one of his own Bills.

LXXIV

"Call Junius!" From the crowd a shadow stalked, 585
And at the name there was a general squeeze,
So that the very ghosts no longer walked
In comfort, at their own aërial ease,
But were all rammed, and jammed (but to be balked,
As we shall see), and jostled hands and knees, 590
Like wind compressed and pent within a bladder,
Or like a human colic, which is sadder.

LXXV

The shadow came—a tall, thin, grey-haired figure,
That looked as it had been a shade on earth;
Quick in its motions, with an air of vigour, 595
But nought to mark its breeding or its birth;
Now it waxed little, then again grew bigger,
With now an air of gloom, or savage mirth;
But as you gazed upon its features, they
Changed every instant—to what, none could say. 600

LXXVI

The more intently the ghosts gazed, the less
Could they distinguish whose the features were;
The Devil himself seemed puzzled even to guess;
They varied like a dream—now here, now there;
And several people swore from out the press,
They knew him perfectly; and one could swear 605
He was his father; upon which another
Was sure he was his mother's cousin's brother:

LXXVII

Another, that he was a duke, or knight,
An orator, a lawyer, or a priest, 610

A nabob, a man-midwife; but the wight
   Mysterious changed his countenance at least
As oft as they their minds: though in full sight
   He stood, the puzzle only was increased;
The man was a phantasmagoria in   615
Himself—he was so volatile and thin.

LXXVIII

The moment that you had pronounced him one,
   Presto! his face changed, and he was another;
And when that change was hardly well put on,
   It varied, till I don't think his own mother   620
(If that he had a mother) would her son
   Have known, he shifted so from one to t'other;
Till guessing from a pleasure grew a task,
At this epistolary "Iron Mask."

LXXIX

For sometimes he like Cerberus would seem—   625
   "Three gentlemen at once" (as sagely says
Good Mrs. Malaprop); then you might deem
   That he was not even one; now many rays
Were flashing round him; and now a thick steam
   Hid him from sight—like fogs on London days: 630
Now Burke, now Tooke, he grew to people's fancies
And certes often like Sir Philip Francis.

LXXX

I've an hypothesis—'tis quite my own;
   I never let it out till now, for fear
Of doing people harm about the throne,   635
   And injuring some minister or peer,
On whom the stigma might perhaps be blown;
   It is—my gentle public, lend thine ear!
'Tis, that what Junius we are wont to call,
Was *really—truly*—nobody at all.   640

LXXXI

I don't see wherefore letters should not be
  Written without hands, since we daily view
Them written without heads; and books, we see,
  Are filled as well without the latter too:
And really till we fix on somebody   645
  For certain sure to claim them as his due,
Their author, like the Niger's mouth, will bother
The world to say if *there* be mouth or author.

LXXXII

"And who and what art thou?" the Archangel said.
  "For *that* you may consult my title-page,"   650
Replied this mighty shadow of a shade:
  "If I have kept my secret half an age,
I scarce shall tell it now."—"Canst thou upbraid,"
  Continued Michael, "George Rex, or allege
Aught further?" Junius answered, "You had better   655
First ask him for *his* answer to my letter:

LXXXIII

"My charges upon record will outlast
  The brass of both his epitaph and tomb."
"Repent'st thou not," said Michael, "of some past
  Exaggeration? something which may doom   660
Thyself if false, as him if true? Thou wast
  Too bitter—is it not so?—in thy gloom
Of passion?"—"Passion!" cried the phantom dim,
"I loved my country, and I hated him.

LXXXIV

"What I have written, I have written: let   665
  The rest be on his head or mine!" So spoke
Old "Nominis Umbra;" and while speaking yet,
  Away he melted in celestial smoke.
Then Satan said to Michael, "Don't forget
  To call George Washington, and John Horne Tooke,   670

And Franklin;"—but at this time there was heard
A cry for room, though not a phantom stirred.

LXXXV

At length with jostling, elbowing, and the aid
    Of Cherubim appointed to that post,
The devil Asmodeus to the circle made   675
    His way, and looked as if his journey cost
Some trouble. When his burden down he laid,
    "What's this?" cried Michael; "why, 'tis not a ghost?"
"I know it," quoth the Incubus; "but he
Shall be one, if you leave the affair to me.   680

LXXXVI

"Confound the renegado! I have sprained
    My left wing, he's so heavy; one would think
Some of his works about his neck were chained.
    But to the point; while hovering o'er the brink
Of Skiddaw (where as usual it still rained),   685
    I saw a taper, far below me, wink,
And stooping, caught this fellow at a libel—
No less on History—than the Holy Bible.

LXXXVII

"The former is the Devil's scripture, and
    The latter yours, good Michael: so the affair   690
Belongs to all of us, you understand.
    I snatched him up just as you see him there,
And brought him off for sentence out of hand:
    I've scarcely been ten minutes in the air—
At least a quarter it can hardly be:
I dare say that his wife is still at tea."   695

LXXXVIII

Here Satan said, "I know this man of old,
    And have expected him for some time here;
A sillier fellow you will scarce behold,
    Or more conceited in his petty sphere: 700

But surely it was not worth while to fold
  Such trash below your wing, Asmodeus dear:
We had the poor wretch safe (without being bored
With carriage) coming of his own accord.

LXXXIX

"But since he's here, let's see what he has done."   705
  "Done!" cried Asmodeus, "he anticipates
The very business you are now upon,
  And scribbles as if head clerk to the Fates.
Who knows to what his ribaldry may run,
  When such an ass as this, like Balaam's, prates?"   710
"Let's hear," quoth Michael, "what he has to say:
You know we're bound to that in every way."

XC

Now the bard, glad to get an audience, which
  By no means often was his case below,
Began to cough, and hawk, and hem, and pitch   715
  His voice into that awful note of woe
To all unhappy hearers within reach
  Of poets when the tide of rhyme's in flow;
But stuck fast with his first hexameter,
Not one of all whose gouty feet would stir.   720

XCI

But ere the spavined dactyls could be spurred
  Into recitative, in great dismay
Both Cherubim and Seraphim were heard
  To murmur loudly through their long array;
And Michael rose ere he could get a word   725
  Of all his foundered verses under way,
And cried, "For God's sake stop, my friend! 'twere best—
'Non Di, non homines'—you know the rest."

XCII

A general bustle spread throughout the throng,
  Which seemed to hold all verse in detestation;   730

The Angels had of course enough of song
    When upon service; and the generation
Of ghosts had heard too much in life, not long
    Before, to profit by a new occasion:
The Monarch, mute till then, exclaimed, "What! what! 735
Pye come again? No more—no more of that!"

XCIII

The tumult grew; an universal cough
    Convulsed the skies, as during a debate,
When Castlereagh has been up long enough
    (Before he was first minister of state,   740
I mean—the *slaves hear now);* some cried "Off, off!"
    As at a farce; till, grown quite desperate,
The Bard Saint Peter prayed to interpose
(Himself an author) only for his prose.

XCIV

The varlet was not an ill-favoured knave;   745
    A good deal like a vulture in the face,
With a hook nose and a hawk's eye, which gave
    A smart and sharper-looking sort of grace
To his whole aspect, which, though rather grave,
    Was by no means so ugly as his case;   750
But that, indeed, was hopeless as can be,
Quite a poetic felony "de se."

XCV

Then Michael blew his trump, and stilled the noise
    With one still greater, as is yet the mode
On earth besides; except some grumbling voice,   755
    Which now and then will make a slight inroad
Upon decorous silence, few will twice
    Lift up their lungs when fairly overcrowed;
And now the Bard could plead his own bad cause,
With all the attitudes of self-applause.   760

XCVI

He said—(I only give the heads)—he said,
  He meant no harm in scribbling; 'twas his way
Upon all topics; 'twas, besides, his bread,
  Of which he buttered both sides; 'twould delay
Too long the assembly (he was pleased to dread),   765
  And take up rather more time than a day,
To name his works—he would but cite a few—
"Wat Tyler"—"Rhymes on Blenheim"—"Waterloo."

XCVII

He had written praises of a Regicide;
  He had written praises of all kings whatever;   770
He had written for republics far and wide,
  And then against them bitterer than ever;
For pantisocracy he once had cried
  Aloud, a scheme less moral than 'twas clever;
Then grew a hearty anti-jacobin—   775
Had turned his coat—and would have turned his skin.

XCVIII

He had sung against all battles, and again
  In their high praise and glory; he had called
Reviewing "the ungentle craft," and then
  Became as base a critic as e'er crawled—   780
Fed, paid, and pampered by the very men
  By whom his muse and morals had been mauled:
He had written much blank verse, and blanker prose,
And more of both than any body knows.

XCIX

He had written Wesley's life:—here turning round   785
  To Satan, "Sir, I'm ready to write yours,
In two octavo volumes, nicely bound,
  With notes and preface, all that most allures
The pious purchaser; and there's no ground
  For fear, for I can choose my own reviewers: 790

So let me have the proper documents,
That I may add you to my other saints."

C

Satan bowed, and was silent. "Well, if you,
  With amiable modesty, decline
My offer, what says Michael? There are few   795
  Whose memoirs could be rendered more divine.
Mine is a pen of all work; not so new
  As it was once, but I would make you shine
Like your own trumpet. By the way, my own
Has more of brass in it, and is as well blown.   800

CI

"But talking about trumpets, here's my 'Vision!'
  Now you shall judge, all people—yes—you shall
Judge with my judgment! and by my decision
  Be guided who shall enter heaven or fall.
I settle all these things by intuition,   805
  Times present, past, to come—Heaven—Hell—and all,
Like King Alfonso. When I thus see double,
I save the Deity some worlds of trouble."

CII

He ceased, and drew forth an MS.; and no
  Persuasion on the part of Devils, Saints,   810
Or Angels, now could stop the torrent; so
  He read the first three lines of the contents;
But at the fourth, the whole spiritual show
  Had vanished, with variety of scents,
Ambrosial and sulphureous, as they sprang,   815
Like lightning, off from his "melodious twang."

CIII

Those grand heroics acted as a spell;
  The Angels stopped their ears and plied their pinions;
The Devils ran howling, deafened, down to Hell;
  The ghosts fled, gibbering, for their own dominions— 820

(For 'tis not yet decided where they dwell,
  And I leave every man to his opinions);
Michael took refuge in his trump—but, lo!
His teeth were set on edge, he could not blow!

CIV

Saint Peter, who has hitherto been known   825
  For an impetuous saint, upraised his keys,
And at the fifth line knocked the poet down;
  Who fell like Phaeton, but more at ease,
Into his lake, for there he did not drown;
  A different web being by the Destinies   830
Woven for the Laureate's final wreath, whene'er
Reform shall happen either here or there.

CV

He first sank to the bottom—like his works,
  But soon rose to the surface—like himself;
For all corrupted things are buoyed like corks,   835
  By their own rottenness, light as an elf,
Or wisp that flits o'er a morass: he lurks,
  It may be, still, like dull books on a shelf,
In his own den, to scrawl some "Life" or "Vision,"
As Welborn says—"the Devil turned precisian."   840

CVI

As for the rest, to come to the conclusion
  Of this true dream, the telescope is gone
Which kept my optics free from all delusion,
  And showed me what I in my turn have shown;
All I saw farther, in the last confusion,   845
  Was, that King George slipped into Heaven for one;
And when the tumult dwindled to a calm,
I left him practising the hundredth psalm.
    [1821]

STANZAS WRITTEN ON THE ROAD BETWEEN
FLORENCE AND PISA

1

Oh, talk not to me of a name great in story—
The days of our Youth are the days of our glory;
And the myrtle and ivy of sweet two-and-twenty
Are worth all your laurels, though ever so plenty.

2

What are garlands and crowns to the brow that is
    wrinkled?   5
'Tis but as a dead flower May-dew besprinkled:
Then away with all such from the head that is hoary,
What care I for the wreaths that can *only* give glory?

3

Oh Fame!—if I e'er took delight in thy praises,
'Twas less for the sake of thy high-sounding phrases,   10
Than to see the bright eyes of the dear One discover,
She thought that I was not unworthy to love her.

4

There chiefly I sought thee, *there* only I found thee;
Her Glance was the best of the rays that surround thee,
When it sparkled o'er aught that was bright in my story,   15
I knew it was Love, and I felt it was Glory.
    [1821]

DON JUAN

CANTO THE TWELFTH

I

Of all the barbarous middle ages, that
　Which is most barbarous is the middle age
Of man! it is—I really scarce know what;
　But when we hover between fool and sage,
And don't know justly what we would be at—   5
　A period something like a printed page,
Black letter upon foolscap, while our hair
Grows grizzled, and we are not what we were;—

II

Too old for Youth,—too young, at thirty-five,
　To herd with boys, or hoard with good threescore,—   10
I wonder people should be left alive;
　But since they are, that epoch is a bore:
Love lingers still, although 't were late to wive:
　And as for other love, the illusion 's o'er;
And Money, that most pure imagination,   15
Gleams only through the dawn of its creation.

III

O Gold! Why call we misers miserable?
　Theirs is the pleasure that can never pall;
Theirs is the best bower anchor, the chain cable
　Which holds fast other pleasures great and small.
Ye who but see the saving man at table,   20
　And scorn his temperate board, as none at all,
And wonder how the wealthy can be sparing,
Know not what visions spring from each cheese-paring.

IV

Love or lust makes Man sick, and wine much sicker;   25
　Ambition rends, and gaming gains a loss;

But making money, slowly first, then quicker,
  And adding still a little through each cross
(Which will come over things), beats Love or liquor,
  The gamester's counter, or the statesman's dross.   30
O Gold! I still prefer thee unto paper,
Which makes bank credit like a bank of vapour.

V

Who hold the balance of the World? Who reign
  O'er congress, whether royalist or liberal?
Who rouse the shirtless patriots of Spain?   35
  (That make old Europe's journals "squeak and gibber"
    all)
Who keep the World, both old and new, in pain
  Or pleasure? Who make politics run glibber all?
The shade of Buonaparte's noble daring?—
Jew Rothschild, and his fellow-Christian, Baring.   40

VI

Those, and the truly liberal Lafitte,
  Are the true Lords of Europe. Every loan
Is not a merely speculative hit,
  But seats a Nation or upsets a Throne
Republics also get involved a bit;   45
  Columbia's stock hath holders not unknown
On 'Change; and even thy silver soil, Peru,
Must get itself discounted by a Jew.

VII

Why call the miser miserable? as
  I said before: the frugal life is his,   50
Which in a saint or cynic ever was
  The theme of praise: a hermit would not miss
Canonization for the self-same cause,
  And wherefore blame gaunt Wealth's austerities?
Because, you'll say, nought calls for such a trial;—   55
Then there's more merit in his self-denial.

VIII

He is your only poet;—Passion, pure
   And sparkling on from heap to heap, displays,
Possessed, the ore, of which mere hopes allure
   Nations athwart the deep: the golden rays   60
Flash up in ingots from the mine obscure:
   On him the Diamond pours its brilliant blaze,
While the mild Emerald's beam shades down the dies
Of other stones, to soothe the miser's eyes.

IX

The lands on either side are his; the ship   65
   From Ceylon, Inde, or far Cathay, unloads
For him the fragrant produce of each trip;
   Beneath his cars of Ceres groan the roads,
And the vine blushes like Aurora's lip;
   His very cellars might be Kings' abodes;   70
While he, despising every sensual call,
Commands—the intellectual Lord of all.

X

Perhaps he hath great projects in his mind,
   To build a college, or to found a race,
A hospital, a church,—and leave behind   75
   Some dome surmounted by his meagre face:
Perhaps he fain would liberate Mankind
   Even with the very ore which makes them base;
Perhaps he would be wealthiest of his nation,
Or revel in the joys of calculation.   80

XI

But whether all, or each, or none of these
   May be the hoarder's principle of action,
The fool will call such mania a disease:—
   What is his own? Go—look at each transaction,
Wars, revels, loves—do these bring men more ease   85
   Than the mere plodding through each "vulgar fraction?"

Or do they benefit Mankind? Lean Miser!
Let spendthrifts' heirs inquire of yours—who 's wiser?

XII

How beauteous are rouleaus! how charming chests
    Containing ingots, bags of dollars, coins   90
(Not of old victors, all whose heads and crests
    Weigh not the thin ore where their visage shines,
But) of fine unclipped gold, where dully rests
    Some likeness, which the glittering cirque confines,
Of modern, reigning, sterling, stupid stamp!—   95
Yes! ready money *is* Aladdin's lamp.

XIII

"Love rules the Camp, the Court, the Grove,—for Love
    Is Heaven, and Heaven is Love:"—so sings the bard;
Which it were rather difficult to prove
    (A thing with poetry in general hard).   100
Perhaps there may be something in "the Grove,"
    At least it rhymes to "Love:" but I'm prepared
To doubt (no less than landlords of their rental)
If "Courts" and "Camps" be quite so sentimental.

XIV

But if Love don't, *Cash* does, and Cash alone: 105
    Cash rules the Grove, and fells it too besides;
Without cash, camps were thin, and courts were none;
    Without cash, Malthus tells you—"take no brides."
So Cash rules Love the ruler, on his own
    High ground, as virgin Cynthia sways the tides: 110
And as for "Heaven being Love," why not say honey
Is wax? Heaven is not Love, 't is Matrimony.

XV

Is not all Love prohibited whatever,
    Excepting Marriage? which is Love, no doubt,
After a sort; but somehow people never   115
    With the same thought the two words have helped out.

Love may exist *with* Marriage, and *should* ever,
   And Marriage also may exist without;
But Love *sans* banns is both a sin and shame,
And ought to go by quite another name.   120

XVI

Now if the "Court," and "Camp," and "Grove," be not
   Recruited all with constant married men,
Who never coveted their neighbour's lot,
   I say *that* line's a lapsus of the pen;—
Strange too in my *buon camerado* Scott,   125
   So celebrated for his morals, when
My Jeffrey held him up as an example
To me;—of whom these morals are a sample.

XVII

Well, if I don't succeed, I *have* succeeded,
   And that's enough; succeeded in my youth,   130
The only time when much success is needed:
   And my success produced what I, in sooth,
Cared most about; it need not now be pleaded—
   Whate'er it was, 'twas mine; I've paid, in truth,
Of late, the penalty of such success,   135
But have not learned to wish it any less.

XVIII

That suit in Chancery,—which some persons plead
   In an appeal to the unborn, whom they,
In the faith of their procreative creed,
   Baptize Posterity, or future clay,—   140
To me seems but a dubious kind of reed
   To lean on for support in any way;
Since odds are that Posterity will know
No more of them, than they of her, I trow.

XIX

Why, I 'm Posterity—and so are you;   145
   And whom do we remember? Not a hundred.
Were every memory written down all true,
   The tenth or twentieth name would be but blundered;

Even Plutarch's Lives have but picked out a few,
  And 'gainst those few your annalists have thundered;   150
And Mitford in the nineteenth century
Gives, with Greek truth, the good old Greek the lie.

XX

Good people all, of every degree,
  Ye gentle readers and ungentle writers,
In this twelfth Canto 't is my wish to be   155
  As serious as if I had for inditers
Malthus and Wilberforce:—the last set free
  The Negroes, and is worth a million fighters;
While Wellington has but enslaved the Whites,
And Malthus does the thing 'gainst which he writes. 160

XXI

I 'm serious—so are all men upon paper;
  And why should I not form my speculation,
And hold up to the Sun my little taper?
  Mankind just now seem wrapped in meditation
On constitutions and steam-boats of vapour;   165
  While sages write against all procreation,
Unless a man can calculate his means
Of feeding brats the moment his wife weans.

XXII

That 's noble! That 's romantic! For my part,
  I think that "Philo-genitiveness" is—   170
(Now here 's a word quite after my own heart,
  Though there 's a shorter a good deal than this,
If that politeness set it not apart;
  But I 'm resolved to say nought that 's amiss)—
I say, methinks that "Philo-genitiveness"   175
Might meet from men a little more forgiveness.

XXIII

And now to business.—O my gentle Juan!
  Thou art in London—in that pleasant place,

Where every kind of mischief 's daily brewing,
　Which can await warm Youth in its wild race.　　　180
'T is true, that thy career is not a new one;
　Thou art no novice in the headlong chase
Of early life; but this is a new land,
Which foreigners can never understand.

XXIV

What with a small diversity of climate,　　　　　185
　Of hot or cold, mercurial or sedate,
I could send forth my mandate like a Primate
　Upon the rest of Europe's social state;
But thou art the most difficult to rhyme at,
　Great Britain, which the Muse may penetrate.　　190
All countries have their "Lions," but in thee
There is but one superb menagerie.

XXV

But I am sick of politics. Begin—
　"Paulo Majora." Juan, undecided
Amongst the paths of being "taken in,"　　　　195
　Above the ice had like a skater glided:
When tired of play, he flirted without sin
　With some of those fair creatures who have prided
Themselves on innocent tantalisation,
And hate all vice except its reputation.　　　　200

XXVI

But these are few, and in the end they make
　Some devilish escapade or stir, which shows
That even the purest people may mistake
　Their way through Virtue's primrose paths of snows;
And then men stare, as if a new ass spake　　　205
　To Balaam, and from tongue to ear o'erflows
Quicksilver small talk, ending (if you note it)
With the kind World's Amen—"Who would have
　　thought it?"

XXVII

The little Leila, with her Orient eyes,
   And taciturn Asiatic disposition,   210
(Which saw all Western things with small surprise,
   To the surprise of people of condition,
Who think that novelties are butterflies
   To be pursued as food for inanition,)
Her charming figure and romantic history   215
Became a kind of fashionable mystery.

XXVIII

The women much divided—as is usual
   Amongst the sex in little things or great—
Think not, fair creatures, that I mean to abuse you all,
   I have always liked you better than I state—   220
Since I've grown moral, still I must accuse you all
   Of being apt to talk at a great rate;
And now there was a general sensation
Amongst you, about Leila's education.

XXIX

In one point only were you settled—and   225
   You had reason; 'twas that a young child of grace,
As beautiful as her own native land,
   And far away, the last bud of her race,
Howe'er our friend Don Juan might command
   Himself for five, four, three, or two years' space,   230
Would be much better taught beneath the eye
Of peeresses whose follies had run dry.

XXX

So first there was a generous emulation,
   And then there was a general competition,
To undertake the orphan's education: 235
   As Juan was a person of condition,
It had been an affront on this occasion
   To talk of a subscription or petition;

But sixteen dowagers, ten unwed she sages
Whose tale belongs to "Hallam's Middle Ages,"   240

XXXI

And one or two sad, separate wives, without
    A fruit to bloom upon their withering bough—
Begged to bring up the little girl, and "out,"—
    For that's the phrase that settles all things now,
Meaning a virgin's first blush at a rout,
    And all her points as thorough bred to show: 245
And I assure you, that like virgin honey
Tastes their first season (mostly if they have money).

XXXII

How all the needy honourable misters,
    Each out-at-elbow peer, or desperate dandy,
The watchful mothers, and the careful sisters,   250
    (Who, by the by, when clever, are more handy
At making matches, where "'t is gold that glisters,"
    Than their *he* relatives), like flies o'er candy
Buzz round "the Fortune" with their busy battery,   255
To turn her head with waltzing and with flattery!

XXXIII

Each aunt, each cousin, hath her speculation;
    Nay, married dames will now and then discover
Such pure disinterestedness of passion,
    I 've known them court an heiress for their lover.   260
"Tantane!" Such the virtues of high station,
    Even in the hopeful Isle, whose outlet 's "Dover!"
While the poor rich wretch, object of these cares,
Has cause to wish her sire had had male heirs.

XXXIV

Some are soon bagged, and some reject three dozen: 265
    'T is fine to see them scattering refusals
And wild dismay o'er every angry cousin
    (Friends of the party), who begin accusals,

Such as—"Unless Miss Blank meant to have chosen
    Poor Frederick, why did she accord perusals   270
To his billets? Why waltz with him? Why, I pray,
Look 'Yes' last night, and yet say 'No' to-day?

xxxv

"Why?—Why?—Besides, Fred really was *attached*;
    'T was not her fortune—he has enough without;
The time will come she 'll wish that she had snatched 275
    So good an opportunity, no doubt:—
But the old Marchioness some plan had hatched,
    As I 'll tell Aurea at to-morrow's rout:
And after all poor Frederick may do better—
Pray did you see her answer to his letter?"   280

xxxvi

Smart uniforms and sparkling coronets
    Are spurned in turn, until her turn arrives,
After male loss of time, and hearts, and bets
    Upon the sweepstakes for substantial wives;
And when at last the pretty creature gets   285
    Some gentleman, who fights, or writes, or drives,
It soothes the awkward squad of the rejected
To find how very badly she selected.

xxxvii

For sometimes they accept some long pursuer,
    Worn out with importunity; or fall   290
(But here perhaps the instances are fewer)
    To the lot of him who scarce pursued at all.
A hazy widower turned of forty 's sure
    (If 't is not vain examples to recall)
To draw a high prize: now, howe'er he got her, I   295
See nought more strange in this than t' other lottery.

xxxviii

I, for my part—(one "modern instance" more,
    "True, 't is a pity—pity 't is, 't is true")—
Was chosen from out an amatory score,

Albeit my years were less discreet than few;   300
But though I also had reformed before
  Those became one who soon were to be two,
I 'll not gainsay the generous public's voice,
That the young lady made a monstrous choice.

XXXIX

Oh, pardon my digression—or at least   305
  Peruse! 'T is always with a moral end
That I dissert, like grace before a feast:
  For like an agéd aunt, or tiresome friend,
A rigid guardian, or a zealous priest,
  My Muse by exhortation means to mend   310
All people, at all times, and in most places,
Which puts my Pegasus to these grave paces.

XL

But now I 'm going to be immoral; now
  I mean to show things really as they are,
Not as they ought to be: for I avow,   315
  That till we see what 's what in fact, we 're far
From much improvement with that virtuous plough
  Which skims the surface, leaving scarce a scar
Upon the black loam long manured by Vice,
Only to keep its corn at the old price.   320

XLI

But first of little Leila we'll dispose,
  For like a day-dawn she was young and pure—
Or like the old comparison of snows,
  (Which are more pure than pleasant, to be sure,
Like many people everybody knows),—   325
  Don Juan was delighted to secure
A goodly guardian for his infant charge,
Who might not profit much by being at large.

XLII

Besides, he had found out he was no tutor
  (I wish that others would find out the same),   330

And rather wished in such things to stand neuter,
   For silly wards will bring their guardians blame:
So when he saw each ancient dame a suitor
   To make his little wild Asiatic tame,
Consulting "the Society for Vice   335
Suppression," Lady Pinchbeck was his choice.

XLIII

Olden she was—but had been very young;
   Virtuous she was—and had been, I believe;
Although the World has such an evil tongue
   That—but my chaster ear will not receive   340
An echo of a syllable that 's wrong:
   In fact, there 's nothing makes me so much grieve,
As that abominable tittle-tattle,
Which is the cud eschewed by human cattle.

XLIV

Moreover I 've remarked (and I was once   345
   A slight observer in a modest way),
And so may every one except a dunce,
   That ladies in their youth a little gay,
Besides their knowledge of the World, and sense
   Of the sad consequence of going astray,   350
Are wiser in their warnings 'gainst the woe
Which the mere passionless can never know.

XLV

While the harsh prude indemnifies her virtue
   By railing at the unknown and envied passion,
Seeking far less to save you than to hurt you,   355
   Or, what 's still worse, to put you out of fashion,—
The kinder veteran with calm words will court you,
   Entreating you to pause before you dash on;
Expounding and illustrating the riddle
Of epic Love's beginning—end—and middle.   360

XLVI

Now whether it be thus, or that they are stricter,
   As better knowing why they should be so,

I think you 'll find from many a family picture,
  That daughters of such mothers as may know
The World by experience rather than by lecture,   365
  Turn out much better for the Smithfield Show
Of vestals brought into the marriage mart,
Than those bred up by prudes without a heart.

XLVII

I said that Lady Pinchbeck had been talked about—
  As who has not, if female, young, and pretty?   370
But now no more the ghost of Scandal stalked about;
  She merely was deemed amiable and witty,
And several of her best bons-mots were hawked about:
  Then she was given to charity and pity,
And passed (at least the latter years of life)   375
For being a most exemplary wife.

XLVIII

High in high circles, gentle in her own,
  She was the mild reprover of the young,
Whenever—which means every day—they 'd shown
  An awkward inclination to go wrong.   380
The quantity of good she did 's unknown,
  Or at the least would lengthen out my song:
In brief, the little orphan of the East
Had raised an interest in her,—which increased.

XLIX

Juan, too, was a sort of favourite with her,   385
  Because she thought him a good heart at bottom,
A little spoiled, but not so altogether;
  Which was a wonder, if you think who got him,
And how he had been tossed, he scarce knew whither:
  Though this might ruin others, it did not him,   390
At least entirely—for he had seen too many
Changes in Youth, to be surprised at any.

L

And these vicissitudes tell best in youth;
  For when they happen at a riper age,

People are apt to blame the Fates, forsooth,   395
    And wonder Providence is not more sage.
Adversity is the first path to Truth:
    He who hath proved War—Storm—or Woman's rage,
Whether his winters be eighteen or eighty,
Hath won the experience which is deemed so weighty.   400

LI

How far it profits is another matter.—
    Our hero gladly saw his little charge
Safe with a lady, whose last grown-up daughter
    Being long married, and thus set at large,
Had left all the accomplishments she taught her   405
    To be transmitted, like the Lord Mayor's barge,
To the next comer; or—as it will tell
More Muse-like—like to Cytherea's shell.

LII

I call such things transmission; for there is
    A floating balance of accomplishment,   410
Which forms a pedigree from Miss to Miss,
    According as their minds or backs are bent.
Some waltz—some draw—some fathom the abyss
    Of Metaphysics; others are content
With Music; the most moderate shine as wits;—   415
While others have a genius turned for fits.

LIII

But whether fits, or wits, or harpsichords—
    Theology—fine arts—or finer stays,
May be the baits for Gentlemen or Lords
    With regular descent, in these our days,   420
The last year to the new transfers its hoards;
    New vestals claim men's eyes with the same praise
Of "elegant" et cætera, in fresh batches—
All matchless creatures—and yet bent on matches.

LIV

But now I will begin my poem. 'Tis   425
    Perhaps a little strange, if not quite new,

That from the first of Cantos up to this
  I 've not begun what we have to go through.
These first twelve books are merely flourishes,
  Preludios, trying just a string or two   430
Upon my lyre, or making the pegs sure;
  And when so, you shall have the overture.

LV

My Muses do not care a pinch of rosin
  About what 's called success, or not succeeding:
Such thoughts are quite below the strain they have chosen; 435
  'T is a "great moral lesson" they are reading.
I thought, at setting off, about two dozen
  Cantos would do; but at Apollo's pleading,
If that my Pegasus should not be foundered,
I think to canter gently through a hundred.   440

LVI

Don Juan saw that Microcosm on stilts,
  Yclept the Great World; for it is the least,
Although the highest: but as swords have hilts
  By which their power of mischief is increased,
When Man in battle or in quarrel tilts,   445
  Thus the low world, north, south, or west, or east,
Must still obey the high—which is their handle,
Their Moon, their Sun, their gas, their farthing candle.

LVII

He had many friends who had many wives, and was
  Well looked upon by both, to that extent   450
Of friendship which you may accept or pass,
  It does nor good nor harm; being merely meant
To keep the wheels going of the higher class,
  And draw them nightly when a ticket 's sent;
And what with masquerades, and fêtes, and balls, 455
For the first season such a life scarce palls.

LVIII

A young unmarried man, with a good name
  And fortune, has an awkward part to play;

For good society is but a game,
  "The royal game of Goose," as I may say,   460
Where everybody has some separate aim,
  An end to answer, or a plan to lay—
The single ladies wishing to be double,
The married ones to save the virgins trouble.

LIX

I don't mean this as general, but particular   465
  Examples may be found of such pursuits:
Though several also keep their perpendicular
  Like poplars, with good principles for roots;
Yet many have a method more reticular—
  "Fishers for men," like Sirens with soft lutes: 470
For talk six times with the same single lady,
And you may get the wedding-dresses ready.

LX

Perhaps you 'll have a letter from the mother,
  To say her daughter's feelings are trepanned;
Perhaps you 'll have a visit from the brother,   475
  All strut, and stays, and whiskers, to demand
What "your intentions are?"—One way or other
  It seems the virgin's heart expects your hand:
And between pity for her case and yours,
You 'll add to Matrimony's list of cures.   480

LXI

I 've known a dozen weddings made even thus,
  And some of them high names: I have also known
Young men who—though they hated to discuss
  Pretensions which they never dreamed to have shown—
Yet neither frightened by a female fuss,   485
  Nor by mustachios moved, were let alone,
And lived, as did the broken-hearted fair,
In happier plight than if they formed a pair.

LXII

There 's also nightly, to the uninitiated,
  A peril—not indeed like Love or Marriage,   490

But not the less for this to be depreciated:
   It is—I meant and mean not to disparage
The show of Virtue even in the vitiated—
   It adds an outward grace unto their carriage—
But to denounce the amphibious sort of harlot,   495
Couleur de rose, who 's neither white nor scarlet.

LXIII

Such is your cold coquette, who can't say "No,"
   And won't say "Yes," and keeps you on and off-ing
On a lee-shore, till it begins to blow—
   Then sees your heart wrecked, with an inward scoffing.   500
This works a world of sentimental woe,
   And sends new Werters yearly to their coffin;
But yet is merely innocent flirtation,
Not quite adultery, but adulteration.

LXIV

"Ye gods, I grow a talker!" Let us prate.   505
   The next of perils, though I place it sternest,
Is when, without regard to Church or State,
   A wife makes or takes love in upright earnest.
Abroad, such things decide few women's fate—
   (Such, early Traveller! is the truth thou learnest)— 510
But in old England, when a young bride errs,
Poor thing! Eve's was a trifling case to hers.

LXV

For 't is a low, newspaper, humdrum, lawsuit
   Country, where a young couple of the same ages
Can't form a friendship, but the world o'erawes it.   515
   Then there 's the vulgar trick of those d—d damages!
A verdict—grievous foe to those who cause it!—
   Forms a sad climax to romantic homages;
Besides those soothing speeches of the pleaders,
And evidences which regale all readers.   520

LXVI

But they who blunder thus are raw beginners;
   A little genial sprinkling of hypocrisy

Has saved the fame of thousand splendid sinners,
   The loveliest oligarchs of our Gynocracy;
You may see such at all the balls and dinners,   525
   Among the proudest of our aristocracy,
So gentle, charming, charitable, chaste—
And all by having *tact* as well as taste.

LXVII

Juan, who did not stand in the predicament
   Of a mere novice, had one safeguard more;   530
For he was sick——no, 't was not the word *sick* I meant—
   But he had seen so much good love before,
That he was not in heart so very weak;—I meant
   But thus much, and no sneer against the shore
Of white cliffs, white necks, blue eyes, bluer stockings—   535
Tithes, taxes, duns—and doors with double knockings.

LXVIII

But coming young from lands and scenes romantic,
   Where lives, not lawsuits, must be risked for Passion
And Passion's self must have a spice of frantic,
   Into a country where 't is half a fashion,   540
Seemed to him half commercial, half pedantic,
   Howe'er he might esteem this moral nation:
Besides (alas! his taste—forgive and pity!)
At *first* he did not think the women pretty.

LXIX

I say at *first*—for he found out at *last*,   545
   But by degrees, that they were fairer far
Than the more glowing dames whose lot is cast
   Beneath the influence of the Eastern Star.
A further proof we should not judge in haste;
   Yet inexperience could not be his bar   550
To taste:—the truth is, if men would confess,
That novelties *please* less than they *impress.*

LXX

Though travelled, I have never had the luck to
   Trace up those shuffling negroes, Nile or Niger,

To that impracticable place Timbuctoo, 555
  Where Geography finds no one to oblige her
With such a chart as may be safely stuck to—
  For Europe ploughs in Afric like "*bos piger:*"
But if I *had been* at Timbuctoo, there
  No doubt I should be told that black is fair. 560

LXXI

It is. I will not swear that black is white,
  But I suspect in fact that white is black,
And the whole matter rests upon eye-sight:—
  Ask a blind man, the best judge. You 'll attack
Perhaps this new position—but I 'm right; 565
  Or if I 'm wrong, I 'll not be ta'en aback:—
He hath no morn nor night, but all is dark
Within—and what seest thou? A dubious spark!

LXXII

But I 'm relapsing into Metaphysics,
  That labyrinth, whose clue is of the same 570
Construction as your cures for hectic phthisics,
  Those bright moths fluttering round a dying flame:
And this reflection brings me to plain Physics,
  And to the beauties of a foreign dame,
Compared with those of our pure pearls of price, 575
Those polar summers, *all* Sun, and some ice.

LXXIII

Or say they are like virtuous mermaids, whose
  Beginnings are fair faces, ends mere fishes;—
Not that there 's not a quantity of those
  Who have a due respect for their own wishes. 580
Like Russians rushing from hot baths to snows
  Are they, at bottom virtuous even when vicious:
They warm into a scrape, but keep of course,
As a reserve, a plunge into remorse.

LXXIV

But this has nought to do with their outsides. 585
  I said that Juan did not think them pretty

At the first blush; for a fair Briton hides
    Half her attractions—probably from pity—
And rather calmly into the heart glides,
    Than storms it as a foe would take a city;   590
But once *there* (if you doubt this, prithee try)
She keeps it for you like a true ally.

LXXV

She cannot step as does an Arab barb,
    Or Andalusian girl from mass returning,
Nor wear as gracefully as Gauls her garb,   595
    Nor in her eye Ausonia's glance is burning;
Her voice, though sweet, is not so fit to war-
    ble those *bravuras* (which I still am learning
To like, though I have been seven years in Italy,
And have, or had, an ear that served me prettily);—   600

LXXVI

She cannot do these things, nor one or two
    Others, in that off-hand and dashing style
Which takes so much—to give the Devil his due;
    Nor is she quite so ready with her smile,
Nor settles all things in one interview,   605
    (A thing approved as saving time and toil);—
But though the soil may give you time and trouble,
Well cultivated, it will render double.

LXXVII

And if in fact she takes to a *grande passion,*
    It is a very serious thing indeed: 610
Nine times in ten 't is but caprice or fashion,
    Coquetry, or a wish to take the lead,
The pride of a mere child with a new sash on,
    Or wish to make a rival's bosom bleed:
But the *tenth* instance will be a tornado,   615
For there 's no saying what they will or may do.

LXXVIII

The reason 's obvious: if there 's an *éclat,*
    They lose their caste at once, as do the Parias;

And when the delicacies of the Law
   Have filled their papers with their comments various, 620
Society, that china without flaw,
   (The Hypocrite!) will banish them like Marius,
To sit amidst the ruins of their guilt:
For Fame 's a Carthage not so soon rebuilt.

LXXIX

Perhaps this is as it should be;—it is   625
   A comment on the Gospel's "Sin no more,
And be thy sins forgiven:"—but upon this
   I leave the Saints to settle their own score.
Abroad, though doubtless they do much amiss,
   An erring woman finds an opener door   630
For her return to Virtue—as they call
That Lady, who should be at home to all.

LXXX

For me, I leave the matter where I find it,
   Knowing that such uneasy virtue leads
People some ten times less in fact to mind it,   635
   And care but for discoveries, and not deeds.
And as for Chastity, you 'll never bind it
   By all the laws the strictest lawyer pleads,
But aggravate the crime you have not prevented,
By rendering desperate those who had else repented.   640

LXXXI

But Juan was no casuist, nor had pondered
   Upon the moral lessons of mankind:
Besides, he had not seen of several hundred
   A lady altogether to his mind.
A little *blasé*—'t is not to be wondered   645
   At, that his heart had got a tougher rind:
And though not vainer from his past success,
No doubt his sensibilities were less.

LXXXII

He also had been busy seeing sights—
   The Parliament and all the other houses;   650

Had sat beneath the Gallery at nights,
    To hear debates whose thunder roused (not rouses)
The World to gaze upon those Northern Lights,
    Which flashed as far as where the musk-bull browses;
He had also stood at times behind the Throne—   655
But Grey was not arrived, and Chatham gone.

LXXXIII

He saw, however, at the closing session,
    That noble sight, when really free the nation,
A King in constitutional possession
    Of such a Throne as is the proudest station,   660
Though Despots know it not—till the progression
    Of Freedom shall complete their education.
'T is not mere Splendour makes the show august
To eye or heart—it is the People's trust.

LXXXIV

There, too, he saw (whate'er he may be now)   665
    A Prince, the prince of Princes at the time,
With fascination in his very bow,
    And full of promise, as the spring of prime.
Though Royalty was written on his brow,
    He had then the grace, too, rare in every clime,   670
Of being, without alloy of fop or beau,
A finished Gentleman from top to toe.

LXXXV

And Juan was received, as hath been said,
    Into the best society; and there
Occurred what often happens, I 'm afraid,   675
    However disciplined and debonnaire:—
The talent and good humour he displayed,
    Besides the marked distinction of his air,
Exposed him, as was natural, to temptation,
Even though himself avoided the occasion.   680

LXXXVI

But what, and where, with whom, and when, and why,
    Is not to be put hastily together;

And as my object is Morality
  (Whatever people say), I don't know whether
I 'll leave a single reader's eyelid dry,
  But harrow up his feelings till they wither,   685
And hew out a huge monument of pathos,
As Philip's son proposed to do with Athos.

LXXXVII

Here the twelfth canto of our Introduction
  Ends. When the body of the Book 's begun,   690
You 'll find it of a different construction
  From what some people say 't will be when done;
The plan at present 's simply in concoction.
  I can't oblige you, reader, to read on;
That 's your affair, not mine: a real spirit   695
Should neither court neglect, nor dread to bear it.

LXXXVIII

And if my thunderbolt not always rattles,
  Remember, reader! you have had before,
The worst of tempests and the best of battles,
  That e'er were brewed from elements or gore,   700
Besides the most sublime of—Heaven knows what else;
  An usurer could scarce expect much more—
But my best canto—save one on astronomy—
Will turn upon "Political Economy."

LXXXIX

That is your present theme for popularity: 705
  Now that the public hedge hath scarce a stake,
It grows an act of patriotic charity,
  To show the people the best way to break.
My plan (but I, if but for singularity,
  Reserve it) will be very sure to take.   710
Meantime, read all the National-Debt sinkers,
And tell me what you think of our great thinkers.
  [1822]

ON THIS DAY I COMPLETE MY THIRTY-SIXTH YEAR

1

'T is time this heart should be unmoved,
  Since others it hath ceased to move:
Yet, though I cannot be beloved,
    Still let me love!

2

My days are in the yellow leaf;   5
  The flowers and fruits of Love are gone;
The worm, the canker, and the grief
    Are mine alone!

3

The fire that on my bosom preys
  Is lone as some Volcanic isle;   10
No torch is kindled at its blaze—
    A funeral pile.

4

The hope, the fear, the jealous care,
  The exalted portion of the pain
And power of love, I cannot share,   15
    But wear the chain.

5

But 't is not *thus*—and 't is not *here*—
  Such thoughts should shake my soul, nor *now*
Where Glory decks the hero's bier,
    Or binds his brow.   20

6

The Sword, the Banner, and the Field,
  Glory and Greece, around me see!

The Spartan, borne upon his shield,
    Was not more free.

7

Awake! (not Greece—she *is* awake!)   25
    Awake, my spirit! Think through *whom*
Thy life-blood tracks its parent lake,
    And then strike home!

8

Tread those reviving passions down,
    Unworthy manhood!—unto thee   30
Indifferent should the smile or frown
    Of Beauty be.

9

If thou regret'st thy youth, *why live?*
    The land of honourable death
Is here:—up to the Field, and give   35
    Away thy breath!

10

Seek out—less often sought than found—
    A soldier's grave, for thee the best;
Then look around, and choose thy ground,
    And take thy Rest.   40
  [1824]

Percy Bysshe Shelley

1792=1822

Percy Bysshe Shelley

PERCY BYSSHE SHELLEY was born near Horsham, Sussex, on August 4, 1792. His grandfather was Bysshe Shelley, an eccentric old man whose principal desire was to establish his family with wealth and position, and who lived in a house in the town of Horsham and allowed his son Timothy, the poet's father, to occupy the family estate of Field Place. Here Shelley remained until he was ten, when he entered Syon House Academy, a respectable but uninspiring school located outside of London near Brentford. Two years later he went to Eton College, the ancient school situated across the Thames from Windsor Castle, where he remained until the summer of 1810. Shelley's intellectual capacities, which were apparent early in his life, combined with unconventional behavior to set him quickly apart from his less intelligent and sensitive fellows at both Syon House and Eton. Within the curricular frame he was a good Latinist, but he soon developed strong interests in scientific experiment and hypothesis, metaphysics and social theory. In March 1810, *Zastrozzi*, a rather commonplace Gothic novel, appeared as the first of Shelley's publications.

When Shelley later entered Oxford in 1810, he was left largely on his own, free to pursue scientific experiments in his own quarters rather than attend lectures. His principal friend was Thomas Jefferson Hogg, a young man of good family who shared Shelley's increasingly radical opinions, and the book that had the greatest influence upon Shelley at this time was William Godwin's *Political Justice* (1793), a work built upon the rationalism and philosophic perfectibilism characteristic of many Enlightenment thinkers. The Godwinian influences simply intensified Shelley's growing belief that established religion

merely served the purposes of the wealthy and powerful, thus
encouraging Shelley in his support of radical causes. The final
result so far as Oxford, though not the world, was concerned,
was a pamphlet rather deceptively and alarmingly entitled
"The Necessity of Atheism," in which Shelley argued that
belief cannot be based upon empirical and logical grounds.
(The term *agnosticism*, to be invented by Thomas Henry
Huxley in the last third of the nineteenth century, would have
better served Shelley.) Shelley and Hogg surreptitiously placed
copies of the privately printed work in the window of an
Oxford bookseller, thereby initiating a process that inevitably
concluded with their expulsion from the University on March
25, 1811.

Shelley proceeded with Hogg to London, but, after seemingly interminable negotiations with his outraged father, he
returned to an uneasy life at Field Place. He had by this time
met Harriet Westbrook, daughter of a well-to-do middle class
family and schoolmate of Shelley's sister Elizabeth. Harriet's
apparently forced confinement at the school struck Shelley
as an instance of injustice and aroused his sympathies to the
point that he set forth to rescue her in the summer of 1811.
In August they eloped to Edinburgh, where they were subsequently married under Scottish law. Soon burdened with
financial difficulties, expectedly intensified by the fresh anger
of Shelley's father, they remained in Edinburgh, where Hogg
joined them. For a while Shelley spent his time in reading and
study, but in time he became bored, and they set forth on
travels which took them to York, Sussex and Keswick. The
financial strain continued until the Duke of Norfolk, Whig
leader and friend of Timothy Shelley, mediated, with the
result that both Shelley's father and Harriet's agreed to con-
tribute toward the couple's support.

Shelley's radicalism was not diminished by his marriage. In
February 1812, he and his wife set forth for Ireland with the
full intention, at least on his part, of aiding the Irish people in
their struggle for liberty by bringing to them the Godwinian
doctrines of reason and non-violent opposition. Shelley soon
published two pamphlets on Irish affairs, "Address to the Irish
People" and "Proposals for an Association," but these drew
slight response from either the Irish populace or the British
Government. In most of his activities in Ireland Shelley simply
overlooked strong human factors at work among the people,

with whom he became disillusioned. In April he and Harriet returned to England.

Early in 1812, Shelley had written a letter of introduction to William Godwin, at this time a small London publisher largely forgotten despite the enormous influence that *Political Justice* had exerted upon English radical opinion during the middle years of the French Revolution. Later that year, after the disheartening experience in Ireland, Shelley was frequently associated with Godwin; however, at this time his reading was slowly carrying him beyond Godwin's rationalistic position toward that of the late eighteenth-century idealists. In May 1813, "Queen Mab," Shelley's long didactic poem with full notes—one of which incorporated "The Necessity of Atheism"—was in the press. Though Shelley made only a token distribution of copies, the poem, a monument to the influence of late eighteenth-century rationalism upon the emerging nineteenth-century mind, was to serve him disadvantageously on subsequent occasions during the remaining nine years of his life.

Shelley's marriage had been built upon something more akin to pity than mature love. There was but slight intellectual rapport between Harriet and himself, and the strong influence that Harriet's older sister, Eliza Westbrook, exerted upon her could only weaken what emotional bonds existed between the couple. By 1814, the marriage had obviously though gradually deteriorated. In November 1812, Shelley and Harriet had briefly met Mary Godwin—daughter of the philosopher and his first wife, the feminist leader Mary Wollstonecraft—then a girl of fifteen, attractive and intelligent. Nearly a year and a half later Shelley was thrown into constant association with the Godwin household in London, and by late June he realized that he was in love with Mary. In mid-July he revealed the fact to Harriet, who quite naturally refused to accept the situation. Things nevertheless came to a climax several weeks later when Shelley and Mary eloped to the Continent, from which they did not return until September. In November, Harriet gave birth to their second child, a son, and though she remained unreconciled to the loss of her husband, Shelley and she moved further apart until he was no longer in her life in any way. She committed suicide late in 1816.

In 1815, Shelley's grandfather, Bysshe, who had been made

a baronet in 1806, died, leaving a considerable fortune. By accident, one part of the estate was not entailed by Sir Bysshe's will; consequently, by selling the reversion of this to his father, Shelley received an income for life. Though financial matters always constituted a problem for him, now there was to be at least a degree of economic security for Shelley and Mary and for Harriet and Shelley's two children as well.

After Harriet's death, Shelley and Mary were married in a London church, seeking what protection the law might offer in the custody of their child, William, born early in 1816, and any other children they might have (Clara was to be born in September 1817). Despite Shelley's attempts to take possession of his children by the first marriage, they remained in Eliza Westbrook's hands, and early in 1817 the Westbrooks instituted Chancery proceedings to deprive Shelley permanently of their custody. Fairly or not, the opinions expressed in the privately printed "Queen Mab" were successfully used against him in the proceedings.

In the late spring and summer of 1816 Shelley and Mary traveled to Geneva, where they met Byron, who, following his separation from Lady Byron, had now become "The Pilgrim of Eternity," as Shelley was to call him five years later in Adonais (xxx). Together the poets spent many hours walking, boating and talking; it was the beginning of an association which, sometimes intense and frequently uneven, was to be a major part of Shelley's life. Shelley wrote his "Hymn to Intellectual Beauty" during the Genevan interval, and Mary developed the idea from which came her novel Frankenstein (1817).

Following their return to England, Shelley touched upon the circle that gathered around Leigh Hunt, the minor poet and critic and the editor of the radical newspaper The Examiner. This group included such figures as John Keats, William Hazlitt, John Hamilton Reynolds, and the artist Benjamin Robert Haydon; for Shelley it was the start of a strong friendship with Hunt. In 1817, Shelley published the pamphlet "A Proposal for Putting Reform to a Vote throughout the Kingdom" and the long poem "The Revolt of Islam," both strong repudiations of the revolutionary principles of which Shelley was accused by many of his contemporaries.

Late in 1817, primarily because of Shelley's uncertain health, he and Mary decided to go with their children to

Italy, and early the following year Shelley left England for the last time. The family passed the summer at the Baths of Lucca, sixty miles from Leghorn. In August, Shelley journeyed to Venice, where he was reunited with Byron, now in one of his most active poetic phases and, according to stories that were then current, one of the most irresponsible periods in his personal life. In September, Clara, the Shelleys' younger child, died. The parents went as planned to spend the winter in Naples, where an intense depression quite expectedly fell over both, reflected most clearly in the poem "Stanzas, Written in Dejection, Near Naples." In Rome during the spring of 1819, Shelley wrote the second and third acts of *Prometheus Unbound*, which he had begun in the late summer of the previous year. At this time he composed the moderate prose work *A Philosophical View of Reform*, which, unfortunately for his reputation in the nineteenth century, was not published until 1926. In June 1819, William, their other child, sickened and died, leaving Shelley and Mary in a deep dejection which was in part alleviated only by the birth of their last child, Percy Florence, in November of that year. (He was to live until 1889.) From early October 1819 to late January 1820, they were in Florence, where Shelley composed the fourth act of *Prometheus Unbound* and the "Ode to the West Wind." From here they moved to Pisa, near which Shelley was to spend the remaining two and a half years of his life.

In most instances the reviews of Shelley's poems published during these years were expectedly unsympathetic. Not only were most of the critics hostile to what they regarded as Shelley's extreme politics—they frequently judged this more by "Queen Mab" than by the later poems—but for the most part they failed to comprehend the dimensions of Shelleian idealism. The level of Shelley's poetic production in 1820 fell off from that of 1819, sometimes called his "Annus Mirabilis," but 1821 brought forth the two relatively long and complex expressions of his later idealism, "Epipsychidion" and "Adonais," together with the prose piece "A Defence of Poetry" (which was not to be published until 1840), wherein Shelley defined his essential literary position.

In August 1821, Shelley journeyed briefly to Ravenna to visit Byron, who at this time suggested the plan that was to culminate in the publication of *The Liberal* in October

1822, three months after Shelley's death. For the moment Shelley was at the center of a group of friends in Pisa, many of them with literary interests, such as Dante's translator John Taaffe and Byron and Shelley's subsequent memorialists Thomas Medwin and Edward John Trelawny. Byron joined the group in October 1821, establishing himself and his large ménage in the Casa Lanfranchi, which had been leased for him. Leigh Hunt, who was to edit the proposed periodical, was expected almost daily with his wife and numerous children. 1821 wore on into 1822, and Hunt, delayed for one reason after another, did not arrive. Byron was growing restless and Shelley anxious. At this time he wrote, among other poems, "With a Guitar: To Jane," addressed to the wife of his friend Edward Ellerker Williams, and also worked on "The Triumph of Life," a poem in which he pursued his idealism beyond the point proposed in "Adonais," that earthly life itself is but a shadow of reality, but this poem was never to be completed.

In the spring, the Shelley and Williams families moved to Casa Magni, San Terenzo, a two-story house on the Gulf of Spezia, which was well situated for the summer sailing that they anticipated in Shelley's boat, the "Don Juan." After Shelley had settled Leigh Hunt and his family on the first floor of Byron's Casa Lanfranchi, it was to this spot that he and Williams were sailing on July 8, 1822, when the "Don Juan" went down off Viareggio and they were drowned.

II

Shelley's intellectual development can be usefully divided into two phases. The first, represented principally by the didactic poem "Queen Mab," reveals the influence of Enlightenment thinking upon him, especially in his subscription to the idea of a rationalistic basis for external order and of the ultimate possibility for perfection of society. The second, represented initially by "Alastor" and fully by *Prometheus Unbound*, reflects Shelley's subsequent awareness that rational systems do not solve the problems of organic life and his concomitant concern with the self as the basis of reality. In no way, however, must these two phases be regarded as the result of a break in Shelley's development: The philosophic antecedents of his idealism lay in his early rationalism.

Clearly, his most successful poems belong to the second phase. In "Queen Mab," characteristically a poem of indoctrination, Shelley subordinated all other elements to the thesis. Although the poem is consequently of secondary value, it is worth considering the thesis itself in order that the point from which Shelley moved toward his idealism might be more readily seen.

Quite simply, "Queen Mab" illustrates that the "Spirit of Nature," the only non-material force co-existent and co-eternal with phenomena, is Necessity, expressed by an "uninterrupted chain of causes and effects." Once an evil cause has been introduced into the cycle, further evil will necessarily result. Thus, in his present state, man, though potentially rational and good, is afflicted with crime and pain: the past reveals only the monuments of man's own inhumanity and the present binds him with institutions and practices of his own creation—tyranny, war, commerce—by which the strong oppress the weak and the unjust the just. However, since man is potentially a reasoning being, there is hope; when properly motivated to exercise reason by such causes within the "chain" as rational poems and treatises, he can recognize the universal presence of Necessity and bring about the regeneration of himself and of the world which he inhabits.

The inability of the system underlying "Queen Mab" to solve the problems of organic (rather than mechanical) existence soon became apparent to Shelley. But in 1815, when he wrote "Alastor," he did not reject the system so much as assimilate it into a larger construct: he still allowed that matter, existing in time and space, could be described in terms of cause and effect; however, the cohesiveness of the universe and the function of the mind of man must be attributed to a force transcending what Shelley had earlier called Necessity. In turning from the mechanistic system dominating "Queen Mab" to the organic values implicit in "Alastor," Shelley passed in his thought from a point of view characteristic of the Enlightenment toward full Romanticism.

Such a passage, however, is never fully conscious. "Alastor" is, in the main, a poem about self-realization: the poet-protagonist—though "He lived, he died, he sung in solitude"—seeks in this world the embodiment of a vision that has come to him in a dream, whose "voice was like the voice of his own soul." At length he finds it only in death, toward which the Spirit summons him and he goes "at peace and faintly smiling." In the Preface to the poem, Shelley put a construction upon his work which, as has been perceptively pointed out in our own time, is not consistent with the triumphant resolution in the poem: the poet-protagonist is here described as the object of punishment by the avenging Spirit of Solitude because he has lived away from mankind "in self-centred seclusion." Thus, "his mind is at length suddenly awakened and thirsts for intercourse with an intelligence similar to itself," and in the image of "the Being whom he loves" he joins all aspects of the Ideal; seeking "in vain for a prototype of his conception," he suffers disappointment and "descends to an untimely grave." The discrepancy between the statement in the Preface to "Alastor" and what actually develops in the poem itself can perhaps usefully be explained in terms of the difference between Shelley's earlier mechanistic conception of the universe, of which he was fully conscious, and the organicism toward which he was moving. The Preface really suggests that the poem allegorically represents an unchanging universe to which the poet-protagonist must adjust himself, whereas the poem "Alastor" itself symbolically illustrates the developing Shelleian view that for man the universe must derive its meaning from the act by which man achieves self-realization: the poet-protagonist does not die in disappointment but in a sense of fulfillment.

As "Alastor" might suggest, in the emerging idealism of Shelley, though reality is not inherent in *things*, neither is it simply an aspect of *mind*. Instead, reality is to be found in act itself, in the mind's searching after truth and the self's seeking the meaning of its own existence, in terms of which the outer world might be understood. In the poem "Mont Blanc" (1816), the speaker's act of contemplating the scene itself constitutes reality for him. In the "Hymn to Intellectual Beauty" (1816), the speaker seeks a sustaining awareness of the elusive Spirit which, by the act of quest itself, he achieves. Similarly, the conclusion of the "Ode to the West Wind" (1819) expresses hope for inspiration from the intellectual beauty which the wind itself symbolizes: poetic activity is a form of reality, so that by using the wind symbolically the speaker gives value to its literal existence. Conversely, in "Stanzas, Written in Dejection, Near Naples," the speaker describes the failure to become one with reality, for in his dejection he himself has fallen into inaction and, consequently, alienation from all forms of value or truth.

In "The Defence of Poetry," which Shelley wrote in 1821, he proposed a distinction, in terms of which the quest for reality can be viewed. This distinction was between *reason*— "mind contemplating the relations borne by one thought to another, however produced"—and *imagination*—"mind acting upon those thoughts so as to color them with its own light, and composing from them, as from elements, other thoughts, each containing within itself the principle of its own integrity." Reason is purely quantitative by this distinction, imagination qualitative, and poetry itself becomes "the expression of the imagination." The true poet "participates in the eternal, the infinite, and the one." It is not surprising therefore that in "Adonais"—written on the occasion of John Keats' death—by adapting the conventions of the pastoral elegy to his needs, Shelley made one of his most forceful assertions about the quest for reality. By poetic activity itself, the speaker in the poem reaches that point where he can propose that there is meaning and order in a universe that permits Adonais to pass from earthly life:

> The One remains, the many change and pass;
> Heaven's light forever shines, Earth's shadows fly;
> Life, like a dome of many-coloured glass,
> Stains the white radiance of Eternity,
> Until Death tramples it to fragments.—Die,
> If thou wouldst be with that which thou dost seek!
> Follow where all is fled!

Paradoxically, in his full assertion of himself as poet, the speaker in the poem loses all sense of individuality; he participates in the universality that Adonais has attained; he dies and thereby lives. In full activity all poets become one, since any distinction is absorbed by the reality which they thereby achieve; or, as Shelley wrote in the prose fragment "On Life": "The words *I*, *you*, *they*, are not signs of any actual differences subsisting between the assemblage of thoughts thus indicated, but merely marks employed to denote the different modifications of the one mind."

The lyrical drama *Prometheus Unbound*, Shelley's most

complex work, reveals more firmly than any other the nature of his later idealism. In the Preface to his play he admitted the "license" which he had taken in adapting the Æschylean model to his own purposes:

> The *Prometheus Unbound* of Æschylus supposed the reconciliation of Jupiter with his victim as the price of the disclosure of the danger threatened to his empire by the consummation of his marriage with Thetis. Thetis, according to this view of the subject, was given in marriage to Peleus, and Prometheus, by the permission of Jupiter, delivered from his captivity by Hercules. Had I framed my story on this model, I should have done no more than have attempted to restore the lost drama of Æschylus. . . . But, in truth, I was averse from a catastrophe so feeble as that of reconciling the Champion with the Oppressor of mankind. The moral interest of the fable, which is so powerfully sustained by the sufferings and endurance of Prometheus, would be annihilated if we could conceive of him as unsaying his high language and quailing before his successful and perfidious adversary.

Shelley could do nothing else. In *Prometheus Unbound,* as elsewhere in his later writings, the "One," on which all universal activity depends, is identifiable with Love. This is an absolute and cannot be precisely defined, but at the same time it is a force in which all men can participate by a variety of means. In "The Defence of Poetry" Shelley proposed:

> The great secret of morals is love; or a going out of our own nature, and an identification of ourselves with the beautiful which exists in thought, action, or person, not our own. A man, to be greatly good, must imagine intensely and comprehensively; he must put himself in the place of another and of many others; the pains and pleasures of his species must become his own. The great instrument of moral good is the imagination.

Among all other values that he symbolizes, Prometheus represents the mind of man, the human spirit itself. At the opening of the drama he has been indefinitely bound ("Three thousand years" must in no sense be taken literally), osten-

sibly because Jupiter—in the universe the source of evil and
of power based upon injustice—has ordered his confinement.
Actually, Prometheus has been bound since the time that
he first admitted hatred—present only when there is de-
ficiency of Love—to his mind and spirit: Prometheus cursed
Jupiter and thereby gave the tyrant the power over the human soul—in other words, recognition by the mind of man
—that he had previously lacked. As he reveals in his initial
speech, during the confinement Prometheus has withstood
the physical tortures inflicted upon him at Jupiter's direc-
tion, ultimately triumphing over his hatred and thereby de-
priving Jupiter of reality in the human mind. Prometheus
has thus been prepared to recall his curse upon Jupiter. Love
moves the universe, and when the human spirit participates
in Love, evil ceases to be. The fall of Jupiter, which Prometheus now foretells, is inherent in Prometheus' act of Love.
Demogorgon, appearing for the first time in the second act,
explicitly stands for Eternity or, to use an older Shelleian
term, Necessity, to which all things in time and space are
subject. But Eternity itself is subject to Love, so that at the
moment of Prometheus' regeneration, Demogorgon is motivated and becomes the instrument for the inevitable downfall of Jupiter.

Such is Prometheus' secret, that one of "the wingless, crawling hours" shall bring the destruction of the "cruel King."
Jupiter, whose viewpoint is derived entirely from his evil substance, can understand nothing of Love ("He who is evil
can receive no good," remarks Prometheus) and confidently
plans that the "fatal child" to be born of his union with
Thetis shall break the spirit of Prometheus, who will then,
if he has not done so before, yield the secret which he holds.
Nevertheless, Jupiter would know Prometheus' secret now,
and thus he sends Mercury and the attending Furies to ex-
tract it from Prometheus by spiritual rather than merely
physical tortures. Supposedly to induce despair, Mercury and
the Furies assume the form of visions, one of the crucifixion
of Christ and the other of the French Revolution. They represent the futility of other endeavors to bring about the triumph
of the good over the powerful—a futility which is only apparent, as Prometheus knows. He does not yield to his tor-
mentors, of course, for by the very nature of the secret which
he possesses, derived as it is from the regenerate and free con-

dition of his mind, paradoxically he could not succumb, or even will to succumb, to despair. Mercury and the Furies depart, to be replaced by the Spirits of the human mind who, with Prometheus, celebrate the inevitable triumph of truth and humanity.

Panthea, who speaks last in the first act, appears early in the second before the solitary Asia. No one can define with precision the symbolic relation between Prometheus and Asia. Certainly, as he represents the intellectual principle, she represents the æsthetic, but because the play is a work of symbolism rather than an allegory, each reveals indefinite possibilities of meaning. Together they represent Love in its various forms, and for this reason each implies the other. In this respect Panthea, one of the central symbols, images each lover to the other, appearing in the first act to Prometheus and in the second to Asia, who says to her: "Oh, lift/ Thine eyes, that I may read his written soul!"

Together the sisters proceed to the Cave of Demogorgon, who makes the distinction for them between the idea of good —Love—and the image of the momentary ruler of the universe—Jupiter—soon to be banished from the mind of man. Upon the firm foundations of Prometheus' utterances in the first act and Demogorgon's pronouncements in the second, the action of the third act is built. This is followed by the lyrical celebration of the regeneration of man and the resuscitation of nature in the fourth.

Prometheus is the ideal of every man rather than, in some limited allegorical sense, Everyman. His triumph becomes the model for individual man, recurring moment by moment in human life. Man achieves his close contact with reality only by participation in Love through the activity of the imagination: such is the nature of Shelleian self-realization, by which the individual being can impose meaning and order on the world existing outside the self.

Percy Bysshe Shelley

ALASTOR

OR, THE SPIRIT OF SOLITUDE

Earth, ocean, air, beloved brotherhood!
If our great Mother have imbued my soul
With aught of natural piety to feel
Your love, and recompense the boon with mine;
If dewy morn, and odorous noon, and even,   5
With sunset and its gorgeous ministers,
And solemn midnight's tingling silentness;
If autumn's hollow sighs in the sere wood,
And winter robing with pure snow and crowns
Of starry ice the grey grass and bare boughs;   10
If spring's voluptuous pantings when she breathes
Her first sweet kisses, have been dear to me;
If no bright bird, insect, or gentle beast
I consciously have injured, but still loved
And cherished these my kindred; then forgive   15
This boast, beloved brethren, and withdraw
No portion of your wonted favour now!

  Mother of this unfathomable world!
Favour my solemn song, for I have loved
Thee ever, and thee only; I have watched   20
Thy shadow, and the darkness of thy steps,
And my heart ever gazes on the depth
Of thy deep mysteries. I have made my bed
In charnels and on coffins, where black death
Keeps record of the trophies won from thee,   25
Hoping to still these obstinate questionings
Of thee and thine, by forcing some lone ghost
Thy messenger, to render up the tale
Of what we are. In lone and silent hours,
When night makes a weird round of its own stillness,   30
Like an inspired and desperate alchymist
Staking his very life on some dark hope,
Have I mixed awful talk and asking looks
With my most innocent love, until strange tears
Uniting with those breathless kisses, made   35

Such magic as compels the charmed night
To render up thy charge: . . . and, though ne'er yet
Thou hast unveil'd thy inmost sanctuary;
Enough from incommunicable dream,
And twilight phantasms, and deep noonday thought,   40
Has shone within me, that serenely now
And moveless, as a long-forgotten lyre
Suspended in the solitary dome
Of some mysterious and deserted fane,
I wait thy breath, Great Parent, that my strain   45
May modulate with murmurs of the air,
And motions of the forests and the sea,
And voice of living beings, and woven hymns
Of night and day, and the deep heart of man.

There was a Poet whose untimely tomb   50
No human hands with pious reverence reared,
But the charmed eddies of autumnal winds
Built o'er his mouldering bones a pyramid
Of mouldering leaves in the waste wilderness;—
A lovely youth,—no mourning maiden decked   55
With weeping flowers, or votive cypress wreath,
The lone couch of his everlasting sleep:—
Gentle, and brave, and generous,—no lorn bard
Breathed o'er his dark fate one melodious sigh:
He lived, he died, he sung, in solitude.   60
Strangers have wept to hear his passionate notes,
And virgins, as unknown he passed, have pined
And wasted for fond love of his wild eyes.
The fire of those soft orbs has eased to burn,
And Silence, too enamoured of that voice,   65
Locks its mute music in her rugged cell.

By solemn vision and bright silver dream,
His infancy was nurtured. Every sight
And sound from the vast earth and ambient air,
Sent to his heart its choicest impulses.   70
The fountains of divine philosophy
Fled not his thirsting lips, and all of great,
Or good, or lovely, which the sacred past
In truth or fable consecrates, he felt
And knew. When early youth had past, he left   75

His cold fireside and alienated home
To seek strange truths in undiscovered lands.
Many a wide waste and tangled wilderness
Has lured his fearless steps; and he has bought
With his sweet voice and eyes, from savage men,   80
His rest and food. Nature's most secret steps
He like her shadow has pursued, where'er
The red volcano overcanopies
Its fields of snow and pinnacles of ice
With burning smoke, or where bitumen lakes   85
On black bare pointed islets ever beat
With sluggish surge, or where the secret caves
Rugged and dark, winding among the springs
Of fire and poison, inaccessible
To avarice or pride, their starry domes   90
Of diamond and of gold expand above
Numberless and immeasurable halls,
Frequent with crystal column, and clear shrines
Of pearl, and thrones radiant with chrysolite.
Nor had that scene of ampler majesty   95
Than gems or gold, the varying roof of heaven
And the green earth lost in his heart its claims
To love and wonder; he would linger long
In lonesome vales, making the wild his home,
Until the doves and squirrels would partake   100
From his innocuous hand his bloodless food,
Lured by the gentle meaning of his looks,
And the wild antelope, that starts whene'er
The dry leaf rustles in the brake, suspend
Her timid steps to gaze upon a form   105
More graceful than her own.

                        His wandering step,
Obedient to high thoughts, has visited
The awful ruins of the days of old:
Athens, and Tyre, and Balbec, and the waste
Where stood Jerusalem, the fallen towers   110
Of Babylon, the eternal pyramids,
Memphis and Thebes, and whatsoe'er of strange
Sculptured on alabaster obelisk,
Or jasper tomb, or mutilated sphinx,
Dark Ethiopia in her desert hills   115

Conceals. Among the ruined temples there,
Stupendous columns, and wild images
Of more than man, where marble dæmons watch
The Zodiac's brazen mystery, and dead men
Hang their mute thoughts on the mute walls around,   120
He lingered, poring on memorials
Of the world's youth, through the long burning day
Gazed on those speechless shapes, nor, when the moon
Filled the mysterious halls with floating shades
Suspended he that task, but ever gazed   125
And gazed, till meaning on his vacant mind
Flashed like strong inspiration, and he saw
The thrilling secrets of the birth of time.

Meanwhile an Arab maiden brought his food,
Her daily portion, from her father's tent,   130
And spread her matting for his couch, and stole
From duties and repose to tend his steps:—
Enamoured, yet not daring for deep awe
To speak her love:—and watched his nightly sleep,
Sleepless herself, to gaze upon his lips   135
Parted in slumber, whence the regular breath
Of innocent dreams arose: then, when red morn
Made paler the pale moon, to her cold home,
Wildered, and wan, and panting, she returned.

The Poet wandering on, through Arabie   140
And Persia, and the wild Carmanian waste,
And o'er the aërial mountains which pour down
Indus and Oxus from their icy caves,
In joy and exultation held his way;
Till in the vale of Cashmire, far within   145
Its loneliest dell, where odorous plants entwine
Beneath the hollow rocks a natural bower,
Beside a sparkling rivulet he stretched
His languid limbs. A vision on his sleep
There came, a dream of hopes that never yet   150
Had flushed his cheek. He dreamed a veiled maid
Sate near him, talking in low solemn tones.
Her voice was like the voice of his own soul
Heard in the calm of thought; its music long,
Like woven sounds of streams and breezes, held   155

His inmost sense suspended in its web
Of many-coloured woof and shifting hues.
Knowledge and truth and virtue were her theme,
And lofty hopes of divine liberty,
Thoughts the most dear to him, and poesy,   160
Himself a poet. Soon the solemn mood
Of her pure mind kindled through all her frame
A permeating fire: wild numbers then
She raised, with voice stifled in tremulous sobs
Subdued by its own pathos: her fair hands   165
Were bare alone, sweeping from some strange harp
Strange symphony, and in their branching veins
The eloquent blood told an ineffable tale.
The beating of her heart was heard to fill
The pauses of her music, and her breath   170
Tumultuously accorded with those fits
Of intermitted song. Sudden she rose,
As if her heart impatiently endured
Its bursting burthen: at the sound he turned,
And saw by the warm light of their own life   175
Her glowing limbs beneath the sinuous veil
Of woven wind, her outspread arms now bare,
Her dark locks floating in the breath of night,
Her beamy bending eyes, her parted lips
Outstretched, and pale, and quivering eagerly.   180
His strong heart sunk and sickened with excess
Of love. He reared his shuddering limbs, and quelled
His gasping breath, and spread his arms to meet
Her panting bosom; . . . she drew back a while,
Then, yielding to the irresistible joy,   185
With frantic gesture and short breathless cry
Folded his frame in her dissolving arms.
Now blackness veiled his dizzy eyes, and night
Involved and swallowed up the vision; sleep,
Like a dark flood suspended in its course,   190
Rolled back its impulse on his vacant brain.

Roused by the shock he started from his trance—
The cold white light of morning, the blue moon
Low in the west, the clear and garish hills,
The distinct valley and the vacant woods,   195
Spread round him where he stood. Whither have fled

The hues of heaven that canopied his bower
Of yesternight? The sounds that soothed his sleep,
The mystery and the majesty of Earth,
The joy, the exultation? His wan eyes   200
Gaze on the empty scene as vacantly
As ocean's moon looks on the moon in heaven.
The spirit of sweet human love has sent
A vision to the sleep of him who spurned
Her choicest gifts. He eagerly pursues   205
Beyond the realms of dream that fleeting shade;
He overleaps the bounds. Alas! alas!
Were limbs and breath and being intertwined
Thus treacherously? Lost, lost, for ever lost,
In the wide pathless desert of dim sleep,   210
That beautiful shape! Does the dark gate of death
Conduct to thy mysterious paradise,
O Sleep? Does the bright arch of rainbow clouds,
And pendent mountains seen in the calm lake,
Lead only to a black and watery depth,   215
While death's blue vault, with loathliest vapours hung,
Where every shade which the foul grave exhales
Hides its dead eye from the detested day,
Conduct, O Sleep, to thy delightful realms?
This doubt with sudden tide flowed on his heart,   220
The insatiate hope which it awakened, stung
His brain even like despair.

                    While daylight held
The sky, the Poet kept mute conference
With his still soul. At night the passion came,
Like the fierce fiend of a distempered dream,   225
And shook him from his rest, and led him forth
Into the darkness.—As an eagle grasped
In folds of the green serpent, feels her breast
Burn with the poison, and precipitates
Through night and day, tempest, and calm and cloud,   230
Frantic with dizzying anguish, her blind flight
O'er the wide aëry wilderness: thus driven
By the bright shadow of that lovely dream,
Beneath the cold glare of the desolate night,
Through tangled swamps and deep precipitous dells,   235
Startling with careless step the moon-light snake,

He fled. Red morning dawned upon his flight,
Shedding the mockery of its vital hues
Upon his cheek of death. He wandered on,
Till vast Aornos, seen from Petra's steep,   240
Hung o'er the low horizon like a cloud;
Through Balk, and where the desolated tombs
Of Parthian kings scatter to every wind
Their wasting dust, wildly he wandered on,
Day after day, a weary waste of hours,   245
Bearing within his life the brooding care
That ever fed on its decaying flame.
And now his limbs were lean; his scattered hair
Sered by the autumn of strange suffering,
Sung dirges in the wind; his listless hand   250
Hung like dead bone within its withered skin;
Life, and the lustre that consumed it, shone
As in a furnace burning secretly
From his dark eyes alone. The cottagers,
Who ministered with human charity   255
His human wants, beheld with wondering awe
Their fleeting visitant. The mountaineer,
Encountering on some dizzy precipice
That spectral form, deemed that the Spirit of wind
With lightning eyes, and eager breath, and feet   260
Disturbing not the drifted snow, had paused
In his career: the infant would conceal
His troubled visage in his mother's robe
In terror at the glare of those wild eyes,
To remember their strange light in many a dream   265
Of after times; but youthful maidens, taught
By nature, would interpret half the woe
That wasted him, would call him with false names
Brother, and friend, would press his pallid hand
At parting, and watch, dim through tears, the path   270
Of his departure from their father's door.

At length upon the lone Chorasmian shore
He paused, a wide and melancholy waste
Of putrid marshes. A strong impulse urged
His steps to the sea-shore. A swan was there,   275
Beside a sluggish stream among the reeds.
It rose as he approached, and with strong wings

Scaling the upward sky, bent its bright course
High over the immeasurable main.
His eyes pursued its flight:—"Thou hast a home,   280
Beautiful bird! thou voyagest to thine home,
Where thy sweet mate will twine her downy neck
With thine, and welcome thy return with eyes
Bright in the lustre of their own fond joy.
And what am I that I should linger here,   285
With voice far sweeter than thy dying notes,
Spirit more vast than thine, frame more attuned
To beauty, wasting these surpassing powers
In the deaf air, to the blind earth, and heaven
That echoes not my thoughts?" A gloomy smile   290
Of desperate hope wrinkled his quivering lips.
For sleep, he knew, kept most relentlessly
Its precious charge, and silent death exposed,
Faithless perhaps as sleep, a shadowy lure,
With doubtful smile mocking its own strange charms.   295

   Startled by his own thoughts, he looked around.
There was no fair fiend near him, not a sight
Or sound of awe but in his own deep mind.
A little shallop floating near the shore
Caught the impatient wandering of his gaze.   300
It had been long abandoned, for its sides
Gaped wide with many a rift, and its frail joints
Swayed with the undulations of the tide.
A restless impulse urged him to embark
And meet lone Death on the drear ocean's waste;   305
For well he knew that mighty Shadow loves
The slimy caverns of the populous deep.

   The day was fair and sunny: sea and sky
Drank its inspiring radiance, and the wind
Swept strongly from the shore, blackening the waves.   310
Following his eager soul, the wanderer
Leaped in the boat, he spread his cloak aloft
On the bare mast, and took his lonely seat,
And felt the boat speed o'er the tranquil sea
Like a torn cloud before the hurricane.   315

As one that in a silver vision floats
Obedient to the sweep of odorous winds
Upon resplendent clouds, so rapidly
Along the dark and ruffled waters fled
The straining boat.—A whirlwind swept it on,   320
With fierce gusts and precipitating force,
Through the white ridges of the chafed sea.
The waves arose. Higher and higher still
Their fierce necks writhed beneath the tempest's scourge
Like serpents struggling in a vulture's grasp.   325
Calm and rejoicing in the fearful war
Of wave ruining on wave, and blast on blast
Descending, and black flood on whirlpool driven
With dark obliterating course, he sate:
As if their genii were the ministers   330
Appointed to conduct him to the light
Of those beloved eyes, the Poet sate
Holding the steady helm. Evening came on,
The beams of sunset hung their rainbow hues
High 'mid the shifting domes of sheeted spray   335
That canopied his path o'er the waste deep;
Twilight, ascending slowly from the east,
Entwin'd in duskier wreaths her braided locks
O'er the fair front and radiant eyes of day;
Night followed, clad with stars. On every side   340
More horribly the multitudinous streams
Of ocean's mountainous waste to mutual war
Rushed in dark tumult thundering, as to mock
The calm and spangled sky. The little boat
Still fled before the storm; still fled, like foam   345
Down the steep cataract of a wintry river;
Now pausing on the edge of the riven wave;
Now leaving far behind the bursting mass
That fell, convulsing ocean. Safely fled—
As if that frail and wasted human form   350
Had been an elemental god.

At midnight
The moon arose: and lo! the etherial cliffs
Of Caucasus, whose icy summits shone
Among the stars like sunlight, and around
Whose cavern'd base the whirlpools and the waves   355

Bursting and eddying irresistibly
Rage and resound for ever.—Who shall save?—
The boat fled on,—the boiling torrent drove,—
The crags closed round with black and jagged arms,
The shattered mountains overhung the sea,   360
And faster still, beyond all human speed,
Suspended on the sweep of the smooth wave,
The little boat was driven. A cavern there
Yawned, and amid its slant and winding depths
Ingulfed the rushing sea. The boat fled on   365
With unrelaxing speed.—"Vision and Love!"
The Poet cried aloud, "I have beheld
The path of thy departure. Sleep and death
Shall not divide us long!"

                    The boat pursued
The windings of the cavern. Day-light shone   370
At length upon that gloomy river's flow;
Now, where the fiercest war among the waves
Is calm, on the unfathomable stream
The boat moved slowly. Where the mountain, riven,
Exposed those black depths to the azure sky,   375
Ere yet the flood's enormous volume fell
Even to the base of Caucasus, with sound
That shook the everlasting rocks, the mass
Filled with one whirlpool all that ample chasm;
Stair above stair the eddying waters rose,   380
Circling immeasurably fast, and laved
With alternating dash the knarled roots
Of mighty trees, that stretched their giant arms
In darkness over it. I' the midst was left,
Reflecting, yet distorting every cloud,   385
A pool of treacherous and tremendous calm,
Seized by the sway of the ascending stream,
With dizzy swiftness, round, and round, and round,
Ridge after ridge the straining boat arose,
Till on the verge of the extremest curve,   390
Where, through an opening of the rocky bank,
The waters overflow, and a smooth spot
Of glassy quiet mid those battling tides
Is left, the boat paused shuddering. Shall it sink—
Down the abyss? Shall the reverting stress   395

Of that resistless gulf embosom it?
Now shall it fall? A wandering stream of wind,
Breathed from the west, has caught the expanded sail,
And, lo! with gentle motion between banks
Of mossy slope, and on a placid stream,   400
Beneath a woven grove, it sails, and, hark!
The ghastly torrent mingles its far roar,
With the breeze murmuring in the musical woods.
Where the embowering trees recede, and leave
A little space of green expanse, the cove   405
Is closed by meeting banks, whose yellow flowers
For ever gaze on their own drooping eyes,
Reflected in the crystal calm. The wave
Of the boat's motion marred their pensive task,
Which nought but vagrant bird, or wanton wind,   410
Or falling spear-grass, or their own decay
Had e'er disturbed before. The Poet longed
To deck with their bright hues his withered hair,
But on his heart its solitude returned,
And he forbore. Not the strong impulse hid   415
In those flushed cheeks, bent eyes, and shadowy frame
Had yet performed its ministry: it hung
Upon his life, as lightning in a cloud
Gleams, hovering ere it vanish, ere the floods
Of night close over it.   420

           The noonday sun
Now shone upon the forest, one vast mass
Of mingling shade, whose brown magnificence
A narrow vale embosoms. There, huge caves,
Scooped in the dark base of their aëry rocks
Mocking its moans, respond and roar for ever.   425
The meeting boughs and implicated leaves
Wove twilight o'er the Poet's path, as led
By love, or dream, or god, or mightier Death,
He sought in Nature's dearest haunt, some bank,
Her cradle, and his sepulchre. More dark   430
And dark the shades accumulate. The oak,
Expanding its immense and knotty arms,
Embraces the light beech. The pyramids
Of the tall cedar overarching, frame
Most solemn domes within, and far below,   435

Like clouds suspended in an emerald sky,
The ash and the acacia floating hang
Tremulous and pale. Like restless serpents, clothed
In rainbow and in fire, the parasites,
Starr'd with ten thousand blossoms, flow around   440
The grey trunks, and, as gamesome infants' eyes,
With gentle meanings, and most innocent wiles,
Fold their beams round the hearts of those that love,
These twine their tendrils with the wedded boughs
Uniting their close union; the woven leaves   445
Make net-work of the dark blue light of day,
And the night's noontide clearness, mutable
As shapes in the weird clouds. Soft mossy lawns
Beneath these canopies extend their swells,
Fragrant with perfumed herbs, and eyed with blooms   450
Minute, yet beautiful. One darkest glen
Sends from its woods of musk-rose, twined with jasmine,
A soul-dissolving odour, to invite
To some more lovely mystery. Through the dell,
Silence and Twilight here, twin-sisters, keep   455
Their noonday watch, and sail among the shades,
Like vaporous shapes half seen; beyond, a well,
Dark, gleaming, and of most translucent wave,
Images all the woven boughs above,
And each depending leaf, and every speck   460
Of azure sky, darting between their chasms;
Nor aught else in the liquid mirror laves
Its portraiture, but some inconstant star
Between one foliaged lattice twinkling fair,
Or painted bird, sleeping beneath the moon,   465
Or gorgeous insect floating motionless,
Unconscious of the day, ere yet his wings
Have spread their glories to the gaze of noon.

  Hither the Poet came. His eyes beheld
Their own wan light through the reflected lines   470
Of his thin hair, distinct in the dark depth
Of that still fountain; as the human heart,
Gazing in dreams over the gloomy grave,
Sees its own treacherous likeness there. He heard
The motion of the leaves, the grass that sprung   475

Startled and glanced and trembled even to feel
An unaccustomed presence, and the sound
Of the sweet brook that from the secret springs
Of that dark fountain rose. A Spirit seemed
To stand beside him—clothed in no bright robes   480
Of shadowy silver or enshrining light,
Borrow'd from aught the visible world affords
Of grace, or majesty, or mystery;—
But, undulating woods, and silent well,
And leaping rivulet, and evening gloom   485
Now deepening the dark shades, for speech assuming
Held commune with him, as if he and it
Were all that was,—only . . . when his regard
Was raised by intense pensiveness, . . . two eyes,
Two starry eyes, hung in the gloom of thought,   490
And seemed with their serene and azure smiles
To beckon him.

          Obedient to the light
That shone within his soul, he went, pursuing
The windings of the dell.—The rivulet
Wanton and wild, through many a green ravine   495
Beneath the forest flowed. Sometimes it fell
Among the moss, with hollow harmony
Dark and profound. Now on the polished stones
It danced; like childhood laughing as it went:
Then, through the plain in tranquil wanderings crept,   500
Reflecting every herb and drooping bud
That overhung its quietness.—"O stream!
Whose source is inaccessibly profound,
Whither do thy mysterious waters tend?
Thou imagest my life. Thy darksome stillness,   505
Thy dazzling waves, thy loud and hollow gulphs,
Thy searchless fountain, and invisible course
Have each their type in me: And the wide sky,
And measureless ocean may declare as soon
What oozy cavern or what wandering cloud   510
Contains thy waters, as the universe
Tell where these living thoughts reside, when stretched
Upon thy flowers my bloodless limbs shall waste
I' the passing wind!"

Beside the grassy shore
Of the small stream he went; he did impress   515
On the green moss his tremulous step, that caught
Strong shuddering from his burning limbs. As one
Roused by some joyous madness from the couch
Of fever, he did move; yet, not like him,
Forgetful of the grave, where, when the flame   520
Of his frail exultation shall be spent,
He must descend. With rapid steps he went
Beneath the shade of trees, beside the flow
Of the wild babbling rivulet; and now
The forest's solemn canopies were changed   525
For the uniform and lightsome evening sky.
Grey rocks did peep from the spare moss, and stemmed
The struggling brook: tall spires of windlestrae
Threw their thin shadows down the rugged slope,
And nought but knarled roots of ancient pines   530
Branchless and blasted, clenched with grasping roots
The unwilling soil. A gradual change was here,
Yet ghastly. For, as fast years flow away,
The smooth brow gathers, and the hair grows thin
And white; and where irradiate dewy eyes   535
Had shone, gleam stony orbs: so from his steps
Bright flowers departed, and the beautiful shade
Of the green groves, with all their odorous winds
And musical motions. Calm, he still pursued
The stream, that with a larger volume now   540
Rolled through the labyrinthine dell; and there
Fretted a path through its descending curves
With its wintry speed. On every side now rose
Rocks, which, in unimaginable forms,
Lifted their black and barren pinnacles   545
In the light of evening, and its precipice
Obscuring the ravine, disclosed above,
'Mid toppling stones, black gulfs, and yawning caves,
Whose windings gave ten thousand various tongues
To the loud stream. Lo! where the pass expands   550
Its stony jaws, the abrupt mountain breaks,
And seems, with its accumulated crags,
To overhang the world: for wide expand
Beneath the wan stars and descending moon
Islanded seas, blue mountains, mighty streams,   555

Dim tracts and vast, robed in the lustrous gloom
Of leaden-coloured even, and fiery hills
Mingling their flames with twilight, on the verge
Of the remote horizon. The near scene,
In naked and severe simplicity, 560
Made contrast with the universe. A pine,
Rock-rooted, stretched athwart the vacancy
Its swinging boughs, to each inconstant blast
Yielding one only response, at each pause,
In most familiar cadence, with the howl 565
The thunder and the hiss of homeless streams
Mingling its solemn song, whilst the broad river,
Foaming and hurrying o'er its rugged path,
Fell into that immeasurable void,
Scattering its waters to the passing winds. 570

　　Yet the grey precipice, and solemn pine
And torrent, were not all;—one silent nook
Was there. Even on the edge of that vast mountain,
Upheld by knotty roots and fallen rocks,
It overlooked in its serenity 575
The dark earth, and the bending vault of stars.
It was a tranquil spot, that seemed to smile
Even in the lap of horror. Ivy clasped
The fissured stones with its entwining arms,
And did embower with leaves forever green, 580
And berries dark, the smooth and even space
Of its inviolated floor, and here
The children of the autumnal whirlwind bore,
In wanton sport, those bright leaves, whose decay,
Red, yellow, or ethereally pale, 585
Rivals the pride of summer. 'Tis the haunt
Of every gentle wind, whose breath can teach
The wilds to love tranquillity. One step,
One human step alone, has ever broken
The stillness of its solitude:—one voice 590
Alone inspired its echoes;—even that voice
Which hither came, floating among the winds,
And led the loveliest among human forms
To make their wild haunts the depository
Of all the grace and beauty that endued 595
Its motions, render up its majesty,

Scatter its music on the unfeeling storm,
And to the damp leaves and blue cavern mould,
Nurses of rainbow flowers and branching moss,
Commit the colours of that varying cheek,   600
That snowy breast, those dark and drooping eyes.

  The dim and horned moon hung low, and poured
A sea of lustre on the horizon's verge
That overflowed its mountains. Yellow mist
Filled the unbounded atmosphere, and drank   605
Wan moonlight even to fulness: not a star
Shone, not a sound was heard; the very winds,
Danger's grim playmates, on that precipice
Slept, clasped in his embrace.—O, storm of death!
Whose sightless speed divides this sullen night: 610
And thou, colossal Skeleton, that, still
Guiding its irresistible career
In thy devastating omnipotence,
Art king of this frail world, from the red field
Of slaughter, from the reeking hospital,   615
The patriot's sacred couch, the snowy bed
Of innocence, the scaffold and the throne,
A mighty voice invokes thee. Ruin calls
His brother Death. A rare and regal prey
He hath prepared, prowling around the world;   620
Glutted with which thou mayst repose, and men
Go to their graves like flowers or creeping worms,
Nor ever more offer at thy dark shrine
The unheeded tribute of a broken heart.

  When on the threshold of the green recess   625
The wanderer's footsteps fell, he knew that death
Was on him. Yet a little, ere it fled,
Did he resign his high and holy soul
To images of the majestic past,
That paused within his passive being now,   630
Like winds that bear sweet music, when they breathe
Through some dim latticed chamber. He did place
His pale lean hand upon the rugged trunk
Of the old pine. Upon an ivied stone
Reclined his languid head, his limbs did rest,   635
Diffused and motionless, on the smooth brink

Of that obscurest chasm;—and thus he lay,
Surrendering to their final impulses
The hovering powers of life. Hope and despair,
The torturers, slept: no mortal pain or fear   640
Marred his repose, the influxes of sense,
And his own being unalloyed by pain,
Yet feebler and more feeble, calmly fed
The stream of thought, till he lay breathing there
At peace, and faintly smiling:—his last sight   645
Was the great moon, which o'er the western line
Of the wide world her mighty horn suspended,
With those dun beams inwoven darkness seemed
To mingle. Now upon the jagged hills
It rests, and still as the divided frame   650
Of the vast meteor sunk, the Poet's blood,
That ever beat in mystic sympathy
With nature's ebb and flow, grew feebler still:
And when two lessening points of light alone
Gleamed through the darkness, the alternate gasp   655
Of his faint respiration scarce did stir
The stagnate night:—till the minutest ray
Was quenched, the pulse yet lingered in his heart.
It paused—it fluttered. But when heaven remained
Utterly black, the murky shades involved   660
An image, silent, cold, and motionless,
As their own voiceless earth and vacant air.
Even as a vapour fed with golden beams
That ministered on sunlight, ere the west
Eclipses it, was now that wondrous frame—   665
No sense, no motion, no divinity—
A fragile lute, on whose harmonious strings
The breath of heaven did wander—a bright stream
Once fed with many-voiced waves—a dream
Of youth, which night and time have quenched for ever, 670
Still, dark, and dry, and unremembered now.

O, for Medea's wondrous alchymy,
Which wheresoe'er it fell made the earth gleam
With bright flowers, and the wintry boughs exhale
From vernal blooms fresh fragrance! O, that God,   675
Profuse of poisons, would concede the chalice
Which but one living man has drained, who now,

Vessel of deathless wrath, a slave that feels
No proud exemption in the blighting curse
He bears, over the world wanders for ever,   680
Lone as incarnate death! O, that the dream
Of dark magician in his visioned cave,
Raking the cinders of a crucible
For life and power, even when his feeble hand
Shakes in its last decay, were the true law   685
Of this so lovely world! But thou art fled
Like some frail exhalation, which the dawn
Robes in its golden beams,—ah! thou hast fled!
The brave, the gentle, and the beautiful,
The child of grace and genius. Heartless things   690
Are done and said i' the world, and many worms
And beasts and men live on, and mighty Earth
From sea and mountain, city and wilderness,
In vesper low or joyous orison,
Lifts still its solemn voice:—but thou art fled—   695
Thou canst no longer know or love the shapes
Of this phantasmal scene, who have to thee
Been purest ministers, who are, alas!
Now thou art not. Upon those pallid lips
So sweet even in their silence, on those eyes   700
That image sleep in death, upon that form
Yet safe from the worm's outrage, let no tear
Be shed—not even in thought. Nor, when those hues
Are gone, and those divinest lineaments,
Worn by the senseless wind, shall live alone   705
In the frail pauses of this simple strain,
Let not high verse, mourning the memory
Of that which is no more, or painting's woe
Or sculpture, speak in feeble imagery
Their own cold powers. Art and eloquence,   710
And all the shews o' the world, are frail and vain
To weep a loss that turns their lights to shade.
It is a woe "too deep for tears," when all
Is reft at once, when some surpassing Spirit,
Whose light adorned the world around it, leaves   715
Those who remain behind, not sobs or groans,
The passionate tumult of a clinging hope;
But pale despair and cold tranquillity,

Nature's vast frame, the web of human things,
Birth and the grave, that are not as they were.   720
[1815]

MONT BLANC

LINES WRITTEN IN THE VALE OF CHAMOUNI

I

The everlasting universe of things
Flows through the mind, and rolls its rapid waves,
Now dark—now glittering—now reflecting gloom—
Now lending splendour, where from secret springs
The source of human thought its tribute brings   5
Of waters,—with a sound but half its own,
Such as a feeble brook will oft assume
In the wild woods, among the mountains lone,
Where waterfalls around it leap for ever,
Where woods and winds contend, and a vast river   10
Over its rocks ceaselessly bursts and raves.

II

Thus thou, Ravine of Arve—dark, deep Ravine—
Thou many-coloured, many-voiced vale,
Over whose pines, and crags, and caverns sail
Fast cloud shadows and sunbeams: awful scene,   15
Where Power in likeness of the Arve comes down
From the ice gulphs that gird his secret throne,
Bursting thro' these dark mountains like the flame
Of lightning thro' the tempest;—thou dost lie,
Thy giant brood of pines around thee clinging,   20
Children of elder time, in whose devotion
The chainless winds still come and ever came
To drink their odours, and their mighty swinging
To hear—an old and solemn harmony;
Thine earthly rainbows stretched across the sweep   25
Of the ethereal waterfall, whose veil
Robes some unsculptured image; the strange sleep
Which when the voices of the desert fail

Wraps all in its own deep eternity;—
Thy caverns echoing to the Arve's commotion,   30
A loud, lone sound no other sound can tame;
Thou art pervaded with that ceaseless motion,
Thou art the path of that unresting sound—
Dizzy Ravine! and when I gaze on thee
I seem as in a trance sublime and strange   35
To muse on my own separate phantasy,
My own, my human mind, which passively
Now renders and receives fast influencings,
Holding an unremitting interchange
With the clear universe of things around;   40
One legion of wild thoughts, whose wandering wings
Now float above thy darkness, and now rest
Where that or thou art no unbidden guest,
In the still cave of the witch Poesy,
Seeking among the shadows that pass by   45
Ghosts of all things that are, some shade of thee,
Some phantom, some faint image; till the breast
From which they fled recalls them, thou art there!

III

Some say that gleams of a remoter world
Visit the soul in sleep,—that death is slumber,   50
And that its shapes the busy thoughts outnumber
Of those who wake and live.—I look on high;
Has some unknown omnipotence unfurled
The veil of life and death? or do I lie
In dream, and does the mightier world of sleep   55
Spread far around and inaccessibly
Its circles? For the very spirit fails,
Driven like a homeless cloud from steep to steep
That vanishes among the viewless gales!
Far, far above, piercing the infinite sky,   60
Mont Blanc appears,—still, snowy, and serene—
Its subject mountains their unearthly forms
Pile around it, ice and rock; broad vales between
Of frozen floods, unfathomable deeps,
Blue as the overhanging heaven, that spread   65
And wind among the accumulated steeps;
A desert peopled by the storms alone,

Save when the eagle brings some hunter's bone,
And the wolf tracks her there—how hideously
Its shapes are heaped around! rude, bare, and high,   70
Ghastly, and scarred, and riven.—Is this the scene
Where the old Earthquake-dæmon taught her young
Ruin? Were these their toys? or did a sea
Of fire envelop once this silent snow?
None can reply—all seems eternal now.   75
The wilderness has a mysterious tongue
Which teaches awful doubt, or faith so mild,
So solemn, so serene, that man may be,
But for such faith, with nature reconciled;
Thou hast a voice, great Mountain, to repeal   80
Large codes of fraud and woe; not understood
By all, but which the wise, and great, and good
Interpret, or make felt, or deeply feel.

IV

The fields, the lakes, the forests, and the streams,
Ocean, and all the living things that dwell   85
Within the dædal earth; lightning, and rain,
Earthquake, and fiery flood, and hurricane,
The torpor of the year when feeble dreams
Visit the hidden buds, or dreamless sleep
Holds every future leaf and flower;—the bound   90
With which from that detested trance they leap;
The works and ways of man, their death and birth,
And that of him and all that his may be;
All things that move and breathe with toil and sound
Are born and die; revolve, subside, and swell.   95
Power dwells apart in its tranquillity,
Remote, serene, and inaccessible:
And *this*, the naked countenance of earth,
On which I gaze, even these primæval mountains
Teach the adverting mind. The glaciers creep   100
Like snakes that watch their prey, from their far fountains,
Slow rolling on; there, many a precipice,
Frost and the Sun in scorn of mortal power
Have piled: dome, pyramid, and pinnacle,
A city of death, distinct with many a tower   105
And wall impregnable of beaming ice.

Yet not a city, but a flood of ruin
Is there, that from the boundaries of the sky
Rolls its perpetual stream; vast pines are strewing
Its destined path, or in the mangled soil   110
Branchless and shattered stand; the rocks, drawn down
From yon remotest waste, have overthrown
The limits of the dead and living world,
Never to be reclaimed. The dwelling-place
Of insects, beasts, and birds, becomes its spoil;   115
Their food and their retreat for ever gone,
So much of life and joy is lost. The race
Of man flies far in dread; his work and dwelling
Vanish, like smoke before the tempest's stream,
And their place is not known. Below, vast caves   120
Shine in the rushing torrents' restless gleam,
Which from those secret chasms in tumult welling
Meet in the vale, and one majestic River,
The breath and blood of distant lands, for ever
Rolls its loud waters to the ocean waves,   125
Breathes its swift vapours to the circling air.

v

Mont Blanc yet gleams on high;—the power is there,
The still and solemn power of many sights,
And many sounds, and much of life and death.
In the calm darkness of the moonless nights,   130
In the lone glare of day, the snows descend
Upon that Mountain; none beholds them there,
Nor when the flakes burn in the sinking sun,
Or the star-beams dart through them:—Winds contend
Silently there, and heap the snow with breath   135
Rapid and strong, but silently! Its home
The voiceless lightning in these solitudes
Keeps innocently, and like vapour broods
Over the snow. The secret Strength of things
Which governs thought, and to the infinite dome   140
Of heaven is as a law, inhabits thee!
And what were thou, and earth, and stars, and sea,
If to the human mind's imaginings
Silence and solitude were vacancy?
        [1816]

HYMN TO INTELLECTUAL BEAUTY

The awful shadow of some unseen Power
  Floats tho' unseen among us; visiting
  This various world with as inconstant wing
As summer winds that creep from flower to flower;
Like moonbeams that behind some piny mountain shower,   5
    It visits with inconstant glance
  Each human heart and countenance;
Like hues and harmonies of evening,
    Like clouds in starlight widely spread,
    Like memory of music fled,   10
    Like aught that for its grace may be
Dear, and yet dearer for its mystery.

Spirit of BEAUTY, that dost consecrate
  With thine own hues all thou dost shine upon
  Of human thought or form, where art thou gone?   15
Why dost thou pass away and leave our state,
This dim vast vale of tears, vacant and desolate?
    Ask why the sunlight not forever
    Weaves rainbows o'er yon mountain river
Why aught should fail and fade that once is shown;   20
    Why fear and dream and death and birth
    Cast on the daylight of this earth
    Such gloom, why man has such a scope
For love and hate, despondency and hope?

No voice from some sublimer world hath ever   25
    To sage or poet these responses given:
    Therefore the names of Demon, Ghost, and Heaven,
Remain the records of their vain endeavour:
Frail spells, whose uttered charm might not avail to sever,
    From all we hear and all we see,   30
    Doubt, chance, and mutability.
Thy light alone, like mist o'er mountains driven,
    Or music by the night wind sent
    Thro' strings of some still instrument,
    Or moonlight on a midnight stream,   35
Gives grace and truth to life's unquiet dream.

Love, Hope, and Self-esteem, like clouds, depart
    And come, for some uncertain moments lent.
    Man were immortal and omnipotent,
Didst thou, unknown and awful as thou art,   40
Keep with thy glorious train firm state within his heart.
    Thou messenger of sympathies,
    That wax and wane in lovers' eyes;
Thou, that to human thought art nourishment,
    Like darkness to a dying flame!   45
    Depart not as thy shadow came:
    Depart not, lest the grave should be,
Like life and fear, a dark reality.

While yet a boy I sought for ghosts, and sped
    Thro' many a listening chamber, cave, and ruin,   50
    And starlight wood, with fearful steps pursuing
Hopes of high talk with the departed dead.
I called on poisonous names with which our youth is fed:
    I was not heard: I saw them not:
    When musing deeply on the lot   55
Of life, at that sweet time when winds are wooing
    All vital things that wake to bring
    News of birds and blossoming,
    Sudden, thy shadow fell on me;
I shrieked, and clasped my hands in extacy!   60

I vowed that I would dedicate my powers
    To thee and thine: have I not kept the vow?
    With beating heart and streaming eyes, even now
I call the phantoms of a thousand hours
Each from his voiceless grave: they have in visioned bowers   65
    Of studious zeal or love's delight
    Outwatched with me the envious night:
They know that never joy illumed my brow,
    Unlinked with hope that thou wouldst free
    This world from its dark slavery,   70
    That thou, O awful LOVELINESS,
Wouldst give whate'er these words cannot express.

The day becomes more solemn and serene
    When noon is past: there is a harmony
    In autumn, and a lustre in its sky,   75

Which thro' the summer is not heard or seen,
As if it could not be, as if it had not been!
 Thus let thy power, which like the truth
 Of nature on my passive youth
Descended, to my outward life supply
  Its calm, to one who worships thee,   80
  And every form containing thee,
 Whom, SPIRIT fair, thy spells did bind
To fear himself, and love all human kind.
 [1816]

OZYMANDIAS

I met a traveller from an antique land
Who said: Two vast and trunkless legs of stone
Stand in the desert. Near them, on the sand,
Half sunk, a shattered visage lies, whose frown,
And wrinkled lip, and sneer of cold command,   5
Tell that its sculptor well those passions read
Which yet survive, stamped on these lifeless things,
The hand that mocked them and the heart that fed;
And on the pedestal these words appear:
"My name is Ozymandias, king of kings;   10
Look on my works, ye Mighty, and despair!"
Nothing beside remains. Round the decay
Of that colossal wreck, boundless and bare
The lone and level sands stretch far away.
 [1817]

LINES TO A CRITIC

Honey from silk-worms who can gather,
 Or silk from the yellow bee?
The grass may grow in winter weather
 As soon as hate in me.

Hate men who cant, and men who pray,   5
    And men who rail like thee;
An equal passion to repay
    They are not coy like me.

Or seek some slave of power and gold,
    To be thy dear heart's mate;   10
Thy love will move that bigot cold,
    Sooner than me, thy hate.

A passion like the one I prove
    Cannot divided be;
I hate thy want of truth and love—   15
    How should I then hate thee?
        [1817]

STANZAS,

WRITTEN IN DEJECTION, NEAR NAPLES

The sun is warm, the sky is clear,
    The waves are dancing fast and bright,
Blue isles and snowy mountains wear
    The purple noon's transparent might:
The breath of the moist air is light,   5
    Around its unexpanded buds;
Like many a voice of one delight,
    The winds, the birds, the ocean floods,
The City's voice itself, is soft like Solitude's.

I see the Deep's untrampled floor   10
    With green and purple sea-weeds strown;
I see the waves upon the shore,
    Like light dissolved in star-showers, thrown:
I sit upon the sands alone,
    The lightning of the noon-tide ocean   15
Is flashing round me, and a tone
    Arises from its measured motion,
How sweet! did any heart now share in my emotion.

Alas! I have nor hope nor health,
  Nor peace within nor calm around,   20
Nor that content surpassing wealth
  The sage in meditation found,
And walked with inward glory crowned—
  Nor fame, nor power, nor love, nor leisure.
Others I see whom these surround—   25
  Smiling they live, and call life pleasure;
To me that cup has been dealt in another measure.

Yet now despair itself is mild,
  Even as the winds and waters are;
I could lie down like a tired child,   30
  And weep away the life of care
Which I have borne, and yet must bear,
  Till death like sleep might steal on me,
And I might feel in the warm air
  My cheek grow cold, and hear the sea   35
Breathe o'er my dying brain its last monotony.

Some might lament that I were cold,
  As I, when this sweet day is gone,
Which my lost heart, too soon grown old,
  Insults with this untimely moan;   40
They might lament—for I am one
  Whom men love not,—and yet regret,
Unlike this day, which, when the sun
  Shall on its stainless glory set,
Will linger, though enjoyed, like joy in memory yet.   45
  [1818]

PROMETHEUS UNBOUND:

A Lyrical Drama in Four Acts

DRAMATIS PERSONÆ

PROMETHEUS
DEMOGORGON
JUPITER
THE EARTH
OCEAN
APOLLO
MERCURY
HERCULES
PANTHEA ⎫
IONE ⎬ *Oceanides*
ASIA ⎭
THE PHANTASM OF JUPITER
THE SPIRIT OF THE EARTH
THE SPIRIT OF THE MOON
SPIRITS OF THE HOURS
SPIRITS. ECHOES. FAUNS
FURIES

ACT I.

Scene: A Ravine of Icy Rocks in the Indian Caucasus. PROMETHEUS is discovered bound to the Precipice. PANTHEA and IONE are seated at his feet. Time, Night. During the Scene, Morning slowly breaks.

PROMETHEUS. Monarch of Gods and Dæmons, and all
    Spirits
But One, who throng those bright and rolling worlds
Which Thou and I alone of living things
Behold with sleepless eyes! regard this Earth
Made multitudinous with thy slaves, whom thou   5
Requitest for knee-worship, prayer, and praise,
And toil, and hecatombs of broken hearts,
With fear and self-contempt and barren hope.
Whilst me, who am thy foe, eyeless in hate,
Hast thou made reign and triumph, to thy scorn,   10
O'er mine own misery and thy vain revenge.
Three thousand years of sleep-unsheltered hours,
And moments aye divided by keen pangs
Till they seemed years, torture and solitude,
Scorn and despair,—these are mine empire.   15
More glorious far than that which thou surveyest
From thine unenvied throne, O, Mighty God!
Almighty, had I deigned to share the shame
Of thine ill tyranny, and hung not here
Nailed to this wall of eagle-baffling mountain,   20
Black, wintry, dead, unmeasured; without herb,
Insect, or beast, or shape or sound of life.
Ah me, alas! pain, pain ever, for ever!

No change, no pause, no hope! Yet I endure.
I ask the Earth, have not the mountains felt?   25
I ask yon Heaven, the all-beholden Sun,
Has it not seen? The Sea, in storm or calm,
Heaven's ever-changing Shadow, spread below,
Have its deaf waves not heard my agony?
Ah me! alas, pain, pain ever, for ever!   30

The crawling glaciers pierce me with the spears
Of their moon-freezing crystals, the bright chains
Eat with their burning cold into my bones.
Heaven's winged hound, polluting from thy lips
His beak in poison not his own, tears up   35
My heart; and shapeless sights come wandering by,
The ghastly people of the realm of dream,
Mocking me: and the Earthquake-fiends are charged
To wrench the rivets from my quivering wounds
When the rocks split and close again behind: 40
While from their loud abysses howling throng
The genii of the storm, urging the rage
Of whirlwind, and afflict me with keen hail.
And yet to me welcome is day and night,
Whether one breaks the hoar frost of the morn,   45
Or starry, dim, and slow, the other climbs
The leaden-coloured east; for then they lead
Their wingless, crawling hours, one among whom
—As some dark Priest hales the reluctant victim—
Shall drag thee, cruel King, to kiss the blood   50
From these pale feet, which then might trample thee
If they disdained not such a prostrate slave.
Disdain! Ah no! I pity thee. What ruin
Will hunt thee undefended thro' wide Heaven!
How will thy soul, cloven to its depth with terror,   55
Gape like a hell within! I speak in grief,
Not exultation, for I hate no more,
As then ere misery made me wise. The curse
Once breathed on thee I would recall. Ye Mountains,
Whose many-voiced Echoes, through the mist   60
Of cataracts, flung the thunder of that spell!
Ye icy Springs, stagnant with wrinkling frost,
Which vibrated to hear me, and then crept
Shuddering thro' India! Thou serenest Air,
Thro' which the Sun walks burning without beams!   65
And ye swift Whirlwinds, who on poised wings
Hung mute and moveless o'er yon hushed abyss,
As thunder, louder than your own, made rock
The orbed world! If then my words had power,
Though I am changed so that aught evil wish   70
Is dead within; although no memory be

Of what is hate, let them not lose it now!
What was that curse? for ye all heard me speak.

FIRST VOICE *(from the mountains).*

> Thrice three hundred thousand years
>> O'er the Earthquake's couch we stood: 75
> Oft, as men convulsed with fears,
>> We trembled in our multitude.

SECOND VOICE *(from the springs).*

> Thunderbolts had parched our water,
>> We had been stained with bitter blood,
> And had run mute, 'mid shrieks of slaughter,   80
>> Thro' a city and a solitude.

THIRD VOICE *(from the air).*

> I had clothed, since Earth uprose,
>> Its wastes in colours not their own,
> And oft had my serene repose
>> Been cloven by many a rending groan.   85

FOURTH VOICE *(from the whirlwinds).*

> We had soared beneath these mountains
>> Unresting ages; nor had thunder,
> Nor yon volcano's flaming fountains,
>> Nor any power above or under
> Ever made us mute with wonder.   90

FIRST VOICE.

> But never bowed our snowy crest
> As at the voice of thine unrest.

SECOND VOICE.

> Never such a sound before
> To the Indian waves we bore.
> A pilot asleep on the howling sea
> Leaped up from the deck in agony,   95
> And heard, and cried, "Ah, woe is me!"
> And died as mad as the wild waves be.

THIRD VOICE.

> By such dread words from Earth to Heaven
> My still realm was never riven: 100
> When its wound was closed, there stood
> Darkness o'er the day like blood.

FOURTH VOICE.

> And we shrank back: for dreams of ruin
> To frozen caves our flight pursuing
> Made us keep silence—thus—and thus—   105
> Though silence is as hell to us.

THE EARTH. The tongueless Caverns of the craggy hills
Cried, 'Misery!' then; the hollow Heaven replied,
'Misery!' And the Ocean's purple waves,
Climbing the land, howled to the lashing winds,   110
And the pale nations heard it, 'Misery!'
PROMETHEUS. I hear a sound of voices: not the voice
Which I gave forth. Mother, thy sons and thou
Scorn him, without whose all-enduring will
Beneath the fierce omnipotence of Jove,   115
Both they and thou had vanished, like thin mist
Unrolled on the morning wind. Know ye not me,
The Titan? He who made his agony
The barrier to your else all-conquering foe?
Oh, rock-embosomed lawns, and snow-fed streams,   120
Now seen athwart frore vapours, deep below,
Thro' whose o'ershadowing woods I wandered once
   With Asia, drinking life from her loved eyes;
Why scorns the spirit which informs ye, now
To commune with me? me alone, who check'd,   125
As one who checks a fiend-drawn charioteer,
The falsehood and the force of him who reigns
Supreme, and with the groans of pining slaves
Fills your dim glens and liquid wildernesses:
Why answer ye not, still? Brethren!
THE EARTH.   They dare not.   130
PROMETHEUS. Who dares? for I would hear that curse
   again.
Ha, what an awful whisper rises up!
'Tis scarce like sound: it tingles thro' the frame
As lightning tingles, hovering ere it strike.

Speak, Spirit! from thine inorganic voice   135
I only know that thou art moving near
And love. How cursed I him?
THE EARTH.   How canst thou hear,
Who knowest not the language of the dead?
PROMETHEUS. Thou art a living spirit; speak as they.
THE EARTH. I dare not speak like life, lest Heaven's fell
     King   140
Should hear, and link me to some wheel of pain
More torturing than the one whereon I roll.
Subtle thou art and good, and tho' the Gods
Hear not this voice, yet thou art more than God
Being wise and kind: earnestly hearken now.   145
PROMETHEUS. Obscurely thro' my brain, like shadows dim,
Sweep awful thoughts, rapid and thick. I feel
Faint, like one mingled in entwining love;
Yet 'tis not pleasure.
THE EARTH.   No, thou canst not hear:
Thou art immortal, and this tongue is known   150
Only to those who die.
PROMETHEUS.   And what art thou,
O melancholy Voice?
THE EARTH.   I am the Earth,
Thy mother; she within whose stony veins,
To the last fibre of the loftiest tree
Whose thin leaves trembled in the frozen air,   155
Joy ran, as blood within a living frame,
When thou didst from her bosom, like a cloud
Of glory, arise, a spirit of keen joy!
And at thy voice her pining sons uplifted
Their prostrate brows from the polluting dust,   160
And our almighty Tyrant with fierce dread
Grew pale, until his thunder chained thee here.
Then, see those million worlds which burn and roll
Around us: their inhabitants beheld
My sphered light wane in wide Heaven; the sea   165
Was lifted by strange tempest, and new fire
From earthquake-rifted mountains of bright snow
Shook its portentous hair beneath Heaven's frown;
Lightning and Inundation vexed the plains;
Blue thistles bloomed in cities; foodless toads   170
Within voluptuous chambers panting crawled:

When Plague had fallen on man, and beast, and worm,
And Famine; and black blight on herb and tree;
And in the corn, and vines, and meadow-grass,
Teemed ineradicable poisonous weeds   175
Draining their growth, for my wan breast was dry
With grief; and the thin air, my breath, was stained
With the contagion of a mother's hate
Breathed on her child's destroyer; aye, I heard
Thy curse, the which, if thou rememberest not,   180
Yet my innumerable seas and streams,
Mountains, and caves, and winds, and yon wide air,
And the inarticulate people of the dead,
Preserve, a treasured spell. We meditate
In secret joy and hope those dreadful words   185
But dare not speak them.
PROMETHEUS.   Venerable mother!
All else who live and suffer take from thee
Some comfort; flowers, and fruits, and happy sounds,
And love, though fleeting; these may not be mine.
But mine own words, I pray, deny me not.   190
THE EARTH. They shall be told. Ere Babylon was dust,
The Magus Zoroaster, my dead child,
Met his own image walking in the garden.
That apparition, sole of men, he saw.
For know there are two worlds of life and death: 195
One that which thou beholdest; but the other
Is underneath the grave, where do inhabit
The shadows of all forms that think and live
Till death unite them and they part no more;
Dreams and the light imaginings of men,   200
And all that faith creates or love desires,
Terrible, strange, sublime and beauteous shapes.
There thou art, and dost hang, a writhing shade,
'Mid whirlwind-shaken mountains; all the gods
Are there, and all the powers of nameless worlds,   205
Vast, sceptred phantoms; heroes, men, and beasts;
And Demogorgon, a tremendous gloom;
And he, the supreme Tyrant, on his throne
Of burning gold. Son, one of these shall utter
The curse which all remember. Call at will   210
Thine own ghost, or the ghost of Jupiter,
Hades or Typhon, or what mightier Gods

From all-prolific Evil, since thy ruin
Have sprung, and trampled on my prostrate sons.
Ask, and they must reply: so the revenge   215
Of the Supreme may sweep thro' vacant shades,
As rainy wind thro' the abandoned gate
Of a fallen palace.
PROMETHEUS.   Mother, let not aught
Of that which may be evil, pass again
My lips, or those of aught resembling me.   220
Phantasm of Jupiter, arise, appear!

IONE.

    My wings are folded o'er mine ears:
        My wings are crossed over mine eyes:
    Yet thro' their silver shade appears,
        And thro' their lulling plumes arise,   225
    A Shape, a throng of sounds;
        May it be no ill to thee,
    O thou of many wounds!
Near whom, for our sweet sister's sake,
Ever thus we watch and wake.   230

PANTHEA.

    The sound is of whirlwind underground,
        Earthquake, and fire, and mountains cloven;
    The shape is awful like the sound,
        Clothed in dark purple, star-inwoven.
    A sceptre of pale gold   235
        To stay steps proud, o'er the slow cloud
    His veined hand doth hold.
Cruel he looks, but calm and strong,
Like one who does, not suffers wrong.

PHANTASM OF JUPITER. Why have the secret powers of this
    strange world   240
Driven me, a frail and empty phantom, hither
On direst storms? What unaccustomed sounds
Are hovering on my lips, unlike the voice
With which our pallid race hold ghastly talk
In darkness? And, proud sufferer, who art thou?   245
PROMETHEUS. Tremendous Image, as thou art must be

He whom thou shadowest forth. I am his foe,
The Titan. Speak the words which I would hear,
Although no thought inform thine empty voice.
THE EARTH. Listen! And tho' your echoes must be mute,   250
Grey mountains, and old woods, and haunted springs,
Prophetic caves, and isle-surrounding streams,
Rejoice to hear what yet ye cannot speak.
PHANTASM. A spirit seizes me and speaks within:
It tears me as fire tears a thunder-cloud.   255
PANTHEA. See, how he lifts his mighty looks, the Heaven
Darkens above.
IONE.   He speaks! O shelter me!
PROMETHEUS. I see the curse on gestures proud and cold,
And looks of firm defiance, and calm hate,
And such despair as mocks itself with smiles,   260
Written as on a scroll: yet speak: Oh, speak!

PHANTASM.

    Fiend, I defy thee! with a calm, fixed mind,
        All that thou canst inflict I bid thee do;
    Foul Tyrant both of Gods and Human-kind,
        One only being shalt thou not subdue.   265
    Rain then thy plagues upon me here,
    Ghastly disease and frenzying fear;
    And let alternate frost and fire
    Eat into me, and be thine ire
Lightning, and cutting hail, and legioned forms   270
Of furies, driving by upon the wounding storms.

    Aye, do thy worst. Thou art omnipotent.
        O'er all things but thyself I gave thee power,
    And my own will. Be thy swift mischiefs sent
        To blast mankind, from yon ethereal tower   275
    Let thy malignant spirit move
    In darkness over those I love:
    On me and mine I imprecate
    The utmost torture of thy hate;
And thus devote to sleepless agony,   280
This undeclining head while thou must reign on high.

    But thou, who art the God and Lord: O, thou
        Who fillest with thy soul this world of woe,

To whom all things of Earth and Heaven do bow
   In fear and worship: all-prevailing foe!   285
I curse thee! let a sufferer's curse
Clasp thee, his torturer, like remorse!
Till thine Infinity shall be
A robe of envenomed agony;
And thine Omnipotence a crown of pain,   290
To cling like burning gold round thy dissolving brain.

Heap on thy soul, by virtue of this Curse,
   Ill deeds, then be thou damned, beholding good;
Both infinite as is the universe,
   And thou, and thy self-torturing solitude.   295
An awful image of calm power
Though now thou sittest, let the hour
Come, when thou must appear to be
That which thou art internally.
And after many a false and fruitless crime,   300
Scorn track thy lagging fall thro' boundless space and time.

PROMETHEUS. Were these my words, O Parent?
THE EARTH.   They were thine.
PROMETHEUS. It doth repent me: words are quick and
    vain;
Grief for awhile is blind, and so was mine.
I wish no living thing to suffer pain.   305

THE EARTH.

Misery, Oh misery to me,
That Jove at length should vanquish thee.
Wail, howl aloud, Land and Sea,
The Earth's rent heart shall answer ye.
Howl, Spirits of the living and the dead,   310
Your refuge, your defence lies fallen and vanquished.

FIRST ECHO.

Lies fallen and vanquished?

SECOND ECHO.

Fallen and vanquished!

IONE.

Fear not: 'tis but some passing spasm,
    The Titan is unvanquished still.   315
But see, where thro' the azure chasm
    Of yon forked and snowy hill
Trampling the slant winds on high
    With golden-sandalled feet, that glow
Under plumes of purple dye,   320
Like rose-ensanguined ivory,
    A Shape comes now,
Stretching on high from his right hand
A serpent-cinctured wand.

PANTHEA. 'Tis Jove's world-wandering herald, Mercury. 325

IONE.

And who are those with hydra tresses
    And iron wings that climb the wind,
Whom the frowning God represses
    Like vapours steaming up behind,
Clanging loud, an endless crowd—   330

PANTHEA.

    These are Jove's tempest-walking hounds,
Whom he gluts with groans and blood,
When charioted on sulphurous cloud
    He bursts Heaven's bounds.

IONE.

Are they now led, from the thin dead   335
On new pangs to be fed?

PANTHEA.

The Titan looks as ever, firm, not proud.
FIRST FURY. Ha! I scent life!
SECOND FURY.   Let me but look into his eyes!
THIRD FURY. The hope of torturing him smells like a heap
Of corpses, to a death-bird after battle.   340
FIRST FURY. Darest thou delay, O Herald! take cheer,
    Hounds

Of Hell: what if the Son of Maia soon
Should make us food and sport—who can please long
The Omnipotent?
MERCURY.   Back to your towers of iron,
And gnash beside the streams of fire, and wail   345
Your foodless teeth. Geryon, arise! and Gorgon,
Chimæra, and thou Sphinx, subtlest of fiends,
Who ministered to Thebes Heaven's poisoned wine,
Unnatural love, and more unnatural hate:
These shall perform your task.
FIRST FURY.   Oh, mercy! mercy!   350
We die with our desire: drive us not back!
MERCURY. Crouch then in silence.
                              Awful Sufferer
To thee unwilling, most unwillingly
I come, by the great Father's will driven down,
To execute a doom of new revenge.   355
Alas! I pity thee, and hate myself
That I can do no more: aye from thy sight
Returning, for a season, heaven seems hell,
So thy worn form pursues me night and day,
Smiling reproach. Wise art thou, firm and good,   360
But vainly wouldst stand forth alone in strife
Against the Omnipotent; as yon clear lamps
That measure and divide the weary years
From which there is no refuge, long have taught
And long must teach. Even now thy Torturer arms   365
With the strange might of unimagined pains
The powers who scheme slow agonies in Hell,
And my commission is to lead them here,
Or what more subtle, foul, or savage fiends
People the abyss, and leave them to their task.   370
Be it not so! there is a secret known
To thee, and to none else of living things,
Which may transfer the sceptre of wide Heaven,
The fear of which perplexes the Supreme:
Clothe it in words, and bid it clasp his throne   375
In intercession; bend thy soul in prayer,
And like a suppliant in some gorgeous fane,
Let the will kneel within thy haughty heart:
For benefits and meek submission tame
The fiercest and the mightiest.

PROMETHEUS.   Evil minds   380
Change good to their own nature. I gave all
He has; and in return he chains me here
Years, ages, night and day: whether the Sun
Split my parched skin, or in the moony night
The crystal-winged snow cling round my hair: 385
Whilst my beloved race is trampled down
By his thought-executing ministers.
Such is the tyrant's recompense: 'tis just:
He who is evil can receive no good;
And for a world bestowed, or a friend lost,   390
He can feel hate, fear, shame; not gratitude:
He but requites me for his own misdeed.
Kindness to such is keen reproach, which breaks
With bitter stings the light sleep of Revenge.
Submission, thou dost know I cannot try;   395
For what submission but that fatal word,
The death-seal of mankind's captivity,
Like the Sicilian's hair-suspended sword,
Which trembles o'er his crown, would he accept,
Or could I yield? Which yet I will not yield.   400
Let others flatter Crime, where it sits throned
In brief Omnipotence: secure are they:
For Justice, when triumphant, will weep down
Pity, not punishment, on her own wrongs,
Too much avenged by those who err. I wait,   405
Enduring thus, the retributive hour
Which since we spake is even nearer now.
But hark, the hell-hounds clamour: fear delay:
Behold! Heaven lowers under thy Father's frown.
MERCURY. Oh, that we might be spared: I to inflict 410
And thou to suffer! once more answer me:
Thou knowest not the period of Jove's power?
PROMETHEUS. I know but this, that it must come.
MERCURY.   Alas!
Thou canst not count thy years to come of pain?
PROMETHEUS. They last while Jove must reign; nor more,
    nor less   415
Do I desire or fear.
MERCURY.   Yet pause, and plunge
Into Eternity, where recorded time,
Even all that we imagine, age on age,

Seems but a point, and the reluctant mind
Flags wearily in its unending flight,   420
Till it sink, dizzy, blind, lost, shelterless;
Perchance it has not numbered the slow years
Which thou must spend in torture, unreprieved?
PROMETHEUS. Perchance no thought can count them, yet
    they pass.
MERCURY. If thou might'st dwell among the Gods the 425
    while,
Lapped in voluptuous joy?
PROMETHEUS.   I would not quit
This bleak ravine, these unrepentant pains.
MERCURY. Alas! I wonder at, yet pity thee.
PROMETHEUS. Pity the self-despising slaves of Heaven,
Not me, within whose mind sits peace serene,   430
As light in the sun, throned: how vain is talk!
Call up the fiends
IONE.   O, sister, look! White fire
Has cloven to the roots yon huge snow-loaded cedar;
How fearfully God's thunder howls behind!
MERCURY. I must obey his words and thine: alas!   435
Most heavily remorse hangs at my heart!
PANTHEA. See where the child of Heaven, with winged
    feet,
Runs down the slanted sunlight of the dawn.
IONE. Dear sister, close thy plumes over thine eyes
Lest thou behold and die: they come: they come   440
Blackening the birth of day with countless wings,
And hollow underneath, like death.
FIRST FURY.   Prometheus!
SECOND FURY. Immortal Titan!
THIRD FURY.   Champion of Heaven's slaves!
PROMETHEUS. He whom some dreadful voice invokes is
    here,
Prometheus, the chained Titan. Horrible forms,   445
What and who are ye? Never yet there came
Phantasms so foul thro' monster-teeming Hell
From the all-miscreative brain of Jove;
Whilst I behold such execrable shapes,
Methinks I grow like what I contemplate,   450
And laugh and stare in loathsome sympathy.
FIRST FURY. We are the ministers of pain and fear,

And disappointment, and mistrust, and hate,
And clinging crime; and as lean dogs pursue
Thro' wood and lake some struck and sobbing fawn,   455
We track all things that weep, and bleed, and live,
When the great King betrays them to our will.
PROMETHEUS. Oh! many fearful natures in one name,
I know ye; and these lakes and echoes know
The darkness and the clangour of your wings.   460
But why more hideous than your loathed selves
Gather ye up in legions from the deep?
SECOND FURY. We knew not that: Sisters, rejoice, rejoice!
PROMETHEUS. Can aught exult in its deformity?
SECOND FURY. The beauty of delight makes lovers glad,   465
Gazing on one another: so are we.
As from the rose which the pale priestess kneels
To gather for her festal crown of flowers
The aërial crimson falls, flushing her cheek,
So from our victim's destined agony   470
The shade which is our form invests us round,
Else are we shapeless as our mother Night.
PROMETHEUS. I laugh your power, and his who sent you
        here,
To lowest scorn. Pour forth the cup of pain.
FIRST FURY. Thou thinkest we will rend thee bone from
        bone,   475
And nerve from nerve, working like fire within?
PROMETHEUS. Pain is my element, as hate is thine;
Ye rend me now: I care not.
SECOND FURY.   Dost imagine
We will but laugh into thy lidless eyes?
PROMETHEUS. I weigh not what ye do, but what ye suffer,   480
Being evil. Cruel was the power which called
You, or aught else so wretched, into light.
THIRD FURY. Thou think'st we will live thro' thee, one
        by one,
Like animal life, and tho' we can obscure not
The soul which burns within, that we will dwell   485
Beside it, like a vain loud multitude
Vexing the self-content of wisest men:
That we will be dread thought beneath thy brain,
And foul desire round thine astonished heart,
And blood within thy labyrinthine veins   490

Crawling like agony.
PROMETHEUS.   Why, ye are thus now;
Yet am I king over myself, and rule
The torturing and conflicting throngs within,
As Jove rules you when Hell grows mutinous.

CHORUS OF FURIES.

From the ends of the earth, from the ends of the earth,   495
Where the night has its grave and the morning its birth,
      Come, come, come!
Oh, ye who shake hills with the scream of your mirth,
When cities sink howling in ruin; and ye
Who with wingless footsteps trample the sea,   500
And close upon Shipwreck and Famine's track,
Sit chattering with joy on the foodless wreck;
      Come, come, come!
   Leave the bed, low, cold, and red,
   Strewed beneath a nation dead;   505
   Leave the hatred, as in ashes
    Fire is left for future burning:
  It will burst in bloodier flashes
    When ye stir it, soon returning:
  Leave the self-contempt implanted   510
  In young spirits, sense enchanted,
   Misery's yet unkindled fuel:
Leave Hell's secrets half unchanted
   To the maniac dreamer; cruel
More than ye can be with hate   515
   Is he with fear.
      Come, come, come!
We are steaming up from Hell's wide gate,
  And we burthen the blasts of the atmosphere,
  But vainly we toil till ye come here.   520
IONE. Sister, I hear the thunder of new wings.
PANTHEA. These solid mountains quiver with the sound
Even as the tremulous air: their shadows make
The space within my plumes more black than night.

FIRST FURY.

   Your call was as a winged car,   525
   Driven on whirlwinds fast and far;
   It rapt us from red gulfs of war.

SECOND FURY.

From wide cities, famine-wasted;

THIRD FURY.

Groans half heard, and blood untasted;

FOURTH FURY.

Kingly conclaves stern and cold,   530
Where blood with gold is bought and sold;

FIFTH FURY.

From the furnace, white and hot,
In which—

A FURY.

Speak not: whisper not:
I know all that ye would tell,
But to speak might break the spell   535
Which must bend the Invincible,
    The stern of thought;
He yet defies the deepest power of Hell.

FURY.

Tear the veil!

ANOTHER FURY.

It is torn.

CHORUS.

The pale stars of the morn
Shine on a misery, dire to be borne.   540
Dost thou faint, mighty Titan? We laugh thee to scorn.
Dost thou boast the clear knowledge thou waken'dst for
    man?
Then was kindled within him a thirst which outran
Those perishing waters; a thirst of fierce fever,
Hope, love, doubt, desire, which consume him for ever.   545

One came forth of gentle worth
Smiling on the sanguine earth;
His words outlived him, like swift poison
    Withering up truth, peace, and pity.
Look! where round the wide horizon   550
    Many a million-peopled city
Vomits smoke in the bright air.
Hark that outcry of despair!
    'Tis his mild and gentle ghost
        Wailing for the faith he kindled: 555
Look again, the flames almost
        To a glow-worm's lamp have dwindled:
The survivors round the embers
    Gather in dread.
              Joy, joy, joy!   560
Past ages crowd on thee, but each one remembers,
And the future is dark, and the present is spread
Like a pillow of thorns for thy slumberless head.

SEMICHORUS I.

Drops of bloody agony flow
From his white and quivering brow.   565
Grant a little respite now:
See a disenchanted nation
Springs like day from desolation;
To truth its state is dedicate,
And Freedom leads it forth, her mate;   570
A legioned band of linked brothers,
Whom Love calls children—

SEMICHORUS II.

              'Tis another's:
See how kindred murder kin:
'Tis the vintage-time for death and sin:
Blood, like new wine, bubbles within: 575
    Till Despair smothers
The struggling world, which slaves and tyrants win.
      [All the FURIES vanish, except one.]
IONE. Hark, sister! what a low yet dreadful groan
Quite unsuppressed is tearing up the heart
Of the good Titan, as storms tear the deep,   580

And beasts hear the sea moan in inland caves.
Darest thou observe how the fiends torture him?
PANTHEA. Alas! I looked forth twice, but will no more.
IONE. What didst thou see?
PANTHEA.   A woful sight: a youth
With patient looks nailed to a crucifix.   585
IONE. What next?
PANTHEA.   The heaven around, the earth below
Was peopled with thick shapes of human death,
All horrible, and wrought by human hands,
Tho' some appeared the work of human hearts,
For men were slowly killed by frowns and smiles: 590
And other sights too foul to speak and live
Were wandering by. Let us not tempt worse fear
By looking forth: those groans are grief enough.
FURY. Behold an emblem: those who do endure
Deep wrongs for man, and scorn, and chains, but heap   595
Thousandfold torment on themselves and him.
PROMETHEUS. Remit the anguish of that lighted stare;
Close those wan lips; let that thorn-wounded brow
Stream not with blood; it mingles with thy tears!
Fix, fix those tortured orbs in peace and death,   600
So thy sick throes shake not that crucifix,
So those pale fingers play not with thy gore.
O, horrible! Thy name I will not speak,
It hath become a curse. I see, I see
The wise, the mild, the lofty, and the just,   605
Whom thy slaves hate for being like to thee,
Some hunted by foul lies from their heart's home,
An early-chosen, late-lamented home;
As hooded ounces cling to the driven hind;
Some linked to corpses in unwholesome cells: 610
Some—Hear I not the multitude laugh loud?—
Impaled in lingering fire: and mighty realms
Float by my feet, like sea-uprooted isles,
Whose sons are kneaded down in common blood
By the red light of their own burning homes.   615
FURY. Blood thou canst see, and fire; and canst hear
    groans:
Worse things, unheard, unseen, remain behind.
PROMETHEUS. Worse?
FURY.   In each human heart terror survives

The ravin it has gorged: the loftiest fear
All that they would disdain to think were true: 620
Hypocrisy and custom make their minds
The fanes of many a worship, now outworn.
They dare not devise good for man's estate,
And yet they know not that they do not dare.
The good want power, but to weep barren tears.   625
The powerful goodness want: worse need for them.
The wise want love; and those who love want wisdom;
And all best things are thus confused to ill.
Many are strong and rich, and would be just,
But live among their suffering fellow-men
As if none felt: they know not what they do.   630
PROMETHEUS. Thy words are like a cloud of winged
     snakes;
And yet I pity those they torture not.
FURY. Thou pitiest them? I speak no more!   [Vanishes.]
PROMETHEUS.   Ah woe!
Ah woe! Alas! pain, pain ever, for ever!   635
I close my tearless eyes, but see more clear
Thy works within my woe-illumined mind,
Thou subtle tyrant! Peace is in the grave.
The grave hides all things beautiful and good:
I am a God and cannot find it there,   640
Nor would I seek it: for, though dread revenge,
This is defeat, fierce king, not victory.
The sights with which thou torturest gird my soul
With new endurance, till the hour arrives
When they shall be no types of things which are.   645
PANTHEA. Alas! what sawest thou more?
PROMETHEUS.   There are two woes;
To speak, and to behold; thou spare me one.
Names are there, Nature's sacred watch-words, they
Were borne aloft in bright emblazonry;
The nations thronged around, and cried aloud,   650
As with one voice, Truth, liberty, and love!
Suddenly fierce confusion fell from heaven
Among them: there was strife, deceit, and fear:
Tyrants rushed in, and did divide the spoil.
This was the shadow of the truth I saw.   655
THE EARTH. I felt thy torture, son, with such mixed joy
As pain and virtue give. To cheer thy state

I bid ascend those subtle and fair spirits,
Whose homes are the dim caves of human thought,
And who inhabit, as birds wing the wind,   660
Its world-surrounding ether: they behold
Beyond that twilight realm, as in a glass,
The future: may they speak comfort to thee!
PANTHEA. Look, sister, where a troop of spirits gather,
Like flocks of clouds in spring's delightful weather,   665
Thronging in the blue air!
IONE.   And see! more come,
Like fountain-vapours when the winds are dumb,
That climb up the ravine in scattered lines.
And, hark! is it the music of the pines?
Is it the lake? Is it the waterfall?   670
PANTHEA. 'Tis something sadder, sweeter far than all.

CHORUS OF SPIRITS.

From unremembered ages we
Gentle guides and guardians be
Of heaven-oppressed mortality;
And we breathe, and sicken not,   675
The atmosphere of human thought:
Be it dim, and dank, and grey,
Like a storm-extinguished day,
Travelled o'er by dying gleams;
Be it bright as all between   680
Cloudless skies and windless streams,
Silent, liquid, and serene;
As the birds within the wind,
As the fish within the wave,
As the thoughts of man's own mind   685
Float thro' all above the grave;
We make there our liquid lair,
Voyaging cloudlike and unpent
Thro' the boundless element:
Thence we bear the prophecy   690
Which begins and ends in thee!

IONE. More yet come, one by one: the air around them
Looks radiant as the air around a star.

FIRST SPIRIT.

On a battle-trumpet's blast
I fled hither, fast, fast, fast,
'Mid the darkness upward cast.   695
From the dust of creeds outworn,
From the tyrant's banner torn,
Gathering 'round me, onward borne,
There was mingled many a cry—
Freedom! Hope! Death! Victory!   700
Till they faded thro' the sky;
And one sound, above, around,
One sound beneath, around, above,
Was moving; 'twas the soul of love;   705
'Twas the hope, the prophecy,
Which begins and ends in thee.

SECOND SPIRIT.

A rainbow's arch stood on the sea,
Which rocked beneath, immovably;
And the triumphant storm did flee,   710
Like a conqueror, swift and proud,
Between, with many a captive cloud,
A shapeless, dark and rapid crowd,
Each by lightning riven in half:
I heard the thunder hoarsely laugh: 715
Mighty fleets were strewn like chaff
And spread beneath a hell of death
O'er the white waters. I alit
On a great ship lightning-split,
And speeded hither on the sigh   720
Of one who gave an enemy
His plank, then plunged aside to die.

THIRD SPIRIT.

I sate beside a sage's bed,
And the lamp was burning red
Near the book where he had fed,   725
When a Dream with plumes of flame,
To his pillow hovering came,
And I knew it was the same

Which had kindled long ago
Pity, eloquence, and woe;   730
And the world awhile below
Wore the shade, its lustre made.
It has borne me here as fleet
As Desire's lightning feet:
I must ride it back ere morrow,   735
Or the sage will wake in sorrow.

FOURTH SPIRIT.

On a poet's lips I slept
Dreaming like a love-adept
In the sound his breathing kept;
Nor seeks nor finds he mortal blisses,   740
But feeds on the aërial kisses
Of shapes that haunt thought's wildernesses.
He will watch from dawn to gloom
The lake-reflected sun illume
The yellow bees in the ivy-bloom,   745
Nor heed nor see, what things they be;
But from these create he can
Forms more real than living man,
Nurslings of immortality!
One of these awakened me,   750
And I sped to succour thee.

IONE. Behold'st thou not two shapes from the east and
        west
Come, as two doves to one beloved nest,
Twin nurslings of the all-sustaining air
On swift still wings glide down the atmosphere?   755
And, hark! their sweet sad voices! 'tis despair
Mingled with love and then dissolved in sound.
PANTHEA. Canst thou speak, sister? all my words are
        drowned.
IONE. Their beauty gives me voice. See how they float
On their sustaining wings of skiey grain,   760
Orange and azure deepening into gold:
Their soft smiles light the air like a star's fire.

CHORUS OF SPIRITS.

        Hast thou beheld the form of Love?

FIFTH SPIRIT.

As over wide dominions
I sped, like some swift cloud that wings the wide air's
    wildernesses,
That planet-crested shape swept by on lightning braided
    pinions,   765
Scattering the liquid joy of life from his ambrosial tresses:
His footsteps paved the world with light; but as I past
    'twas fading,
And hollow Ruin yawned behind: great sages bound in
    madness,
And headless patriots, and pale youths who perished, un-
    upbraiding,
Gleamed in the night. I wandered o'er, till thou, O King
    of sadness,   770
Turned by thy smile the worst I saw to recollected glad-
    ness.

SIXTH SPIRIT.

Ah, sister! Desolation is a delicate thing:
It walks not on the earth, it floats not on the air,
But treads with lulling footstep, and fans with silent wing
The tender hopes which in their hearts the best and
    gentlest bear;   775
Who, soothed to false repose by the fanning plumes
    above,
And the music-stirring motion of its soft and busy feet,
Dream visions of aërial joy, and call the monster, Love,
And wake, and find the shadow Pain, as he whom now we
    greet.

CHORUS.

    Tho' Ruin now Love's shadow be,   780
    Following him, destroyingly,
        On Death's white and winged steed,
    Which the fleetest cannot flee,
        Trampling down both flower and weed,
    Man and beast, and foul and fair,   785
    Like a tempest thro' the air;
    Thou shalt quell this horseman grim,
    Woundless though in heart or limb.

PROMETHEUS. Spirits! how know ye this shall be?

CHORUS.

> In the atmosphere we breathe,   790
> As buds grow red when snow-storms flee,
>   From spring gathering up beneath,
> Whose mild winds shake the elder brake,
> And the wandering herdsmen know
> That the white-thorn soon will blow: 795
> Wisdom, Justice, Love, and Peace,
> When they struggle to increase,
>   Are to us as soft winds be
>   To shepherd boys, the prophecy
> Which begins and ends in thee.   800

IONE. Where are the Spirits fled?
PANTHEA.   Only a sense
Remains of them, like the omnipotence
Of music, when the inspired voice and lute
Languish, ere yet the responses are mute,
Which thro' the deep and labyrinthine soul,   805
Like echoes thro' long caverns, wind and roll.
PROMETHEUS. How fair these air-born shapes! and yet I
    feel
Most vain all hope but love; and thou art far,
Asia! who, when my being overflowed,
Wert like a golden chalice to bright wine   810
Which else had sunk into the thirsty dust.
All things are still: alas! how heavily
This quiet morning weighs upon my heart;
Tho' I should dream I could even sleep with grief
If slumber were denied not. I would fain   815
Be what it is my destiny to be,
The saviour and the strength of suffering man,
Or sink into the original gulph of things:
There is no agony, and no solace left;
Earth can console, Heaven can torment no more.   820
PANTHEA. Hast thou forgotten one who watches thee
The cold dark night, and never sleeps but when
The shadow of thy spirit falls on her?
PROMETHEUS. I said all hope was vain but love: thou
    lovest.

PANTHEA. Deeply in truth; but the eastern star looks
     white,   825
And Asia waits in that far Indian vale
The scene of her sad exile; rugged once
And desolate and frozen, like this ravine;
But now invested with fair flowers and herbs,
And haunted by sweet airs and sounds, which flow   830
Among the woods and waters, from the ether
Of her transforming presence, which would fade
If it were mingled not with thine. Farewell!

END OF THE FIRST ACT.

ACT II.

Scene I. Morning. A lovely Vale in the Indian Caucasus.
   ASIA, alone.

ASIA. From all the blasts of heaven thou hast descended:
Yes, like a spirit, like a thought, which makes
Unwonted tears throng to the horny eyes,
And beatings haunt the desolated heart,
Which should have learnt repose: thou has descended   5
Cradled in tempests; thou dost wake, O Spring!
O child of many winds! As suddenly
Thou comest as the memory of a dream,
Which now is sad because it hath been sweet;
Like genius, or like joy which riseth up   10
As from the earth, clothing with golden clouds
The desert of our life.
This is the season, this the day, the hour;
At sunrise thou shouldst come, sweet sister mine,
Too long desired, too long delaying, come!   15
How like death-worms the wingless moments crawl!
The point of one white star is quivering still
Deep in the orange light of widening morn
Beyond the purple mountains: thro' a chasm
Of wind-divided mist the darker lake   20
Reflects it: now it wanes: it gleams again

As the waves fade, and as the burning threads
Of woven cloud unravel in pale air:
'Tis lost! and thro' yon peaks of cloudlike snow
The roseate sun-light quivers: hear I not   25
The Æolian music of her sea-green plumes
Winnowing the crimson dawn?

Panthea enters.

               I feel, I see
Those eyes which burn thro' smiles that fade in tears,
Like stars half quenched in mists of silver dew.
Beloved and most beautiful, who wearest   30
The shadow of that soul by which I live,
How late thou art! the sphered sun had climbed
The sea; my heart was sick with hope, before
The printless air felt thy belated plumes.
Panthea. Pardon, great Sister! but my wings were faint 35
With the delight of a remembered dream,
As are the noon-tide plumes of summer winds
Satiate with sweet flowers. I was wont to sleep
Peacefully, and awake refreshed and calm
Before the sacred Titan's fall, and thy   40
Unhappy love, had made, thro' use and pity,
Both love and woe familiar to my heart
As they had grown to thine: erewhile I slept
Under the glaucous caverns of old Ocean
Within dim bowers of green and purple moss,   45
Our young Ione's soft and milky arms
Locked then, as now, behind my dark, moist hair,
While my shut eyes and cheek were pressed within
The folded depth of her life-breathing bosom:
But not as now, since I am made the wind   50
Which fails beneath the music that I bear
Of thy most wordless converse; since dissolved
Into the sense with which love talks, my rest
Was troubled and yet sweet; my waking hours
Too full of care and pain.
Asia.   Lift up thine eyes,   55
And let me read thy dream.
Panthea.   As I have said
With our sea-sister at his feet I slept.
The mountain mists, condensing at our voice

Under the moon, had spread their snowy flakes,
From the keen ice shielding our linked sleep.   60
Then two dreams came. One, I remember not.
But in the other his pale wound-worn limbs
Fell from Prometheus, and the azure night
Grew radiant with the glory of that form
Which lives unchanged within, and his voice fell   65
Like music which makes giddy the dim brain,
Faint with intoxication of keen joy:
"Sister of her whose footsteps pave the world
"With loveliness—more fair than aught but her,
"Whose shadow thou art—lift thine eyes on me."   70
I lifted them: the overpowering light
Of that immortal shape was shadowed o'er
By love; which, from his soft and flowing limbs,
And passion-parted lips, and keen, faint eyes,
Steamed forth like vaporous fire; an atmosphere   75
Which wrapped me in its all-dissolving power,
As the warm ether of the morning sun
Wraps ere it drinks some cloud of wandering dew.
I saw not, heard not, moved not, only felt
His presence flow and mingle thro' my blood   80
Till it became his life, and his grew mine,
And I was thus absorb'd, until it past,
And like the vapours when the sun sinks down,
Gathering again in drops upon the pines,
And tremulous as they, in the deep night   85
My being was condensed; and as the rays
Of thought were slowly gathered, I could hear
His voice, whose accents lingered ere they died
Like footsteps of far melody: thy name
Among the many 'sounds alone I heard   90
Of what might be articulate; tho' still
I listened through the night when sound was none.
Ione wakened then, and said to me:
"Canst thou divine what troubles me to-night?
"I always knew what I desired before,   95
"Nor ever found delight to wish in vain.
"But now I cannot tell thee what I seek;
"I know not; something sweet, since it is sweet
"Even to desire; it is thy sport, false sister;
"Thou hast discovered some enchantment old,   100

"Whose spells have stolen my spirit as I slept
"And mingled it with thine: for when just now
"We kissed, I felt within thy parted lips
"The sweet air that sustained me, and the warmth
"Of the life-blood, for loss of which I faint,   105
"Quivered between our intertwining arms."
I answered not, far the Eastern star grew pale,
But fled to thee.
ASIA.   Thou speakest, but thy words
Are as the air: I feel them not: Oh, lift
Thine eyes, that I may read his written soul!   110
PANTHEA. I lift them, tho' they droop beneath the load
Of that they would express: what canst thou see
But thine own fairest shadow imaged there?
ASIA. Thine eyes are like the deep, blue, boundless heaven
Contracted to two circles underneath   115
Their long, fine lashes; dark, far, measureless,
Orb within orb, and line thro' line inwoven.
PANTHEA. Why lookest thou as if a spirit past?
ASIA. There is a change: beyond their inmost depth
I see a shade, a shape: 'tis He, arrayed   120
In the soft light of his own smiles, which spread
Like radiance from the cloud-surrounded moon.
Prometheus, it is thine! depart not yet!
Say not those smiles that we shall meet again
Within that bright pavilion which their beams   125
Shall build o'er the waste world? The dream is told.
What shape is that between us? Its rude hair
Roughens the wind that lifts it, its regard
Is wild and quick, yet 'tis a thing of air
For through its grey robe gleams the golden dew   130
Whose stars the noon has quench'd not.
DREAM.   Follow! Follow!
PANTHEA. It is mine other dream.
ASIA.   It disappears.
PANTHEA. It passes now into my mind. Methought
As we sate here, the flower-infolding buds
Burst on yon lightning-blasted almond tree,   135
When swift from the white Scythian wilderness
A wind swept forth wrinkling the Earth with frost:
I looked, and all the blossoms were blown down;
But on each leaf was stamped, as the blue bells

Of Hyacinth tell Apollo's written grief,   140
O, FOLLOW, FOLLOW!
ASIA.   As you speak, your words
Fill, pause by pause, my own forgotten sleep
With shapes. Methought among these lawns together
We wandered, underneath the young grey dawn,
And multitudes of dense white fleecy clouds   145
Were wandering in thick flocks along the mountains
Shepherded by the slow, unwilling wind;
And the white dew on the new bladed grass,
Just piercing the dark earth, hung silently;
And there was more which I remember not: 150
But on the shadows of the moving clouds,
Athwart the purple mountain slope, was written
FOLLOW, O FOLLOW! As they vanished by,
And on each herb, from which Heaven's dew had fallen,
The like was stamped, as with a withering fire,   155
A wind arose among the pines; it shook
The clinging music from their boughs, and then
Low, sweet, faint sounds, like the farewell of ghosts,
Were heard: OH, FOLLOW, FOLLOW, FOLLOW ME!
And then I said, "Panthea, look on me."   160
But in the depth of those beloved eyes
Still I saw, FOLLOW, FOLLOW!
ECHO.   Follow, follow!
PANTHEA. The crags, this clear spring morning, mock our
    voices,
As they were spirit-tongued.
ASIA.   It is some being
Around the crags. What fine clear sounds! Oh, list!   165

ECHOES (unseen).

> Echoes we: listen!
> We cannot stay:
> As dew-stars glisten
> Then fade away—
>   Child of Ocean!   170

ASIA. Hark! Spirits speak. The liquid responses
Of their aërial tongues yet sound.
PANTHEA.   I hear.

ECHOES.

        O, follow, follow,
          As our voice recedeth
        Thro' the caverns hollow,   175
          Where the forest spreadeth;

(MORE DISTANT.)

        O, follow, follow!
        Through the caverns hollow,
      As the song floats thou pursue,
      Where the wild bee never flew,   180
      Thro' the noon-tide darkness deep,
      By the odour-breathing sleep
      Of faint night flowers, and the waves
      At the fountain-lighted caves,
      While our music, wild and sweet,   185
      Mocks thy gently falling feet,
        Child of Ocean!

ASIA. Shall we pursue the sound? It grows more faint
And distant.
PANTHEA.   List! the strain floats nearer now.

ECHOES.

        In the world unknown   190
        Sleeps a voice unspoken;
        By thy step alone
        Can its rest be broken;
          Child of Ocean!

ASIA. How the notes sink upon the ebbing wind!   195

ECHOES.

        O, follow, follow!
        Thro' the caverns hollow,
      As the song floats thou pursue,
      By the woodland noon-tide dew;
      By the forests, lakes, and fountains,   200
      Thro' the many-folded mountains;
      To the rents, and gulphs, and chasms,

Where the Earth reposed from spasms,
On the day when He and thou
Parted, to commingle now;   205
    Child of Ocean!

ASIA. Come, sweet Panthea, link thy hand in mine,
And follow, ere the voices fade away.

Scene II. A Forest, intermingled with Rocks and Caverns.
    ASIA and PANTHEA pass into it. Two young FAUNS
    are sitting on a Rock, listening.

SEMICHORUS I OF SPIRITS.

The path thro' which that lovely twain
    Have past, by cedar, pine, and yew,
    And each dark tree that ever grew,
Is curtained out from Heaven's wide blue;
Nor sun, nor moon, nor wind, nor rain,   5
    Can pierce its interwoven bowers,
    Nor aught, save where some cloud of dew,
Drifted along the earth-creeping breeze,
Between the trunks of the hoar trees,
    Hangs each a pearl in the pale flowers   10
    Of the green laurel, blown anew;
And bends, and then fades silently,
One frail and fair anemone:
Or when some star of many a one
That climbs and wanders thro' steep night,   15
Has found the cleft thro' which alone
Beams fall from high those depths upon
Ere it is borne away, away,
By the swift Heavens that cannot stay,
It scatters drops of golden light,   20
Like lines of rain that ne'er unite:
And the gloom divine is all around;
And underneath is the mossy ground.

SEMICHORUS II.

There the voluptuous nightingales,
    Are awake thro' all the broad noon-day.   25

When one with bliss or sadness fails,
    And thro' the windless ivy-boughs,
    Sick with sweet love, droops dying away
    On its mate's music-panting bosom;
    Another from the swinging blossom,   30
        Watching to catch the languid close
    Of the last strain, then lifts on high
    The wings of the weak melody,
'Till some new strain of feeling bear
    The song, and all the woods are mute;   35
When there is heard thro' the dim air
    The rush of wings, and rising there
    Like many a lake-surrounded flute,
    Sounds overflow the listener's brain
    So sweet, that joy is almost pain.   40

SEMICHORUS I.

There those enchanted eddies play
    Of echoes, music-tongued, which draw,
    By Demogorgon's mighty law,
    With melting rapture, or sweet awe,
All spirits on that secret way;   45
    As inland boats are driven to Ocean
Down streams made strong with mountain-thaw:
        And first there comes a gentle sound
        To those in talk or slumber bound,
    And wakes the destined: soft emotion   50
Attracts, impels them: those who saw
    Say from the breathing earth behind
    There steams a plume-uplifting wind
Which drives them on their path, while they
    Believe their own swift wings and feet   55
The sweet desires within obey:
And so they float upon their way,
    Until, still sweet, but loud and strong,
    The storm of sound is driven along,
        Sucked up and hurrying: as they fleet   60
        Behind, its gathering billows meet
    And to the fatal mountain bear
    Like clouds amid the yielding air.

FIRST FAUN. Canst thou imagine where those spirits live
Which make such delicate music in the woods?   65
We haunt within the lest frequented caves
And closest coverts, and we know these wilds,
Yet never meet them, tho' we hear them oft:
Where may they hide themselves?
SECOND FAUN.   'Tis hard to tell:
I have heard those more skilled in spirits say,   70
The bubbles, which enchantment of the sun
Sucks from the pale faint water-flowers that pave
The oozy bottom of clear lakes and pools,
Are the pavilions where such dwell and float
Under the green and golden atmosphere   75
Which noon-tide kindles thro' the woven leaves;
And when these burst, and the thin fiery air,
The which they breathed within those lucent domes,
Ascends to flow like meteors thro' the night,
They ride on them, and rein their headlong speed,   80
And bow their burning crests, and glide in fire
Under the waters of the earth again.
FIRST FAUN. If such live thus, have others other lives,
Under pink blossoms or within the bells
Of meadow flowers, or folded violets deep,   85
Or on their dying odours, when they die,
Or in the sunlight of the sphered dew?
SECOND FAUN. Ay, many more which we may well divine.
But should we stay to speak, noontide would come,
And thwart Silenus find his goats undrawn,   90
And grudge to sing those wise and lovely songs
Of fate, and chance, and God, and Chaos old,
And Love, and the chained Titan's woful doom,
And how he shall be loosed, and make the earth
One brotherhood: delightful strains which cheer   95
Our solitary twilights, and which charm
To silence the unenvying nightingales.

Scene III. A Pinnacle of Rock among Mountains. ASIA and
    PANTHEA.

PANTHEA. Hither the sound has borne us—to the realm
Of Demogorgon, and the mighty portal,

Like a volcano's meteor-breathing chasm,
Whence the oracular vapour is hurled up
Which lonely men drink wandering in their youth,   5
And call truth, virtue, love, genius, or joy,
That maddening wine of life, whose dregs they drain
To deep intoxication; and uplift,
Like Mænads who cry loud, Evoe! Evoe!
The voice which is contagion to the world.   10
Asia. Fit throne for such a Power! Magnificent!
How glorious art thou, Earth! And if thou be
The shadow of some spirit lovelier still,
Though evil stain its work, and it should be
Like its creation, weak yet beautiful,   15
I could fall down and worship that and thee.
Even now my heart adoreth: Wonderful!
Look, sister, ere the vapour dim thy brain:
Beneath is a wide plain of billowy mist,
As a lake, paving in the morning sky,   20
With azure waves which burst in silver light,
Some Indian vale. Behold it, rolling on
Under the curdling winds, and islanding
The peak whereon we stand, midway, around,
Encinctured by the dark and blooming forests,   25
Dim twilight-lawns and stream-illumined caves,
And wind-enchanted shapes of wandering mist;
And far on high the keen sky-cleaving mountains,
From icy spires of sun-like radiance fling
The dawn, as lifted Ocean's dazzling spray,   30
From some Atlantic islet scattered up,
Spangles the wind with lamp-like water-drops.
The vale is girdled with their walls, a howl
Of cataracts from their thaw-cloven ravines
Satiates the listening wind, continuous, vast,   35
Awful as silence. Hark! the rushing snow!
The sun-awakened avalanche! whose mass,
Thrice sifted by the storm, had gathered there
Flake after flake, in heaven-defying minds
As thought by thought is piled, till some great truth   40
Is loosened, and the nations echo round,
Shaken to their roots, as do the mountains now.
Panthea. Look how the gusty sea of mist is breaking
In crimson foam, even at our feet! it rises

As Ocean at the enchantment of the moon 45
Round foodless men wrecked on some oozy isle.
ASIA. The fragments of the cloud are scattered up;
The wind that lifts them disentwines my hair;
Its billows now sweep o'er mine eyes; my brain
Grows dizzy; See'st thou shapes within the mist? 50
PANTHEA. A countenance with beckoning smiles: there burns
An azure fire within its golden locks!
Another and another: hark! they speak!

SONG OF SPIRITS.

To the deep, to the deep,
Down, down!
Through the shade of sleep, 55
Through the cloudy strife
Of Death and of Life;
Through the veil and the bar
Of things which seem and are 60
Even to the steps of the remotest throne,
Down, down!

While the sound whirls around,
Down, down!
As the fawn draws the hound, 65
As the lightning the vapour,
As a weak moth the taper;
Death, despair; love, sorrow;
Time both! to-day, to-morrow;
As steel obeys the spirit of the stone, 70
Down, down!

Through the grey, void abysm,
Down, down!
Where the air is no prism,
And the moon and stars are not, 75
And the cavern-crags wear not
The radiance of Heaven,
Nor the gloom to Earth given,
Where there is one pervading, one alone,
Down, down! 80

In the depth of the deep
Down, down!
Like veiled lightning asleep,
Like the spark nursed in embers,
The last look Love remembers,   85
Like a diamond, which shines
On the dark wealth of mines,
A spell is treasur'd but for thee alone.
Down, down!

We have bound thee, we guide thee;   90
Down, down!
With the bright form beside thee;
Resist not the weakness,
Such strength is in meekness
That the Eternal, the immortal,   95
Must unloose through life's portal
The snake-like Doom coiled underneath his throne
By that alone.

Scene IV. The Cave of DEMOGORGON. ASIA and PANTHEA.

PANTHEA. What veiled form sits on that ebon throne?
ASIA. The veil has fallen.
PANTHEA.   I see a mighty darkness
Filling the seat of power, and rays of gloom
Dart round, as light from the meridian sun,
Ungazed upon and shapeless; neither limb,   5
Nor form, nor outline; yet we feel it is
A living Spirit.
DEMOGORGON. Ask what thou wouldst know.
ASIA. What canst thou tell?
DEMOGORGON.   All things thou dar'st demand.
ASIA. Who made the living world?
DEMOGORGON.   God.
ASIA.   Who made all
That it contains? thought, passion, reason, will,   10
Imagination?
DEMOGORGON. God: Almighty God.
ASIA. Who made that sense which, when the winds of
    spring

In rarest visitation, or the voice
Of one beloved heard in youth alone,
Fills the faint eyes with falling tears which dim   15
The radiant looks of unbewailing flowers,
And leaves this peopled earth a solitude
When it returns no more?
DEMOGORGON.   Merciful God.
ASIA. And who made terror, madness, crime, remorse,
Which from the links of the great chain of things,   20
To every thought within the mind of man
Sway and drag heavily, and each one reels
Under the load towards the pit of death;
Abandoned hope, and love that turns to hate;
And self-contempt, bitterer to drink than blood;   25
Pain, whose unheeded and familiar speech
Is howling, and keen shrieks, day after day;
And Hell, or the sharp fear of Hell?
DEMOGORGON.   He reigns.
ASIA. Utter his name: a world pining in pain
Asks but his name: curses shall drag him down.   30
DEMOGORGON. He reigns.
ASIA.   I feel, I know it: who?
DEMOGORGON.   He reigns.
ASIA. Who reigns? There was the Heaven and Earth at
     first,
And Light and Love; then Saturn, from whose throne
Time fell, an envious shadow: such the state
Of the earth's primal spirits beneath his sway,   35
As the calm joy of flowers and living leaves
Before the wind or sun has withered them
And semivital worms; but he refused
The birthright of their being, knowledge, power,
The skill which wields the elements, the thought   40
Which pierces this dim universe like light,
Self-empire, and the majesty of love;
For thirst of which they fainted. Then Prometheus
Gave wisdom, which is strength, to Jupiter,
And with this law alone, "Let man be free,"   45
Clothed him with the dominion of wide Heaven.
To know nor faith, nor love, nor law; to be
Omnipotent but friendless is to reign;
And Jove now reigned; for on the race of man

First famine, and then toil, and then disease,   50
Strife, wounds, and ghastly death unseen before,
Fell; and the unseasonable seasons drove
With alternating shafts of frost and fire,
Their shelterless, pale tribes to mountain caves:
And in their desert hearts fierce wants he sent,   55
And mad disquietudes, and shadows idle
Of real good, which levied mutual war,
So ruining the lair wherein they raged.
Prometheus saw, and waked the legioned hopes
Which sleep within folded Elysian flowers,   60
Nepenthe, Moly, Amaranth, fadeless blooms,
That they might hide with thin and rainbow wings
The shape of Death; and Love he sent to bind
The disunited tendrils of that vine
Which bears the wine of life, the human heart;   65
And he tamed fire which, like some beast of prey,
Most terrible, but lovely, played beneath
The frown of man; and tortured to his will
Iron and gold, the slaves and signs of power,
And gems and poisons, and all subtlest forms   70
Hidden beneath the mountains and the waves.
He gave man speech, and speech created thought,
Which is the measure of the universe;
And Science struck the thrones of earth and heaven,
Which shook, but fell not; and the harmonious mind   75
Poured itself forth in all-prophetic song;
And music lifted up the listening spirit
Until it walked, exempt from mortal care,
Godlike, o'er the clear billows of sweet sound;
And human hands first mimicked and then mocked,   80
With moulded limbs more lovely than its own,
The human form, till marble grew divine,
And mothers, gazing, drank the love men see
Reflected in their race, behold, and perish.
He told the hidden power of herbs and springs,   85
And Disease drank and slept. Death grew like sleep.
He taught the implicated orbits woven
Of the wide-wandering stars; and how the sun
Changes his lair, and by what secret spell
The pale moon is transformed, when her broad eye   90
Gazes not on the interlunar sea:

He taught to rule, as life directs the limbs,
The tempest-winged chariots of the Ocean,
And the Celt knew the Indian. Cities then
Were built, and through their snow-like columns flowed　　95
The warm winds, and the azure æther shone,
And the blue sea and shadowy hills were seen.
Such, the alleviations of his state,
Prometheus gave to man, for which he hangs
Withering in destined pain: but who rains down　　100
Evil, the immedicable plague, which, while
Man looks on his creation like a God
And sees that it is glorious, drives him on
The wreck of his own will, the scorn of earth,
The outcast, the abandoned, the alone?　　105
Not Jove: while yet his frown shook heaven, aye when
His adversary from adamantine chains
Cursed him, he trembled like a slave. Declare
Who is his master? Is he too a slave?
DEMOGORGON. All spirits are enslaved which serve things
　　evil:　　110
Thou knowest if Jupiter be such or no.
ASIA. Whom called'st thou God?
DEMOGORGON.　　　　　　　　I spoke but as ye speak,
For Jove is the supreme of living things.
ASIA. Who is the master of the slave?
DEMOGORGON.　　　　　　　　　　If the abysm
Could vomit forth its secrets. But a voice　　115
Is wanting, the deep truth is imageless;
For what would it avail to bid thee gaze
On the revolving world? What to bid speak
Fate, Time, Occasion, Chance and Change? To these
All things are subject but eternal Love.　　120
ASIA. So much I asked before, and my heart gave
The response thou hast given; and of such truths
Each to itself must be the oracle.
One more demand; and do thou answer me
As my own soul would answer, did it know　　125
That which I ask. Prometheus shall arise
Henceforth the sun of this rejoicing world:
When shall the destined hour arrive?
DEMOGORGON.　　　　　　　　　Behold!
ASIA. The rocks are cloven, and through the purple night

I see cars drawn by rainbow-winged steeds   130
Which trample the dim winds: in each there stands
A wild-eyed charioteer urging their flight.
Some look behind, as fiends pursued them there,
And yet I see no shapes but the keen stars:
Others, with burning eyes, lean forth, and drink   135
With eager lips the wind of their own speed,
As if the thing they loved fled on before,
And now, even now, they clasped it. Their bright locks
Stream like a comet's flashing hair: they all
Sweep onward.
DEMOGORGON. These are the immortal Hours,   140
Of whom thou didst demand. One waits for thee.
ASIA. A spirit with a dreadful countenance
Checks its dark chariot by the craggy gulph.
Unlike thy brethren, ghastly charioteer,
Who art thou? Whither wouldst thou bear me? Speak!   145
SPIRIT. I am the shadow of a destiny
More dread than is my aspect: ere yon planet
Has set, the darkness which ascends with me
Shall wrap in lasting night heaven's kingless throne.
ASIA. What meanest thou?
PANTHEA.   That terrible shadow floats   150
Up from its throne, as may the lurid smoke
Of earthquake-ruined cities o'er the sea.
Lo! it ascends the car; the coursers fly
Terrified: watch its path among the stars
Blackening the night!
ASIA.   Thus I am answered: strange!   155
PANTHEA. See, near the verge, another chariot stays;
An ivory shell inlaid with crimson fire,
Which comes and goes within its sculptured rim
Of delicate strange tracery; the young spirit
That guides it has the dove-like eyes of hope;   160
How its soft smiles attract the soul! as light
Lures winged insects thro' the lampless air.

SPIRIT.

My coursers are fed with the lightning,
    They drink of the whirlwind's stream,
And when the red morning is brightning   165

They bathe in the fresh sunbeam;
They have strength for their swiftness I deem,
Then ascend with me, daughter of Ocean.

I desire: and their speed makes night kindle;
I fear: they outstrip the Typhoon; 170
Ere the cloud piled on Atlas can dwindle
We encircle the earth and the moon:
We shall rest from long labours at noon:
Then ascend with me, daughter of Ocean.

Scene V. The Car pauses within a Cloud on the Top of a snowy Mountain.

ASIA, PANTHEA, and the SPIRIT OF THE HOUR.

SPIRIT.

On the brink of the night and the morning
My coursers are wont to respire;
But the Earth has just whispered a warning
That their flight must be swifter than fire:
They shall drink the hot speed of desire! 5

ASIA. Thou breathest on their nostrils, but my breath
Would give them swifter speed.
SPIRIT. Alas! it could not.
PANTHEA. Oh Spirit! pause, and tell whence is the light
Which fills this cloud? the sun is yet unrisen.
SPIRIT. The sun will rise not until noon. Apollo 10
Is held in heaven by wonder; and the light
Which fills this vapour, as the aërial hue
Of fountain-gazing roses fills the water,
Flows from thy mighty sister.
PANTHEA. Yes, I feel—
ASIA. What is it with thee, sister? Thou art pale. 15
PANTHEA. How thou art changed! I dare not look on thee;
I feel but see thee not. I scarce endure
The radiance of thy beauty. Some good change
Is working in the elements, which suffer
Thy presence thus unveiled. The Nereids tell 20

That on the day when the clear hyaline
Was cloven at thine uprise, and thou didst stand
Within a veined shell, which floated on
Over the calm floor of the crystal sea,
Among the Ægean isles, and by the shores   25
Which bear thy name; love, like the atmosphere
Of the sun's fire filling the living world,
Burst from thee, and illumined earth and heaven
And the deep ocean and the sunless caves
And all that dwells within them; till grief cast   30
Eclipse upon the soul from which it came:
Such art thou now; nor is it I alone,
Thy sister, thy companion, thine own chosen one,
But the whole world which seeks thy sympathy.
Hearest thou not sounds i' the air which speak the love   35
Of all articulate beings? Feelest thou not
The inanimate winds enamoured of thee? List!

                                  [*Music.*]

ASIA. Thy words are sweeter than aught else but his
Whose echoes they are: yet all love is sweet,
Given or returned. Common as light is love,   40
And its familiar voice wearies not ever.
Like the wide heaven, the all-sustaining air,
It makes the reptile equal to the God:
They who inspire it most are fortunate,
As I am now; but those who feel it most   45
Are happier still, after long sufferings,
As I shall soon become.
PANTHEA.   List! Spirits, speak.

VOICE (*in the air, singing*).

    Life of Life! thy lips enkindle
      With their love the breath between them;
    And thy smiles before they dwindle   50
      Make the cold air fire; then screen them
    In those looks, where whoso gazes
    Faints, entangled in their mazes.

    Child of Light! thy limbs are burning
      Thro' the vest which seems to hide them;   55

As the radiant lines of morning
   Thro' the clouds ere they divide them;
And this atmosphere divinest
Shrouds thee wheresoe'er thou shinest.

Fair are others; none beholds thee,   60
   But thy voice sounds low and tender
Like the fairest, for it folds thee
   From the sight, that liquid splendour,
And all feel, yet see thee never,
As I feel now, lost for ever!   65

Lamp of Earth! where'er thou movest
   Its dim shapes are clad with brightness,
And the souls of whom thou lovest
   Walk upon the winds with lightness,
Till they fail, as I am failing,   70
Dizzy, lost, yet unbewailing!

ASIA.

   My soul is an enchanted boat,
     Which, like a sleeping swan, doth float
Upon the silver waves of thy sweet singing;
     And thine doth like an angel sit   75
     Beside the helm conducting it,
Whilst all the winds with melody are ringing.
     It seems to float ever, for ever,
     Upon that many-winding river,
     Between mountains, woods, abysses,   80
     A paradise of wildernesses!
Till, like one in slumber bound,
Borne to the ocean, I float down, around,
Into a sea profound, of ever-spreading sound:

     Meanwhile thy spirit lifts its pinions   85
     In music's most serene dominions:
Catching the winds that fan that happy heaven.
     And we sail on, away, afar,
     Without a course, without a star,
But, by the instinct of sweet music driven;   90
     Till through Elysian garden islets

By thee, most beautiful of pilots,
Where never mortal pinnace glided,
The boat of my desire is guided:
Realms where the air we breathe is love,   95
Which in the winds and on the waves doth move,
Harmonizing this earth with what we feel above.

We have pass'd Age's icy caves,
And Manhood's dark and tossing waves,
And Youth's smooth ocean, smiling to betray: 100
Beyond the glassy gulphs we flee
Of shadow-peopled Infancy,
Through Death and Birth, to a diviner day;
A paradise of vaulted bowers
Lit by downward-gazing flowers,   105
And watery paths that wind between
Wildernesses calm and green,
Peopled by shapes too bright to see,
And rest, having beheld: somewhat like thee;
Which walk upon the sea, and chant melodiously!   110

END OF THE SECOND ACT.

ACT III.

Scene I. Heaven. JUPITER on his Throne; THETIS and the
other Deities assembled.

JUPITER. Ye congregated powers of heaven, who share
The glory and the strength of him ye serve,
Rejoice! henceforth I am omnipotent.
All else had been subdued to me; alone
The soul of man, like unextinguished fire,   5
Yet burns towards heaven with fierce reproach, and doubt,
And lamentation, and reluctant prayer,
Hurling up insurrection, which might make
Our antique empire insecure, though built
On eldest faith, and hell's coeval, fear;   10
And tho' my curses thro' the pendulous air,

Like snow on herbless peaks, fall flake by flake,
And cling to it; tho' under my wrath's night
It climb the crags of life, step after step,
Which wound it, as ice wound unsandalled feet,   15
It yet remains supreme o'er misery,
Aspiring, unrepressed, yet soon to fall:
Even now have I begotten a strange wonder,
That fatal child, the terror of the earth,
Who waits but till the destined hour arrive,   20
Bearing from Demogorgon's vacant throne
The dreadful might of ever-living limbs
Which clothed that awful spirit unbeheld,
To redescend, and trample out the spark.

Pour forth heaven's wine, Idæan Ganymede,   25
And let it fill the Dædal cups like fire,
And from the flower-inwoven soul divine,
Ye all-triumphant harmonies arise,
As dew from earth under the twilight stars:
Drink! be the nectar circling thro' your veins   30
The soul of joy, ye ever-living Gods,
Till exultation burst in one wide voice
Like music from Elysian winds.
                        And thou
Ascend beside me, veiled in the light
Of the desire which makes thee one with me,   35
Thetis, bright image of eternity!
When thou didst cry, "Insufferable might!
"God! Spare me! I sustain not the quick flames,
"The penetrating presence; all my being,
"Like him whom the Numidian seps did thaw   40
"Into a dew with poison, is dissolved,
"Sinking thro' its foundations:" even then
Two mighty spirits, mingling, made a third
Mightier than either, which, unbodied now,
Between us floats, felt, although unbeheld,   45
Waiting the incarnation, which ascends,
(Hear ye the thunder of the fiery wheels
Griding the winds?) from Demogorgon's throne.
Victory! victory! Feel'st thou not, O world!
The earthquake of his chariot thundering up   50
Olympus?

The Car of the HOUR *arrives.* DEMOGORGON *descends and
    moves towards the Throne of* JUPITER.
            Awful shape, what are thou? Speak!
DEMOGORGON. Eternity. Demand no direr name.
Descend, and follow me down the abyss.
I am thy child, as thou wert Saturn's child;
Mightier than thee: and we must dwell together   55
Henceforth in darkness. Lift thy lightnings not.
The tyranny of heaven none may retain,
Or reassume, or hold, succeeding thee:
Yet if thou wilt, as 'tis the destiny
Of trodden worms to writhe till they are dead,   60
Put forth thy might.
JUPITER.   Detested prodigy!
Even thus beneath the deep Titanian prisons
I trample thee! thou lingerest?
                        Mercy! mercy!
No pity, no release, no respite! Oh,
That thou wouldst make mine enemy my judge,   65
Even where he hangs, scared by my long revenge,
On Caucasus! he would not doom me thus.
Gentle, and just, and dreadless, is he not
The monarch of the world? What then art thou?
No refuge! no appeal!
                        Sink with me then,   70
We two will sink on the wide waves of ruin,
Even as a vulture and a snake outspent
Drop, twisted in inextricable fight,
Into a shoreless sea. Let hell unlock
Its mounted oceans of tempestuous fire,   75
And whelm on them into the bottomless void
This desolated world, and thee, and me,
The conqueror and the conquered, and the wreck
Of that for which they combated.
                        Ai! Ai!
The elements obey me not. I sink   80
Dizzily down, ever, for ever, down.
And, like a cloud, mine enemy above
Darkens my fall with victory! Ai, Ai!

Scene II. The Mouth of a great River in the Island Atlan-
tis. OCEAN is discovered reclining near the Shore;
APOLLO stands beside him.

OCEAN. He fell, thou sayest, beneath his conqueror's
    frown?
APOLLO. Ay, when the strife was ended which made dim
The orb I rule, and shook the solid stars,
The terrors of his eye illumined heaven
With sanguine light, through the thick ragged skirts   5
Of the victorious darkness, as he fell:
Like the last glare of day's red agony,
Which, from a rent among the fiery clouds,
Burns far along the tempest-wrinkled deep.
OCEAN. He sunk to the abyss? To the dark void?   10
APOLLO. An eagle so caught in some bursting cloud
On Caucasus, his thunder-baffled wings
Entangled in the whirlwind, and his eyes
Which gazed on the undazzling sun, now blinded
By the white lightning, while the ponderous hail   15
Beats on his struggling form, which sinks at length
Prone, and the aërial ice clings over it.
OCEAN. Henceforth the fields of Heaven-reflecting sea
Which are my realm, will heave, unstain'd with blood,
Beneath the uplifting winds, like plains of corn   20
Swayed by the summer air; my streams will flow
Round many-peopled continents, and round
Fortunate isles; and from their glassy thrones
Blue Proteus and his humid nymphs shall mark
The shadow of fair ships, as mortals see   25
The floating bark of the light-laden moon
With that white star, its sightless pilot's crest,
Borne down the rapid sunset's ebbing sea;
Tracking their path no more by blood and groans,
And desolation, and the mingled voice   30
Of slavery and command; but by the light
Of wave-reflected flowers, and floating odours,
And music soft, and mild, free, gentle voices,
That sweetest music, such as spirits love.
APOLLO. And I shall gaze not on the deeds which make   35

My mind obscure with sorrow, as eclipse
Darkens the sphere I guide; but list, I hear
The small, clear, silver lute of the young Spirit
That sits i' the morning star.
OCEAN.   Thou must away;
Thy steeds will pause at even, till when farewell: 40
The loud deep calls me home even now to feed it
With azure calm out of the emerald urns
Which stand for ever full beside my throne.
Behold the Nereids under the green sea,
Their wavering limbs borne on the wind-like stream,   45
Their white arms lifted o'er their streaming hair
With garlands pied and starry sea-flower crowns,
Hastening to grace their mighty sister's joy.
                    [*A sound of waves is heard.*]
It is the unpastured sea hungering for calm.
Peace, monster; I come now. Farewell.
APOLLO.   Farewell.   50

Scene III. Caucasus. PROMETHEUS, HERCULES, IONE, the
    EARTH, SPIRITS, ASIA, and PANTHEA, borne in the Car
    with the SPIRIT OF THE HOUR.

HERCULES *unbinds* PROMETHEUS, *who descends.*

HERCULES. Most glorious among spirits! thus doth
    strength
To wisdom, courage, and long-suffering love,
And thee, who art the form they animate,
Minister like a slave.
PROMETHEUS.   Thy gentle words
Are sweeter even than freedom long desired   5
And long delayed.
                Asia, thou light of life,
Shadow of beauty unbeheld: and ye,
Fair sister nymphs, who made long years of pain
Sweet to remember, thro' your love and care:
Henceforth we will not part. There is a cave,   10
All overgrown with trailing odorous plants,
Which curtain out the day with leaves and flowers,
And paved with veined emerald, and a fountain,

Leaps in the midst with an awakening sound.
From its curved roof the mountain's frozen tears,   15
Like snow, or silver, or long diamond spires,
Hang downward, raining forth a doubtful light:
And there is heard the ever-moving air,
Whispering without from tree to tree, and birds,
And bees; and all around are mossy seats,   20
And the rough walls are clothed with long soft grass;
A simple dwelling, which shall be our own;
Where we will sit and talk of time and change,
As the world ebbs and flows, ourselves unchanged.
What can hide man from mutability?   25
And if ye sigh, then I will smile; and thou,
Ione, shall chaunt fragments of sea-music,
Until I weep, when ye shall smile away
The tears she brought, which yet were sweet to shed.
We will entangle buds and flowers and beams   30
Which twinkle on the fountain's brim, and make
Strange combinations out of common things,
Like human babes in their brief innocence;
And we will search, with looks and words of love,
For hidden thoughts, each lovelier than the last,   35
Our unexhausted spirits; and like lutes
Touched by the skill of the enamoured wind,
Weave harmonies divine, yet ever new,
From difference sweet where discord cannot be;
And hither come, sped on the charmed winds,   40
Which meet from all the points of heaven, as bees
From every flower aërial Enna feeds,
At their known island-homes in Himera,
The echoes of the human world, which tell
Of the low voice of love, almost unheard,   45
And dove-eyed pity's murmured pain, and music,
Itself the echo of the heart, and all
That tempers or improves man's life, now free;
And lovely apparitions, dim at first,
Then radiant, as the mind, arising bright   50
From the embrace of beauty, whence the forms
Of which these are the phantoms, casts on them
The gathered rays which are reality,
Shall visit us, the progeny immortal
Of Painting, Sculpture, and rapt Poesy,   55

And arts, tho' unimagined, yet to be.
The wandering voices and the shadows these
Of all that man becomes, the mediators
Of that best worship love, by him and us
Given and returned; swift shapes and sounds, which grow   60
More fair and soft as man grows wise and kind,
And veil by veil, evil and error fall:
Such virtue has the cave and place around.
                    [*Turning to the* SPIRIT OF THE HOUR.]
For thee, fair Spirit, one toil remains. Ione,
Give her that curved shell, which Proteus old,   65
Made Asia's nuptial boon, breathing within it
A voice to be accomplished, and which thou
Didst hide in grass under the hollow rock.
IONE. Thou most desired Hour, more loved and lovely
Than all thy sisters, this is the mystic shell;   70
See the pale azure fading into silver
Lining it with a soft yet glowing light:
Looks it not like lulled music sleeping there?
SPIRIT. It seems in truth the fairest shell of Ocean:
Its sound must be at once both sweet and strange.   75
PROMETHEUS. Go, borne over the cities of mankind
On whirlwind-footed coursers: once again
Outspeed the sun around the orbed world;
And as thy chariot cleaves the kindling air,
Thou breathe into the many-folded shell,   80
Loosening its mighty music; it shall be
As thunder mingled with clear echoes: then
Return; and thou shalt dwell beside our cave.

And thou, O Mother Earth!—
THE EARTH.   I hear, I feel;
Thy lips are on me, and their touch runs down   85
Even to the adamantine central gloom
Along these marble nerves; 'tis life, 'tis joy,
And, thro' my withered, old, and icy frame
The warmth of an immortal youth shoots down
Circling. Henceforth the many children fair   90
Folded in my sustaining arms; all plants,
And creeping forms, and insects rainbow-winged,
And birds, and beasts, and fish, and human shapes,
Which drew disease and pain from my wan bosom,

Draining the poison of despair, shall take   95
And interchange sweet nutriment; to me
Shall they become like sister-antelopes
By one fair dam, snow-white and swift as wind,
Nursed among lilies near a brimming stream.
The dew-mists of my sunless sleep shall float   100
Under the stars like balm: night-folded flowers
Shall suck unwithering hues in their repose:
And men and beasts in happy dreams shall gather
Strength for the coming day, and all its joy:
And death shall be the last embrace of her   105
Who takes the life she gave, even as a mother,
Folding her child, says, "Leave me not again."
Asia. Oh, mother! wherefore speak the name of death?
Cease they to love, and move, and breathe, and speak,
Who die?
The Earth. It would avail not to reply: 110
Thou art immortal, and this tongue is known
But to the uncommunicating dead.
Death is the veil which those who live call life:
They sleep, and it is lifted: and meanwhile
In mild variety the seasons mild   115
With rainbow-skirted showers, and odorous winds,
And long blue meteors cleansing the dull night,
And the life-kindling shafts of the keen sun's
All-piercing bow, and the dew-mingled rain
Of the calm moonbeams, a soft influence mild,   120
Shall clothe the forests and the fields, aye, even
The crag-built deserts of the barren deep,
With ever-living leaves, and fruits, and flowers.
And thou! There is a cavern where my spirit
Was panted forth in anguish whilst thy pain   125
Made my heart mad, and those who did inhale it
Became mad too, and built a temple there,
And spoke, and were oracular, and lured
The erring nations round to mutual war,
And faithless faith, such as Jove kept with thee;   130
Which breath now rises, as amongst tall weeds
A violet's exhalation, and it fills
With a serener light and crimson air
Intense, yet soft, the rocks and woods around;
It feeds the quick growth of the serpent vine,   135

And the dark linked ivy tangling wild,
And budding, blown, or odour-faded blooms
Which star the winds with points of coloured light,
As they rain thro' them, and bright golden globes
Of fruit, suspended in their own green heaven,   140
And thro' their veined leaves and amber stems
The flowers whose purple and translucid bowls
Stand ever mantling with aërial dew,
The drink of spirits: and it circles round,
Like the soft waving wings of noonday dreams,   145
Inspiring calm and happy thoughts, like mine,
Now thou art thus restored. This cave is thine.
Arise! Appear!
          [A SPIRIT rises in the likeness of a winged child.]
          This is my torch-bearer;
Who let his lamp out in old time with gazing
On eyes from which he kindled it anew   150
With love, which is as fire, sweet daughter mine,
For such is that within thine own. Run, wayward,
And guide this company beyond the peak
Of Bacchic Nysa, Mænad-haunted mountain,
And beyond Indus and its tribute rivers,   155
Trampling the torrent streams and glassy lakes
With feet unwet, unwearied, undelaying,
And up the green ravine, across the vale,
Beside the windless and crystalline pool,
Where ever lies, on unerasing waves,   160
The image of a temple, built above,
Distinct with column, arch, and architrave,
And palm-like capital, and over-wrought,
And populous with most living imagery,
Praxitelean shapes, whose marble smiles   165
Fill the hushed air with everlasting love.
It is deserted now, but once it bore
Thy name, Prometheus; there the emulous youths
Bore to thy honour thro' the divine gloom
The lamp which was thine emblem; even as those   170
Who bear the untransmitted torch of hope
Into the grave, across the night of life,
As thou hast borne it most triumphantly
To this far goal of Time. Depart, farewell.
Beside that temple is the destined cave.   175

Scene IV. A Forest. In the Back-ground a Cave.
PROMETHEUS, ASIA, PANTHEA, IONE, and the SPIRIT
OF THE EARTH.

IONE. Sister, it is not earthly: how it glides
Under the leaves! how on its head there burns
A light, like a green star, whose emerald beams
Are twined with its fair hair! how, as it moves,
The splendour drops in flakes upon the grass!   5
Knowest thou it?
PANTHEA.   It is the delicate spirit
That guides the earth thro' heaven. For afar
The populous constellations call that light
The loveliest of the planets; and sometimes
It floats along the spray of the salt sea,   10
Or makes its chariot of a foggy cloud,
Or walks thro' fields or cities while men sleep,
Or o'er the mountain tops, or down the rivers,
Or thro' the green waste wilderness, as now,
Wondering at all it sees. Before Jove reigned   15
It loved our sister Asia, and it came
Each leisure hour to drink the liquid light
Out of her eyes, for which it said it thirsted
As one bit by a dipsas, and with her
It made its childish confidence, and told her   20
All it had known or seen, for it saw much,
Yet idly reasoned what it saw; and called her,
For whence it sprung it knew not, nor do I,
Mother, dear mother.
THE SPIRIT OF THE EARTH (*running to* ASIA). Mother,
     dearest mother;
May I then talk with thee as I was wont?   25
May I then hide my eyes in thy soft arms,
After thy looks have made them tired of joy?
May I then play beside thee the long noons,
When work is none in the bright silent air?
ASIA. I love thee, gentlest being; and henceforth   30
Can cherish thee unenvied: speak, I pray:
Thy simple talk once solaced, now delights.

SPIRIT OF THE EARTH. Mother, I am grown wiser, though
    a child
Cannot be wise like thee, within this day;
And happier too; happier and wiser both.   35
Thou knowest that toads, and snakes, and loathly worms,
And venomous and malicious beasts, and boughs
That bore ill berries in the woods, were ever
An hindrance to my walks o'er the green world:
And that, among the haunts of humankind,   40
Hard-featured men, or with proud, angry looks,
Or cold, staid gait, or false and hollow smiles,
Or the dull sneer of self-loved ignorance,
Or other such foul masks, with which ill thoughts
Hide that fair being whom we spirits call man;   45
And women too, ugliest of all things evil,
(Tho' fair, even in a world where thou art fair,
When good and kind, free and sincere like thee),
When false or frowning made me sick at heart
To pass them, tho' they slept, and I unseen.   50
Well, my path lately lay thro' a great city
Into the woody hills surrounding it:
A sentinel was sleeping at the gate:
When there was heard a sound, so loud, it shook
The towers amid the moonlight, yet more sweet   55
Than any voice but thine, sweetest of all;
A long, long sound, as it would never end:
And all the inhabitants leapt suddenly
Out of their rest, and gathered in the streets,
Looking in wonder up to Heaven, while yet   60
The music pealed along. I hid myself
Within a fountain in the public square,
Where I lay like the reflex of the moon
Seen in a wave under green leaves; and soon
Those ugly human shapes and visages   65
Of which I spoke as having wrought me pain,
Past floating thro' the air, and fading still
Into the winds that scattered them; and those
From whom they past seemed mild and lovely forms
After some foul disguise had fallen, and all   70
Were somewhat changed, and after a brief surprise
And greetings of delighted wonder, all
Went to their sleep again: and when the dawn

Came, would'st thou think that toads, and snakes, and
    efts,
Could e'er be beautiful? yet so they were,   75
And that with little change of shape or hue:
All things had put their evil nature off:
I cannot tell my joy, when o'er a lake
Upon a drooping bough with night-shade twined,
I saw two azure halcyons clinging downward   80
And thinning one bright bunch of amber berries,
With quick long beaks, and in the deep there lay
Those lovely forms imaged as in a sky;
So with my thoughts full of these happy changes,
We meet again, the happiest change of all.   85
Asia. And never will we part, till thy chaste sister,
Who guides the frozen and inconstant moon,
Will look on thy more warm and equal light
Till her heart thaw like flakes of April snow
And love thee.
Spirit of the Earth. What; as Asia loves Prometheus? 90
Asia. Peace, wanton, thou art yet not old enough.
Think ye by gazing on each other's eyes
To multiply your lovely selves, and fill
With sphered fires the interlunar air?
Spirit of the Earth. Nay, mother, while my sister trims
    her lamp   95
'Tis hard I should go darkling.
Asia.   Listen; look!

        The Spirit of the Hour enters.

Prometheus. We feel what thou hast heard and seen; yet
    speak.
Spirit of the Hour. Soon as the sound had ceased whose
    thunder filled
The abysses of the sky and the wide earth,
There was a change: the impalpable thin air   100
And the all-circling sunlight were transformed,
As if the sense of love dissolved in them
Had folded itself round the sphered world.
My vision then grew clear, and I could see
Into the mysteries of the universe: 105
Dizzy as with delight I floated down,

Winnowing the lightsome air with languid plumes,
My coursers sought their birth-place in the sun,
Where they henceforth will live exempt from toil
Pasturing flowers of vegetable fire.   110
And where my moonlike car will stand within
A temple, gazed upon by Phidian forms
Of thee, and Asia, and the Earth, and me,
And you fair nymphs looking the love we feel;
In memory of the tidings it has borne;   115
Beneath a dome fretted with graven flowers,
Poised on twelve columns of resplendent stone,
And open to the bright and liquid sky.
Yoked to it by an amphisbænic snake
The likeness of those winged steeds will mock   120
The flight from which they find repose. Alas,
Whither has wandered now my partial tongue
When all remains untold which ye would hear?
As I have said, I floated to the earth:
It was, as it is still, the pain of bliss   125
To move, to breathe, to be; I wandering went
Among the haunts and dwellings of mankind,
And first was disappointed not to see
Such mighty change, as I had felt within
Expressed in outward things; but soon I looked,   130
And behold, thrones were kingless, and men walked
One with the other even as spirits do,
None fawned, none trampled; hate, disdain, or fear,
Self-love or self-contempt, on human brows
No more inscribed, as o'er the gate of hell,   135
"All hope abandon ye who enter here;"
None frowned, none trembled, none with eager fear
Gazed on another's eye of cold command,
Until the subject of a tyrant's will
Became, worse fate, the abject of his own,   140
Which spurred him, like an outspent horse, to death.
None wrought his lips in truth-entangling lines
Which smiled the lie his tongue disdained to speak;
None, with firm sneer, trod out in his own heart
The sparks of love and hope till there remained   145
Those bitter ashes, a soul self-consumed,
And the wretch crept a vampire among men,
Infecting all with his own hideous ill;

None talked that common, false, cold hollow talk
Which makes the heart deny the yes it breathes,   150
Yet question that unmeant hypocrisy
With such a self-mistrust as has no name.
And women, too, frank, beautiful, and kind
As the free heaven which rains fresh light and dew
On the wide earth, past; gentle radiant forms,   155
From custom's evil taint exempt and pure;
Speaking the wisdom once they could not think,
Looking emotions once they feared to feel,
And changed to all which once they dared not be,
Yet being now, made earth like heaven; nor pride,   160
Nor jealousy, nor envy, nor ill-shame,
The bitterest of those drops of treasured gall,
Spoilt the sweet taste of the nepenthe, love.

Thrones, altars, judgment-seats, and prisons; wherein,
And beside which, by wretched men were borne   165
Sceptres, tiaras, swords, and chains, and tomes
Of reasoned wrong, glozed on by ignorance,
Were like those monstrous and barbaric shapes,
The ghosts of a no more remembered fame,
Which, from their unworn obelisks, look forth   170
In triumph o'er the palaces and tombs
Of these who were their conquerors: mouldering round
Those imaged to the pride of kings and priests,
A dark yet mighty faith, a power as wide
As is the world it wasted, and are now   175
But an astonishment; even so the tools
And emblems of its last captivity,
Amid the dwellings of the peopled earth,
Stand, not o'erthrown, but unregarded now.
And those foul shapes, abhorred by god and man,   180
Which, under many a name and many a form
Strange, savage, ghastly, dark, and execrable,
Were Jupiter, the tyrant of the world;
And which the nations, panic-stricken, served
With blood, and hearts broken by long hope, and love 185
Dragged to his altars soiled and garlandless,
And slain amid men's unreclaiming tears,
Flattering the thing they feared, which fear was hate,
Frown, mouldering fast, o'er their abandoned shrines:

The painted veil, by those who were, called life,   190
Which mimicked, as with colours idly spread,
All men believed or hoped, is torn aside;
The loathsome mask has fallen, the Man remains,—
Sceptreless, free, uncircumscribed,—but man:
Equal, unclassed, tribeless and nationless,   195
Exempt from awe, worship, degree, the King
Over himself; just, gentle, wise,—but man:
Passionless? no: yet free from guilt or pain,
Which were, for his will made, or suffered them,
Nor yet exempt, tho' ruling them like slaves,   200
From chance, and death, and mutability,
The clogs of that which else might oversoar
The loftiest star of unascended heaven,
Pinnacled dim in the intense inane.

END OF THE THIRD ACT.

ACT IV.

Scene. A part of the Forest near the Cave of PROMETHEUS.
PANTHEA and IONE are sleeping: they awaken
gradually during the first Song.

VOICE OF UNSEEN SPIRITS.

  The pale stars are gone!
  For the sun, their swift shepherd
  To their folds them compelling,
   In the depths of the dawn,
Hastes, in meteor-eclipsing array, and they flee   5
  Beyond his blue dwelling,
  As fawns flee the leopard,
   But where are ye?

A Train of dark Forms and Shadows passes by confusedly
singing.
  Here, oh! here:
  We bear the bier   10
Of the Father of many a cancelled year!

Spectres we
Of the dead Hours be,
We bear Time to his tomb in eternity.

Strew, oh, strew   15
Hair, not yew!
Wet the dusty pall with tears, not dew!
Be the faded flowers
Of Death's bare bowers
Spread on the corpse of the King of Hours!   20

Haste, oh, haste!
As shades are chased,
Trembling, by day, from heaven's blue waste,
We melt away,
Like dissolving spray,   25
From the children of a diviner day,
With the lullaby
Of winds that die
On the bosom of their own harmony!

                                            [*They vanish.*]

IONE.

What dark forms were they?   30

PANTHEA.

The past Hours weak and grey,
With the spoil which their toil
    Raked together
From the conquest but One could foil.

IONE.

Have they past?
PANTHEA.   They have past;   35
    They outspeeded the blast,
    While 'tis said, they are fled:
IONE. Whither, oh, whither?
PANTHEA. To the dark, to the past, to the dead.

Voice of Unseen Spirits.

      Bright clouds float in heaven,   **40**
      Dew-stars gleam on earth,
      Waves assemble on ocean,
      They are gathered and driven
By the storm of delight, by the panic of glee!
      They shake with emotion,   **45**
      They dance in their mirth.
         But where are ye?

      The pine boughs are singing
      Old songs with new gladness,
      The billows and fountains   **50**
      Fresh music are flinging,
Like the notes of a spirit from land and from sea;
      The storms mock the mountains
      With the thunder of gladness,
         But where are ye?   **55**

Ione. What charioteers are these?
Panthea. Where are their chariots?

Semichorus of Hours.

The voice of the Spirits of Air and of Earth
Have drawn back the figured curtain of sleep,
Which covered our being and darkened our birth
In the deep.

A Voice.

         In the deep?

Semichorus II.

             Oh! below the deep.   **60**
Semichorus I.

A hundred ages we had been kept
Cradled in visions of hate and care,
And each one who waked as his brother slept,
Found the truth—

SEMICHORUS II.

> Worse than his visions were!

SEMICHORUS I.

> We have heard the lute of Hope in sleep;   65
> We have known the voice of Love in dreams,
> We have felt the wand of Power, and leap—

SEMICHORUS II.

> As the billows leap in the morning beams!

CHORUS.

> Weave the dance on the floor of the breeze,
>   Pierce with song heaven's silent light,   70
> Enchant the day that too swiftly flees,
>   To check its flight ere the cave of night.
>
> Once the hungry Hours were hounds
>   Which chased the day like a bleeding deer,
> And it limped and stumbled with many wounds   75
>   Through the nightly dells of the desert year.
>
> But now, oh, weave the mystic measure
>   Of music, and dance, and shapes of light,
> Let the Hours, and the spirits of might and pleasure,
>   Like the clouds and sunbeams, unite.

A VOICE.

> Unite!   80

PANTHEA. See, where the Spirits of the human mind
Wrapt in sweet sounds, as in bright veils, approach.

CHORUS OF SPIRITS.

> We join the throng
>   Of the dance and the song,
> By the whirlwind of gladness borne along;   85
>   As the flying-fish leap
>   From the Indian deep,
> And mix with the sea-birds half-asleep.

CHORUS OF HOURS.

> Whence come ye, so wild and so fleet,
> For sandals of lightning are on your feet,   90
> And your wings are soft and swift as thought,
> And your eyes are as love which is veiled not?

CHORUS OF SPIRITS.

> We come from the mind
> Of human kind,
> Which was late so dusk, and obscene, and blind,   95
> Now 'tis an ocean
> Of clear emotion,
> A heaven of serene and mighty motion.
>
> From that deep abyss
> Of wonder and bliss,   100
> Whose caverns are crystal palaces;
> From those skiey towers
> Where Thought's crowned powers
> Sit watching your dance, ye happy Hours!
>
> From the dim recesses   105
> Of woven caresses,
> Where lovers catch ye by your sliding tresses;
> From the azure isles,
> Where sweet Wisdom smiles,
> Delaying your ships with her syren wiles.   110
>
> From the temples high
> Of Man's ear and eye,
> Roofed over Sculpture and Posey;
> From the murmurings
> Of the unsealed springs   115
> Where Science bedews her Dædal wings.
>
> Years after years,
> Through blood, and tears,
> And a thick hell of hatreds, and hopes, and fears;
> We waded and flew,   120
> And the islets were few
> Where the bud-blighted flowers of happiness grew.

Our feet now, every palm,
Are sandalled with calm,
And the dew of our wings is a rain of balm;   125
And, beyond our eyes,
The human love lies,
Which makes all it gazes on Paradise.

CHORUS OF SPIRITS AND HOURS.

Then weave the web of the mystic measure;
From the depths of the sky and the ends of the earth,   130
Come, swift Spirits of might and of pleasure,
Fill the dance and the music of mirth,
As the waves of a thousand streams rush by
To an ocean of splendour and harmony!

CHORUS OF SPIRITS.

Our spoil is won,   135
Our task is done,
We are free to dive, or soar, or run;
Beyond and around,
Or within the bound
Which clips the world with darkness round.   140

We'll pass the eyes
Of the starry skies
Into the hoar deep to colonize:
Death, Chaos, and Night,
From the sound of our flight,   145
Shall flee, like mist from a tempest's might.

And Earth, Air, and Light,
And the Spirit of Might,
Which drives round the stars in their fiery flight;
And Love, Thought, and Breath,   150
The powers that quell Death,
Wherever we soar shall assemble beneath.

And our singing shall build
In the void's loose field
A world for the Spirit of Wisdom to wield;   155

We will take our plan
From the new world of man
And our work shall be called the Promethean.

CHORUS OF HOURS.

Break the dance, and scatter the song;
Let some depart, and some remain.   160

SEMICHORUS I.

We, beyond heaven, are driven along:

SEMICHORUS II.

Us the enchantments of earth retain:

SEMICHORUS I.

Ceaseless, and rapid, and fierce, and free,
With the Spirits which build a new earth and sea,
And a heaven where yet heaven could never be.   165

SEMICHORUS II.

Solemn, and slow, and serene, and bright,
Leading the Day, and outspeeding the Night,
With the powers of a world of perfect light.

SEMICHORUS I.

We whirl, singing loud, round the gathering sphere,
Till the trees, and the beasts, and the clouds appear   170
From its chaos made calm by love, not fear.

SEMICHORUS II.

We encircle the oceans and mountains of earth
And the happy forms of its death and birth
Change to the music of our sweet mirth.

CHORUS OF HOURS AND SPIRITS.

Break the dance, and scatter the song,   175
    Let some depart, and some remain,
Wherever we fly we lead along
In leashes, like starbeams, soft yet strong,
    The clouds that are heavy with love's sweet rain.

PANTHEA. Ha! they are gone!
IONE.   Yet feel you no delight   180
From the past sweetness?
PANTHEA.   As the bare green hill
When some soft cloud vanishes into rain,
Laughs with a thousand drops of sunny water
To the unpavilioned sky!
IONE.   Even whilst we speak
New notes arise. What is that awful sound?   185
PANTHEA. 'Tis the deep music of the rolling world,
Kindling within the strings of the waved air
Æolian modulations.
IONE.   Listen too,
How every pause is filled with under-notes,
Clear, silver, icy, keen awakening tones,   190
Which pierce the sense, and live within the soul,
As the sharp stars pierce winter's crystal air
And gaze upon themselves within the sea.
PANTHEA. But see where, through two openings in the
        forest
Which hanging branches overcanopy,   195
And where two runnels of a rivulet,
Between the close moss, violet-inwoven,
Have made their path of melody, like sisters
Who part with sighs that they may meet in smiles,
Turning their dear disunion to an isle   200
Of lovely grief, a wood of sweet sad thoughts;
Two visions of strange radiance float upon
The ocean-like enchantment of strong sound,
Which flows intenser, keener, deeper yet
Under the ground and through the windless air.   205
IONE. I see a chariot like that thinnest boat,
In which the mother of the months is borne
By ebbing light into her western cave,
When she upsprings from interlunar dreams,
O'er which is curved an orblike canopy   210
Of gentle darkness, and the hills and woods
Distinctly seen through that dusk aery veil,
Regard like shapes in an enchanter's glass;
Its wheels are solid clouds, azure and gold,
Such as the genii of the thunder-storm,   215
Pile on the floor of the illumined sea

When the sun rushes under it; they roll
And move and grow as with an inward wind;
Within it sits a winged infant, white
Its countenance, like the whiteness of bright snow,   220
Its plumes are as feathers of sunny frost,
Its limbs gleam white, through the wind-flowing folds
Of its white robe woof of ætherial pearl.
Its hair is white, the brightness of white light
Scattered in strings; yet its two eyes are heavens   225
Of liquid darkness, which the Deity
Within seems pouring, as a storm is poured
From jagged clouds, out of their arrowy lashes,
Tempering the cold and radiant air around,
With fire that is not brightness; in its hand   230
It sways a quivering moon-beam, from whose point
A guiding power directs the chariot's prow
Over its wheeled clouds, which as they roll
Over the grass, and flowers, and waves, wake sounds,
Sweet as a singing rain of silver dew.   235
PANTHEA. And from the other opening in the wood
Rushes, with loud and whirlwind harmony,
A sphere, which is as many thousand spheres,
Solid as crystal, yet through all its mass
Flow, as through empty space, music and light: 240
Ten thousand orbs involving and involved,
Purple and azure, white and green and golden,
Sphere within sphere; and every space between
Peopled with unimaginable shapes,
Such as ghosts dream dwell in the lampless deep,   245
Yet each inter-transpicuous; and they whirl
Over each other with a thousand motions,
Upon a thousand sightless axles spinning,
And with the force of self-destroying swiftness,
Intensely, slowly, solemnly, roll on,   250
Kindling with mingled sounds, and many tones,
Intelligible words and music wild.
With mighty whirl the multitudinous orb
Grinds the bright brook into an azure mist
Of elemental subtlety, like light;   255
And the wild odour of the forest flowers,
The music of the living grass and air,
The emerald light of leaf-entangled beams

Round its intense yet self-conflicting speed,
Seem kneaded into one aërial mass   260
Which drowns the sense. Within the orb itself,
Pillowed upon its alabaster arms,
Like to a child o'erwearied with sweet toil,
On its own folded wings, and wavy hair,
The Spirit of the Earth is laid asleep,   265
And you can see its little lips are moving,
Amid the changing light of their own smiles,
Like one who talks of what he loves in dream.
IONE. 'Tis only mocking the orb's harmony.
PANTHEA. And from a star upon its forehead, shoot,   270
Like swords of azure fire, or golden spears
With tyrant-quelling myrtle overtwined,
Embleming heaven and earth united now,
Vast beams like spokes of some invisible wheel
Which whirl as the orb whirls, swifter than thought, 275
Filling the abyss with sun-like lightenings,
And perpendicular now, and now transverse,
Pierce the dark soil, and as they pierce and pass,
Make bare the secrets of the earth's deep heart;
Infinite mines of adamant and gold,   280
Valueless stones, and unimagined gems,
And caverns on crystalline columns poised
With vegetable silver overspread;
Wells of unfathomed fire, and water springs
Whence the great sea, even as a child is fed,   285
Whose vapours clothe earth's monarch mountain-tops
With kingly, ermine snow. The beams flash on
And make appear the melancholy ruins
Of cancelled cycles; anchors, beaks of ships;
Planks turned to marble; quivers, helms, and spears,   290
And gorgon-headed targes, and the wheels
Of scythed chariots, and the emblazonry
Of trophies, standards, and armorial beasts,
Round which death laughed, sepulchred emblems
Of dead destruction, ruin within ruin!   295
The wrecks beside of many a city vast,
Whose population which the earth grew over
Was mortal, but not human; see, they lie
Their monstrous works, and uncouth skeletons,
Their statues, homes and fanes; prodigious shapes   300

Huddled in grey annihilation, split,
Jammed in the hard, black deep; and over these,
The anatomies of unknown winged things,
And fishes which were isles of living scale,
And serpents, bony chains, twisted around   305
The iron crags, or within heaps of dust
To which the tortuous strength of their last pangs
Had crushed the iron crags; and over these
The jagged alligator, and the might
Of earth-convulsing behemoth, which once   310
Were monarch beasts, and on the slimy shores,
And weed-overgrown continents of earth,
Increased and multiplied like summer worms
On an abandoned corpse, till the blue globe
Wrapt deluge round it like a cloak, and they   315
Yelled, gaspt, and were abolished; or some God
Whose throne was in a comet, past, and cried,
Be not! And like my words they were no more.

THE EARTH.

The joy, the triumph, the delight, the madness!
The boundless, overflowing, bursting gladness,   320
The vaporous exultation not to be confined!
    Ha! ha! the animation of delight
    Which wraps me, like an atmosphere of light,
And bears me as a cloud is borne by its own wind.

THE MOON.

        Brother mine, calm wanderer,   325
        Happy globe of land and air,
    Some spirit is darted like a beam from thee,
        Which penetrates my frozen frame,
        And passes with the warmth of flame,
    With love, and odour, and deep melody   330
        Through me, through me!

THE EARTH.

Ha! ha! the caverns of my hollow mountains,
My cloven fire-crags, sound-exulting fountains,
Laugh with a vast and inextinguishable laughter.

The oceans, and the deserts, and the abysses   335
Of the deep air's unmeasured wildernesses,
Answer from all their clouds and billows, echoing after.

They cry aloud as I do. Sceptred curse,
Who all our green and azure universe
Threatenedst to muffle round with black destruction,
    sending   340
A solid cloud to rain hot thunder-stones,
And splinter and knead down my children's bones,
All I bring forth, to one void mass battering and blending.

Until each crag-like tower, and storied column,
Palace, and obelisk, and temple solemn,   345
My imperial mountains crowned with cloud, and snow,
    and fire;
My sea-like forests, every blade and blossom
Which finds a grave or cradle in my bosom,
Were stamped by thy strong hate into a lifeless mire.

How art thou sunk, withdrawn, covered, drunk up   350
By thirsty nothing, as the brackish cup
Drained by a desert-troop, a little drop for all;
And from beneath, around, within, above,
Filling thy void annihilation, love
Bursts in like light on caves cloven by the thunder-ball.   355

THE MOON.

The snow upon my lifeless mountains
Is loosened into living fountains,
My solid oceans flow, and sing, and shine:
A spirit from my heart bursts forth,
It clothes with unexpected birth   360
My cold bare bosom: Oh! it must be thine
    On mine, on mine!

Gazing on thee I feel, I know,
Green stalks burst forth, and bright flowers grow,
And living shapes upon my bosom move: 365
Music is in the sea and air,
    Winged clouds soar here and there,
Dark with the rain new buds are dreaming of:
    'Tis love, all love!

THE EARTH.

It interpenetrates my granite mass,   370
    Through tangled roots and trodden clay doth pass,
Into the utmost leaves and delicatest flowers;
    Upon the winds, among the clouds 'tis spread,
    It wakes a life in the forgotten dead,
They breathe a spirit up from their obscurest bowers.   375

And like a storm bursting its cloudy prison
    With thunder, and with whirlwind, has arisen
Out of the lampless caves of unimagined being:
    With earthquake shock and swiftness making shiver
    Thought's stagnant chaos, unremoved for ever,   380
Till hate, and fear, and pain, light-vanquished shadows,
        fleeing,

Leave Man, who was a many-sided mirror,
    Which could distort to many a shape of error,
This true fair world of things, a sea reflecting love;
    Which over all his kind, as the sun's heaven   385
    Gliding o'er ocean, smooth, serene, and even
Darting from starry depths radiance and life, doth move,

Leave Man, even as a leprous child is left,
    Who follows a sick beast to some warm cleft
Of rocks, through which the might of healing springs is 390
        poured;
    Then when it wanders home with rosy smile,
    Unconscious, and its mother fears awhile
It is a spirit, then, weeps on her child restored.

Man, oh, not men! a chain of linked thought,
    Of love and might to be divided not,   395
Compelling the elements with adamantine stress;
    As the sun rules, even with a tyrant's gaze,
    The unquiet republic of the maze
Of planets, struggling fierce towards heaven's free wilder-
        ness.

Man, one harmonious soul of many a soul,   400
    Whose nature is its own divine controul,
Where all things flow to all, as rivers to the sea;

Familiar acts are beautiful through love;
Labour, and pain, and grief, in life's green grove
Sport like tame beasts, none knew how gentle they could
    be!   405

His will, with all mean passions, bad delights,
And selfish cares, its trembling satellites,
A spirit ill to guide, but mighty to obey,
Is as a tempest-winged ship, whose helm
Love rules, through waves which dare not overwhelm,   410
Forcing life's wildest shores to own its sovereigns sway.

All things confess his strength. Through the cold mass
Of marble and of colour his dreams pass;
Bright threads whence mothers weave the robes their chil-
    dren wear;
    Language is a perpetual Orphic song,   415
    Which rules with Dædal harmony a throng
Of thoughts and forms, which else senseless and shapeless
    were.

The lightning is his slave; heaven's utmost deep
Gives up her stars, and like a flock of sheep
They pass before his eye, are numbered, and roll on.   420
    The tempest is his steed, he strides the air;
    And the abyss shouts from her depth laid bare,
Heaven, hast thou secrets? Man unveils me; I have none.

THE MOON.

    The shadow of white death has past
    From my path in heaven at last,   425
A clinging shroud of solid frost and sleep;
    And through my newly-woven bowers,
    Wander happy paramours
Less mighty, but as mild as those who keep
    Thy vales more deep.   430

THE EARTH.

    As the dissolving warmth of dawn may fold
    A half unfrozen dew-globe, green, and gold,
And crystalline, till it becomes a winged mist,

And wanders up the vault of the blue day,
Outlives the noon, and on the sun's last ray   435
Hangs o'er the sea, a fleece of fire and amethyst—

THE MOON.

Thou art folded, thou art lying
In the light which is undying
Of thine own joy, and heaven's smile divine;
All suns and constellations shower   440
On thee a light, a life, a power
Which doth array thy sphere; thou pourest thine
On mine, on mine!

THE EARTH.

I spin beneath my pyramid of night,
Which points into the heavens, dreaming delight,   445
Murmuring victorious joy in my enchanted sleep;
As a youth lulled in love-dreams, faintly sighing,
Under the shadow of his beauty lying,
Which round his rest a watch of light and warmth doth
keep.

THE MOON.

As in the soft and sweet eclipse,   450
When soul meets soul on lovers' lips,
High hearts are calm, and brightest eyes are dull;
So, when thy shadow falls on me,
Then am I mute and still, by thee
Covered; of thy love, Orb most beautiful,   455
Full, oh, too full!

Thou art speeding round the sun,
Brightest world of many a one;
Green and azure sphere which shinest
With a light which is divinest   460
Among all the lamps of Heaven
To whom life and light is given;
I, thy crystal paramour,
Borne beside thee by a power
Like the polar Paradise,   465
Magnet-like, of lovers' eyes;

I, a most enamoured maiden,
Whose weak brain is overladen
With the pleasure of her love,
Maniac-like around thee move   470
Gazing, an insatiate bride,
On thy form from every side
Like a Mænad, round the cup
Which Agave lifted up
In the weird Cadmæan forest.   475
Brother, wheresoe'er thou soarest,
I must hurry, whirl and follow.
Through the heavens wide and hollow,
Sheltered by the warm embrace
Of thy soul from hungry space,   480
Drinking from thy sense and sight
Beauty, majesty, and might,
As a lover or a camelion
Grows like what it looks upon,
As a violet's gentle eye   485
Gazes on the azure sky
Until its hue grows like what it beholds
As a grey and watery mist
Glows like solid amethyst
Athwart the western mountain it enfolds   490
    When the sunset sleeps
        Upon its snow.

THE EARTH.

    And the weak day weeps
        That it should be so.
    Oh, gentle Moon, the voice of thy delight   495
    Falls on me like thy clear and tender light
    Soothing the seaman, borne the summer night
        Through isles for ever calm;
    Oh, gentle Moon, thy crystal accents pierce
    The caverns of my pride's deep universe,   500
    Charming the tiger joy, whose tramplings fierce
        Made wounds which need thy balm.

PANTHEA. I rise as from a bath of sparkling water,
A bath of azure light, among dark rocks,
Out of the stream of sound.

IONE.   Ah me! sweet sister,   505
The stream of sound has ebbed away from us,
And you pretend to rise out of its wave,
Because your words fall like the clear, soft dew
Shaken from a bathing wood-nymph's limbs and hair.
PANTHEA. Peace, peace! a mighty Power, which is as dark-
     ness,   510
Is rising out of Earth, and from the sky
Is showered like night, and from within the air
Bursts, like eclipse which had been gathered up
Into the pores of sunlight: the bright visions,
Wherein the singing spirits rode and shone,   515
Gleam like pale meteors through a watery night.
IONE. There is a sense of words upon mine ear.
PANTHEA. A universal sound like words: Oh, list!

DEMOGORGON.

Thou, Earth, calm empire of a happy soul,
     Spheres of divinest shapes and harmonies,   520
Beautiful orb! gathering as thou dost roll
     The love which paves thy path along the skies:

THE EARTH.

I hear: I am as a drop of dew that dies.

DEMOGORGON.

Thou Moon, which gazest on the nightly Earth
     With wonder, as it gazes upon thee;   525
Whilst each to men, and beasts, and the swift birth
     Of birds, is beauty, love, calm, harmony:

THE MOON.

I hear: I am a leaf shaken by thee!

DEMOGORGON.

Ye kings of suns and stars! Dæmons and Gods,
     Ætherial Dominations! who possess   530
Elysian, windless, fortunate abodes
     Beyond Heaven's constellated wilderness:

A VOICE FROM ABOVE.

Our great Republic hears; we are blest, and bless.

DEMOGORGON.

Ye happy dead, whom beams of brightest verse
    Are clouds to hide, not colours to pourtray,   535
Whether your nature is that universe
    Which once ye saw and suffered—

A VOICE FROM BENEATH.

                            Or as they
Whom we have left, we change and pass away.

DEMOGORGON.

Ye elemental Genii, who have homes
    From man's high mind even to the central stone   540
Of sullen lead; from Heaven's star-fretted domes
    To the dull weed some sea-worm battens on:

A CONFUSED VOICE.

We hear: thy words waken Oblivion.

DEMOGORGON.

Spirits! whose homes are flesh: ye beasts and birds,
    Ye worms and fish; ye living leaves and buds;   545
Lightning and wind; and ye untameable herds,
    Meteors and mists, which throng air's solitudes.

A VOICE.

Thy voice to us is wind among still woods.

DEMOGORGON.

Man, who wert once a despot and a slave;
    A dupe and a deceiver; a decay;   550
A traveller from the cradle to the grave
    Through the dim night of this immortal day:

ALL.

Speak! thy strong words may never pass away.

DEMOGORGON.

This is the day, which down the void abysm
At the Earth-born's spell yawns for Heaven's despotism,   555
   And Conquest is dragged captive through the deep;
Love, from its awful throne of patient power
In the wise heart, from the last giddy hour
   Of dread endurance, from the slippery, steep,
And narrow verge of crag-like agony, springs   560
And folds over the world its healing wings.

   Gentleness, Virtue, Wisdom, and Endurance,
These are the seals of that most firm assurance
   Which bars the pit over Destruction's strength;
And if, with infirm hand, Eternity,   565
Mother of many acts and hours, should free
   The serpent that would clasp her with his length;
These are the spells by which to re-assume
An empire o'er the disentangled doom.

To suffer woes which Hope thinks infinite;   570
To forgive wrongs darker than death or night;
   To defy Power, which seems omnipotent;
To love, and bear; to hope till Hope creates
From its own wreck the thing it contemplates:
   Neither to change, nor falter, nor repent;   575
This, like thy glory, Titan! is to be
Good, great and joyous, beautiful and free;
This is alone Life, Joy, Empire, and Victory!
     [1818–19]

THE INDIAN SERENADE

I

I arise from dreams of thee
In the first sweet sleep of night,
When the winds are breathing low,
And the stars are burning bright:

I arise from dreams of thee,   5
And a spirit in my feet
Has led me—who knows how?
To thy chamber window—Sweet!

II

The wandering airs they faint
On the dark, the silent stream—   10
The Champak odours fail
Like sweet thoughts in a dream;
The Nightingale's complaint—
It dies upon her heart
As I must die on thine,   15
Oh belovéd as thou art!

III

Oh! lift me from the grass!
I die, I faint, I fail!
Let thy love in kisses rain
On my lips and eyelids pale.   20
My cheek is cold and white, alas!
My heart beats loud and fast,
Oh! press it close to thine again,
Where it must break at last.
[1819]

LOVE'S PHILOSOPHY

I

The fountains mingle with the river,
    And the rivers with the ocean;
The winds of Heaven mix for ever
    With a sweet emotion;
Nothing in the world is single;   5
    All things by a law divine
In one another's being mingle—
    Why not I with thine?

II

See the mountains kiss high Heaven,
    And the waves clasp one another;   10
No sister flower would be forgiven
    If it disdained its brother;
And the sunlight clasps the earth,
    And the moonbeams kiss the sea:
What are all these kissings worth,   15
    If thou kiss not me?
[1819]

ODE TO THE WEST WIND

I

O wild West Wind, thou breath of Autumn's being,
Thou, from whose unseen presence the leaves dead
Are driven, like ghosts from an enchanter fleeing,

Yellow, and black, and pale, and hectic red,
Pestilence-stricken multitudes: O thou,   5
Who chariotest to their dark wintry bed

The winged seeds, where they lie cold and low,
Each like a corpse within its grave, until
Thine azure sister of the spring shall blow

Her clarion o'er the dreaming earth, and fill   10
(Driving sweet buds like flocks to feed in air)
With living hues and odours plain and hill:

Wild Spirit, which art moving every where;
Destroyer and preserver; hear, O, hear!

II

Thou on whose stream, 'mid the steep sky's commotion,   15
Loose clouds like earth's decaying leaves are shed,
Shook from the tangled boughs of Heaven and Ocean,

Angels of rain and lightning: there are spread
On the blue surface of thine airy surge,
Like the bright hair uplifted from the head   20

Of some fierce Mænad, even from the dim verge
Of the horizon to the zenith's height
The locks of the approaching storm. Thou dirge

Of the dying year, to which this closing night
Will be the dome of a vast sepulchre,   25
Vaulted with all thy congregated might

Of vapours, from whose solid atmosphere
Black rain, and fire, and hail will burst: O, hear!

III

Thou who didst waken from his summer dreams
The blue Mediterranean, where he lay,   30
Lulled by the coil of his crystalline streams,

Beside a pumice isle in Baiæ's bay,
And saw in sleep dim palaces and towers
Quivering within the wave's intenser lay,

All overgrown with azure moss and flowers   35
So sweet, the sense faints picturing them! Thou
For whose path the Atlantic's level powers

Cleave themselves into chasms, while far below
The sea-blooms and the oozy woods which wear
The sapless foliage of the ocean, know   40

Thy voice, and suddenly grow grey with fear,
And tremble and despoil themselves: O, hear!

IV

If I were a dead leaf thou mightest bear;
If I were a swift cloud to fly with thee;
A wave to pant beneath thy power, and share   45

The impulse of thy strength, only less free
Than thou, O uncontroulable! If even
I were as in my boyhood, and could be

The comrade of thy wanderings over heaven,
As then, when to outstrip thy skiey speed   50
Scarce seemed a vision, I would ne'er have striven

As thus with thee in prayer in my sore need.
Oh! lift me as a wave, a leaf, a cloud!
I fall upon the thorns of life! I bleed!

A heavy weight of hours has chained and bowed   55
One too like thee: tameless, and swift, and proud.

v

Make me thy lyre, even as the forest is:
What if my leaves are falling like its own!
The tumult of thy mighty harmonies

Will take from both a deep, autumnal tone,   60
Sweet though in sadness. Be thou, spirit fierce,
My spirit! Be thou me, impetuous one!

Drive my dead thoughts over the universe
Like withered leaves to quicken a new birth!
And, by the incantation of this verse,   65

Scatter, as from an unextinguished hearth
Ashes and sparks, my words among mankind!
Be through my lips to unawakened earth

The trumpet of a prophecy! O, wind,
If Winter comes, can Spring be far behind?   70
[1819]

THE CLOUD

I

I bring fresh showers for the thirsting flowers,
    From the seas and the streams;
I bear light shade for the leaves when laid
    In their noon-day dreams.
From my wings are shaken the dews that waken   5
    The sweet buds every one,
When rocked to rest on their mother's breast,
    As she dances about the sun.
I wield the flail of the lashing hail,
    And whiten the green plains under,   10
And then again I dissolve it in rain,
    And laugh as I pass in thunder.

II

I sift the snow on the mountains below,
    And their great pines groan aghast;
And all the night 'tis my pillow white,
    While I sleep in the arms of the blast.   15
Sublime on the towers of my skiey bowers,
    Lightning my pilot sits,
In a cavern under is fettered the thunder,
    It struggles and howls at fits;
Over earth and ocean, with gentle motion,   20
    This pilot is guiding me,
Lured by the love of the genii that move
    In the depths of the purple sea;
Over the rills, and the crags, and the hills,
    Over the lakes and the plains,   25
Wherever he dream, under mountain or stream,
    The Spirit he loves remains;
And I all the while bask in heaven's blue smile,
    Whilst he is dissolving in rains.   30

III

The sanguine sunrise, with his meteor eyes,
    And his burning plumes outspread,
Leaps on the back of my sailing rack,
    When the morning star shines dead;
As on the jag of a mountain crag,   **35**
    Which an earthquake rocks and swings,
An eagle alit one moment may sit
    In the light of its golden wings.
And when sunset may breathe, from the lit sea beneath,
    Its ardours of rest and of love,   **40**
And the crimson pall of eve may fall
    From the depth of heaven above,
With wings folded I rest, on mine airy nest,
    As still as a brooding dove.

IV

That orbed maiden with white fire laden,   **45**
    Whom mortals call the moon,
Guides glimmering o'er my fleece-like floor,
    By the midnight breezes strewn;
And wherever the beat of her unseen feet,
    Which only the angels hear,   **50**
May have broken the woof of my tent's thin roof,
    The stars peep behind her and peer;
And I laugh to see them whirl and flee,
    Like a swarm of golden bees,
When I widen the rent in my wind-built tent,   **55**
    Till the calm rivers, lakes, and seas,
Like strips of the sky fallen through me on high,
    Are each paved with the moon and these.

V

I bind the sun's throne with a burning zone,
    And the moon's with a girdle of pearl;   **60**
The volcanoes are dim, and the stars reel and swim,
    When the whirlwinds my banner unfurl.
From cape to cape, with a bridge-like shape,
    Over a torrent sea,

Sunbeam-proof, I hang like a roof,   65
    The mountains its columns be.
The triumphal arch through which I march,
    With hurricane, fire, and snow,
When the powers of the air are chained to my chair,
    Is the million-coloured bow;   70
The sphere-fire above its soft colours wove,
    While the moist earth was laughing below.

VI

I am the daughter of earth and water,
    And the nursling of the sky;
I pass through the pores of the ocean and shores;   75
    I change, but I cannot die.
For after the rain when with never a stain,
    The pavilion of heaven is bare,
And the winds and sunbeams with their convex gleams,
    Build up the blue dome of air,   80
I silently laugh at my own cenotaph,
    And out of the caverns of rain,
Like a child from the womb, like a ghost from the tomb,
    I arise and unbuild it again.
    [1820]

TO A SKYLARK

I

Hail to thee, blithe Spirit!
    Bird thou never wert,
That from Heaven, or near it,
    Pourest thy full heart
In profuse strains of unpremeditated art.   5

II

Higher still and higher
    From the earth thou springest
Like a cloud of fire;
    The blue deep thou wingest,
And singing still dost soar, and soaring ever singest.   10

III

In the golden lightning
　　Of the sunken Sun,
O'er which clouds are brightning,
　　Thou dost float and run;
Like an unbodied joy whose race is just begun.　　15

IV

The pale purple even
　　Melts around thy flight;
Like a star of Heaven,
　　In the broad day-light
Thou art unseen, but yet I hear thy shrill delight,　　20

V

Keen as are the arrows
　　Of that silver sphere,
Whose intense lamp narrows
　　In the white dawn clear,
Until we hardly see, we feel that it is there.　　25

VI

All the earth and air
　　With thy voice is loud,
As, when Night is bare,
　　From one lonely cloud
The moon rains out her beams, and Heaven is overflowed.　　30

VII

What thou art we know not;
　　What is most like thee?
From rainbow clouds there flow not
　　Drops so bright to see,
As from thy presence showers a rain of melody.　　35

VIII

Like a poet hidden
In the light of thought,
Singing hymns unbidden,
Till the world is wrought
To sympathy with hopes and fears it heeded not: 40

IX

Like a high-born maiden
In a palace-tower,
Soothing her love-laden
Soul in secret hour
With music sweet as love, which overflows her bower;   45

X

Like a glow-worm golden
In a dell of dew,
Scattering unbeholden
Its aërial hue
Among the flowers and grass, which screen it from the
view: 50

XI

Like a rose embowered
In its own green leaves,
By warm winds deflowered,
Till the scent it gives
Makes faint with too much sweet those heavy-winged
thieves: 55

XII

Sound of vernal showers
On the twinkling grass,
Rain-awakened flowers,
All that ever was
Joyous, and clear, and fresh, thy music doth surpass.   60

XIII

Teach us, Sprite or Bird,
   What sweet thoughts are thine:
I have never heard
   Praise of love or wine
That panted forth a flood of rapture so divine.   65

XIV

Chorus Hymeneal,
   Or triumphant chaunt,
Matched with thine would be all
   But an empty vaunt,
A thing wherein we feel there is some hidden want.   70

XV

What objects are the fountains
   Of thy happy strain?
What fields, or waves, or mountains?
   What shapes of sky or plain?
What love of thine own kind? what ignorance of pain?   75

XVI

With thy clear keen joyance
   Languor cannot be:
Shadow of annoyance
   Never came near thee:
Thou lovest; but ne'er knew love's sad satiety.   80

XVII

Waking or asleep,
   Thou of death must deem
Things more true and deep
   Than we mortals dream,
Or how could thy notes flow in such a crystal stream?   85

XVIII

We look before and after,
   And pine for what is not:

Our sincerest laughter
With some pain is fraught;
Our sweetest songs are those that tell of saddest thought. 90

XIX

Yet if we could scorn
Hate, and pride, and fear;
If we were things born
Not to shed a tear,
I know not how thy joy we ever should come near. 95

XX

Better than all measures
Of delightful sound,
Better than all treasures
That in books are found,
Thy skill to poet were, thou scorner of the ground! 100

XXI

Teach me half the gladness
That thy brain must know;
Such harmonious madness
From my lips would flow,
The world should listen then, as I am listening now. 105
   [1820]

TO ——

Music, when soft voices die,
Vibrates in the memory—
Odours, when sweet violets sicken,
Live within the sense they quicken.

Rose leaves, when the rose is dead, 5
Are heaped for the belovéd's bed;
And so thy thoughts, when thou art gone,
Love itself shall slumber on.
   [1821]

MUTABILITY

I

The flower that smiles to-day
    To-morrow dies;
All that we wish to stay,
    Tempts and then flies.
What is this world's delight?   5
Lightning that mocks the night,
    Brief even as bright.

II

Virtue, how frail it is!
    Friendship how rare!
Love, how it sells poor bliss   10
    For proud despair!
But we, though soon they fall,
Survive their joy, and all
    Which ours we call.

III

Whilst skies are blue and bright,   15
    Whilst flowers are gay,
Whilst eyes that change ere night
    Make glad the day;
Whilst yet the calm hours creep,
Dream thou—and from thy sleep   20
    Then wake to weep.

[1821]

ADONAIS

I

I weep for ADONAIS—he is dead!
Oh, weep for Adonais! though our tears

Thaw not the frost which binds so dear a head!
And thou, sad Hour, selected from all years
To mourn our loss, rouse thy obscure compeers, 5
And teach them thine own sorrow, say: with me
Died Adonais; till the Future dares
Forget the Past, his fate and fame shall be
An echo and a light unto eternity!

II

Where wert thou mighty Mother, when he lay, 10
When thy Son lay, pierced by the shaft which flies
In darkness? where was lorn Urania
When Adonais died? With veiled eyes,
'Mid listening Echoes, in her Paradise
She sate, while one, with soft enamoured breath, 15
Rekindled all the fading melodies,
With which, like flowers that mock the corse beneath,
He had adorned and hid the coming bulk of death.

III

Oh, weep for Adonais—he is dead!
Wake, melancholy Mother, wake and weep! 20
Yet wherefore? Quench within their burning bed
Thy fiery tears, and let thy loud heart keep
Like his, a mute and uncomplaining sleep;
For he is gone, where all things wise and fair
Descend:—oh, dream not that the amorous Deep 25
Will yet restore him to the vital air;
Death feeds on his mute voice, and laughs at our despair.

IV

Most musical of mourners, weep again!
Lament anew, Urania!—He died,
Who was the Sire of an immortal strain, 30
Blind, old, and lonely, when his country's pride,
The priest, the slave, and the liberticide,
Trampled and mocked with many a loathed rite
Of lust and blood; he went, unterrified,
Into the gulf of death; but his clear Sprite 35
Yet reigns o'er earth; the third among the sons of light.

V

Most musical of mourners, weep anew!
Not all to that bright station dared to climb;
And happier they their happiness who knew,
Whose tapers yet burn through that night of time   40
In which suns perished; others more sublime,
Struck by the envious wrath of man or God,
Have sunk, extinct in their refulgent prime;
And some yet live, treading the thorny road,
Which leads, through toil and hate, to Fame's serene
      abode.   45

VI

But now, thy youngest, dearest one, has perished,
The nursling of thy widowhood, who grew,
Like a pale flower by some sad maiden cherished,
And fed with true love tears, instead of dew;
Most musical of mourners, weep anew!   50
Thy extreme hope, the loveliest and the last,
The bloom, whose petals nipt before they blew
Died on the promise of the fruit, is waste;
The broken lily lies—the storm is overpast.

VII

To that high Capital, where kingly Death   55
Keeps his pale court in beauty and decay,
He came; and bought, with price of purest breath,
A grave among the eternal.—Come away!
Haste, while the vault of blue Italian day
Is yet his fitting charnel-roof! while still   60
He lies, as if in dewy sleep he lay;
Awake him not! surely he takes his fill
Of deep and liquid rest, forgetful of all ill.

VIII

He will awake no more, oh, never more!—
Within the twilight chamber spreads apace,   65

The shadow of white Death, and at the door
Invisible Corruption waits to trace
His extreme way to her dim dwelling-place;
The eternal Hunger sits, but pity and awe
Soothe her pale rage, nor dares she to deface   70
So fair a prey, till darkness and the law
Of change, shall o'er his sleep the mortal curtain draw.

IX

Oh, weep for Adonais!—The quick Dreams,
The passion-winged Ministers of thought,
Who were his flocks, whom near the living streams   75
Of his young spirit he fed, and whom he taught
The love which was its music, wander not,—
Wander no more, from kindling brain to brain,
But droop there, whence they sprung; and mourn their
     lot
Round the cold heart, where, after their sweet pain,   80
They ne'er will gather strength, or find a home again.

X

And one with trembling hand clasps his cold head,
And fans him with her moonlight wings, and cries,
"Our love, our hope, our sorrow, is not dead;
"See, on the silken fringe of his faint eyes,   85
"Like dew upon a sleeping flower, there lies
"A tear some Dream has loosened from his brain."
Lost Angel of a ruined Paradise!
She knew not 'twas her own; as with no stain
She faded, like a cloud which had outwept its rain.   90

XI

One from a lucid urn of starry dew
Washed his light limbs as if embalming them;
Another clipt her profuse locks, and threw
The wreath upon him, like an anadem,
Which frozen tears instead of pearls begem;   95
Another in her wilful grief would break
Her bow and winged reeds, as if to stem

A greater loss with one which was more weak;
And dull the barbed fire against his frozen cheek.

XII

Another Splendour on his mouth alit,   100
That mouth, whence it was wont to draw the breath
Which gave it strength to pierce the guarded wit,
And pass into the panting heart beneath
With lightning and with music: the damp death
Quenched its caress upon its icy lips;   105
And, as a dying meteor stains a wreath
Of moonlight vapour, which the cold night clips,
It flushed through his pale limbs, and passed to its eclipse.

XIII

And others came . . . Desires and Adorations,
Winged Persuasions and veiled Destinies,   110
Splendours, and Glooms, and glimmering Incarnations
Of hopes and fears, and twilight Phantasies;
And Sorrow, with her family of Sighs,
And Pleasure, blind with tears, led by the gleam
Of her own dying smile instead of eyes,   115
Came in slow pomp;—the moving pomp might seem
Like pageantry of mist on an autumnal stream.

XIV

All he had loved, and moulded into thought
From shape, and hue, and odour, and sweet sound,
Lamented Adonais. Morning sought   120
Her eastern watch-tower, and her hair unbound,
Wet with the tears which should adorn the ground,
Dimmed the aërial eyes that kindle day;
Afar the melancholy thunder moaned,
Pale Ocean in unquiet slumber lay,   125
And the wild winds flew round, sobbing in their dismay.

XV

Lost Echo sits amid the voiceless mountains,
And feeds her grief with his remembered lay,

And will no more reply to winds or fountains,
Or amorous birds perched on the young green spray,   130
Or herdsman's horn, or bell at closing day;
Since she can mimic not his lips, more dear
Than those for whose disdain she pined away
Into a shadow of all sounds:—a drear
Murmur, between their songs, is all the woodmen hear.   135

XVI

Grief made the young Spring wild, and she threw down
Her kindling buds, as if she Autumn were,
Or they dead leaves; since her delight is flown
For whom should she have waked the sullen year?
To Phœbus was not Hyacinth so dear,   140
Nor to himself Narcissus, as to both
Thou Adonais; wan they stand and sere
Amid the faint companions of their youth,
With dew all turned to tears; odour, to sighing ruth.

XVII

Thy spirit's sister, the lorn nightingale,   145
Mourns not her mate with such melodious pain;
Not so the eagle, who like thee could scale
Heaven, and could nourish in the sun's domain
Her mighty youth, with morning, doth complain,
Soaring and screaming round her empty nest,   150
As Albion wails for thee: the curse of Cain
Light on his head who pierced thy innocent breast,
And scared the angel soul that was its earthly guest!

XVIII

Ah woe is me! Winter is come and gone,
But grief returns with the revolving year;   155
The airs and streams renew their joyous tone;
The ants, the bees, the swallows reappear;
Fresh leaves and flowers deck the dead Season's bier;
The amorous birds now pair in every brake,
And build their mossy homes in field and brere;   160
And the green lizard, and the golden snake,
Like unimprisoned flames, out of their trance awake.

XIX

Through wood and stream and field and hill and Ocean,
A quickening life from the Earth's heart has burst
As it has ever done, with change and motion,   165
From the great morning of the world when first
God dawned on Chaos; in its stream immersed
The lamps of Heaven flash with a softer light;
All baser things pant with life's sacred thirst;
Diffuse themselves; and spend in love's delight,   170
The beauty and the joy of their renewed might.

XX

The leprous corpse touched by this spirit tender
Exhales itself in flowers of gentle breath;
Like incarnations of the stars, when splendour
Is changed to fragrance, they illumine death   175
And mock the merry worm that wakes beneath;
Nought we know, dies. Shall that alone which knows
Be as a sword consumed before the sheath
By sightless lightning?—th' intense atom glows
A moment, then is quenched in a most cold repose.   180

XXI

Alas! that all we loved of him should be,
But for our grief, as if it had not been.
And grief itself be mortal! Woe is me!
Whence are we, and why are we? of what scene
The actors or spectators? Great and mean   185
Meet massed in death, who lends what life must borrow.
As long as skies are blue, and fields are green,
Evening must usher night, night urge the morrow,
Month follow month with woe, and year wake year to
    sorrow.

XXII

He will awake no more, oh, never more!   190
"Wake thou," cried Misery, "childless Mother, rise

"Out of thy sleep, and slake, in thy heart's core,
"A wound more fierce than his with tears and sighs."
And all the Dreams that watched Urania's eyes,
And all the Echoes whom their sister's song   195
Had held in holy silence, cried, "Arise!"
Swift as a Thought by the snake Memory stung,
From her ambrosial rest the fading Splendour sprung.

XXIII

She rose like an autumnal Night, that springs
Out of the East, and follows wild and drear   200
The golden Day, which, on eternal wings,
Even as a ghost abandoning a bier,
Has left the Earth a corpse. Sorrow and fear
So struck, so roused, so rapt; Urania
So saddened round her like an atmosphere   205
Of stormy mist; so swept her on her way
Even to the mournful place where Adonais lay.

XXIV

Out of her secret Paradise she sped,
Through camps and cities rough with stone, and steel,
And human hearts, which to her aëry tread   210
Yielding not, wounded the invisible
Palms of her tender feet where'er they fell:
And barbed tongues, and thoughts more sharp than
        they
Rent the soft Form they never could repel,
Whose sacred blood, like the young tears of May,   215
Paved with eternal flowers that undeserving way.

XXV

In the death-chamber for a moment Death,
Shamed by the presence of that living Might
Blushed to annihilation, and the breath
Revisited those lips, and life's pale light   220
Flashed through those limbs, so late her dear delight.
"Leave me not wild and drear and comfortless,
"As silent lightning leaves the starless night!

"Leave me not!" cried Urania: her distress
Roused Death: Death rose and smiled, and met her vain
 caress. 225

XXVI

"Stay yet awhile! speak to me once again;
"Kiss me, so long but as a kiss may live;
"And in my heartless breast and burning brain
"That word, that kiss shall all thoughts else survive,
"With food of saddest memory kept alive, 230
"Now thou art dead, as if it were a part
"Of thee, my Adonais! I would give
"All that I am to be as thou now art,
"But I am chained to Time, and cannot thence depart!

XXVII

"O gentle child, beautiful as thou wert, 235
"Why didst thou leave the trodden paths of men
"Too soon, and with weak hands though mighty heart
"Dare the unpastured dragon in his den?
"Defenceless as thou wert, oh! where was then
"Wisdom the mirror'd shield, or scorn the spear? 240
"Or hadst thou waited the full cycle, when
"Thy spirit should have filled its crescent sphere,
"The monsters of life's waste had fled from thee like deer.

XXVIII

"The herded wolves, bold only to pursue;
"The obscene ravens, clamorous o'er the dead; 245
"The vultures, to the conqueror's banner true,
"Who feed where Desolation first has fed,
"And whose wings rain contagion;—how they fled,
"When like Apollo, from his golden bow,
"The Pythian of the age one arrow sped 250
"And smiled!—The spoilers tempt no second blow,
"They fawn on the proud feet that spurn them lying low.

XXIX

"The sun comes forth, and many reptiles spawn;
"He sets, and each ephemeral insect then

"Is gathered into death without a dawn,   255
"And the immortal stars awake again;
"So is it in the world of living men:
"A godlike mind soars forth, in its delight
"Making earth bare and veiling heaven, and when
"It sinks, the swarms that dimmed or shared its light   260
"Leave to its kindred lamps the spirit's awful night."

XXX

Thus ceased she: and the mountain shepherds came
Their garlands sere, their magic mantles rent;
The Pilgrim of Eternity, whose fame
Over his living head like Heaven is bent,   265
An early but enduring monument,
Came, veiling all the lightnings of his song
In sorrow; from her wilds Ierne sent
The sweetest lyrist of her saddest wrong,
And love taught grief to fall like music from his tongue. 270

XXXI

Midst others of less note, came one frail Form,
A phantom among men; companionless
As the last cloud of an expiring storm,
Whose thunder is its knell; he, as I guess,
Had gazed on Nature's naked loveliness,   275
Actæon-like, and now he fled astray
With feeble steps o'er the world's wilderness,
And his own thoughts, along that rugged way,
Pursued, like raging hounds, their father and their prey.

XXXII

A pardlike Spirit beautiful and swift—   280
A Love in desolation masked;—a Power
Girt round with weakness;—it can scarce uplift
The weight of the superincumbent hour;
It is a dying lamp, a falling shower,
A breaking billow;—even whilst we speak   285
Is it not broken? On the withering flower
The killing sun smiles brightly: on a cheek
The life can burn in blood, even while the heart may
     break.

XXXIII

His head was bound with pansies overblown,
And faded violets, white, and pied, and blue;   290
And a light spear topped with a cypress cone,
Round whose rude shaft dark ivy-tresses grew
Yet dripping with the forest's noon-day dew,
Vibrated, as the ever-beating heart
Shook the weak hand that grasped it; of that crew   295
He came the last, neglected and apart;
A herd-abandoned deer, struck by the hunter's dart.

XXXIV

All stood aloof, and at his partial moan
Smiled through their tears; well knew that gentle band
Who in another's fate now wept his own;   300
As in the accents of an unknown land,
He sung new sorrow; sad Urania scanned
The Stranger's mien, and murmured: "Who art thou?"
He answered not, but with a sudden hand
Made bare his branded and ensanguined brow,   305
Which was like Cain's or Christ's.—Oh! that it should
      be so!

XXXV

What softer voice is hushed over the dead?
Athwart what brow is that dark mantle thrown?
What form leans sadly o'er the white death-bed,
In mockery of monumental stone,   310
The heavy heart heaving without a moan?
If it be He, who, gentlest of the wise,
Taught, soothed, loved, honoured the departed one;
Let me not vex, with inharmonious sighs,
The silence of that heart's accepted sacrifice.   315

XXXVI

Our Adonais has drunk poison—oh!
What deaf and viperous murderer could crown
Life's early cup with such a draught of woe?
The nameless worm would now itself disown:

It felt, yet could escape the magic tone   320
Whose prelude held all envy, hate and wrong,
But what was howling in one breast alone,
Silent with expectation of the song,
Whose master's hand is cold, whose silver lyre unstrung.

XXXVII

Live thou, whose infamy is not thy fame!   325
Live! fear no heavier chastisement from me,
Thou noteless blot on a remembered name!
But be thyself, and know thyself to be!
And ever at thy season be thou free
To spill the venom when thy fangs o'erflow: 330
Remorse and Self-contempt shall cling to thee;
Hot Shame shall burn upon thy secret brow,
And like a beaten hound tremble thou shalt—as now.

XXXVIII

Not let us weep that our delight is fled
Far from these carrion kites that scream below;   335
He wakes or sleeps with the enduring dead;
Thou canst not soar where he is sitting now.—
Dust to the dust! but the pure spirit shall flow
Back to the burning fountain whence it came,
A portion of the Eternal, which must glow   340
Through time and change, unquenchably the same,
Whilst thy cold embers choke the sordid hearth of shame.

XXXIX

Peace, peace! he is not dead, he doth not sleep—
He hath awakened from the dream of life—
'Tis we, who lost in stormy visions, keep   345
With phantoms an unprofitable strife,
And in mad trance strike with our spirit's knife
Invulnerable nothings—We decay
Like corpses in a charnel; fear and grief
Convulse us and consume us day by day,   350
And cold hopes swarm like worms within our living clay.

XL

He has outsoared the shadow of our night;
Envy and calumny and hate and pain,
And that unrest which men miscall delight,
Can touch him not and torture not again;   355
From the contagion of the world's slow stain
He is secure, and now can never mourn
A heart grown cold, a head grown grey in vain;
Nor, when the spirit's self has ceased to burn,
With sparkless ashes load an unlamented urn.   360

XLI

He lives, he wakes—'tis Death is dead, not he;
Mourn not for Adonais.—Thou young Dawn,
Turn all thy dew to splendour, for from thee
The spirit thou lamentest is not gone;
Ye caverns and ye forests, cease to moan!   365
Cease ye faint flowers and fountains, and thou Air,
Which like a morning veil thy scarf hadst thrown
O'er the abandoned Earth, now leave it bare
Even to the joyous stars which smile on its despair!

XLII

He is made one with Nature: there is·heard   370
His voice in all her music, from the moan
Of thunder, to the song of night's sweet bird;
He is a presence to be felt and known
In darkness and in light, from herb and stone,
Spreading itself where'er that Power may move   375
Which has withdrawn his being to its own;
Which wields the world with never wearied love,
Sustains it from beneath, and kindles it above.

XLIII

He is a portion of the loveliness
Which once he made more lovely: he doth bear   380
His part, while the one Spirit's plastic stress

Sweeps through the dull dense world, compelling there
All new successions to the forms they wear;
Torturing th' unwilling dross that checks its flight
To its own likeness, as each mass may bear;   385
And bursting in its beauty and its might
From trees and beasts and men into the Heaven's light.

XLIV

The splendours of the firmament of time
May be eclipsed, but are extinguished not;
Like stars to their appointed height they climb,   390
And death is a low mist which cannot blot
The brightness it may veil. When lofty thought
Lifts a young heart above its mortal lair,
And love and life contend in it, for what
Shall be its earthly doom, the dead live there   395
And move like winds of light on dark and stormy air.

XLV

The inheritors of unfulfilled renown
Rose from their thrones, built beyond mortal thought,
Far in the Unapparent. Chatterton
Rose pale, his solemn agony had not   400
Yet faded from him; Sidney, as he fought
And as he fell and as he lived and loved
Sublimely mild, a Spirit without spot,
Arose; and Lucan, by his death approved:
Oblivion as they rose shrank like a thing reproved.   405

XLVI

And many more, whose names on Earth are dark
But whose transmitted effluence cannot die
So long as fire outlives the parent spark,
Rose, robed in dazzling immortality.
"Thou art become as one of us," they cry,   410
"It was for thee yon kingless sphere has long
"Swung blind in unascended majesty,
"Silent alone amid an Heaven of Song.
"Assume thy winged throne, thou Vesper of our throng!"

XLVII

Who mourns for Adonais? oh come forth,   415
Fond wretch! and know thyself and him aright.
Clasp with thy panting soul the pendulous Earth;
As from a centre, dart thy spirit's light
Beyond all worlds, until its spacious might
Satiate the void circumference: then shrink   420
Even to a point within our day and night;
And keep thy heart light lest it make thee sink
When hope has kindled hope, and lured thee to the
    brink.

XLVIII

Or go to Rome, which is the sepulchre
Oh, not of him, but of our joy: 'tis nought   425
That ages, empires, and religions there
Lie buried in the ravage they have wrought;
For such as he can lend,—they borrow not
Glory from those who made the world their prey;
And he is gathered to the kings of thought   430
Who waged contention with their time's decay,
And of the past are all that cannot pass away.

XLIX

Go thou to Rome,—at once the Paradise,
The grave, the city, and the wilderness;
And where its wrecks like shattered mountains rise,   435
And flowering weeds, and fragrant copses dress
The bones of Desolation's nakedness
Pass, till the Spirit of the spot shall lead
Thy footsteps to a slope of green access
Where, like an infant's smile, over the dead   440
A light of laughing flowers along the grass is spread,

L

And grey walls moulder round, on which dull Time
Feeds, like slow fire upon a hoary brand;
And one keen pyramid with wedge sublime,

Pavilioning the dust of him who planned   445
This refuge for his memory, doth stand
Like flame transformed to marble; and beneath,
A field is spread, on which a newer band
Have pitched in Heaven's smile their camp of death,
Welcoming him we lose with scarce extinguished breath.   450

LI

Here pause: these graves are all too young as yet
To have outgrown the sorrow which consigned
Its charge to each; and if the seal is set,
Here, on one fountain of a mourning mind,
Break it not thou! too surely shalt thou find   455
Thine own well full, if thou returnest home,
Of tears and gall. From the world's bitter wind
Seek shelter in the shadow of the tomb.
What Adonais is, why fear we to become?

LII

The One remains, the many change and pass;   460
Heaven's light forever shines, Earth's shadows fly;
Life, like a dome of many-coloured glass,
Stains the white radiance of Eternity,
Until Death tramples it to fragments.—Die,
If thou wouldst be with that which thou dost seek!   465
Follow where all is fled!—Rome's azure sky,
Flowers, ruins, statues, music, words, are weak
The glory they transfuse with fitting truth to speak.

LIII

Why linger, why turn back, why shrink, my Heart?
Thy hopes are gone before: from all things here   470
They have departed; thou shouldst now depart!
A light is past from the revolving year,
And man, and woman; and what still is dear
Attracts to crush, repels to make thee wither.
The soft sky smiles,—the low wind whispers near: 475
'Tis Adonais calls! oh, hasten thither,
No more let life divide what Death can join together.

LIV

That Light whose smile kindles the Universe,
That Beauty in which all things work and move,
That Benediction which the eclipsing Curse   480
Of birth can quench not, that sustaining Love
Which through the web of being blindly wove
By man and beast and earth and air and sea,
Burns bright or dim, as each are mirrors of
The fire for which all thirst; now beams on me,   485
Consuming the last clouds of cold mortality.

LV

The breath whose might I have invoked in song
Descends on me; my spirit's bark is driven,
Far from the shore, far from the trembling throng
Whose sails were never to the tempest given;   490
The massy earth and sphered skies are riven!
I am borne darkly, fearfully, afar;
Whilst burning through the inmost veil of Heaven,
The soul of Adonais, like a star,
Beacons from the abode where the Eternal are.   495
    [1821]

LINES

I

When the lamp is shattered,
The light in the dust lies dead—
When the cloud is scattered,
The rainbow's glory is shed.
When the lute is broken,   5
Sweet tones are remembered not;
When the lips have spoken,
Loved accents are soon forgot.

II

As music and splendour
Survive not the lamp and the lute,   10
The heart's echoes render
No song when the spirit is mute:—
No song but sad dirges,
Like the wind through a ruined cell,
Or the mournful surges   15
That ring the dead seaman's knell.

III

When hearts have once mingled,
Love first leaves the well-built nest;
The weak one is singled
To endure what it once possesst.   20
O, Love! who bewailest
The frailty of all things here,
Why choose you the frailest
For your cradle, your home, and your bier?

IV

Its passions will rock thee,   25
As the storms rock the ravens on high:
Bright reason will mock thee,
Like the sun from a wintry sky.
From thy nest every rafter
Will rot, and thine eagle home   30
Leave thee naked to laughter,
When leaves fall and cold winds come.
[1822]

WITH A GUITAR: TO JANE

ARIEL to MIRANDA:—Take
This slave of music, for the sake

Of him, who is the slave of thee;
And teach it all the harmony
In which thou canst, and only thou,   5
Make the delighted spirit glow,
Till joy denies itself again,
And, too intense, is turned to pain;
For by permission and command
Of thine own Prince Ferdinand,   10
Poor Ariel sends this silent token
Of love that never can be spoken;
Your guardian spirit, Ariel, who
From life to life must still pursue
Your happiness, for thus alone   15
Can Ariel ever find his own.
From Prospero's enchanted cell,
As the mighty verses tell,
To the throne of Naples he
Lit you o'er the trackless sea,   20
Flitting on, your prow before,
Like a living meteor.
When you die, the silent Moon,
In her interlunar swoon,
Is not sadder in her cell   25
Than deserted Ariel;
When you live again on Earth,
Like an unseen Star of birth,
Ariel guides you o'er the sea
Of life from your nativity;   30
Many changes have been run
Since Ferdinand and you begun
Your course of love, and Ariel still
Has tracked your steps and served your will.
Now, in humbler, happier lot,   35
This is all remembered not;
And now, alas! the poor sprite is
Imprisoned for some fault of his
In a body like a grave.—
From you, he only dares to crave   40
For his service and his sorrow,
A smile to day, a song to morrow.

The artist who this idol wrought
To echo all harmonious thought,
Felled a tree, while on the steep   45
The woods were in their winter sleep,
Rocked in that repose divine
On the wind-swept Apennine;
And dreaming, some of autumn past,
And some of spring approaching fast,   50
And some of April birds and showers,
And some of songs in July bowers,
And all of love,—and so this tree—
O that such our death may be—
Died in sleep, and felt no pain   55
To live in happier form again,
From which, beneath Heaven's fairest star,
The artist wrought this lov'd guitar,
And taught it justly to reply
To all who question skilfully,   60
In language gentle as thine own;
Whispering in enamoured tone
Sweet oracles of woods and dells
And summer winds in sylvan cells;
For it had learnt all harmonies   65
Of the plains and of the skies,
Of the forests and the mountains,
And the many-voicéd fountains,
The clearest echoes of the hills,
The softest notes of falling rills,   70
The melodies of birds and bees,
The murmuring of summer seas,
And pattering rain and breathing dew
And airs of evening; and it knew
That seldom-heard mysterious sound,   75
Which, driven on its diurnal round
As it floats through boundless day,
Our world enkindles on its way—
All this it knows, but will not tell
To those who cannot question well   80
The spirit that inhabits it:
It talks according to the wit
Of its companions, and no more
Is heard than has been felt before

By those who tempt it to betray   85
These secrets of an elder day.—
But, sweetly as its answers will
Flatter hands of perfect skill,
It keeps its highest, holiest tone
For our belovèd Jane alone.—   90
[1822]

John Keats

1795=1821

John Keats

JOHN KEATS, the eldest of the five children of Thomas and Frances Keats, was born just outside of London on October 31, 1795. His father—head ostler to John Jennings, Mrs. Keats' own father—died when John was not yet nine years old, leaving an estate of some value for a man in his position. After his mother's remarriage, John and the other three surviving children lived with their maternal grandmother, Mrs. Jennings, who took them to Edmonton after the death of her own husband in 1805. In 1810, John's mother died following a long separation from her apparently opportunistic second husband, and Mrs. Jennings appointed two men guardians to the children. Of these, Richard Abbey, a tea-dealer whose image has come down to us quite tarnished, took charge of the children after the grandmother's death in 1814.

The younger children suffered under Abbey more than John did. In 1803, he had entered nearby Enfield School, run by the humane and courageous John Clarke, whose son, Charles Cowden Clarke, a lifelong friend of literary men, was one of Keats' most important associates. At Enfield Keats received all the formal education he was to have in an atmosphere of kindness and individual attention not characteristic of the English grammar schools of the early nineteenth century. However, this education was enough to move him rapidly to "the realms of gold" on which he was to draw for his poetry. In 1811, John Keats left school to be bound as an apprentice to a surgeon-apothecary, whom he left in 1815 to become an apothecary student in Guy's Hospital, London. In July of the following year he passed his examination and was licensed as an apothecary in the United Kingdom.

Ironically, however, during his months at Guy's Hospital, John Keats was approaching the end rather than the beginning of his medical career. His early literary interests continued to develop, and in the spring of 1816 his meeting with Leigh Hunt—editor of the newspaper *The Examiner*, recently released from a two-year imprisonment for his supposed libel on the Prince Regent—accelerated his motion toward the decision to abandon medical work and devote himself fully to his literary activity—a decision he was to make the following spring. On May 5, 1816, Keats' first publication, the sonnet beginning "O Solitude! if I must with thee dwell," appeared in *The Examiner*. On December 1 of that year, Hunt published an article upon the "Young Poets" in his paper in which he celebrated the emergence of several poets. He included Shelley but emphasized Keats, whose sonnet "On First Looking into Chapman's Homer" was quoted in full. Keats now came to know others of similar interest, such as the painter Benjamin Robert Haydon, whom he met through Hunt, and, more casually, William Hazlitt and Charles Lamb, whom he then met through Haydon. His associations with Shelley were slight, and apparently any hopes which Leigh Hunt might have held for their friendship were bound to be unfulfilled. Keats was in all probability somewhat overwhelmed by Shelley's greater productivity at this time, and, as Hunt himself later observed, he regarded Shelley's higher social position with some suspicion. John Keats' brother George, apprenticed in 1811 in Mr. Abbey's counting house and now a businessman in his own right, remained beside John when he decided to abandon medicine in 1817 (Mr. Abbey was expectedly horrified) and, like the literary men with whom John Keats was now associated, encouraged him in the publication of the volume of *Poems* in the spring of 1817.

The volume contained seventeen sonnets, including those already published, three verse epistles, the two poems in which Keats presented some of his ideas about poetry—"I Stood Tip-toe" and "Sleep and Poetry"—and a variety of lesser works. The quality is uneven, but the book represents a far more promising beginning than many poets of Keats' ultimate stature have shown. His friends were intensely hopeful for the volume, but they were to be disappointed: The sale was limited, and the reviews in the periodicals, though frequently just, did not confirm their expectations. On occasion, of course, Keats himself rather than his poems was condemned by the reviewers, and then because of his association with Hunt and the supposedly radical young intellectuals around him.

Later in 1817, Keats visited the Isle of Wight and Canterbury and then returned to the London suburbs. He finished "Endymion," which was to be his longest poem, in late November. For several weeks during the winter he served as drama critic of *The Champion*. His friendship ripened with Charles Armitage Brown, who was to be one of his more important contemporary biographers. At this time he saw something of William Wordsworth, who had by this time passed through the transformation of his former self.

In March 1818, John went to Teignemouth in South Devon, where he might be with his younger brother Tom. Teignemouth was in a mild climate, which was considered necessary to cure the consumption from which Tom was acutely suffering. "Endymion" was published in April, and in May John brought Tom back to London, where George was waiting to be married at the end of the month and to emigrate to America in June. John Keats and Charles Armitage Brown accompanied George and his wife to Liverpool, from which they were to sail. The two men then proceeded on a walking tour northward, passing through Lancaster and the Lake District, into Scotland, across the North Channel to Belfast, then back to Scotland. At Cromarty, on Moray Firth, Keats succumbed to a persisting sore throat and consulted a physician, who advised that he sail back to England, allowing Brown to proceed alone with the tour. He returned to London in late August, to find his brother Tom perceptibly sinking.

On September 1, 1818, *Blackwood's Edinburgh Magazine*, the most vitriolic though perhaps the most humorous of the extreme Tory periodicals, published—in one of six articles running from 1817 to 1819 directed principally against Hunt and entitled "On the Cockney School of Poetry"—its review of "Endymion" and a personal attack upon Keats himself. Later that month *The Quarterly Review* followed in the attack. There were other reviews, but these two are most important; their total effect upon Keats' health has long been a matter of rumor and speculation. Although Keats himself remarked in a letter that such notice as this merely brought him more public attention, he was clearly sensitive to this kind of severe criticism; yet it is unlikely that he was emotionally and physically destroyed by these attacks, as Shelley in part suggested in "Adonais" and Byron in a flippant verse beginning, " 'Who killed John Keats?'/'I,' says the *Quarterly.*" Whatever emotional and physical effect there was, Tom Keats' death on December 1 clearly intensified it.

In the autumn of 1818, Keats met Fanny Brawne, a young woman of eighteen. Apparently more sensitive, more aware of the particular kind of man John Keats was than history has often depicted her, Fanny came to love Keats very much; they were engaged on Christmas Day of that year. Although their engagement lasted into 1820, about the time that Keats made his journey to Italy, it was probably apparent to him, and possibly to her, from late 1819, that a happy life together was not to be theirs.

Despite all else, however, 1819 was John Keats' "Annus Mirabilis." It was then that he achieved his greatest poetic intensity, writing the major odes—"To a Nightingale," "On a Grecian Urn," "To Psyche," "On Melancholy" and "On Indolence"—as well as "The Eve of St. Agnes," "La Belle Dame Sans Merci" and "Lamia." These, with the earlier poem "Isabella, or the Pot of Basil" and several others, were published in 1820 as *Lamia, Isabella, The Eve of St. Agnes, and Other Poems* by John Keats, Author of "Endymion." The publication brought forth the inevitable reviews, but this time even the short notice in *Blackwood's* was tempered, and the other Tory journals that had abused Keats on the earlier occasions now displayed moderation, admitting his genius and blaming what faults he possessed only on his association with Leigh Hunt. Francis Jeffrey, the editor of the Whig *Edinburgh Review,* wrote an article which appeared in August 1820 on both "Endymion" and the present poems. In this article he described Keats' work as among the richest and sweetest of the blossoms that marked "a second spring in our poetry." Public recognition was beginning to move toward Keats, but at this time he had only a few months to live.

Toward the end of the year 1819, there were signs of weariness and decline both in his physical being and in the quality of his work. Keats' mood was frequently bitter, and at times his thoughts morbid. Early in February he had a severe seizure, the inevitable meaning of which could not escape him; from this time forth he wrote no more poetry. He was confined to his room for some weeks, though toward the end of March

1820 he was permitted to attend a private showing of Haydon's massive picture, at last finished, *Christ's Entry into Jerusalem*, in which Keats' face, like those of Wordsworth and Hazlitt, appears among the crowds. His dark moods intensified, and in his letters to Fanny Brawne he frequently displayed irrational anger and suspicion. In the spring he suffered further hemorrhages, and his physician concluded that the only chance for prolonging his life lay in his spending the winter in Italy. Shelley, hearing of Keats' situation, generously offered to share the Shelleys' Pisan residence with him, but of course in his emotional state Keats was hardly susceptible to this suggestion from one whom he had originally regarded without warmth. In mid-September, with little hope for the success of his journey and with intense pain at leaving Fanny Brawne, John Keats, accompanied by the painter Joseph Severn, sailed for Naples on the ship *Maria Crowther*.

The story of Keats' last months is one of anguish and hopelessness, revealing no pattern except the gradual realization of the inevitable. Severn remained with him, tireless and uncomplaining to the end, assuring himself a place in the history of man's humanity, regardless of what his meager talents prevented him from achieving in the history of man's art. After a long journey, they reached Naples in October 1820, where they were quarantined for the last ten days of the month. From Naples they proceeded to Rome, where a house had been arranged for them at 26 Piazza di Spagna, next to the steps leading up to the Church of the Trinità on the Pincian Hill. Here Keats had another severe hemorrhage on December 10, followed by further decline and a serious attack in late January. He died shortly before midnight on February 23, 1821. On the stone above Keats' grave, located in the Protestant Cemetery of Rome near the Tomb of Caius Cestius and not far from the spot where Shelley is buried, the ironic words appear, "Here lies One/Whose Name was writ in Water."

II

All true poems should "explain themselves . . . without comment," John Keats wrote on one occasion. The tendency during much of the nineteenth century was to take this and similar utterances with complete literalism. There was no realization that the critical remarks as well as the poems of Keats—perhaps more than those of any other of the major English Romantic poets—communicate at more than one level of meaning. Keats' comment, "We hate poetry that has a palpable design upon us," emphasizes his rejection of didactic poetry as a form of art, of poetry that was to serve any purpose other than its own. His somewhat exaggerated remark elsewhere—"I have never yet been able to perceive how any thing can be known for truth by consequitive reasoning—and yet it must be. . . . However it may be, O for a Life of Sensations rather than of Thoughts"—does indeed stress the large part played by experience and sensation in Keats' world view. However, this remark was taken as evidence of the poet's absolute anti-intellectualism by many Victorian and Edwardian Keatsians. Until the last thirty-five years or so it has been generally believed that in his poetry Keats used merely sensuous effects which defy analysis or objective comment. Clearly, if we read his poems only at this level, we shall come to similar conclusions, but then we are overlooking all other levels of possible communication in the poems themselves. To propose that as a poet Keats was not intellectual may be to confuse *prescriptive* with *intellectual* poetry, in this instance to ignore the fact that though Keats did not subordinate his poetry to any intellectual purpose—to the support of a philosophic system, for example—he worked from a complex æsthetic viewpoint and employed techniques that are themselves far from simple and frequently paradoxical.

For Keats, as for other Romantic thinkers, the world in which man lives is manifestly imperfect and in itself not perfectible: "In truth I do not believe in . . . perfectibility—the nature of the world will not admit of it," he wrote on one occasion. Man's lot is limited, for "the inhabitants of the world will correspond to itself." Rejecting the neat systems that supported Enlightenment thought, Keats did not conceive of reason as leading man toward perfection—personal or social. He used an analogy: "Let the fish philosophise the ice away from the Rivers in winter time and they shall be at continual play in the tepid delight of summer." Man's province is experience, and a significant part of experience is suffering: "Until we are sick, we understand not"; maturity comes with the acceptance of pain as an essential attribute of life. The world is, to use Keats' term, "the vale of Soul-making," which he explained by distinguishing "Soul" from "an Intelligence":

> There may be intelligences or sparks of the divinity in millions—but they are not Souls till they acquire identities, till each one is personally itself. I[n]telligences are atoms of perception—they know and they see and they are pure, in short they are God—how then are Souls to be made? . . . How but by the medium of a world like this? . . . Do you not see how necessary a World of Pains and troubles is to school an Intelligence and make it a soul? A place where the heart must feel and suffer in a thousand diverse ways!

In short, soul-making is the identity of the self. It is the development of the reality of the inner world from which, in characteristic Romantic form, the meaning of the outer world is derived: "My own being which I know to be becomes of more consequence to me than the crowds of Shadows in the Shape of Man and women that inhabit a kingdom. The Soul is a world of itself and has enough to do in its own home."

The dynamic nature of man's being causes him to strive toward soul-making or self-identity which, in its fulfillment, brings him moments of truth. These strivings are necessarily paradoxical, however, because they emphasize to man his own ephemeral existence, the very futility of his attempting to hold forever in this life these same visions of truth. Here Keats accepted the paradox of imperfection, proposing simply that although perfection is not possible for man in "the vale of Soul-making," he should act as if it were, striving for these brief moments of truth, whatever pain they may bring with them. The speaker in the "Ode on a Grecian Urn" is representative: He exists in time and must succumb to it, but in his contemplation of the timeless figures on the time-defying urn he experiences a moment of truth which intensifies his own awareness that it is but a *moment*. More precisely, the figures on the urn—cast in a circle, the traditional symbol of perfection—illustrate the paradox of imperfection, for the lovers eternally approach the maidens without the possibility of fulfillment.

Keats' acceptance of the paradox of imperfection lies at

the heart of his proposal concerning the nature of what he calls "negative capability":

> at once it struck me, what quality went to form a Man of Achievement especially in Literature & which Shakespeare possessed so enormously—I mean *Negative Capability*, that is when man is capable of being in uncertainties, Mysteries, doubts, without any irritable reaching after fact & reason. . . . This pursued through Volumes would perhaps take us no further than this, that with a great poet the sense of Beauty overcomes every other consideration, or rather obliterates all consideration.

The poet, unable to discover truth by rational means, seeks it by the assertion of self, which is essentially paradoxical: the only way by which the poet can achieve full assertion—or identity—of the self is by losing all awareness of the self in the object of contemplation, in the subject of his poem and in the poem itself. Only by losing his identity as an *individual* can the real poet become aware of—feel—the identity of others and thereby discover his identity as a *poet*. It is from this point of view that in 1818 Keats wrote in a letter, "I feel more and more every day, as my imagination strengthens, that I do not live in this world alone but in a thousand worlds." In this sense, "the poetical Character . . . . has no self—it is every thing and nothing—It has no character." The quality required for the poetic act, in effect the essence of the poetic being, is imagination. Unlike Coleridge, Keats made no attempt to analyze or define imagination, except that, like Shelley, he distinguished it from reason. Imagination is a pure act, recognized in its achievement rather than in its components, defying explanation in terms of cause and effect: "I am certain of nothing but of the holiness of the Heart's affections and the truth of Imagination." Here truth is to be found neither in rational propositions nor in baldly perceived experience, but rather in the awareness of beauty: "What the imagination seizes as Beauty must be truth—whether it existed before or not." Obviously, reality is potentially within the poet, who brings it to the objects of contemplation by losing himself in these objects and thereby creating a poem that transcends both the poet and the subject of his poem.

At the heart of the poetic experience, the measure of its success, is what Keats called its "intensity, capable of making all disagreeables evaporate, from their being in close relationship with Beauty & Truth." For the poet, for Keats specifically, intensity is to be achieved in art by the concentration upon physical detail. The poem "Isabella, or The Pot of Basil," for example, must be read, in part at least, as the story of one kind of quest for beauty, but it is always sensuous beauty, which Isabella momentarily achieves because she eliminates the ordinary human distinction between life and death and—in an act that is in its way poetic—by her suffering and through her intensity she synthesizes elements not usually considered beautiful. However, as a poem "Isabella" is also a self-conscious illustration of the Keatsian achievement in creating a work of art from the discordant elements of unhappy experience. A similar intensity informs the poem "Ode on Melancholy": Here the speaker, by contemplating the paradox that for man Melancholy is at the heart of his brief vision of Beauty, creates the self-absorbing poem, a work of art and thus a form of beauty that will defy time; from the joylessness of his first recognition he derives joy in art and a moment of truth, at the heart of which perception he again finds his melancholy recognition of his own human impermanence. In its outward forms beauty is related to the sensuous, truth to the spiritual; they become identical for the moment that the poet loses self-awareness entirely in the object which he contemplates. In this sense Keats wrote at one point, "I never can feel certain of any truth but from a clear perception of its Beauty." Thus, the speaker in the "Ode on a Grecian Urn," who is a poet as well as an observer, can justifiably conclude his contemplation of the urn, in which he has momentarily lost all self-awareness, with the frequently quoted but sometimes puzzling couplet: "Beauty is truth, truth beauty,—that is all/ Ye know on earth, and all ye need to know."

These lines suggest another element in the Keatsian æsthetic. To this point the speaker has used the pronoun *thou* in addressing the contemplated urn, but he concludes with *ye*, clearly implying the reality of the reader, one who, like the poet in front of the urn, contemplates the poem and loses self-awareness in it. For Keats the reader was essential. In axioms that he proposed in 1818, concerning the nature of good poetry, he was much concerned with means of affecting the reader. Although in the poem itself the poet expresses an intensity of experience, the poem contains nothing that is reducible to a verbal proposition, and its value must ultimately be derived from the reader's own response to it. The urn has not communicated to the poet but, instead, revealed to him what he himself has brought to his contemplations of the urn; consequently, the poem evokes from the reader what he carries to the experience of reading it. There can of course be a mutually comprehended basis for the activity of a symbol, such as that suggested by the word *hyacinth* in the eleventh stanza of the poem "Isabella," but the total achievement of a poem depends upon the complex interaction of symbols— the implicit allusions of which may not all be equally apparent to everyone concerned with the poem—by which each symbol accumulates value and function. Put quite simply, a poem is not ultimately a "meaning" or "message." This is essentially the point that Keats wished to make when he rejected the proposition that poetry "must have a purpose."

For Keats, in other words, a real poem was essentially far more than an allegory. His own poem "Lamia" is not, as we might first be disposed to regard it, an examination of the conflict between mind and body. Instead, it explores the experience of self-fulfillment through the loss of self-awareness— in this instance as Lycius surrenders to his intense response to Lamia—in effect, the poetic experience, which by its very nature must, in "the vale of Soul-making," be momentary. In this poem, as in one way or another throughout his major work, Keats was essentially concerned with the human condition, revealing its paradoxical nature with all the intensity that his imagination could achieve. Though life in its individual forms must pass away, the poetry which it evokes is enduring; or, as Keats himself wrote in a somewhat more dramatic context in one of his sonnets, "The poetry of earth is never dead."

John Keats

WRITTEN ON THE DAY THAT MR. LEIGH HUNT LEFT PRISON

What though, for showing truth to flatter'd state,
  Kind Hunt was shut in prison, yet has he,
  In his immortal spirit, been as free
As the sky-searching lark, and as elate.
Minion of grandeur! think you he did wait?   5
  Think you he nought but prison walls did see,
  Till, so unwilling, thou unturn'dst the key?
Ah, no! far happier, nobler was his fate!
In Spenser's halls he strayed, and bowers fair,
  Culling enchanted flowers; and he flew   10
With daring Milton through the fields of air:
  To regions of his own his genius true
Took happy flights. Who shall his fame impair
  When thou art dead, and all thy wretched crew?
[1815]

I STOOD TIP-TOE UPON A LITTLE HILL

I stood tip-toe upon a little hill,
The air was cooling, and so very still,
That the sweet buds which with a modest pride
Pull droopingly, in slanting curve aside,
Their scantly leaved, and finely tapering stems,   5
Had not yet lost those starry diadems
Caught from the early sobbing of the morn.
The clouds were pure and white as flocks new shorn,
And fresh from the clear brook; sweetly they slept
On the blue fields of heaven, and then there crept   10
A little noiseless noise among the leaves,
Born of the very sigh that silence heaves:
For not the faintest motion could be seen
Of all the shades that slanted o'er the green.
There was wide wand'ring for the greediest eye,   15
To peer about upon variety;
Far round the horizon's crystal air to skim,

And trace the dwindled edgings of its brim;
To picture out the quaint, and curious bending
Of a fresh woodland alley, never ending;   20
Or by the bowery clefts, and leafy shelves,
Guess where the jaunty streams refresh themselves.
I gazed awhile, and felt as light, and free
As though the fanning wings of Mercury
Had played upon my heels: I was light-hearted,   25
And many pleasures to my vision started;
So I straightway began to pluck a posey
Of luxuries bright, milky, soft and rosy.

A bush of May flowers with the bees about them;
Ah, sure no tasteful nook would be without them;   30
And let a lush laburnum oversweep them,
And let long grass grow round the roots to keep them
Moist, cool and green; and shade the violets,
That they may bind the moss in leafy nets.

A filbert hedge with wild briar overtwined,   35
And clumps of woodbine taking the soft wind
Upon their summer thrones; there too should be
The frequent chequer of a youngling tree,
That with a score of light green brethren shoots
From the quaint mossiness of aged roots: 40
Round which is heard a spring-head of clear waters
Babbling so wildly of its lovely daughters
The spreading blue bells: it may haply mourn
That such fair clusters should be rudely torn
From their fresh beds, and scattered thoughtlessly   45
By infant hands, left on the path to die.
Open afresh your round of starry folds,
Ye ardent marigolds!
Dry up the moisture from your golden lids,
For great Apollo bids   50
That in these days your praises should be sung
On many harps, which he has lately strung;
And when again your dewiness he kisses,
Tell him, I have you in my world of blisses:
So haply when I rove in some far vale,   55
His mighty voice may come upon the gale.

Here are sweet peas, on tip-toe for a flight:
With wings of gentle flush o'er delicate white,
And taper fingers catching at all things,
To bind them all about with tiny rings.   60

Linger awhile upon some bending planks
That lean against a streamlet's rushy banks,
And watch intently Nature's gentle doings:
They will be found softer than ring-dove's cooings.
How silent comes the water round that bend;   65
Not the minutest whisper does it send
To the o'erchanging sallows: blades of grass
Slowly across the chequer'd shadows pass.
Why, you might read two sonnets, ere they reach
To where the hurrying freshnesses aye preach   70
A natural sermon o'er their pebbly beds;
Where swarms of minnows show their little heads,
Staying their wavy bodies 'gainst the streams,
To taste the luxury of sunny beams
Temper'd with coolness. How they ever wrestle   75
With their own sweet delight, and ever nestle
Their silver bellies on the pebbly sand.
If you but scantily hold out the hand,
That very instant not one will remain;
But turn your eye, and they are there again.   80
The ripples seem right glad to reach those cresses,
And cool themselves among the em'rald tresses;
The while they cool themselves, they freshness give,
And moisture, that the bowery green may live:
So keeping up an interchange of favours,   85
Like good men in the truth of their behaviours.
Sometimes goldfinches one by one will drop
From low hung branches; little space they stop;
But sip, and twitter, and their feathers sleek;
Then off at once, as in a wanton freak: 90
Or perhaps, to show their black, and golden wings,
Pausing upon their yellow flutterings.
Were I in such a place, I sure should pray
That nought less sweet might call my thoughts away,
Than the soft rustle of a maiden's gown   95
Fanning away the dandelion's down;
Than the light music of her nimble toes

Patting against the sorrel as she goes.
How she would start, and blush, thus to be caught
Playing in all her innocence of thought.   100
O let me lead her gently o'er the brook,
Watch her half-smiling lips, and downward look;
O let me for one moment touch her wrist;
Let me one moment to her breathing list;
And as she leaves me may she often turn   105
Her fair eyes looking through her locks aubùrne.
What next? A tuft of evening primroses,
O'er which the mind may hover till it dozes;
O'er which it well might take a pleasant sleep,
But that 'tis ever startled by the leap   110
Of buds into ripe flowers; or by the flitting
Of diverse moths, that aye their rest are quitting;
Or by the moon lifting her silver rim
Above a cloud, and with a gradual swim
Coming into the blue with all her light.   115
O Maker of sweet poets, dear delight
Of this fair world, and all its gentle livers;
Spangler of clouds, halo of crystal rivers,
Mingler with leaves, and dew and tumbling streams,
Closer of lovely eyes to lovely dreams,   120
Lover of loneliness, and wandering,
Of upcast eye, and tender pondering!
Thee must I praise above all other glories
That smile us on to tell delightful stories.
For what has made the sage or poet write   125
But the fair paradise of Nature's light?
In the calm grandeur of a sober line,
We see the waving of the mountain pine;
And when a tale is beautifully staid,
We feel the safety of a hawthorn glade: 130
When it is moving on luxurious wings,
The soul is lost in pleasant smotherings:
Fair dewy roses brush against our faces,
And flowering laurels spring from diamond vases;
O'er head we see the jasmine and sweet briar,   135
And bloomy grapes laughing from green attire;
While at our feet, the voice of crystal bubbles
Charms us at once away from all our troubles:
So that we feel uplifted from the world,

Walking upon the white clouds wreath'd and curl'd. 140
So felt he, who first told, how Psyche went
On the smooth wind to realms of wonderment;
What Psyche felt, and Love, when their full lips
First touch'd; what amorous, and fondling nips
They gave each other's cheeks; with all their sighs,   145
And how they kist each other's tremulous eyes:
The silver lamp,—the ravishment,—the wonder—
The darkness,—loneliness,—the fearful thunder;
Their woes gone by, and both to heaven upflown,
To bow for gratitude before Jove's throne.   150
So did he feel, who pull'd the boughs aside,
That we might look into a forest wide,
To catch a glimpse of Fawns, and Dryades
Coming with softest rustle through the trees;
And garlands woven of flowers wild, and sweet,   155
Upheld on ivory wrists, or sporting feet:
Telling us how fair, trembling Syrinx fled
Arcadian Pan, with such a fearful dread.
Poor nymph,—poor Pan,—how he did weep to find,
Nought but a lovely sighing of the wind   160
Along the reedy stream; a half heard strain,
Full of sweet desolation—balmy pain.

What first inspired a bard of old to sing
Narcissus pining o'er the untainted spring?
In some delicious ramble, he had found   165
A little space, with boughs all woven round;
And in the midst of all, a clearer pool
Than e'er reflected in its pleasant cool
The blue sky here, and there, serenely peeping
Through tendril wreaths fantastically creeping.   170
And on the bank a lonely flower he spied,
A meek and forlorn flower, with naught of pride,
Drooping its beauty o'er the watery clearness,
To woo its own sad image into nearness:
Deaf to light Zephyrus it would not move;   175
But still would seem to droop, to pine, to love
So while the Poet stood in this sweet spot,
Some fainter gleamings o'er his fancy shot;
Nor was it long ere he had told the tale
Of young Narcissus, and sad Echo's bale.   180

Where had he been, from whose warm head out-flew
That sweetest of all songs, that ever new,
That aye refreshing, pure deliciousness,
Coming ever to bless
The wanderer by moonlight? to him bringing   **185**
Shapes from the invisible world, unearthly singing
From out the middle air, from flowery nests,
And from the pillowy silkiness that rests
Full in the speculation of the stars.
Ah! surely he had burst our mortal bars;   **190**
Into some wond'rous region he had gone,
To search for thee, divine Endymion!

He was a Poet, sure a lover too,
Who stood on Latmus' top, what time there blew
Soft breezes from the myrtle vale below;   **195**
And brought in faintness solemn, sweet, and slow
A hymn from Dian's temple; while upswelling,
The incense went to her own starry dwelling.
But though her face was clear as infant's eyes,
Though she stood smiling o'er the sacrifice,   **200**
The Poet wept at her so piteous fate,
Wept that such beauty should be desolate:
So in fine wrath some golden sounds he won,
And gave meek Cynthia her Endymion.

Queen of the wide air; thou most lovely queen   **205**
Of all the brightness that mine eyes have seen!
As thou exceedest all things in thy shine,
So every tale, does this sweet tale of thine.
O for three words of honey, that I might
Tell but one wonder of thy bridal night!   **210**

Where distant ships do seem to show their keels,
Phoebus awhile delayed his mighty wheels,
And turned to smile upon thy bashful eyes,
Ere he his unseen pomp would solemnize.
The evening weather was so bright, and clear,   **215**
That men of health were of unusual cheer;
Stepping like Homer at the trumpet's call,
Or young Apollo on the pedestal:
And lovely women were as fair and warm,

As Venus looking sideways in alarm.   220
The breezes were ethereal, and pure,
And crept through half closed lattices to cure
The languid sick; it cool'd their fever'd sleep,
And soothed them into slumbers full and deep.
Soon they awoke clear eyed: nor burnt with thirsting,   225
Nor with hot fingers, nor with temples bursting:
And springing up, they met the wond'ring sight
Of their dear friends, nigh foolish with delight;
Who feel their arms, and breasts, and kiss and stare,
And on their placid foreheads part the hair.   230
Young men, and maidens at each other gaz'd
With hands held back, and motionless, amaz'd
To see the brightness in each other's eyes;
And so they stood, fill'd with a sweet surprise,
Until their tongues were loos'd in poesy.   235
Therefore no lover did of anguish die:
But the soft numbers, in that moment spoken,
Made silken ties, that never may be broken.
Cynthia! I cannot tell the greater blisses,
That follow'd thine, and thy dear shepherd's kisses: 240
Was there a Poet born?—but now no more,
My wand'ring spirit must no further soar.—
     [1816]

from EPISTLES

TO MY BROTHER GEORGE

Full many a dreary hour have I past,
My brain bewilder'd, and my mind o'ercast
With heaviness; in seasons when I've thought
No spherey strains by me could e'er be caught
From the blue dome, though I to dimness gaze   5
On the far depth where sheeted lightning plays;
Or, on the wavy grass outstretch'd supinely,
Pry 'mong the stars, to strive to think divinely:
That I should never hear Apollo's song,
Though feathery clouds were floating all along   10
The purple west, and, two bright streaks between,

The golden lyre itself were dimly seen:
That the still murmur of the honey bee
Would never teach a rural song to me:
That the bright glance from beauty's eyelids slanting   15
Would never make a lay of mine enchanting,
Or warm my breast with ardour to unfold
Some tale of love and arms in time of old.

But there are times, when those that love the bay,
Fly from all sorrowing far, far away;   20
A sudden glow comes on them, naught they see
In water, earth, or air, but poesy.
It has been said, dear George, and true I hold it,
(For knightly Spenser to Libertas told it,)
That when a Poet is in such a trance,   25
In air he sees white coursers paw, and prance,
Bestridden of gay knights, in gay apparel,
Who at each other tilt in playful quarrel,
And what we, ignorantly, sheet-lightning call,
Is the swift opening of their wide portal,   30
When the bright warder blows his trumpet clear,
Whose tones reach naught on earth but Poet's ear.
When these enchanted portals open wide,
And through the light the horsemen swiftly glide,
The Poet's eye can reach those golden halls,   35
And view the glory of their festivals:
Their ladies fair, that in the distance seem
Fit for the silv'ring of a seraph's dream;
Their rich brimm'd goblets, that incessant run
Like the bright spots that move about the sun;   40
And, when upheld, the wine from each bright jar
Pours with the lustre of a falling star.
Yet further off, are dimly seen their bowers,
Of which, no mortal eye can reach the flowers;
And 'tis right just, for well Apollo knows   45
'Twould make the Poet quarrel with the rose.
All that's reveal'd from that far seat of blisses,
Is, the clear fountains' interchanging kisses,
As gracefully descending, light and thin,
Like silver streaks across a dolphin's fin,   50
When he upswimmeth from the coral caves,
And sports with half his tail above the waves.

These wonders strange he sees, and many more,
Whose head is pregnant with poetic lore.
Should he upon an evening ramble fare   55
With forehead to the soothing breezes bare,
Would he naught see but the dark, silent blue
With all its diamonds trembling through and through?
Or the coy moon, when in the waviness
Of whitest clouds she does her beauty dress,   60
And staidly paces higher up, and higher,
Like a sweet nun in holy-day attire?
Ah, yes! much more would start into his sight—
The revelries, and mysteries of night:
And should I ever see them, I will tell you   65
Such tales as needs must with amazement spell you.

These are the living pleasures of the bard:
But richer far posterity's award.
What does he murmur with his latest breath,
While his proud eye looks through the film of death? 70
"What though I leave this dull, and earthly mould,
"Yet shall my spirit lofty converse hold
"With after times.—The patriot shall feel
"My stern alarum, and unsheath his steel;
"Or, in the senate thunder out my numbers   75
"To startle princes from their easy slumbers.
"The sage will mingle with each moral theme
"My happy thoughts sententious; he will teem
"With lofty periods when my verses fire him,
"And then I'll stoop from heaven to inspire him.   80
"Lays have I left of such a dear delight
"That maids will sing them on their bridal night.
"Gay villagers, upon a morn of May,
"When they have tried their gentle limbs with play,
"And form'd a snowy circle on the grass,   85
"And plac'd in midst of all that lovely lass
"Who chosen is their queen,—with her fine head
"Crowned with flowers purple, white, and red:
"For there the lily, and the musk-rose, sighing,
"Are emblems true of hapless lovers dying: 90
"Between her breasts, that never yet felt trouble,
"A bunch of violets full blown, and double,
"Serenely sleep:—she from a casket takes

"A little book,—and then a joy awakes
"About each youthful heart,—with stifled cries,   95
"And rubbing of white hands, and sparkling eyes:
"For she 's to read a tale of hopes, and fears;
"One that I foster'd in my youthful years:
"The pearls, that on each glist'ning circlet sleep,
"Gush ever and anon with silent creep,   100
"Lured by the innocent dimples. To sweet rest
"Shall the dear babe, upon its mother's breast,
"Be lull'd with songs of mine. Fair world, adieu!
"Thy dales, and hills, are fading from my view:
"Swiftly I mount, upon wide spreading pinions,   105
"Far from the narrow bounds of thy dominions.
"Full joy I feel, while thus I cleave the air,
"That my soft verse will charm thy daughters fair,
"And warm thy sons!" Ah, my dear friend and brother,
Could I, at once, my mad ambition smother,   110
For tasting joys like these, sure I should be
Happier, and dearer to society.
At times, 'tis true, I've felt relief from pain
When some bright thought has darted through my brain:
Through all that day I've felt a greater pleasure   115
Than if I'd brought to light a hidden treasure.
As to my sonnets, though none else should heed them,
I feel delighted, still, that you should read them.
Of late, too, I have had much calm enjoyment,
Stretch'd on the grass at my best lov'd employment   120
Of scribbling lines for you. These things I thought
While, in my face, the freshest breeze I caught.
E'en now I'm pillow'd on a bed of flowers
That crowns a lofty clift, which proudly towers
Above the ocean-waves. The stalks, and blades,   125
Chequer my tablet with their quivering shades.
On one side is a field of drooping oats,
Through which the poppies show their scarlet coats;
So pert and useless, that they bring to mind
The scarlet coats that pester human-kind.   130
And on the other side, outspread, is seen
Ocean's blue mantle streak'd with purple, and green.
Now 'tis I see a canvass'd ship, and now
Mark the bright silver curling round her prow.
I see the lark down-dropping to his nest,   135

And the broad winged sea-gull never at rest;
For when no more he spreads his feathers free,
His breast is dancing on the restless sea.
Now I direct my eyes into the west,
Which at this moment is in sunbeams drest: 140
Why westward turn? 'Twas but to say adieu!
'Twas but to kiss my hand, dear George, to you!
  [1816]

HOW MANY BARDS GILD THE LAPSES OF TIME

How many bards gild the lapses of time!
  A few of them have ever been the food
  Of my delighted fancy,—I could brood
Over their beauties, earthly, or sublime:
And often, when I sit me down to rhyme,   5
  These will in throngs before my mind intrude:
  But no confusion, no disturbance rude
Do they occasion; 'tis a pleasing chime.
So the unnumber'd sounds that evening store;
  The songs of birds—the whisp'ring of the leaves—   10
The voice of waters—the great bell that heaves
  With solemn sound,—and thousand others more,
That distance of recognizance bereaves,
  Make pleasing music, and not wild uproar.
    [1816]

O SOLITUDE! IF I MUST WITH THEE DWELL

O Solitude! if I must with thee dwell,
  Let it be among the jumbled heap
  Of murkey buildings; climb with me the steep,—
Nature's observatory—whence the dell,
Its flowery slopes, its river's crystal swell,   5
  May seem a span; let me thy vigils keep
  'Mongst boughs pavillion'd, where the deer's swift leap

Startles the wild bee from the fox-glove bell.
But though I'll gladly trace these scenes with thee,
  Yet the sweet converse of an innocent mind,   10
Whose words are images of thoughts refin'd,
  Is my soul's pleasure; and it sure must be
Almost the highest bliss of human kind,
  When to thy haunts two kindred spirits flee.
      [1816]

KEEN, FITFUL GUSTS ARE WHISP'RING HERE AND THERE

  Keen, fitful gusts are whisp'ring here and there
    Among the bushes half leafless, and dry;
    The stars look very cold about the sky,
  And I have many miles on foot to fare.
  Yet feel I little of the cool bleak air,   5
    Or of the dead leaves rustling drearily,
    Or of those silver lamps that burn on high,
  Or of the distance from home's pleasant lair:
  For I am brimfull of the friendliness
    That in a little cottage I have found;   10
  Of fair-hair'd Milton's eloquent distress,
    And all his love for gentle Lycid drown'd;
  Of lovely Laura in her light green dress,
    And faithful Petrarch gloriously crown'd.
      [1816]

TO ONE WHO HAS BEEN LONG IN CITY PENT

  To one who has been long in city pent,
    'Tis very sweet to look into the fair
    And open face of heaven,—to breathe a prayer
  Full in the smile of the blue firmament.
  Who is more happy, when, with heart's content,   5
    Fatigued he sinks into some pleasant lair
    Of wavy grass, and reads a debonair

And gentle tale of love and languishment?
Returning home at evening, with an ear
    Catching the notes of Philomel,—an eye   10
Watching the sailing cloudlet's bright career,
    He mourns that day so soon has glided by:
E'en like the passage of an angel's tear
That falls through the clear ether silently.
    [1816]

ON FIRST LOOKING INTO CHAPMAN'S HOMER

Much have I travell'd in the realms of gold,
    And many goodly states and kingdoms seen;
    Round many western islands have I been
Which bards in fealty to Apollo hold.
Oft of one wide expanse had I been told   5
    That deep-brow'd Homer ruled as his demesne;
    Yet did I never breathe its pure serene
Till I heard Chapman speak out loud and bold:
Then felt I like some watcher of the skies
    When a new planet swims into his ken;   10
Or like stout Cortez when with eagle eyes
    He stare 'd at the Pacific—and all his men
Look 'd at each other with a wild surmise—
    Silent, upon a peak in Darien.
    [1816]

ON LEAVING SOME FRIENDS AT AN EARLY HOUR

Give me a golden pen, and let me lean
    On heap'd up flowers, in regions clear, and far;
    Bring me a tablet whiter than a star,
Or hand of hymning angel, when 'tis seen
The silver strings of heavenly harp atween: 5
    And let there glide by many a pearly car,
    Pink robes, and wavy hair, and diamond jar,

And half discovered wings, and glances keen.
The while let music wander round my ears,
    And as it reaches each delicious ending,   10
        Let me write down a line of glorious tone,
And full of many wonders of the spheres:
    For what a height my spirit is contending!
        'Tis not content so soon to be alone.
       [1816]

ADDRESSED TO HAYDON

Highmindedness, a jealousy for good,
    A loving-kindness for the great man's fame,
    Dwells here and there with people of no name,
In noisome alley, and in pathless wood:
And where we think the truth least understood,   5
    Oft may be found a "singleness of aim",
    That ought to frighten into hooded shame
A money-mong'ring, pitiable brood.
How glorious this affection for the cause
    Of stedfast genius, toiling gallantly!   10
What when a stout unbending champion awes
    Envy, and Malice to their native sty?
Unnumber'd souls breathe out a still applause,
    Proud to behold him in his country's eye.
       [1816]

ADDRESSED TO THE SAME

Great spirits now on earth are sojourning;
    He of the cloud, the cataract, the lake,
Who on Helvellyn's summit, wide awake,
Catches his freshness from Archangel's wing:
He of the rose, the violet, the spring,   5
    The social smile, the chain for Freedom's sake:
    And lo!—whose stedfastness would never take

A meaner sound than Raphael's whispering.
And other spirits there are standing apart
   Upon the forehead of the age to come;   10
These, these will give the world another heart,
   And other pulses. Hear ye not the hum
Of mighty workings?——
   Listen awhile ye nations, and be dumb.
      [1816]

ON THE GRASSHOPPER AND THE CRICKET

The poetry of earth is never dead:
   When all the birds are faint with the hot sun,
   And hide in cooling trees, a voice will run
From hedge to hedge about the new-mown mead;
That is the Grasshopper's—he takes the lead   5
   In summer luxury,—he has never done
   With his delights; for when tired out with fun
He rests at ease beneath some pleasant weed.
The poetry of earth is ceasing never:
   On a lone winter evening, when the frost   10
      Has wrought a silence, from the stove there shrills
The Cricket's song, in warmth increasing ever,
   And seems to one in drowsiness half lost,
      The Grasshopper's among some grassy hills.
      [1816]

TO KOSCIUSKO

Good Kosciusko, thy great name alone
   Is a full harvest whence to reap high feeling;
   It comes upon us like the glorious pealing
Of the wide spheres—an everlasting tone.
And now it tells me, that in worlds unknown,   5
   The names of heroes, burst from clouds concealing,
   Are changed to harmonies, for ever stealing

Through cloudless blue, and round each silver throne.
It tells me too, that on a happy day,
   When some good spirit walks upon the earth,   10
   Thy name with Alfred's, and the great of yore
Gently commingling, gives tremendous birth
To a loud hymn, that sounds far, far away
   To where the great God lives for evermore.
     [1816]

HAPPY IS ENGLAND

Happy is England! I could be content
   To see no other verdure than its own;
   To feel no other breezes than are blown
Through its tall woods with high romances blent:
Yet do I sometimes feel a languishment   5
   For skies Italian, and an inward groan
   To sit upon an Alp as on a throne,
And half forget what world or worldling meant.
Happy is England, sweet her artless daughters;
   Enough their simple loveliness for me,   10
      Enough their whitest arms in silence clinging:
   Yet do I often warmly burn to see
      Beauties of deeper glance, and hear their singing,
And float with them about the summer waters.
     [1816]

SLEEP AND POETRY

     As I lay in my bed slepe full unmete
    'Was unto me, but why that I ne might
    'Rest I ne wist, for there n'as erthly wight
    '[As I suppose] had more of hertis ese
    'Than I, for I n'ad sicknesse nor disese.'
                      CHAUCER.

What is more gentle than a wind in summer?
What is more soothing than the pretty hummer

That stays one moment in an open flower,
And buzzes cheerily from bower to bower?
What is more tranquil than a musk-rose blowing   5
In a green island, far from all men's knowing?
More healthful than the leafiness of dales?
More secret than a nest of nightingales?
More serene than Cordelia's countenance?
More full of visions than a high romance?   10
What, but thee, Sleep? Soft closer of our eyes!
Low murmurer of tender lullabies!
Light hoverer around our happy pillows!
Wreather of poppy buds, and weeping willows!
Silent entangler of a beauty's tresses!   15
Most happy listener! when the morning blesses
Thee for enlivening all the cheerful eyes
That glance so brightly at the new sun-rise.

But what is higher beyond thought than thee?
Fresher than berries of a mountain tree?   20
More strange, more beautiful, more smooth, more regal,
Than wings of swans, than doves, than dim-seen eagle?
What is it? And to what shall I compare it?
It has a glory, and nought else can share it:
The thought thereof is awful, sweet, and holy,   25
Chacing away all worldliness and folly;
Coming sometimes like fearful claps of thunder,
Or the low rumblings earth's regions under;
And sometimes like a gentle whispering
Of all the secrets of some wond'rous thing   30
That breathes about us in the vacant air;
So that we look around with prying stare,
Perhaps to see shapes of light, aerial lymning,
And catch soft floatings from a faint-heard hymning;
To see the laurel wreath, on high suspended,   35
That is to crown our name when life is ended.
Sometimes it gives a glory to the voice,
And from the heart up-springs 'Rejoice! rejoice!'
Sounds which will reach the Framer of all things,
And die away in ardent mutterings.   40

No one who once the glorious sun has seen,
And all the clouds, and felt his bosom clean

For his great Maker's presence, but must know
What 'tis I mean, and feel his being glow:
Therefore no insult will I give his spirit   45
By telling what he sees from native merit.

O Poesy! for thee I hold my pen
That am not yet a glorious denizen
Of thy wide heaven—Should I rather kneel
Upon some mountain-top until I feel   50
A glowing splendour round about me hung,
And echo back the voice of thine own tongue?
O Poesy! for thee I grasp my pen
That am not yet a glorious denizen
Of thy wide heaven; yet, to my ardent prayer,   55
Yield from thy sanctuary some clear air,
Smoothed for intoxication by the breath
Of flowering bays, that I may die a death
Of luxury, and my young spirit follow
The morning sun-beams to the great Apollo   60
Like a fresh sacrifice; or, if I can bear
The o'erwhelming sweets, 'twill bring to me the fair
Visions of all places: a bowery nook
Will be elysium—an eternal book
Whence I may copy many a lovely saying   65
About the leaves, and flowers—about the playing
Of nymphs in woods, and fountains; and the shade
Keeping a silence round a sleeping maid;
And many a verse from so strange influence
That we must ever wonder how, and whence   70
It came. Also imaginings will hover
Round my fire-side, and haply there discover
Vistas of solemn beauty, where I'd wander
In happy silence, like the clear Meander
Through its lone vales; and where I found a spot   75
Of awfuller shade, or an enchanted grot,
Or a green hill o'erspread with chequered dress
Of flowers, and fearful from its loveliness,
Write on my tablets all that was permitted,
All that was for our human senses fitted.   80
Then the events of this wide world I'd seize
Like a strong giant, and my spirit teaze

Till at its shoulders it should proudly see
Wings to find out an immortality.

Stop and consider! life is but a day;   85
A fragile dew-drop on its perilous way
From a tree's summit; a poor Indian's sleep
While his boat hastens to the monstrous steep
Of Montmorenci. Why so sad a moan?
Life is the rose's hope while yet unblown;   90
The reading of an ever-changing tale;
The light uplifting of a maiden's veil;
A pigeon tumbling in clear summer air;
A laughing school-boy, without grief or care,
Riding the springy branches of an elm.   95

O for ten years, that I may overwhelm
Myself in poesy; so I may do the deed
That my own soul has to itself decreed.
Then will I pass the countries that I see
In long perspective, and continually   100
Taste their pure fountains. First the realm I'll pass
Of Flora, and old Pan: sleep in the grass,
Feed upon apples red, and strawberries,
And choose each pleasure that my fancy sees;
Catch the white-handed nymphs in shady places,   105
To woo sweet kisses from averted faces,—
Play with their fingers, touch their shoulders white
Into a pretty shrinking with a bite
As hard as lips can make it: till agreed,
A lovely tale of human life we'll read.   110
And one will teach a tame dove how it best
May fan the cool air gently o'er my rest;
Another, bending o'er her nimble tread,
Will set a green robe floating round her head,
And still will dance with ever varied ease,   115
Smiling upon the flowers and the trees:
Another will entice me on, and on
Through almond blossoms and rich cinnamon;
Till in the bosom of a leafy world
We rest in silence, like two gems upcurl'd   120
In the recesses of a pearly shell.

And can I ever bid these joys farewell?
Yes, I must pass them for a nobler life,
Where I may find the agonies, the strife
Of human hearts: for lo! I see afar,   125
O'er-sailing the blue cragginess, a car
And steeds with streamy manes—the charioteer
Looks out upon the winds with glorious fear:
And now the numerous tramplings quiver lightly
Along a huge cloud's ridge; and now with sprightly   130
Wheel downward come they into fresher skies,
Tipt round with silver from the sun's bright eyes.
Still downward with capacious whirl they glide;
And now I see them on a green-hill's side
In breezy rest among the nodding stalks.   135
The charioteer with wond'rous gesture talks
To the trees and mountains; and there soon appear
Shapes of delight, of mystery, and fear,
Passing along before a dusky space
Made by some mighty oaks: as they would chase   140
Some ever-fleeting music on they sweep.
Lo! how they murmur, laugh, and smile, and weep:
Some with upholden hand and mouth severe;
Some with their faces muffled to the ear
Between their arms; some, clear in youthful bloom,   145
Go glad and smilingly athwart the gloom;
Some looking back, and some with upward gaze;
Yes, thousands in a thousand different ways
Flit onward—now a lovely wreath of girls
Dancing their sleek hair into tangled curls;   150
And now broad wings. Most awfully intent
The driver of those steeds is forward bent,
And seems to listen: O that I might know
All that he writes with such a hurrying glow.

The visions all are fled—the car is fled   155
Into the light of heaven, and in their stead
A sense of real things comes doubly strong,
And, like a muddy stream, would bear along
My soul to nothingness: but I will strive
Against all doubtings, and will keep alive   160
The thought of that same chariot, and the strange
Journey it went.

         Is there so small a range
In the present strength of manhood, that the high
Imagination cannot freely fly
As she was wont of old? prepare her steeds,   165
Paw up against the light, and do strange deeds
Upon the clouds? Has she not shewn us all?
From the clear space of ether, to the small
Breath of new buds unfolding? From the meaning
Of Jove's large eye-brow, to the tender greening   170
Of April meadows? Here her altar shone,
E'en in this isle; and who could paragon
The fervid choir that lifted up a noise
Of harmony, to where it aye will poise
Its mighty self of convoluting sound,   175
Huge as a planet, and like that roll round,
Eternally around a dizzy void?
Ay, in those days the Muses were nigh cloy'd
With honors; nor had any other care
Than to sing out and sooth their wavy hair.   180

Could all this be forgotten? Yes, a schism
Nurtured by foppery and barbarism,
Made great Apollo blush for this his land.
Men were thought wise who could not understand
His glories: with a puling infant's force   185
They sway'd about upon a rocking horse,
And thought it Pegasus. Ah dismal soul'd!
The winds of heaven blew, the ocean roll'd
Its gathering waves—ye felt it not. The blue
Bared its eternal bosom, and the dew   190
Of summer nights collected still to make
The morning precious: beauty was awake!
Why were ye not awake? But ye were dead
To things ye knew not of,—were closely wed
To musty laws lined out with wretched rule   195
And compass vile: so that ye taught a school
Of dolts to smooth, inlay, and clip, and fit,
Till, like the certain wands of Jacob's wit,
Their verses tallied. Easy was the task:
A thousand handicraftsmen wore the mask   200
Of Poesy. Ill-fated, impious race!
That blasphemed the bright Lyrist to his face,

And did not know it,—no, they went about,
Holding a poor, decrepid standard out
Mark'd with most flimsy mottos, and in large   205
The name of one Boileau!

                              O ye whose charge
It is to hover round our pleasant hills!
Whose congregated majesty so fills
My boundly reverence, that I cannot trace
Your hallowed names, in this unholy place,   210
So near those common folk; did not their shames
Affright you? Did our old lamenting Thames
Delight you? Did ye never cluster round
Delicious Avon, with a mournful sound,
And weep? Or did ye wholly bid adieu   215
To regions where no more the laurel grew?
Or did ye stay to give a welcoming
To some lone spirits who could proudly sing
Their youth away, and die? 'Twas even so:
But let me think away those times of woe: 220
Now 'tis a fairer season; ye have breathed
Rich benedictions o'er us; ye have wreathed
Fresh garlands: for sweet music has been heard
In many places;—some has been upstirr'd
From out its crystal dwelling in a lake,   225
By a swan's ebon bill; from a thick brake,
Nested and quiet in a valley mild,
Bubbles a pipe; fine sounds are floating wild
About the earth: happy are ye and glad.

These things are doubtless: yet in truth we've had   230
Strange thunders from the potency of song;
Mingled indeed with what is sweet and strong,
From majesty: but in clear truth the themes
Are ugly clubs, the Poets Polyphemes
Disturbing the grand sea. A drainless shower   235
Of light is poesy; 'tis the supreme of power;
'Tis might half slumb'ring on its own right arm.
The very archings of her eye-lids charm
A thousand willing agents to obey,
And still she governs with the mildest sway: 240
But strength alone though of the Muses born

Is like a fallen angel: trees uptorn,
Darkness, and worms, and shrouds, and sepulchres
Delight it; for it feeds upon the burrs,
And thorns of life; forgetting the great end   245
Of poesy, that it should be a friend
To sooth the cares, and lift the thoughts of man.

Yet I rejoice: a myrtle fairer than
E'er grew in Paphos, from the bitter weeds
Lifts its sweet head into the air, and feeds   250
A silent space with ever sprouting green.
All tenderest birds there find a pleasant screen,
Creep through the shade with jaunty fluttering,
Nibble the little cupped flowers and sing.
Then let us clear away the choaking thorns   255
From round its gentle stem; let the young fawns,
Yeaned in after times, when we are flown,
Find a fresh sward beneath it, overgrown
With simple flowers: let there nothing be
More boisterous than a lover's bended knee;   260
Nought more ungentle than the placid look
Of one who leans upon a closed book;
Nought more untranquil than the grassy slopes
Between two hills. All hail delightful hopes!
As she was wont, th' imagination   265
Into most lovely labyrinths will be gone,
And they shall be accounted poet kings
Who simply tell the most heart-easing things.
O may these joys be ripe before I die.

Will not some say that I presumptuously   270
Have spoken? that from hastening disgrace
'Twere better far to hide my foolish face?
That whining boyhood should with reverence bow
Ere the dread thunderbolt could reach? How!
If I do hide myself, it sure shall be   275
In the very fane, the light of Poesy:
If I do fall, at least I will be laid
Beneath the silence of a poplar shade;
And over me the grass shall be smooth shaven;
And there shall be a kind memorial graven.   280
But off Despondence! miserable bane!

They should not know thee, who athirst to gain
A noble end, are thirsty every hour.
What though I am not wealthy in the dower
Of spanning wisdom; though I do not know   285
The shiftings of the mighty winds that blow
Hither and thither all the changing thoughts
Of man: though no great minist'ring reason sorts
Out the dark mysteries of human souls
To clear conceiving: yet there ever rolls   290
A vast idea before me, and I glean
Therefrom my liberty; thence too I've seen
The end and aim of Poesy. 'Tis clear
As any thing most true; as that the year
Is made of the four seasons—manifest   295
As a large cross, some old cathedral's crest,
Lifted to the white clouds. Therefore should I
Be but the essence of deformity,
A coward, did my very eye-lids 'wink
At speaking out what I have dared to think.   300
Ah! rather let me like a madman run
Over some precipice; let the hot sun
Melt my Dedalian wings, and drive me down
Convuls'd and headlong! Stay! an inward frown
Of conscience bide me be more calm awhile.   305
An ocean dim, sprinkled with many an isle,
Spreads awfully before me. How much toil!
How many days! what desperate turmoil!
Ere I can have explored its widenesses.
Ah, what a task! upon my bended knees,   310
I could unsay those—no, impossible!
Impossible!

       For sweet relief I'll dwell
On humbler thoughts, and let this strange assay
Begun in gentleness die so away.
E'en now all tumult from my bosom fades: 315
I turn full hearted to the friendly aids
That smooth the path of honour; brotherhood,
And friendliness the nurse of mutual good.
The hearty grasp that sends a pleasant sonnet
Into the brain ere one can think upon it;   320
The silence when some rhymes are coming out;

And when they're come, the very pleasant rout:
The message certain to be done to-morrow—
'Tis perhaps as well that it should be to borrow
Some precious book from out its snug retreat,   325
To cluster round it when we next shall meet.
Scarce can I scribble on; for lovely airs
Are fluttering round the room like doves in pairs;
Many delights of that glad day recalling,
When first my senses caught their tender falling.   330
And with these airs come forms of elegance
Stooping their shoulders o'er a horse's prance,
Careless, and grand—fingers soft and round
Parting luxuriant curls;—and the swift bound
Of Bacchus from his chariot, when his eye   335
Made Ariadne's cheek look blushingly.
Thus I remember all the pleasant flow
Of words at opening a portfolio.

Things such as these are ever harbingers
To trains of peaceful images: the stirs   340
Of a swan's neck unseen among the rushes:
A linnet starting all about the bushes:
A butterfly, with golden wings broad parted,
Nestling a rose, convuls'd as though it smarted
With over pleasure—many, many more,   345
Might I indulge at large in all my store
Of luxuries: yet I must not forget
Sleep, quiet with his poppy coronet:
For what there may be worthy in these rhymes
I partly owe to him—and thus: The chimes   350
Of friendly voices had just given place
To as sweet a silence, when I 'gan retrace
The pleasant day, upon a couch at ease.
It was a poet's house who keeps the keys
Of Pleasure's temple. Round about were hung   355
The glorious features of the bards who sung
In other ages—cold and sacred busts
Smiled at each other. Happy he who trusts
To clear Futurity his darling fame!
Then there were fauns and satyrs taking aim   360
At swelling apples with a frisky leap
And reaching fingers, 'mid a luscious heap

Of vine leaves. Then there rose to view a fane
Of liny marble, and thereto a train
Of nymphs approaching fairly o'er the sward: 365
One, loveliest, holding her white hand toward
The dazzling sun-rise: two sisters sweet
Bending their graceful figures till they meet
Over the trippings of a little child:
And some are hearing, eagerly, the wild   370
Thrilling liquidity of dewy piping.
See, in another picture, nymphs are wiping
Cherishingly Diana's timorous limbs;—
A fold of lawny mantle dabbling swims
At the bath's edge, and keeps a gentle motion   375
With the subsiding crystal: as when ocean
Heaves calmly its broad swelling smoothness o'er
Its rocky marge, and balances once more
The patient weeds; that now unshent by foam
Feel all about their undulating home.   380

Sappho's meek head was there half smiling down
At nothing; just as though the earnest frown
Of over thinking had that moment gone
From off her brow, and left her all alone.

Great Alfred's too, with anxious, pitying eyes,   385
As if he always listened to the sighs
Of the goaded world; and Kosciusko's worn
By horrid suffrance—mightily forlorn.

Petrarch, outstepping from the shady green,
Starts at the sight of Laura; nor can wean   390
His eyes from her sweet face. Most happy they!
For over them was seen a free display
Of out-spread wings, and from between them shone
The face of Poesy: from off her throne
She overlook'd things that I scarce could tell.   395
The very sense of where I was might well
Keep Sleep aloof: but more than that there came
Thought after thought to nourish up the flame
Within my breast; so that the morning light
Surprised me even from a sleepless night;   400

And up I rose refresh'd, and glad, and gay,
Resolving to begin that very day
These lines; and howsoever they be done,
I leave them as a father does his son.

[1816]

from ENDYMION

BOOK I

A thing of beauty is a joy for ever:
Its loveliness increases; it will never
Pass into nothingness; but still will keep
A bower quiet for us, and a sleep
Full of sweet dreams, and health, and quiet breathing.   5
Therefore, on every morrow, are we wreathing
A flowery band to bind us to the earth,
Spite of despondence, of the inhuman dearth
Of noble natures, of the gloomy days,
Of all the unhealthy and o'er-darkened ways   10
Made for our searching: yes, in spite of all,
Some shape of beauty moves away the pall
From our dark spirits. Such the sun, the moon,
Trees old, and young sprouting a shady boon
For simple sheep; and such are daffodils   15
With the green world they live in; and clear rills
That for themselves a cooling covert make
'Gainst the hot season; the mid forest brake,
Rich with a sprinkling of fair musk-rose blooms:
And such too is the grandeur of the dooms   20
We have imagined for the mighty dead;
All lovely tales that we have heard or read:
An endless fountain of immortal drink,
Pouring unto us from the heaven's brink.

Nor do we merely feel these essences   25
For one short hour; no, even as the trees
That whisper round a temple become soon
Dear as the temple's self, so does the moon,

The passion poesy, glories infinite,
Haunt us till they become a cheering light 30
Unto our souls, and bound to us so fast,
That, whether there be shine, or gloom o'ercast,
They always must be with us, or we die.
[1817–18]

WHEN I HAVE FEARS THAT I MAY CEASE TO BE

When I have fears that I may cease to be
  Before my pen has glean'd my teeming brain,
Before high-piled books, in charact'ry,
  Hold like rich garners the full-ripen'd grain;
When I behold, upon the night's starr'd face, 5
  Huge cloudy symbols of a high romance,
And think that I may never live to trace
  Their shadows, with the magic hand of chance;
And when I feel, fair creature of an hour!
  That I shall never look upon thee more, 10
Never have relish in the faery power
  Of unreflecting love!—then on the shore
Of the wide world I stand alone, and think
Till love and fame to nothingness do sink.
[1818]

LINES ON THE MERMAID TAVERN

Souls of Poets dead and gone,
What Elysium have ye known,
Happy field or mossy cavern,
Choicer than the Mermaid Tavern?
Have ye tippled drink more fine 5
Than mine host's Canary wine?
Or are fruits of Paradise
Sweeter than those dainty pies
Of venison? O generous food!

Drest as though bold Robin Hood   10
Would, with his maid Marian,
Sup and bowse from horn and can.

    I have heard that on a day
Mine host's sign-board flew away,
Nobody knew whither, till   15
An astrologer's old quill
To a sheepskin gave the story,
Said he saw you in your glory,
Underneath a new-old sign
Sipping beverage divine,   20
And pledging with contented smack
The Mermaid in the Zodiac.

    Souls of Poets dead and gone,
What Elysium have ye known,
Happy field or mossy cavern,   25
Choicer than the Mermaid Tavern?
     [1818]

ISABELLA

OR,

THE POT OF BASIL

I

Fair Isabel, poor simple Isabel!
  Lorenzo, a young palmer in Love's eye!
They could not in the self-same mansion dwell
  Without some stir of heart, some malady;
They could not sit at meals but feel how well   5
  It soothed each to be the other by;
They could not, sure, beneath the same roof sleep
But to each other dream, and nightly weep.

II

With every morn their love grew tenderer,
　With every eve deeper and tenderer still;　　　　　10
He might not in house, field, or garden stir,
　But her full shape would all his seeing fill;
And his continual voice was pleasanter
　To her, than noise of trees or hidden rill;
Her lute-string gave an echo of his name,　　　　　15
She spoilt her half-done broidery with the same.

III

He knew whose gentle hand was at the latch,
　Before the door had given her to his eyes;
And from her chamber-window he would catch
　Her beauty farther than the falcon spies;　　　　　20
And constant as her vespers would he watch,
　Because her face was turn'd to the same skies;
And with sick longing all the night outwear,
To hear her morning-step upon the stair.

IV

A whole long month of May in this sad plight　　　　　25
　Made their cheeks paler by the break of June:
'To-morrow will I bow to my delight,
　'To-morrow will I ask my lady's boon.'—
'O may I never see another night,
　'Lorenzo, if thy lips breathe not love's tune.'—　　　　　30
So spake they to their pillows; but, alas,
Honeyless days and days did he let pass;

V

Until sweet Isabella's untouch'd cheek
　Fell sick within the rose's just domain,
Fell thin as a young mother's, who doth seek　　　　　35
　By every lull to cool her infant's pain:
'How ill she is,' said he, 'I may not speak,
　'And yet I will, and tell my love all plain:
'If looks speak love-laws, I will drink her tears,
'And at the least 'twill startle off her cares.'　　　　　40

VI

So said he one fair morning, and all day
   His heart beat awfully against his side;
And to his heart he inwardly did pray
   For power to speak; but still the ruddy tide
Stifled his voice, and puls'd resolve away—   45
   Fever'd his high conceit of such a bride,
Yet brought him to the meekness of a child:
Alas! when passion is both meek and wild!

VII

So once more he had wak'd and anguished
   A dreary night of love and misery,   50
If Isabel's quick eye had not been wed
   To every symbol on his forehead high;
She saw it waxing very pale and·dead,
   And straight all flush'd; so, lisped tenderly,
'Lorenzo!'—here she ceas'd her timid quest,   55
But in her tone and look he read the rest.

VIII

'O Isabella, I can half perceive
   'That I may speak my grief into thine ear;
'If thou didst ever any thing believe,
   'Believe how I love thee, believe how near   60
'My soul is to its doom: I would not grieve
   'Thy hand by unwelcome pressing, would not fear
'Thine eyes by gazing; but I cannot live
'Another night, and not my passion shrive.

IX

'Love! thou art leading me from wintry cold,   65
   'Lady! thou leadest me to summer clime,
'And I must taste the blossoms that unfold
   'In its ripe warmth this gracious morning time.'
So said, his erewhile timid lips grew bold,
   And poesied with hers in dewy rhyme: 70
Great bliss was with them, and great happiness
Grew, like a lusty flower in June's caress.

X

Parting they seem'd to tread upon the air,
  Twin roses by the zephyr blown apart
Only to meet again more close, and share   **75**
  The inward fragrance of each other's heart.
She, to her chamber gone, a ditty fair
  Sang, of delicious love and honey'd dart;
He with light steps went up a western hill,
And bade the sun farewell, and joy'd his fill.   **80**

XI

All close they met again, before the dusk
  Had taken from the stars its pleasant veil,
All close they met, all eves, before the dusk
  Had taken from the stars its pleasant veil,
Close in a bower of hyacinth and musk,   **85**
  Unknown of any, free from whispering tale.
Ah! better had it been for ever so,
Than idle ears should pleasure in their woe.

XII

Were they unhappy then?—It cannot be—
  Too many tears for lovers have been shed,   **90**
Too many sighs give we to them in fee,
  Too much of pity after they are dead,
Too many doleful stories do we see,
  Whose matter in bright gold were best be read;
Except in such a page where Theseus' spouse   **95**
Over the pathless waves towards him bows.

XIII

But, for the general award of love,
  The little sweet doth kill much bitterness;
Though Dido silent is in under-grove,
  And Isabella's was a great distress,   **100**
Though young Lorenzo in warm Indian clove
  Was not embalm'd, this truth is not the less
Even bees, the little almsmen of spring-bowers,
Know there is richest juice in poison-flowers.

XIV

With her two brothers this fair lady dwelt,   105
  Enriched from ancestral merchandize,
And for them many a weary hand did swelt
  In torched mines and noisy factories,
And many once proud-quiver'd loins did melt
  In blood from stinging whip;—with hollow eyes   110
Many all day in dazzling river stood,
To take the rich-ored driftings of the flood.

XV

For them the Ceylon diver held his breath,
  And went all naked to the hungry shark;
For them his ears gush'd blood; for them in death   115
  The seal on the cold ice with piteous bark
Lay full of darts; for them alone did seethe
  A thousand men in troubles wide and dark:
Half-ignorant, they turn'd an easy wheel,
That set sharp racks at work, to pinch and peel.   120

XVI

Why were they proud? Because their marble founts
  Gush'd with more pride than do a wretch's tears?—
Why were they proud? Because fair orange-mounts
  Were of more soft ascent than lazar stairs?—
Why were they proud? Because red-lin'd accounts   125
  Were richer than the songs of Grecian years?—
Why were they proud? again we ask aloud,
Why in the name of Glory were they proud?

XVII

Yet were these Florentines as self-retired
  In hungry pride and gainful cowardice,   130
As two close Hebrews in that land inspired,
  Paled in and vineyarded from beggar-spies
The hawks of ship-mast forests—the untired
  And pannier'd mules for ducats and old lies—
Quick cat's-paws on the generous stray-away,—   135
Great wits in Spanish, Tuscan, and Malay.

XVIII

How was it these same ledger-men could spy
   Fair Isabella in her downy nest?
How could they find out in Lorenzo's eye
   A straying from his toil? Hot Egypt's pest   140
Into their vision covetous and sly!
   How could these money-bags see east and west?—
Yet so they did—and every dealer fair
Must see behind, as doth the hunted hare.

XIX

O eloquent and famed Boccaccio!   145
   Of thee we now should ask forgiving boon,
And of thy spicy myrtles as they blow,
   And of thy roses amorous of the moon,
And of thy lilies, that do paler grow
   Now they can no more hear thy ghittern's tune,   150
For venturing syllables that ill beseem
The quiet glooms of such a piteous theme.

XX

Grant thou a pardon here, and then the tale
   Shall move on soberly, as it is meet;
There is no other crime, no mad assail   155
   To make old prose in modern rhyme more sweet:
But it is done—succeed the verse or fail—
   To honour thee, and thy gone spirit greet;
To stead thee as a verse in English tongue,
An echo of thee in the north-wind sung.   160

XXI

These brethren having found by many signs
   What love Lorenzo for their sister had,
And how she lov'd him too, each unconfines
   His bitter thoughts to other, well nigh mad
That he, the servant of their trade designs,   165
   Should in their sister's love be blithe and glad,
When 'twas their plan to coax her by degrees
To some high noble and his olive-trees.

XXII

And many a jealous conference had they,
   And many times they bit their lips alone,   170
Before they fix'd upon a surest way
   To make the youngster for his crime atone;
And at the last, these men of cruel clay
   Cut Mercy with a sharp knife to the bone;
For they resolved in some forest dim   175
To kill Lorenzo, and there bury him.

XXIII

So on a pleasant morning, as he leant
   Into the sun-rise, o'er the balustrade
Of the garden-terrace, towards him they bent
   Their footing through the dews; and to him said,   180
'You seem there in the quiet of content,
   'Lorenzo, and we are most loth to invade
'Calm speculation; but if you are wise,
'Bestride your steed while cold is in the skies.

XXIV

'To-day we purpose, ay, this hour we mount   185
   'To spur three leagues towards the Apennine;
'Come down, we pray thee, ere the hot sun count
   'His dewy rosary on the eglantine.'
Lorenzo, courteously as he was wont,
   Bow'd a fair greeting to these serpents' whine;   190
And went in haste, to get in readiness,
With belt, and spur, and bracing huntsman's dress.

XXV

And as he to the court-yard pass'd along,
   Each third step did he pause, and listen'd oft
If he could hear his lady's matin-song,   195
   Or the light whisper of her footstep soft;
And as he thus over his passion hung,
   He heard a laugh full musical aloft;
When, looking up, he saw her features bright
Smile through an in-door lattice, all delight.   200

XXVI

'Love, Isabel!' said he, 'I was in pain
   'Lest I should miss to bid thee a good morrow
'Ah! what if I should lose thee, when so fain
   'I am to stifle all the heavy sorrow
'Of a poor three hours' absence? but we'll gain   205
   'Out of the amorous dark what day doth borrow.
'Good bye! I'll soon be back.'—'Good bye!' said she:—
And as he went she chanted merrily.

XXVII

So the two brothers and their murder'd man
   Rode past fair Florence, to where Arno's stream   210
Gurgles through straiten'd banks, and still doth fan
   Itself with dancing bulrush, and the bream
Keeps head against the freshets. Sick and wan
   The brothers' faces in the ford did seem,
Lorenzo's flush with love.—They pass'd the water   215
Into a forest quiet for the slaughter.

XXVIII

There was Lorenzo slain and buried in,
   There in that forest did his great love cease;
Ah! when a soul doth thus its freedom win,
   It aches in loneliness—is ill at peace   220
As the break-covert blood-hounds of such sin:
   They dipp'd their swords in the water, and did tease
Their horses homeward, with convulsed spur,
Each richer by his being a murderer.

XXIX

They told their sister how, with sudden speed,   225
   Lorenzo had ta'en ship for foreign lands,
Because of some great urgency and need
   In their affairs, requiring trusty hands.
Poor Girl! put on thy stifling widow's weed,
   And 'scape at once from Hope's accursed bands;   230
To-day thou wilt not see him, nor to-morrow,
And the next day will be a day of sorrow.

XXX

She weeps alone for pleasures not to be;
  Sorely she wept until the night came on,
And then, instead of love, O misery!   235
  She brooded o'er the luxury alone:
His image in the dusk she seem'd to see,
  And to the silence made a gentle moan,
Spreading her perfect arms upon the air,
And on her couch low murmuring 'Where? O Where?' 240

XXXI

But Selfishness, Love's cousin, held not long
  Its fiery vigil in her single breast;
She fretted for the golden hour, and hung
  Upon the time with feverish unrest—
Not long—for soon into her heart a throng   245
  Of higher occupants, a richer zest,
Came tragic; passion not to be subdued,
And sorrow for her love in travels rude.

XXXII

In the mid days of autumn, on their eves,
  The breath of Winter comes from far away,   250
And the sick west continually bereaves
  Of some gold tinges, and plays a roundelay
Of death among the bushes and the leaves
  To make all bare before he dares to stray
From his north cavern. So sweet Isabel   255
By gradual decay from beauty fell,

XXXIII

Because Lorenzo came not. Oftentimes
  She ask'd her brothers, with an eye all pale,
Striving to be itself, what dungeon climes
  Could keep him off so long? They spake a tale   260
Time after time, to quiet her. Their crimes
  Came on them, like a smoke from Hinnom's vale;
And every night in dreams they groan'd aloud,
To see their sister in her snowy shroud.

XXXIV

And she had died in drowsy ignorance,   265
    But for a thing more deadly dark than all;
It came like a fierce potion, drunk by chance,
    Which saves a sick man from the feather'd pall
For some few gasping moments; like a lance,
    Waking an Indian from his cloudy hall   270
With cruel pierce, and bringing him again
Sense of the gnawing fire at heart and brain.

XXXV

It was a vision.—In the drowsy gloom,
    The dull of midnight, at her couch's foot
Lorenzo stood, and wept: the forest tomb   275
    Had marr'd his glossy hair which once could shoot
Lustre into the sun, and put cold doom
    Upon his lips, and taken the soft lute
From his lorn voice, and past his loamed ears
Had made a miry channel for his tears.   280

XXXVI

Strange sound it was, when the pale shadow spake;
    For there was striving, in its piteous tongue,
To speak as when on earth it was awake,
    And Isabella on its music hung:
Languor there was in it, and tremulous shake,   285
    As in a palsied Druid's harp unstrung;
And through it moan'd a ghostly under-song,
Like hoarse night-gusts sepulchral briars among.

XXXVII

Its eyes, though wild, were still all dewy bright
    With love, and kept all phantom fear aloof   290
From the poor girl by magic of their light,
    The while it did unthread the horrid woof
Of the late darken'd time,—the murderous spite
    Of pride and avarice,—the dark pine roof
In the forest,—and the sodden turfed dell,   295
Where, without any word, from stabs he fell.

XXXVIII

Saying moreover, 'Isabel, my sweet!
  'Red whortle-berries droop above my head,
'And a large flint-stone weighs upon my feet;
    'Around me beeches and high chestnuts shed   300
'Their leaves and prickly nuts; a sheep-fold bleat
    'Comes from beyond the river to my bed:
'Go, shed one tear upon my heather-bloom,
'And it shall comfort me within the tomb.

XXXIX

'I am a shadow now, alas! alas!   305
  'Upon the skirts of human-nature dwelling
'Alone: I chant alone the holy mass,
    'While little sounds of life are round me knelling,
'And glossy bees at noon do fieldward pass,
    'And many a chapel bell the hour is telling,   310
'Paining me through: those sounds grow strange to me,
'And thou art distant in Humanity.

XL

'I know what was, I feel full well what is,
  'And I should rage, if spirits could go mad;
'Though I forget the taste of earthly bliss,   315
    'That paleness warms my grave, as though I had
'A Seraph chosen from the bright abyss
    'To be my spouse: thy paleness makes me glad;
'Thy beauty grows upon me, and I feel
'A greater love through all my essence steal.'   320

XLI

The Spirit mourn'd 'Adieu!'—dissolv'd, and left
  The atom darkness in a slow turmoil;
As when of healthful midnight sleep bereft,
  Thinking on rugged hours and fruitless toil,
We put our eyes into a pillowy cleft,   325
  And see the spangly gloom froth up and boil:
It made sad Isabella's eyelids ache,
And in the dawn she started up awake;

XLII

'Ha! ha!' said she, 'I knew not this hard life,
   'I thought the worst was simple misery;   **330**
'I thought some Fate with pleasure or with strife
   'Portion'd us—happy days, or else to die;
'But there is crime—a brother's bloody knife!
   'Sweet Spirit, thou hast school'd my infancy:
'I'll visit thee for this, and kiss thine eyes,   **335**
'And greet thee morn and even in the skies.'

XLIII

When the full morning came, she had devised
   How she might secret to the forest hie;
How she might find the clay, so dearly prized,
   And sing to it one latest lullaby;   **340**
How her short absence might be unsurmised,
   While she the inmost of the dream would try.
Resolv'd, she took with her an aged nurse,
And went into that dismal forest-hearse.

XLIV

See, as they creep along the river side,   **345**
   How she doth whisper to that aged Dame,
And, after looking round the champaign wide,
   Shows her a knife.—'What feverous hectic flame
'Burns in thee, child?—What good can thee betide,
   'That thou should'st smile again?'—The evening came, **350**
And they had found Lorenzo's earthy bed;
The flint was there, the berries at his head.

XLV

Who hath not loiter'd in a green church-yard,
   And let his spirit, like a demon-mole,
Work through the clayey soil and gravel hard,   **355**
   So see scull, coffin'd bones, and funeral stole;
Pitying each form that hungry Death hath marr'd,
   And filling it once more with human soul?
Ah! this is holiday to what was felt
When Isabella by Lorenzo knelt.   **360**

XLVI

She gaz'd into the fresh-thrown mould, as though
　　One glance did fully all its secrets tell;
Clearly she saw, as other eyes would know
　　Pale limbs at bottom of a crystal well;
Upon the murderous spot she seem'd to grow,　　　　365
　　Like to a native lily of the dell:
Then with her knife, all sudden, she began
To dig more fervently than misers can.

XLVII

Soon she turn'd up a soiled glove, whereon
　　Her silk had play'd in purple phantasies,　　　　370
She kiss'd it with a lip more chill than stone,
　　And put it in her bosom, where it dries
And freezes utterly unto the bone
　　Those dainties made to still an infant's cries:
Then 'gan she work again; nor stay'd her care,　　　375
But to throw back at times her veiling hair.

XLVIII

That old nurse stood beside her wondering,
　　Until her heart felt pity to the core
At sight of such a dismal labouring,
　　And so she kneeled, with her locks all hoar,　　　380
And put her lean hands to the horrid thing:
　　Three hours they labour'd at this travail sore;
At last they felt the kernel of the grave,
And Isabella did not stamp and rave.

XLIX

Ah! wherefore all this wormy circumstance?　　　　385
　　Why linger at the yawning tomb so long?
O for the gentleness of old Romance,
　　The simple plaining of a minstrel's song!
Fair reader, at the old tale take a glance,
　　For here, in truth, it doth not well belong　　　390
To speak:—O turn thee to the very tale,
And taste the music of that vision pale.

L

With duller steel than the Persèan sword
    They cut away no formless monster's head,
But one, whose gentleness did well accord   **395**
    With death, as life. The ancient harps have said,
Love never dies, but lives, immortal Lord:
    If Love impersonate was ever dead,
Pale Isabella kiss'd it, and low moan'd.
'Twas love; cold,—dead indeed, but not dethroned.   **400**

LI

In anxious secrecy they took it home,
    And then the prize was all for Isabel:
She calm'd its wild hair with a golden comb,
    And all around each eye's sepulchral cell
Pointed each fringed lash; the smeared loam   **405**
    With tears, as chilly as a dripping well,
She drench'd away:—and still she comb'd, and kept
Sighing all day—and still she kiss'd, and wept.

LII

Then in a silken scarf,—sweet with the dews
    Of precious flowers pluck'd in Araby,   **410**
And divine liquids come with odorous ooze
    Through the cold serpent-pipe refreshfully,—
She wrapp'd it up; and for its tomb did choose
    A garden-pot, wherein she laid it by,
And cover'd it with mould, and o'er it set   **415**
Sweet basil, which her tears kept ever wet.

LIII

And she forgot the stars, the moon, and sun,
    And she forgot the blue above the trees,
And she forgot the dells where waters run,
    And she forgot the chilly autumn breeze;   **420**
She had no knowledge when the day was done,
    And the new morn she saw not: but in peace
Hung over her sweet basil evermore,
And moisten'd it with tears unto the core.

LIV

And so she ever fed it with thin tears,   425
   Whence thick, and green, and beautiful it grew,
So that it smelt more balmy than its peers
   Of basil-tufts in Florence; for it drew
Nurture besides, and life, from human fears,
   From the fast mouldering head there shut from view: 430
So that the jewel, safely casketed,
Came forth, and in perfumed leafits spread.

LV

O Melancholy, linger here awhile!
   O Music, Music, breathe despondingly!
O Echo, Echo, from some sombre isle,   435
   Unknown, Lethean, sigh to us—O sigh!
Spirits in grief, lift up your heads, and smile;
   Lift up your heads, sweet Spirits, heavily,
And make a pale light in your cypress glooms,
Tinting with silver wan your marble tombs.   440

LVI

Moan hither, all ye syllables of woe,
   From the deep throat of sad Melpomene!
Through bronzed lyre in tragic order go,
   And touch the strings into a mystery;
Sound mournfully upon the winds and low;   445
   For simple Isabel is soon to be
Among the dead: She withers, like a palm
Cut by an Indian for its juicy balm.

LVII

O leave the palm to wither by itself;
   Let not quick Winter chill its dying hour!—   450
It may not be—those Baälites of pelf,
   Her brethren, noted the continual shower
From her dead eyes; and many a curious elf,
   Among her kindred, wonder'd that such dower
Of youth and beauty should be thrown aside   455
By one mark'd out to be a Noble's bride.

LVIII

And, furthermore, her brethren wonder'd much
　　Why she sat drooping by the basil green,
And why it flourish'd, as by magic touch;
　　Greatly they wonder'd what the thing might mean: 460
They could not surely give belief, that such
　　A very nothing would have power to wean
Her from her own fair youth, and pleasures gay,
And even remembrance of her love's delay.

LIX

Therefore they watch'd a time when they might sift 465
　　This hidden whim; and long they watch'd in vain;
For seldom did she go to chapel-shrift,
　　And seldom felt she any hunger pain;
And when she left, she hurried back, as swift
　　As bird on wing to breast its eggs again;　　　470
And, patient as a hen-bird, sat her there
Beside her basil, weeping through her hair.

LX

Yet they contriv'd to steal the basil-pot,
　　And to examine it in secret place:
The thing was vile with green and livid spot,　　475
　　And yet they knew it was Lorenzo's face:
The guerdon of their murder they had got,
　　And so left Florence in a moment's space,
Never to turn again.—Away they went,
With blood upon their heads, to banishment.　　480

LXI

O Melancholy, turn thine eyes away!
　　O Music, Music, breathe despondingly!
O Echo, Echo, on some other day,
　　From isles Lethean, sigh to us—O sigh!
Spirits of grief, sing not you 'Well-a-way!'　　485
　　For Isabel, sweet Isabel, will die;
Will die a death too lone and incomplete,
Now they have ta'en away her basil sweet.

LXII

Piteous she look'd on dead and senseless things,
  Asking for her lost basil amorously;   490
And with melodious chuckle in the strings
  Of her lorn voice, she oftentimes would cry
After the Pilgrim in his wanderings,
  To ask him where her basil was; and why
Twas hid from her: 'For cruel 'tis,' said she,   495
'To steal my basil-pot away from me.'

LXIII

And so she pined, and so she died forlorn,
  Imploring for her basil to the last.
No heart was there in Florence but did mourn
  In pity of her love, so overcast.   500
And a sad ditty of this story born
  From mouth to mouth through all the country pass'd:
Still is the burthen sung—'O cruelty,
'To steal my basil-pot away from me!'
       [1818]

BRIGHT STAR! WOULD I WERE STEADFAST AS THOU ART

Bright star! would I were steadfast as thou art—
  Not in lone splendour hung aloft the night
And watching, with eternal lids apart,
  Like nature's patient, sleepless Eremite,
The moving waters at their priestlike task   5
  Of pure ablution round earth's human shores,
Or gazing on the new soft fallen mask
  Of snow upon the mountains and the moors—
No—yet still steadfast, still unchangeable,
  Pillow'd upon my fair love's ripening breast,   10
To feel for ever its soft fall and swell,
  Awake for ever in a sweet unrest,
Still, still to hear her tender-taken breath,
And so live ever—or else swoon to death.
       [1819]

THE EVE OF ST. AGNES

I

St. Agnes' Eve—Ah, bitter chill it was!
The owl, for all his feathers, was a-cold;
The hare limp'd trembling through the frozen grass,
And silent was the flock in woolly fold:
Numb were the Beadsman's fingers, while he told   5
His rosary, and while his frosted breath,
Like pious incense from a censer old,
Seem'd taking flight for heaven, without a death,
Past the sweet Virgin's picture, while his prayer he saith.

II

His prayer he saith, this patient, holy man;   10
Then takes his lamp, and riseth from his knees,
And back returneth, meagre, barefoot, wan,
Along the chapel aisle by slow degrees:
The sculptur'd dead, on each side, seem to freeze,
Emprison'd in black, purgatorial rails: 15
Knights, ladies, praying in dumb orat'ries,
He passeth by; and his weak spirit fails
To think how they may ache in icy hoods and mails.

III

Northward he turneth through a little door,
And scarce three steps, ere Music's golden tongue   20
Flatter'd to tears this aged man and poor;
But no—already had his deathbell rung;
The joys of all his life were said and sung:
His was harsh penance on St. Agnes' Eve:
Another way he went, and soon among   25
Rough ashes sat he for his soul's reprieve,
And all night kept awake, for sinners' sake to grieve.

IV

That ancient Beadsman heard the prelude soft;
And so it chanc'd, for many a door was wide,

From hurry to and fro. Soon, up aloft,   30
The silver, snarling trumpets 'gan to chide:
The level chambers, ready with their pride,
Were glowing to receive a thousand guests:
The carved angels, ever eager-eyed,
Star'd, where upon their heads the cornice rests,   35
With hair blown back, and wing put cross-wise on their
    breasts.

V

At length burst in the argent revelry,
With plume, tiara, and all rich array,
Numerous as shadows haunting fairily
The brain, new stuff'd, in youth, with triumphs gay   40
Of old romance. These let us wish away,
And turn, sole-thoughted, to one Lady there,
Whose heart had brooded, all that wintry day,
On love, and wing'd St. Agnes' saintly care,
As she had heard old dames full many times declare.   45

VI

They told her how, upon St. Agnes' Eve,
Young virgins might have visions of delight,
And soft adorings from their loves receive
Upon the honey'd middle of the night,
If ceremonies due they did aright;   50
As, supperless to bed they must retire,
And couch supine their beauties, lily white;
Nor look behind, nor sideways, but require
Of Heaven with upward eyes for all that they desire.

VII

Full of this whim was thoughtful Madeline: 55
The music, yearning like a God in pain,
She scarcely heard: her maiden eyes divine,
Fix'd on the floor, saw many a sweeping train
Pass by—she heeded not at all: in vain
Came many a tiptoe, amorous cavalier,   60
And back retir'd; not cool'd by high disdain,
But she saw not: her heart was otherwhere:
She sigh'd for Agnes' dreams, the sweetest of the year.

VIII

She danc'd along with vague, regardless eyes,
Anxious her lips, her breathing quick and short: 65
The hallow'd hour was near at hand: she sighs
Amid the timbrels, and the throng'd resort
Of whisperers in anger, or in sport;
'Mid looks of love, defiance, hate, and scorn,
Hoodwink'd with faery fancy; all amort,   70
Save to St. Agnes and her lambs unshorn,
And all the bliss to be before to-morrow morn.

IX

So, purposing each moment to retire,
She linger'd still. Meantime, across the moors,
Had come young Porphyro, with heart on fire   75
For Madeline. Beside the portal doors,
Buttress'd from moonlight, stands he, and implores
All saints to give him sight of Madeline,
But for one moment in the tedious hours,
That he might gaze and worship all unseen;   80
Perchance speak, kneel, touch, kiss—in sooth such things
        have been.

X

He ventures in: let not buzz'd whisper tell:
All eyes be muffled, or a hundred swords
Will storm his heart, Love's fev'rous citadel:
For him, those chambers held barbarian hordes,   85
Hyena foemen, and hot-blooded lords,
Whose very dogs would execrations howl
Against his lineage: not one breast affords
Him any mercy, in that mansion foul,
Save one old beldame, weak in body and in soul.   90

XI

Ah, happy chance! the aged creature came,
Shuffling along with ivory-headed wand,
To where he stood, hid from the torch's flame,
Behind a broad hall-pillar, far beyond

The sound of merriment and chorus bland: 95
He startled her; but soon she knew his face,
And grasp'd his fingers in her palsied hand,
Saying, 'Mercy, Porphyro! hie thee from this place;
'They are all here to-night, the whole blood-thirsty race!

XII

'Get hence! get hence! there's dwarfish Hildebrand;   100
'He had a fever late, and in the fit
'He cursed thee and thine, both house and land:
'Then there's that old Lord Maurice, not a whit
'More tame for his gray hairs—Alas me! flit!
'Flit like a ghost away.'—'Ah, Gossip dear,   105
'We're safe enough; here in this arm-chair sit,
'And tell me how'—'Good Saints! not here, not here;
'Follow me, child, or else these stones will be thy bier.'

XIII

He follow'd through a lowly arched way,
Brushing the cobwebs with his lofty plume,   110
And as she mutter'd 'Well-a—well-a-day!'
He found him in a little moonlight room,
Pale, lattic'd, chill, and silent as a tomb.
'Now tell me where is Madeline,' said he,
'O tell me, Angela, by the holy loom   115
'Which none but secret sisterhood may see,
'When they St. Agnes' wool are weaving piously.'

XIV

'St. Agnes! Ah! it is St. Agnes' Eve—
'Yet men will murder upon holy days;
'Thou must hold water in a witch's sieve,   120
'And be liege-lord of all the Elves and Fays,
'To venture so: it fills me with amaze
'To see thee, Porphyro!—St. Agnes' Eve!
'God's help! my lady fair the conjuror plays
'This very night: good angels her deceive!   125
'But let me laugh awhile, I've mickle time to grieve."

XV

Feebly she laugheth in the languid moon,
While Porphyro upon her face doth look,
Like puzzled urchin on an aged crone
Who keepeth clos'd a wond'rous riddle-book,   130
As spectacled she sits in chimney nook.
But soon his eyes grew brilliant, when she told
His lady's purpose; and he scarce could brook
Tears, at the thought of those enchantments cold
And Madeline asleep in lap of legends old.   135

XVI

Sudden a thought came like a full-blown rose,
Flushing his brow, and in his pained heart
Made purple riot: then doth he propose
A stratagem, that makes the beldame start:
'A cruel man and impious thou art: 140
'Sweet lady, let her pray, and sleep, and dream
'Alone with her good angels, far apart
'From wicked men like thee. Go, go!—I deem
'Thou canst not surely be the same that thou didst seem.

XVII

'I will not harm her, by all saints I swear,'   145
Quoth Porphyro: 'O may I ne'er find grace
'When my weak voice shall whisper its last prayer,
'If one of her soft ringlets I displace,
'Or look with ruffian passion in her face:
'Good Angela, believe me by these tears;   150
'Or I will, even in a moment's space,
'Awake, with horrid shout, my foemen's ears,
'And beard them, though they be more fang'd than wolves
        and bears.'

XVIII

'Ah! why wilt thou affright a feeble soul?
'A poor, weak, palsy-stricken, churchyard thing,   155
'Whose passing-bell may ere the midnight toll;
'Whose prayers for thee, each morn and evening,

'Were never miss'd.'—Thus plaining, doth she bring
A gentler speech from burning Porphyro;
So woful, and of such deep sorrowing,   160
That Angela gives promise she will do
Whatever he shall wish, betide her weal or woe.

XIX

Which was, to lead him, in close secrecy,
Even to Madeline's chamber, and there hide
Him in a closet, of such privacy   165
That he might see her beauty unespied,
And win perhaps that night a peerless bride,
While legion'd fairies pac'd the coverlet,
And pale enchantment held her sleepy-eyed.
Never on such a night have lovers met,   170
Since Merlin paid his Demon all the monstrous debt.

XX

'It shall be as thou wishest,' said the Dame:
"All cates and dainties shall be stored there
'Quickly on this feast-night: by the tambour frame
'Her own lute thou wilt see: no time to spare,   175
'For I am slow and feeble, and scarce dare
'On such a catering trust my dizzy head.
'Wait here, my child, with patience; kneel in prayer
'The while: Ah! thou must needs the lady wed,
'Or may I never leave my grave among the dead.'   180

XXI

So saying, she hobbled off with busy fear.
The lover's endless minutes slowly pass'd;
The dame return'd, and whisper'd in his ear
To follow her; with aged eyes aghast
From fright of dim espial. Safe at last,   185
Through many a dusky gallery, they gain
The maiden's chamber, silken, hush'd, and chaste;
Where Porphyro took covert, pleas'd amain.
His poor guide hurried back with agues in her brain.

XXII

Her falt'ring hand upon the balustrade,   190
Old Angela was feeling for the stair,
When Madeline, St. Agnes' charmed maid,
Rose, like a mission'd spirit, unaware:
With silver taper's light, and pious care,
She turn'd, and down the aged gossip led   195
To a safe level matting. Now prepare,
Young Porphyro, for gazing on that bed;
She comes, she comes again, like ring-dove fray'd and fled.

XXIII

Out went the taper as she hurried in;
Its little smoke, in pallid moonshine, died: 200
She clos'd the door, she panted, all akin
To spirits of the air, and visions wide:
No uttered syllable, or, woe betide!
But to her heart, her heart was voluble,
Paining with eloquence her balmy side;   205
As though a tongueless nightingale should swell
Her throat in vain, and die, heart-stifled, in her dell.

XXIV

A casement high and triple-arch'd there was,
All garlanded with carven imag'ries
Of fruits, and flowers, and bunches of knot-grass,   210
And diamonded with panes of quaint device,
Innumerable of stains and splendid dyes,
As are the tiger-moth's deep-damask'd wings;
And in the midst, 'mong thousand heraldries,
And twilight saints, and dim emblazonings,   215
A shielded scutcheon blush'd with blood of queens and
    kings.

XXV

Full on this casement shone the wintry moon,
And threw warm gules on Madeline's fair breast,
As down she knelt for heaven's grace and boon;
Rose-bloom fell on her hands, together prest,   220

And on her silver cross soft amethyst,
And on her hair a glory, like a saint:
She seem'd a splendid angel, newly drest,
Save wings, for heaven:—Porphyro grew faint:
She knelt, so pure a thing, so free from mortal taint.   225

XXVI

Anon his heart revives: her vespers done,
Of all its wreathed pearls her hair she frees;
Unclasps her warmed jewels one by one;
Loosens her fragrant boddice; by degrees
Her rich attire creeps rustling to her knees: 230
Half-hidden, like a mermaid in sea-weed,
Pensive awhile she dreams awake, and sees,
In fancy, fair St. Agnes in her bed,
But dares not look behind, or all the charm is fled.

XXVII

Soon, trembling in her soft and chilly nest,   235
In sort of wakeful swoon, perplex'd she lay,
Until the poppied warmth of sleep oppress'd
Her soothed limbs, and soul fatigued away;
Flown, like a thought, until the morrow-day;
Blissfully haven'd both from joy and pain;   240
Clasp'd like a missal where swart Paynims pray;
Blinded alike from sunshine and from rain,
As though a rose should shut, and be a bud again.

XXVIII

Stol'n to this paradise, and so entranced,
Porphyro gazed upon her empty dress,   245
And listen'd to her breathing, if it chanced
To wake into a slumberous tenderness;
Which when he heard, that minute did he bless,
And breath'd himself: then from the closet crept,
Noiseless as fear in a wide wilderness,   250
And over the hush'd carpet, silent, stept,
And 'tween the curtains peep'd, where, lo!—how fast she
slept.

XXIX

Then by the bed-side, where the faded moon
Made a dim, silver twilight, soft he set
A table, and, half anguish'd, threw thereon   255
A cloth of woven crimson, gold, and jet:—
O for some drowsy Morphean amulet!
The boisterous, midnight, festive clarion,
The kettle-drum, and far-heard clarionet,
Affray his ears, though but in dying tone:—   260
The hall door shuts again, and all the noise is gone.

XXX

And still she slept an azure-lidded sleep,
In blanched linen, smooth, and lavender'd,
While he from forth the closet brought a heap
Of candied apple, quince, and plum, and gourd   265
With jellies soother than the creamy curd,
And lucent syrops, tinct with cinnamon;
Manna and dates, in argosy transferr'd
From Fez; and spiced dainties, every one,
From silken Samarcand to cedar'd Lebanon.   270

XXXI

These delicates he heap'd with glowing hand
On golden dishes and in baskets bright
Of wreathed silver: sumptuous they stand
In the retired quiet of the night,
Filling the chilly room with perfume light.—   275
'And now, my love, my seraph fair, awake!
'Thou art my heaven, and I thine eremite:
'Open thine eyes, for meek St. Agnes' sake,
'Or I shall drowse beside thee, so my soul doth ache.'

XXXII

Thus whispering, his warm, unnerved arm   280
Sank in her pillow. Shaded was her dream
By the dusk curtains:—'twas a midnight charm
Impossible to melt as iced stream:
The lustrous salvers in the moonlight gleam;

Broad golden fringe upon the carpet lies: 285
It seem'd he never, never could redeem
From such a stedfast spell his lady's eyes;
So mus'd awhile, entoil'd in woofed phantasies.

XXXIII

Awakening up, he took her hollow lute,—
Tumultuous,—and, in chords that tenderest be,   290
He play'd an ancient ditty, long since mute,
In Provence call'd, 'La belle dame sans mercy:'
Close to her ear touching the melody;—
Wherewith disturb'd, she utter'd a soft moan:
He ceased—she panted quick—and suddenly   295
Her blue affrayed eyes wide open shone:
Upon his knees he sank, pale as smooth-sculptured stone.

XXXIV

Her eyes were open, but she still beheld,
Now wide awake, the vision of her sleep:
There was a painful change, that nigh expell'd   300
The blisses of her dream so pure and deep
At which fair Madeline began to weep,
And moan forth witless words with many a sigh;
While still her gaze on Porphyro would keep;
Who knelt, with joined hands and piteous eye,   305
Fearing to move or speak, she look'd so dreamingly.

XXXV

'Ah, Porphyro!' said she, 'but even now
'Thy voice was at sweet tremble in mine ear,
'Made tuneable with every sweetest vow;
'And those sad eyes were spiritual clear: 310
'How chang'd thou art! how pallid, chill, and drear!
'Give me that voice again, my Porphyro,
'Those looks immortal, those complainings dear!
'Oh leave me not in this eternal woe,
'For if thou diest, my Love, I know not where to go.'   315

XXXVI

Beyond a mortal man impassion'd far
At these voluptuous accents, he arose,

Ethereal, flush'd, and like a throbbing star
Seen mid the sapphire heaven's deep repose
Into her dream he melted, as the rose   320
Blendeth its odour with the violet,—
Solution sweet: meantime the frost-wind blows
Like Love's alarum pattering the sharp sleet
Against the window-panes; St. Agnes' moon hath set.

XXXVII

'Tis dark: quick pattereth the flaw-blown sleet: 325
'This is no dream, my bride, my Madeline!'
'Tis dark: the iced gusts still rave and beat:
'No dream, alas! alas! and woe is mine!
'Porphyro will leave me here to fade and pine.—
'Cruel! what traitor could thee hither bring?   330
'I curse not, for my heart is lost in thine
'Though thou forsakest a deceived thing;—
'A dove forlorn and lost with sick unpruned wing.'

XXXVIII

'My Madeline! sweet dreamer! lovely bride!
'Say, may I be for aye thy vassal blest?   335
'Thy beauty's shield, heart-shap'd and vermeil dyed?
'Ah, silver shrine, here will I take my rest
'After so many hours of toil and quest,
'A famish'd pilgrim,—saved by miracle.
'Though I have found, I will not rob thy nest   340
'Saving of thy sweet self; if thou think'st well
'To trust, fair Madeline, to no rude infidel.'

XXXIX

'Hark! 'tis an elfin-storm from faery land,
'Of haggard seeming, but a boon indeed;
'Arise—arise! the morning is at hand;—   345
'The bloated wassaillers will never heed:—
'Let us away, my love, with happy speed;
'There are no ears to hear, or eyes to see,—
'Drown'd all in Rhenish and the sleepy mead:
'Awake! arise! my love, and fearless be,   350
'For o'er the southern moors I have a home for thee.'

XL

She hurried at his words, beset with fears,
For there were sleeping dragons all around,
At glaring watch, perhaps, with ready spears—
Down the wide stairs a darkling way they found.—   355
In all the house was heard no human sound.
A chain-droop'd lamp was flickering by each door;
The arras, rich with horseman, hawk, and hound,
Flutter'd in the besieging wind's uproar;
And the long carpets rose along the gusty floor.   360

XLI

They glide, like phantoms, into the wide hall;
Like phantoms, to the iron porch, they glide;
Where lay the Porter, in uneasy sprawl,
With a huge empty flaggon by his side:
The wakeful bloodhound rose, and shook his hide,   365
But his sagacious eye an inmate owns:
By one, and one, the bolts full easy slide:—
The chains lie silent on the footworn stones;—
The key turns, and the door upon its hinges groans.

XLII

And they are gone: ay, ages long ago   370
These lovers fled away into the storm.
That night the Baron dreamt of many a woe,
And all his warrior-guests, with shade and form
Of witch, and demon, and large coffin-worm,
Were long be-nightmar'd. Angela the old   375
Died palsy-twitch'd, with meagre face deform;
The Beadsman, after thousand aves told,
For aye unsought for slept among his ashes cold.
[1819]

LAMIA

PART I

Upon a time, before the faery broods
Drove Nymph and Satyr from the prosperous woods,
Before King Oberon's bright diadem,
Sceptre, and mantle, clasp'd with dewy gem,
Frighted away the Dryads and the Fauns   5
From rushes green, and brakes, and cowslip'd lawns,
The ever-smitten Hermes empty left
His golden throne, bent warm on amorous theft:
From high Olympus had he stolen light,
On this side of Jove's clouds, to escape the sight   10
Of his great summoner, and made retreat
Into a forest on the shores of Crete.
For somewhere in that sacred island dwelt
A nymph, to whom all hoofed Satyrs knelt;
At whose white feet the languid Tritons poured   15
Pearls, while on land they wither'd and adored.
Fast by the springs where she to bathe was wont,
And in those meads where sometime she might haunt,
Were strewn rich gifts, unknown to any Muse,
Though Fancy's casket were unlock'd to choose.   20
Ah, what a world of love was at her feet!
So Hermes thought, and a celestial heat
Burnt from his winged heels to either ear,
That from a whiteness, as the lily clear,
Blush'd into roses 'mid his golden hair,   25
Fallen in jealous curls about his shoulders bare.
From vale to vale, from wood to wood, he flew,
Breathing upon the flowers his passion new,
And wound with many a river to its head,
To find where this sweet nymph prepar'd her secret bed: 30
In vain; the sweet nymph might nowhere be found,
And so he rested, on the lonely ground,
Pensive, and full of painful jealousies
Of the Wood-Gods, and even the very trees.
There as he stood, he heard a mournful voice,   35
Such as once heard, in gentle heart, destroys,

All pain but pity: thus the lone voice spake:
'When from this wreathed tomb shall I awake!
'When move in a sweet body fit for life,
'And love, and pleasure, and the ruddy strife   40
'Of hearts and lips! Ah, miserable me!'
The God, dove-footed, glided silently
Round bush and tree, soft-brushing, in his speed,
The taller grasses and full-flowering weed,
Until he found a palpitating snake,   45
Bright, and cirque-couchant in a dusky brake.

    She was a gordian shape of dazzling hue,
Vermilion-spotted, golden, green, and blue;
Striped like a zebra, freckled like a pard,
Eyed like a peacock, and all crimson barr'd;   50
And full of silver moons, that, as she breathed,
Dissolv'd, or brighter shone, or interwreathed
Their lustres with the gloomier tapestries—
So rainbow-sided, touch'd with miseries,
She seem'd, at once, some penanced lady elf,   55
Some demon's mistress, or the demon's self.
Upon her crest she wore a wannish fire
Sprinkled with stars, like Ariadne's tiar:
Her head was serpent, but ah, bitter-sweet!
She had a woman's mouth with all its pearls complete: 60
And for her eyes: what could such eyes do there
But weep, and weep, that they were born so fair?
As Proserpine still weeps for her Sicilian air.
Her throat was serpent, but the words she spake
Came, as through bubbling honey, for Love's sake,   65
And thus; while Hermes on his pinions lay,
Like a stoop'd falcon ere he takes his prey.

    'Fair Hermes, crown'd with feathers, fluttering light,
'I had a splendid dream of thee last night:
'I saw thee sitting, on a throne of gold,   70
'Among the Gods, upon Olympus old,
'The only sad one; for thou didst not hear
'The soft, lute-finger'd Muses chaunting clear,
'Nor even Apollo when he sang alone,
'Deaf to his throbbing throat's long, long melodious moan.   75
'I dreamt I saw thee, robed in purple flakes,

'Break amorous through the clouds, as morning breaks,
'And, swiftly as a bright Phœbean dart,
'Strike for the Cretan isle; and here thou art!
'Too gentle Hermes, hast thou found the maid?'   80
Whereat the star of Lethe not delay'd
His rosy eloquence, and thus inquired:
'Thou smooth-lipp'd serpent, surely high inspired!
'Thou beauteous wreath, with melancholy eyes,
'Possess whatever bliss thou canst devise,   85
'Telling me only where my nymph is fled,—
'Where she doth breathe!' 'Bright planet, thou hast said,'
Return'd the snake, 'but seal with oaths, fair God!'
'I swear,' said Hermes, 'by my serpent rod,
'And by thine eyes, and by thy starry crown!'   90
Light flew his earnest words, among the blossoms blown.
Then thus again the brilliance feminine:
'Too frail of heart! for this lost nymph of thine,
'Free as the air, invisibly, she strays
'About these thornless wilds; her pleasant days   95
'She tastes unseen; unseen her nimble feet
'Leave traces in the grass and flowers sweet;
'From weary tendrils, and bow'd branches green,
'She plucks the fruit unseen, she bathes unseen:
'And by my power is her beauty veil'd   100
'To keep it unaffronted, unassail'd
'By the love-glances of unlovely eyes,
'Of Satyrs, Fauns, and blear'd Silenus' sighs.
'Pale grew her immortality, for woe
'Of all these lovers, and she grieved so   105
'I took compassion on her, bade her steep
'Her hair in weird syrops, that would keep
'Her loveliness invisible, yet free
'To wander as she loves, in liberty.
'Thou shalt behold her, Hermes, thou alone,   110
'If thou wilt, as thou swearest, grant my boon!'
Then, once again, the charmed God began
An oath, and through the serpent's ears it ran
Warm, tremulous, devout, psalterian.
Ravish'd, she lifted her Circean head,   115
Blush'd a live damask, and swift-lisping said,
'I was a woman, let me have once more
'A woman's shape, and charming as before.

'I love a youth of Corinth—O the bliss!
'Give me any woman's form, and place me where he is.   **120**
'Stoop, Hermes, let me breathe upon thy brow,
'And thou shalt see thy sweet nymph even now.'
The God on half-shut feathers sank serene,
She breath'd upon his eyes, and swift was seen
Of both the guarded nymph near-smiling on the green.   **125**
It was no dream; or say a dream it was,
Real are the dreams of Gods, and smoothly pass
Their pleasures in a long immortal dream.
One warm, flush'd moment, hovering, it might seem
Dash'd by the wood-nymph's beauty, so he burn'd;   **130**
Then, lighting on the printless verdure, turn'd
To the swoon'd serpent, and with languid arm,
Delicate, put to proof the lythe Caducean charm.
So done, upon the nymph his eyes he bent
Full of adoring tears and blandishment,   **135**
And towards her stept: she, like a moon in wane,
Faded before him, cower'd, nor could restrain
Her fearful sobs, self-folding like a flower
That faints into itself at evening hour:
But the God fostering her chilled hand,   **140**
She felt the warmth, her eyelids open'd bland,
And, like new flowers at morning song of bees,
Bloom'd, and gave up her honey to the lees.
Into the green-recessed woods they flew;
Nor grew they pale, as mortal lovers do.   **145**

  Left to herself, the serpent now began
To change; her elfin blood in madness ran,
Her mouth foam'd, and the grass, therewith besprent,
Wither'd at dew so sweet and virulent;
Her eyes in torture fix'd, and anguish drear,   **150**
Hot, glaz'd, and wide, with lid-lashes all sear,
Flash'd phosphor and sharp sparks, without one cooling
        tear.
The colours all inflam'd throughout her train,
She writh'd about, convuls'd with scarlet pain:
A deep volcanian yellow took the place   **155**
Of all her milder-mooned body's grace;
And, as the lava ravishes the mead,
Spoilt all her silver mail, and golden brede,

Made gloom of all her frecklings, streaks and bars,
Eclips'd her crescents, and lick'd up her stars: 160
So that, in moments few, she was undrest
Of all her sapphires, greens, and amethyst,
And rubious-argent: of all these bereft,
Nothing but pain and ugliness were left.
Still shone her crown; that vanish'd, also she   165
Melted and disappear'd as suddenly;
And in the air, her new voice luting soft,
Cried, 'Lycius! gentle Lycius!'—Borne aloft
With the bright mists about the mountains hoar
These words dissolv'd: Crete's forests heard no more.   170

Whither fled Lamia, now a lady bright,
A full-born beauty new and exquisite?
She fled into that valley they pass o'er
Who go to Corinth from Cenchreas' shore;
And rested at the foot of those wild hills,   175
The rugged founts of the Peræan rills,
And of that other ridge whose barren back
Stretches, with all its mist and cloudy rack,
South-westward to Cleone. There she stood
About a young bird's flutter from a wood,   180
Fair, on a sloping green of mossy tread,
By a clear pool, wherein she passioned
To see herself escap'd from so sore ills,
While her robes flaunted with the daffodils.

Ah, happy Lycius!—for she was a maid   185
More beautiful than ever twisted braid,
Or sigh'd, or blush'd, or on spring-flowered lea
Spread a green kirtle to the minstrelsy:
A virgin purest lipp'd, yet in the lore
Of love deep learned to the red heart's core: 190
Not one hour old, yet of sciential brain
To unperplex bliss from its neighbour pain;
Define their pettish limits, and estrange
Their points of contact, and swift counterchange;
Intrigue with the specious chaos, and dispart   195
Its most ambiguous atoms with sure art;
As though in Cupid's college she had spent

Sweet days a lovely graduate, still unshent,
And kept his rosy terms in idle languishment.

Why this fair creature chose so fairily   200
By the wayside to linger, we shall see;
But first 'tis fit to tell how she could muse
And dream, when in the serpent prison-house,
Of all she list, strange or magnificent:
How, ever, where she will'd, her spirit went;   205
Whether to faint Elysium, or where
Down through tress-lifting waves the Nereids fair
Wind into Thetis' bower by many a pearly stair;
Or where God Bacchus drains his cups divine,
Stretch'd out, at ease, beneath a glutinous pine;   210
Or where in Pluto's gardens palatine
Mulciber's columns gleam in far piazzian line.
And sometimes into cities she would send
Her dream, with feast and rioting to blend;
And once, while among mortals dreaming thus,   215
She saw the young Corinthian Lycius
Charioting foremost in the envious race,
Like a young Jove with calm uneager face,
And fell into a swooning love of him.
Now on the moth-time of that evening dim   220
He would return that way, as well she knew,
To Corinth from the shore; for freshly blew
The eastern soft wind, and his galley now
Grated the quaystones with her brazen prow
In port Cenchreas, from Egina isle   225
Fresh anchor'd; whither he had been awhile
To sacrifice to Jove, whose temple there
Waits with high marble doors for blood and incense rare.
Jove heard his vows, and better'd his desire;
For by some freakful chance he made retire   230
From his companions, and set forth to walk,
Perhaps grown wearied of their Corinth talk:
Over the solitary hills he fared,
Thoughtless at first, but ere eve's star appeared
His phantasy was lost, where reason fades,   235
In the calm'd twilight of Platonic shades.
Lamia beheld him coming, near, more near—
Close to her passing, in indifference drear,

His silent sandals swept the mossy green;
So neighbour'd to him, and yet so unseen   240
She stood: he pass'd, shut up in mysteries,
His mind wrapp'd like his mantle, while her eyes
Follow'd his steps, and her neck regal white
Turn'd—syllabling thus, 'Ah, Lycius bright,
'And will you leave me on the hills alone?   245
'Lycius, look back! and be some pity shown.'
He did; not with cold wonder fearingly,
But Orpheus-like at an Eurydice;
For so delicious were the words she sung,
It seem'd he had lov'd them a whole summer long: 250
And soon his eyes had drunk her beauty up,
Leaving no drop in the bewildering cup,
And still the cup was full,—while he, afraid
Lest she should vanish ere his lip had paid
Due adoration, thus began to adore;   255
Her soft look growing coy, she saw his chain so sure:
'Leave thee alone! Look back! Ah, Goddess, see
'Whether my eyes can ever turn from thee!
'For pity do not this sad heart belie—
'Even as thou vanishest so I shall die.   260
'Stay! though a Naiad of the rivers, stay!
'To thy far wishes will thy streams obey:
'Stay! though the greenest woods be thy domain,
'Alone they can drink up the morning rain:
'Though a descended Pleiad, will not one   265
'Of thine harmonious sisters keep in tune
'Thy spheres, and as thy silver proxy shine?
'So sweetly to these ravish'd ears of mine
'Came thy sweet greeting, that if thou shouldst fade
'Thy memory will waste me to a shade:—   270
'For pity do not melt!'—'If I should stay,'
Said Lamia, 'here, upon this floor of clay,
'And pain my steps upon these flowers too rough,
'What canst thou say or do of charm enough
'To dull the nice remembrance of my home?   275
'Thou canst not ask me with thee here to roam
'Over these hills and vales, where no joy is,—
'Empty of immortality and bliss!
'Thou art a scholar, Lycius, and must know
'That finer spirits cannot breathe below   280

'In human climes, and live: Alas! poor youth,
'What taste of purer air hast thou to soothe
'My essence? What serener palaces,
'Where I may all my many senses please,
'And by mysterious sleights a hundred thirsts appease?   285
'It cannot be—Adieu!' So said, she rose
Tiptoe with white arms spread. He, sick to lose
The amorous promise of her lone complain,
Swoon'd, murmuring of love, and pale with pain.
The cruel lady, without any show   290
Of sorrow for her tender favourite's woe,
But rather, if her eyes could brighter be,
With brighter eyes and slow amenity,
Put her new lips to his, and gave afresh
The life she had so tangled in her mesh: 295
And as he from one trance was wakening
Into another, she began to sing,
Happy in beauty, life, and love, and every thing,
A song of love, too sweet for earthly lyres,
While, like held breath, the stars drew in their panting
          fires.   300
And then she whisper'd in such trembling tone,
As those who, safe together met alone
For the first time through many anguish'd days,
Use other speech than looks; bidding him raise
His drooping head, and clear his soul of doubt,   305
For that she was a woman, and without
Any more subtle fluid in her veins
Than throbbing blood, and that the self-same pains
Inhabited her frail-strung heart as his.
And next she wonder'd how his eyes could miss   310
Her face so long in Corinth, where, she said,
She dwelt but half retir'd, and there had led
Days happy as the gold coin could invent
Without the aid of love; yet in content
Till she saw him, as once she pass'd him by,   315
Where 'gainst a column he leant thoughtfully
At Venus' temple porch, 'mid baskets heap'd
Of amorous herbs and flowers, newly reap'd
Late on that eve, as 'twas the night before
The Adonian feast; whereof she saw no more,   320
But wept alone those days, for why should she adore?

Lycius from death awoke into amaze,
To see her still, and singing so sweet lays;
Then from amaze into delight he fell
To hear her whisper woman's lore so well;   325
And every word she spake entic'd him on
To unperplex'd delight and pleasure known.
Let the mad poets say whate'er they please
Of the sweets of Fairies, Peris, Goddesses,
There is not such a treat among them all,   330
Haunters of cavern, lake, and waterfall,
As a real woman, lineal indeed
From Pyrrha's pebbles or old Adam's seed.
Thus gentle Lamia judg'd, and judg'd aright,
That Lycius could not love in half a fright,   335
So threw the goddess off, and won his heart
More pleasantly by playing woman's part,
With no more awe than what her beauty gave,
That, while it smote, still guaranteed to save.
Lycius to all made eloquent reply,   340
Marrying to every word a twinborn sigh;
And last, pointing to Corinth, ask'd her sweet,
If 'twas too far that night for her soft feet.
The way was short, for Lamia's eagerness
Made, by a spell, the triple league decrease   345
To a few paces; not at all surmised
By blinded Lycius, so in her comprized.
They pass'd the city gates, he knew not how,
So noiseless, and he never thought to know.

   As men talk in a dream, so Corinth all,   350
Throughout her palaces imperial,
And all her populous streets and temples lewd,
Mutter'd, like tempest in the distance brew'd,
To the wide-spreaded night above her towers.
Men, women, rich and poor, in the cool hours,   355
Shuffled their sandals o'er the pavement white,
Companion'd or alone; while many a light
Flared, here and there, from wealthy festivals,
And threw their moving shadows on the walls,
Or found them cluster'd in the corniced shade   360
Of some arch'd temple door, or dusky colonnade.

Muffling his face, of greeting friends in fear,
Her fingers he press'd hard, as one came near
With curl'd gray beard, sharp eyes, and smooth bald
    crown,
Slow-stepp'd, and robed in philosophic gown: 365
Lycius shrank closer, as they met and past,
Into his mantle, adding wings to haste,
While hurried Lamia trembled: 'Ah,' said he,
'Why do you shudder, love, so ruefully?
'Why does your tender palm dissolve in dew?'—   370
'I'm wearied,' said fair Lamia: 'tell me who
'Is that old man? I cannot bring to mind
'His features:—Lycius! wherefore did you blind
'Yourself from his quick eyes?' Lycius replied,
' 'Tis Apollonius sage, my trusty guide   375
'And good instructor; but to-night he seems
'The ghost of folly haunting my sweet dreams.'

    While yet he spake they had arrived before
A pillar'd porch, with lofty portal door,
Where hung a silver lamp, whose phosphor glow   380
Reflected in the slabbed steps below,
Mild as a star in water; for so new,
And so unsullied was the marble hue,
So through the crystal polish, liquid fine,
Ran the dark veins, that none but feet divine   385
Could e'er have touch'd there. Sounds Æolian
Breath'd from the hinges, as the ample span
Of the wide doors disclos'd a place unknown
Some time to any, but those two alone,
And a few Persian mutes, who that same year   390
Were seen about the markets: none knew where
They could inhabit; the most curious
Were foil'd, who watch'd to trace them to their house:
And but the flitter-winged verse must tell
For truth's sake, what woe afterwards befel,   395
'Twould humour many a heart to leave them thus,
Shut from the busy world of more incredulous.

PART II

Love in a hut, with water and a crust,
Is—Love, forgive us!—cinders, ashes, dust;
Love in a palace is perhaps at last
More grievous torment than a hermit's fast:—
That is a doubtful tale from faery land,   5
Hard for the non-elect to understand.
Had Lycius liv'd to hand his story down,
He might have given the moral a fresh frown,
Or clench'd it quite: but too short was their bliss
To breed distrust and hate, that make the soft voice hiss.   10
Besides, there, nightly, with terrific glare,
Love, jealous grown of so complete a pair,
Hover'd and buzz'd his wings, with fearful roar,
Above the lintel of their chamber door,
And down the passage cast a glow upon the floor.   15

    For all this came a ruin: side by side
They were enthroned, in the even tide,
Upon a couch, near to a curtaining
Whose airy texture, from a golden string,
Floated into the room, and let appear   20
Unveil'd the summer heaven, blue and clear,
Betwixt two marble shafts:—there they reposed,
Where use had made it sweet, with eyelids closed,
Saving a tythe which love still open kept,
That they might see each other while they almost slept;   25
When from the slope side of a suburb hill,
Deafening the swallow's twitter, came a thrill
Of trumpets—Lycius started—the sounds fled,
But left a thought a-buzzing in his head.
For the first time, since first he harbour'd in   30
That purple-lined palace of sweet sin,
His spirit pass'd beyond its golden bourn
Into the noisy world almost forsworn.
The lady, ever watchful, penetrant,
Saw this with pain, so arguing a want   35
Of something more, more than her empery
Of joys; and she began to moan and sigh

Because he mused beyond her, knowing well
That but a moment's thought is passion's passing bell.
'Why do you sigh, fair creature!' whisper'd he: 40
'Why do you think?' return'd she tenderly:
'You have deserted me;—where am I now?
'Not in your heart while care weighs on your brow:
'No, no, you have dismiss'd me; and I go
'From your breast houseless: ay, it must be so.'   45
He answer'd, bending to her open eyes,
Where he was mirror'd small in paradise,
'My silver planet, both of eve and morn!
'Why will you plead yourself so sad forlorn,
'While I am striving how to fill my heart   50
'With deeper crimson, and a double smart?
'How to entangle, trammel up and snare
'Your soul in mine, and labyrinth you there
'Like the hid scent in an unbudded rose?
'Ay, a sweet kiss—you see your mighty woes.   55
'My thoughts! shall I unveil them? Listen then!
'What mortal hath a prize, that other men
'May be confounded and abash'd withal,
'But lets it sometimes pace abroad majestical,
'And triumph, as in thee I should rejoice   60
'Amid the hoarse alarm of Corinth's voice.
'Let my foes choke, and my friends shout afar,
'While through the thronged streets your bridal car
'Wheels round its dazzling spokes.'—The lady's cheek
Trembled; she nothing said, but, pale and meek,   65
Arose and knelt before him, wept a rain
Of sorrows at his words; at last with pain
Beseeching him, the while his hand she wrung,
To change his purpose. He thereat was stung,
Perverse, with stronger fancy to reclaim   70
Her wild and timid nature to his aim:
Besides, for all his love, in self despite
Against his better self, he took delight
Luxurious in her sorrows, soft and new.
His passion, cruel grown, took on a hue   75
Fierce and sanguineous as 'twas possible
In one whose brow had no dark veins to swell.
Fine was the mitigated fury, like
Apollo's presence when in act to strike

The serpent—Ha, the serpent; certes, she   80
Was none. She burnt, she lov'd the tyranny,
And, all subdued, consented to the hour
When to the bridal he should lead his paramour.
Whispering in midnight silence, said the youth,
'Sure some sweet name thou hast, though, by my truth,   85
'I have not ask'd it, ever thinking thee
'Not mortal, but of heavenly progeny,
'As still I do. Hast any mortal name,
'Fit appellation for this dazzling frame?
'Or friends or kinsfolk on the citied earth,   90
'To share our marriage feast and nuptial mirth?'
'I have no friends,' said Lamia, 'no, not one;
'My presence in wide Corinth hardly known:
'My parents' bones are in their dusty urns
'Sepulchred, where no kindled incense burns,   95
'Seeing all their luckless race are dead, save me,
'And I neglect the holy rite for thee.
'Even as you list invite your many guests;
'But if, as now it seems, your vision rests
'With any pleasure on me, do not bid   100
'Old Apollonius—from him keep me hid.'
Lycius, perplex'd at words so blind and blank,
Made close inquiry; from whose touch she shrank,
Feigning a sleep; and he to the dull shade
Of deep sleep in a moment was betray'd.   105

    It was the custom then to bring away
The bride from home at blushing shut of day,
Veil'd, in a chariot, heralded along
By strewn flowers, torches, and a marriage song,
With other pageants: but this fair unknown   110
Had not a friend. So being left alone,
(Lycius was gone to summon all his kin)
And knowing surely she could never win
His foolish heart from its mad pompousness,
She set herself, high-thoughted, how to dress   115
The misery in fit magnificence.
She did so, but 'tis doubtful how and whence
Came, and who were her subtle servitors.
About the halls, and to and from the doors,
There was a noise of wings, till in short space   120

The glowing banquet-room shone with wide-arched grace.
A haunting music, sole perhaps and lone
Supportress of the faery-roof, made moan
Throughout, as fearful the whole charm might fade.
Fresh carved cedar, mimicking a glade   125
Of palm and plantain, met from either side,
High in the midst, in honour of the bride:
Two palms and then two plantains, and so on,
From either side their stems branch'd one to one
All down the aisled place; and beneath all   130
There ran a stream of lamps straight on from wall to wall.
So canopied, lay an untasted feast
Teeming with odours. Lamia, regal drest,
Silently paced about, and as she went,
In pale contented sort of discontent,   135
Mission'd her viewless servants to enrich
The fretted splendour of each nook and niche.
Between the tree-stems, marbled plain at first,
Came jasper pannels; then, anon, there burst
Forth creeping imagery of slighter trees,   140
And with the larger wove in small intricacies.
Approving all, she faded at self-will,
And shut the chamber up, close, hush'd and still.
Complete and ready for the revels rude,
When dreadful guests would come to spoil her solitude.   145

   The day appear'd, and all the gossip rout.
O senseless Lycius! Madman! wherefore flout
The silent-blessing fate, warm cloister'd hours,
And show to common eyes these secret bowers?
The herd approach'd; each guest, with busy brain,   150
Arriving at the portal, gaz'd amain,
And enter'd marveling: for they knew the street,
Remember'd it from childhood all complete
Without a gap, yet ne'er before had seen
That royal porch, that high-built fair demesne;   155
So in they hurried all, maz'd, curious and keen:
Save one, who look'd thereon with eye severe,
And with calm-planted steps walk'd in austere;
'Twas Apollonius: something too he laugh'd,
As though some knotty problem, that had daft   160

His patient thought, had now begun to thaw,
And solve and melt:—'twas just as he foresaw.

He met within the murmurous vestibule
His young disciple. 'Tis no common rule,
'Lycius,' said he, 'for uninvited guest   165
'To force himself upon you, and infest
'With an unbidden presence the bright throng
'Of younger friends; yet must I do this wrong,
'And you forgive me.' Lycius blush'd, and led
The old man through the inner doors broad-spread;   170
With reconciling words and courteous mien
Turning into sweet milk the sophist's spleen.

Of wealthy lustre was the banquet-room,
Fill'd with pervading brilliance and perfume:
Before each lucid pannel fuming stood   175
A censer fed with myrrh and spiced wood,
Each by a sacred tripod held aloft,
Whose slender feet wide-swerv'd upon the soft
Wool-woofed carpets: fifty wreaths of smoke
From fifty censers their light voyage took   180
To the high roof, still mimick'd as they rose
Along the mirror'd walls by twin-clouds odorous.
Twelve sphered tables, by silk seats insphered,
High as the level of a man's breast rear'd
On libbard's paws, upheld the heavy gold   185
Of cups and goblets, and the store thrice told
Of Ceres' horn, and, in huge vessels, wine
Come from the gloomy tun with merry shine.
Thus loaded with a feast the tables stood,
Each shrining in the midst the image of a God.   190

When in an antichamber every guest
Had felt the cold full sponge to pleasure press'd,
By minist'ring slaves, upon his hands and feet,
And fragrant oils with ceremony meet
Pour'd on his hair, they all mov'd to the feast   195
In white robes, and themselves in order placed
Around the silken couches, wondering
Whence all this mighty cost and blaze of wealth could
        spring.

Soft went the music the soft air along,
While fluent Greek a vowel'd undersong   200
Kept up among the guests, discoursing low
At first, for scarcely was the wine at flow;
But when the happy vintage touch'd their brains,
Louder they talk, and louder come the strains
Of powerful instruments:—the gorgeous dyes,   205
The space, the splendour of the draperies,
The roof of awful richness, nectarous cheer,
Beautiful slaves, and Lamia's self, appear,
Now, when the wine has done its rosy deed,
And every soul from human trammels freed,   210
No more so strange; for merry wine, sweet wine,
Will make Elysian shades not too fair, too divine.
Soon was God Bacchus at meridian height;
Flush'd were their cheeks, and bright eyes double bright:
Garlands of every green, and every scent   215
From vales deflower'd, or forest-trees branch-rent,
In baskets of bright osier'd gold were brought
High as the handles heap'd, to suit the thought
Of every guest; that each, as he did please,
Might fancy-fit his brows, silk-pillow'd at his ease.   220

What wreath for Lamia? What for Lycius?
What for the sage, old Apollonius?
Upon her aching forehead be there hung
The leaves of willow and of adder's tongue;
And for the youth, quick, let us strip for him   225
The thyrsus, that his watching eyes may swim
Into forgetfulness; and, for the sage,
Let spear-grass and the spiteful thistle wage
War on his temples. Do not all charms fly
At the mere touch of cold philosophy?   230
There was an awful rainbow once in heaven:
We know her woof, her texture; she is given
In the dull catalogue of common things.
Philosophy will clip an Angel's wings,
Conquer all mysteries by rule and line,   235
Empty the haunted air, and gnomed mine—
Unweave a rainbow, as it erewhile made
The tender-person'd Lamia melt into a shade.

By her glad Lycius sitting, in chief place,
Scarce saw in all the room another face,   240
Till, checking his love trance, a cup he took
Full brimm'd, and opposite-sent forth a look
'Cross the broad table, to beseech a glance
From his old teacher's wrinkled countenance,
And pledge him. The bald-head philosopher   245
Had fix'd his eye, without a twinkle or stir
Full on the alarmed beauty of the bride,
Brow-beating her fair form, and troubling her sweet pride.
Lycius then press'd her hand, with devout touch,
As pale it lay upon the rosy couch: 250
'Twas icy, and the cold ran through his veins;
Then sudden it grew hot, and all the pains
Of an unnatural heat shot to his heart.
'Lamia, what means this? Wherefore dost thou start?
'Know'st thou that man?' Poor Lamia answer'd not.   255
He gaz'd into her eyes, and not a jot
Own'd they the lovelorn piteous appeal:
More, more he gaz'd: his human senses reel:
Some hungry spell that loveliness absorbs;
There was no recognition in those orbs.   260
'Lamia!' he cried—and no soft-toned reply.
The many heard, and the loud revelry
Grew hush; the stately music no more breathes;
The myrtle sicken'd in a thousand wreaths.
By faint degrees, voice, lute, and pleasure ceased;   265
A deadly silence step by step increased,
Until it seem'd a horrid presence there,
And not a man but felt the terror in his hair.
'Lamia!' he shriek'd; and nothing but the shriek
With its sad echo did the silence break.   270
'Begone, foul dream!' he cried, gazing again
In the bride's face, where now no azure vein
Wander'd on fair-spaced temples; no soft bloom
Misted the cheek; no passion to illume
The deep-recessed vision:—all was blight;   275
Lamia, no longer fair, there sat a deadly white.
'Shut, shut those juggling eyes, thou ruthless man!
'Turn them aside, wretch! or the righteous ban
'Of all the Gods, whose dreadful images
'Here represent their shadowy presences,   280

'May pierce them on the sudden with the thorn
'Of painful blindness; leaving thee forlorn,
'In trembling dotage to the feeblest fright
'Of conscience, for their long offended might,
'For all thine impious proud-heart sophistries,   285
'Unlawful magic, and enticing lies.
'Corinthians! look upon that gray-beard wretch!
'Mark how, possess'd, his lashless eyelids stretch
'Around his demon eyes! Corinthians, see!
'My sweet bride withers at their potency.'   290
'Fool!' said the sophist, in an under-tone
Gruff with contempt; which a death-nighing moan
From Lycius answer'd, as heart-struck and lost,
He sank supine beside the aching ghost.
'Fool! Fool!' repeated he, while his eyes still   295
Relented not, nor mov'd; 'from every ill
'Of life have I preserv'd thee to this day,
'And shall I see thee made a serpent's prey?'
Then Lamia breath'd death breath; the sophist's eye,
Like a sharp spear, went through her utterly,   300
Keen, cruel, perceant, stinging: she, as well
As her weak hand could any meaning tell,
Motion'd him to be silent; vainly so,
He look'd and look'd again a level—No!
'A Serpent!' echoed he; no sooner said,   305
Than with a frightful scream she vanished:
And Lycius' arms were empty of delight,
As were his limbs of life, from that same night.
On the high couch he lay!—his friends came round—
Supported him—no pulse, or breath they found,   310
And, in its marriage robe, the heavy body wound.
            [1819]

            ODE TO A NIGHTINGALE

                        1

My heart aches, and a drowsy numbness pains
    My sense, as though of hemlock I had drunk,

Or emptied some dull opiate to the drains
  One minute past, and Lethe-wards had sunk:
'Tis not through envy of thy happy lot,   5
  But being too happy in thine happiness,—
    That thou, light-winged Dryad of the trees,
      In some melodious plot
  Of beechen green, and shadows numberless,
    Singest of summer in full-throated ease.   10

                        2

O, for a draught of vintage! that hath been
  Cool'd a long age in the deep-delved earth,
Tasting of Flora and the country green,
  Dance, and Provençal song, and sunburnt mirth!
O for a beaker full of the warm South,   15
  Full of the true, the blushful Hippocrene,
    With beaded bubbles winking at the brim,
      And purple-stained mouth;
  That I might drink, and leave the world unseen,
    And with thee fade away into the forest dim: 20

                        3

Fade far away, dissolve, and quite forget
  What thou among the leaves hast never known,
The weariness, the fever, and the fret
  Here, where men sit and hear each other groan;
Where palsy shakes a few, sad, last gray hairs,   25
  Where youth grows pale, and spectre-thin, and dies;
    Where but to think is to be full of sorrow
      And leaden-eyed despairs,
  Where Beauty cannot keep her lustrous eyes,
    Or new Love pine at them beyond to-morrow.   30

                        4

Away! away! for I will fly to thee,
  Not charioted by Bacchus and his pards,
But on the viewless wings of Poesy,
  Though the dull brain perplexes and retards:
Already with thee! tender is the night,   35
  And haply the Queen-Moon is on her throne,

Cluster'd around by all her starry Fays;
    But here there is no light,
Save what from heaven is with the breezes blown
    Through verdurous glooms and winding mossy ways.   40

5

I cannot see what flowers are at my feet,
    Nor what soft incense hangs upon the boughs,
But, in embalmed darkness, guess each sweet
    Wherewith the seasonable month endows
The grass, the thicket, and the fruit-tree wild;   45
    White hawthorn, and the pastoral eglantine;
        Fast fading violets cover'd up in leaves;
        And mid-May's eldest child,
The coming musk-rose, full of dewy wine,
    The murmurous haunt of flies on summer eves.   50

6

Darkling I listen; and, for many a time
    I have been half in love with easeful Death,
Call'd him soft names in many a mused rhyme,
    To take into the air my quiet breath;
Now more than ever seems it rich to die,   55
    To cease upon the midnight with no pain,
        While thou art pouring forth thy soul abroad
        In such an ecstasy!
Still wouldst thou sing, and I have ears in vain—
    To thy high requiem become a sod.   60

7

Thou wast not born for death, immortal Bird!
    No hungry generations tread thee down;
The voice I hear this passing night was heard
    In ancient days by emperor and clown:
Perhaps the self-same song that found a path   65
    Through the sad heart of Ruth, when, sick for home,
        She stood in tears amid the alien corn;
        The same that oft-times hath
Charm'd magic casements, opening on the foam
    Of perilous seas, in faery lands forlorn.   70

8

Forlorn! the very word is like a bell
    To toll me back from thee to my sole self!
Adieu! the fancy cannot cheat so well
    As she is fam'd to do, deceiving elf.
Adieu! adieu! thy plaintive anthem fades   75
    Past the near meadows, over the still stream,
        Up the hill-side; and now 'tis buried deep
            In the next valley-glades:
Was it a vision, or a waking dream?
    Fled is that music:—Do I wake or sleep?   80
    [1819]

ODE ON A GRECIAN URN

1

Thou still unravish'd bride of quietness,
    Thou foster-child of silence and slow time,
Sylvan historian, who canst thus express
    A flowery tale more sweetly than our rhyme:
What leaf-fring'd legend haunts about thy shape   5
    Of deities or mortals, or of both,
        In Tempe or the dales of Arcady?
What men or gods are these? What maidens loth?
    What mad pursuit? What struggle to escape?
        What pipes and timbrels? What wild ecstasy?   10

2

Heard melodies are sweet, but those unheard
    Are sweeter; therefore, ye soft pipes, play on;
Not to the sensual ear, but, more endear'd,
    Pipe to the spirit ditties of no tone:
Fair youth, beneath the trees, thou canst not leave!   15
    Thy song, nor ever can those trees be bare;
        Bold Lover, never, never canst thou kiss,

Though winning near the goal—yet, do not grieve;
 She cannot fade, though thou hast not thy bliss,
  For ever wilt thou love, and she be fair!   20

3

Ah, happy, happy boughs! that cannot shed
 Your leaves, nor ever bid the Spring adieu;
And, happy melodist, unwearied,
 For ever piping songs for ever new;
More happy love! more happy, happy love!   25
 For ever warm and still to be enjoy'd,
  For ever panting, and for ever young;
All breathing human passion far above,
 That leaves a heart high-sorrowful and cloy'd,
  A burning forehead, and a parching tongue.   30

4

Who are these coming to the sacrifice?
 To what green altar, O mysterious priest,
Lead'st thou that heifer lowing at the skies,
 And all her silken flanks with garlands drest?
What little town by river or sea shore,   35
 Or mountain-built with peaceful citadel,
  Is emptied of this folk, this pious morn?
And, little town, thy streets for evermore
 Will silent be; and not a soul to tell
  Why thou art desolate, can e'er return.   40

5

O Attic shape! Fair attitude! with brede
 Of marble men and maidens overwrought,
With forest branches and the trodden weed;
 Thou, silent form, dost tease us out of thought
As doth eternity: Cold Pastoral!   45
 When old age shall this generation waste,
  Thou shalt remain, in midst of other woe
Than ours, a friend to man, to whom thou say'st,
 Beauty is truth, truth beauty,—that is all
  Ye know on earth, and all ye need to know.   50
  [1819]

ODE TO PSYCHE

O Goddess! hear these tuneless numbers, wrung
    By sweet enforcement and remembrance dear,
And pardon that thy secrets should be sung
    Even into thine own soft-conched ear:
Surely I dreamt to-day, or did I see   5
    The winged Psyche with awaken'd eyes?
I wander'd in a forest, thoughtlessly,
    And, on the sudden, fainting with surprise,
Saw two fair creatures, couched side by side
    In deepest grass, beneath the whisp'ring roof   10
    Of leaves and trembled blossoms, where there ran
        A brooklet, scarce espied:
'Mid hush'd, cool-rooted flowers, fragrant-eyed,
    Blue, silver-white, and budded Tyrian,

They lay calm-breathing on the bedded grass;   15
    Their arms embraced, and their pinions too;
    Their lips touch'd not, but had not bid adieu,
As if disjoined by soft-handed slumber,
And ready still past kisses to outnumber
    At tender eye-dawn of aurorean love: 20
        The winged boy I knew;
But who wast thou, O happy, happy dove?
        His Psyche true!

O latest born and loveliest vision far
    Of all Olympus' faded hierarchy!   25
Fairer than Phœbe's sapphire-region'd star,
    Or Vesper, amorous glow-worm of the sky;
Fairer than these, though temple thou hast none,
    Nor altar heap'd with flowers;
Nor virgin-choir to make delicious moan   30
    Upon the midnight hours;
No voice, no lute, no pipe, no incense sweet
    From chain-swung censer teeming;
No shrine, no grove, no oracle, no heat
    Of pale-mouth'd prophet dreaming.   35

O brightest! though too late for antique vows,
   Too, too late for the fond believing lyre,
When holy were the haunted forest boughs,
   Holy the air, the water, and the fire;
Yet even in these days so far retir'd   40
   From happy pieties, thy lucent fans,
   Fluttering among the faint Olympians,
I see, and sing, by my own eyes inspired.
So let me be thy choir, and make a moan
     Upon the midnight hours;   45
Thy voice, thy lute, thy pipe, thy incense sweet
   From swinged censer teeming;
Thy shrine, thy grove, thy oracle, thy heat
   Of pale-mouth'd prophet dreaming.

Yes, I will be thy priest, and build a fane   50
   In some untrodden region of my mind,
Where branched thoughts, new grown with pleasant pain,
   Instead of pines shall murmur in the wind:
Far, far around shall those dark-cluster'd trees
   Fledge the wild-ridged mountains steep by steep;   55
And there by zephyrs, streams, and birds, and bees,
   The moss-lain Dryads shall be lull'd to sleep;
And in the midst of this wide quietness
A rosy sanctuary will I dress
With the wreath'd trellis of a working brain,   60
   With buds, and bells, and stars without a name,
With all the gardener Fancy e'er could feign,
   Who breeding flowers, will never breed the same:
And there shall be for thee all soft delight
   That shadowy thought can win,   65
A bright torch, and a casement ope at night,
   To let the warm Love in!
     [1819]

ODE

Bards of Passion and of Mirth,
Ye have left your souls on earth!

Have ye souls in heaven too,
Double-lived in regions new?
Yes, and those of heaven commune   5
With the spheres of sun and moon,
With the noise of fountains wond'rous,
And the parle of voices thund'rous;
With the whisper of heaven's trees
And one another, in soft ease   10
Seated on Elysian lawns
Brows'd by none but Dian's fawns
Underneath large blue-bells tented,
Where the daisies are rose-scented,
And the rose herself has got   15
Perfume which on earth is not;
Where the nightingale doth sing
Not a senseless, tranced thing,
But divine melodious truth;
Philosophic numbers smooth;   20
Tales and golden histories
Of heaven and its mysteries.

Thus ye live on high, and then
On the earth ye live again;
And the souls ye left behind you   25
Teach us, here, the way to find you,
Where your other souls are joying,
Never slumber'd, never cloying.
Here, your earth-born souls still speak
To mortals, of their little week;   30
Of their sorrows and delights;
Of their passions and their spites;
Of their glory and their shame;
What does strengthen and what maim.
Thus ye teach us, every day,   35
Wisdom, though fled far away.

Bards of Passion and of Mirth,
Ye have left your souls on earth!
Ye have souls in heaven too,
Double-lived in regions new!   40
[1819]

TO AUTUMN

1

Season of mists and mellow fruitfulness,
  Close bosom-friend of the maturing sun;
Conspiring with him how to load and bless
  With fruit the vines that round the thatch-eves run;
To bend with apples the moss'd cottage-trees,   5
  And fill all fruit with ripeness to the core;
    To swell the gourd, and plump the hazel shells
With a sweet kernel; to set budding more,
  And still more, later flowers for the bees,
  Until they think warm days will never cease,   10
    For Summer has o'er-brimm'd their clammy cells.

2

Who hath not seen thee oft amid thy store?
  Sometimes whoever seeks abroad may find
Thee sitting careless on a granary floor,
  Thy hair soft-lifted by the winnowing wind;   15
Or on a half-reap'd furrow sound asleep,
  Drows'd with the fume of poppies, while thy hook
    Spares the next swath and all its twined flowers:
And sometimes like a gleaner thou dost keep
  Steady thy laden head across a brook;   20
  Or by a cyder-press, with patient look,
    Thou watchest the last oozings hours by hours.

3

Where are the songs of Spring? Ay, where are they?
  Think not of them, thou hast thy music too,—
While barred clouds bloom the soft-dying day,   25
  And touch the stubble-plains with rosy hue;
Then in a wailful choir the small gnats mourn
  Among the river shallows, borne aloft
    Or sinking as the light wind lives or dies;
And full-grown lambs loud bleat from hilly bourn;   30
  Hedge-crickets sing; and now with treble soft

The red-breast whistles from a garden-croft;
    And gathering swallows twitter in the skies.
        [1819]

ODE ON MELANCHOLY

1

No, no, go not to Lethe, neither twist
    Wolf's-bane, tight-rooted, for its poisonous wine;
Nor suffer thy pale forehead to be kiss'd
    By nightshade, ruby grape of Proserpine;
Make not your rosary of yew-berries,   5
    Nor let the beetle, nor the death-moth be
        Your mournful Psyche, nor the downy owl
A partner in your sorrow's mysteries;
    For shade to shade will come too drowsily,
        And drown the wakeful anguish of the soul.   10

2

But when the melancholy fit shall fall
    Sudden from heaven like a weeping cloud,
That fosters the droop-headed flowers all,
    And hides the green hill in an April shroud;
Then glut thy sorrow on a morning rose,   15
    Or on the rainbow of the salt sand-wave,
        Or on the wealth of globed peonies;
Or if thy mistress some rich anger shows,
    Emprison her soft hand, and let her rave,
        And feed deep, deep upon her peerless eyes.   20

3

She dwells with Beauty—Beauty that must die;
    And Joy, whose hand is ever at his lips
Bidding adieu; and aching Pleasure nigh,
    Turning to poison while the bee-mouth sips:
Ay, in the very temple of Delight   25
    Veil'd Melancholy has her sovran shrine,
        Though seen of none save him whose strenuous
            tongue

Can burst Joy's grape against his palate fine;
　His soul shall taste the sadness of her might,
　And be among her cloudy trophies hung.　　　　30
　　[1819]

ODE ON INDOLENCE

'They toil not, neither do they spin.' [*Matthew*, vi:28]

I

One morn before me were three figures seen,
　With bowed necks, and joined hands, side-faced;
And one behind the other stepp'd serene,
　In placid sandals, and in white robes graced;
They pass'd, like figures on a marble urn,　　　　5
　When shifted round to see the other side;
　　They came again; as when the urn once more
Is shifted round, the first seen shades return;
　And they were strange to me, as may betide
　With vases, to one deep in Phidian lore.　　　　10

II

How is it, Shadows! that I knew ye not?
　How came ye muffled in so hush a masque?
Was it a silent deep-disguised plot
　To steal away, and leave without a task
My idle days? Ripe was the drowsy hour;　　　　15
　The blissful cloud of summer-indolence
　　Benumb'd my eyes; my pulse grew less and less;
Pain had no sting, and pleasure's wreath no flower:
　O, why did ye not melt, and leave my sense
　Unhaunted quite of all but—nothingness?　　　　20

III

A third time came they by;—alas! wherefore?
　My sleep had been embroider'd with dim dreams;

My soul had been a lawn besprinkled o'er
   With flowers, and stirring shades, and baffled beams:
The morn was clouded, but no shower fell,   25
   Tho' in her lids hung the sweet tears of May;
     The open casement press'd a new-leav'd vine,
Let in the budding warmth and throstle's lay;
   O Shadows! 'twas a time to bid farewell!
     Upon your skirts had fallen no tears of mine.   30

IV

A third time pass'd they by, and, passing, turn'd
   Each one the face a moment whiles to me;
Then faded, and to follow them I burn'd
   And ached for wings because I knew the three;
The first was a fair Maid, and Love her name;   35
   The second was Ambition, pale of cheek,
     And ever watchful with fatigued eye;
The last, whom I love more, the more of blame
   Is heap'd upon her, maiden most unmeek,—
     I knew to be my demon Poesy.   40

V

They faded, and, forsooth! I wanted wings:
   O folly! What is Love! and where is it?
And for that poor Ambition—it springs
   From a man's little heart's short fever-fit;
For Poesy!—no,—she has not a joy,—   45
   At least for me,—so sweet as drowsy noons,
     And evenings steep'd in honied indolence;
Or, for an age so shelter'd from annoy,
     That I may never know how change the moons,
     Or hear the voice of busy common-sense!   50

VI

So, ye three Ghosts, adieu! Ye cannot raise
   My head cool-bedded in the flowery grass;
For I would not be dieted with praise,
   A pet-lamb in a sentimental farce!
Fade softly from my eyes, and be once more   55
   In masque-like figures on the dreamy urn;

Farewell! I yet have visions for the night,
And for the day faint visions there is store;
  Vanish, ye Phantoms! from my idle spright,
  Into the clouds, and never more return!   60
      [1819]

THE EVE OF ST. MARK

Upon a Sabbath-day it fell;
Twice holy was the Sabbath-bell,
That call'd the folk to evening prayer;
The city streets were clean and fair
From wholesome drench of April rains;   5
And, on the western window panes,
The chilly sunset faintly told
Of unmatured green vallies cold,
Of the green thorny bloomless hedge,
Of rivers new with spring-like sedge,   10
Of primroses by shelter'd rills,
And daisies on the aguish hills.
Twice holy was the Sabbath-bell:
The silent streets were crowded well
With staid and pious companies,   15
Warm from their fire-side orat'ries;
And moving, with demurest air,
To even-song, and vesper prayer.
Each arched porch, and entry low,
Was fill'd with patient folk and slow,   20
With whispers hush, and shuffling feet,
While play'd the organ loud and sweet.

The bells had ceased, the prayers begun,
And Bertha had not yet half done
A curious volume, patch'd and torn,   25
That all day long, from earliest morn,
Had taken captive her two eyes,
Among its golden broideries;
Perplex'd with a thousand things,—
The stars of Heaven, and angels' wings,   30

Martyrs in a fiery blaze,
Azure saints in silver rays,
Aaron's breastplate, and the seven
Candlesticks John saw in Heaven,
The winged Lion of Saint Mark,   35
And the Covenantal Ark,
With its many mysteries,
Cherubim and golden mice.

Bertha was a maiden fair,
Dwelling in the old Minster-square;   40
From her fire-side she could see,
Sidelong, its rich antiquity,
Far as the Bishop's garden-wall;
Where sycamores and elm-trees tall,
Full-leaved, the forest had outstript,   45
By no sharp north-wind ever nipt,
So shelter'd by the mighty pile.
Bertha arose, and read awhile,
With forehead 'gainst the window-pane.
Again she tried, and then again,   50
Until the dusk eve left her dark
Upon the legend of St. Mark.
From plaited lawn-frill, fine and thin,
She lifted up her soft warm chin,
With aching neck and swimming eyes,   55
And dazed with saintly imag'ries.

All was gloom, and silent all,
Save now and then the still foot-fall
Of one returning homewards late,
Past the echoing minster-gate.   60

The clamorous daws, that all the day
Above tree-tops and towers play,
Pair by pair had gone to rest,
Each in its ancient belfrey-nest,
Where asleep they fall betimes,   65
To music of the drowsy chimes.

All was silent, all was gloom,
Abroad and in the homely room:
Down she sat, poor cheated soul!
And struck a lamp from a dismal coal;   70

Leaned forward, with bright drooping hair
And slant book, full against the glare.
Her shadow, in uneasy guise,
Hover'd about, a giant size,
On ceiling-beam and old oak chair,   75
The parrot's cage, and panel square;
And the warm angled winter screen,
On which were many monsters seen,
Call'd doves of Siam, Lima mice,
And legless birds of Paradise,   80
Macaw, the tender Av'davat,
And silken-furr'd Angora cat.
Untired she read, her shadow still
Glower'd about, as it would fill
The room with wildest forms and shades,   85
As though some ghostly queen of spades
Had come to mock behind her back,
And dance, and ruffle her garments black.
Untired she read the legend page,
Of holy Mark, from youth to age,   90
On land, on sea, in pagan chains,
Rejoicing for his many pains.
Sometimes the learned eremite,
With golden star, or dagger bright,
Referr'd to pious poesies   95
Written in smallest crow-quill size
Beneath the text; and thus the rhyme
Was parcell'd out from time to time:
'Gif ye wol stonden hardie wight—   a
Amiddes of the blacke night—   b
Righte in the churche porch, pardie   c
Ye wol behold a companie   d
Appouchen thee full dolourouse   e
For sooth to sain from everich house   f
Be it City or village   g
Wol come the Phantom and image   h
Of ilka gent and ilka carle   i
Whom coldè Deathè hath in parle   j
And wol some day that very year   k
Touchen with foulè venìme spear   l
And sadly do them all to die—   m
Hem all shalt thou see verilie—   n

And everichon shall by the[e] pass   o
All who must die that year Alas   p
——Als writith he of swevenis,
Men han beforne they wake in bliss,   100
Whanne that hir friendes thinke hem bound
In crimped shroude farre under grounde;
And how a litling child mote be
A saint er its nativitie,
Gif that the modre (God her blesse!)   105
Kepen in solitarinesse,
And kissen devoute the holy croce.
Of Goddes love, and Sathan's force,—
He writith; and thinges many mo:
Of swiche thinges I may not show.   110
Bot I must tellen verilie
Somdel of Saintè Cicilie,
And chieflie what he auctorethe
Of Saintè Markis life and dethe:'

At length her constant eyelids come   115
Upon the fervent martyrdom;
Then lastly to his holy shrine,
Exalt amid the tapers' shine
At Venice.—
        [1819]

LA BELLE DAME SANS MERCI

A BALLAD

I

O what can ail thee, knight-at-arms,
    Alone and palely loitering?
The sedge has wither'd from the lake,
    And no birds sing.

II

O what can ail thee, knight-at-arms,   5
    So haggard and so woe-begone?
The squirrel's granary is full,
    And the harvest's done.

III

I see a lilly on thy brow,
 With anguish moist and fever dew,   10
And on thy cheeks a fading rose
 Fast withereth too.

IV

I met a lady in the meads,
 Full beautiful—a faery's child,
Her hair was long, her foot was light,   15
 And her eyes were wild.

V

I made a garland for her head,
 And bracelets too, and fragrant zone;
She look'd at me as she did love,
 And made sweet moan.   20

VI

I set her on my pacing steed,
 And nothing else saw all day long,
For sidelong would she bend, and sing
 A faery's song.

VII

She found me roots of relish sweet,   25
 And honey wild, and manna dew,
And sure in language strange she said—
 'I love thee true'.

VIII

She took me to her elfin grot,
 And there she wept, and sigh'd full sore,   30
And there I shut her wild wild eyes
 With kisses four.

IX

And there she lulled me asleep,
  And there I dream'd—Ah! woe betide!
The latest dream I ever dream'd   35
  On the cold hill side.

X

I saw pale kings and princes too,
  Pale warriors, death-pale were they all;
They cried—'La Belle Dame sans Merci
  Hath thee in thrall!'   40

XI

I saw their starved lips in the gloam,
  With horrid warning gaped wide,
And I awoke and found me here,
  On the cold hill's side.

XII

And this is why I sojourn here,   45
  Alone and palely loitering,
Though the sedge has wither'd from the lake,
  And no birds sing.
    [1819]

Bibliographies

BIBLIOGRAPHIES

THE BIBLIOGRAPHIES which follow are necessarily selective. For the most part, they include titles of major twentieth-century books concerning the Romantic Movement and the five poets who appear here; intrinsic value and accessibility have been the primary criteria in their selection. For obvious reasons I have not included any of the innumerable articles in the professional journals or the less easily procured works written about the poets in their own time. It is likely that any reader venturing at all far in the use of the books listed here will rapidly become aware of the enormous possibilities that exist for the further study of the English Romantic poets.

THE ROMANTIC MOVEMENT

Bibliographies

Bernbaum, Ernest. *Guide through the Romantic Movement.* New York: Ronald Press, 1930; second edition, 1949.

Raysor, Thomas M. (ed.). *The English Romantic Poets: A Review of Research.* New York: Modern Language Association, 1950; revised edition, 1956.

"Current Bibliography [Keats, Shelley, Byron]," *Keats-Shelley Journal,* I (1952)————.

"The Romantic Movement: A Selective and Critical Bibliography," *ELH: A Journal of English Literary History,* IV-XVI (1937-49); *Philological Quarterly,* XXIX (1950)————.

Literary History

Chew, Samuel C. "The Nineteenth Century and After (1789-1939)," *A Literary History of England,* ed. Albert C. Baugh. New York: Appleton-Century-Crofts, 1948, pp. 1109-1605.

Historical Background

Brinton, Crane. *English Political Thought in the Nineteenth Century.* London: Ernest Benn, 1933; New York: Harper Torchbooks, 1962.

Bryant, Arthur. *The Age of Elegance, 1815-1822.* London: Collins, 1950.

Darvall, Frank Ongley. *Popular Disturbances and Public Order in Regency England.* London: Oxford University Press, 1934.

Dowden, Edward. *The French Revolution and English Literature.* New York: Scribner's, 1897.

Feiling, Keith Grahame. *The Second Tory Party, 1714-1832.* New York: Macmillan, 1938.

Herford, C. H. *The Age of Wordsworth.* New York: Macmillan, 1897.

Jaeger, Muriel. *Before Victoria: Changing Standards and Behaviour, 1787-1837.* London: Chatto and Windus, 1956.

Mowat, R. B. *The Romantic Age. Europe in the Early Nineteenth Century.* London: Harrap, 1937.

Quinlan, Maurice J. *Victorian Prelude, A History of English Manners, 1700-1830.* New York: Columbia University Press, 1941.

Wain, John (ed.). *Contemporary Reviews of Romantic Poetry.* New York: Barnes and Noble, 1953.

Romanticism

Abercrombie, Lascelles. *Romanticism.* London: Secker and Warburg, 1926.

Abrams, M. H. *The Mirror and the Lamp: Romantic Theory and the Critical Tradition.* New York: Oxford, 1953; Norton, 1958.

Babbitt, Irving. *Rousseau and Romanticism.* Boston: Houghton Mifflin, 1919; New York: Meridian, 1957.

Barzun, Jacques. *Romanticism and the Modern Ego.* Boston: Little, Brown, 1943; republished with revisions as *Classic, Romantic, and Modern.* Garden City: Doubleday Anchor Books, 1961.

Bowra, C. M. *The Romantic Imagination.* Cambridge, Massachusetts: Harvard University Press, 1949; New York: Galaxy Books, 1961.

Bush, Douglas. *Mythology and the Romantic Tradition in English Poetry*. Cambridge, Massachusetts: Harvard University Press, 1937; New York: Norton, 1963.

Clive, Geoffrey. *The Romantic Enlightenment*. New York: Meridian, 1960.

Comfort, Alex. *Art and Social Responsibility: Lectures in the Ideology of Romanticism*. London: Falcon, 1946.

Fairchild, Hoxie Neale. *The Romantic Quest*. New York: Columbia University Press, 1931.

Fausset, Hugh l'Anson. *The Proving of Psyche*. New York: Harcourt, Brace, 1929.

Foakes, R. A. *The Romantic Assertion: A Study in the Language of Nineteenth-Century Poetry*. New Haven: Yale University Press, 1958.

Frye, Northrop (ed.). *Romanticism Reconsidered. Selected Papers from the English Institute*. New York: Columbia University Press, 1963.

Gérard, Albert. *L'Idée romantique de la Poésie en Angleterre*. Paris: Les Belles Lettres, 1955.

Gleckner, Robert F., and Gerald E. Enscoe (eds.). *Romanticism. Points of View*. Englewood Cliffs, New Jersey: Prentice-Hall, 1962.

Kermode, Frank. *Romantic Image*. London: Routledge and Kegan Paul, 1957.

Lovejoy, Arthur O. *The Great Chain of Being. A Study of the History of an Idea*. Cambridge, Massachusetts: Harvard University Press, 1936; New York: Torch, 1960.

Lucas, F. L. *The Decline and Fall of the Romantic Ideal*. New York: Macmillan, 1936; second edition, 1949.

Peckham, Morse. *Beyond the Tragic Vision. The Quest for Identity in the Nineteenth Century*. New York: George Braziller, 1962.

Piper, H. W. *The Active Universe: Pantheism and the Concept of Imagination in the English Romantic Poets*. New York: Oxford University Press, 1962.

Praz, Mario. *The Romantic Agony*, trans. Angus Davidson. London: Oxford University Press, second edition, 1951; New York: Meridian, 1956.

Tuveson, Ernest Lee. *The Imagination as a Means of Grace; Locke and the Aesthetics of Romanticism*. Berkeley: University of California Press, 1960.

Wellek, René. *A History of Modern Criticism: 1750-1950.*
Vols. I and II. New Haven: Yale University Press, 1955.

Discussions of the Poets

Abrams, M. H. (ed.). *English Romantic Poets: Modern
Essays in Criticism.* New York: Galaxy, 1960.

Benziger, James. *Images of Eternity: Studies in the Poetry
of Religious Vision from Wordsworth to T. S. Eliot.*
Carbondale: Southern Illinois University Press, 1962.

Blackstone, Bernard. *The Lost Travellers: A Romantic
Theme with Variations,* London: Longmans, 1962.

Bloom, Harold. *The Visionary Company.* Garden City:
Doubleday, 1961.

Bostetter, Edward E. *The Romantic Ventriloquists:
Wordsworth, Coleridge, Keats, Shelley, Byron.* Seattle:
University of Washington Press, 1963.

Fairchild, Hoxie Neale. *Religious Trends in English Poetry.*
Vol. III: *1780-1830: Romantic Faith.* New York: Columbia University Press, 1949.

Kroeber, Karl. *The Artifice of Reality: Poetic Style in
Wordsworth, Foscolo, Keats, and Leopardi.* Madison
and Milwaukee: The University of Wisconsin Press,
1964.

————. *Romantic Narrative Art.* Madison: University of
Wisconsin Press, 1960.

Thrope, Clarence D., Carlos Baker, and Bennett Weaver
(eds.). *The Major English Romantic Poets: A Sympo-
sium in Reappraisal.* Carbondale: Southern Illinois University Press, 1957.

COLERIDGE

Bibliographies

Haney, John Louis (ed.). *A Bibliography of Samuel Taylor
Coleridge.* Philadelphia: For Private Circulation, 1903.

Kennedy, Virginia Wadlow, and Mary Neill Barton (eds.).
Samuel Taylor Coleridge: A Selected Bibliography. Baltimore: Enoch Pratt Free Library, 1935.

Concordance

Logan, Sister Eugenia (ed.). *A Concordance to the Poetry*

Anima Poetæ, from the Unpublished Notebooks of Samuel Taylor Coleridge, ed. Ernest Hartley Coleridge. Boston: Houghton Mifflin, 1895.

Biographia Literaria, ed. J. Shawcross. 2 vols. London: Oxford University Press, 1907; reprinted photographically, 1939, 1949; with corrections, 1954, 1958.

Coleridge's Miscellaneous Criticism, ed. Thomas Middleton Raysor. London: Constable, 1936.

Coleridge's Shakespearean Criticism, ed. Thomas Middleton Raysor. 2 vols. Cambridge, Massachusetts: Harvard University Press, 1930.

Confessions of an Inquiring Spirit, ed. H. St. J. Hart. Stanford: Stanford University Press, 1957.

Essays on His Own Times, ed. Sara Coleridge. 3 vols. London: William Pickering, 1850.

Notes on the English Divines, ed. Derwent Coleridge. 2 vols. London: Edward Moxon, 1853.

The Philosophical Lectures of Samuel Taylor Coleridge, ed. Kathleen Coburn. London: Pilot Press, 1949.

S. T. Coleridge's Treatise on Method as Published in the Encyclopedia Metropolitana, ed. Alice D. Snyder. London: Constable, 1934.

II

Letters of Samuel Taylor Coleridge, ed. Ernest Hartley Coleridge. 2 vols. London: Heinemann, 1895.

Unpublished Letters of Samuel Taylor Coleridge, ed. Earl Leslie Griggs. 2 vols. New Haven: Yale University Press, 1933.

Collected Letters of Samuel Taylor Coleridge, ed. Earl Leslie Griggs. Vols. I-IV (1785-1819). Oxford: Clarendon Press, 1956-59.

The Notebooks of Samuel Taylor Coleridge, ed. Kathleen Coburn. Vols. I and II (1794-1808). Bollingen Series L. New York: Pantheon, 1957-61.

Biographies and Related Sources

I

Campbell, James Dykes. *Samuel Taylor Coleridge: A Narrative of the Events of His Life.* New York: Macmillan, 1894.

Carpenter, Maurice. *The Indifferent Horseman: The Divine Comedy of Samuel Taylor Coleridge*. London: Elek, 1954.

Chambers, E. K. *Samuel Taylor Coleridge: A Biographical Study*. Oxford: Clarendon Press, 1938.

Charpentier, John. *Coleridge, the Sublime Somnambulist*, trans. M. V. Nugent. New York: Dodd, Mead, 1929.

Fausset, Hugh l'Anson. *Samuel Taylor Coleridge*. New York: Harcourt, Brace, 1926.

Suther, Marshall. *The Dark Night of Samuel Taylor Coleridge*. New York: Columbia University Press, 1960.

II

Hanson, Lawrence. *The Life of S. T. Coleridge: The Early Years*. New York: Oxford University Press, 1939.

Margoliouth, H. M. *Wordsworth and Coleridge, 1795-1834*. New York: Oxford University Press, 1953.

Potter, Stephen. *Coleridge and STC*. London: Jonathan Cape, 1938.

Schneider, Elisabeth. *Coleridge, Opium, and Kubla Khan*. Chicago: University of Chicago Press, 1953.

Whalley, George. *Coleridge and Sara Hutchinson and the Asra Poems*. London: Routledge and Kegan Paul, 1955.

III

Coleridge the Talker: A Series of Contemporary Descriptions and Comments, ed. Richard W. Armour and Raymond F. Howes. Ithaca: Cornell University Press, 1940.

Minnow among Tritons: Mrs. S. T. Coleridge's Letters to Thomas Poole, 1799-1834, ed. Stephen Potter. Bloomsbury: Nonesuch Press, 1934.

Criticism and Commentary

Baker, James V. *The Sacred River: Coleridge's Theory of the Imagination*. Baton Rouge: Louisiana State University Press, 1957.

Beer, J. B. *Coleridge the Visionary*. London: Chatto and Windus, 1959; New York: Collier, 1962.

Bodkin, Maud. *Archetypal Patterns in Poetry*. London: Oxford University Press, 1934; New York: Vintage, 1958.

Bonjour, Adrien. *Coleridge's "Hymn Before Sunrise." A Study of Facts and Problems Connected with the Poem.* Lausanne: Imprimerie la Concorde, 1942.

Boulger, James D. *Coleridge as Religious Thinker.* New Haven: Yale University Press, 1961.

Colmer, John A. *Coleridge: Critic of Society.* Oxford: Clarendon Press, 1959.

Fogle, Richard Harter. *The Idea of Coleridge's Criticism.* Berkeley and Los Angeles: University of California Press, 1962.

Gettmann, Royal A. (ed.). *The Rime of the Ancient Mariner: A Handbook.* San Francisco: Wadsworth, 1961.

House, Humphry. *Coleridge.* London: Rupert Hart-Davis, 1953.

Lowes, John Livingston. *The Road to Xanadu: A Study in the Ways of the Imagination.* Boston: Houghton Mifflin, 1927; revised, 1930; New York: Vintage, 1959.

Muirhead, John H. *Coleridge as Philosopher.* New York: Humanities, 1930.

Nethercot, Arthur H. *The Road to Tryermaine.* Chicago: University of Chicago Press, 1939.

Read, Herbert. *Coleridge as Critic.* London: Faber and Faber, 1949.

Richards, I. A. *Coleridge on Imagination.* London: Kegan Paul, 1934; Bloomington, Indiana: Midland Books, 1960.

Sanders, Charles R. *Coleridge and the Broad Church Movement.* Durham, North Carolina: Duke University Press, 1942.

Schulz, Max F. *The Poetic Voices of Coleridge. A Study of His Desire for Spontaneity and Passion for Order.* Detroit: Wayne State University Press, 1963.

Sherwood, Margaret. *Coleridge's Imaginative Concept of Imagination.* Wellesley, Massachusetts: Wellesley College Press, 1937, 1960.

Snyder, Alice D. *Coleridge on Logic and Learning, with Selections from the Unpublished Manuscripts.* New Haven: Yale University Press, 1929.

Tillyard, E. M. W. *Five Poems, 1470-1870.* London: Chatto and Windus, 1948.

Warren, Robert Penn (ed.). *The Rime of the Ancient Mariner.* New York: Reynal & Hitchcock, 1946.

Willey, Basil. *Nineteenth Century Studies. Coleridge to*

Sanders, Charles R. *Coleridge and the Broad Church Movement*. Durham, North Carolina: Duke University Press, 1942.

Schulz, Max F. *The Poetic Voices of Coleridge. A Study of His Desire for Spontaneity and Passion for Order*. Detroit: Wayne State University Press, 1963.

Sherwood, Margaret. *Coleridge's Imaginative Concept of Imagination*. Wellesley, Massachusetts: Wellesley College Press, 1937, 1960.

Snyder, Alice D. *Coleridge on Logic and Learning, with Sections from the Unpublished Manuscripts*. New Haven: Yale University Press, 1929.

Tillyard, E. M. W. *Five Poems, 1470-1870*. London: Chatto and Windus, 1948.

Warren, Robert Penn (ed.). *The Rime of the Ancient Mariner*. New York: Reynal & Hitchcock, 1946.

Willey, Basil. *Nineteenth Century Studies. Coleridge to Matthew Arnold*. New York: Columbia University Press, 1949.

Woodring, Carl R. *Politics in the Poetry of Coleridge*. Madison: University of Wisconsin Press, 1961.

WORDSWORTH

Bibliographies

Henley, Elton F., and David H. Stam (eds.). *Wordsworthian Criticism, 1945-1959. An Annotated Bibliography*. New York: New York Public Library, 1960.

Logan, James V. (ed.). *Wordsworthian Criticism, A Guide and Bibliography*. Columbus: Ohio State University Press, 1947, 1961.

Concordance

Cooper, Lane (ed.). *A Concordance to the Poems of Wordsworth*. New York: E. P. Dutton, 1911.

Editions

I

Lyrical Ballads. The Text of the 1798 Edition, with the Additional 1800 Poems and the Prefaces, ed. R. L. Brett and A. R. Jones. New York: Barnes and Noble, 1963.

Herford, C. H. *Wordsworth*. New York: E. P. Dutton, 1930.

Raleigh, Walter. *Wordsworth*. London: E. Arnold, 1912.

II

Beatty, Frederika. *William Wordsworth of Rydal Mount*. New York: E. P. Dutton, 1939.

de Selincourt, Ernest. *Dorothy Wordsworth*. Oxford: Clarendon Press, 1933.

————. *The Early Wordsworth*. London: English Association Pamphlet, 1936.

Legouis, Emil. *The Early Life of Wordsworth, 1770-1798; A Study of The Prelude*, trans. J. W. Matthews. New York: E. P. Dutton, 1897; third edition, 1932.

————. *William Wordsworth and Annette Vallon*. New York: E. P. Dutton, 1922.

Maclean, Catherine Macdonald. *Dorothy Wordsworth, The Early Years*. New York: Viking, 1932.

Margoliouth, H. M. *Wordsworth and Coleridge, 1795-1834*. New York: Oxford University Press, 1953.

Meyer, George Wilbur. *Wordsworth's Formative Years*. Ann Arbor: University of Michigan Press, 1943.

Moorman, Mary. *William Wordsworth: A Biography. The Early Years, 1770-1803*. Oxford: Clarendon Press, 1957.

III

The Correspondence of Crabb Robinson with the Wordsworth Circle, ed. Edith J. Morley. 2 vols. Oxford: Clarendon Press, 1927.

The Journals of Dorothy Wordsworth, ed. Ernest de Selincourt. 2 vols. New York: Macmillan, 1941.

Some Letters of the Wordsworth Family, Now First Published, with a Few Unpublished Letters of Coleridge, Southey and Others, ed. Leslie N. Broughton. Ithaca: Cornell University Press, 1942.

Criticism and Commentary

Bateson, F. W. *Wordsworth: A Re-Interpretation*. New York: Longmans, 1954; second edition, 1956.

Batho, Edith C. *The Later Wordsworth*. Cambridge: Cambridge University Press, 1933.

III

The Correspondence of Crabb Robinson with the Wordsworth Circle, ed. Edith J. Morley. 2 vols. Oxford: Clarendon Press, 1927.

The Journals of Dorothy Wordsworth, ed. Ernest de Selincourt. 2 vols. New York: Macmillan, 1941.

Some Letters of the Wordsworth Family, Now First Pub-
lished, with a Few Unpublished Letters of Coleridge,
Southey and Others, ed. Leslie N. Broughton. Ithaca:
Cornell University Press, 1942.

Criticism and Commentary

Bateson, F. W. Wordsworth: A Re-Interpretation. New
York: Longmans, 1954; second edition, 1956.

Batho, Edith C. The Later Wordsworth. Cambridge: Cambridge University Press, 1933.

Beatty, Arthur. William Wordsworth: His Doctrine and
Art in Their Historical Relations. Madison: University of
Wisconsin Press, second edition, 1927; University of
Wisconsin Paperbacks, 1960.

Bradley, A. C. Oxford Lectures on Poetry. New York: St.
Martin's, second edition, 1955; Bloomington, Indiana:
Midland Books, 1961.

Burton, Mary E. The One Wordsworth. Chapel Hill: University of North Carolina Press, 1942.

Clarke, Colin. Romantic Paradox: An Essay on the Poetry
of Wordsworth. New York: Barnes and Noble, 1963.

Danby, John F. The Simple Wordsworth: Studies in the
Poems 1797-1807. New York: Barnes and Noble, 1961.

————. William Wordsworth: The Prelude and Other
Poems: Great Neck, New York: Barron's Educational
Series, 1963.

Darbishire, Helen. The Poet Wordsworth. Oxford: Clarendon Press, 1950.

Ferry, David. The Limits of Mortality: An Essay on Wordsworth's Major Poems. Middletown, Connecticut: Wes-
leyan University Press, 1959.

Havens, Raymond Dexter. The Mind of a Poet: A Study of
Wordsworth's Thought with Particular Reference to
"The Prelude." Baltimore: The Johns Hopkins Press,
1941.

Durham, North Carolina: Duke University Press, 1945; Bloomington: Indiana University Press, second edition, 1958.

Todd, F. M. *Politics and the Poet: A Study of Wordsworth.* London: Methuen, 1957.

BYRON

Bibliographies

Chew, Samuel C. *Byron in England: His Fame and After-Fame.* London: John Murray, 1924.

Escarpit, Robert. *Lord Byron: Un Tempérament Littéraire.* 2 vols. Paris: Le Cercle du Livre, 1957.

Editions

I

Byron's *Don Juan: A Variorum Edition*, ed. Truman Guy Steffan and Willis W. Pratt. 4 vols. Austin: University of Texas Press, 1957.

The Works of Lord Byron: Poetry, ed. Ernest Hartley Coleridge. 7 vols. London: John Murray; New York: Scribner's, 1898-1904.

II

Lord Byron's Correspondence, Chiefly with Lady Melbourne, Mr. Hobhouse, The Hon. Douglas Kinnaird, and P. B. Shelley, ed. John Murray. 2 vols. New York: Scribner's, 1922.

The Works of Lord Byron: Letters and Journals, ed. Rowland E. Prothero. 6 vols. London: John Murray; New York: Scribner's, 1898-1901.

Concordance

Young, Ione (ed.) *A Concordance To The Poetry of Byron.* 4 vols. Austen: The Pemberton Press, 1965.

Biographies and Related Sources

I

Drinkwater, John. *The Pilgrim of Eternity; Byron—A Conflict.* New York: George H. Doran, 1925.

Marchand, Leslie A. *Byron: A Biography.* 3 vols. New York: Knopf, 1957.

Maurois, André. *Byron*, trans. Hamish Miles. New York: D. Appleton, 1930.

Mayne, Ethel Colburn. *Byron*. 2 vols. New York: Scribner's, 1912; rev., 1 vol., 1924.

II

Borst, William A. *Lord Byron's First Pilgrimage*. New Haven: Yale University Press, 1948.

Cline, C. L. *Byron, Shelley and their Pisan Circle*. Cambridge, Massachusetts: Harvard University Press, 1952.

Elwin, Malcom. *Lord Byron's Wife*. New York: Harcourt, Brace & World, 1963.

Fox, Sir John C. *The Byron Mystery*. London: Grant Richards, 1924.

Grylls, Rosalie Glynn. *Claire Clairmont, Mother of Byron's Allegra*. London: John Murray, 1939.

———. *Trelawny*. London: Constable, 1950.

Joyce, Michael. *"My Friend H"*: *John Cam Hobhouse, Baron Broughton of Broughton de Gyfford*. London: John Murray, 1948.

Knight, G. Wilson. *Lord Byron. Christian Virtues*. New York: Oxford University Press, 1953.

Lovelace, Ralph Milbanke, Earl of. *Astarte, A Fragment of Truth concerning George Gordon Byron, Sixth Lord Byron*. London: Christophers, 1905; revised, Mary, Countess of Lovelace, 1921.

Lovell, Ernest J., Jr. *Captain Medwin, Friend of Byron and Shelley*. Austin: University of Texas Press, 1962.

——— (ed.). *His Very Self and Voice. Collected Conversations of Lord Byron*. New York: Macmillan, 1954.

Marshall, William H. *Byron, Shelley, Hunt, and The Liberal*. Philadelphia: University of Pennsylvania Press, 1960.

Mayne, Ethel Colburn. *The Life and Letters of Anne Isabella, Lady Noel Byron*. New York: Scribner's, 1929.

Moore, Doris Langley. *The Late Lord Byron*. Philadelphia: Lippincott, 1961.

Nicolson, Harold. *Byron: The Last Journey, April 1823—April 1824*. London: Constable, 1924; revised, 1948.

Origo, Iris. *The Last Attachment: The Story of Byron and Teresa Guiccioli*. New York: Scribner's, 1949.

Knight, G. Wilson. *Lord Byron. Christian Virtues.* New York: Oxford University Press, 1953.

Lovelace, Ralph Milbanke, Earl of. *Astarte, A Fragment of Truth concerning George Gordon Byron, Sixth Lord Byron.* London: Christophers, 1905; revised, Mary, Countess of Lovelace, 1921.

Lovell, Ernest J., Jr. *Captain Medwin, Friend of Byron and Shelley.* Austin: University of Texas Press, 1962.

———— (ed.). *His Very Self and Voice. Collected Conversations of Lord Byron.* New York: Macmillan, 1954.

Marshall, William H. *Byron, Shelley, Hunt, and The Liberal.* Philadelphia: University of Pennsylvania Press, 1960.

Mayne, Ethel Colburn. *The Life and Letters of Anne Isabella, Lady Noel Byron.* New York: Scribner's, 1929.

Moore, Doris Langley. *The Late Lord Byron.* Philadelphia: Lippincott, 1961.

Nicolson, Harold. *Byron: The Last Journey, April 1823- April 1824.* London: Constable, 1924; revised, 1948.

Origo, Iris. *The Last Attachment: The Story of Byron and Teresa Guiccioli.* New York: Scribner's, 1949.

Pratt, Willis W. *Byron at Southwell: The Making of a Poet.* Austin: University of Texas Press, 1948.

Quennell, Peter. *Byron in Italy.* New York: Viking, 1941; Compass, 1957.

————. *Byron: The Years of Fame.* New York: Viking, 1935.

Criticism and Commentary

Boyd, Elizabeth French. *Byron's "Don Juan": A Critical Study.* New Brunswick: Rutgers University Press, 1945; New York: Humanities, 1958.

Calvert, William J. *Byron: Romantic Paradox.* Chapel Hill: University of North Carolina Press, 1935.

Chew, Samuel C. *The Dramas of Lord Byron, A Critical Study.* Baltimore: The Johns Hopkins Press, 1915.

Fuess, Claude M. *Lord Byron as a Satirist in Verse.* New York: Columbia University Press, 1912.

Goode, Clement Tyson. *Byron as Critic.* Weimar: R. Wagner sohn, 1923.

Lovell, Ernest J., Jr. Byron: *The Record of a Quest. Studies in a Poet's Concept and Treatment of Nature.* Austin: University of Texas Press, 1949.

Marshall, William H. *The Structure of Byron's Major Poems.* Philadelphia: University of Pennsylvania Press, 1962.

Ridenour, George M. *The Style of Don Juan.* New Haven: Yale University Press, 1960.

Rutherford, Andrew. *Byron: A Critical Study.* Stanford: Stanford University Press, 1961.

Thorslev, Peter L., Jr., *The Byronic Hero. Types and Prototypes.* Minneapolis: University of Minnesota Press, 1962.

Trueblood, Paul Graham. *The Flowering of Byron's Genius: Studies in Byron's Don Juan.* Stanford: Stanford University Press, 1945; Russell and Russell, 1962.

Vulliamy, C. E. Byron, *With a View of the Kingdom of Cant and a Dissection of the Byronic Ego.* London: Michael Joseph, 1948.

West, Paul. *Byron and the Spoiler's Art.* New York: St. Martin's, 1960.

SHELLEY

Concordance

Ellis, Frederick S. (ed.). *A Lexical Concordance to the Poetical Works of Shelley.* London: Bernard Quaritch, 1892.

Editions

I

The Complete Poetical Works of Percy Bysshe Shelley, ed. Thomas Hutchinson; introduction, Benjamin Kurtz. New York: Oxford University Press, 1933.

The Complete Poetical Works of Shelley, ed. George E. Woodberry. Boston: Houghton Mifflin, 1901.

The Complete Works of Percy Bysshe Shelley, ed. Roger Ingpen and Walter E. Peck. 10 vols. London: Ernest Benn; New York: Scribner's, 1926-30. The "Julian Edition": prose, poetry, letters.

II

New Shelley Letters, ed. W. S. Scott. London: Bodley Head, 1948.

The Letters of Percy Bysshe Shelley, ed. Frederick L. Jones. 2 vols. Oxford: The Clarendon Press, 1964.
Shelley's Lost Letters to Harriet, ed. Leslie Hotson. Boston: Atlantic Monthly, 1930.

Biographies and Related Sources

I

Blunden, Edmund. *Shelley: A Life Story*. New York: Viking, 1947.
Boas, Louise Schutz. *Harriet Shelley: Five Long Years*. New York: Oxford University Press, 1962.
Brock, Arthur Clutton. *Shelley, the Man and the Poet*. New York: G. P. Putnam's, 1909; revised, 1923.
Dowden, Edward. *The Life of Shelley*. 2 vols. London: K. Paul, Trench, 1887; revised, 1 vol., 1932.
Peck, Walter E. *Shelley: His Life and Work*. 2 vols. Boston: Houghton Mifflin, 1927.
White, Newman Ivey. *Shelley*. 2 vols. New York: Knopf, 1940, 1947; revised, 1 vol., as *Portrait of Shelley*, 1945.

II

Brailsford, Henry N. *Shelley, Godwin and Their Circle*. New York: Henry Holt, 1913; New York: Oxford University Press, second edition, 1951.
Cameron, Kenneth Neill. *The Young Shelley: The Genesis of a Radical*. New York: Macmillan, 1950; Collier, 1962.
Cline, C. L. *Byron, Shelley and their Pisan Circle*. Cambridge, Massachusetts: Harvard University Press, 1952.
Grabo, Carl. *Shelley's Eccentricities*. Albuquerque: University of New Mexico Press, 1950.
Grylls, R. Glynn. *Mary Shelley: A Biography*. New York: Oxford University Press, 1938.
Hughes, A. M. D. *The Nascent Mind of Shelley*. New York: Oxford University Press, 1947.
Lovell, Ernest J., Jr. *Captain Medwin, Friend of Byron and Shelley*. Austin: University of Texas Press, 1962.
Marshall, William H. *Byron, Shelley, Hunt, and The Liberal*. Philadelphia: University of Pennsylvania Press, 1960.

Shelley and His Circle, 1773-1822, Being an Edition of
the Manuscripts of Percy Bysshe Shelley . . . [etc] between 1773 and 1822 in The Carl H. Pforzheimer Library, ed. Kenneth Neill Cameron. Vols. I and II. Cambridge, Massachusetts: Harvard University Press, 1961.

Criticism and Commentary

Baker, Carlos. *Shelley's Major Poetry: The Fabric of a
Vision.* Princeton: Princeton University Press, 1948; New
York: Russell and Russell, 1961.

Barnard, Ellsworth. *Shelley's Religion.* Minneapolis: University of Minnesota Press, 1937.

Barrell, Joseph. *Shelley and the Thought of His Time: A
Study in the History of Ideas.* New Haven: Yale University Press, 1947.

Bloom, Harold. *Shelley's Mythmaking.* New Haven: Yale
University Press, 1959.

Butter, Peter. *Shelley's Idols of the Cave.* Edinburgh: University Press, 1954.

Campbell, Olwen Ward. *Shelley and the Unromantics.* New
York: Scribner's, 1924.

Fogle, Richard Harter. *The Imagery of Keats and Shelley: A
Comparative Study.* Chapel Hill: University of North
Carolina Press, 1949.

Grabo, Carl. *The Magic Plant. The Growth of Shelley's
Mind.* Chapel Hill: University of North Carolina Press,
1936.

————. *The Meaning of The Witch of Atlas.* Chapel Hill:
University of North Carolina Press, 1935.

————. *A Newton among Poets: Shelley's Use of Science
in "Prometheus Unbound."* Chapel Hill: University of
North Carolina Press, 1930.

————. *Prometheus Unbound: An Interpretation.* Chapel
Hill: University of North Carolina Press, 1935.

Hoffman, Harold Leroy. *An Odyssey of the Soul: Shelley's
"Alastor."* New York: Columbia University Press, 1933.

King-Hele, Desmond. *Shelley: His Thought and Work.* New
York: Thomas Yoseloff, 1960.

Kurtz, Benjamin P. *The Pursuit of Death: A Study of
Shelley's Poetry.* New York: Oxford University Press,
1933.

Lemaître, Hélène. *Shelley, Poète des Eléments.* Paris: Didier, 1962.

Notopoulos, James A. *The Platonism of Shelley: A Study of Platonism and the Poetic Mind.* Durham, North Carolina: Duke University Press, 1949.

Perkins, David. *The Quest for Permanence: The Symbolism of Wordsworth, Shelley, and Keats.* Cambridge, Massachusetts: Harvard University Press, 1959.

Pulos, C. E. *The Deep Truth: A Study of Shelley's Scepticism.* Lincoln: University of Nebraska Press, 1954; Bison Books, 1962.

Rogers, Neville. *Shelley at Work: A Critical Inquiry.* Oxford: Clarendon Press, 1956.

Solve, Melvin T. *Shelley: His Theory of Poetry.* Chicago: University of Chicago Press, 1927.

Stovall, Floyd. *Desire and Restraint in Shelley.* Durham, North Carolina: Duke University Press, 1931.

Wasserman, Earl R. *The Subtler Language: Critical Readings of Neoclassic and Romantic Poetry.* Baltimore: Johns Hopkins Press, 1959.

Weaver, Bennett. *Prometheus Unbound.* Ann Arbor: University of Michigan Press, 1957.

————. *Toward the Understanding of Shelley.* Ann Arbor: University of Michigan Press, 1932.

Wilson, Milton. *Shelley's Later Poetry: A Study of His Prophetic Imagination.* New York: Columbia University Press, 1959.

Zillman, Lawrence John (ed.). *Shelley's Prometheus Unbound, A Variorum Edition.* Seattle: University of Washington Press, 1959.

KEATS

Bibliography

MacGillivray, J.R. (ed.). *Keats. A Bibliography and Reference Guide, with an Essay on Keats' Reputation.* Toronto: University of Toronto Press, 1949.

Concordance

Baldwin, Dane Lewis, Leslie Nathan Broughton [et al.]

Weaver, Bennett. *Prometheus Unbound*. Ann Arbor: University of Michigan Press, 1957.
————. *Toward the Understanding of Shelley*. Ann Arbor: University of Michigan Press, 1932.
Wilson, Milton. *Shelley's Later Poetry: A Study of His Prophetic Imagination*. New York: Columbia University Press, 1959.
Zillman, Lawrence John (ed.). *Shelley's Prometheus Unbound, A Variorum Edition*. Seattle: University of Washington Press, 1959.

KEATS

Bibliography
MacGillivray, J.R. (ed.). *Keats. A Bibliography and Reference Guide, with an Essay on Keats' Reputation*. Toronto: University of Toronto Press, 1949.

Concordance
Baldwin, Dane Lewis, Leslie Nathan Broughton [et al.] (eds.). *A Concordance to the Poems of John Keats*. Washington, D. C.: Carnegie Institution, 1917.

Editions

I

The Poetical Works of John Keats, ed. H. W. Garrod. Oxford: Clarendon Press, 1939; second edition, 1958.

II

The Letters of John Keats, 1814-1821, ed. Hyder Edward Rollins. 2 vols. Cambridge, Massachusetts: Harvard University Press, 1958.
Bate, Walter Jackson. *John Keats*. Cambridge, Massachusetts: Harvard University Press, 1963.

Biographies and Related Sources

I

Colvin, Sir Sidney. *John Keats: His Life and Poetry, His Friends, Critics, and After-Fame*. New York: Scribner's, third edition, 1925.

Hewlett, Dorothy. *Adonais: A Life of John Keats.* New York: Bobbs-Merrill, 1937; enlarged as *A Life of John Keats.* New York: Barnes and Noble, 1950.

Lowell, Amy. *John Keats.* 2 vols. Boston: Houghton Mifflin, 1925.

Ward, Aileen. *John Keats: The Making of a Poet.* New York: Viking, 1963.

II

Birkenhead, Sheila. *Against Oblivion. The Life of Joseph Severn.* London: Cassell, 1943.

Brown, Charles Armitage. *Life of Keats,* ed. Dorothy M. Bodurtha and Willard Bissell Pope. New York: Oxford University Press, 1937.

Ford, George H. *Keats and the Victorians. A Study of His Influence and Rise to Fame, 1821-1895.* New Haven: Yale University Press, 1944.

Gittings, Robert. *John Keats: The Living Year, 21 September 1818 to 21 September 1819.* Cambridge, Massachusetts: Harvard University Press, 1954.

Hunt, Leigh. *Autobiography,* ed. J. E. Morpurgo. London: Cresset Press, 1949.

Richardson, Joanna. *Fanny Brawne: A Biography.* New York: Vanguard, 1952.

Rollins, Hyder Edward, and Stephen Maxfield Parrish. *Keats and the Bostonians.* Cambridge, Massachusetts: Harvard University Press, 1951.

III

The Keats Circle: Letters and Papers, 1816-1878, ed. Hyder Edward Rollins. 2 vols. Cambridge, Massachusetts: Harvard University Press, 1948.

Letters of Fanny Brawne to Fanny Keats, 1820-1824, ed. Fred Edgcumbe. London: Oxford University Press, 1936.

More Letters and Poems of the Keats Circle, ed. Hyder Edward Rollins. Cambridge, Massachusetts: Harvard University Press, 1955.

Balslev, Thora. *Keats and Wordsworth: A Comparative Study.* Copenhagen: Munksgaard, 1962.

Criticism and Commentary

Bate, Walter Jackson. *Negative Capability. The Intuitive Approach in Keats.* Cambridge, Massachusetts: Harvard University Press, 1939.

————. *The Stylistic Development of Keats.* New York: Modern Language Association, 1945.

Blackstone, Bernard. *The Consecrated Urn: An Interpretation of Keats in Terms of Growth and Form.* New York: Longmans, Green, 1959.

Blunden, Edmund. *John Keats.* New York: Longmans, Green, 1950.

Crawford, Alexander W. *The Genius of Keats: An Interpretation.* London: A. A. Stockwell, 1932.

Finney, Claude L. *The Evolution of Keats's Poetry,* 2 vols. Cambridge, Massachusetts: Harvard University Press, 1936.

Fogle, Richard Harter. *The Imagery of Keats and Shelley: A Comparative Study.* Chapel Hill: University of North Carolina Press, 1949.

Ford, Newell F. *The Prefigurative Imagination of John Keats.* Stanford: Stanford University Press, 1951.

Garrod, H. W. *Keats.* Oxford: Clarendon Press, 1926; second edition, 1939.

Gittings, Robert. *The Mask of Keats: A Study of Problems.* Cambridge, Massachusetts: Harvard University Press, 1956.

Marilla, E. L. *Three Odes of Keats.* Copenhagen: Munksgaard, 1962.

Muir, Kenneth. (ed.). *John Keats: A Reassessment.* Liverpool: Liverpool University Press, 1958.

Murry, John Middleton. *Keats and Shakespeare. A Study of Keats' Poetic Life from 1816 to 1820.* London: Oxford University Press, 1925.

————. *Studies in Keats.* New York: Oxford University Press, second edition, 1939.

Perkins, David. *The Quest for Permanence. The Symbolism of Wordsworth, Shelley, and Keats.* Cambridge, Massachusetts: Harvard University Press, 1959.

Pettet, E. C. *On the Poetry of Keats.* Cambridge: Cambridge University Press, 1957.

Ridley, M. R. *Keats' Craftsmanship. A Study in Poetic Development.* Oxford: Clarendon Press, 1933.

Slote, Bernice. *Keats and the Dramatic Principle.* Lincoln: University of Nebraska Press, 1958.

Thorp, Clarence D. *The Mind of John Keats.* New York: Oxford University Press, 1926.

Wasserman, Earl R. *The Finer Tone. Keats' Major Poems.* Baltimore: The Johns Hopkins Press, 1953.

Zillman, Lawrence John. *John Keats and the Sonnet Tradition: A Critical and Comparative Study.* Los Angeles: Lymanhouse, 1939.

Index
of
Titles and Authors

Index of Titles and Authors

Index of First Lines

Index of First Lines

DATE DUE

GAYLORD

PRINTED IN U.S.A.